Mauritius

Rodrigues • Réunion

the Bradt Travel Guide

Alexandra Richards
Royston Ellis
Derek Schuurman

edition
6

www.bradtguides.com

Bradt Travel Guides Ltd, UK
The Globe Pequot Press Inc, USA

D0292587

Mascarene Islands
Don't miss…

Culture
Statue at the Tamil temple
at St Aubin, Mauritius
(AR) page 22

Amazing landscapes
Cirque de Cilaos, Réunion
(AR) page 313

Beautiful beaches
Secluded beach at
Trou d'Argent,
Rodrigues
(AR) page 215

Spectacular lava formations
The volcano's recent
lava spill, Réunion
(AR) page 219

Flora and fauna
Anthurium flowers
Anthurium andraeanum
(AR) page 26

top **Notre Dame Auxiliatrice, Cap Malheureux, Mauritius** (AR)
centre **Creole house, Réunion** (AR) page 232
below left **Tamil pilgrims, Thaipoosam Cavadee festival, Mauritius** (AR) page 70
below right **Hindu woman at prayer, Grand Bassin, Mauritius** (AR)

above **Market stall, Port Louis, Mauritius** (AR) page 106
below left **Rodrigues child ready for school** (AR)
below right **Conical baskets, St-Pierre, Réunion** (AR) page 284

top left **Pink pigeon, Macchabée Forest, Mauritius** (NG) page 29
top right **Mauritius kestrel, Black River Gorges National Park, Mauritius** (PG) page 29
above left **Green heron, on giant waterlily, Pamplemousses Botanical Gardens, Mauritius** (AR) page 133
above right **Rodrigues fruit bat** (AR) page 191
below **Giant Aldabra tortoises, Mauritius** (AR)

top **Cascade de Grand-Galet, Réunion** (AR) page 283
centre **Tea picking, Bois Chéri Tea Estate, Mauritius** (AR) page 16
right *Butea monosperma,* **Mauritius** (AR)
far right **Sugarcane** *Saccharum officinarum* (AR) page 14

above left Waterfall abseiling or 'canyoning', Cirque de Ciliaos, Réunion (AR) page 318
above right Boats over the Mauritian coral reefs (PG) page 37
below Hiking area of Cirque de Mafate viewed from Piton Maïdo, Réunion (AR) page 305

Authors

Alexandra Richards graduated from Durham University in 2000, where she read modern European languages. During her studies she spent a year teaching English in Réunion and took the opportunity to travel in the Mascarenes. She has kept in touch with many of the friends that she made on the islands and returns as often as possible. Having worked in the travel industry, she is now a freelance travel writer with a passion for photography, natural history and adventure. Alex is currently living in Australia.

Royston Ellis is a travel writer, biographer and novelist who has visited Mauritius regularly since 1983. He contributes features on Indian Ocean destinations to major British newspapers and magazines worldwide and also lectures about the region on cruise liners. He is the author of over 40 books, including some best-selling historical novels, several set in Mauritius, under the pseudonym of Richard Tresillian. He has written the Bradt travel guides to Maldives and Sri Lanka.

Derek Schuurman is a freelance travel writer, author and keen naturalist. He first visited Mauritius in 1986. Subsequently he has returned to all the Mascarene Islands as a specialist tour operator and on press assignments. He now works in London for the specialist tour operator, Rainbow Tours. His other books include *Madagascar Wildlife: A Visitor's Guide* with Nick Garbutt and Hilary Bradt.

FEEDBACK REQUEST

Thank you to those readers who sent in their observations on the fifth edition. Your feedback certainly helped me in updating the guidebook this time around.

Even in the ostensibly slow-paced Mascarene Islands things are constantly changing and all too soon I will once again find myself there hiking up mountains, sampling goat curries, photographing fruit bats and being chased by monkeys in my quest to keep this guidebook accurate and current.

In the meantime, if you spot anything in this edition that is inaccurate or out of date, or if you simply want to provide some feedback, please contact me c/o Bradt Travel Guides 23 High Street, Chalfont St Peter, Bucks, SL9 9QE; **e** info@bradtguides.com

PUBLISHER'S FOREWORD

Hilary Bradt

The first Bradt travel guide was written in 1974 by George and Hilary Bradt on a river barge floating down a tributary of the Amazon. In the 1980s and '90s the focus shifted away from hiking to broader-based guides covering new destinations – usually the first to be published about these places. In the 21st century Bradt continues to publish such ground-breaking guides, as well as others to established holiday destinations, incorporating in-depth information on culture and natural history with the nuts and bolts of where to stay and what to see.

Bradt authors support responsible travel, and provide advice not only on minimum impact but also on how to give something back through local charities. In this way a true synergy is achieved between the traveller and local communities.

My association with Royston Ellis goes back to the mid 1980s when he approached me as a possible publisher for a guide to Mauritius, an island he knew intimately since many of his novels were set there. I saw the book as a partner for my own Madagascar guide which was in the pipeline, so we agreed to go ahead. And anyway, how could I resist a writer who had, in 1960, performed his beat poetry with a group he dubbed The Beatles? This group went on to greater things, keeping Royston's spelling of their name. Now the book is under the equally expert and knowledgeable authorship of Alexandra Richards, a former resident of Réunion, who has restructured, updated and expanded the guide through two editions, and added her own personal stamp on the contents.

Sixth edition May 2006 First published 1988

Bradt Travel Guides Ltd
23 High Street, Chalfont St Peter, Bucks SL9 9QE, England. www.bradtguides.com

Published in the USA by The Globe Pequot Press Inc, 246 Goose Lane,
PO Box 480, Guilford, Connecticut 06475-0480

British Library Cataloguing in Publication Data
A catalogue record for this book is available from the British Library
ISBN-10: 1 84162 151 X   ISBN-13: 978 1 84162 151 7

Photographs Alexandra Richards (AR), Nick Garbutt (NG), Peter Goodman (PG)
Front cover Young Mauritian girl, Cap Malheureux, Mauritius (AR)
Back cover Anthurium flowers (AR), Tamil pilgrims, Mauritius (AR)
Title page Butea monosperma, Mauritius (AR), Beach at Trou d'Argent, Rodrigues (AR), Tamil temple, Mauritius (AR)
Illustrations Carole Vincer   **Maps** Terence Crump

Typeset from the author's disc by Wakewing
Printed and bound in Italy by Legoprint SpA, Trento

Acknowledgements

For the time and effort that they devoted to this sixth edition, I am very grateful to the staff of White Sand Tours, in particular Joan Barry Duval. My thanks also go to the Mauritius Tourism Promotion Authority, to Air Mauritius, to the Mauritius High Commission in Canberra, and to the following for their help with the maps: B&T Directories, Kartaplus and Option Service Ltd.

I am grateful to the Durrell Wildlife Conservation Trust and the Mauritius Wildlife Foundation for showing me their work and for their contributions to the sections on natural history and conservation.

For his assistance with the chapters on Rodrigues, I would like to thank Paul Draper. My thanks and best wishes go to everyone at Craft CARE-Co – a truly inspirational team.

For their assistance with the section on Réunion, I would like to thank the Comité du Tourisme de la Réunion. My heartfelt thanks go to my dear Réunionnais friends, Dominique Vendôme and Richard Thesée, for their help and companionship, and for making living in Réunion such fun.

For their help I must thank Alf and June Wallis, and Chris and Cleo Campbell. I also thank Jan and Martin Williams and, of course, Noel for many years of unstinting support. My thanks go to my parents for not forcing me to get a 'proper job' just yet and I must acknowledge my mother's role in holding my household together while I was absorbed with writing this guide.

My sincere thanks to my Australian friends, in particular Ian, Brian, Gary, Laurence and Lyn. My thanks to Eric for keeping my French up to speed and to Mike for the countless hours he devoted to helping me.

Finally, for his invaluable help, I am (once again) hugely indebted to Ian Hayes – economist, cartographer and baggage carrier!

Alexandra Richards

My desire to write this guide grew out of my own enjoyment at visiting Mauritius. To all those who helped with the first three editions, now completely rewritten, I am grateful for their advice and assistance, especially to Suzy Edouard and Roselyne Hauchler, of the then Mauritius Government Tourist Office, to Marcello Giobbe, and to my old friend in Mauritius, Lindsay Genave. New friends Alain O'Reilly and Alain Maderbocus were extraordinarily kind and helpful. My thanks also to the Sri Lankan photographer, Gemunu Amarasinghe, who accompanied me on two visits to Mauritius and assisted me in preparing the text.

Royston Ellis

For their valuable assistance with the chapter on Rodrigues, I should like to thank Shalene Johnson (Mauritius Tourist Information Service, South Africa); Willy Auguste (Hotel Mourouk Ebony, Rodrigues); Paul Draper and Suzanne Auguste (Craft Aid Project, Port Mathurin); Dr Lee Durrell and John Hartley (Durrell Wildlife Conservation Trust); botanists Colin Barbery and Alex Malcovic; James Bowyer; Rita Bachmann (Unusual Destinations, Johannesburg); Paula Leufai and photographer Andrew Bannister; and Wendy Bashford (Inside Edge).

Without the help of the following people, to whom I am equally grateful, the section on Réunion could not have been completed: Didier Annette (formerly Réunion Promotion International, Johannesburg); Greta du Bois (Air Austral); Lisa Trepp (Anthurium Indian Ocean); Alice Deligey; Jeremy Saville; Duncan Guy; Philip Schedler; Sylvia Magid; Stephan Ulliac and Raoul Vincent (Comité du Tourisme de la Réunion); Alain Chung Wee; Ian Sinclair and Nicci Wood.

Derek Schuurman

Contents

LIST OF MAPS

KEY TO STANDARD SYMBOLS

Bradt

International boundary
National park, game reserve, etc
Market
Airport
Bus station etc
Car park
Main road (unpaved)
Other road
Track (4x4 etc)
Featured trek
Footpath
Picnic area
Cave
Mountain peak
Hotel, inn with restaurant, café
Pharmacy
Hospital/clinic/ health centre
Historic castle/fortification
Telephone

Bank
Statue/monument
Cathedral/church
Mosque
Hindu temple
Pagoda
Museum/art gallery
Tourist information
Stadium
Garden/botanical site
Scenic viewpoint
Stables
Bird nesting
Other place of interest
Petrol station, garage
Hilltop/summit
Post office
Internet café
Embassy
Theatre
Volcanic crater

Introduction

Whenever my mother is struggling for an answer (usually prompted by a particularly tricky question on a television game show), she turns to one of her enormous collection of ancient books and invariably comes up with the goods. I had always dismissed this practice as pure eccentricity. However, after fumbling for some time for inspiration for this introduction, I gave in and reluctantly asked if she had any old books that may help. It didn't surprise me in the least that she happened to have handy a copy of the 1879 edition of *The Illustrated Globe Encyclopaedia of Universal Information*.

I searched for a little-known gem of information on the Mascarene Isles, as Mauritius, Rodrigues and Réunion are known, and came up with this authoritative pronouncement on Réunion: 'The climate of late has greatly deteriorated, and is now very deadly to Europeans.'

Having just returned fit and healthy from the Indian Ocean, I can assure you that this is not the case, either in Réunion or any of the Mascarenes. And just in case you think mine was a fluke escape, official statistics show that hundreds of thousands of Europeans visit the Mascarenes each year and survive to bore friends and relatives with their holiday photos.

Mauritius, in particular, has become a 'dream holiday' destination, especially popular with honeymooners and couples wishing to tie the knot on a classic white-sand beach. It is easy to see why: luxurious hotels, a tropical climate, a glorious coastline, excellent diving and fascinating flora and fauna combine to make this island idyllic. In fact, sooner or later someone in Mauritius will tell you that when God made the island he liked it so much that he fashioned paradise in its image. Mark Twain is responsible for perpetuating that idea and I am grateful to the label on a bottle of the local Green Island Rum for the complete quotation:

> You gather the idea that Mauritius was made first and then heaven, and that heaven was copied after Mauritius.

Like heaven, Mauritius exudes an air of exclusivity, partly because the government does not allow charter flights and pursues a tourism policy of quality not quantity. However, holidays to Mauritius needn't be expensive, as I hope to show in this guide.

By contrast, the island of Rodrigues, although part of Mauritius, is a place of simple charm. I was struck by the tremendous sense of community and the laid-back way of life is a lesson to us all. I am told that it resembles the Mauritius of 30 years ago. Tourism in Rodrigues isn't only in its infancy – it has barely left the maternity ward. Although development of the island's tourism potential has begun, with the expansion of the airport and creation of the island's first 'four-star' hotel, tourists are still a novelty here and receive an incredibly warm welcome. My advice is to get to Rodrigues as soon as possible, before it all changes.

Réunion is an island of contrasts. Officially part of France, and therefore part of the European Union, it is inhabited by a cocktail of people of African, Indian, European and Chinese origin. The Creole culture is strong here and séga (a traditional dance with African roots), sorcery and occasional cockfights contrast with the ubiquitous croissants, Citroëns and pétanque tournaments.

Réunion was my home for almost a year. It is a kind of user-friendly, flat-packed paradise, where life is exotic yet easy and familiar. The atmosphere is tropical, yet the roads, doctors' surgeries and hospitals are of a reassuringly European quality.

Whilst Réunion's beaches may not rival those of Mauritius, its natural beauty is world class. The rugged, mountainous interior attracts hikers, naturalists and adventure sports enthusiasts from around the globe.

Each of the Mascarenes has its own trump card, as I am sure you will discover. However, in combination they are unrivalled. If you visit just one you'll love it, but if you can take in all three you'll be smitten.

I leave you with the thought that you shouldn't believe everything you read in an encyclopaedia and wish you a very enjoyable trip to the Mascarenes.

Alexandra Richards

Part One

MAURITIUS: GENERAL INFORMATION

Country Mauritius is an independent state, consisting of the islands of Mauritius, Rodrigues and dependencies; it is known as Ile Maurice in French.

Location In the Indian Ocean, south of the Equator and just north of the Tropic of Capricorn.

Size Mauritius 1,864km²; total area with dependencies 2,045km²

History Discovered by Arabs, then the Portuguese, Mauritius was first settled by the Dutch in 1598. It was claimed by the French in 1715 as Ile de France and captured by the British in 1810. It was a British colony until 1968 when it became an independent member of the Commonwealth. It became a republic in 1992.

Climate Hot summers (November to April) with average coastal temperatures of 30°C; warm winters (May to October), averaging 24°C. Interior temperatures are 3–5°C lower. Rainy season January to May; possibility of a stray cyclone from January to March.

Nature Mountainous with plateaux; flowers, forests and crops; rare wildlife and nothing dangerous; fine beaches within coral reefs.

Visitors Tourists come all the year around; November to January and August most popular months; May and October most pleasant.

Capital Port Louis

Government Parliamentary democracy based on the Westminster model of government. The president is the head of state but the prime minister and cabinet have constitutional power.

Population 1,300,000 of Indian, African, European and Chinese origin

Economy Based on industrial and agricultural exports, tourism and financial services

Language Official language English, but Creole most widely used. Most people speak (and read) French, with Hindi, Tamil and Chinese as the main alternatives.

Religion Hindusim, Islam, Christianity, and also Confucianism and Buddhism

Currency Mauritian rupee (Rs), which is divided into 100 cents (cs). The international exchange rate fluctuates daily, linked to a basketful of currencies.

Rate of exchange £1 = Rs55, US$1 = Rs31, €1 = Rs38 (April 2006)

International telephone code +230

Time GMT +4

Electricity 220 volts

Weights and measures The metric system was officially introduced in 1985.

Accommodation Rates for dbl room per night, B&B: Category A from Rs17,000, Category B Rs7,000–17,000, Category C Rs2,500–7,000, Category D Rs70–2,500

Background Information

GEOGRAPHY

Its isolated location kept Mauritius from being settled until 1598 and even today, many people don't know where it is. Rarely does it feature in the news and even the extraordinary result of the 1995 general election, in which the ruling party failed to win a single seat, went unreported internationally. On a world map, it is an insignificant dot in that vast expanse of ocean between southern Africa and Australia, at longitude 57°E, latitude 20°S, overshadowed by its much larger neighbour, Madagascar, 855km to the west.

Africa is the nearest continent, with Mombasa some 1,800km away. Perth is 6,000km from Mauritius and London is 9,755km away.

Mauritius is part of the Mascarene Archipelago, together with its closest neighbour, the French island of Réunion (161km away), and its own territory, Rodrigues, which lies 560km to the east, a mountainous, barren island only 108km² in size. The Cargados Garayos Archipelago, also known as the St Brandon Islands, 395km northeast of Mauritius, and the two Agalega Islands, 1,200km to the north, are Mauritian dependencies.

Mauritius also claims Tromelin Island, although this is currently occupied by France, and would like to reclaim the Six Islands, Peros Banhos, Salomon, Trois Frères and Diego Garcia, which have, since 1965, been the British Indian Ocean Territory (BIOT).

The island of Mauritius is 65km long at its longest, and 45km across at its widest. There are 160km of coastline, almost entirely surrounded by coral reefs, while the centre is a great plateau punctuated by impressive mountains. The whole state, including its dependencies, has a land area of only 2,045km², although, because the islands are so spread out, its sea area is vast.

Around Mauritius itself there are more than 15 islets lying in their own lagoons, whilst north of the island, uninhabited except for wildlife, are six small islands: Serpent, Round, Flat, Gabriel, Amber and Coin de Mire.

The origins of the island of Mauritius date back some 13 million years, when masses of molten lava bubbled up beneath the ocean floor. It took five million years to surface through the activity of two volcanic craters. The weathered crater rims of these once enormous peaks still remain as the mountain ranges of Black River, Grand Port and Moka.

Further volcanic activity followed four million years later, opening up the craters of Trou aux Cerfs, Bassin Blánc and Kanaka. The island's volcanoes have now been extinct for 200,000 years, although odd lava flows may have occurred up to 10,000 years ago. The first colonisers were marine plants and the larvae of sedentary marine animals. Lichens encrusted the bare rocks and, as a powdery soil was formed, plants brought by winds, sea and birds began to take root.

The island's rugged profile is a constant reminder of these cataclysms. The jagged volcanic peaks tower over coastal plains smothered in sugarcane, leaves waving like long green ribbons in the wind. The broad plain of the north rises to an extensive, fertile plateau, itself broken by more volcanic steeples and gorges. This tableland (600m/1,970ft high) is bordered by mountains which roll down to the crags of the southern coastline. In some areas there are deep, and seldom explored, lava caves.

It is not the height of the mountains that is impressive, but the sheer oddity of their shape. The highest is Piton de la Petite Rivière Noire at 828m (2,717ft). Pieter Both is next at 823m (2,699ft) with Pouce – the thumb-shaped mountain looming behind Port Louis – at 812m (2,664ft).

Despite the mountains and a rainfall on the windward slopes of the central plateau that can amount to 5m (197in) a year, Mauritius is not an island of great rivers. There are some 60 small rivers and streams, many degenerating as they reach the coast into rubbish-clogged trickles through cement ditches and culverts. The Grande Rivière Sud-est is the largest at 39.4km long.

The main harbour is at Port Louis, the capital, on the west coast. The airport is at the opposite side of the island to the capital, at Plaisance, not far from the old east coast harbour of Grand Port, 45km from Port Louis.

The island is divided into the same nine districts as it was when the British captured it in 1810. In a clockwise direction from the capital, these districts are: Port Louis, Pamplemousses, Rivière du Rempart, Flacq, Grand Port, Savanne and Black River, with Plaines Wilhems and Moka in the centre. Rodrigues is a district in its own right.

The eccentric terrain of Mauritius means that the island is blessed with a diversity of scenery not usually found in such a small area, and since there are good roads, travel is not time consuming. When the brashness of the northwest coast is too much, sanctuary is easily found in the tranquillity of the southwest or the dramatic coastline of the south.

CLIMATE

Basically, there are two seasons: summer is hot and wet (November to April), whilst winter is warm and dry (May to October).

Its proximity to the Tropic of Capricorn assures Mauritius of a subtropical climate that is typically warm and humid. Temperatures during summer range from 24°C at dawn to 30°C at noon on the coast, and during winter from about 18°C at dawn to 24°C at noon. On the central plateau it is normally about three to five degrees cooler. The western and northern regions are slightly drier and warmer than the east and the south.

Winter brings the trade winds, which are predominantly southeasterly and are at their strongest in July and August. The south and east coasts can be unpleasantly windy at this time of year, while in summer the sea breezes offer welcome relief from the humidity. The rainy season is roughly January to May, although rain is spasmodic, not a constant downpour for the entire five months. On the west coast the rainfall is about 1m or less a year, whilst the central plateau and windward slopes can have up to 5m in a year.

Mauritius, Réunion and Madagascar are prone to cyclones between January and March. A cyclone is a violent tropical storm that can have a devastating effect on vegetation, insecure buildings and roads. It is a tropical zone low-pressure system with winds circulating in a clockwise direction, spiralling with force towards a centre, or eye, around 4km wide. They usually form in the southwest Indian Ocean, north of Mauritius, embracing the island as they move southwards. Gusts can reach over 250km/h.

Around the centre of a cyclone, where most uplift occurs, are torrential rains (up to 50cm per day). The cyclone season starts in November with the onset of summer. An average of ten storms is tracked in each summer period but few ever represent a threat to Mauritius. Each is given a name, beginning at 'A' then working through the alphabet. Cyclones used to be given men's names; now they are dubbed with female ones. Since the name change, cyclones have been curiously erratic in behaviour, perhaps – mused one chauvinist – because men know where to go and women aren't so sure.

The lifecycle of a cyclone is around nine days but its effect on the island lasts only a day or two, according to its velocity. It moves at a speed of 8–15km/h. Damage is caused by continuous winds and gusts, and flooding.

Mauritius has a well-structured system of cyclone warnings and procedures. The warnings range from Class I, preliminary precautions (usually 36–48 hours before the cyclone strikes), to Class IV, striking moment, when people are confined to indoors.

The Mauritius Meteorological Service has a website giving up-to-date weather information, which is particularly useful when a cyclone is approaching (*http://ncb.intnet.mu/meteo.htm*).

HISTORY

The delightful *mélange* that is Mauritius has its origins in a mixed-up history. It was Dutch ... French ... and finally British until the country's independence in 1968.

DISCOVERY The first recorded discovery of Mauritius was by Islamic colonisers, when, in AD975, Hasan ibn Ali, a mercurial leader from Shiraz, Iran, left his homeland with a fleet of seven ships and a band of followers.

Most of them eventually settled in Mombasa and Pemba, although one of their ships went as far as the Comoros. From there they reached Madagascar and the islands to the east of it. In 15th-century maps, these were shown as *Dina Arobi* (Mauritius), *Dina Margabim* (Réunion) and *Dina Moraze* (Rodrigues).

It is unlikely that the colonisers actually settled in *Dina Arobi*. The island was uninhabited then and no evidence of Arab settlements has ever been found. Its neighbour, Madagascar, was inhabited but according to a 12th-century observer, Idrisi, its inhabitants had no boats capable of crossing the sea.

THE ARRIVAL OF THE EUROPEANS In the wake of Vasco da Gama's penetration of the Indian Ocean via the Cape of Good Hope, came the Portuguese *conquistadores*. While they progressed along the African and Indian coasts, they never tried to establish themselves properly in Madagascar and neighbouring islands. Pedro Mascarenhas (after whom the Mascarenes were named) is credited with the European discovery of Réunion in 1512 and Mauritius is said to have been discovered by navigator Domingo Fernandez in about 1511, although there is some doubt that he ever saw the island. No Portuguese settlement was started despite the island's ideal situation on the route from the Cape to India.

Mauritius became known on Portuguese maps as *Ilha do Cirne*, Island of the Swan, possibly after the 'land swan' which then inhabited the island: the dodo. A more prosaic theory is that the name was derived from that of a Portuguese vessel.

In 1528, Diego Rodriguez gave his name to the island still known as Rodrigues. Portuguese names have also survived on other neighbouring islands including Diego Garcia in the Chagos Archipelago, which was named after another Portuguese navigator.

If the Portuguese did visit Mauritius, it was infrequently. On their way to and from India they preferred to use the Mozambique Channel, staying close to the African coast rather than risking the open sea. Mauritius remained uninhabited except by bats and tropical birds, many of which, like the dodo, are now extinct.

The great bay on the southeast corner of the island, now known as Grand Port, was a natural haven for ships. During the latter part of the 16th century, Swan Island was probably used by pirates who preyed on the pilgrim route between India and Jeddah. Vessels from a Dutch fleet on its way from Amsterdam to Java sailed in during a violent storm in September 1598. Many of the crew were suffering from scurvy and the landfall was seen as a godsend.

Admiral Wybrandt van Warwyck was in command of the fleet and he arrogantly named the bay Warwyck Haven, a name immediately forgotten. His choice of a name for the island, however, had a catchier ring to it – he claimed possession for the Stadtholder of the Netherlands, Prince Mauritius van Nassau.

The Dutch were fascinated by the island, especially by the trusting curiosity of the birds which had yet to learn fear and allowed themselves to be knocked down with a club. In Grant's *History of Mauritius*, published in London in 1801, the dodo is described as 'a feathered tortoise' whose sluggish movements made it an easy target for the laziest hunter. Although the Dutch called occasionally for shelter, food and fresh water they took little interest in developing the island.

The French and British, too, began to see possibilities for both trade and strategy in the Mascarenes and sent out expeditions in 1638. Their ships arrived too late. In May 1638, Cornelius Simonsz Gooyer had set up the first permanent Dutch settlement in Mauritius. He was sent by the Netherlands East India Company and became the first governor, over a population of 25 colonists who planned to exploit the island's resources of ebony and ambergris, as well as rearing cattle and growing tobacco.

Over the next few years, a hundred slaves were imported from Madagascar and convicts sent over from Batavia (now Jakarta). The convicts were Europeans, Indonesians and Indians and were employed in cutting ebony. The free colonists came from Baltic and North Sea ports, hardened men who were settlers out of desperation and coercion rather than through brave ideals. From its very first settlement, Mauritius had a mix of races that was to set a pattern for its future.

The settlers supported themselves by raising vegetables and livestock, which they sold to the company or, for more profit, to the crews of visiting French, English and pirate ships. Yet although the settlement grew to 500, it did not prosper.

The slaves from Madagascar escaped to the forest and began to exact revenge for Dutch cruelties by destroying their crops and slaughtering their cattle. Invasions by hungry rats added to the problems of the settlement. The lack of interest shown by the Dutch East India Company finally demoralised the colonists.

A few years after the Dutch founded a colony at the Cape of Good Hope in 1652, the island was abandoned completely, the European market for ebony being glutted. Only the sugarcane that had been introduced from Batavia and the runaway Malagasy slaves in the forests remained.

The Dutch tried again in 1664, starting a settlement under the aegis of the Cape colony. They were more ambitious this time with attempts at agriculture on a commercial scale, including tobacco, sugarcane, indigo and maize. Deer, introduced from Java, thrived in the forests and were hunted for food and pelts. Forts were built on the eastern coast, forests cleared and domestic animals raised.

Legend has it that the Dutch were driven off for a second time in 1710 by the rats they had themselves accidentally introduced. Resentment at colonial bureaucracy also played its part, since the colony at the Cape received preferential treatment from the Dutch authorities. The settlers were ill suited to be colonists – they suffered from the heat, were undisciplined, lazy and prone to drunkenness.

Meanwhile, a new state was forming in Madagascar. Called Libertalia, it was a pirate republic founded by a French adventurer and a defrocked Italian monk. There was no shortage of tough men, mostly pirates from every nation, who made Libertalia their home. From there they successfully plundered shipping throughout the Indian Ocean and their community thrived. These men were to contribute to the new colonisation of Mauritius.

FRENCH RULE The French East India Company had already occupied Bourbon (now Réunion) as a trading centre, but although the island had fertile soil and attracted as settlers a great number of pirates and their offspring by Malagasy women, it lacked harbours. The attraction of a vacant Mauritius with its well-protected bays was irresistible.

A preliminary expedition led by Guillaume Dufresne d'Arsel took possession of Mauritius in the name of King Louis XV of France in September 1715, naming it Ile de France so its ownership would be in no doubt. D'Arsel placed the French flag near what is now Port Louis, drew up a document witnessed by his officers declaring the island French and, after three days, sailed away.

Nearly seven years passed before the French East India Company actually occupied the island. In 1721, a motley crew of company officials, settlers and slaves from Madagascar, Mozambique and west Africa landed. Swiss mercenaries made up the garrison; pirates and their women accompanied them. More women were rounded up on the waterfronts of St Malo and Bordeaux and shipped out to swell the island's population. It was hoped that a grant of land, a sum of money and the prospect of an imported wife would be enough to tempt men to settle.

For the first 14 years, the French colony followed the dismal experience of the Dutch. Only the most desperate and toughest of settlers survived, eking out a living from the pittance they earned from the company. Their appallingly treated slaves escaped to become *marrons*, living in the forest and sabotaging the plantations.

A forlorn settlement of palm-thatched cabins sprang up near the west coast harbour of Port Louis, where the French East India Company decided to build the capital. The company, however, maintained its headquarters in Bourbon, despairing of ever controlling their reluctant settlers or making a profit on their investment in Ile de France.

The solution was an inspired one. As the new Governor of Ile de France and Ile Bourbon, the French East India Company appointed an aristocratic sea captain, Bertrand François Mahé de Labourdonnais. He was 38 and full of ambition when he sailed into Port Louis harbour in 1735.

The wretched conditions of the settlers dismayed Labourdonnais. There were 190 whites on the island and 648 blacks, most of them African or Malagasy slaves, together with a few Indians.

Labourdonnais transformed the island from a colony of malcontents into 'the star and key of the Indian Ocean'. He was a born leader and as a naval man understood the lusty spirit of men with pirate blood flowing in their veins. Despite – or was it because of? – his own blue blood, he had an affinity with the struggling colonisers. He began by giving them self-respect and ambition.

He ordered that the seat of government of the two colonies be transferred from Bourbon, which was better established, to Ile de France and set up a council to administer the islands. He channelled the seafaring abilities of his settlers back to the sea, deliberately creating a navy of buccaneers.

The thatched hovels were demolished and in their place rose forts, barracks, warehouses, hospitals and houses, many of which survive in part of Port Louis today. Government House was built of coral blocks, roads were opened throughout the island and a shipbuilding industry commenced.

Although he had to import slaves, Labourdonnais made their lot easier by also importing ox-carts so slaves could be utilised for more skilled tasks. He turned many of them into artisans to make up for the lack of skilled men among the settlers. He also pushed through an agriculture programme that concentrated on feeding the islanders and on marketable produce. On his own estates he grew sugarcane, encouraging new settlers to start plantations of cotton, indigo, coffee and manioc. The first sugar factory was opened at Villebague in 1744, a salt pan was started and he even tried to rear silkworms.

Gradually a civilised life evolved in Port Louis, attracting colonisers from Bourbon, and even from good French families. Labourdonnais is known today as the father of the colony.

In 1746, with England and France at war, Labourdonnais led an expedition of nine ships from Ile de France to India. There they defeated a British squadron and captured Madras, the most important British outpost.

Labourdonnais's actions resulted in a conflict with Dupleix, his superior in India and caused his downfall. Dupleix wanted Madras razed to the ground but Labourdonnais refused because he knew the British would pay a ransom to get Madras back. He was accused of accepting a bribe to preserve Madras and was replaced as Governor of Ile de France. On his return to France he was thrown into the Bastille. Although in 1751 he was found innocent, he died a broken man two years later, aged 54. His statue stands in Port Louis facing out across the harbour. The town of Mahébourg (started in 1805) is named after him. So, too, is Mahé, capital of the Seychelles.

In 1764, the French East India Company, brought to bankruptcy by the Seven Years War, made over its assets, including the Ile de France, to the French king. In 1767, the Royal Government was established on the island. At that time there was a population of 18,773 that included 3,163 Europeans and 587 free blacks, mostly Hindus. The rest were slaves.

The appositely named Pierre Poivre (Peter Pepper) was picked as administrator. He introduced varieties of plants from South America, including pepper, and even offered tax incentives to planters to grow them. Under his influence, the colony developed as an agricultural and trading centre.

A French nobleman, Vicomte de Souillac, was made governor (1779–87), bringing an era of extravagance to the colony. Port Louis became renowned for its bright social life, duelling, gambling, and hunting. Public affairs were neglected; fraud, corruption and dishonesty were commonplace and land speculation and scandals were rife.

In January 1790, a packet-boat arrived in Port Louis harbour from France, flying a new flag, the Tricolour. It brought news of the revolution. An elected assembly and municipal councils were set up and tribunals replaced courts of justice. A National Guard was formed, streets were renamed and revolutionary clubs started. Church property was confiscated and white, red and blue cockades were sported with delight. A guillotine was even erected in the Champ de Mars but its only victim was a dog (some historians say a goat), decapitated to try it out.

The colonists' enthusiasm for the revolutionary principles of liberty, equality and fraternity faltered when in 1796 two agents of the Directoire, wearing splendid orange cloaks, arrived from France and informed the startled colonists that slavery was abolished. The news was received with anger and the agents had to flee for their lives.

The last French governor of Ile de France was appointed by Napoleon Bonaparte in 1803 to bring the colony back to order after 13 years of autonomy. With such a task, it was inevitable that the governor, General Charles Decaen, would be unpopular. He dissolved all the elected councils and adopted a dictatorial attitude to administration.

BRITISH RULE Meanwhile, the British were expanding their influence in the Indian Ocean and in 1809, British forces from both the Cape and India occupied Rodrigues from where they prepared their attack on all the Mascarenes. Bourbon, which had been renamed Réunion during the revolutionary years, was taken. A major battle was fought between the French and British fleets off Grand Port in August 1810. After prolonged fighting, the French won a victory that no-one expected.

In December 1810, 70 British vessels and 11,500 soldiers set sail from Rodrigues for the north of Ile de France. Their aim was not colonisation, but to neutralise the island so that it wouldn't be used as a base for French attacks on British vessels bound for India. British spies and reconnaissance had found a passage near Coin de Mire. Decaen was taken by surprise as he awaited the invasion in Port Louis. The British forces under General Abercrombie marched on the capital, meeting only token resistance.

Faced with the might of the British forces and the indifference of the settlers to remaining French, Decaen surrendered.

Soldiers were allowed to leave the island and settlers who did not want to stay under a British administrator were permitted to return to France with all their possessions. These generous capitulation terms also included British pledges to preserve the island's laws, customs, language, religion and property.

The majority of settlers remained. Perhaps some expected the colony to be restored to France in peace time. The Treaty of Paris did restore Réunion in 1814 but Mauritius was confirmed as a British possession.

A dashing, unorthodox personality in the Labourdonnais mould, Robert Farquhar became the first British governor in 1810. He soon revealed himself as remarkably independent of the British government in London, taking advantage of the long time it took for despatches from London to reach Mauritius to act as he thought best.

Farquhar quickly won over the French settlers, particularly through his scrupulous interpretation of the capitulation terms. Since the settlers were allowed their customs, he permitted them to continue with the slave trade despite the British law of 1807, which prohibited trading in slaves in the British Empire.

Farquhar had to contend with many calamities during his administration, including an outbreak of smallpox in 1811 and of rabies in 1813. There was a disastrous fire in Port Louis in 1816 when 700 houses, mostly wooden, were destroyed, which resulted in new ones being built of stone. A cholera epidemic broke out in 1819, and there were fierce cyclones in 1818 and 1819.

Farquhar campaigned for reliance on sugarcane because it was the only money-making crop able to withstand cyclones, encouraging the planters to abandon coffee, cotton and their other crops. He also established Port Louis as a free port, open to ships of all nations, and stimulated food production and road building. He proved to the inhabitants that there were distinct economic advantages in being British rather than French.

He mixed with everyone and opened dialogue with non-white leaders. Although his stance on slavery seemed ambivalent, he believed in attacking the slave trade at its source (in this case Madagascar) and worked for its elimination there as a way of ending the trade to Mauritius. He set up an office for the registration of slaves and tried to improve their conditions in the face of hostility from their owners.

Yet like Labourdonnais before him, Farquhar ran foul of his home government and was recalled to England in 1817. He returned to Mauritius, though, in 1820 as Sir Robert and governed for a further three years.

The attempts by the British government to abolish slavery in Mauritius met with resistance from the planters who, having been persuaded to concentrate on sugar as an income-earning export crop, relied on slave labour to produce it. The arrival of Attorney General John Jeremy in 1832 to force through emancipation led to clashes and Jeremy was obliged to flee the island.

This time the planters' triumph was short-lived and slavery was abolished on 1 February 1835. The planters were paid over two million pounds compensation. They considered this to be half the total value of their 68,613 registered slaves.

For the slaves the pleasure of emancipation was dulled by the imposition of a four-year period of apprenticeship during which they were supposed to work for their former masters in return for meagre wages. Not surprisingly, the scheme failed and slaves took up residence in unpopulated coastal areas where they suffered years of neglect. The wily planters turned to an alternative source of compliant labour: Indian migrants, known in Mauritius as 'the coolie trade'.

INDIAN MIGRATION Indian migrants had been in Mauritius since 1736 when Labourdonnais brought in 40 artisans from Pondicherry. In 1835, the planters began to recruit workers in India to replace the labour lost to them by emancipation. By 1838, there were 24,000 Indians in Mauritius and over 200,000 were brought in between 1840 and 1870 to meet the insatiable demands of the rapidly expanding sugar industry.

Recruitment ended in 1907, by which time the impact of Indian immigration had changed the course of the island's history. Now the majority, they came to wield influence in all spheres, not only by their contribution of an efficient workforce that sustained the economy, but also by a vigorous intellectual force in politics.

The political reforms of 1886, however, excluded the Indian population, although they launched the beginning of a parliamentary democracy. Universal franchise was finally granted only in 1959.

In 1901, Mohandas Gandhi (later Mahatma Gandhi) visited Mauritius and as a result sent Manillal Doctor, an Indian lawyer, to Port Louis in 1907 to organise the indentured labourers who had no say in politics and no civil rights. A Royal Commission from Britain visited in 1907 and made wide-ranging recommendations for the reorganisation of agriculture, the civil service, education and the constitution, under which only 2% of the population were then qualified to register as electors.

THE 20TH CENTURY AND POLITICAL CHANGE Party politics followed the constitutional reforms of 1886 with the 'Oligarques' of the conservative Parti de l'Ordre dominant over the 'democrats' of Action Libérale until the early 1920s. The socialist Mauritius Labour Party (MLP) founded in 1936 represented one side of the traditional two-party system with the Railliement Mauricien on the right. A multi-party system based on ethnic as well as political appeal evolved after 1950.

World War I brought suffering to the island with drastic cuts in shipping causing food shortages and price rises. There was a local campaign after the war for Mauritius to be returned to France but the so-called 'retrocessionist' candidates were heavily defeated in the 1921 general election.

World War II brought infrastructural development. The British based a fleet at Port Louis and Grand Port, as well as building an airport at Plaisance and a seaplane base at Baie du Tombeau. A large telecommunication station was built at Vacoas, although the first underwater telephone cable, linking South Africa to Australia, had been laid to Mauritius in 1901.

In the election held after the war, the MLP won the majority of seats in the Legislative Council set up under the 1948 constitution. This success was repeated in 1953. After the 1959 election (the first held following the introduction of universal adult franchise), Hindu doctor (later Sir) Seewoosagur Ramgoolam, leader of the MLP, became chief minister, then premier in 1965, holding the post until 1982. In 1968, Mauritius became an independent country within the Commonwealth of Nations, with Queen Elizabeth II as Head of State represented by a governor general.

In 1971, social and industrial unrest led by the Mouvement Militant Mauricien (MMM) resulted in a state of emergency. The party's leaders, including Paul Berenger, a Franco-Mauritian born in 1945, were jailed for a year.

In the election of 1982, the MMM, with Paul Berenger as general secretary and a Hindu, British-trained lawyer, Aneerood Jugnauth, as president, captured all 62 directly elected seats. Aneerood Jugnauth became prime minister with Berenger as his finance minister.

Tensions among the ministers resulted in a break when Berenger resigned with ten of his cabinet colleagues. Jugnauth formed a new party, the Mouvement Socialiste Militant (MSM), drawing on defectors from other parties and allying himself with Sir Seewoosagur's MLP and the Parti Mauricien Social Démocrate (PMSD).

The new alliance scored a victory that gave them 41 of the directly elected seats and five of the eight 'best loser' seats. (The 'best loser' system was devised by the British to ensure that every ethnic group has adequate representation.) Sir Seewoosagur became governor general.

Following the defection of some party members and the resignation of six parliamentarians because of a drug smuggling scandal, the next general election was held a year early, on 30 August 1987. This resulted in a win for the alliance of parties led by Prime Minister Aneerood Jugnauth. Knighted in 1988, Sir Aneerood Jugnauth became prime minister again after a general election in 1991, when he led an alliance of the MSM and MMM. In March 1992, Mauritius became a republic within the Commonwealth and later that year M Cassam Uteem, a former minister, was nominated as president.

At the general election held in December 1995, there was a curious repeat of history when, as in 1982, the opposition captured all the 60 seats on Mauritius and allies took the two seats on Rodrigues. The victors were an opposition coalition and their leader, Dr Navin Chandra Ramgoolam, son of the much-revered Sir Seewoosagur Ramgoolam, became prime minister.

Born in 1947, Dr Navin Ramgoolam is a Dublin-qualified medical practitioner and a barrister called to the Bar in London in 1993. He became leader of the Labour Party in 1990 and was elected to the National Assembly in 1991. In 1994, he formed an alliance with the MMM of Paul Berenger and it was this alliance that captured all the elected seats. However, on 18 June 1997, the Labour Party and MMM split from one another. The Labour Party ruled the country while the MMM headed the opposition.

By the time of the September 2000 elections, Navin Ramgoolam's popularity had fallen considerably. Many Mauritians felt he was out of touch with the island, having spent much of his life abroad, and allegations of corruption plagued his time in government. The elections saw Ramgoolam defeated by an alliance of the MSM and MMM, who won 50 seats in the parliament. In an unusual step, it was agreed that Aneerood Jugnauth would be prime minister for the first three years of the parliamentary term, followed by Paul Berenger for the second three.

February 2002 saw another unexpected shake-up for Mauritian politics. President Cassam Uteem, a Mauritian Muslim, was forced to resign after refusing to give his assent to the proposed prevention of terrorism legislation in the wake of the 11 September 2001 terrorist attacks in New York. His vice-president also resigned and on 25 February 2002 Karl Auguste Offman was sworn in as the third president of the Republic of Mauritius. Offman's term as president lasted just over a year, with Anerood Jugnauth assuming the role of president when Berenger became prime minister.

When he became prime minister in 2003, Paul Berenger was not only the first white but also the first non-Hindu prime minister since independence in 1968. His time as prime minister came to an end in July 2005, when his party was defeated by the newly formed Socialist Alliance and Dr Navin Ramgoolam once more became prime minister. The result was not unexpected with rising unemployment in the sugar and textile industries, high-profile figures resigning from the government to join the opposition alliance and allegations of corruption all conspiring against the governing MSM–MMM coalition.

GOVERNMENT AND POLITICS

Mauritius is a parliamentary democracy, with 62 members of parliament elected every five years by universal suffrage.

The role of the president, although important, is limited in powers to official and ceremonial procedures. Authority is delegated by him to the Council of Ministers, a body of ministers headed by the prime minister.

The prime minister is the member of the National Assembly (parliament) who appears to the president to command the support of the majority of its members.

Government by coalition is a common feature of Mauritian politics and reflects the way of life of the people. The class divisions and communal differences of the post-war period are gradually crumbling as the economic situation improves. Education, industrialisation and the improving prosperity have also helped people attain better status and heightened their aspirations.

This (or it could be due to religious restraint) seems to have created a willingness to avoid disruptive influences to the national and political well-being, thereby allowing for the compromises of coalition.

One of the main challenges facing any government of Mauritius is the constant effort that must be made to maintain harmony between the island's various ethnic groups. The growth of tourism has made this an even greater priority. It is no secret that many Mauritians of African descent feel disadvantaged and under-represented in politics. You only to have to visit the southwest of the island, the most Creole area, to see that this is one of the poorest parts of Mauritius. The social unrest that occurred following the death of the popular Creole singer, Kaya, in February 1999, is a reminder of how dangerous underlying discontent can be. (See box *Kaya*, page 166.)

NATIONAL FLAG The flag of Mauritius consists of four equal-width horizontal stripes. In descending order these are red, blue, yellow and green, so when the flag is flying, red is at the top. The colours have been interpreted as red for freedom and independence; blue for the Indian Ocean; yellow representing the light of independence shining over the nation; and green standing for the agriculture of Mauritius and showing the country's colour throughout the 12 months of the year.

A second interpretation maintains that the colours stand for the island's different religious and ethnic groups. Red represents the Hindus, blue the Catholic population, yellow the Tamils and green the Muslims.

Crest The crest of Mauritius reflects its past more than its present, flanked by a dodo and a stag, both clutching shoots of sugarcane. The shield portrays a medieval ship, presumably representing the island's discoverers, and three stylistic trees.

There is also a key and a shining star, depicting the country's motto that appears below it: STELLA CLAVISQUE MARIS INDICI (Star and key of the Indian Ocean).

The influence on the economy of Sir Robert Farquhar, the first British governor, only waned 168 years after his departure from Mauritius. Farquhar realised the value of an export-oriented economy but encouraged a reliance on one export only: sugar. It was not until 1985 that sugar was displaced as the country's main foreign exchange earner by the manufacturing sector.

The reliance on a one-crop economy meant that the prosperity of Mauritius depended on the world demand for sugar and on home climatic conditions. When both were favourable, Mauritius benefited.

This is what happened in the early 1970s when economic growth averaged 9% per year. The standard of living improved visibly; new houses were built of concrete blocks and electricity served 90% of the island's dwellings. However, the pace of economic advance slowed as the sugar boom fizzled out.

The salvation was the Export Processing Zone (EPZ) set up in 1970 to attract foreign, as well as to encourage local, investment. According to the 1995 report of the Chamber of Commerce, 'The EPZ which has been the main engine of growth for a decade is giving way to an economic growth supported more and more by local demand'. The report noted that, from a macro-economic point of view, there was an urgent need to reduce consumption and increase savings and investment. This was based on the observation that 'new shopping centres with modern concepts have been well received by the population. Their immediate success is evidence of the aspirations of the population for better services and greater choice'.

Inflation, which was 14.5% in 1981, dropped to 6.7% in 1985 and was running at 3.9% in 2003. Unemployment, which reached 25% of the registered workforce in 1983, had fallen to 8.8% in 2000 but has been rising steadily since then, reaching 11% in December 2004. There is no unemployment benefit.

There are currently about 500,000 people in full employment, and approximately a third of them are women. Unemployment is often through choice and since 1993 it has been necessary to import labour from abroad, mainly from Taiwan and Sri Lanka, for the construction and textile industries.

The challenge for the Mauritian economy as the 21st century begins is to look for new areas which can drive economic growth. Although sugar, textiles and tourism are likely to remain important, new avenues are opening up which take advantage of Mauritius's greatest natural asset: its skilled and multi-lingual workforce.

Offshore banking (see pages 82–3), pharmaceuticals, communications, publishing and information technology have already started to gain a foothold and it is perhaps these new industries that will direct Mauritius's economic development over the coming decades.

INDUSTRY When industrialisation began in the 1960s the objective was to produce locally the goods that were being imported, creating jobs and saving on foreign exchange. Small industries were set up by local entrepreneurs, encouraged by fiscal incentives. Scope for profitable expansion was limited, however, by the size and buying power of the local market.

The Yaoundé Convention, allowing African countries associated with the European Economic Community (EEC) to have access to European markets for their goods, provided the fillip Mauritius needed. An Export Processing Zone (the EPZ) was set up in 1970 and policy switched to the labour-intensive production of goods for export.

A package of fiscal incentives, including exemption from certain taxes and duties, freedom to repatriate capital and profits, and a guarantee against state takeovers was offered. Investors saw other advantages in the adaptability of an amenable workforce and in the network of sophisticated Mauritian entrepreneurs with whom to associate.

The scheme attracted investors from around the world, including the UK, France, Germany, Holland, India, South Africa, Hong Kong, Singapore, Taiwan and Australia.

In actual fact, more than half the companies set up under the EPZ legislation (and 50% of the capital invested) are under Mauritian, not foreign, control. New factories have opened up throughout the island with the benefits of employment in industry spreading to all areas.

The EPZ produces 95% of all Mauritius's industrial exports. Nearly 540 enterprises have been established under its banner and about 70,000 new jobs have been created. Nearly half the workforce are engaged in the knitwear industry.

The manufacturing sector is the largest employer in the country, with some 128,000 employees, and contributes 21% of the GDP. Although a variety of goods are produced, the textile industry dominates the manufacturing sector, accounting for 80% of its total earnings. In fact, Mauritius is amongst the world's largest exporters of woollen knitwear and produces clothing for numerous famous brands, such as BHS and Littlewoods in the UK. However, this sector is coming under pressure from cheaper producers such as China and Bangladesh. This is forcing textile companies like Floréal Knitwear to shift from producing basic products to more upmarket, niche products, as well as moving some of its production to countries with lower labour costs, such as Madagascar.

After the success of the EPZ, concern was expressed that the concentration on textiles could be as risky as the reliance on sugar had been. The industrial development strategy now aims for diversification and new target areas include electronics, information technology, jewellery and printing and publishing.

Meanwhile Mauritius has become world famous as a reliable supplier of manufactured goods. The 'made in Mauritius' label is familiar and much sought-after as the country gains a reputation for high standards of quality.

The Mauritius Export Development and Investment Authority (MEDIA) was opened in 1985 by government and private sector officials to promote the industrialisation process of the country, help industries find new markets for their products and attract the right type of entrepreneur to the EPZ. This has now been replaced by the Mauritius Investment and Development Authority (MIDA), which promotes the export of goods and services from Mauritius. For further information see *Chapter 3, Business*, pages 81–3. The success in displacing sugar's importance to the economic base of Mauritius was crucial. The industrialisation of sugar itself is also taking place with such by-products as molasses, rum, ethyl alcohol and acetic acid.

AGRICULTURE AND FISHING

Sugar When the sugarcane is fully grown, the roads of the flat lands in the north of Mauritius are like tunnels through the cane fields. With nothing to be seen except the blue sky above and the green ribbons of cane waving in the wind, it is easy to imagine that the whole of the island is one vast sugar plantation.

While the overall economy may be less reliant on sugar than it once was, it still dominates the agricultural sector with nearly 90% of agricultural land being used for sugarcane. However, the proportion of land devoted to sugarcane is in decline. Recently, some of the large sugar estates have begun to diversify, establishing so-called Integrated Resource Schemes (IRS) consisting of hotels, luxury villas and golf courses (see page 46). Bel Ombre in the south and Médine in the west are two such examples.

The number of sugar factories has also been in steady decline for some years. In the 19th century there were 250 sugar factories. Now tall, crumbling chimney stacks are all that remain – monuments to the early days of the industry that made Mauritius.

Sugarcane was introduced from Batavia (Jakarta) by the Dutch in 1639. A plaque recording the date can be seen set into a portion of stone wall standing in a palm grove on the Ferney Sugar Estate near Vieux Grand Port.

It was the French Governor, Labourdonnais, who began sugar production in earnest. He set up the first sugar factory at Villebague in the centre of the island in 1744, using slave labour. By the time the British arrived in 1810 there were 10,000 acres under cultivation. The British Governor, Farquhar, persuaded the settlers to expand their cane cultivation because of the crop's ability to withstand cyclones.

It was not until the abolition of duties on Mauritius-grown sugar in 1825, which allowed it to be imported into Britain on the same terms as sugar from the Caribbean, that the industry really began to thrive.

The early sugar mills relied on slaves and oxen to turn the rollers to crush the cane. The juice was extracted and collected in cauldrons where foreign matter was skimmed off. Then it was boiled, using the *bagasse* (crushed cane) as fuel, and the syrup was cooled until it crystallised into sugar. A copy of an early sugar mill showing how sugar was produced in 1770 can be seen in action at Domaine les Pailles (see page 180).

Animal-driven mills were gradually replaced by machinery, with the last one closing in 1853. The last sugar windmill was decommissioned in 1862, by which time production had risen to 130,000 tonnes.

Owing to the island's volcanic beginnings, which caused the soil to be strewn with boulders and stones, every inch of the land used for cane growing has had to be cleared by hand. The gaunt piles of rock in the midst of the cane fields are a forceful reminder of the toil of the men and women who worked in the blisteringly hot sun to clean these patches in the volcanic blanket.

The stony nature of the soil still restricts mechanical harvesting, although tractors and forklifts are used to transport the cut cane for processing. The ox-carts that can be seen on country lanes are carrying cane for smallholders.

The success of the sugar industry is the reason for the complicated network of roads in the island, in which strangers invariably get lost. Originally, sugar was shipped around the coast to Port Louis by boat. Trails were opened up so the inland estates could send their sugar for shipment by cart. These trails became makeshift roads and then gave way to railways.

The first railway line was between Port Louis and the north and opened in 1864. Six branch lines were in operation by 1904. Smaller railways ran between the rows of cane to link with the main lines. The main railway system operated until 1964, when it was closed down as being uneconomic, since its use for profitable freight was confined to the crop season. One of the few remaining locomotives used to haul the sugarcane trolleys rests in splendour on public display in the unusual setting of La Vanille Réserve des Mascareignes (see pages 155–6).

The soil and climate of Mauritius are ideally suited to sugar production; even the rains that fringe the cyclones are beneficial. The sight of cane labourers wearing enormous floppy hats, their arms and legs swathed in protective clothing as they patiently tend the fields, reveals their extreme dedication.

New cane is planted in cycles to be harvested after 14 to 18 months. The ratoons (shoots) appear from the second year onward. They are harvested every 12 months during the June to December cropping period.

When cane is cut, it is transported as soon as possible to the nearest factory where it is bulk fed into mechanical crushers. A constant supply of cane is needed to maintain production, so the pace is frenetic. On one occasion a load of cane was fed into the crushers so quickly that a labourer's bicycle was gobbled up by the machinery too, causing considerable damage to the plant.

The factories are self-powered, as they were in the 19th century, only now it is more scientific. The *bagasse* is used to produce electricity, not only for the factories but to augment the national supply.

The factories that remain have become ultra-efficient in sugar production and highly adaptable. They are also required to cultivate other crops, such as potatoes and tomatoes, which are planted between the rows of cane. Some estates have branched out into growing flowers, particularly the red, wax-like anthuriums (*Anthurium andraeanum*) for export, and into pineapple and watercress cultivation, hotel development and other projects.

Although sugar's importance in the economy may be dwindling, it still plays a vital role, representing about 22% of exports and about 6% of GDP. However, the industry is now facing one of its most challenging periods. Over the next few years, the European Union is due to steadily reduce the price it pays for sugar. This, coupled with an increasingly competitive international environment, will undoubtedly cause further sugar mills to close and increased unemployment.

Not surprisingly, a typical Mauritian has a sweet tooth. From childhood, sugar has been an accepted part of the daily diet. Brightly coloured sugar confections shaped like the mountains of Mauritius are sold by hawkers in every town and village. Tea is always served with sugar. While its importance to the economy may be diminishing, sugar's popularity with Mauritians is unlikely to turn sour.

The history of the sugar industry and the processes of sugar production are brilliantly explained at l'Aventure du Sucre, a museum housed in the former Beau Plan sugar factory near Pamplemousses (see page 135).

Tea The tea you drink in Mauritius is produced on the island and comes in a variety of locally inspired flavours, such as vanilla and coconut.

Teas with the best flavour are grown at heights greater than the altitude of the tea plantations in Mauritius. However, the Mauritius tea is popular for blending and it is the island's second major crop. Much of Mauritius's tea is exported, while the balance is sold on the local market.

The central highlands around Curepipe are the main plantation area. The cooler temperatures and the greater rainfall of the highland plateau suit tea. Being a plant that grows as a sturdy bush with deep roots and a long life, it can withstand winds of cyclonic force.

Tea's roots in Mauritius actually go back to the 18th century, when it was grown by settlers for their own use. From the early 1960s, extensive planting was pursued until, 25 years later, there were 40km² of land under tea.

The crew-cut tops of the bushes have a uniform appearance, thanks to the nimble fingers of tea pickers and to an electric shearer. The picking is done with incredible dexterity early in the morning, mainly by women. Only the top two or three young leaves are removed from the branches. The green leaf is then bagged and transported to a factory where it dries, ferments and is sorted and prepared for packing.

In recent years the fortunes of the tea industry have fluctuated, with its demise seeming likely in the late 1970s. Then the Tea Development Authority was reconstructed, factories expanded with new processing equipment, tea plantation land was rehabilitated and inducements offered for improved cultivation methods. By the mid 1990s, with tea prices dropping and sugar prices rising, some tea bushes were being torn up to be replaced by sugar. Tea, being labour intensive, used to be regarded as a good crop when there was an abundance of labour. With labour in short supply and with Mauritian tea having to compete with that produced by traditional tea-growing countries like Sri Lanka, its value to the economy of Mauritius is doubtful.

It is worth taking the time to visit the working tea factory of Bois Chéri, near Curepipe, and see the production in progress (see page 157).

Tobacco Tobacco has been grown in Mauritius since the days of the Dutch and for the past 80 years has been a major local industry. In 1926, the British American Tobacco Company established itself in Mauritius and today their factory is on the outskirts of Port Louis just north of Camp Yoloff.

Although it is a major crop, tobacco is not exported and often falls short of local demand. Most of the tobacco is Virginia flue-cured, although Amarello air-cured is also produced. It is grown on small plantations by private planters under the supervision of the state-controlled Tobacco Board. The main areas are in the northern districts of the island.

In recent years, tobacco production has declined and the volume of imported tobacco has increased. At the same time, smoking in Mauritius has been in decline.

Other crops The staple diet of Mauritians is rice, which has to be imported. However, enough potatoes for local demand are now grown, in excess of 20,000 tons a year. Maize production is increasing, although a substantial proportion has to be imported.

Groundnuts, onions, garlic, manioc, various leaf vegetables and spices are grown locally, as well as the tiny, round Mauritian tomato known quaintly as *pomme d'amour* (love apple). The growing of pulses such as peas and beans is being encouraged.

Fruits abound, especially pineapples, which are offered, already peeled in spirals, for sale at every major street corner and bus station. Bananas, papayas and traditional tropical fruit such as mangoes, lychees, watermelons, coconuts and citrus thrive and are of commercial importance.

Coffee is grown only on a small scale because it is in flower during the risky cyclone season. It can be found in the Chamarel area of the south, growing in sheltered places by the ridges of the hillsides.

Enough poultry and eggs are produced for domestic needs. Cattle-rearing has been developed on some sugar estates as part of the diversification policy but meat is still imported. Goat meat is popular and is produced commercially. Pigs and sheep are also raised, but in smaller numbers than cattle or goats. Venison, too, is farm reared.

Fishing The romantic sight of a small rowing boat, bobbing peacefully in a sun-drenched lagoon while its crew pull up a net full of fish, is a glimpse of the tradition behind an expanding fishing industry. Mauritius has 1.7 million km² of marine surface area, known as its Exclusive Economic Zone (EEZ), which it is intent on developing.

Since the first settlers came to Mauritius, fishing has been confined to the lagoon and offshore lagoon areas. Most fishermen, being Creoles of small means, do not have the equipment or the inclination for fishing far beyond the reefs. They use traditional methods, with wooden (or sometimes fibreglass) boats of 6–7m in length. The crew fish with handlines, basket traps, seines, gill nets and harpoons. These artisanal fishing grounds, the only source of fresh fish supply, spread over an area of 1,020km² for Mauritius and 1,380km² for Rodrigues.

Banks fishery is conducted by motherships using small dories with outboard motors, operated by a crew of three. The mother vessel remains at sea for 35 to 55 days with the dories bringing in their catch for gutting and freezing twice a day.

The mothership's load is landed at the fishing port of Trou Fanfaron in Port Louis as frozen fish, more than 90% of it *Lethrinus mahsena* (or *Sanguineus*), known locally as Dame Berri.

The areas fished are the St Brandon, Nazareth and Saya de Malha banks on the Mauritius/Seychelles ridge, and the Chagos Bank around the Chagos Archipelago submarine plateaux, which lie 20–25m below the surface.

Tuna fishing for mainly skipjack (*Katsuwonus pelamis*) and yellow-fin tuna (*Thunnus albacares*) is a major industrial activity. Tuna canning started in 1972 when most of the fish had to be imported from the Maldives.

International big-game fishing competitions are held frequently and are popular with tourists who pay high fees to participate. The catch is mainly marlin (*makaira*) and swordfish (*Xiphias gladius*). Smoked marlin is a delicious delicacy served in most upmarket hotels and restaurants.

If you like eating fish, look out for Mama Rouge (orange rock cod: *Cephalopholis aurantius*), a grouper. It is much in demand, with a flesh that tastes like crab. Mauritian cooks complain that it is priced beyond their pockets or exported to Réunion where people pay more for it. A fish frequently to be found on menus is Capitaine (*Lethrinus nebulosos*), a snapper sold frozen as *poisson la Perle*.

Fish farming is an old tradition, using *barachois*, or artificial sea ponds, to breed finfish, crabs and oysters. The local oyster (*Crassostrea cuculata*) lives in brackish water on rocks and mangrove roots. Efforts to introduce faster-growing species from the USA were tried without success.

A few species of seaweed with commercial importance for the food, cosmetic and medical industries have been identified, as have four marine shrimp species with potential for commercial aquaculture.

The growing of freshwater fish is another possibility. Mauritius, being an oceanic island remote from continental land masses, is limited in endemic freshwater fauna and does not have any freshwater fish or crustaceans suitable for culture, but researchers are experimenting with introducing a wide variety of species for commercial cultivation.

Sea salt, incidentally, is produced in Mauritius, with salt pans along the coast in the Black River district, in the area known as Les Salines. The salt is used for local consumption only.

Development of the EEZ is at present confined to the expansion of all sections of the fishing industry. For the future, however, studies have revealed a wealth of minerals on the ocean floor and there is also the possibility of ocean thermal energy conversion. It all seems a long way from the tranquil sight, beloved by tourists, of a fisherman casting his net in a picturesque lagoon.

TOURISM The first tourists to arrive in Mauritius by air were 50 passengers and crew on a Qantas flight from Australia to South Africa, who landed in 1952. The airline agents were asked in advance to find overnight accommodation for them and, seeing the possibilities, bought a colonial mansion in Curepipe. This became the Park Hotel and is now the administrative offices of the island's Beachcomber group of hotels.

Today, tourism is the island's third-largest foreign-exchange earner after the EPZ and sugar. The industry provides employment for nearly 20,000 people. Since earnings from tourism circulate very quickly into the economy, the impact is considerable. However, tourism has also been a factor in the increase in imports, especially foodstuffs.

In 2004, Mauritius attracted about 720,000 tourists. Of these, 13.4% came from Réunion, 12.9% came from the UK, 7.3% from Germany, 7.3% from South Africa and 5.7% from Italy. France (excluding Réunion) topped the charts with 29.3% of tourist arrivals.

The popularity of Mauritius with French tourists is not only because of the common language; with cheap flights from France to Réunion and a separate ticket on to Mauritius, the French can reach Mauritius at much less expense than their European neighbours flying direct. For them, too, the cost of living in Mauritius is remarkably low compared with that of France and Réunion. Many – whether affluent middle-aged or youthful backpackers – visit as independent travellers and keep the non-package hotels and guesthouses and self-catering units in business.

Studies have been made on the careful development of tourism in the future and the prospects are, with careful management, that tourism will continue to be an asset and not a blight on the island.

At present the government policy of preserving Mauritius as an upmarket destination continues. Charter flights are not allowed and the emphasis throughout the industry is on quality rather than quantity.

The future of the tourist industry looks bright in view of the island's obvious attractions. Many of the hotels are expanding their capacity and there seems to be a natural limit on new hotels being built because of the shortage of sites. By maximising the use of hotels with a year-round season, the industry can still grow without becoming a monster that swallows the very attractions that make Mauritius worth visiting. However, because of competition from other holiday destinations, hoteliers and their staff will have to avoid complacency to prevent Mauritius losing its image as a genuinely pleasant place to stay and becoming, perhaps, as charmless as some of the Caribbean islands.

The Mauritius Tourism Promotion Authority is responsible for marketing the country as a tourist destination. As well as offices in Port Louis, the MTPA have representatives in many counties worldwide (see *Chapter 3, Gathering information*, pages 42–3).

INFORMATION TECHNOLOGY In an attempt to reduce its dependence on sugar and textiles, the government has launched an ambitious project to make Mauritius a 'cyber island'. A few kilometres outside Port Louis, Cyber City is gradually rising out of the sugarcane fields. Plans are to build a telecommunications network linking Portugal and Malaysia, via South Africa and Mauritius. Cyber City will provide computing on demand, an internet data centre to back up data and servers for web-hosting, e-commerce and financial transactions. The project is backed by some big names in the IT world, including Hewlett Packard.

It is early days for this industry in Mauritius and there will need to be considerable investment in IT education if the local population is to benefit from the jobs that are created. Nevertheless, Mauritius is seen as relatively secure and stable, which will encourage companies to take advantage of Cyber City's facilities.

PEOPLE

With an estimated population of 1.3 million, you would expect Mauritius to feel crowded, but it doesn't. Although the main towns are frequently teeming with pedestrians and the roads jammed with cars, deserted areas of beach and forest are easy to find.

The population is overwhelmingly young with about 25% being under 15 years of age and only 6.5% over 65. In 2003, life expectancy at birth was 68.7 years for a man and 75.6 years for a woman.

INTOXICATING MIXTURE In the enthusiastic prose of the MTPA, 'the people are unique for their sheer diversity – Indians, Africans, Europeans, Chinese and an intoxicating range of mixtures'.

It is potentially an explosive mixture, although few tensions are apparent to the visitor. Instead there is an admirable respect for the beliefs and lifestyles of others.

Mauritians are usually delighted to speak to visitors, although the stranger may have to start up the conversation. The ethnic diversity means that, unless dressed like a typical tourist, you won't stand out and can wander around without being the object of curiosity outside the tourist areas. If people approach to talk to you, it will probably be a genuine offer of help or hospitality, rather than a sales ploy.

Since all Mauritians are descended from immigrants (many have grandparents who were born in another country), the ethnic groups are distinctive in appearance, religion and language, although the distinctions are getting blurred and the many ethnic labels have now been whittled down to the General Population, the Indo-Mauritians and the Sino-Mauritians.

General Population The General Population (those who can't be tagged as being of Indian or Chinese descent) makes up about 30% of the islanders. They are the whites and the Creoles (people of mixed European and African origin), with European influences of culture and religion.

Mauritian Creoles are a diverse group, the result of intermarriage that cuts across class and ethnic considerations. They constitute about a quarter of the total population and form a large working class. Their influence is a unifying one and their language, Creole, is the *lingua franca* of the entire population, spoken by all races.

The whites are descended from European, mostly French, settlers. Curiously, despite 158 years of British presence, only a handful of families think of themselves as Anglo-Mauritian. Franco-Mauritians make up only 2–3% of the population but hold much of the island's private wealth and dominate the professions and management.

Indo-Mauritians Indian immigrants arrived in numbers after the emancipation of slaves in 1835, although some came later from the Indian subcontinent. By 1861, the Indian population outnumbered the whites and Creoles by 192,634 to 117,416, forming the ethnic and cultural majority. They now make up 68% of the population.

There are two major groups by religious definition: Hindus (some of whom are actually Tamils) and Muslims. Many of the Muslims migrated independently from India and Pakistan as traders.

To confuse the situation, intermarriage has resulted in an Indo-Mauritian element being introduced into the (Christian) General Population as well.

As well as forming the backbone of the labouring and agricultural communities, the Indo-Mauritians have developed through a history of industrial and political agitation to take vital roles in the economic and political life of the island.

Sino-Mauritians Mauritians of Chinese origin are a small but ubiquitous ethnic community forming about 3% of the population. The first Chinese migrants came from Canton in the 19th century but the largest group is the Hakkas, from the province of Honan in northeast China.

There is a large Chinese quarter in Port Louis but Sino-Mauritians are to be found throughout the island, mostly as retailers or traders.

Their noticeable contribution to the development and unification of Mauritius is Chinese cuisine, which is found in private homes, as well as in restaurants and food stalls.

In spite of this wide variety of peoples, one of the attractions of Mauritius is its ethnic mix, not its ethnic division. Former Prime Minister of Mauritius, Sir

Anerood Jugnauth, summed up his people aptly when he said: 'The single great wealth of this island nation is its people, a multi-national group with an amazing blend of cultures, a political maturity admired by friend and foe alike and a jealously guarded freedom … The hospitality of Mauritians is legendary and spontaneous.'

LANGUAGE

The official language of Mauritius is English, although most Mauritians are more comfortable speaking French. The language of the people, however, is Creole.

Although the Mauritians working in the tourism industry speak good English, the English-speaking visitor should not count on being understood everywhere on the island. English is the medium of teaching in schools and the working language of government and business, but beyond school and work it is rarely used. Fewer than 3,000 Mauritians speak English at home.

French, however, is spoken at home by about 35,000 Mauritians. It is used in polite and formal circumstances, although not at government level. The daily newspapers are predominantly in French with occasional articles in English.

Creole is the *lingua franca* of Mauritius, understood and spoken by all Mauritians. It is the home language of about 52% of the population but, incredibly, is neither taught in schools nor officially recognised as a language, and has no popular written form. It is a *patois*, structurally distinct from French but borrowing most of its vocabulary from that tongue, although pronunciation is different. It evolved from the pidgin used by the French masters of the 18th century to communicate with their slaves, also incorporating words from African and Malagasy dialects.

Its popularity stems from the ease with which it can be learnt. Since the African population was disinclined to learn Indian or Chinese languages, the new immigrants of the 19th century took to Creole as a simple means of communicating. It requires little intellectual effort to speak, and English, French and Indian words can be adapted by 'Creolising' them. There are no grammatical rules and foreigners settling in Mauritius soon speak it without embarrassment at making errors.

Creole's lowly origins have caused the language to be treated with contempt in the past but its unifying value as the one language that all Mauritians speak and understand is clear. While it shares characteristics with the Creole spoken in the Caribbean and the Bayous of Louisiana, a Mauritian would not immediately understand, for example, the Creole of Dominica. Even the Creole of neighbouring Réunion is not identical.

For the visitor wanting to speak Creole, there are several locally printed Creole phrase books on sale in Mauritius. The language is written phonetically and the hardest part seems to be to understand the odd spelling used, such as *ahn-kohr* (meaning 'more'). Although it sounds an aggressive language it is very colourful, rich in clichés and ribaldry. For useful phrases, see *Appendix 1, Language*, pages 325–6.

The main mother tongue of the country's largest ethnic group is Hindi and is spoken at home by over 100,000 people. While Hindi is the medium for religious ceremonies and is looked on as a sign of education and prestige, the Indian equivalent of Creole is Bhojpuri, spoken by more than 200,000. Tamil was actually the first Indian language spoken in Mauritius and today is spoken at home by about 35,000 people. Other Indian languages spoken as mother tongues are Urdu, Telegu, Marathi and Gujarathi.

Arabic is also spoken, although most of the preaching in the mosques is in Creole. Less than a third of the Chinese community (about 6,000) speak Chinese languages, including Hakka, Mandarin and Cantonese.

Today, there are 22 languages spoken in Mauritius, an extraordinary number for little over a million people.

RELIGION

There are nearly 90 different religious denominations represented in Mauritius. Since there is complete freedom of religion, new sects or groupings have emerged within the main religions of Hinduism, Christianity and Islam. Throughout Mauritius there are Gothic-style churches, high-domed temples, minareted mosques and ornate pagodas in the most unlikely places – the middle of a sugarcane field, by the racecourse – testifying to the strong Mauritian belief in religion. It is not fanaticism but an enduring way of life, which Mauritians relish.

HINDUISM About 52% of Mauritians are followers of one of the many Hindu sects, the majority being Sanatanists, or Orthodox Hindus.

Devout Hindus proclaim their faith with small shrines and red or white pennants fluttering outside their homes. Several villages have Hindu temples, the largest being at Triolet. Saints of other religions, especially the Roman Catholic Père Laval, whose shrine is at Sainte Croix, are also worshipped by Hindus.

Local Tamils have their own religion which has evolved since 1771, when the French granted permission for a Tamil temple in Port Louis. The reformist movement of Arya Samaj, in which worship is of the spirit Brahma and not of statues or idols, took hold from 1910, when the first 'Samaj' was opened in Port Louis. Tamils sometimes indulge in spectacular forms of worship in honour of different deities, such as fire-walking and piercing their flesh with enormous needles (see *Chapter 3, Working hours, public holidays and festivals*, pages 69–72). As with Christianity, there is a variety of sects including Kabir Panthis, a reformist group, Rabidass, and the Hare Rama Krishna sect.

CHRISTIANITY Christianity was the first religion in Mauritius and is now the religion both of the General Population and of more than 80% of the Sino-Mauritians. Roman Catholicism became the official religion of the Ile de France in 1721, spreading with the French conversion of their slaves and still permitted to flourish after the British arrived. There is a Roman Catholic cathedral, St Louis, in Port Louis.

Anglicans, Presbyterians, and the evangelical Christian religions such as the Assembly of God and Adventists all play a part in society, as do at least a dozen other denominations including Jehovah's Witnesses, Methodists and Swedenborgians.

With its various sects, Christianity is the second-largest faith in the country, and about 30% of the population are Christians of some kind. In Rodrigues, 97% of the population is Roman Catholic.

ISLAM The Muslims of Mauritius form about 16% of the total population. The majority consists of Sunni Muslims and is divided into three subgroups: Sunni Hanfites, Sunni Surtis and Meimons. The Meimons are a small aristocracy with responsibility for the best-known mosque in Mauritius, the Jummah (Friday) Mosque in Port Louis.

The Shi'ite Muslims are very few and are subdivided into groups. One is the Cocknies from Cochin in the southwest of India, who came as boat builders to Mauritius. Since intermarrying with Creoles they have created a people known as Creole Lascars.

CHINESE RELIGIONS The Chinese religions are almost dying out since the majority of Sino-Mauritians have embraced Roman Catholicism. However, Buddhism and Confucianism are still practised by around 2% of the population.

The first Chinese temple was opened in Port Louis in 1846. Other temples have since been opened by the Cantonese Nam Shun Fooye Koon society and the Hakka Heeh Foh society.

EDUCATION

The education system in Mauritius is based on the British model and is free up to university level. Education up to the age of 16 was recently made compulsory. The literacy rate among the younger generation is high and over 95% of all children attend school.

The education boom began in the 1960s, with the opening of scores of private colleges. Free education at secondary level was introduced in 1977 with an immediate doubling of the number of students enrolled, and with new schools being opened by the government.

The majority of schools are state run, but a significant number are controlled by the Roman Catholic Education Authority and the Hindu Education Authority.

Lessons are conducted mostly in English, whilst French is taught. Pupils also have the opportunity to learn Indian and Chinese languages. The majority of papers for public examinations are marked in the UK.

The University of Mauritius at Le Réduit was opened in 1965, originally to train civil servants in preparation for independence. It now runs schools of Administration, Agriculture and Technology. The Mauritius Institute of Education trains the country's schoolteachers and is responsible for the national certificate of primary education. The Mahatma Gandhi Institute at Moka concentrates on African and Asian studies.

CULTURE

Each of Mauritius's ethnic groups and religions brings its own unique qualities to the island's rich and varied culture. An exciting variety of cuisine, musical styles and languages are a part of everyday life.

MUSIC Mauritians grow up with music and dancing playing an important role in their lives: at family gatherings, festivals and celebrations.

Ubiquitous is the *séga* (pronounced *say-ga*), which evolved from the spontaneous dances of African and Malagasy slaves. At night, after a day's toiling in the cane fields, slaves used improvised instruments to create a primitive music to which they could dance and forget their woes. At times, this meant defying their masters' prohibition of music and dancing, which aimed to sever the slaves from their African and Malagasy roots.

Songs were often about the slaves' plight and were highly critical of their masters. Girls danced to songs composed and sung by their admirers while the spectators encouraged them with hand clapping, foot stomping and chanting. The more impassioned the lyrics, the more heated the music and the more tempestuous the dancing.

On Mauritius's accession to independence, *séga* was adopted as the national dance and it has been flourishing and evolving ever since. Traditional *séga* is a courtship drama, beginning slowly with couples dancing apart from each other. As the beat intensifies, they shuffle closer together, hips swinging in time, but they never quite touch. The girl will sink to her knees at the cry of *en bas*, leaning back

23

in the manner of a limbo dancer passing under a pole. Her partner leans over her, still not touching, as they both shimmer and shake, while the music races to a crescendo. The music slows and the partners retreat. What makes *séga* unique is the combination of musical influences it has absorbed over the centuries, until it has assumed its own immediately recognisable beat. Like the *ka-danse* or *zouk* music of the French West Indies, also sung in Creole *patois*, it has a similarity to Latin American music in its jaunty rhythms. *Séga* is as prolific on Rodrigues and Réunion as it is in Mauritius, but each of the islands has developed its own distinctive version.

Descendents of the primitive instruments used by the slaves can still be seen in *séga* bands today. Vital to *séga* is the distinctive drum beat provided by the *ravane*, a goatskin tambourine. The *maravane* is a container (either wooden or fashioned from a gourd) filled with seeds or pebbles, which is shaken like the *maracas*. A triangle beaten with vigour adds a carillon voice echo, just as a cowbell does in *ka-danse*.

Séga is a fantastic dance with a wonderful, joyful music that seizes spectators with an urge to join in, which they are encouraged to do at hotel performances. At hotel shows, the men will usually wear the traditional pedal pushers and a colourful shirt, while the women are sensational in a billowing skirt.

Kaya, the popular Creole singer who was found dead in a police cell in February 1999, pioneered a new musical style in the late 1980s: *séggae*, a blend of *reggae* and *séga*. Kaya's work has been continued by his fellow Creole musicians and the mellow *séggae* is now popular throughout the western Indian Ocean islands (see box *Kaya*, page 166).

ARCHITECTURE Creole architecture can be appreciated both in small, simple dwellings and in grand colonial mansions, such as Eureka (see page 180). A charming characteristic feature of such buildings is the carved wooden or metal fringes that decorate the roof, the *lambrequin*. Sadly, examples of colonial architecture, such as Government House in Port Louis, are sometimes overwhelmed by the modern monstrosities erected next to them.

Contemporary architecture in Mauritius mostly finds expression in new hotels since new houses tend to be standard, cyclone-proof concrete boxes. The Curepipe market building, with concrete culverts upturned like gigantic organ pipes, is a most remarkable example of modern public architecture. More pleasing is the rustic style of the Royal Palm, Dinarobin and Casuarina Village hotels, which are a tribute to the ingenuity of Mauritian architect Maurice Giraud.

2

Natural History and Conservation

VOLCANIC ORIGINS OF FRAGILE ECOSYSTEMS

Around 7½ million years ago, the lava that created Mauritius rose above sea level, throwing up the mountain ranges of Grand Port, Moka and Black River. Later, light grey rock, also of volcanic origin, was scattered across the island in a northeast–southwest axis, giving rise to Bassin Blanc, Trou aux Cerfs and the Kanaka Crater. For 200,000 years, the island's volcanoes have been extinct and fragile ecosystems evolved gently in a predator-free haven.

First to appear on the lava formations were pioneer plants, like lichens, mosses and ferns. These were followed by other plants, seeds of which were brought by birds or washed on to the shores by the sea. In time, most of the island was swathed in lush rainforest. Where rainfall was lower, palm savanna replaced forest.

Some invertebrates, birds and bats found their way to Mauritius deliberately; others came accidentally due to gale-force winds. Reptiles (and more invertebrates) arrived by means of floating logs or driftwood. In time these evolved into a myriad of species unique to Mauritius. When examining Mauritian fauna in terms of its links elsewhere, connections with the other Indian Ocean islands, Africa and Asia are apparent.

Man's arrival in the Mascarenes signalled a wave of extinctions paralleled only by that which occurred in the Hawaiian archipelago. Magnificent tropical hardwood forests were felled for construction, export and agriculture. It is not clear exactly how many endemic plant species were lost. Today, only token remnants of the original forests remain, mostly in the Black River Gorges National Park. But even there, fast-growing introduced plants have swamped the indigenous species.

With the original forests went a remarkable ensemble of animals, the most famed of which is the dodo (*dronte*). Also wiped out quickly – as in the other Mascarenes – were herds of giant tortoises and, offshore, the gentle, vulnerable dugong. Apart from the dodo, at least 20 species of endemic birds were exterminated.

The situation was worsened considerably by the introduction of man's ghastly, invasive animal entourage: dogs, cats, rats, monkeys, rabbits, wild pigs, goats and deer all wreaked havoc on the island ecosystem, just as they have done on other islands around the globe. Further introductions were tenrecs (similar to hedgehogs) from Madagascar, mongooses and musk shrews, all of which have affected native fauna adversely. Snakes were also introduced, along with a host of birds, most of which now far outnumber the few remaining indigenous varieties.

By 1970, the situation for the remaining endemic Mauritian plants and animals looked horribly bleak. Some conservation organisations abroad wrote the Mascarenes off as 'paradise lost'. In the mid 1970s, the Durrell Wildlife Conservation Trust (then the Jersey Wildlife Preservation Trust) and the Mauritian government stepped in. (See box on page 192 for details of the DWCT's work.)

ENDEMIC AND INDIGENOUS FLORA with Dr Ehsan Dulloo

The published figure for plant species endemic to the Mascarenes is 700, but this is likely to change following current revision of certain families. Of these, about 311 species are endemic to Mauritius only (Strahm, 1994).

Widespread habitat destruction has rendered many endemic plants extremely rare: some species are now down to just one or two specimens. Indigenous species, which are shared with Réunion and/or Rodrigues, have stood a better chance of survival. However, as on Réunion and Rodrigues, most of the flora you'll see on Mauritius is of introduced species.

To find examples of the impressive tropical hardwood trees that once covered much of Mauritius, go to the Black River Gorges National Park, where many are still represented. Only approximately 1.9% of Mauritius's virgin forest remains, and most of it is found in this national park.

ISLAND COMMUNITIES

Jonathan Hughes

Remote islands throughout the world house rather special communities of animals and plants. In order to colonise an isolated island a species must pass three great challenges. The first challenge is to arrange transportation, the second to establish a stable population upon arrival, and the third to adapt to the island's habitats. At each stage the chance of failure is high, but with luck, and a certain degree of 'evolutionary skill', some inevitably succeed.

Species arrive on remote islands either by 'active' means, such as swimming or flying, or by 'passive' means, such as floating with ocean and air currents or hitching a ride on or in another individual. This degree of mobility is not available to all animal and plant groups, hence on isolated archipelagos there is often a characteristic assemblage of flying animals such as birds, bats and insects, light animals such as spiders and micro-organisms, buoyant animals such as tortoises and snakes, and plants employing edible seeds such as fruit trees, airborne seeds such as grasses, or floating seeds such as the coconut palm. Large land mammals, amphibians and freshwater fish have obvious difficulties in colonising remote islands and are therefore often absent, unless introduced by humans.

Assuming the problem of transport is overcome, there is then the task of establishing a permanent population on the island. Pioneers with the highest chance of success are single pregnant females, or in the case of plants, individuals able to self-fertilise. Flying species may arrive en masse, while species carried by currents must chance successive landings on the same island.

As populations establish, the animal and plant community begins to exploit the island's resources, and some animals take on very unusual roles in the community, but one role that is left vacant is that of the large, fierce predator at the top of the food chain. Large predators need a lot of space and a lot of resources. Without an extensive range there simply isn't enough food to support a population of such animals. Hence, on all but the largest of islands, large predators are absent, leaving meat-eating to smaller, less demanding species.

The absence of large predators has a profound effect on species that are normally on their menu – their worries are over. Ground-foraging birds, with no need for a quick escape, tend to lose the ability to fly, marooning themselves in the process. The downfall of Mauritius's most famous former resident, the dodo, was a lack of fear, evidence of its worry-free lifestyle. Even where flightless birds are absent today, most remote islands have had them in the past. Island giants, such as the giant tortoises which used to wander through the Mauritius scrub, are also indications of a short food chain. Free from

Undoubtedly the island's best-known hardwood, the Mauritius ebony (*Diospyros tesselaria*) was in particularly high demand because it has the darkest wood of any tree. Its congener on Réunion (*D. borbonica*) is still quite plentiful but the Mauritian species was almost wiped out. Other impressive protected hardwoods found in Black River Gorges include various species of the genera *Mimusops* and *Sideroxylon*, as well as *Labourdonnaisia glauca*. Quite a few of the rare, slow-growing hardwoods are shared with Réunion, such as the takamaka (*Calophyllum tacamahaca*), the 'guinea-fowl' tree (*Tarenna borbonica*) and the 'bois blanc' (*Hernandia mascarenensis*).

There are 89 species of orchid found in Mauritius. Of those, 94% are endemic to the Mascarenes/Madagascar region. Nine species are endemic to Mauritius only. Certain orchids, like *Oenillia aphrodite* and *Angraecum eburneum*, have become rare, so attempts are being made to conserve them on Ile aux Aigrettes, where they can be seen in the wild. (For details of visits to Ile aux Aigrettes, see page 154.)

predators, but in stiff competition with each other, the bigger, stronger individuals tend to survive and the smaller, meeker ones don't, so that, over time, the population attains giant proportions.

Although a remote island offers unusual opportunities, it cannot carry an infinite number of animals and plants. As each new population arrives, the competition for food and space increases, and the community has to adjust. The pressure to adapt is intense and species change their characteristics dramatically in a short time. Less mobile species such as inland birds and plants, isolated from their mainland ancestors, soon spread throughout the various habitats found on the island and gradually adapt to each one; after a period of time the original founding species evolves into a string of new species. This explains why many of the animals and plants found on remote islands are endemics – types found nowhere else in the world.

Inevitably, at some point, after repeated immigrations, an island 'fills up' – the diversity of species reaches a maximum and there is literally 'no room at the inn'. Biologists have found that the number of species that any one island can support depends on several factors. The size of the island is the most influential of these. Larger islands, not surprisingly, can cater for more species, but the number of different habitats is also important. Islands that have forests, lagoons, lakes, scrub and cliffs, simply offer more opportunities than those covered in one type of vegetation, and consequently sustain more species. Nevertheless, at some point the island will be full, and from this moment on any new arrival will either perish from lack of food or be forced to usurp one of the residents – an act that leads to extinction. The rate at which species immigrate and cause such disruption is determined by the remoteness of the island. Islands distant from other lands experience few new arrivals and hence suffer extinctions less frequently. Islands near to a mainland have far more disruption, receiving new species and losing old ones at a daunting rate.

The remoteness of the Mascarenes protected the islands from excessive immigrations for millions of years, while the size of Mauritius and Réunion nurtured a diverse community. Then we arrived, in a wave similar to any other immigration. Like large predators, we needed space and resources too, but unlike the predators, we made sure that we got what we needed. We chopped down forests and introduced our favourite species, animals and plants that would never have been able to overcome the three challenges of island colonisation. Exposed to the new, advanced species from the mainland, the island community quickly lost many of its older residents in an event more profoundly disruptive than any witnessed by these islands since their abrupt beginnings.

Seven species of palm are endemic to Mauritius. Most of these are in cultivation because in the wild they are all gravely threatened. Two palms – *Hyophorbe amaricaulis* and *Dyctosperma album* var. *conjugatum* – are down to a single wild individual each. The latter, which is sought after for heart-of-palm salad, has been cultivated successfully by the Mauritius Wildlife Foundation as part of a project to rescue all endangered flora. However, the species *Hyophorbe amaricaulis* appears to be doomed.

A problem facing botanists and conservationists currently is lack of information about the indigenous flora. For instance, very little is known about pollinator agents. The MWF and Aarhus University of Denmark have been engaged in studies of Mauritian plant pollinators: bats, invertebrates like hawk moths, butterflies and beetles, passerine birds and reptiles like *Phelsuma* geckos. Where plants have been decimated, their pollinators suffer likewise, particularly those that are specifically associated with one or two plant species.

In terms of flowering plants, one of the most impressive endemics is the 'bois bouquet banane' (*Ochna mauritania*). In summer (November to January), this small deciduous shrub can be seen covered in a display of white flowers, at Pétrin and in Black River Gorges National Park.

Of the various plants with medicinal properties, the best known is the 'bois de ronde' (*Erythroxylon laurifolium*), the bark of which is used to treat kidney stones.

Finally, the national flower of Mauritius is the rare and beautiful *Trochetia boutoniana* (or 'boucle d'oreille', which means 'earring') of the *Serculiaceae* family. Forget about seeing this stunner in the wild, though – it is confined to a single, privately owned mountaintop. But being the national flower, it is cultivated in various sites, for example at the Special Mobile Force Museum in Vacoas and in the grounds of the Forestry Service. The closely related (and just as beautiful) *Trochetia blackburniana* is a little more plentiful and can be seen along the road at Plaine Champagne. It also has lovely pinkish-crimson flowers.

Dr Ehsan Dulloo has worked in plant conservation in Mauritius for almost 20 years. He was formerly plant conservation manager for the MWF.

FAUNA with Richard Gibson

The sole endemic mammal is the striking Mauritius fruit bat (*Pteropus niger*), which still exists in fair numbers. Like its endangered cousin, the Rodrigues fruit bat (*P. rodericensis*), the much darker Mauritius fruit bat roosts in large trees by day and forages for fruit and flowers at night. These fruit bats belong to a predominantly Asian genus also present in Madagascar and the Comoros, where they reach their westernmost limit. A third Mascarene fruit bat, *Pteropus subniger* is sadly extinct.

Fruit bats are endearing creatures, with fox-like faces (hence the popular name of 'flying fox'), large eyes and striking fur on their heads and mantles. Thanks to the Durrell Wildlife Conservation Trust's intervention during a single incident of 'bat bashing', local youths no longer molest the animals as much as they used to. Here's why: traditionally, whenever a cyclone struck, youths would knock disorientated fruit bats out of the sky just for fun. Seeing a bat on the ground about to be bludgeoned one day, the Mauritius Programme Director grabbed the animal and ran, chased by the mob. At the breeding aviaries, he locked himself in one of the cages and delivered a lecture on fruit bats. Now, children collect the bats after cyclones and bring them to the aviaries for rehabilitation and release. To see fruit bats, go to Black River Gorges, Savannah or the Grand Port Mountains.

BIRDS Birdwatchers visiting Mauritius are in for a treat. Although only eight endemic species still remain, they include some of the world's rarest birds.

NARCOTIC INDULGENCES OF THE PINK PIGEON

The pink pigeon's continued existence has left some naturalists puzzled. It has been questioned why this bird survived, when the similarly sized Mauritius blue pigeon, with which it shared its habitat, was exterminated.

The answer seems to lie in the pink pigeon's dietary preferences. Apparently, its favoured food was the white berry of the 'fandamane' shrub (*Aphloeia mauritana*), a relative of the coca bush from which cocaine is derived. It is said that when fandamane berries were in season, the pink pigeons would gorge themselves and flop to the ground in a drug-induced daze. As such, they were an even easier target for hunters. However, the Dutch soon realised that every time they ate a pink pigeon pie, they felt quite dreadful. So the pink pigeons were left alone and are still around today, whilst the last Mauritius blue pigeon (*Alectroenas nitidissima*) was shot as long ago as 1826.

By 1974, the fabulous pink pigeon (*Nesoenas mayeri*) was down to some 24 individuals. Following intensive captive-breeding efforts by the DWCT and MWF, this gorgeous pigeon (yes, it really is pink!) is now more plentiful, numbering some 350 birds. A substantial population is held in various captive-breeding centres and large numbers of captive-bred birds have been reintroduced into the wild. Successful predator-control programmes, carried out in woodland where wild pink pigeons nest, help tremendously. What was once the world's rarest pigeon can now be seen in its natural habitat at Black River Gorges National Park and Ile aux Aigrettes.

Another rarity which the DWCT and MWF have saved from certain extinction is the sole surviving Mauritian raptor, the Mauritius kestrel (*Falco punctatus*). In 1973, when only four individuals could be found, it was declared the world's rarest bird. Causes for its dramatic decline included the extensive use of DDT, which was sprayed everywhere except for Black River Gorges. No other conservation organisation was prepared to tackle a project aimed at rescuing this kestrel from oblivion.

Captive breeding of the Mauritian kestrel started in very basic and primitive conditions in 1974 but was hampered by lack of knowledge about the bird. By 1978, the situation had become desperate and so little progress had been made that Carl Jones of the MWF was sent to close down the project. Fortunately his keen interest in hawks and his enthusiasm saw him revive the project and restart the captive breeding, which has led to such spectacular results.

Zoologist Nick Garbutt, who worked on the project from 1990 to 1992, was involved in the release of many young kestrels back into the wild (the release process is called 'hacking'). According to Garbutt, young kestrels are at their most vulnerable for the first ten days after being released, but they soon develop into proficient hunters. By the time they are 100 days old, their reliance on food handouts should have diminished and they should be independent. Garbutt personally released the 200th captive-bred kestrel into the wild. Today, between 800 and 1,000 kestrels are estimated to be flying around Mauritius and some are even nesting in people's gardens.

The phenomenal success which the DWCT had with the pink pigeon and Mauritius kestrel meant they could turn their attention to yet another Mauritian endemic in dire straits – the echo parakeet (*Psittacula echo*). By the 1990s, about 15 birds remained, all in the upland forest of Macchabée ridge. It was regarded as the world's rarest wild breeding bird. Progress with the echo parakeets has been slightly more gradual, but lately has accelerated. In 2001/02, 21 hand-reared birds were released into the wild and management of wild nests allowed a further 21 birds to fledge naturally. The wild population now stands at over 250 birds.

For four of the five remaining endemic birds, all passerines (songbirds), things do not look too rosy at present. The Mauritius cuckoo-shrike (*Coracina typica*), Mauritius bulbul (*Hypsipetes olivaceous*), Mauritius olive white-eye (*Zosterops chloronothus*) and Mauritius fody (*Foudia rubra*) have all suffered heavy losses, caused by introduced predators (rats, mongooses, cats and monkeys) raiding their nests. All are classified as 'uncommon' in the definitive field guide *Birds of the Indian Ocean Islands* (Olivier Langrand and Ian Sinclair, 1998). At present there is particular concern for the striking Mauritius fody and olive white-eye, both of which have declined to fewer than 150 birds. In breeding plumage, the male fody is a living jewel, with a ruby-red head and upper breast and dark green underparts. All of these threatened birds can be seen in the Black River Gorges National Park, their last stronghold. In November 2003, the MWF released the Mauritius fody on Ile aux Aigrettes. It seems to have taken to its new home and there are now nearly 90 birds on the island.

Strangely enough, one endemic, the Mauritius grey white-eye (*Zosterops mauritanus*, locally known as 'zozo maniok' or 'pic pic'), has adapted very successfully to man's encroachment of its habitat. It is very common all over the island, entering hotel gardens freely, as its near relative on Réunion does there.

The Mascarene swiftlet (*Collocalia francica*) and Mascarene paradise flycatcher (*Terpsiphone bourbonnensis*) are shared with Réunion, where both are more plentiful than on Mauritius. Also shared with Réunion (and with Madagascar) is the larger Mascarene martin (*Phedina borbonica*).

Finally, of great interest to visiting birders are two small seabirds, one of which is the Round Island petrel (*Pterodroma arminjoniana*), also referred to as the Trinidade petrel. Amazingly, it is found only around Round Island (where it nests) and on the other side of the globe, around Trinidade Island. Some authorities consider it a full species (separate from the birds of Trinidade), in which case another endemic can be added to the list for Mauritius. However, recent work suggests that it may be a hybrid form in a species complex, and research by the MWF is ongoing. It is endangered but, thanks to all the rehabilitation work that has been conducted on Round Island, its chances for survival have been improved significantly. The second, shared with Mauritius and the Comoros, is the very localised and poorly understood Mascarene shearwater (*Puffinus atrodorsalis*), which may quite easily be confused in the field with the much more common and widespread Audubon's shearwater (*Puffinus iherminieri*).

REPTILES The endemic birds – and to a lesser extent, plants – of Mauritius have received much international press coverage, but few people know that a fascinating ensemble of endangered reptiles exists there also, most significantly on a small chunk of volcanic rock called Round Island, 22km north of Mauritius.

Other offshore islets and the mainland itself support four endemic day geckos (genus *Phelsuma*), two more night geckos (genus *Nactus*), and two small skink species (genus *Gongylomorphus*), one as yet undescribed by science.

Round Island is a tilted volcanic cone rising 278m above the sea. Its surface area covers 151ha. Surrounded by rough seas and often buffeted by strong winds, the island has remained uninhabited by man, allowing reptiles, seabirds and plants that have perished elsewhere to survive. Five of Round Island's eight reptile species are now endemic to the island and endangered: the large Telfair's skink (*Leiolopisma telfairi*); the strangely nocturnal Round Island 'day' gecko (*Phelsuma guentheri*); the tiny nocturnal Durrell's night gecko (*Nactus durrelli*); and the remarkable keel-scaled boa (*Casarea dussumieri*). The fifth, the Round Island burrowing boa (*Bolyeria*

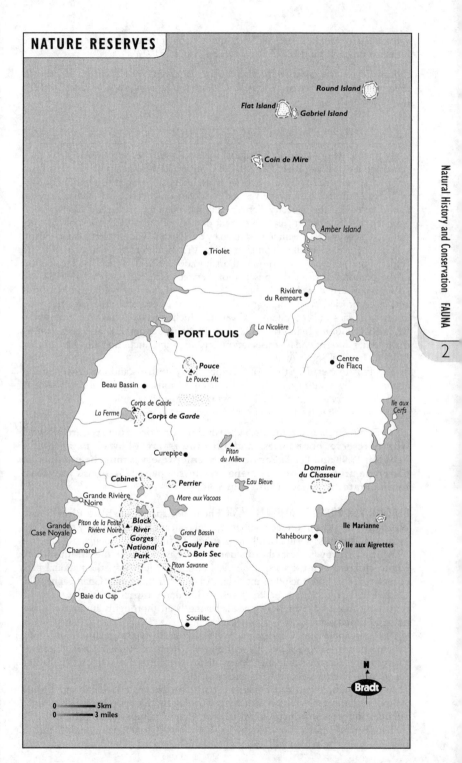

NATURE RESERVES

Round Island

Flat Island   Gabriel Island

Coin de Mire

Amber Island

Triolet

Rivière
du Rempart

La Nicolière

PORT LOUIS

Centre
de Flacq

Pouce
Le Pouce Mt

Beau Bassin

Corps de Garde

La Ferme   **Corps de Garde**

Ile aux
Cerfs

Curepipe

Piton
du Milieu

**Domaine
du Chasseur**

Cabinet   **Perrier**   Eau Bleue

Grande Rivière
Noire   Mare aux Vacoas

Grande
Case Noyale   Piton de la Petite
Rivière Noire   **Black
River
Gorges
National
Park**

Grand Bassin

Ile Marianne

Chamarel

**Gouly Père
Bois Sec**

Mahébourg

Ile aux Aigrettes

Piton Savanne

Baie du Cap

Souillac

N

Bradt

0 ——— 5km
0 ——— 3 miles

multocarinata), was last seen in 1975 and is sadly presumed extinct. (For more information on Round Island, see pages 34–5 and 131–2.)

Richard Gibson was fauna conservation manager for the MWF and directed their animal recovery programmes. Previously, he worked for nine years as herpetology curator at DWCT's Jersey Zoo.

NATURE RESERVES AND CONSERVATION

Only fragments of Mauritius's original forests – estimates vary from 1% to 4% – remain today, at Black River Gorges, Bel Ombre and the Kanaka Crater. The palm savanna, which used to feature in drier areas, has been reduced to a hectare or two.

Today, Mauritian nature reserves and national park cover over 6,500ha. They are administered by the Forestry Service and the National Parks and Conservation Service (NPCS). Incidentally, the current director of the NPCS, Yousoof Mugroo, was the first overseas student to be trained by the Durrell Wildlife Conservation Trust.

The Mauritian Wildlife Foundation (MWF, formerly the Mauritian Wildlife Appeal Fund) is a non-governmental organisation (NGO) which has the support of the National Parks and Conservation Service (NPCS). Founded in 1984, the MWF is concerned exclusively with conservation of endemic wildlife in Mauritius and its territories, co-ordinating and administering projects aimed at preserving endemic species and ecosystem biodiversity. Much of its work has been done in the Black River Gorges National Park. Over the years, support has also been lent by many other international conservation organisations, including the Endangered Wildlife Trust of South Africa.

The full-time staff of the MWF comprises Mauritians and expatriates, and is augmented by volunteers who come from various countries abroad, seeking valuable conservation experience after graduating at universities.

The following rules apply to people visiting nature reserves:

NOTE: No firearms, animals, rubbish dumping or structures are allowed within reserve boundaries, and no visitors are allowed in a reserve between 18.00 and 06.00. Permission to enter reserves must be obtained in Curepipe, from the Forestry Department (see page 175), or ask your local tour operator to organise entry for you.

BLACK RIVER GORGES NATIONAL PARK The importance of the Black River Gorges National Park is that it protects a phenomenal concentration of gravely endangered animals and plants. Visitors will not struggle to find its rare denizens, many of which have narrowly escaped extinction. If there is one place in Mauritius which nature enthusiasts must visit, this is it. Set in the southwest, the national park covers 6,574ha and includes the Macchabée, Pétrin, Plaine Champagne, Bel Ombre and Montagne Cocotte forests. But don't expect pristine forest: the remaining forest is severely degraded, having been thoroughly invaded by fast-growing exotic plants.

At Pétrin and Plaine Champagne, you'll find heath-type vegetation flourishing on porous soil (keep a lookout for the lovely *Trochettia blackburniana*). Pandanus thrives where terrain is marshier. A very distinctive tree is the weird, umbrella-like *bois de natte*, often festooned with epiphytes.

At Bel Ombre, you can study the transition between lowland and upland evergreen rainforest, whilst at Montagne Cocotte, there's a good example of high-altitude rainforest, in which shorter trees are draped in mosses and lichens.

The Pétrin Information Centre is open 09.00–16.00 daily, and there's a boardwalk nearby, which will lead you into the heathland. There are several well-

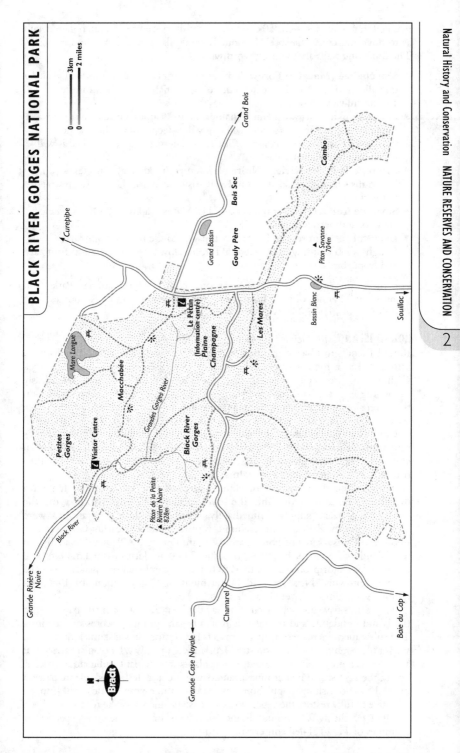

BLACK RIVER GORGES NATIONAL PARK

mapped trails covering some 50km and at the visitors' centre you can obtain details as to how the reserve has been laid out. There's also a picnic spot and campsite. The following trails are the most worthwhile:

- **Macchabée (Macabe) Forest** 7km return from Pétrin (moderate). This loop trail allows visitors the best experience of Mauritian tropical rainforest. Wonderful views, good birding.
- **Parakeet** 6km one-way: Plaine Champagne to Visitor Centre (tough). This is for adventurous, fit hikers, who will enjoy the steep trail joining Plaine Champagne with the gorges area. The really energetic can combine this with Macchabée for a 15km hike.
- **Piton de la Petite Rivière Noire** 6km return (moderate). This takes you to Mauritius's highest peak, at 828m. Fairly easy except for the last, steep stretch to the top.
- **Savanne** 6km return, from the end of Les Mares road (easy). Offers scenic views of southern Mauritius.
- **Bel Ombre** 12km return, Plaine Champagne to the reserve boundary (tough). Good birding in the tropical forest at lower elevations. Also, fruit bats and tropic birds.

For more information about the reserve, contact the National Parks and Conservation Service of the Ministry of Agriculture and Natural Resources at Le Réduit (✆ 464 4016; ℻ 464 2993).

ROUND ISLAND *with Richard Gibson*

Round Island's troubles began in the 19th century, when goats and rabbits were introduced as a food source for fishermen, seabird-egg hunters and shipwreck victims. True to their form, these animals multiplied like flies, relentlessly munching away the hardwood forest on the upper slopes and the palm savanna on the lower slopes, which resembled that present in the drier areas of Mauritius, circa 1500.

Conservationists realised that urgent action had to be taken if Round Island's remaining plants and animals were to be saved. In 1976, the late Gerald Durrell and John Hartley made their first visit there. They were aghast at what they found: only eight hurricane palms and two Round Island bottle palms remained. The three species of skink and three species of gecko fed on a dwindling insect supply, and the two species of primitive boa on the diminishing lizard supply. Immediately, captive-breeding programmes were started at Jersey Zoo for the endemic reptiles. The Mauritius Government, under the Conservator of Forests and Wildlife Director A Wahab Owadally, rid the island of its goats by 1979. But the 3,000 undernourished rabbits still presented a major problem. So, the DWCT finally enlisted the assistance of the equally renowned New Zealand Department of Conservation. In 1986, the rabbits were completely eradicated.

The results have been spectacular, to say the least. Almost immediately, most of the island's endemic and indigenous plants began sprouting scores of seedlings. The subsequent increase of fruit and insects has resulted in substantial increases in the reptile populations. The Forestry Department and a WWF botanist carried out an extensive programme to weed exotic plants and replant indigenous species. Today, the keel-scaled boa, Round Island day gecko and Telfair's skink are present in healthy, flourishing populations and a new three-year World Bank-funded initiative to fully restore the vegetation of the island and study the reptiles has been initiated by the MWF. Round Island represents one of the most spectacular examples of a DWCT-led conservation triumph.

British zoologist/author Nick Garbutt, who visited Round Island several times while working in Mauritius, provides a fascinating report:

I was surprised at the density of vegetation, for despite the rugged nature of the slopes and the apparent lack of soil, latan palms (*Latania loddigesii*) and pandanus or screwpines (*Pandanus vandermeerschi*) covered the majority of the western slopes. I recalled photographs of these same slopes looking barren and lifeless, taken in previous years, when the goats and rabbits were still present. The difference was absolutely remarkable and it was clear that the palm savanna was beginning to recover. The helicopter swung in over the south coast and landed on the one flat piece of rock on the island. It was not long before I spotted our first visitor, a Telfair's skink, scurrying over a hot rock surface towards the camp. It was followed by three more, then a further four from various directions. This large skink often reaches a length of 1ft. It is very bold, showing no fear of man, and congregates around visitors. Because they are highly adept at locating any food, all supplies had to be stored in 'skink-proof' boxes well above the ground. The skinks also prey on smaller lizards present, namely Bojer's skinks, night geckos and ornate day geckos.

Bojer's skink (*Gongylomorphus bojeri*) is the island's most common reptile, also being present on Coin de Mire, Flat and Gabriel islands, and was probably exterminated on Mauritius by introduced rats, mongooses and Indian wolf snakes (*Lycodon aulica*).

Another skink found on Round Island is the pan-tropical Bouton's skink (*Cryptoblepharus boutonii*). Because of its long legs and claws, it is capable of staying on a rock while raging whitewater crashes over it. The ornate day gecko (*Phelsuma ornata*) remains common on Mauritius and Round Island. It forages by day for insects and nectar. The endemic Round Island day gecko (*P. guentheri*), is unusual among day geckos in that it is most active at night and is not brightly coloured like its relatives. Reaching a total length of nearly 300mm (1ft), it is the largest day gecko which still exists. They are often to be seen foraging in latan palms, for which they are important pollinators. Another gecko to be found on Round Island is the diminutive Durrell's night gecko (*Nactus durrelli*).

Round Island is best known among zoological circles for its two endemic snakes, which are so distinctive taxonomically that they have been accorded a family of their own, the *Bolyeridae*. Intriguingly, the only other animal family unique to the Mascarenes is the *Raphidae* – the remarkable dodo and solitaires – all of which are extinct. The considerable regeneration of native vegetation on Round Island following the rabbit eradication means that the keel-scaled boa is now thriving and there may just be a faint glimmer of hope for the Round Island burrowing boa. The keel-scaled boa is largely nocturnal, preying wholly on lizards. During the day, the boas tend to curl up in rock crevices or between fallen latan palm fronds. Sadly, no-one knows what the burrowing boa ate or how it lived.

The importance of Round Island as a refuge for a unique group of reptiles and plants cannot be overstated.

ILE AUX AIGRETTES Ile aux Aigrettes is a 25ha reef-ringed coral islet about 1km off the southeast coast. It contains the last remaining traces of the lowland ebony forest that once dominated much of coastal Mauritius, as well as numerous other endemic animal and plant species threatened with extinction.

Since the MWF obtained the long-term lease of the islet in 1985, they've been engaged in extensive rehabilitation of the ecosystem there, which had been severely damaged over 400 years. The aim is that Ile aux Aigrettes should one day resemble its original state as closely as possible. To this end, the MWF has been weeding the islet and replanting with native plants, restoring the forest and reintroducing endemic birds and reptiles known to have once lived there. As the

The poor Mascarene ecosystems! Not only have they been hammered by man and his animal followers, but they're riddled with invasive alien plants. Most of what you'll see in terms of animals and plants are species which have been introduced, and which have subsequently run rampant to the detriment of indigenous flora and fauna.

Very prominent introductions include the 'filao' (casuarina) tree (*Casuarina equisetifolia*), which often lines beaches and is useful as a windbreak. It originates in Malaysia. Great banyan trees (*Ficus benghalensis*) were brought from India, recognisable by their weird root systems dangling from their branches to the ground. Two distinctive Malagasy introductions are the flamboyant tree (*Delonix regia*) and the fan-shaped ravenala palm (*Ravenala madagascariensis*).

Privet and Chinese guava (goyavier) have spread at an alarming rate in the montane rainforests, often choking seedlings of slow-growing indigenous hardwoods. A horribly invasive bush is *Lantana camara*, the worst nightmare of conservationists. It is native to tropical America and has spread like wildfire in the Mascarenes.

Other tropical American invaders include sisal (*Furcraea foetida*), the morning glory creeper (*Ipomoea purpurea*), the prickly-pear cactus (*Opuntia vulgaris*) and the unmistakable poinsettia (*Euphorbia pulcherrima*).

In marshy areas, pampas grass (*Saccharum officinarum*), introduced from southeast Asia, is common. The originally Asian elephant ear (*Colocasea esculenta*) also frequents damp places. The staghorn fern (*Platycerium bifurcatum*), which one sees on so many rainforest trees, is actually Australian. Two of the most commonly used ornamentals, the bougainvillea (*Bougainvillea glabra*) and the frangipani (*Plumeria alba*), are tropical American species.

When the earlier settlers arrived in Mauritius, they introduced a selection of destructive animals, intentionally and by accident. A truly senseless introduction was the southeast Asian long-tailed macaque monkey (*Macaca fasicularis*), courtesy of the Dutch back in 1606. These primates are now abundant in Mauritius, where eradicating them is very difficult because Indo-Mauritians consider them sacred. They pose a very real threat to the endemic birds, reptiles, invertebrates and flora.

Wild pigs (*Sus scrofra*), of Asian origin, abound too, but are very secretive and wary. No doubt they don't do terrestrial fauna much good, being the highly adaptable omnivores that they are, and are very destructive in native forests.

threat from highly invasive plants, such as giant acacia, is very real, general maintenance weeding will continue for years to come. Reintroductions of fauna will also continue.

Visitors can enjoy fascinating guided tours of the islet, see some very rare flora and fauna and witness conservation work in process. It is one of the best places to see the rare pink pigeon and the Mauritius fody, and the only place in the Mascarenes where giant Aldabra tortoises roam completely freely. Two tortoise species are known to have existed in Mauritius; both are now extinct, having been used as a source of protein by passing sailors. The giant Aldabra tortoises, which can weigh as much as 200kg, are native to the Seychelles but have been introduced to the island as the closest surviving relative of the lost species. Visitors are also likely to see colourful day geckos basking in the sun. Tours last around two hours and the guide will take the time to explain the geology and history of the island (for details see page 154).

OTHER PROTECTED AREAS North of Black River are two small mountain forest reserves, **Corps de Garde** and **Le Pouce**. The island's smallest reserve, **Perrier**, is only 1.5ha and is between Curepipe and the Mare aux Vacoas reservoir. It

Brown rats and black rats arrived by means of ships and thoroughly invaded all the Mascarenes. Other introductions include the musk shrew, the black-naped hare (*Lepus nigricollis*) and the wild rabbit (*Oryctolagus cuniculus*), which was eradicated on Round Island after severely damaging the ecosystem there. The lesser Indian mongoose (*Herpestes javanicus*) is fairly often seen bolting across rural roads and was introduced in 1900 to reduce rats. It also munched its way through native bird populations.

Of the reptile introductions, the aggressive Indian wolf snake (*Lycodon aulicus*) is most often seen. We can only imagine what species this reptile wiped out while establishing itself in Mauritius, where it is now quite common.

Many birds have been introduced and those that established themselves are generally common and highly successful species. They are the birds you'll see in hotel gardens, parks and towns. Sadly, where they have an endemic relative, they far outnumber that species; like the red-whiskered bulbul, an Asian introduction, which is numerous, while the endemic Mauritius bulbul is uncommon.

The aggressive Indian mynah is to be seen in any urban centre, as are the house sparrow and house crow. Also regularly seen and heard is the zebra dove. The ring-neck parakeet (*Psittacula krameri*) can be confused with its endangered, endemic relative, the echo parakeet. However, their calls differ and both sexes of the ring-neck have red beaks, whilst only female echoes have black beaks.

Three small passerines (an order of birds characterised by the perching habit) from Africa are the spotted-backed weaver, the common waxbill and the yellow-eyed canary, all of which are now abundant. The bright red Madagascar fody has colonised all the Mascarenes. Seeing this little weaverbird is guaranteed, but not so its rare native congener, the Mauritius fody, which has never adapted to manmade conditions.

Some of the introduced birds have been far less invasive and are actually quite interesting. The Meller's duck (*Anas melleri*) is uncommon in its native Madagascar and is known to breed in Mauritius, where there are no other wild ducks or geese left. The common quail, grey francolin and Madagascar partridge are said to be present in grasslands, though none of them is plentiful by any means. More often seen are the Madagascar buttonquail and the Madagascar turtledove.

protects a small remnant parcel of transition forest between lowland and montane rainforest and harbours a large number of endemic plants.

Domaine du Chasseur, in southeast Mauritius, also appears on a map of the island's reserves. It has impressive tracts of upland rainforest on the highest reaches of steep slopes and is a favourite haunt of the Mauritius kestrel. (For information about visiting the reserve, see page 143.)

Other nature reserves include Bois Sec, Cabinet, Combo, Flat Island, Gabriel Island, Coin de Mire, Gouly Père, Les Mares, Marianne Islet and Serpent Island.

MARINE LIFE

The marine life of Mauritius has also suffered since man's arrival, although it is still an important attraction for visitors.

It is easy to visit coral gardens in depths of 7–20m through hotel diving centres (see *Chapter 4, Scuba diving*, pages 93–4). The range of fish to be seen, especially those engaging in antics like the boxfish with their curious sculling action and the trumpet fish with their darting movements, is fascinating.

MARINE ENVIRONMENTAL AWARENESS

with Tom Hooper

By following a few simple guidelines you can enjoy the wonderful marine environment of the Mascarenes without damaging it.

BE CAREFUL WHERE YOU WALK There are many delicate organisms on the reef edge and shoreline which will break or be crushed if you walk on them. Corals are particularly vulnerable and are likely to die from being touched or smothered by silt. When you are diving and snorkelling be especially careful with your fins to make sure you don't break corals.

DON'T BUY SHELLS There are good reasons for not buying shells. The most beautiful and pristine shells are very rarely collected dead. They are taken live from the seabed and the animal inside is killed. While looking for and collecting shells there is also damage to the surrounding marine life. Lastly, even empty shells serve a useful purpose as homes for hermit crabs or a hard substrate for new growths of coral.

DON'T BUY CORALS, TURTLE SHELLS OR OTHER MARINE CURIOS Creating a market in these organisms leads to them being targeted for capture and the destruction of their surroundings during collection.

DISPOSE OF YOUR LITTER CAREFULLY A single piece of litter can destroy the illusion of wild remoteness and ruin a beach walk. With the introduction of cans and plastic bottles, wrappers and bags, even the coastlines of Rodrigues are beginning to suffer from the eyesore of scattered litter. Some of these items will take tens or hundreds of years to biodegrade.

SEAFOOD The demand for particular types of seafood can set a marine ecosystem off balance. In addition, some harvesting techniques are particularly damaging to the environment. Octopus populations are currently vulnerable in Rodrigues and the collection method damages the marine environment. Good fish to eat are the herbivorous fish which are caught in basket traps such as unicorn and rabbit fish. These have a delicate taste and are excellent grilled.

AVOID EATING SHARK World populations of shark are in serious decline and as the top predators this has led to an imbalance in marine food chains. Areas of the Caribbean and Far East still use the lamentable practice of finning, which involves cutting fins from sharks for use in shark fin soup, and then throwing them back alive.

The appeal of the reef is enhanced by the variety of the coral that is among the most beautiful in the world. Because of the sunlight that filters through sea of the right salinity and temperature, the coral thrives better in the waters of Mauritius than elsewhere. There are notable coral gardens at the southern corners of Mauritius, off La Morne Brabant and Blue Bay.

Shell collecting has been rapacious since the 1960s and the Mauritius Scuba Diving Association now considers collecting unacceptable. To meet demand for souvenirs, shells are imported from the Philippines to be sold to tourists who want something pretty.

The rarest and most valuable shells in the world, such as the several varieties of conus, *Lambis violacea* and *Cyproe onyx-nymphal*, have been found off Mauritius. There is an extensive collection of shells at the Mauritius Museum Council in Port

Louis (see page 114). A model of the rare cone (*Conus milneedwardsi*) can be seen among the exhibits. This was brought up in a fisherman's basket net from a depth of 40 fathoms, off the coast of Black River. Also exhibited is a giant clam (*Tridacna gigas*), the largest clam ever evolved.

Cone and cowrie shells, while delightful, can be deadly if of the *Conus aulieus*, *geographicus*, *marmoreus*, *rattus*, *textile* or *tulipa* species. Poison injected from their sharp ends can bring death within 150 minutes, with no known antidote. There have been 105 species recorded. Harp shells, four species with ribs resembling the strings of a harp, are attractive to collectors, especially the double harp (*Harpa costata*), which is not found outside Mauritian waters. There are 135 species of mitre shells (*Mitridae*), which are spindle- to oval-shaped and notched in front. Murex shells, such as *Murex tenuispina* with its elongated, jagged stem, are popular. The purple fluid secreted by them was used in ancient times as a dye.

Starfish are common and the presence of the crown of thorns (*Star achantaster*) is destructive to coral. An excellent specimen of the very rare *Acanthocidaris curvatispinis*, which is known only in Mauritius, is on display at the Institute Museum. The collection of *echinoderms* there also contains a remarkable specimen of *Chondrocidaris gigantea*, exhibited in a special showcase as it is considered to be the most beautiful sea urchin in the world.

Trochetia boutoniana

3

Practical Information

WHEN TO VISIT

Mauritius is a place to visit at any time of the year for someone from northern climes who craves tropical beauty and warmth. The one time which may not be ideal is January–March, when cyclones are most likely to occur. They don't happen every year but the cyclonic rains, which can last for several days, are an annual event. Humidity is high then and it can be a depressing, unsettling time. See *Chapter 1, Climate*, pages 4–5 for more information.

The high season for tourism, when holiday packages cost more, is November to early January. Hefty peak season supplements are charged over Christmas and Easter. Flights should be less crowded outside European school holiday periods and hotels are noticeably so.

December is the time when local fruits are in abundance: it's summer and the temperature on the coast is about 30°C. The weather is cooler from June to September with the temperature at sea level being about 24°C. Package holiday prices are lower and hotels tend to host conference and incentive groups. October and early November are perhaps the best times to travel as the weather is good but high season prices and crowds have not yet set in.

If climate is not the governing factor, choose when to visit according to your interests. For instance, the horse racing season is from May to late November and the best deep-sea fishing is from November to May.

There are many websites which offer useful tips and information to help you prepare for your visit. For details see *Appendix 3, Further Information*, pages 332–3.

HIGHLIGHTS

Mauritius is small enough for you to base yourself in one place and explore the island's highlights. **Natural history** enthusiasts and hikers should head to the **Black River Gorges National Park**. There are **hiking trails** of varying difficulty, where glimpses of the rare **Mauritius Pink Pigeon** and **Mauritius Kestrel** are possible. Also worth a visit is **Ile aux Aigrettes**, a coral island off the south coast, which the Mauritius Wildlife Foundation is working hard to restore to its natural state.

The **markets at Port Louis** are not to be missed. The hustle and bustle amidst the colourful displays of fruit, vegetables, spices and souvenirs represents an unforgettable snapshot of everyday life in the island's capital. For a **shopping** experience of a different kind, visit one of the upmarket shopping centres where tourists are tempted at every turn by diamonds, clothing and model ships. You may as well make the most of Mauritius being a **duty-free island**.

One of the island's newest attractions is **L'Aventure du Sucre** (Sugar World), a former sugar factory which has been transformed into a museum telling the story of the industry on which the island was built. Equally fascinating are guided tours of the **Bois Chéri Tea Factory**, which are followed by a tasting. The tour can also be done as part of **La Route du Thé** (The Tea Route), which takes in three sites linked to the Bois Chéri Tea Estate.

Mauritius's 'melting pot' of ethnicities provides a wealth of opportunities to experience local **culture**. Most organised tours will include a stop at **Grand Bassin**, where visitors can learn about this sacred Hindu lake and watch the worshippers who flock to its shores. The Tamil festivals are colourful and fascinating – if you have a chance to watch **fire-walking** or the **Thaipoosam Cavadee** pilgrimage, don't miss it.

I couldn't write about the highlights of Mauritius without mentioning the **beaches** – and, yes they really are as good as they look in the holiday brochures. Belle Mare, Trou aux Biches and Flic en Flac are considered by locals to be among the islands' finest.

Beyond the beaches all manner of **watersports** are on offer, from kayaking to kitesurfing. Non-motorised watersports may well be included in your accommodation package. Under the waves there are colourful coral reefs and a wealth of **diving and snorkelling sites**. For those who wish to explore the underwater world without getting wet, there are **submersible vessels** – a great option for children and non-divers.

Sailing, **deep-sea fishing** and **dolphin-watching** cruises are all popular with visitors. **Golf** is also flourishing on the island, with several world-class courses now available.

A trip to the island of **Rodrigues** is an ideal add-on to a stay in Mauritius. It is not a beach-lovers' paradise but an opportunity to stray well off the beaten track and retreat into a world where simplicity rules.

i GATHERING INFORMATION

The **Mauritius Tourist Promotion Authority** (MTPA) is the best source of information both prior to your trip and during it. They publish information booklets on the island and have a website that is packed with useful information and links.

MTPA Head Office 11th Fl, Air Mauritius Centre, President John F Kennedy St, Port Louis; ☎ 208 1545; f 212 5142; e mtpa@intnet.mu;

www.mauritius.net. They have information desks at the airport in Plaisance, ☎ 637 3635 and on the Caudan Waterfront, ☎ 208 6397

The MTPA also has offices in the UK and France:

UK MTPA London, 32–33 Elvaston Pl, London SW7 5NW; ☎ 020 7584 3666; f 020 7225 1135; e mtpa@btinternet.com

France MTPA Paris, 124 Bd Haussman, 75008, Paris; ☎ +33 01 44 69 34 50; f +33 01 44 69 34 51; e mtpa@wanadoo.fr

Information and public relations offices in other countries are as follows:

Germany Mauritius Informationsburo, GCI Hering Schuppener, Corporate & Public Relations Beratung GmbH, Grüneburgweg 64 D-60322, Frankfurt; ☎ 0700 6287 48487; f +49 69 9218 7431; e mauritius@gcihsf.de
India Mauritius Tourist Information Service, c/o TRAC Representation Pvt. Ltd, A-61, 6th Fl, Himalays Hse K G Marg, New Delhi 110001; ☎ +91 11

2335 2550; f +91 11 2335 0270; e mtpaindia@tracrep.com
Italy Ufficio del Turismo delle Isole Mauritius, c/o GIGA SRL, Piazza Caiazzo 1, 20124 Milan; ☎ +39 02 6707 4703; f +39 02 6692 648; e mtpa@gigacomunicazione.com
South Africa Mauritius Tourism Information Service, c/o Inside Edge, Suite 2A, Glenashley Views, 36

Newport Av, Glenashley, Durban; ✆ +27 31 562 1320; f +27 31 562 1383; e mauritius@ie.co.za
Switzerland/Austria Mauritius Tourist Information

Service, c/o PRW Public Relations & Werbe AG, Kirchenweg 5, 8032 Zurich; ✆ +41 1 383 8788; f +41 1 383 5124; e info@prw.ch

TOUR OPERATORS

Below is a non-exhaustive list of tour operators that feature Mauritius:

UK

Aardvark Safaris RBL Hse, Ordnance Rd, Tidworth, Hampshire SP9 7QD; ✆ 01980 849160; f 01980 849161; e mail@aardvarksafaris.com; www.aardvarksafaris.com

Beachcomber Tours Direction Hse, 186 High St, Guildford, Surrey GU1 3HW; ✆ 01483 445621; www.beachcombertours.co.uk

Partnership Travel Marlborough Hse, 298 Regents Park Rd, London N3 2TJ; ✆ 020 8343 3446; f 020 8349 3439; e info@partnershiptravel.co.uk; www.partnershiptravel.co.uk

Rainbow Tours 305 Upper St, London N1 2TU; ✆ 020 7226 1004; f 020 7226 1004; e info@rainbowtours.co.uk; www.rainbowtours.co.uk

Somak Holidays Harrovian Business Village, Bessborough Rd, Harrow on the Hill, Middlesex HA1 3EX; ✆ 020 8423 3000; f 020 8423 7700; e holidays@somak.co.uk; www.somak.co.uk

Sunset Faraway Holidays 4 Abbeville Mews, 88 Clapham Park Rd, London SW4 7BX; ✆ 020 7498 9922; f 020 7978 1337; e info@sunsettravel.co.uk; www.sunsetfaraway.co.uk

Australia

Abercrombie & Kent Level 1, Suite 6, 3 Spring St, Sydney, NSW 2000; ✆ +61 2 9241 3213; f +61 2 9241 3813; e info@abercrombiekent.com.au; www.abercrombiekent.com.au

Beachcomber Tours 1344 Gympie Rd, Aspley, QLD 4034; ✆ +61 7 3353 6204; f +61 7 3353 6214; e info@beachcomber.com.au; www.beachcomber.com.au

Mauritius Holidays 163a East Boundary Rd, Bentleigh East, VIC 3165; ✆ +61 3 9563 7022

France

Havas Voyages 6–8 Pl Jean Zay, 923594 Levallois-

Perret; ✆ +33 01 46 39 75 95; f +33 01 46 39 75 99

Nouvelles Frontières 34 Rue du Commerce, 75015 Paris; ✆ +33 0825 000 747

Germany

Escape Tours Grandlstrasse 26, 81247 Munich; ✆ +49 89 8299 480; f +49 89 8299 4897

Trauminsel Reisen Summerstrasse 8, D-82211, Herrsching; ✆ +49 08152 93190; f +49 08152 931920; e info@trauminselreisen.de; www.trauminselreisen.de

Italy

Caesar Tour Geometria Viaggi Roma, Via della Magliana, 179a/b – 00146 Rome; ✆ +39 06 5526 2616; infoviaggi@caesartour.it; www.caesartour.it

I Viaggi Dell'airone Sede di Milano, Via Trivulziana, 16/c, 20097 S Donato Milanese; ✆ +39 02 5162 1662; f +39 02 510 695; e milano@iviaggidellairone.com; www.iviaggidellairone.com

South Africa

Recreational Tours PO Box 79, Cramerview 2060, Johannesburg; ✆ +27 011 807 9195; f +27 011 803 4853; e safaris@iafrica.com; www.recreational-tours.co.za

Unusual Destinations 12 George St, Bryanston, Johannesburg; ✆ +27 011 706 1991; f +27 011 463 1469; e info@unusualdestinations.com; www.unusualdestinations.com

Switzerland

Nouvelles Frontières 10 Rue de Chantepoulet, 1201 Geneva; ✆ +41 022 906 8080; f +41 022 906 8090; e geneve@nouvelles-frontieres.ch; www.nouvelles-frontieres.ch

RED TAPE

ENTRY REQUIREMENTS A full passport is required to enter Mauritius. However, holders of a Certificate of Identity issued by the Government of Mauritius or of a *Laissez Passer* issued by the United Nations will be admitted without passports.

British passport holders and citizens of other European Union countries (including new members of the EU such as Poland and Hungary) and of the US, Canada, Australia, New Zealand, South Africa and Scandinavia, can enter visa-free. Holders of passports from the following countries are granted a stay of two weeks on arrival: Albania, Bulgaria, Comoros, Fiji, Madagascar, Romania and the ex-USSR Commonwealth of Independent States. Visitors from India, China, Jordan and Lebanon require a visa only if they are intending to stay for more than 15 days, are visiting for social or religious purposes or are intending to look for employment. However, they also have to satisfy certain conditions, which include, but are not limited to, having a return air ticket, confirmed accommodation and evidence of sufficient funds.

Bona fide visitors are usually granted a stay of up to one month or for the duration of their visit if less. Entry requirements change so, if you are in doubt, check with your nearest Mauritius representative.

VISA ISSUE Visas can be obtained from Mauritian embassies and high commissions (see page 47). If there is no diplomatic representation in your country, your application should be submitted to an Air Mauritius office and failing that, your contact in Mauritius, or you, should request an application form from the Passport and Immigration Office (*Stirling Hse, 11–12 Lislet Geoffrey St, Port Louis;* ❭ *210 9312;* f *210 9322;* e *poimain@mail.gov.mu; http://passport.gov.mu*). There is also a Passport and Immigration Office at the airport. The application has to be filled out and submitted with two photographs. A letter of approval will be issued, free of charge, which you have to show to immigration at the airport. If you need a visa and have not got one (and if you manage to get on a flight to Mauritius), entry will be refused.

IMMIGRATION During your flight to Mauritius you should be given an international embarkation/disembarkation card. This needs to be filled in before you join the immigration queue. Have it ready, together with your return air ticket and passport. The process may require some patience on your part.

You will be required to provide the address where you intend to stay or at least the name of your hotel. If you don't know where you're going to stay, expect questions, since immigration needs an address for you. If you intend to camp bear in mind that there are no official campsites and camping is not encouraged.

You must have a return air ticket otherwise you may be asked to purchase one on the spot. You may also be asked to provide proof that you have sufficient funds to cover your stay. The amount of money that you have in your possession is not the sole criterion: your access to funds in an emergency is important too.

The visitor who comes on a package holiday does not raise the same doubts that independent travellers do because the package tourist has prepaid accommodation and is under the auspices of the tour company. However, providing the independent traveller is a genuine tourist who will not take up 'gainful employment', which is forbidden, entry is granted after the short interview at the desk.

There is a list of undesirable types who will not be admitted to Mauritius. Anyone who is likely to be a charge on public funds will be refused entry, as will chronic alcoholics, so don't overdo the drinks on the plane.

The second desk you come to is manned by a Ministry of Health official, who may ask whether you are carrying any plant or animal material and whether you have visited a farm recently. This is part of the continual campaign to prevent malaria returning to Mauritius. If you have come from a malaria-infected country you could be asked to give a blood sample for precautionary analysis within a few days of your arrival.

CUSTOMS The red and green channel system operates in Mauritius but even if you opt for the green channel, you may be questioned before being allowed through.

Incoming visitors aged 16 and over are allowed to import free of duty:

Tobacco	up to 250g
Spirits	1 litre
Wine	2 litres of wine, ale or beer
Perfume	10cl of perfume and 25cl of eau de toilette
Goods for personal use	up to the value of Rs15,000 (Mauritian passport holder), Rs7,000 (Mauritian passport holder under 12 years of age), Rs7,500 (foreign passport holder)

The following goods are either restricted or prohibited: arms and ammunition, including underwater fishing guns, drugs, publications, films or videos of an obscene nature, sugarcane cuttings, vegetables, flowers and plants, live or stuffed animals, water scooters and cigarette paper.

Prescription drugs If you are carrying prescription drugs, they may be illegal for import into Mauritius. It is advisable to keep them in the manufacturer's box with your prescription. Be prepared to present them for inspection to the customs officials.

Plants and animals Be careful! All plants and plant material must be declared to customs and will be subject to inspection. A plant-import permit must be obtained in advance from the Ministry of Agriculture, even for cuttings, bulbs, fresh fruit, vegetables and seeds. It is illegal to import sugarcane, soil or micro-organisms. Inspection will take place at the airport offices of the Plant Pathology Division of the Ministry of Agriculture (*637 3194*).

The same procedure of import permits must also be followed for animals and animal material, which must be accompanied by a health certificate issued by the veterinary authorities of the exporting country. Animals must be declared on arrival. Dogs and cats undergo a six-month quarantine period, birds and other animals two months. The import of dogs and cats from areas within 100km radius of anywhere rabies occurred in the previous 12 months is prohibited; so too are invertebrate animals. The cost is met by the importer.

Animal and plant import permits are available from Agricultural Services (*Head Office, Port Louis;* *454 1091*).

Money There is no published guideline on the minimum amount of spending money a visitor must possess before being allowed into Mauritius. However, immigration officials may require proof of sufficient funds if they don't like the look of you. There is no restriction on the importation of foreign or Mauritian currency.

Drugs The penalties for trafficking drugs of any kind are severe. Don't risk it.

STAYING ON

Visa extensions Each application to stay longer than the period written by the immigration officer in a visitor's passport is treated according to the individual visitor's circumstances, not by standard published guidelines.

Applications are dealt with by the Passport and Immigration Office, which in January 1999 moved from the Line Barracks to new modern offices in Stirling

House (*11–12 Lislet Geoffrey St, Port Louis;* ↘ *210 9312;* f *210 9322;* e *piomain@intnet.mu; http://passport.gov.mu; open Mon–Fri 10.00–12.00*).

You will need to take with you a letter addressed to the Officer In Charge, Passport and Immigration Office, in which you explain your reason for wanting to stay longer, and until what date you want to stay. You should state also that you have a ticket out of Mauritius and give details of your confirmed reservation to leave. Include details of where you are staying and of the amount of funds you have available to cover your costs, including lodging and personal expenses. Be prepared to furnish proof of everything you say in the letter.

If your case is genuine and you satisfy the examining officer that you do not intend to work and will not become a charge on public funds, an extension can be granted for up to six months for one visit.

Work permits Because Mauritius is developing with the aid of considerable private foreign investment, the authorities accept the need of those foreign investors to employ foreign personnel (usually as directors or financial controllers) to represent their interests. Expatriates with technical or professional ability are also likely to be granted work permits where qualified nationals are not available. So if you want to stay and work in Mauritius, it *is* possible, as long as you can find employment with a foreign company at director level or have a skill that is in short supply.

Your potential employer will apply for the work permit and pay the fee, which rises for each year of employment. It is likely to take several weeks before it comes through. If you plan on being self-employed, a permit is still required, as is a local referee.

Residence permits Application for a residence permit has to be made to the Prime Minister's Office. Each application is investigated thoroughly and if it is from a foreigner wishing to invest in Mauritius, it is considered in conjunction with the proposed investment project.

An individual not involved in an investment project who wants to reside in Mauritius has to satisfy the authorities that maintenance will be provided wholly from funds outside Mauritius. A deposit in some form for maintenance support or repatriation may be required. A foreigner who is the spouse of a citizen can achieve the status of resident after a protracted process.

Integrated Resort Schemes In a significant relaxing of the rules, non-Mauritian individuals or companies are now allowed to purchase properties that are part of an Integrated Resort Scheme (IRS). An IRS must have certain characteristics, but broadly speaking, in return for purchasing a luxury villa which is part of an IRS and costs a minimum of US$500,000, the individual is entitled to acquire Mauritian residence for the duration of the villa ownership. There is no restriction on the length of time that the villa can be rented out.

The first project of this type is being built on the Médine Sugar Estate in the west, between Port Louis and Flic en Flac. The Tamarina Golf Estate and Beach Club will comprise 119 luxury villas, a championship 18-hole golf course and a private beach club. The villas will be marketed at an average selling price of US$750,000.

ATTITUDE OF OFFICIALS Generally positive. The police, in a uniform of dark blue trousers and lighter blue shirts, are not menacing. The legacy of British colonial training lingers on and they seem polite and helpful, if unobtrusive, to visitors and law-abiding citizens. Bureaucrats, too, once convinced of a visitor's genuine need for help, are forthcoming as people rather than as regulation-bound civil servants.

High commissions, embassies and consulates can also provide information on Mauritius and deal with visa or work permit enquiries. (See also *Red tape*, page 43.)

Australia Mauritius High Commission, 2 Beale Crescent, Deakin, ACT 2600, Canberra; ↘ 2 6281 1203; f 2 6282 3235

Belgium Mauritius Embassy, 68 Rue des Bollandistes, Etterbeek, 1040 Brussels; ↘ 2 733 9988; f 2 734 4021

China Apartment 2–62, San Li Tung Bldg, San Li Tu Chao Yang District, Beijing 100600; ↘ 10 653 25695; f 10 653 25706

Egypt Mauritius Embassy, 156 El Sudan St, Mohandeseen, Cairo; ↘ 2 361 8102; f 2 361 8101

France Mauritius Embassy, 127 Rue de Tocqueville, 75017 Paris; ↘ 01 4227 3019; f 01 4053 0291

India Mauritius High Commission, 5 Kautilya Marg, Chanakyapuri, New Delhi 110021; ↘ 11 301 1112; f 11 301 9925: Mauritius Consulate, Mittal Tower C, Office 115, 11th Fl, Nariman Point, Mumbai 400021; ↘ 22 2284 1410; f 22 2284 5468

Italy Mauritius Consulate, Via G B Morgagni 6/A, 00161 Rome; ↘ 06 4424 5652; f 06 4424 5659

Madagascar Mauritius Embassy, Route Circulaire, Anjahana, Antananarivo 101; ↘ 20 223 2157; f 20 222 1939

Malaysia Mauritius High Commission, Lot W17-B1 & C1, 17th Fl, West Block, Wisma Selangor Dredging, Jalan Ampang, 50450 Kuala Lumpur; ↘ 603 2163 6306; f 603 2163 6294

Pakistan Mauritius Embassy, Hse No 13, St No 26, Sector F-6/2, Islamabad; ↘ 51 2828 985; f 51 2824 656

South Africa Mauritius High Commission, 1163 Pretorius St, Hatfield 0083, Pretoria; ↘ 12 342 1283; f 12 342 1286

UK Mauritius High Commission, 32–33 Elvaston Pl, London SW7 5NW; ↘ 020 7581 0294; f 020 7823 8437

United Nations (Switzerland) Mauritius Mission to the United Nations, 37–39 Rue de Vermont, CH - 1211 Geneva 20; ↘ 22 734 8550; f 22 734 8630

United Nations (US) Mauritius Mission, 211 East 43rd St, New York, NY 10017; ↘ 212 949 0190; f 212 697 3829

US Mauritius Embassy, 4301 Connecticut Av, NW, Suite 441, Washington DC 2008; ↘ 202 244 1491; f 202 966 0983

GETTING THERE AND AWAY

A package including flights and hotel accommodation is one of the most cost-efficient ways of visiting Mauritius as tour operators are able to negotiate special fares with airlines and hotels. It has become a very popular destination with tour operators so prices are usually competitive. Many offer visits to Mauritius in combination with another destination; particularly popular is a stay in Mauritius after a safari in Africa. Going on a package holiday need not restrict your freedom to explore the island since you are not obliged to eat, or even sleep, in the hotel although anything extra you do is, of course, at your expense and there is no refund for meals, or nights, not taken.

✈ **BY AIR** 'We can't tow Mauritius closer to Europe' is the answer someone was given when he commented to the tourist office about the high price of flying to Mauritius. The fact that it is a long way from anywhere (except Réunion) and that there are no cheap charter flights has helped Mauritius preserve the qualities that make it attractive. It also makes getting there the biggest expense of a visit. There is some talk of allowing low-cost airlines to fly to Mauritius, but this is unlikely to happen in the short term.

From Europe Probably the least expensive way of flying to Mauritius on direct flights from Europe, without buying a flights and accommodation package, is by buying a round-trip ticket from an airline ticket consolidator. A consolidator sells seats from the allocation reserved for holiday companies, offering only the seat instead of the complete holiday package. A return ticket from the UK is likely to cost around £700.

UK Air Mauritius offers six non-stop flights weekly from London Heathrow, depending on the season, along with two codeshare services operated by Air Seychelles. British Airways operates three direct flights weekly from London Heathrow.

In London, the travel organisation WEXAS (*45–49 Brompton Rd, Knightsbridge, London SW3 1DE;* ☏ *020 7589 3315;* f *020 7589 8418;* e *mship@wexas.com; www.wexas.com*), open to membership worldwide, can provide tickets to Mauritius (and other places) at a lot less than scheduled fares. Payment of a membership fee entitles you to discounted flights, hotels, car hire and travel advice.

France Air Mauritius and Air France operate frequent codeshare flights, some via Réunion, all from Paris Charles de Gaulle.

Germany Condor and Air Mauritius each fly once a week from Frankfurt and Munich.
Air Mauritius also offers weekly flights from **Rome**, **Milan**, **Zurich**, **Geneva**, **Vienna** and **Brussels**.

From Africa The closest mainland gateways are those in Africa. From **Johannesburg**, **Durban** and **Cape Town** there are flights by Air Mauritius and South African Airways. Air Mauritius and British Airways operate flights from **Nairobi**, whilst Air Zimbabwe flies once a week from **Harare**. Regular Air Mauritius and Air Madagascar flights link **Madagascar** and Mauritius.

LONG-HAUL FLIGHTS, CLOTS AND DVT

Dr Jane Wilson-Howarth

Long-haul air travel increases the risk of deep vein thrombosis. Although recent research has suggested that many of us develop clots when immobilised, most resolve without us ever having been aware of them. In certain susceptible individuals, though, large clots form and these can break away and lodge in the lungs. This is dangerous but happens in a tiny minority of passengers.

Studies have shown that flights of over five-and-a-half-hours are significant, and that people who take lots of shorter flights over a short space of time form clots. People at highest risk are:

- Those who have had a clot before – unless they are now taking warfarin
- People over 80 years of age
- Anyone who has recently undergone a major operation or surgery for varicose veins
- Someone who has had a hip or knee replacement in the last three months
- Cancer sufferers
- Those who have ever had a stroke
- People with heart disease
- Those with a close blood relative who has had a clot

Those with a slightly increased risk:

- People over 40
- Women who are pregnant or have had a baby in the last couple of weeks
- People taking female hormones or other oestrogen therapy
- Heavy smokers
- Those who have very severe varicose veins
- The very obese
- People who are very tall (over 6ft/1.8m) or short (under 5ft/1.5m)

From other Indian Ocean islands There are several flights a day between **Réunion** (Roland Garros and Pierrefonds) and Mauritius, with Air Austral and Air Mauritius. Air Seychelles and Air Mauritius provide six flights per week linking the **Seychelles** and Mauritius. There are several Air Mauritius flights a day between Mauritius and **Rodrigues**.

A new airline, Catovair (✆ 800 9000), was launched in September 2005 by IBL Aviation, part of the IBL Group. The intention is that the airline will serve the Indian Ocean islands, including the first to link Mauritius to **Agalega**, where IBL is building the island's first hotel complex. At the time of writing, the airline was offering six flights per week to **Rodrigues**.

From the US Air Mauritius (*US Contact: 560 Sylvan Av, Englewood Cliffs, New Jersey 07362;* ✆ *201 871 8382;* f *201 871 6983;* e *airmkusa@concentric.net*) doesn't fly to/from the US itself, but offers a range of packages using Virgin Atlantic via Europe.

From Australia Air Mauritius operates weekly flights from **Sydney and Melbourne** and twice-weekly flights from **Perth**.

From the Middle East Air Mauritius operates four weekly direct flights in a codeshare arrangement from **Dubai** with Emirates Airlines.

From Asia Air Mauritius operates flights from **Mumbai** (Bombay), **Delhi** and **Chennai** in a codeshare arrangement with Air India. Air Mauritius also flies to

A deep vein thrombosis (DVT) is a blood clot that forms in the deep leg veins. This is very different from irritating but harmless superficial phlebitis. DVT causes swelling and redness of one leg, usually with heat and pain in one calf and sometimes the thigh. A DVT is only dangerous if a clot breaks away and travels to the lungs (pulmonary embolus). Symptoms of a pulmonary embolus (PE) include chest pain that is worse on breathing in deeply, shortness of breath, and sometimes coughing up small amounts of blood. The symptoms commonly start three to ten days after a long flight. Anyone who thinks that they might have a DVT needs to see a doctor immediately who will arrange a scan. Warfarin tablets (to thin the blood) are then taken for at least six months.

PREVENTION OF DVT Several conditions make the problem more likely. Immobility is the key, and factors like reduced oxygen in cabin air and dehydration may also contribute. To reduce the risk of thrombosis on a long journey:

- Exercise before and after the flight
- Keep mobile before and during the flight; move around every couple of hours
- During the flight drink plenty of water or juices
- Avoid taking sleeping pills and excessive tea, coffee and alcohol
- Perform exercises that mimic walking and tense the calf muscles
- Consider wearing flight socks or support stockings (see www.legshealth.com)
- Taking a meal of oily fish (mackerel, trout, salmon, sardines, etc) in the 24 hours before departure reduces blood clotability and thus DVT risk
- The jury is still out on whether it is worth taking an aspirin before flying, but this can be discussed with your GP

If you think you are at increased risk of a clot, ask your doctor if it is safe to travel.

Singapore and **Hong Kong** and, in a codeshare arrangement with Malaysian Airlines, to **Kuala Lumpur**.

Whichever way you fly to Mauritius, it is absolutely essential that you have a confirmed return, or onward, ticket in your possession when you arrive. Passengers without a valid ticket to leave Mauritius aren't welcome and won't be allowed in until they buy one. There is more on the immigration requirements in *Red tape*, pages 43–7.

Air Mauritius: the nation's airline

When Air Mauritius began in 1968, it was an airline without an aircraft. It has remained small ever since although it is known in international aviation circles for doing big things. In 1987, it became the first airline in the world to order higher gross weight 767/200 Extended Range jetliners from Boeing which entered service in 1988. This philosophy continued with the introduction in 1994 of Airbus A340-300 aircraft to replace the airline's ageing Boeing 747SPs. The Airbus 300 version can carry 301 passengers in three classes. The next additions to the fleet will be three Airbus A340E aircraft, which are due to enter service in October 2006 and 2007.

In 2005, the fleet consisted of five Airbus A340-300s, two Boeing 767-200ERs, two Airbus A319s, one ATR 72-500, two ATR 42-500s (used on the Réunion and Rodrigues routes) and three Bell 206 Jet Ranger helicopters (available for charter).

By 2005, Air Mauritius was serving 29 destinations on four continents. The airline also acts as the ground handling agent for all other airlines at the international airport.

I have heard very few negative reports from passengers flying with Air Mauritius. As a rule, the cabin crew are professional and friendly. As airline food goes, the quality is good in all classes, but don't forget to make the airline aware of any special dietary requirements at the time of booking. First- and business-class passengers have a choice of three main courses, whilst economy passengers can choose from two dishes. Drinks are free in economy class, except for champagne. The Airbuses have a satisfactory seat pitch of 81cm (32in) in economy class, personal video screens and in-seat telephones in all classes. All flights are non-smoking.

You are allowed 23kg (50.6lb) of checked baggage in economy class, but only 15kg (33lb) on flights to/from Rodrigues. The business-class allowance is 30kg (66lb) and the first-class allowance is 40kg (88lb). A small extra allowance is provided for sports equipment. There is no hanging space for wedding dresses; they can either be stowed in the overhead lockers or boxed and checked in as hold baggage.

The majority of the shares in Air Mauritius are owned by the Government of Mauritius with shares also held by Air France, British Airways, Air India and Rogers & Co of Port Louis.

The airline's head office is located in President John F Kennedy Street in Port Louis. There is a very efficient ticketing office on the ground floor (take a number from the dispenser and wait for it to be flashed on a screen for your turn), as well as several shops, some selling airline souvenirs.

If you do choose to fly Air Mauritius, the in-flight magazine, *Islander*, is worth a read as it frequently contains worthwhile articles on culture, activities, tourist attractions, shopping, etc.

Air Mauritius offices

Mauritius Air Mauritius Centre, President John F Kennedy St, Port Louis; ☎ 207 7070; f 208 8331; reservations and reconfirmation of tickets; ☎ 207 7575; f 211 4014; e contact@airmauritius.com
Air Mauritius, SSR International Airport, Plaisance; ☎ 603 3030; f 637 3266
Air Mauritius Cargo, New Warehouse Complex, FFC, Plaine Magnien; ☎ 603 3698; f 637 8851; e cargo@airmauritius.com

Australia Ground Fl, 276 Pitt St, Sydney, NSW 2000; ☎ 02 8262 6500; f 02 9269 0747; e mksydney@airmauritius.com; Level 10, 43-51 Queen St, Melbourne, VIC 3000; ☎ 03 9611 0010; f 03 9620 9155; e mkmelbourne@airmauritius.com; Level 1, Ashton Chambers, 189 Georges Terrace, Perth, WA 6000; ☎ 08 9486 9133; f 08 9486 9144; e mkperth@airmauritius.com

France 1st Fl, 5 Bd de la Madeleine, 75001, Paris; ☎ 01 44 51 15 63; f 01 49 24 04 25; e mkparis@airmauritius.com

Germany Poststrasse 2–4, 60329 Frankfurt; ☎ 69 2400 1999; f 69 2400 1919; e info@airmauritius.de

Hong Kong Room 608, St George's Bldg, 2 Ice Hse St; ☎ 852 2523 1114; f 852 2525 0910; e mkhongkong@airmauritius.com.hk

India Ground Fl, Express Towers, Nariman Point, Mumbai 400021; ☎ 2202 6430; f 2202 5340;206–7 Arunachal Bldg, 19 Barakhamba Rd, New Delhi 110001; ☎ 2373 1534; f 2373 1545; e delssmk@satyam.net.in

Italy Via Barberini 68, 3rd Fl, 00187 Rome; ☎ 06 4200 7533; f 06 482 5252; e sales.rome@airmauritius.it

Kenya International Life Hse, Mezzanine Fl, Mama Ngina St, PO Box 45270, Nairobi; ☎ 02 229 166; f 02 221 006; e airmauritius@net2000ke.com

Madagascar ARIO Lalana, Solombavambahoaka, Frantsay, 77, Antsahalova, Antananarivo BP 3673; ☎ 020 2235 990; f 020 2235 773; e ariomad@bow.dts.mg

Malaysia CP 05, Suite 2201, 2nd Fl, Central Plaza, 88 Jalan Sultan Ismail, 50200 Kuala Lumpur; ☎ 2142 9161; f 2144 0230; e mkkul@tm.net.my

Réunion 13 Rue Charles Gounod, 97400 St-Denis;

☎ 0262 948383; f 0262 412326; e airmauritius@wanadoo.fr: 7 Rue François de Mahy, 97410 St-Pierre; ☎ 0262 960600; f 0262 962747; e ariosp@guetali.fr

Rodrigues ADS Bldg, Douglas St, Port Mathurin; ☎ 831 1558; f 831 1959; e jhung@airmauritius.com

Seychelles Kings Gate Travel Centre, Independence Av, PO Box 356, Mahé; ☎ 322 414; f 323 951

Singapore 80 Robinson Rd, 22–30, Singapore 068898; ☎ 06 222 3033; f 06 323 5386

South Africa Grayston Ridge Office Park, Ground Fl, South Wing, Block A, Sandown 2196, Johannesburg; ☎ 011 444 4600; f 011 444 4413; e jnbmk@airmauritius.co.za: Holiday Aviation Pty Ltd, Town Office, 3rd Fl, Sanclare Bldg, Dreyer St, Claremont, Cape Town; ☎ 021 671 5225; f 021 683 3359; e mk@holidaycpt.co.za

Switzerland 1–3 Rue de Chantepoulet, Case Postale 1060, 1201 Geneva; ☎ 22 732 0560; f 22 716 3471; e gvakkmk@airmauritius.ch

United Arab Emirates PO Box 1520, Al Maktoum St, Dubai; ☎ 04 221 4455; f 04 221 3378; e jhummun@emirates.net.ae

UK 49 Conduit St, London W1S 2YS; ☎ 020 7434 4375; f 020 7439 4101; e information@airmauritiusuk.com; at London Heathrow: Room 3514/15, South Wing, Terminal 3, Hounslow, Middlesex; ☎ 020 8897 3545; f 020 8283 0209; e mklhr@airmauritius.com

US 560 Sylvan Av, Englewood Cliffs, New Jersey 07632; ☎ 201 871 8382; f 201 871 6983; e sales@airmauritius.us

The Air Mauritius website (*www.airmauritius.com*) is excellent and very informative, and includes timetables, descriptions of the packages they offer and the hotels used.

Airline offices in Mauritius

The following companies act as general sales agents for a number of airlines:

Air Mauritius Air Mauritius Centre, President John F Kennedy St, Port Louis; ☎ 207 7171. General sales agents for Air India, SAS, SwissAir, Thai Airways.

Airworld Blendax Hse, Dumas St, Port Louis; ☎ 208 4935. General sales agents for Malaysian Airlines, Kenya Airways.

Currimjee Jeewanjee & Co 5 Duke of Edinburgh Av, Port Louis; ☎ 208 7695. General sales agents for Singapore Airlines.

Harel Mallac & Co Harel Mallac Bldg, Edith Cavell St,

Port Louis; ☎ 207 3000. General sales agents for Condor, Lufthansa, Japan Airlines.

Ireland Blyth IBL Hse, Caudan Waterfront, Port Louis; ☎ 202 8000. General sales agents for British Airways, ☎ 203 2152; Cathay Pacific Airways, ☎ 203 2152; Emirates, ☎ 203 2154; Air Madagascar, ☎ 203 2150; Catovair, ☎ 800 9000.

IKS Aviation IKS Bldg, cnr La Paix and Farquhar Sts, Port Louis; ☎ 216 4467. General sales agents for Air Zimbabwe, ☎ 241 1573 and Air Tanzania, ☎ 241 1573.

Rogers Travel Rogers Hse, President John F Kennedy St, Port Louis; ↘ 202 6655. General sales agents for Air France, ↘ 202 6747; Air Seychelles, ↘ 202 6727; South African Airways, ↘ 202 6737; Air Austral, ↘ 202 6688.

BY SEA Cruise liners occasionally call at Mauritius, either on round-the-world voyages or on cruises from southern and eastern Africa. However, the island's location rules it out as a call for wintering yachts from Europe. Cargo ships come frequently but since few of them carry passengers you would need to sign on as a crew member to join them.

There are regular passenger sailings between Mauritius and Réunion and between Mauritius and Rodrigues. For detailed information contact the Mauritius Shipping Corporation (*Suite 417–18, St James Court, Saint Denis St, Port Louis;* ↘ *210 5944;* f *210 5176;* e *info@msc.intnet.mu; www.mauritiusshipping.intnet.mu*).

Réunion *Spirit of Port Louis* is a catamaran which sails two or three times per week between Mauritius and Réunion. It leaves from the Customs Steps at the Port Louis Waterfront and the crossing takes just five hours. Return tickets cost US$66 (Rs2,000) per person, or US$41 (Rs1,250) one-way and baggage is limited to 50kg. Prices include a cold lunch. For reservations and more information in Mauritius, contact the Concorde Travel Agency (*La Chaussée St, Port Louis;* ↘ *208 5041;* f *212 2582;* e *concord@bow.intnet.mu*).

Mauritius Pride, operated by Mauritius Shipping Corporation (↘ *210 5944*), sails at least five times a month between Mauritius and Réunion. The crossing takes 12 hours. For non-residents of Mauritius, seats cost from US$90 (Rs2,700) per person return and cabins are US$135 (Rs4,050) per person return. *Mauritius Trochetia* is a new, well-equipped ship with first- and second-class cabins and suites. Facilities include a pool, gym, shop and restaurants. It sails at least four times a month between Mauritius and Réunion. Cabins cost from US$115 (Rs3,450) per person return.

Rodrigues See page 200.

HEALTH

The only proof of vaccination required is against yellow fever for those over one year of age arriving from an infected area. It's good for ten years. Infected areas are those areas which according to the World Health Organisation are included in the endemic zones. Endemic areas include Kenya and Tanzania so you will need a yellow-fever jab if you plan to visit or actually originate your journey there. However, passengers in transit through Nairobi or Dar Es Salaam who do not leave the airport don't need proof of vaccination. Yellow fever vaccine may not be suitable for everyone. Take advice from either your GP or a travel specialist. If you cannot take the vaccine then you should obtain an exemption certificate before travel.

The traveller to any tropical country will benefit from the following vaccinations: tetanus, diphtheria and polio, which are effective for ten years; hepatitis A (as Avaxim or Havrix Monodose), which lasts for one year and can be boosted to last for ten; and typhoid (as Typhim Vi). For longer trips, ie: four weeks or more, hepatitis B and rabies vaccines should also be considered. Both these vaccines consist of three injections given over a minimum of 21 days. You are advised to visit your doctor well in advance of your trip to plan the vaccine schedule.

According to the Mauritian authorities, there is no malaria risk in Mauritius or Rodrigues. Doctors in your home country may try to persuade you that you need prophylaxis, but thousands of visitors travel to the island each year without them and the Mauritian government employs stringent measures to keep Mauritius malaria-free. If you arrive from a country where malaria exists, you may be asked to provide a blood sample for testing.

To combat the annoyance of mosquitoes during the night, I recommend mosquito coils in preference to electric gadgetry, creams or heavy nets suspended from the ceiling. Coils can be bought in Mauritius. They are made of some form of pyrethrum, compacted so it burns for six to eight hours. They give off a smoke which mosquitoes hate. So do some humans, but it is harmless to us and deadly to them. Remember also that there may be day-biting mosquitoes which can carry disease such as dengue fever. You should use a DEET-containing repellent (minimum content 20%) if you spot them about. Remember to re-apply after swimming – repellents are never as waterproof as the manufacturers claim!

Although the water in Mauritius is officially safe to drink in most places, water, especially ice, can be the cause of minor upsets. A sensible precaution is to drink only bottled water (obtainable everywhere) and to do without ice in your drinks. Bottled soft drinks, mixers and soda water are usually served cold. Do not drink tap water during or after a cyclone or heavy rains as nasties can be washed into the water supply and treatment problems may occur.

For those who are looking for it, romance is easy to find in Mauritius. However, AIDS is present on the island and visitors should be aware of the dangers.

TRAVEL CLINICS AND HEALTH INFORMATION A full list of current travel clinic websites worldwide is available on www.istm.org. For other journey preparation information, consult www.tripprep.com.

UK

British Airways Travel Clinics There are now only 2 BA clinics, both in London: one is at 213 Piccadilly St, London W1J 9HQ and operates a walk-in service Mon–Fri 09.30–17.30 and Sat 10.00–15.30. The other is at 101 Cheapside St, London, EC2V 6DT and offers appointments Mon–Fri 09.00–16.00. For further information and bookings ☏ 0845 600 2236 or visit www.britishairways.com/travelclinics. They also sell a variety of health-related goods.

Fleet Street Travel Clinic 29 Fleet St, London EC4Y 1AA; ☏ 020 7353 5678; f 020 7353 5500; e info@fleetstreetclinic.com; www.fleetstreetclinic.com

Hospital for Tropical Diseases Travel Clinic Capper St (off Tottenham Ct Rd), London WC1E 6AU; ☏ 020 7388 9600; f 020 7383 4817; www.thehtd.org. Offers consultations and advice, and is able to provide all necessary drugs and vaccines for travellers. Runs a healthline, ☏ 09061 337733 for country-specific information and health hazards. Calls cost 50p per min and should last 5–8 mins. Also stocks nets, water purification equipment and personal protection measures.

MASTA Travel Clinics A network of independent travel clinics in the UK. Unfortunately, there is not a central phone number so you will need to go to www.masta.org to find your nearest clinic and their

phone number. The website also has an excellent Health Library and an online travel shop.

NHS travel website www.fitfortravel.scot.nhs.uk, provides country-by-country advice on immunisation and malaria, plus details of recent developments, and a list of relevant health organisations.

Nomad Travel Clinics Have 5 clinics: Bristol, ☏ 0117 922 6567; e bristolclinic@nomadtravel.co.uk; Southampton, ☏ 02380 234920; and 3 in London at Victoria, ☏ 020 7823 5823; Russell Sq, ☏ 020 7833 4114; e russellclinic@nomadtravel.co.uk; and Turnpike Lane, ☏ 020 8889 7014; e turnpike@nomadtravel.co.uk. They also have Travel Health Line, ☏ 09068 633414 where you can speak to a health professional (calls cost 60p per min). Their website, www.nomadtravel.co.uk, also contains lots of health advice and sells products online.

Trailfinders Immunisation Centre 194 Kensington High St, London W8 7RG; ☏ 020 7938 3999; www.trailfinders.com

Travelpharm The Travelpharm website, www.travelpharm.com, offers up-to-date guidance on travel-related health and has a range of medications available through their online mini-pharmacy. You can also order products on 01395 233771.

Irish Republic

Tropical Medical Bureau ☎ 1850 487 674; www.tmb.ie. Has clinics throughout Ireland and an excellent website specific to tropical destinations.

US

Centers for Disease Control 1600 Clifton Rd, Atlanta, GA 30333; ☎ 1800 311 3435; e cdcinfo@cdc.gov; www.cdc.gov/travel. The central source of travel information in the USA. Each summer they publish the invaluable *Health Information for International Travel*, available from the Division of Quarantine at the above address.

Connaught Laboratories PO Box 187, Swiftwater, PA 18370; ☎ 800 822 2463. They will send a free list of specialist tropical-medicine physicians in your state.

IAMAT (International Association for Medical Assistance to Travellers) 1623 Military Rd #279, Niagara Falls, NY 14304-1745; ☎ 716 754 4883; www.iamat.org. A non-profit organisation that maintains a network of doctors around the world who will treat IAMAT members. The doctors are all English speaking and have received training in either the US or Europe. There is no charge for membership of IAMAT, but a donation is appreciated.

Canada

IAMAT (International Association for Medical Assistance to Travellers) Suite 1, 1287 St Clair Av West, Toronto, Ontario M6E 1B8; ☎ 416 652 0137; www.iamat.org

Travel Medicine Centre 700 Bay St, Suite 609,

Toronto, Ontario M5G 1Z6; ☎ 416 340 8222; e pscap@idirect.com; www.travelclin.com

Australia, New Zealand

TMVC (Travellers Medical & Vaccination Centre) ☎ 1300 65 88 44; www.tmvc.com.au. Has 25 clinics in Australia and New Zealand including: *Auckland:* Canterbury Arcade, 170 Queen St, Auckland City; ☎ 373 3531; e auckland@traveldoctor.co.nz; *Gold Coast:* Level 2, The Vision Centre, 95 Nerang St, Southport, QLD 4215; ☎ 07 5526 4444; e gcoast@traveldoctor.com.au; *Melbourne:* 393 Little Bourke St, 2nd Fl, Melbourne, VIC 3000; ☎ 03 9602 5788; f 03 9670 8394; e melbourne@traveldoctor.com.au; *Sydney:* Dymocks Bldg, 7th Fl, 428 George St, Sydney, NSW 2000; ☎ 02 9221 7133; f 02 9221 8401; e sydney@traveldoctor.com.au

South Africa

SAA-Netcare Travel Clinics PO Box 786692, Sandton 2146; ☎ +27 11 883 3801; f +27 11 883 3803; www.travelclinic.co.za or www.malaria.co.za. Clinics throughout South Africa.

TMVC (Travellers Medical & Vaccination Centre); www.tmvc.com.au. Has 13 clinics throughout South Africa.

Switzerland

IAMAT (International Association for Medical Assistance to Travellers) 57 Chemin des Voirets, 1212 Grand Lancy, Geneva; www.iamat.org

MEDICAL SERVICES IN MAURITIUS Wherever you are staying, the management will recommend the nearest doctor or dentist for an emergency. The larger hotels have a nurse and small dispensary on their premises, and a roster of doctors on call.

Medical facilities in Mauritius are good, with private clinics and public hospitals available if a doctor advises hospitalisation. The standard is the equivalent of developed countries and the cost of treatment will be a lot less than private treatment in Europe. However, medical services in Rodrigues are limited and many patients are sent to Mauritius for treatment. (See *Chapter 12, Health and safety*, pages 197–8.)

Main hospitals

Dr Jeetoo Hospital Volcy Pougnet St, Port Louis; ☎ 212 3201; f 212 8958

Princess Margaret Orthopaedic Hospital Candos; ☎ 425 3031; f 425 7693

Sir Seewoosagur Ramgoolam National Hospital Pamplemousses; ☎ 243 3661; f 243 3740

Moka Eye Hospital Moka; ☎ 433 4015

Private clinics

City Clinic Sir Edgar Laurent St, Port Louis; ☎ 241 2951; f 240 7042

Clinique du Bon Pasteur Thomy Pitot St, Rose Hill;

☎ 464 7238

Clinique Darné G Guibert St, Floréal; ☎ 686 1477; f 696 3612

Clinique Ferrière College Lane, Curepipe; ☎ 676 1973
Clinique de Lorette Higginson St, Curepipe; ☎ 675 2911; f 676 2695
Clinique Mauricienne Le Réduit; ☎ 454 3063
Clinique du Nord Coast Rd, Baie du Tombeau;
☎ 247 2532; f 247 1254
Clinique de Quatre Bornes Stevenson Av, Quatre Bornes; ☎ 425 0429
Med Point Clinic Sayed Hossen Av, Phoenix;
☎ 426 7777, (ambulance) 426 8888; f 426 5050

Vaccination centres

International Vaccination Centre Mutual Aid Bldg, Victoria Sq, Port Louis; ☎ 212 4464
Air Mauritius Clinic 1st Fl, Air Mauritius Centre,
5 President John F Kennedy St, Port Louis; ☎ 207 7201

Pharmacies Pharmacies are well stocked with European/US proprietary medicines, are open in the evenings in most towns, and there are dispensaries and health centres in most villages. There is a Social Hygiene Clinic at Dr Bouloux Health Centre, Cassis (☎ *212 0811*). The Malaria Eradication Unit is at Victoria Square, Port Louis (☎ *212 1162*).

SAFETY

Although Mauritius enjoys a relatively low crime rate, petty crime is on the increase. Many attribute this to an increase in drug taking. Pickpockets have begun to target tourists in busy areas such as Port Louis market and Grand Baie, whilst self-caterers should be aware of the increase in reports of housebreaking.

Lone women travellers receive a fair amount of attention from males. It is usually well-meaning curiosity but don't take chances that you would not take in your home country. For instance, don't accept a lift from a lone male or group of men. Don't walk alone at night and try to avoid dimly lit areas, such as beaches. Even during the day, make sure that you are not too isolated on a beach.

A vast army of dogs wanders the streets and beaches of Mauritius: some are strays but others simply have careless owners. There is always the possibility of confrontation, particularly as they often go around in packs. I was told by a friend

---

CHIKUNGUNYA VIRUS INFECTION

Dr Felicity Nicholson

Chikungunya is a viral disease that is transmitted by mosquitoes. It is endemic to large parts of Africa, the Middle East, India and southeast Asia, and has some similarities to dengue fever, which is widespread in most tropical regions.

During 2006 there have been increased numbers of cases of chikungunya reported in Réunion, Mauritius and the Seychelles, with over 1,100 cases reported in Mauritius by March 2006. The main preventive measure taken by the authorities is to spray against mosquitoes and to reduce their breeding grounds.

Symptoms appear between four and seven days after a bite by the infected mosquito. A high fever and headache occur, with significant pains in the joints (eg: ankles and wrists). Most patients recover fully over a period of a few weeks, although 5–10% of patients will experience joint symptoms that can persist for a year or more. The virus is rarely fatal.

There is no vaccine available to protect against chikungunya. Travellers are advised to take precautions against insect bites (ie: use insect repellent on areas of exposed skin), particularly during daylight hours when these mosquitoes are active. Pregnant women and those with chronic illnesses should seek specific expert advice before travelling.

living locally that the best defence while walking alone is an umbrella. If a dog with dubious intentions approaches, simply erect the umbrella in its direction and its shield-like appearance should be enough to deter the beast. Take care whilst driving as the roads are not well lit and dogs tend to appear from nowhere.

A relatively new danger is that presented by speedboats, which now roar along the coasts in front of hotels. There have been reports of swimmers being seriously injured, so be vigilant or stick to marked bathing areas.

Don't let all this spoil your holiday, simply use common sense and don't take unnecessary risks.

DISABLED TRAVELLERS

I was very disappointed by the discoveries I made regarding facilities for disabled travellers to Mauritius and Rodrigues. There is no requirement for hotels to construct rooms equipped for the disabled. Even large modern hotels built in the last few years lack specially designed rooms.

However, most hotels claim that they can accommodate disabled guests by giving them a room on the ground floor. This is all very well but many hotels have numerous steps linking their facilities and lifts are not always on hand. I would advise disabled travellers to contact the hotel direct in order to gather as much information as possible.

Hotels which have rooms equipped for the disabled include Hilton Mauritius Resort and Spa, Marina Resort, Le Preskil, One&Only Le Touessrok, One&Only Le St Géran, Sugar Beach Resort and the Indian Resort. Domaine les Pailles is one tourist attraction that has full wheelchair access and even holds conferences for the disabled.

Pavements are adequate in large towns, such as Port Louis and Curepipe. However, the coastal resorts tend to be quite spread out and frequently lack pavements.

WHAT TO TAKE

The glib answer is lots of travellers' cheques. Credit cards too are widely accepted and there are plenty of ATMs.

Apart from difficult personal items like prescription medicines or designer accessories, you should be able to get everything you need.

For clothes, casual elegance is a good watchword. On the coast at any time of the year, you will need lightweight, preferably cotton clothing. In the highlands something warmer will be necessary in the evenings. Hotel boutiques and shops in Port Louis and Curepipe have an excellent range of clothing appropriate for the climate. Don't forget most hotels require men to wear trousers and shirts in the restaurant in the evenings. If you plan to do some hiking, sturdy trainers are sufficient for the trails in Mauritius.

Suncream, insect repellent, camera film and other such essentials are very expensive in hotel shops and are certainly not cheap even in local shops. It is best to take a supply with you.

Three-pin and continental two-pin sockets are both used, so take the appropriate adaptors if you need to. Modern buildings and hotels tend to have three-pin plugs, whilst budget hotels and self-catering accommodation often have two-pin plugs. Occasional power failures do occur so it is prudent to carry a pocket torch.

Since imported liquor is expensive, you may want to take in your full duty-free spirit allowance. Locally made cigarettes are cheap but if you are hooked on a special brand, take it with you.

Finally, don't forget adequate travel insurance.

MAPS There are several small maps available as part of the tourist office literature and some picturesque French maps of Mauritius can be bought at hotels and bookshops. The most detailed map is the one published in English by the UK Government's Directorate of Overseas Surveys for the Mauritius Government, which includes a map of Rodrigues. It is available for a fee from the Plans and Records Office within the Ministry of Housing (*3rd Fl, SILWF Bldg, Edith Cavell St, Port Louis;* \ *208 2831, extension 204*) or from Stanfords (*12–14 Long Acre, London WC2E 9LP;* \ *020 7836 1321*).

More practical for the general tourist is the booklet published by Multimedia Océan Indien and Option Service Ltd, which includes maps of Mauritius and Rodrigues and town plans of Port Louis, the Caudan Waterfront, Grand Baie, Curepipe, Rose Hill and Vacoas/Phoenix. It is available from the MTPA (see pages 42–3).

For hikers, a map of the Black River Gorges National Park is available from the Forestry Department.

$ MONEY AND BANKING

The legal unit of currency is the Mauritian rupee (Rs), which is divided into 100 cents. There are banks with automatic teller machines (ATMs) in most towns around the island, including several in Grand Baie and Flic en Flac. Banking hours are Monday–Thursday 09.15–15.15, Friday 09.15–15.30 and Saturday 09.15–11.15. Banks are closed on Sundays and public holidays. Foreign exchange counters in tourist areas often have longer opening hours.

The Bank of Mauritius (the Central Bank) oversees the proper functioning of the banking system and implements the financial and monetary policies of the government. It used to administer exchange control but since 1983 the rupee has been linked to a basket of currencies relevant to foreign trade. The exchange rate fluctuates daily and is determined by the Central Bank.

Although the rate of foreign exchange is the same in all banks and the commission charged is similar, the method of exchange is not the same. Some banks require a lot of form filling to exchange travellers' cheques and then tell you to join a queue at another counter to collect the rupees. The Mauritius Commercial Bank (MCB) is one of the most efficient.

Some mid-range and all luxury and upmarket hotels offer foreign exchange services, where guests can change travellers' cheques and cash, although the commission may be higher than at banks.

Credit cards, such as Visa and MasterCard, are widely accepted in Mauritius and can also be used to withdraw cash from ATMs, which are found in the main towns. Most upmarket and luxury hotels will also accept American Express.

Currency exchange rates in April 2006 were as follows: £1 = Rs55; US$1 = Rs31; €1 = Rs38.

BUDGETING The thrifty, independent traveller staying in cheap, basic accommodation and eating in budget restaurants, travelling by bus, and enjoying free outdoor pursuits instead of spending liberally in bars and casinos, could live on £25 per day. I tend to underestimate my own probable expenses because I overlook that urge to be extravagant after a period of scrimping. Since there is bound to be a time during your stay when you will want to do or buy something you haven't anticipated, allow extra.

If you are on a package holiday at an upmarket beach resort, you will have the cost of extra meals (even lunch can cost over £20 in some places), drinks, tea, tips and tours to worry about, so you will need more than the independent traveller.

If you're staying in prepaid self-catering accommodation you should find the cost of household items and food averaging out at less than at home.

Taxis have meters but drivers will only use them if you insist. It is often better to negotiate the fare before the journey, but it will still be high. Taxi drivers know their value, especially as resort hotels are isolated and a taxi is usually the only way to reach or leave them, so allow extra cash for unexpected taxi journeys, particularly since the excellent island-wide bus service stops running early in the evening.

There is a 15% government tax on hotel accommodation but this is usually included in the room rate. There is also a tax of 15% on meals in restaurants and this may or may not be included in the prices on the menu. A footnote will explain if it is.

TIPPING Tipping in restaurants is usually left to your discretion, although you should check that a service charge is not going to be added to the bill before you dish out tips. In restaurants where no service charge is added, you could leave 5–10% of the bill, according to your satisfaction with the service. In basic eateries tipping is not expected.

Porters should be tipped according to what they do for you, although hotel porters do not linger waiting for a tip. Rs20–40 is about right for airport porters. Taxi drivers don't expect tips but they are gratefully received.

GETTING MARRIED

In keeping with the romantic ambience of Mauritius, the island has become a popular place for visitors to get married – not to Mauritians, but to each other. Wedding packages feature in the brochures of most overseas tour operators, whose local representatives handle the arrangements.

Most wedding packages mean that many of the administrative formalities are carried out for you. The tour operator will usually arrange a special licence to allow you to be married within two days of arrival but a visit to the Ministry in Port Louis is necessary before your wedding day to obtain special dispensation under Mauritian law. Divorced ladies must allow a minimum 300-day gap between the divorce and new wedding date, or a pregnancy test taken locally must be negative.

It is possible to arrange a wedding independently. Vital is a certificate issued under the authority of the Prime Minister to the effect that the couple are not citizens or residents of Mauritius. This is obtainable on application (at least ten days before the date of the proposed wedding) to the Registrar of Civil Status (*7th Level, Emmanuel Anquetil Bldg, Port Louis;* ⎱ *201 1727;* f *211 2420*). The documents needed for the application are two photocopies of each birth certificate and two photocopies of the pages showing the issuing authority and personal details of each passport, and any other documents in case of proving divorce, or demise of former spouse. This certificate has to be produced to the Civil Status Officer at the time of publication, and the marriage may be celebrated on the day immediately following the day of publication.

A couple can choose to be married at the Civil Status Office or in their hotel, in which case the ceremony is performed by the Civil Status Officer of the locality where the couple are staying. It is possible for a couple (if both parties are Roman Catholic) to have the wedding in a Roman Catholic church in Mauritius. Full details of the procedure are available from the Episcopate of Port Louis (*Monseigneur Gonin St, Port Louis;* ⎱ *208 3068;* f *208 6607*). Information should also be obtained from the diocese in which they normally reside.

Air Mauritius aircraft have no hanging space for wedding dresses. The airline recommends that they are either rolled and packed in the overhead lockers or boxed and checked in as hold baggage.

Information on getting married abroad is available at www.weddings.co.uk.

ON ARRIVAL/DEPARTURE

SIR SEEWOOSAGUR RAMGOOLAM INTERNATIONAL AIRPORT The airport at Plaisance, in the southeast of the island, is small but modern with good facilities.

There are duty-free shops both on arrival and on departure. Restaurants are located in the main hall of the airport and in the departure area. Also in the main hall are shops selling local goods, from handicrafts to smoked marlin. Money can be changed at the bank counters, which are open during all international arrivals.

The public are not allowed to enter the check-in departure area and baggage security screening is done at the entrance to the building.

For more information about the airport, visit http://mauritius-airport.intnet.mu.

LUGGAGE Delivery of luggage is usually prompt unless there are several aircraft arriving at the same time and there are usually plenty of trolleys available. If you use the services of the porters, who wait outside the arrivals lobby, you may want to give a small tip, say about Rs20–40.

GETTING TO YOUR HOTEL All the major car-hire companies have desks at the airport. If a friend is meeting you, they will have to wait outside since the general public are not allowed into the arrivals lobby and have to congregate with the taxi drivers, beyond the doors. Tour operators and hotel representatives wait inside the lobby.

If you need a taxi it helps to know the current fare to your destination and the tourist information counter at the airport should be able to tell you. At night you could well be charged double. It is best to agree the price before starting your journey.

There are public bus services from the airport to Mahébourg and Curepipe, from where buses serve other parts of the island.

See *Getting around*, below, for further information on car hire, bus services and driving.

GETTING AROUND

INBOUND TOUR OPERATORS If you are happy to forego your independence for a while, the easiest way to get around and see the sights of Mauritius is by taking one of the conducted tours run by a tour operator. They provide an instant introduction to the island, enabling the visitor to discover places that they can return to later and explore independently. Inbound tour operators meet arrivals at the airport on behalf of the hotels and overseas tour operators. They provide leaflets about their services to incoming guests and many have desks at the major hotels.

The larger tour operators, listed below, can organise almost anything, including car hire, private driver/guide and all manner of activities and excursions. They can also provide guides fluent in a range of languages. Group excursions last either a half or full day and most include lunch and entrance fees to the attractions visited.

White Sand Tours is a wholly owned subsidiary of Destination Management Limited (DML), which also operates the Avis franchise in Mauritius. It employs lots of highly competent staff and has its own fleet of well-maintained vehicles. It was the first destination management company in the Indian Ocean to obtain the ISO9002 certificate, an internationally recognised quality assurance standard. As well as the usual tours, either chauffeur-driven or in groups, the company can arrange activities such as deep-sea fishing, helicopter flights, horseriding, mountain climbing and trekking.

Smaller tour operators usually specialise in a few organised group tours and most are to be found around Grand Baie and Trou d'Eau Douce. Their prices may not include entrance fees.

GBTT (Grand Baie Travel & Tours) Coastal Rd, Trou aux Biches; ⟍ 265 5261; f 265 5798; e resagbtt@intnet.mu; www.gbtt.com
Mauritours S Venkatesananda St, Rose Hill; ⟍ 467 9700; f 454 1682; e mauritours@mauritours.intnet.mu; www.mauritours.net
MTTB-Mautourco 84 Gustave Colin St, Forest Side; ⟍ 670 4301; f 675 6425; e mtco@mautourco.com;

www.mttb-mautourco.com
SummerTimes 5 Av Bernardin de St Pierre, Quatre Bornes; ⟍ 427 1111; f 427 1010; e summer@summertimes.intnet.mu; www.summer-times.com
White Sand Tours M1 Motorway, Port Louis; ⟍ 212 3712; f 208 8664; e wst@whitesandtours.com; www.whitesandtours.com

DRIVING There are over 1,830km of good, tarred roads throughout Mauritius. The motorways and the road between Port Louis and Curepipe are the best; little-used country roads are not in such good condition. Driving is on the left.

Although the standard of driving is generally good (higher than in neighbouring Réunion), drivers are not courteous. Do not expect other drivers to give way or to stop at pedestrian crossings. Outside the towns, there are stretches of open road without traffic, which make driving pleasant. However, roads are not well lit at night so watch out for pedestrians and stray dogs. Take care to observe the speed limit of 80km/h on the motorway and 50km/h in built-up areas; police operate on-the-spot fines.

Negotiating Port Louis by car requires patience as traffic builds up to horrendous proportions during the day, complicated by the trucks and handcarts which stop to unload goods from the port at warehouses in the city centre, and by the vans that come at the same time to collect the goods for distribution to the country districts. Most of the streets are one-way, which adds to the confusion for the uninitiated.

Parking zones exist in Port Louis, Rose Hill, Quatre Bornes and Curepipe between 09.00 and 16.30. Parking tickets must be purchased in advance from a filling station and displayed inside the windscreen. There are car parks near the Caudan Waterfront, such as the Granary, where you can simply buy a ticket on arrival.

The system of car registration shows by the number plate the month and the year in which a car was first registered. The car's number is followed by an alphabetical abbreviation indicating the month and a number for the year, thus 670 DC 99 indicates a car registered in December 1999. Private cars have black number plates, taxis white, hire cars yellow and diplomatic cars blue.

There are several vehicle spare parts shops and a wide range of cars are driven, with Japanese makes predominant. Both petrol and diesel are readily available at filling stations throughout the country, but it is worth keeping your tank full, especially for distance driving at night.

🚗 Car hire Car hire in Mauritius is expensive. Cars can be rented from independent companies, especially those in the Grand Baie area, for a few rupees a day less than the large firms.

Cars can usually be delivered and recovered anywhere on the island and there are car-hire desks at the airport. Some companies keep cars available at the major hotels.

The minimum age for hiring a self-drive car varies from 20 to 23 years, according to the hire company. Independent ones are not so fussy. All companies require that the driver has been in possession of a valid driver's licence for at least one year. Since an international driving licence is valid for only one year it is advisable to carry either your own home-country licence as well, or an old International Licence as proof of more than a year's driving experience.

The rental must be paid in advance. Payment of a daily premium reduces the insurance excess and a daily driver and passenger personal accident insurance is available. As an example of daily rates, Budget charge €56 (about Rs1,960) per day (one to six days) for a Renault Clio with unlimited mileage (fuel and 15% VAT are not included). Vehicles range from two-door jeeps to executive-class saloon cars with air conditioning.

If you don't want to drive yourself, the car-hire companies will provide a driver. Not only does this save you having to cope with local driving conditions but there is also the bonus of having a private guide too. A chauffeur-driven service provided by the three main companies will add around Rs450 per eight-hour day to your bill. Smaller companies charge less. Overtime, Sundays and public holidays are extra.

If it is important to you to have rear seat belts, do check with the hire company. Not all hire cars have rear seat belts as the wearing of seat belts is compulsory only in the front seats.

Car-hire companies

ABC Car Rental Albion Docks Bldg, Trou Fanfaron, Port Louis; ↘ 242 8957; f 242 8958; e abccar@intnet.mu; www.abc-carrental.com
Avis DML Bldg, M1 Motorway, Port Louis; ↘ 208 6031; f 211 1420; e avis@avismauritius.com; www.avismauritius.com
BBL Car Rental Balance Rd, Surinam; ↘ 625 6104
Budget Rent a Car S Venkatesananda St, Rose Hill; ↘ 467 9700; f 454 1682; e budget@mauritours.net; www.budget-maurice.com
Colony Car Rental Colonie St, Mahébourg; ↘ 631 7062; f 631 1403
Dodo Touring & Co Ltd St Jean Rd, Quatre Bornes; ↘ 425 6810; f 424 4309
Europcar Av Michael Leal, Les Pailles; ↘ 286 0140; f 286 4705; e europcar@intnet.mu; www.europcar.com
Hertz Gustave Colin St, Forest Side; ↘ 674 3695;

f 675 6425; e hertz@mautourco.com; www.hertz.com
Kevtrav Ltd 3rd Fl, Discovery Hse, St Jean Rd, Quatre Bornes; ↘ 465 4458; f 464 3777; e keldt@intnet.mu; www.kevtrav.com
Moon Patrol Royal Rd, Mahébourg; ↘ 631 9507
National Car Rental 217 Royal Rd, Curepipe; ↘ 570 0660; f 670 2137; e national@intnet.mu; www.nationalcar.com
Société J H A Arnulphy & Cie Labourdonnais St, Mahébourg; ↘ 631 9806; f 631 9991
Sunny Beach Tours Ltd 57 Etienne Pellereau St, Sheahfar Bldg, Port Louis; ↘ 240 5245; f 241 3685
Tourismo Travel & Tours Coastal Rd, Grand Baie; ↘ 263 8755; f 263 8775
Waterlily Travel & Tours 15 Malartic St, Curepipe; ↘ 676 1496; f 676 1494

Motorbike hire Motorbikes and mopeds are available for hire. The best area to look is Grand Baie where GBTT (see opposite) acts as an agent for individual motorbike owners and can arrange rental from Rs280 a day. Crash helmets are compulsory when driving or riding a motorbike or moped.

Bicycle hire Bicycles can be hired from the major hotels by the hour, half day and day. The cost is from Rs60 per day and several hotels organise group bicycle tours. Some agencies in Grand Baie and most inbound tour operators can arrange bicycle hire. Cycling is regarded as a diversion rather than a means of getting around the island.

TAXIS A visitor who had been in Mauritius for a week walked into the tourist office in Port Louis and looked around the room for a few minutes.

'I must congratulate you,' he said to the girls at the information counter. 'Yours is the first tourist office I have visited which has a portrait of a taxi driver on its walls.'

The girls were puzzled until the tourist pointed mockingly to the stuffed head of a shark hanging above the counter.

Taxi drivers in Mauritius won a reputation for being rapacious because their charges were governed by outdated guidelines that were simply ignored. The reputation lingers even though taxis now sport nifty modern meters with figures in red which seem to mount alarmingly quickly. Knowing that visitors like to bargain, taxi drivers will negotiate 'special fares' for round-trip journeys (usually boosted to include waiting time), but this is not always to the tourists' advantage. Drivers, though, are generally helpful.

The fares set by government decree in 1994 vary according to where you get your taxi. If you intend retaining the taxi and returning in it, you have the right to ask for Tariff 2 to be programmed into the meter. However, most drivers operate on Tariff 1 which really only applies for a one-way journey and includes the fee for the driver to return to his base.

Locals who know the distance and approximate price usually fix the fare with the driver and don't use the meter at all, since they believe (usually correctly) that it will cost them more. While taxis are obliged by law to have meters, they are not obliged to use them.

Most hotels have a taxi stand and display the fares agreed with the drivers at reception. However, if you take a taxi from a stand not linked to a hotel and negotiate a price, you will often find it is even cheaper than hotel taxi prices.

In most towns taxis are to be found close to the bus station but tend to be available only at conventional times (06.00–20.00). They can also be telephoned (there are two dozen companies listed in the phone directory) and there are 24-hour and night services. Many drivers have mobile phones with numbers also listed in the directory. There is a number of private cars operating as illegal taxis (*taxi marron*).

Taxi trains tout for custom among passengers queuing for buses or follow regular routes, picking up passengers on the way and charging little more than the bus fare for a seat in a shared car. These taxis are usually old boneshakers but they do offer a cheap alternative and will operate late into the night on popular routes.

HELICOPTER HIRE The Air Mauritius Bell Jet Ranger helicopter, with seats for four passengers, is available for hire with pilot for sightseeing and for transfers from/to the airport.

In 2005, the cost of transfer from the airport to hotels in the north of the island was Rs9,500 per person and to hotels the east, south and west US$148 (Rs7,500). Sightseeing helicopter flights start at Rs9,500 (one or two people) for 15 minutes, rising to Rs25,000 (one or two people) for one hour.

Bookings should be possible through your hotel or tour operator. Alternatively, contact Air Mauritius directly (✆ *603 3754;* f *637 4104;* e *helicopter@airmauritius.com*).

BUS Mauritius is blessed with an excellent bus service, a boon to the independent traveller. It is run on a co-operative basis by different operators: the National Transport Corporation (NTC) (✆ *426 2938*); Rose Hill Transport (RHT) (✆ *464 1221*); United Bus Service (UBS) (✆ *212 2026*); Triolet Bus Service (TBS) (✆ *261 6516*); Mauritius Bus Transport (MTB) (✆ *245 2539*); and individual operators. Since so many people live outside the towns where they work, they depend on the bus service for transportation and their patronage keeps it flourishing.

Compared with the bus services of Africa and Asia it is a disciplined, well-run operation. Tickets are issued from a machine-roll by conductors and there are comfortable seats in the coach-type vehicles, which generally carry about 46 seated passengers and 18 standing. Overloading is not typical.

Express buses are not non-stop but take a shorter route between points, although they charge the same fare as the slower buses. The fares are low, with a trip across the island from Port Louis to Mahébourg (which involves a change) costing Rs30 or so. It is important when getting on a bus to ask the conductor where it is going since the town on the front is not necessarily its destination. As the usual flow of passenger traffic is to Port Louis in the morning and out of Port Louis in the evening, making a connection in country districts sometimes takes ages.

Buses operate from 05.30 to 20.00 in urban areas and from 06.30 to 18.30 in rural areas. There is a late-night service until 23.00 between Port Louis and Curepipe via Rose Hill, Quatre Bornes and Vacoas. During the day, services tend to operate as the bus fills up, rather than to a strict timetable.

Bus itineraries This list is not complete, as new services are introduced, or disappear, from time to time. Departures are listed according to point of origin, not the departure point of the return journey.

From Port Louis (Victoria Square)

1	to Place Margéot, Rose Hill; via Coromandel, Beau Bassin
1A	to St Patrick, Rose Hill; via Coromandel, Buckingham, Hugnin St
1B	to Place Margéot, Rose Hill; via Balfour Garden, Vandermeersch
2&2A	to Curepipe, with extension to Forest Side; via Beau Bassin, Place Margéot, Rose Hill, Phoenix
3	to Vacoas; via Rose Hill, Quatre Bornes
3A	to Rose Hill
102	to Curepipe; via Rose Hill, St Paul, Floréal
103	to Nouvelle Découverte; via St Pierre
162	to Forest Side (express)
163	to Vacoas (express)
170	to Curepipe

From Port Louis (Immigration Sq)

19&19A	to Crève Coeur; via Montagne Longue
20	to St François; via Triolet, Mont Choisy, Grand Baie, Cap Malheureux
20A	to Grande Pointe; via Triolet, Quatre Bornes, Vacoas
20C	to St Antoine; via Triolet, Trou aux Biches, Grand Baie, Pereybère
21	to Goodlands; via SSRN Hospital
22	to Grand Gaube; via Pamplemousses, St Antoine
36	to Ste Croix Church
41	to Vallée des Prêtres with extension to Caroline
48A	to Ste Croix; via Cité La Cure

51	to Pointe aux Sables; via Grande Rivière Nord Ouest
52	to Médine; via Petite Rivière, Bambous
71	to Poudre d'Or; via Cottage
82	to St François; via Triolet, Trou aux Biches, Cap Malheureux, Baie du Tombeau
86	to Rivière du Rempart; via SSRN Hospital
112	to Centre de Flacq; via Bon Accueil, Lalmatie, Constance
126	to Rivière du Rempart; via Ile d'Ambre
171	to Grande Pointe aux Piments; via SSRN Hospital
190	to Victoria Sq

From Plaine Verte

33A	to Plaine Lauzun; via SSR St

From Pailles

150	to Vallée Pitot
165	to Immigration Sq, Port Louis; via Cassis

From Plaine Lauzun

152	to Baie du Tombeau; via Plaine Verte

From Vallée des Prêtres

160	to Plaine Lauzun; via SSR St

From Triolet

75	to Pamplemousses

From St Antoine

26	to Centre de Flacq; via Poste Lafayette

From Rivière du Rempart

27A	to Roches Noires
27B	to Plaine des Roches

From Piton

29	to Grand Baie; via Fond du Sac, Sottise

From SSRN Hospital, Pamplemousses

75A	to Pamplemousses Centre
175	to Crève Coeur; via St Pierre

From Place Margéot, Rose Hill

13	to St Pierre; via Montagne Ory
13A&13B	to Nouvelle Découverte; via St Pierre
15	to Centre de Flacq; via Quartier Militaire, Providence

From St Antoine

95	to Pamplemousses; via Grand Gaube, Cap Malheureux, Mont Choisy, Triolet

From Edward VII Street, Rose Hill

45	to Albion; via Mont Roches

From Quatre Bornes

4A	to Jan Palach Sq, Curepipe; via Floréal
5	to Baie du Cap; via Bambous
57	to Wolmar; via Bambous, Flic en Flac

From Jan Palach Sq, Curepipe

6	to Chemin Grenier; via Rivière des Anguilles

9&9A	to Mahébourg; via Rose Belle, Airport
17	to Centre de Flacq; via Quartier Militaire
142	to Souillac; via Beau Bois
168	to Grand Bassin; via Bois Chéri
179A	to Wolmar; via Floréal

From Flic en Flac

123	to Port Louis

From Grand Baie

215	to Port Louis

From Mahébourg

195	to Port Louis

From Centre de Flacq

18	to Mahébourg; via Grand Sable
54	to Palmar; via Quatre Cocos
55	to Trou d'Eau Douce; via Boulet Rouge
101A	to SSRN Hospital, Pamplemousses; via Lalmatie

From Baie du Cap

5A	to Ste Anne; via Chamarel

From Souillac

8	to Baie du Cap; via Rivière des Galets

From Mahébourg

10	to Souillac; via L'Escalier
11	to Le Val
46	to Blue Bay; via Cité la Chaux

HITCHHIKING Hitchhiking is seldom practised by Mauritians. With the bus service reaching the depths of nearly every village, Mauritians are knowledgeable about how to get around their island easily and inexpensively. Foreigners do hitchhike though and cars will stop. Hitchhiking is not disapproved of by the police but it is difficult to assess what Mauritians themselves think of it. As with hitchhiking in any country, you should be wary, particularly at night, and women should definitely not hitchhike alone.

ACCOMMODATION

Mauritius provides a vast range of accommodation, from budget guesthouses to some of the world's most luxurious hotels; camping, however, is not encouraged and there are no official campsites.

Service throughout Mauritius is superb, a fact which owes much to the Hotel School of Mauritius. The school offers courses for all hospitality and tourism personnel, from chefs to airline cabin staff.

There is no official rating or classification system for hotels in Mauritius. Therefore, for the purposes of this guide, we have divided accommodation into four categories, determined principally by the hotel's public rates. The categories, which are defined below, are: luxury, upmarket, mid range and budget.

Many of the hotels, particularly those that are part of a chain, publish their rates in euro only as most of their guests are Europeans and the euro is considered more stable than the Mauritian rupee. Where this is the case, the rates appear in euro in the book.

CATEGORY A: LUXURY A new category for this edition of the guidebook to cater for the growing number of exclusive resorts on the island. These hotels and resorts regard themselves as six-star properties. Rooms will be spacious and superbly finished with all the facilities that you would expect – a large en-suite bathroom, air conditioning, satellite television, DVD, international direct dial (IDD) telephone, minibar and safe. Many will include 24-hour private butler service. Luxury villas and presidential suites with rooms for staff are often a feature of these resorts. There will be a choice of restaurants and bars offering world-class cuisine and at least one of the restaurants is likely to be endorsed by a renowned chef. Facilities will be extensive, usually including numerous free watersports, a dive centre, several pools, tennis, a gym and a kids' club. Many of these resorts will have their own golf course or offer access to one nearby. No luxury hotel would be complete without a spa, offering a variety of massages and treatments, as well as saunas, steam rooms, jacuzzis and relaxation areas. Double rooms will be priced from Rs17,000 or €485 per night, based on two people sharing on a bed and breakfast basis. On half board, double rooms will be priced from around Rs18,000 or €515.

CATEGORY B: UPMARKET Equates roughly to four- and five-star international standards. Rooms will be en suite and equipped with air conditioning, television (including some satellite channels), IDD telephone, minibar and safe. There will be excellent resort-style facilities, usually including free, non-motorised watersports, such as snorkelling, glass-bottom boat trips, pedaloes and kayaks. Many hotels also offer free water skiing but this is sometimes limited to a certain number of hours. These hotels typically feature a spa, several pools, a dive centre, a gym, tennis courts and a kids' club. Some of these resorts will have their own golf course or offer access to one nearby. There will be regular evening entertainment and activities are often organised during the day. At such hotels there is typically a choice of restaurants and bars, and the standard of cuisine is high. Double rooms will be priced from Rs7,000 to Rs17,000, or €200 to €485, per night, based on two people sharing on a bed and breakfast basis. On half board, double rooms will be priced from around Rs8,000 to Rs18,000, or €230 to €515.

CATEGORY C: MID RANGE A wide selection of acceptable hotels offering comfortable accommodation. Many of the large hotels in this category, particularly those owned by the main hotel groups, such as Beachcomber and Naiade, have extensive facilities. Rooms will be en suite and typically have air conditioning, television, IDD telephone and safe. Hotels by the coast will usually offer some free non-motorised watersports, such as pedaloes, kayaks and snorkelling. Other watersports may be payable. Double rooms will be priced from Rs2,500 to Rs7,000, or €70 to €200, per night, based on two people sharing on a bed and breakfast basis. On half board, rooms will be priced from around Rs3,200 to Rs8,000, or €90 to €230.

CATEGORY D: BUDGET No frills but usually fun, ranging from boarding houses with shared bathroom and self-catering accommodation to medium-sized hotels offering basic facilities. Double rooms will be priced at less than Rs2,500 or €70 per night, based on two people sharing on a bed and breakfast basis. On half board, rooms will usually be priced at less than Rs3,200 or €90.

PRICES AND TERMS

AI   means all-inclusive: breakfast, lunch, dinner, snacks and drinks are included in the room rate. Usually available only as part of a package at a resort hotel.

FB   means full board: breakfast, lunch and dinner (meals are often buffets or table d'hôte menus) are included in the room rate.

HB   means half board: breakfast and dinner are included in the room rate. Few hotels allow you to change to breakfast and lunch.

BB   means bed and breakfast is included in the room rate.

RO   means room only: no meals are included in the room rate.

Please bear in mind that the prices given are only a guideline and rates do change regularly, according to season and demand. It is therefore better to judge a hotel by its description than by the price. In any case, if the hotel is booked as part of a package holiday including flights, the public rate is never what you, the guest, actually pay. Even for those who make their own hotel bookings direct, there could be significant discounts on the public rates at luxury, upmarket and mid-range properties. The vast majority of hotels offer considerable discounts for children and infants are often accommodated free of charge. It is worth visiting the websites of hotels as many, particularly the larger ones, publish special offers on the internet.

The prices given at the end of the hotel descriptions are the lowest public rates offered by the hotel, ie: if the hotel has several room categories, the rate applies to the lowest one unless otherwise specified, and all rates are applicable during the low season. Most of the public rates shown include 15% tax; however, some of the smaller budget hotels may add the tax separately.

✖ EATING

Just thinking about the food I've eaten in Mauritius makes my mouth water, from the crusty French-bread rolls served with local coffee for breakfast to the delight of *salade de palmiste* (heart of palm salad) and the beguiling taste of *fish vindaye* (fish curry) for lunch, then a dinner of *samoussas* and Chinese soup from a street stall.

If you have your meals only in your hotel, you'll wonder what I mean. However exceptional its standards, by definition a hotel catering for tourists has to serve international dishes that are familiar to guests and with a taste that is tolerable to nervous palates. The adventure of eating in Mauritius is for the streetwise since so many delicious – and cheap – dishes are available from pavement hawkers or in noisy dives. Of course, the culinary skills of Mauritian cooks are to be found in private homes too, and not only in the wealthy ones. There are also restaurants that specialise in Mauritian ('Creole') food or European dishes with a local zest.

The influences of Creole cuisine are African and Indian, with a dash of French. The recipes of slaves and indentured labourers have been blended with French ingenuity to produce an array of irresistible dishes, most of which are mildly spiced. The Chinese influence has been confined to particular areas, such as *mine* (noodles) and the ever-popular fried rice.

Street-corner cookery is fascinating to watch as well as to taste. Mauritians are addicted to snacks and from early morning the gutter cooks are crouched beside their charcoal fires. At the Immigration Square bus station I once saw a youth in shorts sitting behind his mobile stall with ribbons of prepared dough draped over his bare thigh. He was nonchalantly dabbing chilli filling into each strip before folding the dough into the triangular packets that are *samoussas*. His companion was using his hands to shape dough mixed with ground *dholl* (split peas) and green chillies into small balls for deep frying to make the golden *gâteaux piments*. If you have a sensitive stomach such eateries are perhaps best avoided.

There is a street corner in Port Louis (at the intersection of Bourbon Street and Ollier Street, although it does change), which is renowned for its *dholl purées*. These are like thin pancakes, made from wheat flour dough and ground split peas and cooked on a griddle. They are served plain, or rolled around a spoonful of *rougaille* or *brèdes*, and wrapped in paper. The Indian-originating *purée*, with its African/French filling, is an example of the successful blend of culinary traditions. *Rougaille* is a spicy tomato-based mixture often made with *pommes d'amour*, the tiny cherry tomatoes that are grown and eaten all over the island. *Brèdes* are part of the daily diet of Mauritian country dwellers, cooked either plain or with meat or fish. They are green leaves – such as watercress, spinach, the leaves of tuber plants and Chinese cabbage – tossed with onions, garlic and red chillies in hot oil until the water has evaporated.

More substantial meals are also available from street sellers, such as *poisson vindaye*, seasoned fried fish coated with a *masala* of mustard seeds, green chillies, garlic and turmeric, often eaten cold with bread. *Achards légumes*, pickled vegetables which have been cooked *al dente* and mixed with spicy paste and vinegar, are also sometimes eaten with bread.

The sweet tooth is catered for with many Tamil specialities, such as *gâteau batate*, a wafer-like pastry of sweet potato and coconut. There is an abundance of tropical fruit too, especially the small pineapples dextrously peeled into spirals, with the stem remaining as a handle.

All street eating costs little since office and shop workers on small salaries are the main customers. Some workers carry their lunch with them in plaited reed baskets, dainty square boxes suspended from a string handle with a cover concealing the contents. These containers, called *tentes*, are made from vacoas leaves. They are sold in the markets and make unusual souvenirs.

Mauritians do not only eat in the street. There are inexpensive eateries in all the towns, where the typical dishes will be meat, chicken or fish served either as *carri* (curry), *daube* (stewed with potatoes and peas) or *kalya* (cooked with saffron and ginger/garlic). Snacks, called *gadjacks*, are served in bars on small saucers, like Spanish *tapas*, to accompany drinks. The range is generous, from *rougaille ourite* (octopus in tomato) to *croquettes volaille* (chicken bites).

Snoeck rougaille (salted fish in tomato) is a frequent standby if fresh fish is not available, and shrimps or lobster are also sometimes served in *rougaille*. *Camarons* (freshwater crayfish) served with watercress salad are a favourite with Franco-Mauritians. Wild boar, hare and venison are widely available in restaurants, even out of the hunting season. Goat (*cabri*) is sold in the meat markets in the way that mutton is sold in Europe and is served in curry. The exotic *palmiste* (for which miniature palm trees are especially cultivated to yield their hearts) is sometimes served boiled instead of in a salad, with a Creole sauce.

Most restaurant menus do not contain many options for vegetarians. However, the majority of establishments will proudly create a dish especially for you, usually *carri de légumes* (vegetable curry). If you eat fish you'll be spoilt for choice, with delicious red snapper, dorado, tuna and swordfish on offer. One of the highlights is, of course, *marlin fumé* (smoked marlin), served as an expensive but superb starter.

Restaurant prices may not include 15% tax, so be prepared for it to be added to your final bill.

♀ DRINKING

A popular Mauritian drink is *alooda*, sold on the streets and in markets by energetic salesmen praising their own product. It consists of dissolved, boiled china grass (*agar agar*) and sugar, which has been strained and allowed to set and then grated, to which is added water, milk, rose syrup and soaked *tookmaria* (falooda) seeds. The mixture is refrigerated and served cold in tall glasses.

Local beer is excellent and inexpensive in a corner bar, or shops, but much dearer in hotels and restaurants. There are several local rums, of which connoisseurs rate Rum of Mauritius, in its plain glass bottle with stencilled red labelling, as the best. It is also known as Goodwill. Don't be surprised if your Mauritian host deliberately spills a little of a new bottle on the floor before pouring drinks. It is a custom to appease the other spirits. Since wines are also produced locally, as are local versions of spirits such as gin, whisky and brandy, the tippler is as well served as the gourmand.

Basic drinking is done in corner bars, many of them housed in solid 19th-century buildings with thick granite walls and little comfort. Payment is made to the cashier who oversees the operation and makes a note of every drink you consume, with the help of a commentary in Creole from the barman. You pay when you leave. These are lively, convivial places with snacks (*gadjacks*) on sale at the counter and lots of noise. They are safe for visitors even if they look a bit disreputable.

BEER At the beginning of the 1960s, Pierre Hugnin listened to the suggestion of a friend from Tahiti that he should start a brewery. At the time, 18,000 hectolitres of beer were imported into Mauritius annually. While going into the figures for the project, Hugnin had the well water at his proposed site in Phoenix analysed and found it ideal.

The first Mauritian beer, Phoenix, was brewed by Mauritius Breweries Limited in August 1963. With beer seen as an acceptable drink in multi-religious Mauritius, MBL launched a second beer, Stella, two years later and began to distribute Guinness, which has been brewed under licence since 1975. Phoenix (5% vol) has become synonymous with beer for Mauritians and is the company's bestseller. MBL also produce Blue Marlin, a stronger beer (6% vol) and Phoenix Export, a premium brand (5% vol).

Mauritius beer has won many international awards for its quality, including gold medals for Phoenix (1989) and Blue Marlin (1993). Mauritius sugar is used in the production of beer (where other breweries might use maize or rice) since it produces a beer that is more digestible. Top-quality hops come from the UK, Germany and the Czech Republic. The beer has a clean and refreshing taste with lots of flavour. (*Mauritius Breweries Ltd, Pont Fer, Phoenix,* ↘ *601 2000.*)

SPIRITS Over 150 years ago, a commentator on Mauritius complained: 'The facility with which spirits, especially arrack of inferior quality, are to be procured is more fatal to the soldiers than exposure to the sun, or any other effect of the climate.'

Rum-making on the island dates back to 1639, following the introduction of sugarcane by the Dutch, when it was made from cane juice even before people knew how to extract the crystals. Alcohol is now the most successful by-product of sugar, obtained by turning molasses into fine spirit.

There are many rums produced in Mauritius, including the mellow Rum of Mauritius and the romantic-sounding Green Island Rum. Most households and bars keep a variety of *rhum arrangé*, made by adding their own choice of fruit and/or spices to a large bottle of rum.

WINE In a tasting of rosé wines from South Africa, France and Portugal conducted by a wine writer in South Africa a few years ago, a bottle of Château Bel Ombre featured well. It was determined by half the tasters as being South African in origin and by others as being from Southern France or Portugal. Everyone was flabbergasted when they learned it came from Mauritius, produced by E C Oxenham & Co Ltd (*St Jean Rd, Phoenix;* ℡ *696 7950;* f *696 7953;* e *eureka@intnet.mu; www.oxenham.bz*).

The absence of vineyards in Mauritius has led sceptics to dismiss Oxenham's wines as being obtained through the fermentation of Mauritian fruits. Not so. The wine is made from grape must, concentrated for travel, and imported into Mauritius in plastic blowpacks.

Edward Clark Oxenham, a descendant of British colonials, was a pioneer who tried to grow grapes on his farm in Rodrigues. He failed, but with help from the Pasteur Institute of Paris started to produce wine from dried grapes and local fruits in 1931. He moved to Mauritius and in 1932 founded the company that now bears his name.

Mauritian white and rosé wines can be drunk young, but the red is stored in oak vats to mature. The Oxenham range begins with Eureka, the everyday wine of Mauritians, through the pleasant and inexpensive Rosé Chaptalin, to finer wines with the St Nicholas label, as well as the full-bodied Mon Hussard red.

Wines produced in Mauritius have the added attraction for the drinker of their low retail price, although hotel or restaurant mark-up can increase the price by as much as five times.

WORKING HOURS, PUBLIC HOLIDAYS AND FESTIVALS

For the public sector, working hours are Monday–Friday 09.00–16.00 and Saturday 09.00–12.00. The number of staff is reduced on Saturdays, so for the sake of your sanity it is advisable to carry out administrative formalities on weekdays.

Private enterprises are usually open Monday–Friday 08.30–16.15 and on Saturday 09.00–12.00.

PUBLIC HOLIDAYS Public holidays for religious and state occasions threatened to overwhelm working life in Mauritius, multiplying until there were 28 official days off work a year, in addition to weekends. Now the number of statutory public holidays has been reduced to 15. These are as follows:

New Year's Day	1 January
New Year	2 January
Chinese Spring Festival	variable (January/February)
Thaipoosam Cavadee	variable (January/February)
Abolition of Slavery	1 February
Maha Shivaratree	variable (February/March)
National Day	12 March
Ougadi	variable (March/April)
Labour Day	1 May
Assumption	15 August
Ganesh Chaturthi	variable (August/September)
Divali	variable (October/November)
Arrival of Indentured Labourers	2 November
Id El Fitr	variable (November/December)
Christmas Day	25 December

Employees are also permitted to have two additional days' leave a year to celebrate religious festivals that are no longer official public holidays. Leave is granted at the employee's request even if the employee doesn't belong to the religion celebrating the festival. Some of these festivals are so popular with everyone, regardless of their religion, that they become like public holidays, with shops and businesses closed.

3

Since many of these festivals depend on different religious calendars, the days on which they are held vary each year and will not always be in the months shown below.

FESTIVALS

Sankranti	January
Holi	March
Mehraj Shariff (Muslim)	March
Varusha Pirappu (Tamil New Year)	April
Shabbe Baraat (Muslim)	April
Good Friday	March/April
Easter Monday	March/April
Seemadree Appana Parsa (Telegu)	May
Sittarai Cavadee (Tamil)	May
Corpus Christi	May/June
Id El Adha (Muslim)	August
Raksha Bandhan (Hindu)	August
Anniversary of Père Laval's Death	9 September
Mid Autumn Festival (Chinese)	October
All Saints' Day	1 November
Yaum Un Nabi	November
Ganga Asnan	November
Boxing Day	26 December

Sankranti The first of the year's religious festivals, it is celebrated in the beginning of the Tamil month Thai, and is also known as Thai Pongal. It is an occasion of thanksgiving for the harvest which is represented by the ceremonial boiling of rice. It is customary to wear new clothes at this time.

Chinese Spring Festival This is New Year's Day and spring-cleaning combined. The festival begins on the eve of the Chinese New Year with an explosion of firecrackers to chase away evil spirits. It takes place in January or February and does not fall on the same day every year because of the irregularity of the lunar month.

During the week before New Year's Day there is a thorough spring-cleaning of the home. Traditionalists visit pagodas on New Year's Eve with offerings and prayers of thanksgiving. Neither scissors nor knives are used on the Day and the colour red, symbolic of happiness, is favoured. Food is displayed in an honoured place in the home in the hope of abundance in the coming year. Cakes made of rice flour and honey, called wax cakes because of their texture, are shared with relatives and friends. Many of the Chinese community celebrate by spending a few days at a beach hotel.

Thaipoosam Cavadee This Tamil ritual is named after the wooden yoke – the *cavadee* – decorated with flowers and palm leaves and with a pot of milk suspended from each end, which a devotee fulfilling a vow carries across his/her shoulders in procession to their temple. There it is placed before the deity when, despite the long, hot ordeal, the milk should not be curdled.

The *cavadee* procession, while colourful and spectacular, is awe-inspiring because of the penance undergone by the participants who walk with their bodies pierced with needles, hooks hanging from their flesh and skewers threaded through their tongues and cheeks.

Maha Shivaratree The Great Night of Shiva is a solemn occasion for Hindus which begins with a night-long vigil in worship of the god Shiva. The following day, devotees dressed in pure white carry the *kanwar*, a wooden arch decorated with flowers, paper and tiny mirrors, in procession to the sacred lake, Grand Bassin.

The Hindus carry water from the lake home to their temple. *Poojas* (worship with food) are celebrated that night in the temples dotting the banks of the lake, the air heavy with the sweet smell of burning incense sticks and reverberating with prayers broadcast from loudspeakers.

This is reputed to be the largest Hindu festival celebrated outside India and is reminiscent of the great rituals on the banks of the holy Ganges. Worshippers believe the lights they launch on the lake on banana leaves and their offerings of flowers will float somehow to the Ganges.

Holi A happy time for Hindus when greetings are exchanged and revelry erupts with the squirting of coloured water and the spraying of coloured powder on one another, and on everyone else the revellers come across. A noisy and cheerful festival.

Ougadi Telegu New Year.

Id El Fitr The annual month of fasting (Ramadan) by Muslims, during which they neither eat nor drink between sunrise and sunset, comes to an end with this festival. Prayers are offered at mosques during the day.

Ganesh Chaturthi Celebrated on the fourth day of the lunar month of August/September by Hindus of Marathi faith as the birthday of Ganesh, the god of wisdom and remover of all obstacles. In Baie du Cap processions are held with devotees escorting pink, elephant-nosed effigies to the sea and dusting onlookers with scarlet powder.

Corpus Christi Devout Roman Catholics join in a procession through the streets of Port Louis in May or June on the occasion of Corpus Christi.

Id El Adha Sheep and goats are sacrificed in ceremonial slaughter for this Muslim festival and the meat is shared with family and friends. The day commemorates the sacrifice by Abraham of his son and the events symbolise the Muslim ideal of sacrifice and dedication.

Père Laval Pilgrims of all faiths gather at the tomb of Father Jacques Desiré Laval throughout September, but particularly on 9 September, the anniversary of his death. Many come in hope of a miracle cure. (For more information see page 116.)

Divali Clay oil lamps and paper lanterns with candles in them are placed in front of every Hindu and Tamil home on this Festival of Lights. Hills and valleys sparkle in the night as lights burn to celebrate the victory of Rama over Ravana, and Krishna's destruction of the demon Narakasuran, the victory of good over evil.

All Saints' Day The day on which cemetery cleaning takes place and flowers are placed by Roman Catholics on the graves of the dead.

Yaum Un Nabi The birth and death anniversaries of the Prophet Mohammed are commemorated on the Prophet's Day, following 12 days during which the faithful gather in mosques throughout the island, devoting themselves to religious study.

Ganga Asnan For Hindus this is the time of ceremonial bathing in the sea for purification, since they believe the holy water of the Ganges will be able to purify them through it. At the beaches of Albion, Belle Mare, Baie du Tombeau, Blue Bay, Flic en Flac, Mont Choisy, Pereybère, Pte aux Roches, Pte aux Sables and Tamarin, special lifeguard units are set up to ensure the safety of bathers.

Muharram An important Muslim festival known in Mauritius as Yamsey, featuring figures and towers called *ghoons*, carried in procession through the streets in commemoration of the death of the grandson of the Prophet.

Firewalking At the Tamil temple in Terre Rouge and at other temples in predominantly Tamil areas, *Teemeedee* (firewalking) takes place between October and March. Worshippers walk over beds of red-hot embers which represent the outstretched sari of Draupadee. They prepare for the ordeal by fasting, ritual bathing and a blessing before walking unscathed on the glowing embers to the accompaniment of chants from supporters.

Details of where to see firewalking, and the dates each year of the religious festivals and public holidays, are given in a leaflet about 'Coming Events' available bi-monthly from the tourist office.

CHURCHES

For Christians there are both Roman Catholic and Anglican cathedrals in Port Louis with Presbyterian and Evangelical churches close by and churches of all denominations throughout the island. Hotels display details of religious services held near them on their notice boards. The following churches regularly conduct services in English: St Joseph's Chapel, Rose Hill (⟍ *464 2944*) – Roman Catholic Mass; St Paul's Church, Vacoas (⟍ *686 4819*) – Anglican Mass; St Columba's Church, Phoenix (⟍ *696 4404*) – Presbyterian Sunday Service.

SHOPPING

Mauritius is billed as a 'shopping paradise' and a lot of money could be spent buying intricately carved model ships, duty-free diamonds and designer clothing. Many tourists find it hard to resist the clothing factory outlets, where the clothes produced in Mauritius for export are sold at heavily discounted prices. Although such shops are found throughout Mauritius, they are concentrated around Curepipe, Floréal and Quatre Bornes. A shopping trip to these areas can be organised by most tour operators.

The government is doing all it can to promote shopping in Mauritius. In 2005, it announced plans to become one of the world's few duty-free islands by abolishing, over the next four years, its 80% tax on 1,850 different types of goods, including clothing, electronics and jewellery. It is also going to offer incentives for investors to build large retail centres and shopping malls. The new shopping complex at Rivière Noire, Ruisseau Creole, is already proving popular with locals and tourists alike.

Shops in Port Louis sell everything from the latest electronic goods to coconut husks for polishing wooden floors. Near the harbour, the large and modern **Caudan Waterfront** (⟍ *211 6560;* e *caudan@intnet.mu*) offers something for everyone with duty-free jewellery and carpets, clothing boutiques, bookshops, model ship shops and an excellent craft market, where local artisans can be seen at work. Many of the handicrafts on sale in Mauritius are imported, mostly from Madagascar. However, if you head to one of the National Handicraft Promotion Agency (NHPA) shops, you can be sure not only that the handicrafts you are buying are made in Mauritius, but also that a percentage of the proceeds goes to the artisan. For more information see *Giving something back*, pages 84–5.

Shops in Port Louis open on weekdays at 09.00 and close at 17.00. On Saturday they close at midday and only a few shops open on Sunday mornings. Shops in Curepipe and Quatre Bornes are open 10.00–17.30 daily except Thursday and Sunday, when they close at midday.

Discounts on marked prices may be available if you have the courage to ask, although it's usually Mauritians who are successful. Bargaining on unmarked prices is acceptable if you have time, but do not expect to lower the price significantly since it's more a game than an essential part of the deal. Never agree to purchase anything until you know its price.

MARKETS Markets are good places to shop, as prices tend to be lower than in shops. Self-caterers will find a good range of fresh fruit and vegetables. They are held in the following towns:

Port Louis	daily
Curepipe	Wednesday and Saturday
Quatre Bornes	Thursday and Sunday
Vacoas	Tuesday and Friday
Mahébourg	Monday
Centre de Flacq	Wednesday and Sunday
Plaine Verte	Tuesday and Saturday

DUTY-FREE GOODS The duty-free shops in Mauritius primarily sell jewellery and watches, with diamonds on sale from US$100 to US$40,000. Under the current system for all duty-free purchases, buyers need to show a foreign passport and air ticket in the same name, so remember to take both when you go shopping. Payment must be made with foreign currency, travellers' cheques or credit card, and at least 48 hours before the purchaser's intended departure. However, this is likely to change when the island as a whole becomes duty free.

Some shops that lure customers in with signs proclaiming they sell duty-free products, especially watches, don't, since their prices include an import levy and sales tax. It is genuinely duty free if you cannot take it with you and have to collect your purchases at the airport on departure. However, some locally produced, high-class souvenirs are claimed to be duty free since the material used to make them was imported free of duty.

Since the production of jewellery for export has become a thriving industry, jewellers are not a rare sight and are even found in some upmarket hotels. Recommended to me by a lady who knows is **Charles Lee** (*21 bis Sir Winston Churchill St, Curepipe;* \ *675 2288*) whose creations are available at duty-free prices. For handmade work – even to your own design – try the award-winning **Ravior** (*88 St Jean Rd, Quatre Bornes;* \ *454 3229;* e *ravior@intnet.mu; www.ravior.com*). The Duke of York visited there in October 1987 and signed the clan book of the owner, himself a descendant of Gujarathi royalty. Whether he bought one of the superb range of stones on display there is 'a professional secret'. Ravior have also opened a shop at Ruisseau Creole in Rivière Noire and at the airport.

Adamas has a diamond showroom in Mangalkhan, Floréal (\ *686 5783;* e *adamas@intnet.mu*) and has been selling duty-free jewellery since 1983. It is attached to a workshop operating under the EPZ laws, importing rough diamonds which are then cut, polished and exported. It also has an outlet at the Palm Beach Boutique, Belle Mare (\ *415 5356*). In Port Louis, **Shiv Jewels** has a boutique at the Caudan Waterfront (*Shop C14, Le Pavillon, Caudan Waterfront;* \ *211 7294;* e *shivor@intnet.mu*).

MODEL SHIPS The model shipbuilding industry started small but has become so successful that the original craftsmen split up and there are now several workshops on the island.

The 60 or so different models available include famous ships such as the *Golden Hind*, *Victory*, *Mayflower*, USS *Constitution* and *Cutty Sark*. Each is made by hand exactly to scale, using camphor or teak: camphor for the keel, hard *bois de natté* for the masts, yards and pulley blocks, soft lilac for the helm and capstan. Prices are generally high, but range from Rs400 to over Rs20,000. Model ships can be sent worldwide, or packed for taking in the hold, as checked baggage, on the plane home (a surcharge may apply). Many of the workshops also produce fine furniture.

Curepipe seems to be the centre of the model ship industry. One of the best-known manufacturers is **Comajora** at La Brasserie Road, Forest Side (✎ 676 5345), which has a shop just outside Curepipe. **Bobato** (formerly **La Flotte**) was started some 15 years ago and has a showroom in Sir John Pope Hennessy Street, Curepipe (✎ 675 2899) and a factory in Vacoas (✎ 696 6052). **First Fleet Reproductions** is at 74–76 Royal Road, Phoenix (✎ 698 0161; e *fstfleet@intnet.mu; www.firstfleetreproductions.com*). **Palais d'Orient** has several shops around Mauritius, in the Salaffa Arcade, Curepipe (✎ 675 2375; e *rngpo@hotmail.com*), in Floréal (✎ 697 8090) and in Grand Baie (✎ 263 5738). **Stop Marine** at Coastal Road, Trou d'Eau Douce (✎ 419 5290) sells a variety of goods including model ships. On the west coast, there are two model ship shops on the way into Flic en Flac, **Pirate Ship Models** (✎ 453 9028) and next door, **Superbe Ship Shop**. **Historic Marine** in Goodlands (✎ 283 9304; e *hismar@intnet.mu; www.historic-marine.com*) has been producing model ships since 1982. The company now makes 2,000 models per year. Visitors can visit the model ship workshop and buy the finished articles on site (see page 133).

MAURITIUS GLASS GALLERY The aim of the Mauritius Glass Gallery is to produce handmade glass objects from recycled glass and promote environmental awareness. The workshop at Pont Fer, Phoenix, is open to the public and there are regular glass-blowing demonstrations (for details see page 179). The products can be bought at Pont Fer (✎ 696 3360; e *mgg@intnet.mu*), in the craft market at the Caudan Waterfront (✎ 210 1181), at the Super U Commercial Centre in Grand Baie (✎ 269 0376) and at the airport. A glass dodo costs around Rs112, a paperweight is about Rs195 and lamps are around Rs900.

TEXTILES Textiles are now one of the largest industries in Mauritius. While most of the finished goods are exported to Europe, once the manufacturers have completed their quotas, the remainder can be sold at home, at very attractive prices.

The island has made a name for itself in the knitwear field and shops can be found all across Mauritius. In the Floréal Square, there is a number of shops that sell clothes at factory prices, as well as a textile museum (see page 180).

If you want custom-made clothing, dressmakers and tailors can run up garments in 24 hours but better work takes longer. Short-term visitors should commission the work on arrival to ensure that it is ready in time for departure.

SOUVENIRS Those looking for a reminder of Mauritius to take home with them are spoilt for choice. The wax-like anthuriums grown in Mauritius make a delightful present and are sold packed in cardboard boxes for travelling. They should keep for a few weeks when you get them home.

Smoked marlin can be purchased at the airport just before you leave and is a treat for anyone. Also at the airport are packs of Bois Chéri tea, which are ideal as they weigh very little. Spices are also easy to transport and are inexpensive in markets. A bottle of local rum may create a stir back home and they can be bought quite cheaply at supermarkets, although they need to be carefully packed.

The **National Handicraft Promotion Agency** sells a range of souvenirs made in Mauritius and Rodrigues. Buying souvenirs from its outlets is a good way of supporting the local economy. For more information see *Giving something back*, pages 84–5.

THE ARTS

The arts flourish in Mauritius despite a lack of appreciation and encouragement from the outside world. Local authors and poets who want to be published have to pay for the printing of their own works unless they can find sponsorship from foreign cultural organisations.

The **Alliance-Française** (*1 Victor Hugo St, Bell Village, Port Louis;* 212 2949; e *afim@intnet.mu; www.afmccf.com*) is very active in its encouragement of the arts and the French language, so much so that the British Council (*Royal Rd, Rose Hill;* 454 9550; e *general.enquiries@mu.britishcouncil.org; www.britishcouncil.org/mauritius*), which had slumped into inactivity, was revived at the end of 1987 with the appointment of a new representative.

LITERATURE Several slim volumes of verse, *belles-lettres* and travelogues by local authors are to be found hidden away in Mauritian bookshops. Robert Edward Hart, who died in 1954, was Mauritius's most renowned poet, and was awarded the OBE and the French *Légion d'Honneur*. His house at Souillac is now a museum (see pages 156–7).

Shelf-loads of books, mostly in French, have been written about Mauritius, many with slavery as their theme. The island has been the setting for novels, too, the most famous being the pastoral French novel, *Paul et Virginie*, by Bernadin de Saint Pierre, which was first published in 1773 and is still in print, with English translations available in bookshops. Its sentimental tale of love and heartbreak, based on the wrecking of the *St-Géran* in 1744, is remarkable for the accuracy of its nature notes and description of an idyllic Mauritius when it resembled a garden of Eden. Joseph Conrad set a short story, *A Smile of Fortune*, in Mauritius and Sir Walter Besant, a teacher in Mauritius from 1861 to 1867, used the island as a setting for two novels, *My Little Girl* and *They Were Married*. A trio of plantation novels, the *Black River* saga, and a historical romance, *Giselle*, by Richard Tresillian, all set in Mauritius, were published as paperbacks in the UK in the 1980s.

Bookshops For its population and high literacy rate, Mauritius is poorly served for bookshops. While there is a number of *libraries* on the island, most of these combine stationery supplies with a stock of books for students and a few general volumes in French and some in English. Although there is no duty levied on the import of books into Mauritius, prices are high. The best bookshops are in Curepipe and Port Louis.

THEATRE, DANCE AND ART There are some local folklore and dramatic societies that occasionally perform cultural shows and plays. The old opera house in Port Louis (*Municipal Theatre;* 212 1090), built in 1822, has been lovingly restored and is a fine setting for local drama, although seldom used. The Plaza Theatre (*Royal Rd, Rose Hill;* 424 1145) is part of the Beau Bassin/Rose Hill town hall complex, a Baroque 1920s creation by Coultrac Mazérieux which has become a prestigious venue for Mauritian and foreign cultural activities.

An art gallery also at the Beau Bassin/Rose Hill town hall complex is named after the Mauritian artist, Max Boullé (✎ *454 9500*), and often features exhibitions by local artists.

In Port Louis there is the Galérie d'Art de Port Louis in Mallefille Street, just behind the Mauritius Museum Council, which holds occasional exhibitions of local artists' work. Commercial art galleries are found in Quatre Bornes, Grand Baie, Pointe aux Cannoniers and Port Louis (see page 114).

☆ ENTERTAINMENT

NIGHTLIFE For most tourists, nightlife will centre around their hotel since the hotels themselves are isolated on the coast and far from whatever local action there is. Hotel evening entertainment is of good (but not international) standard, with live bands, floor shows, discotheques and occasional concert parties and fashion shows organised by the hotel's 'animation' staff. Most hotels feature weekly *séga* shows.

Nightclubbers who want to meet young Mauritians enjoying themselves should head on Saturday nights to **The Palladium** (✎ *454 6168*), an extraordinary building with a mock Roman villa façade, on the left at Trianon, just before the St Jean's Church roundabout on the drive from Port Louis. You'll need your own transport or a pre-arranged taxi since there are no buses at night.

There are other discos near tourist resorts, mostly around Grand Baie, many of which are open on Wednesday and Thursday, as well as Friday and Saturday evenings. Expect an entrance charge (Rs100–150), although entry is sometimes free for women.

CASINOS Mauritians love to gamble. Most casinos offer fruit machines as well as a variety of tables (roulette, blackjack etc). Dress standards call for more than beachwear. The casinos are generally open from early evening for playing the slot machines, but only from 21.00 for gambling at the tables. On Sundays, they open at about 15.00, when they are popular with wealthier residents, particularly the Chinese.

The following hotels have casinos: Trou aux Biches, Le St Géran, La Pirogue and Berjaya Le Morne. Gamblers can also indulge their passion at:

Le Grand Casino du Domaine Domaine Les Pailles; ✎ 211 0452
Le Casino du Caudan Port Louis Waterfront; ✎ 210 4090

Casino de Maurice Teste de Buch St, Curepipe; ✎ 675 5012

SOCIAL ORGANISATIONS The **Rotary Club** of Port Louis meets every Wednesday, while the Citadel branch of the club meets on Tuesdays. In Curepipe, the meeting is held on Thursdays and in Grand Baie on Tuesdays. Other Rotary Clubs are in Quatre Bornes, Beau Bassin/Rose Hill, Mahébourg and Black River.

There are **Lions Clubs** in Port Louis, Curepipe and Quatre Bornes. The Mauritius **Round Table** meets on the second Tuesday of every month for lunch. There is also a branch of the **SKAL Club** association of tourism professionals.

PHOTOGRAPHY

Processing of colour print film in 24 hours is available at several outlets in Port Louis and Curepipe. Print, slide and APS films are readily available. The cost of processing and of film may be higher than in your home country. Prints are the 12.5cm x 6.9cm size, not the larger postcard size which is standard in Europe.

Most Mauritians are quite happy to have their photos taken but you should ask permission first. Permits are not required for photography but, officially, you are not allowed to take photographs of the harbour and the airport.

MEDIA AND COMMUNICATIONS

MEDIA Newspapers in Mauritius enjoy a reputation for lively debate and freedom of expression, with the independent press curbed only by self-censorship. The first newspaper was published in 1773 and there have been more than 600 titles since then, including *Le Cernéen*, started in 1832 as the first newspaper that did not have to be submitted to the government for approval.

The most popular daily papers are *Le Mauricien* and *L'Express*, which are published in French, with occasional articles and advertisements in English. There is no English daily newspaper but there are two Chinese dailies. There are also weekly and monthly publications propagating a particular political viewpoint, including one in English. Larger hotels often sell English and other foreign newspapers which are a few days old.

The *Mauritius News* is published monthly in the UK for Mauritians living overseas and is also available in France, Belgium, Switzerland, Australia and Canada. A copy is also held in La Librarie Allot in Curepipe. Five thousand copies are produced each month and the cover price is 60p or £12 for an annual subscription in the UK.

Le Mauricien 8 St Georges St, Port Louis; 208 7808; f 208 7809
L'Express 3 Brown Sequard St, Port Louis; 212 1827; f 208 8174

Mauritius News 583 Wandsworth Rd, London SW8 3JD; 020 7498 3066; e editor@mauritiusnews.co.uk; www.mauritius-news.co.uk

There are estimated to be over 420,000 radio sets in Mauritius. There is one government-controlled radio station, run by the Mauritius Broadcasting Corporation (MBC), which broadcasts in English, French, Creole and Hindi. Mauritius's first private radio station, Radio 1, was officially opened on 11 April 2002. The BBC World Service can be received on MHz 21.47, 11.94, 6.190 and 3.255, while Voice of America is on MHz 21.49, 15.60, 95.25 and 6.035.

There are two television channels run by MBC, whose head office is at Louis Pasteur Street, Forest Side (674 0475; f 675 7332). Programmes are mostly in French, although some are in English and Hindi and there are news summaries in Creole. The local and international news bulletins in English are daily at 07.00 and 21.00. RFO (Réseau France Outre-Mer), with programmes in French, is received from Réunion and there are also some pay-TV channels. Most hotels in the mid-range, upmarket and luxury categories have satellite channels such as BBC World and CNN.

MAIL In 1815, it took 17 weeks for news of Napoleon's defeat to reach Port Louis. Today the postal service is quick and reliable. Mail to/from Europe takes about a week, and approximately ten days to/from the US. Postcards and aerograms to Europe, the US or Australia cost Rs5. A letter to Europe (under 5g) costs Rs6, whilst a letter to the US or Australia is Rs7.

A useful local service is Express Delivery, which can result in a letter mailed before 09.00 being delivered to an address within a radius of three miles a few hours later the same day. Two forms have to be filled in for this service.

There are 93 post offices in Mauritius, so most towns and villages (and the airport) have one. The general post office in Port Louis is a squat Victorian granite-block building in Quay Street, not far from the tourist office on the Caudan Waterfront.

Ariadne Van Zandbergen

EQUIPMENT Although with some thought and an eye for composition you can take reasonable photos with a 'point-and-shoot' camera, you need an SLR camera if you are at all serious about photography. Modern SLRs tend to be very clever, with automatic programmes for almost every possible situation, but remember that these programmes are limited in the sense that the camera cannot think, but only make calculations. Every starting amateur photographer should read a photographic manual for beginners and get to grips with such basics as the relationship between aperture and shutter speed.

Always buy the best lens you can afford. The lens determines the quality of your photo more than the camera body. Fixed fast lenses are ideal, but very costly. Zoom lenses are easier to change composition without changing lenses the whole time. If you carry only one lens, a 28–70mm (digital 17–55mm) or similar zoom should be ideal. For a second lens, a lightweight 80–200mm or 70–300mm (digital 55–200mm) or similar will be excellent for candid shots and varying your composition. Wildlife photography will be very frustrating if you don't have at least a 300mm lens. For a small loss of quality, tele-converters are a cheap and compact way to increase magnification: a 300 lens with a 1.4x converter becomes 420mm, and with a 2x it becomes 600mm. Note, however, that 1.4x and 2x tele-converters reduce the speed of your lens by 1.4 and 2 stops respectively.

For photography from a vehicle, a solid beanbag, which you can make yourself very cheaply, will be necessary to avoid blurred images, and is more useful than a tripod. A clamp with a tripod head screwed on to it can be attached to the vehicle as well. Modern dedicated flash units are easy to use; aside from the obvious need to flash when you photograph at night, you can improve a lot of photos in difficult 'high contrast' or very dull light with some fill-in flash. It pays to have a proper flash unit as opposed to a built-in camera flash.

DIGITAL/FILM Digital photography is now the preference of most amateur and professional photographers, with the resolution of digital cameras improving the whole time. For ordinary prints a 6 megapixel camera is fine. For better results and the possibility to enlarge images and for professional reproduction, higher resolution is available up to 16 megapixels.

Memory space is important. The number of pictures you can fit on a memory card depends on the quality you choose. Calculate in advance how many pictures you can fit on a card and either take enough cards to last for your trip, or take a storage drive on to which you can download the content. A laptop gives the advantage that you can see your pictures properly at the end of each day and edit and delete rejects, but a storage device is lighter and less bulky. These drives come in different capacities up to 80GB.

Interactive kiosks have recently been installed in 24 post offices and are currently being rolled out at the others. These offer local and international phone calls, internet access, email and printing. Prepaid cards to use the kiosks can be purchased at the counters or you can use a credit card.

Mauritius Post offers a Poste Restante facility for visitors who need a temporary mailing address for their incoming mail. Correspondence is kept at the post office for a maximum period of two months for overseas visitors.

Post offices are open Monday–Friday 08.15–16.00 and Saturday 08.15–11.45.

TELEPHONE The IDD code to telephone or fax Mauritius or Rodrigues from overseas is 230, followed by a seven-digit number. To call Rodrigues from

Bear in mind that digital camera batteries, computers and other storage devices need charging, so make sure you have all the chargers, cables and converters with you. Most hotels have charging points, but do enquire about this in advance. When camping you might have to rely on charging from the car battery; a spare battery is invaluable.

If you are shooting film, 100 to 200 ISO print film and 50 to 100 ISO slide film are ideal. Low ISO film is slow but fine grained and gives the best colour saturation, but will need more light, so support in the form of a tripod or monopod is important. You can also bring a few 'fast' 400 ISO films for low-light situations where a tripod or flash is not an option.

DUST AND HEAT Dust and heat are often a problem. Keep your equipment in a sealed bag, stow films in an airtight container (eg: a small cooler bag) and avoid exposing equipment and film to the sun. Digital cameras are prone to collecting dust particles on the sensor which results in spots on the image. The dirt mostly enters the camera when changing lenses, so be careful when doing this. To some extent photos can be 'cleaned' up afterwards in Photoshop, but this is time-consuming. You can have your camera sensor professionally cleaned, or you can do this yourself with special brushes and swabs made for the purpose, but note that touching the sensor might cause damage and should only be done with the greatest care.

LIGHT The most striking outdoor photographs are often taken during the hour or two of 'golden light' after dawn and before sunset. Shooting in low light may enforce the use of very low shutter speeds, in which case a tripod will be required to avoid camera shake.

With careful handling, side lighting and back lighting can produce stunning effects, especially in soft light and at sunrise or sunset. Generally, however, it is best to shoot with the sun behind you. When photographing animals or people in the harsh midday sun, images taken in light but even shade are likely to be more effective than those taken in direct sunlight or patchy shade, since the latter conditions create too much contrast.

PROTOCOL In some countries, it is unacceptable to photograph local people without permission, and many people will refuse to pose or will ask for a donation. In such circumstances, don't try to sneak photographs as you might get yourself into trouble. Even the most willing subject will often pose stiffly when a camera is pointed at them; relax them by making a joke, and take a few shots in quick succession to improve the odds of capturing a natural pose.

Ariadne Van Zandbergen is a professional travel and wildlife photographer specialising in Africa. She runs The Africa Image Library. For photo requests, visit www.africaimagelibrary.co.za or contact her on ariadne@hixnet.co.za.

Mauritius, the code 095 should be used in front of the seven digits.

The telephone system is run by Mauritius Telecom, whose corporate office is at Telecom Tower, Edith Cavell St, Port Louis (℡ *203 7000;* f *208 1070; www.mauritiustelecom.com*).

The tone which indicates that the dialled number is actually ringing is interrupted by long pauses. An engaged number is signalled by short, regular pauses in the ringing tone. If the number is unobtainable, the interruption to the tone is quicker than the busy indicator.

IDD phones are nationwide; just dial 00 followed by the country code, area code and local number. IDD calls are charged on a one-minute minimum basis and in one-minute steps thereafter. An IDD call to the UK, Australia, France, the USA, South Africa, Italy and Germany from Mauritius costs about Rs15 per minute. Hotels, of course, add their own, often considerable, mark-up to the basic cost.

In recent years, a number of companies have launched prepaid phonecards. These offer very attractive call rates to major destinations and can be used from any phone. For example, to call any of the countries listed above using Mauritius Telecom's Sezam Global Prepaid Card costs only Rs6 per minute, although they are only available in Rs150 and Rs250 denominations. Emtel International offer prepaid cards with rates from Rs5.50 that can be purchased in denominations from Rs50 upwards.

Credit card calls can be made using the BT charge card (UK), the Canada credit card, the New Zealand credit card, the South Korea credit card and the AT&T credit card (US).

Payphones using coins or prepaid phonecards are available throughout Mauritius but are not always in working order. Phonecards are sold in the busier places but do not expect them everywhere. For emergencies, it is wise to carry a low-rate card. They come in denominations of Rs30, Rs50, Rs100, Rs200 and Rs400.

If you have a mobile phone, you should be able to use it in Mauritius as coverage is very good in most areas. You will need to inform your service provider prior to travel. However, coverage is not good in Rodrigues.

Emtel Ltd (*1 Boundary Rd, Rose Hill;* ℡ *454 5400;* f *454 1010; hotline: 422 2222*) provides a mobile phone service and phones can be rented on a temporary basis, even just for one day, at around Rs125 per day against a deposit from a non-resident secured by a signed credit card voucher. Call charges are reasonable.

Mauritius Telecom customer service centres can send faxes and have payphones. They are to be found in many towns, including Mahébourg, Rivière du Rempart, Rose Hill, Terre Rouge, Triolet, Vacoas and in Port Mathurin, Rodrigues.

A telephone directory is published at the beginning of every year. It lists telephone and some fax numbers, plus government listings and has a not very helpful nor comprehensive yellow pages section. The directory is in English. The alphabetical listings are confusing since, for example, La Pirogue Hotel is listed under 'L' and not 'P'. Alphabetical order is odd, too, with 'L'Express' and similar words appearing several columns before 'Labour'.

Useful telephone numbers are:

℡ **Operator assistance** 10091	℡ **International directory enquiries** 10090
℡ **National directory enquiries** 150	℡ **International call assistance** 10092

FAX Faxes can be sent through the Mauritius Telecom customer service centres at much less mark-up than that charged by hotels. See above for locations.

ⓔ INTERNET ACCESS/EMAIL Many mid-range, upmarket and luxury hotels offer internet access at a fee, either in your room or in the hotel business centre. If you have a laptop computer and want to access the internet via the telephone point in your hotel room, ask the hotel to link you up to a local server – it is far cheaper.

Mauritius Post are progressively installing interactive kiosks in all post offices, which will include internet access. As of November 2005, 24 of the 93 post offices have a kiosk. You need to purchase a prepaid card from the post office counter or use a credit card.

Internet cafés are not widespread through the island and are usually limited to the main towns and tourist areas. Tariffs for email vary but you can expect to pay around Rs2–4 per minute or around Rs40 for 30 minutes. The following offer internet access:

Port Louis

Zenith Cybercafé Astrolabe Bldg, Port Louis Waterfront; ☎ 208 2213. *Open Mon–Thu 10.00–20.00, Fri–Sat 10.00–22.00, Sun 11.00–16.00.*

Northern Mauritius

Cyber Pirate 1st Fl, Espace Ocean Bldg, Coastal Rd, Grand Baie; ☎ 263 1757; e cyberpirate@intnet.mu. *Also offers photocopying, fax, photos to CD and webcam. Open 09.00–12.00 and 13.00–20.00, closed Wed and Sun.*

Cyberescales La Salette Rd, Grande Baie. Before the Super U supermarket. *Open Mon–Sat 08.30–20.30.*

Eastern Mauritius

Sous le Manguier Coastal Rd, Trou d'Eau Douce; ☎ 480 0192/3855; e slm@intnet.mu. *A tiny restaurant opposite the church, which also has 2 internet terminals and fax facilities. Open daily 09.30–14.30.*

Southern Mauritius

Cybersurf Internet Exchange Rue Labourdonnais, Mahébourg; ☎ 631 4247; e cybersurfmahebourg@yahoo.com. *Cheaper than most at Rs1.10 per min. Open Mon–Sat 09.15–18.30, Sun 09.15–12.00.*

Western Mauritius

Pasanda Internet Café Spa Supermarket, Coastal Rd, Flic en Flac; ☎ 453 5631; e pasadenas@smartnet.mu. *Also offers fax, scanning, photocopying, CD burning and international phonecards. Open Mon–Sat 08.30–20.00, Sun 08.30–18.00.*

Central Mauritius

Orchard Cybercafé Orchard Centre, Quatre Bornes; ☎ 424 0575

The Town Hall Quatre Bornes; ☎ 454 8054. Within the municipal library. *Open Mon–Fri 08.30–16.00.*

Cyber Surfer Av St Paul, Vacoas; ☎ 696 4878; e dabee@intnet.mu. *Open Mon–Sat 10.00–22.00, Sun 10.00–15.00.*

Carnegie Library Elizabeth Av, Curepipe; ☎ 670 4897. *Open Mon–Fri 09.30–17.30, Sat 09.30–16.00.*

COURIERS There are two international courier companies represented in Mauritius:

DHL Mauritius Ltd 14 Mgr Gonin St, Port Louis; ☎ 208 7711; f 208 3908

Federal Express (FEDEX) Grewals Lane, Les Pailles; ☎ 211 5914; f 211 4948

DHL guarantee delivery of letters and parcels to anywhere outside Mauritius within a maximum of 72 hours. The cost varies according to weight.

There is also a national courier service:

Poney Express Mauritius Ltd 18 Kwan Tee St, Caudan, Port Louis; ☎ 211 3262; f 211 3292

BUSINESS Ian Hayes

Over the past three decades Mauritius has successfully followed an economic strategy of diversification and industrialisation. One element of this was to attract direct foreign investment, with the result that Mauritius has developed good facilities for business. There are direct scheduled flights from Europe, Africa, the Far East and Australasia, a reliable infrastructure and sophisticated communication links. Furthermore, the standards of accommodation and service in the upmarket hotels are world class.

BUSINESS ASSISTANCE There is a number of organisations that exist both to develop and promote Mauritius as a centre for business and investment, and also to provide support to existing companies.

Mauritius Chamber of Commerce (MCCI) 3 Royal St, Port Louis; ☎ 208 3301; f 208 0076; e mcci@intnet.mu; www.mcci.org. *Founded in 1850, the MCCI now has 400 members representing a wide* spectrum of economic sectors from commerce and industry to banking, insurance, transport and tourism. Affiliated to the MCCI are the Chinese Chamber of Commerce, the Indian Traders' Association and the Mauritius Chamber of Merchants. The MCCI's activities include constant dialogue with government, trade fair and mission organisation, providing commercial information and defending the economic interests of Mauritius through contact with the European Union. There is a consultancy service for small businesses and computer and system analysis courses are held. Every year the MCCI issues an annual report, essential reading for anyone interested in doing business in Mauritius.

Mauritius Investment and Development Authority (MIDA) BAI Bldg, 25 Pope Hennessy St, Port Louis; ☏ 208 7750; f 208 5965; http://ncb.intnet.mu/mida. Formerly the Mauritius Export Development and Investment Authority (MEDIA), MIDA provides the focal point for export-promotion activities in Mauritius. It is active in searching for new markets for Mauritian products worldwide and owns and operates industrial estates that are leased to investors.

Board of Investment (BOI) Level 10, 1 Cathedral Square Bldg, 16 Jules Koenig St, Port Louis; ☏ 211 4190; f 208 2924; e invest@boi.intnet.mu; www.boimauritius.com. The BOI was established in March 2001 to replace MEDIA as the body responsible for promoting Mauritius as an international investment and business centre. It is

also charged with considering investment proposals and issuing investment certificates.

International Management (Mauritius) Ltd (IMM) Les Cascades Bldg, Edith Cavell St, PO Box 60, Port Louis; ☏ 212 9800; f 212 9833; e services@imm.mu; www.imm.mu. IMM is a wholly owned subsidiary of the Rogers Group, one of the largest and best-known companies in Mauritius. IMM helps clients to set up, manage and administer offshore entities including exempt and ordinary companies, and to liase with the FSC (see below). IMM carries a stock of ready-formed shelf companies and can obtain name approval for new companies within 2 working days. IMM also provides consultancy services to clients wishing to be onshore rather than offshore and provides advice on obtaining residency permits.

Financial Services Commission (FSC) 4th Fl, Harbour Front Bldg, President John F Kennedy St, Port Louis; ☏ 210 7000; f 208 7172; www.fscmauritius.org. The FSC was established in 2001 under the Financial Services Development Act and is the independent regulator of non-bank financial services. The FSC replaced a number of bodies, including the Stock Exchange Commission (SEC) and the Mauritius Offshore Business Activities Authority (MOBAA). The FSC grants licences and supervises the non-banking offshore sector, while co-ordinating government agencies and private organisations dealing with the sector.

OFFSHORE BUSINESS CENTRE As part of its continuing diversification strategy and in order to sustain economic growth, the government initiated offshore business in Mauritius in 1992. Offshore activities include banking, insurance, fund management, trusteeship of offshore trusts, operational headquarters, international consultancy services, shipping and ship management, and aircraft financing and leasing.

Offshore banks operating in Mauritius include Bank of Baroda, Banque Internationale des Mascareignes, Banque Privée Edmond de Rothschild Ltd, BNPI, Barclays Bank plc, Hong Kong Bank (offshore banking unit) and SB International Ltd.

There are considerable incentives for offshore business activities in Mauritius. The corporate tax rate is only 15% for this sector and there are concessionary personal income tax rates for expatriate staff. Furthermore, Mauritius has arranged double taxation agreements with the following countries: Botswana, China, France, Germany, India, Italy, Luxembourg, Madagascar, Malaysia, Namibia, Pakistan, Swaziland, Sweden, the UK and Zimbabwe. Offshore companies can take advantage of those treaties and may obtain a certificate of fiscal residence from the Mauritian tax authorities stating that a company is resident in Mauritius for the purpose of tax.

Other financial institutions which support the development of Mauritius as a financial centre include the Development Bank of Mauritius, State Investment Corporation, Mauritius Leasing Company and Stock Exchange of Mauritius.

Although the **Stock Exchange** (*4th Fl, 1 Cathedral Sq Bldg, 16 Jules Koenig St, Port Louis;* ↘ *212 9541;* f *208 8409,* e *stxbeni@intnet.mu; www.semdex.com*) is of relatively recent origin, it is playing an important role in mobilising funds on behalf of companies listed on the Stock Exchange. Similarly, the offshore banking sector is authorised to provide loans in foreign exchange to the EPZ sector at competitive rates. The Mauritius Leasing Company provides financial leases up to 100% of the value of production equipment for a period of three to seven years.

Mauritius is also a freeport (the only one in the Indian Ocean) which was established in 1992 under the control of the Mauritius Freeport Authority (*Level 10, 1 Cathedral Sq Bldg, 16 Jules Koenig St, Port Louis;* ↘ *211 4190;* f *208 2924;* e *mfa@efreeport.com; www.efreeport.com*). This enables companies that set up storage, assembly and marketing activities to enjoy zero tax on corporate profits, exemption from customs duties on all goods imported into the freeport zone, reduced port charges for all goods designed for re-export, free repatriation of profits, 100% foreign ownership, offshore banking facilities and the opportunity to sell a percentage of total turnover on the local market.

According to *The International*, a financial magazine reviewing offshore centres in 1996: 'If there was an award for busiest offshore centre, Mauritius would be a contender.' As of December 2001, around 14,000 offshore entities were registered with the offshore authority.

However, Mauritius should not be thought of as a tax haven manipulated by 'brass plate' operators. A proven presence locally must be established (for which accountants and company formation firms can be hired) to obtain a tax residence certificate. This enables offshore companies to have an optional zero tax rate and exemption from profit tax, stamp duties and capital gains tax.

BUSINESS ACCOMMODATION Most luxury, upmarket and some upper mid-range hotels cater extremely well for business guests. Business and conference centres provide all the facilities you may need, including secretarial services and assistance with local contacts. Such hotels regularly host conferences and incentive groups. For business accommodation in Port Louis, the **Labourdonnais Waterfront Hotel** (see page 110) and **Le Suffren Hotel & Marina** (see page 110), both near the Caudan Waterfront complex, are popular.

BUSINESS VISA Business visitors to Mauritius do not need a special visa, provided they are nationals of countries for which no tourist visa is required. However, business visitors staying longer than three months will require a work permit. For more information see *Red tape*, pages 43–6.

CULTURAL SENSITIVITIES

Reproduced here (translated from the French by the MTPA) is the Code of Ethics for Tourists, since it shows how great is the concern of Mauritians for the right approach to visitors to their country:

> You are already most welcome in Mauritius. You'll be even more so if you will readily appreciate that our island…
>
> … considers its most important asset is its people. They are well worth meeting and enjoying a friendly chat with;
>
> … possesses a rich capital of cultures, needs and values which it cherishes more than anything else;
>
> … is ready to give you value for money, but is not prepared to sell its soul for it;

... has wealth of its own, which deserves to be preserved;

... treats all its visitors like VIPs, but does not take kindly to those who overact the part;

... is not all lagoon and languor, and boasts a host of many-splendoured sights;

... considers, without being prudish, that nude when flaunted can be provocative and offensive;

... is not a faraway paradise of unlimited licence;

... takes pride in serving you with a smile and would be grateful for a smile in return;

... and will bare its soul willingly if you will handle it with care.

Beachwear is acceptable in tourist resorts but is less so in local towns and villages. Tourists should dress appropriately when visiting religious buildings (no shorts, mini skirts etc). It is a good idea for women to carry a light cardigan or shirt and sarong for this purpose. Shoes should be removed when entering temples and mosques, and you may also be asked to remove leather items at some Hindu temples. At mosques you may be required to cover your head.

Homosexuality has not been legalised in Mauritius and is frowned upon by some locals. Couples should avoid public displays of affection.

In recent years there has been an increase in the number of people begging, including children, particularly around the main commercial centres, markets and tourist attractions. Some have even developed a network of people, such as restaurant staff, to help them. Beggars are not usually aggressive and a gentle refusal to a demand for money, accompanied by a smile, is normally accepted immediately.

Although it should not affect travellers, many Mauritian women are the victims of sexual abuse and domestic violence. There is a hotline for reporting incidents of domestic violence (❦ *211 0725*).

GIVING SOMETHING BACK

I am sure that you will thoroughly enjoy visiting Mauritius and Rodrigues. You may feel that you wish to repay the hospitality you experience by helping the local community in some way. Below is a selection of particularly worthwhile projects and details of how you can lend support.

CARE-CO (RODRIGUES) CARE-Co (Rodrigues), formerly known as Craft Aid Rodrigues, is a wonderful project, giving people with disabilities a vastly improved life and a place in society. I was fortunate enough to visit the CARE-Co workshop in Rodrigues and can assure you that donations are put to excellent use: hearing aids, family support, educational tools, and equipment for the Gonzague Pierre-Louis Special Learning Centre. For further information, see box *CARE-Co*, page 214.

How you can help

- Buy CARE-Co products. They are featured in the catalogues of Tearcraft, Traidcraft and OXFAM in the UK. Write to CARE-Co at the following address if you wish to obtain a list of their UK partners: CARE-Co, Camp du Roi, Rodrigues, Mauritius.
- For coconut jewellery (*bijoux coco*), you can order a full-colour catalogue which has a price list and order form. The catalogue costs £3 to produce so any contributions are very welcome. The cost of the catalogue will be reimbursed on your first order.
- Cheques or donations can be sent in any major currency, or changed at the Mauritius Commercial Bank in Port Mathurin, Rodrigues. Donate to: CARE-Co (Rodrigues), Mauritius Commercial Bank, Port Mathurin; account number 360000940.

- Those who donate any amount exceeding £15 receive direct reports from the Gonzague Pierre-Louis Special Learning Centre.

MAURITIUS WILDLIFE FOUNDATION (MWF) The Mauritius Wildlife Foundation does a fantastic job ensuring that Mauritius's remaining plants and animals do not go the way of the dodo.

How you can help
- Whilst in Mauritius, be sure to book an excursion to Ile aux Aigrettes, which contains the last remnants of native coastal forest and is the probable site of the dodo's extinction. Excursions are offered in most Mauritius hotels and a portion of the tour fees supports wildlife conservation. For further details see pages 35–6 and 104.
- Donations are vital to the continuation of the MWF's work. Donations can be made via the MWF website, or contact the MWF directly (*Mauritius Wildlife Foundation, Grannum Rd, Vacoas;* \ *697 6097;* f *6097 6512;* e *executive@mwf.intnet.mu; www.mauritian-wildlife.org*).
- The MWF is staffed by Mauritians and expatriates, as well as volunteers who come from overseas to gain valuable conservation experience. Should you wish to apply for a volunteer placement with the MWF, please contact Isabelle Lenoir (*MWF, Av Bois des Billes, Royal Road, Black River, Mauritius*).

DURRELL WILDLIFE CONSERVATION TRUST (DWCT) Donations may also be made to the Mauritius programme of the Durrell Wildlife Conservation Trust, which works with the MWF, by sending a cheque in any currency to the Durrell Wildlife Conservation Trust (*Les Augres Manor, Trinity, Jersey JE3 5BP, Channel Islands, UK;* \ *01534 860000;* f *01534 860001;* e *jerseyzoo@durrell.org*). To find out more about the DWCT's fascinating work or to become a member, contact them at the same address.

There is more information about the DWCT in the box on page 192.

SHOALS RODRIGUES Shoals Rodrigues is a non-governmental organisation (NGO) which studies and monitors the marine ecology of Rodrigues and, through various programmes, promotes marine environmental awareness amongst Rodriguans of all ages thus working towards a sustainable development of the lagoon.

The organisation accepts volunteers from around the world on placements. It is a fantastic opportunity to gain experience in marine biology and conservation. If this interests you, or you would like to make a donation to the organisation, please contact Eric Blais at Shoals Rodrigues, Pointe Monier, Rodrigues; \ 831 1225; e director@shoals-rodrigues.org; www.shoals-rodrigues.org.

For more information about their work, see box *Shoals Rodrigues*, page 198.

NATIONAL HANDICRAFT PROMOTION AGENCY (NHPA) The NHPA exists to promote the manufacture and sale of handicrafts in Mauritius and Rodrigues. Buying goods sold in the NHPA outlets means that part of your payment goes to the Mauritian and Rodriguan artisans. Handicrafts sold in other outlets, including the markets, are often imported.

NHPA craft shops can be found at the following locations:

SSR International Airport Plaine Magnien; \ 637 4824
Village Artisanal Mahébourg Museum Compound, Mahébourg; \ 631 8671
Craft Market Caudan Waterfront, Port Louis; \ 210 0139

Astrolabe Centre Caudan Waterfront, Port Louis; \ 211 9972
SILWF Compound Grand Baie; \ 263 9972
Plaine Corail Airport Rodrigues; \ 831 4428

HELP

CONSULAR HELP Embassies, high commissions and their consular offices do not exist as 'minders' or information bureaux. Whereas consuls will help in an emergency, repatriation to your home country at your government's expense is not one of the services generally provided. It is not necessary to register at your consulate unless staying in Mauritius for an extended period.

Embassies/high commissions

Australian High Commission 2nd Fl, Rogers Hse, 5 President John F Kennedy St, Port Louis; ✆ 208 1700; f 208 8878; e austhc@intnet.mu; www.mauritius.embassy.gov.au

British High Commission 7th Fl, Les Cascades Bldg, Edith Cavell St, Port Louis; ✆ 202 9400; f 202 9408; e bhc@bow.intnet.mu

French Embassy 14 St Georges St, Port Louis; ✆ 202 0100; f 202 0120; e ambafr@intnet.mu; www.ambafrance-mu.org

Indian High Commission 6th Fl, LIC Bldg, President

John F Kennedy St, Port Louis; ✆ 208 3775; f 208 6859; http://indiahighcom.intnet.mu

Russian Embassy Queen Mary Av, Floréal; ✆ 696 5533; f 696 5027; e rusemb.mu@intnet.mu

South African High Commission 4th Fl, BAI Bldg, 25 Pope Hennessy St, Port Louis; ✆ 212 6925; f 212 6936; e sahc@intnet.mu

US Embassy 4th Fl, Rogers Hse, 5 John Kennedy St, Port Louis; ✆ 202 4400; f 208 9534; e usembass@intnet.mu

Consulates

Austria 5th Fl, Rogers Hse, 5 President John F Kennedy St, Port Louis; ✆ 202 6800; e vrene.sanson@rogers.mu

Belgium c/o Ireland Blyth Ltd, 10 Dr Ferrière St, Port Louis; ✆ 208 7289; f 211 9561; e fdesmarais@ibl.intnet.mu

Canada c/o Blanche Birger Co Ltd, 18 Jules Koenig St, Port Louis; ✆ 212 5500; f 208 3391; e canada@intnet.mu

Finland 2nd Fl, Rogers Hse, 5 President John F Kennedy St, Port Louis; ✆ 202 6527; e philip.taylor@rogers.mu

Germany 32 bis St Georges St, Port Louis; ✆ 212 4100; f 211 4111

Italy DML Bldg, M1 Motorway, Port Louis; ✆ 211 1427; f 269 0268; e consolato.italia@dmltourism.com

FOREIGN ORGANISATIONS IN MAURITIUS

The British Council PO Box 111, Royal Rd, Rose Hill; ✆ 454 9550; f 454 9553; e general.enquiries@mu.britishcouncil.org; www.britishcouncil.org/mauritius

Delegation of the European Commission 8th Fl, St James Ct, St Denis St, Port Louis; ✆ 207 1515; f 211 6624; www.delmus.cec.eu.int

United Nations Development Programme 6th Fl, Anglo Mauritius Hse, Intendance St, Port Louis; ✆ 212 3726; f 208 4871; e registry.mu@undp.org; http://un.intnet.mu/undp

World Health Organisation 1st Fl, Anglo Mauritius Hse, Intendance St, Port Louis; ✆ 210 7300; f 210 6474; e who@intnet.mu; http://un.intnet.mu/who

EMERGENCY SERVICES

Police/ambulance emergency line	999	Fire service	995

Voice messaging systems for police assistance can be activated by dialling:

Complaints	208 6666	Drugs	208 3333

There are eight 'hotlines' for police assistance (✆ *208 7013 up to 208 7020*). The police headquarters is at Line Barracks in Port Louis (✆ *208 1212*). If reporting theft of property covered by insurance, remember to ask the police for a copy of your report to substantiate your insurance claim.

SOCIAL PROBLEMS There are special 'hotlines' with counselling or for reporting incidents:

Drug addiction	465 4144	Environment hotline	201 1695
Alcoholism	465 4144	Environment SOS	212 5050
Battered children	212 6240	Stray dogs	464 5084
Battered women	211 0725		

UNIFORMS The most frequently seen uniformed personnel are the police who wear light blue shirts and dark blue trousers, with black flat caps. Firemen wear a brown uniform with red belts.

There is no army as such. A paramilitary unit called the Special Mobile Force (SMF) numbers about 1,000 and has its headquarters at Vacoas. It has some tanks, jeeps and other military vehicles. The top soldiers have been trained in Europe and India. French military advisers offer supervision and further training and there is also a lingering British connection. SMF regulars wear khaki, soldier-style uniforms, quite distinct from that of the normal police or riot unit. They have combat and parade uniforms and also wear camouflage overalls.

Other military-style uniforms (blue shirt and darker blue trousers) are worn by members of the Rapid Intervention Brigade. Those men in green overalls with wellington boots belong to the army of street cleaners run by Securiclean.

There is no air force but a small navy unit does exist, as well as a coastguard service.

COMPLAINTS Complaints to achieve redress ought to be made while you are in Mauritius, not after you've returned home. Go to the top and make your complaint in a reasonable manner. Keep copies of any documentation submitted. Usually your comments, if justified, will bring about an acceptable solution.

Letters of complaint addressed to the general manager of the Mauritius Tourist Promotion Authority (*E Anquetil Bldg, Sir S Ramgoolam St, Port Louis;* ℡ *201 1703;* f *212 5142*) will be investigated, especially as the MTPA prides itself on Mauritius being a 'no problem' destination.

Angraecum eburneum

4

Activities

For many visitors, turning over to tan the other side will be the extent of their physical exertion whilst in Mauritius. However, there is plenty to keep the more energetic amused. Activities, watersports in particular, are generally run by the large resort hotels.

SPA TREATMENTS

While many of the upmarket hotels on the island have their own spa (some of which are open to non-hotel residents), those who are staying in smaller establishments without such facilities can take advantage of the growing number of spas opening outside the hotels.

The island's spas are typically operated by well-trained staff and offer a range of massages and treatments. Some even offer comprehensive wellness programmes lasting several days. You can expect to pay around Rs800 for an Indian head massage, Rs1,100 for a body massage.

The following are spas which operate outside the hotels:

Surya Coastal Rd, Pereybère; ✆/f 263 1637; e surya_mauritius@yahoo.co.uk; www.geocities.com/surya_mauritius. This Ayurvedic spa between Grand Baie and Pereybère is run by practitioners from Kerala in southern India. As well as one-off massages and treatments, programmes lasting from 3 days to 3 weeks are available. *Open*

daily 09.00–19.30.
Life Care Spa Club Flic en Flac; ✆ 453 9999; e lifecare@intnet.mu. Specialises in Japanese massages and mud baths.
Spa Viva 102 St Jean Rd, Quatre Bornes; ✆ 467 8907/8; e spaviva@intnet.mu

GOLF

For golfers, there are plenty of courses to choose from, with most located at the upmarket hotels. While some are only open to hotel residents, the following are also open to non-residents on payment of a green fee. Clubs, trolleys and other equipment can usually be hired. The price of club hire varies enormously, but expect to pay Rs500–1,300 for a full set. It is advisable, and often a requirement, to book tee-off times.

18-hole courses

Belle Mare Plage Golf Hotel and Casino Resort Belle Mare; ✆ 402 2600; f 402 2616; e headpro@bellemareplagehotel.com. Two impressive courses designed with both professional and amateur golfers in mind. The Legend is an 18-hole, par-72 course designed by Hugh Baiocchi, with accuracy on the tree-lined fairways the main challenge. The Links is an 18-hole, par-71 championship course designed by Rodney Wright and British player/commentator Peter Alliss, three-time winner of the PGA Championship. A 30-min lesson costs from Rs900, a 3-day package with 2 hours of coaching per day costs from Rs5,800.

Golf du Château Coastal Rd, Bel Ombre; ℡ 601 1500; f 601 1515. An 18-hole, par-72 championship course designed by South African architect, Peter Matkovich, plus a 9-hole course. In a stunning setting on 100 acres sandwiched between hills covered with sugarcane and the ocean. The course was designed to be accessible to a wide range of golfers yet be able to host a championship; it therefore offers 5 tee options. The green fees for non-residents of the Heritage Golf and Spa Resort and Le Telfair are Rs2,300 for 18 holes and Rs1,500 for 9 holes. *Open daily 07.00–16.00.*

Ile aux Cerfs Golf Course One&Only Le Touessrok; ℡ 402 7720; e info@oneandonlyletouessrokgolf.com; www.oneandonlyletouessrokgolf.com. An 18-hole par-72 championship course endorsed by Bernhard Langer and voted tenth in the World's Top One Hundred Courses by *Golf World* magazine. An incredible course on the small offshore island of Ile aux Cerfs – all 18 holes have views of the sea. The 9 lakes and the obvious space limitations of playing on an island make this a challenging course. There is a superb clubhouse, which includes an impressive restaurant and bar with views of the course. *Open daily 06.30–sunset.*

Mauritius Gymkhana Club Suffolk Rd, Vacoas; ℡ 696 1404; f 698 1565; e mgymclub@intnet.mu. An 18-hole par-68 course, the oldest on the island and the only

private club. The charge of Rs1,112 per person per day includes access to the club, green fees and insurance. There is also a compulsory caddy fee of Rs125 per round. Tee-off times must be booked in advance.

Paradis Hotel Le Morne Peninsula; ℡ 401 5050; f 450 5140; e paradis@bchot.com; www.paradis-hotel.com. An 18-hole championship course set against the stunning backdrop of Le Morne. The green fee for non-residents is Rs2,200. A 35-min lesson is Rs550 for 1 person or Rs900 for 2.

Tamarina Golf Estate and Beach Club Médine Sugar Estate. This 18-hole course is due to open in April 2006 between Flic en Flac and Port Louis. No further details were available at the time of writing.

9-hole courses

Trou aux Biches Village Hotel Trou aux Biches; ℡ 204 6565; f 265 6611; e trouauxbiches@bchot.com; www.trouauxbiches-hotel.com. A 9-hole par-32 course. Green fees are Rs550 for non-residents (Rs880 for 18 holes). Caddies are Rs50 for 9 holes, 45-min private lessons cost Rs550 for 1 person or Rs900 for 2. *Open daily 07.00–18.00.*

Le Shandrani Blue Bay; ℡ 603 4343; f 637 4313; e shandrani@bchot.com; www.shandrani-hotel.com. A 9-hole par-30 course. Green fees for non-residents are Rs440.

HORSE RACING

Horse racing takes place at the **Champ de Mars** racecourse in Port Louis every Saturday during the season from May until the end of November/early December. The highlight is the **Maiden Plate**, which is usually run in September. The sport is very popular amongst Mauritians, primarily because they love to gamble, and the centre of the racecourse fills with stalls, snack-bars and bookmakers on race days.

Admission to the course is free but entry to the stands costs Rs120–175, depending on the races being held, and entry to the outside terraces is Rs20. For more information contact the **Mauritius Turf Club**, Eugene Laurent St, Port Louis (℡ 208 6047; e mtc@intnet.mu; www.mauritiusturfclub.com).

HORSERIDING

Most hotels can arrange horseriding, although it is often cheaper to arrange it directly with the stables. The standards of horses and safety vary and, if you are not offered a riding hat, you should ask for one (you may have to insist). Do check that all the equipment is safe before setting off. Jodhpurs and riding boots are not usually available, so suitable clothing (long trousers and sensible, enclosed shoes) must be worn.

Mont Choisy Sugar Estate Grand Baie; \ 265 6159/421 1166 (after hours); e horseriding@montchoisy.com. A highly professional stables offering rides through the estate's private deer park. It is a fantastic, historic setting, featuring a charming traditional home as the centrepiece. The remains of the sugar factory and lime kilns add to the atmosphere and even the horses enjoy stabling in imposing, old, stone buildings. Rides are led by ex-professional racing jockey, Sylvain Ranaivosoa from Madagascar. Riding hats must be worn. There are 17 horses and rides are limited to groups of 10. *1½-hour ride with refreshments from Rs1,650.*

Domaine les Pailles Les Guibies, Pailles; \ 286 4240; e ecurie@intnet.mu; www.domainelespailles.net. Located in the centre of the island, just off the motorway between Port Louis and Moka. Well-managed stables run by qualified and experienced staff. Safety is taken seriously – riding hats must be worn and can be borrowed. Medical insurance is included in the rates. The countryside is beautiful and on early-morning rides you are likely to see monkeys. Reservations should be made at least 24 hours in advance. *One-hour lesson or ride from Rs770, trek with picnic lunch from Rs960.*

Maritim Hotel Turtle Bay, Balaclava; \ 204 1000; f 204 1020; e info.mau@maritim.com; www.maritim.com. Offers riding to hotel residents only. Has 7 horses and riding is along the beach and through the countryside around the hotel. *One-hour lesson from Rs500.*

Le Coco Beach Belle Mare; \ 415 1010; f 415 1888; e infococo@sunresort.com; www.lecocobeach.com. Has about 20 horses and ponies. Offers lessons as well as treks. *One-hour ride from Rs750, half-hour pony ride Rs450.*

Les Ecuries de la Vieille Cheminée Chateaufort, Chamarel; \ 686 5027/725 5546; f 686 1250. Riding is on the 300-acre estate and through the surrounding countryside. Boots and riding hats can be borrowed at no extra cost. No horseriding experience necessary. *One-hour ride from Rs1,200, two-hour ride from Rs1,500, full-day ride with meal from Rs2,000. Open Mon–Sat.*

Le Ranch Chemin Ramdenee, Rivière Noire; \ 483 5478; f 208 8328; e charduc@intnet.mu. Has 17 horses and ponies and offers rides through picturesque, privately owned countryside. Rides are only suitable for experienced riders and there is a minimum age requirement of 13 years. *One-hour ride from Rs800, three-hour ride from Rs1,800.*

HUNTING

Hunting is a status sport in which only wealthy or well-connected Mauritians take part. The traditional season for deer hunting is June to September and the popular area is around Plaine Champagne and Case Noyale in the southwest.

Visitors can hunt at **Domaine du Chasseur** (*Anse Jonchée;* \ *634 5097; f 634 5261; e dchasseur@intnet.mu; www.dchasseur.com*) in the southeast of the island, where 1,500 Javanese deer live in a game reserve of 2,350 acres. As the deer herd has to be culled to keep its natural increase within the ability of the reserve to sustain it, organised hunting is considered a form of conservation. The basic rate starts at €250, rising according to the age and size of deer shot: from €400 for a year-old male to a cool €5,000 for an eight-year-old with antlers of 75cm or more. Guns and guides are included and trophies can be arranged for a fee. Wild boar and hare are hunted all year round.

FOOTBALL

Football is Mauritius's national sport and is played by amateur teams throughout the island. All the main towns have a stadium for local league matches, although unofficial games are played with passion wherever there is a space large enough.

Mauritians are devoted fans of English football and the shirts of English clubs are everywhere. The addiction is perpetuated by the fact that there is more English football on television in Mauritius than in England itself!

The Mauritius Football Association is at Chancery House, Lislet Geoffrey Street, Port Louis (\ *211 5909*).

Mauritius has some of the best deep-sea fishing waters you can find and people come from all over the world just for that reason. World-record catches off Mauritius include the mako shark, blue shark, skipjack tuna and the renowned blue marlin. Although the west coast is regarded as the best area for deep-sea fishing, the northern and eastern coasts can offer equally rewarding trips.

If the primary purpose of your visit to Mauritius is fishing, you may want to take account of the following seasons:

Wahoo/hammerhead shark:	September–December
Blue marlin/sailfish:	November–March
Mako shark:	November–April
Yellow fin tuna:	March–May
Black marlin, skipjack tuna, barracuda:	all year

Most of the deep-sea fishing companies operate modern, well-equipped boats that can reach deep waters in no time at all. The boats usually have three 'fighting' chairs in the stern and outriggers so that five baits can be trolled at a time. Any fish that is caught remains the property of the boat owner, although 'tag and release' is starting to be practised in Mauritius, and is used at Beachcomber hotels.

Almost all hotels will be able to arrange deep-sea fishing and some of the more upmarket ones will have their own fishing centres. Tour operators will also be able to organise trips.

In most cases, the crew of deep-sea fishing boats are incredibly poorly paid, particularly when you consider the amount of skill involved. If you feel that they have looked after you well, a tip will make a lot of difference to them.

The price will vary between boats, but a half-day trip (usually six hours) costs around Rs6,500–9,000 per boat (usually six people) and a full day (usually nine hours) Rs8,000–11,000. This will include all the equipment, snacks and drinks.

DEEP-SEA FISHING OPERATORS

North

Organisation de Pêche du Nord (also known as Corsaire Club) Mont Choisy; ☎ 265 5209; f 265 6267
Sportfisher Sunset Bd Complex, Grand Baie; ☎ 263 8358; ☎/f 263 6309; e karen@intnet.mu

East

Surcouf Trou d'Eau Douce; ☎ 419 3198; f 419 3197

South

Domaine du Pêcheur Vieux Grand Port; ☎ 634 5097; f 634 5261; e dchasseur@intnet.mu

West

Beachcomber Fishing Club Le Morne; ☎ 401 5050; f 483 5919; e challenger@intnet.mu
La Pirogue Big Game Fishing Flic en Flac; ☎ 453 8441; f 453 8449; e info@lapiroguebiggame.com
Morne Anglers Club Black River; ☎ 483 6528; ☎/f 483 5801
Sofitel Imperial Big Game Fishing Wolmar; ☎ 453 8700; f 453 8320; e sofitel@intnet.mu
Island Sports Club Rivière Noire; ☎ 483 5353; f 483 6547

While all deep-sea boats are equipped for anglers, the enthusiast who wants to buy equipment can do so from:

Quay Stores 3 President John F Kennedy St, Port Louis; ☎ 212 1043

Rods & Reels La Preneuse; ☎ 483 6579; f 483 5038; e jphenry@intnet.mu

The reefs off Mauritius offer excellent opportunities for scuba diving and snorkelling: warm, crystal-clear water, calm seas and varied marine life. Although pollution, overfishing, poaching in protected waters and the stealing of shells have taken their toll in some areas, there are still numerous excellent dive sites around. Many experts rate them as better than those to be found around the main Seychelles islands or off Sri Lanka.

Although diving can be done throughout the year, June–July is considered by experienced divers to be the least suitable time, on account of the weather.

Most hotels offer snorkelling equipment and trips, either free of charge or for a small fee. Masks, snorkels and flippers can be bought quite cheaply in tourist areas. The lagoons of the northeast and west coasts are good snorkelling areas, as are the waters around Trou aux Biches and Blue Bay.

There are plenty of scuba diving centres on the island. Instructors should have Professional Association of Diving Instructors (PADI) or Confédération des Activités Subaquatiques (CMAS) qualifications, which ensure that they have undergone professional training and rigorous safety tuition. Many of the dive centres belong to the Mauritian Scuba Diving Association, based at 31 bis, Meldrun Street in Beau Bassin (↘ 454 0011; e msda@intnet.mu).

Prices start at around Rs900 for a single dive including all equipment. For a course of five dives, expect to pay about Rs4,000–5,000 with equipment, and about Rs7,000–10,000 for ten dives. For beginners, many dive centres offer a resort course, which consists of a lesson in a pool followed by a sea dive and these cost around Rs1,650–1,800. Rates do not usually include insurance, so if your travel insurance does not cover diving, you would be advised to pay the additional amount, usually about Rs150–250, for medical insurance. Many dive centres also offer PADI courses and will be able to provide more information and prices.

The Mauritius Underwater Group (MUG, for short), has given rise to the Mauritian Marine Conservation Society, a group actively engaged in conservation of the reef environment. MUG is linked to the Professional Diving Association and to the International Diving Confederation. Members meet on Tuesday and Sunday nights over beers, discussing their latest dive experiences. Visitors are welcome; a week's temporary membership costs about Rs150, but you must be a qualified diver to join. Temporary members can hire equipment from MUG, which is considerably cheaper than at many of the big resorts. The clubhouse is open most days. It is near Phoenix, just off the main Port Louis–Curepipe road.

Divers should not touch any seashells underwater and should remember that it is illegal to remove shells from the sea.

DIVING CENTRES The following list is not exhaustive but covers most of the diving operators. Those marked with an asterisk are members of the Mauritius Scuba Diving Association.

North

Aquarius Diving Centre Veranda Hotel; ↘ 263 6260; f 263 4609

*Atlantis Diving School Trou aux Biches; ↘ 265 7172; f 263 7859

*Blue Water Diving Le Corsaire, Trou aux Biches; ↘/f 265 7186

*Cap Divers Paradise Cove Hotel, Anse La Raie; ↘ 204 4000; f 204 4040

*Diving World Le Canonnier Hotel; ↘ 209 7000; f 263 7864; e divword@intnet.mu. Le Victoria Hotel; ↘ 204 2000; f 263 7888. Le Mauricia Hotel; ↘ 209 1593; f 261 8224.

*Dolphin Diving Centre Pereybère; ↘ 263 9428

*Emperor Diving Marina Village Resort, Anse La Raie; ↘ 262 7651; f 262 7650

*island-diving.com Villas Mon Plaisir, Pointe aux Piments; ↘ 261 7471; m 0786 0554; www.island-diving.com

*Merville Diving Centre Merville Beach Hotel, Grand Baie; ℡ 263 8621; f 263 8146; e mvhotel@intnet.mu

*Nautilus Trou aux Biches Hotel; ℡ 204 6565; f 265 6611

*Paradise Diving Coralia Mont Choisy Hotel, Mont Choisy; ℡ 265 6070; f 265 6749

Pereybère Diving Centre Casa Florida, Pereybère; ℡ 263 6225; f 263 7225

*Turtle Bay Nautics Maritim Hotel, Turtle Bay; ℡ 261 5600; f 261 5670

East

Aquarius Diving Centre Le Coco Beach Hotel, Belle Mare; ℡ 415 5101; f 415 1002

*East Coast Diving Le St Géran Hotel, Poste de Flacq; ℡ 415 1825; f 401 1668

*Neptune Diving Centre Belle Mare Plage Hotel, Belle Mare; ℡ 415 1501; f 415 1993

*Pierre Sport Diving Le Touessrok Hotel, Trou d'Eau Douce; ℡ 419 2451; f 419 2025

*Sea Fan Diving Centre Hotel Ambre, Palmar; ℡ 401 8051; f 415 1182

South

*Coral Dive La Croix du Sud Hotel, Pointe Jérome, Mahébourg; ℡ 631 9505; f 631 9505

*Shandrani Diving Le Shandrani Hotel, Blue Bay; ℡ 603 4343; f 637 4313

West

*Abyss Morcellement Anna, Flic en Flac; ℡/f 453 8109

Aquarius Diving Paradis Hotel, Le Morne; ℡ 450 5050; f 450 5140. Les Pavillons Hotel, Le Morne; ℡ 450 5217; f 450 5248

Easy Dive Berjaya Le Morne Hotel, Le Morne; ℡ 450 5800; f 450 5640; e berjaya@intnet.mu

*Exploration Sous-marine Villas Caroline, Flic en Flac; ℡ 453 8450; f 453 8807

*Klondike Diving Centre Klondike Hotel, Flic en Flac; ℡ 453 8335; f 453 8337

*Punto Blue Pearle Beach Hotel, Flic en Flac; ℡ 453 8428; f 453 8405

*Sofitel Diving Centre Sofitel Imperial Hotel, Wolmar; ℡ 453 8700; f 453 8320; e sofitel@bow.intnet.mu

*Sun Diving La Pirogue Hotel, Wolmar; ℡ 453 8441; f 453 8449; e sundiver@intnet.mu

DIVE SITES The Mascarenes are volcanic isles, so much of the terrain you see whilst diving consists of rock formations like overhangs, walls and caverns. Abundant and diverse corals colonise such formations – some 200 species are said to be present.

The best dive spots include Le Morne in the southwest, the west coast off Flic en Flac and north to Trou aux Biches and Grand Baie. In the southeast, diving is good off Vieux Grand Port. Some of the very best diving, however, is around the northern offshore islets, like Coin de Mire.

The southwest coast Most of the sites in this area are about 30 minutes by boat from the shore and they are all on the seaward side of the barrier reef, where marine life is abundant. You can explore sites like **Needle Hole**, **Jim's Place** and **Anthony**, all of which are shallow dives (12–18m). Highlights include magnificent corals and swarms of fish like sergeant-majors, goldies and surgeonfish, and all boast excellent visibility with exceptional conditions for underwater photography. A deeper dive is **Michel's Place**, at 38m, which features flat corals, lots of clownfish, and triggerfish. Apparently green and hawksbill turtles are also common.

Another deep one is the drop-off called **Cliff** (average depth 22m) opposite Le Paradis Hotel. Conditions can be quite badly affected by a strong tidal surge. Moray eels are seen on most dives.

One of the most beautiful and popular sites in the area is known as the **Japanese Gardens**. At 14–28m, they are so named because of the diversity of corals in the coral garden there. There is very little current and visibility is good. Abundant fish include parrotfish, pipefish and ghost morays.

A flat, horseshoe-shaped reef well known to divers is **Casiers** (average depth 26m), where shoals of barracuda, kingfish and surgeonfish are usually encountered. Tidal influence is a little more pronounced and visibility can be adversely affected by suspensions in the water.

The west coast Ideal for beginners is **Aquarium**, a rocky reef area that harbours the likes of angelfish, clownfish and butterfly fish plus lots of wire coral. The dive starts at 7m and descends to 18m. Visibility is usually good but watch out for poisonous stonefish. This is the site where night dives are conducted for experienced folks.

For some cave diving, try the **Cathedral** (18–27m). The dive takes place on the drop-off, enters a chamber and then a huge underwater cave, in which lionfish, squirrelfish, kingfish and crayfish are often seen. Light filters into the cave through a crack in the ceiling creating the impression of being in a cathedral. Experienced divers rate the site highly.

Also for experienced divers is **Manioc**, a deep dive on rock faces, which begins at 32m and descends to 45m. Game fish, including kingfish, tuna and barracuda often make an appearance. Impressive emperor angelfish abound and white-tipped reef sharks are occasionally seen. Divers are almost guaranteed sharks, rays, tuna and barracuda at **Rempart L'Herbe**, also known as **Shark Place**. The sharks are typically grey reef sharks, although hammerheads occasionally visit the area. It's a deep dive (42–54m) on a pinnacle with steep slopes covered in pink and black coral.

Off the coast opposite the Villas Caroline is the *Kei Sei 113*, a barge which was deliberately sunk in 1988 to form an artificial reef at a depth of 40m. It is partly covered with corals and residents typically include giant moray eels, red snappers and hawkfish.

The north coast The Trou aux Biches area is some 300m from a large reef. This is great for snorkelling, as there's little in the way of surf. From the northwest, you could visit about ten different sites, of which **Coin de Mire** and **Flat Island** are among the best. It takes about 90 minutes to reach Coin de Mire, where the rock walls drop to about 100m. The sites around the island are suitable only for experienced divers because of the tides and currents. Average depth is 10–20m and the dives are usually drift dives. Barracuda, dogtooth tunny, large parrotfish, wahoo and white-tipped shark are common and there are lots of oyster clams, cowries and hermit crabs. To the north of Coin de Mire is Flat Island, but because of strong currents and rough seas this is dived only during the summer and only by highly experienced divers.

There is also a number of sites off Grand Baie. One of the best is **Tortoise** (13m), which lies just 1.5km offshore. The flat reefs are home to a variety of colourful tropical fish, moray eels, octopus, stonefish and lionfish. **Coral Gardens** (average depth 15m), halfway between Grand Baie and Coin de Mire, consists of coral banks between which are sand gullies. The coral and the visibility are generally good, and the site is popular for night dives. Commonly seen are squirrelfish, trumpetfish and goldies. **Night dives** off **Grand Baie** are said to be incredible. At night, colours on the reefs are far brighter than by day and a mass of marine animals emerge from their daytime hideouts.

A good option for novices is the Pereybère site, at only 12m, where tropical reef fish abound. Divers may see octopus, moray eels and stonefish.

In 1987, the *Stella Maru*, a Japanese trawler, was deliberately sunk 1.5km west of Trou aux Biches by the Mauritius Marine Conservation Society. The ship lay on its side until 1992 when a cyclone forced it upright, where it remains. Stonefish, spotted morays and green morays are often seen. This dive, which reaches a depth of 26m, is highly recommended by experienced divers.

The east coast A bit wilder and rather less affected by mass tourism than the other regions, the east coast offers some excellent diving. Drift dives are typical in the area. At **The Pass** (8–25m) you can drift-dive through the 'pass' in the barrier reef, admiring the psychedelic tapestries of coral and reef fishes. Turtles and sharks are often seen.

Lobster Canyon (25m), approximately 1.6km offshore, takes divers through a short cave full of crayfish, along a wall and into a canyon, where sharks and eagle-rays may be seen. At times visibility is limited to 10m due to high levels of plankton.

OTHER UNDERSEA EXPERIENCES

There are plenty of alternatives to diving and snorkelling for those who want a glimpse of underwater life. Most hotels offer trips in **glass-bottom boats**, which sail over the reef. This is a good way for children to see and learn about marine life.

UNDERSEA WALKS Undersea walks involve plodding along the seabed wearing a lead belt, whilst air is pumped into your helmet from the boat above. It is advertised as being suitable for children over seven years of age. Sadly, this activity is damaging the marine environment and thousands of pairs of feet per year gradually destroy what lies beneath them. If you are still interested, walks usually last 20–25 minutes and cost Rs850 per person. Here are some operators:

Captain Nemo's Undersea Walk Coastal Rd, Grand Baie; ↘ 263 7819; e captainnemo@intnet.mu; www.captainnemo-underseawalk.com

Alpha II Grand Baie; ↘ 263 7664
Aquaventure Belle Mare Plage Hotel; ↘ 415 1515

SUBMERSIBLES Submersibles are another option suitable for children and adults alike (although not claustrophobics!).

Blue Safari Submarine Coastal Rd, Grand Baie; ↘ 263 3333; f 263 3334; e bluesaf@intnet.mu; www.blue-safari.com. A 15-min boat trip takes you to the holding ship, from where you board the submarine for the 45-min dive. The submarine can hold 10 people and reaches a depth of 35m. There you can see the coral reef, a shipwreck and tropical fish. The submarine departs every hour 08.30–16.30 in summer and 08.30–15.30 in winter. You need to allow about 2 hours for the whole experience, including time to complete the paperwork etc. *Adult/child Rs2,950/1,600. Reservation essential.*

Blue Safari Submarine also offers 30-min rides on **submersible scooters**. You must be over 16 years of age to drive a scooter and over 12 years to be a passenger. *Double scooter Rs4,000 (2 people), single scooter Rs2,200.*
Le Nessee Centre Sport Nautique, Sunset Bd, Grand Baie; ↘ 263 8017; f 263 5500; e info@centrenautique.com; www.centrenautique.com. A yellow semi-submersible boat with underwater viewing. Departures at 10.00, 12.30 and 14.30. Trips last 1½ hours and include 30 mins of snorkelling. *Adult/child Rs750/375.*

SAILING

Conditions for sailing are usually excellent. The large beach hotels have small sailing dinghies which guests can use within the waters of the lagoon.

Catamaran cruises are popular and full-day trips usually include snorkelling and lunch. They cost around Rs1,400. Sadly, most crews are unaware of the destruction that their actions cause to the marine environment. Many drop their anchors on the coral in the same area each day and it has become such a big business that as many as half a dozen catamarans will be anchored in the same place at the same time for snorkelling. If you hoped to escape the crowds by taking to the sea, a catamaran cruise is not the way to do it. A more expensive but far more pleasurable experience is to charter a yacht.

Grand Baie Yacht Club (☎ *263 8568*), near the Veranda Hotel, has a temporary membership scheme for visitors. **Terres Océanes** in Pereybère specialises in luxury catamarans, which you can sleep on as you sail around the island, stopping off wherever you wish. It costs Rs100,000–140,000 to hire a fully equipped catamaran with a skipper-guide for six people for a week. They can also arrange a variety of other water-based activities. (For contact details, see below).

YACHT/CATAMARAN CHARTER AND CRUISES

Angelo Club Nautique Grand Baie; ☎ 263 3277
Cap Nord La Caravelle, Pereybère; ☎ 422 0101
Catsail Ltd Coastal Rd, Pointe aux Piments; ☎/f 261 1724; e is.advent@intnet.mu
Centre Sport Nautique Sunset Bd, Grand Baie; ☎ 263 8017; f 263 7479
Corail-Evasion Grand Baie; ☎ 250 1565
Croisières Australes Coastal Rd, Grand Baie; ☎ 263 1670; f 263 1671; e cruise@c-australes.com
Croisières Turquoises Coastal Rd, Barachois, Mahébourg; ☎ 631 8347; f 631 1544; e croistur@intnet.mu
Cruises Océane and Aquarelle (Croisières Océanes)
Coastal Rd, Trou d'Eau Douce; ☎/f 480 0743; e oceane@intent.mu; www.easterlies.com
Cruising Experience 9 Nenuphar Complex, Coastal Rd, Flic en Flac; ☎ 453 8888; f 453 9688
Cybèle Charters Blue Bay; ☎/f 674 3596
Gamboro Yacht Charters Coastal Rd, Pointe aux Canonniers; ☎ 263 8117; f 263 8356; e info@gamboro.com
Terres Océanes Chemin de Vieux Moulin, Pereybère; ☎ 262 7188; f 262 7198; e terresoceanes@intnet.mu; www.terresoceanes.com
Yacht Charters Coastal Rd, Grand Baie; ☎ 263 8395; f 263 7814; e yacht@intnet.mu

WINDSURFING

The popularity of windsurfing and the ideal conditions for it have resulted in many competitions, including World Championships, being held in Mauritius. The majority of hotels in the *luxury*, *upmarket* and *mid range* categories will have windsurfers available for their guests and many will also offer instruction (usually payable). Sailing or reef shoes should be worn to prevent coral cuts.

KITESURFING

One of the newer sights to be seen in the waters off Mauritius is kitesurfers, who skim along the water on a small board while attached to a large kite and float into the air intermittently, performing a variety of impressive mid-air acrobatics. It is advisable not to attempt kitesurfing unless you are a good swimmer, and have some experience of surfing, windsurfing, paragliding and kiting. The best spots for kitesurfing are Le Morne (not for novices) and La Prairie (good for beginners) in the southwest, Belle Mare and Pointe d'Esny in the east, Cap Malheureux and Grand Gaube in the north. Kitesurfing schools are found at Le Shandrani Hotel in Blue Bay (see page 148) and at Indian Resort at Le Morne Peninsula (see page 161).
    For information on kitesurfing in Mauritius visit www.mauritiussurf.com.

WATER SKIING

With its calm lagoons, Mauritius is an ideal location for water skiing, particularly for beginners. At *luxury*, *upmarket* and some of the better *mid-range* hotels, water skiing is free, although it may be limited. Other *mid-range* hotels may offer water skiing at a fee.

🚶 HIKING AND ADVENTURE SPORTS

While you can arrange hiking excursions independently, it is probably better to do so through a reputable local tour operator, such as White Sand Tours or Mauritours, or one of the companies that specialise in hiking. Speak to your operator about places like the Black River Gorges National Park, Combo Forest or Bassin Blanc – all of which have great potential as hiking venues. (For information on hiking in the Black River Gorges National Park, see pages 32–4.)

Many of the island's best hiking spots are found in nature reserves and permission from the Forestry Department (↘ 675 4966) is required to enter these. Their offices are next to the Botanical Gardens in Curepipe. They can also provide maps. A growing number of the island's private estates or *domaines* are opening up to the public and typically offer **guided nature walks** and **hiking**, as well as **quad biking** and **4x4 tours** (see below).

As you would for hiking anywhere, be sure to take appropriate footwear, water, rain gear, suncream and protective wear for the tropical sun. The Mauritian mountains really don't require any special skills and you need only an average level of fitness to attempt them. However, to avoid the risk of getting lost, it's advisable to contact your tour operator about arranging a local guide for you.

There are some impressive **caves** in Mauritius, many of which were used as shelters by runaway slaves or by pirates in days gone by, but these should never be explored alone. Again, speak to a local tour operator if you wish to visit any of them. They should be able to arrange transport, entry permission and an experienced local guide.

Adventure sports, like **canyoning**, **climbing**, **mountain biking** and **off-road driving**, are not as big in Mauritius as they are in Réunion. Nevertheless, there is a number of companies that offer these types of activities:

Vertical World PO Box 289, Curepipe; ↘ 254 6607; f 395 3207; e vertical@verticalworldltd.com; www.verticalworldltd.com. Specialises in hiking, canyoning and rock climbing.

Yemaya ↘ 752 0046/283 8187; e haberland@intnet.mu; www.yemayaadventures.com. Specialises in hiking, mountain biking and sea kayaking.

Espace Adventure MTTB-Mautourco, 84 Rue Gustave Colin, Forest Side; ↘ 670 4301; f 674 3720; e nbd@mttb-mautourco.com; www.mttb-mautourco.com. Guided off-road driving in specially designed air-conditioned Land Rovers.

La Fleche Domaine de Chamarel, Chamarel; ↘ 251 1094; f 683 6481. Offers hikes around Chamarel.

Kart Loisir La Joliette, Petite Rivière; ↘ 233 2223; f 233 2225; e kartloisir@intnet.mu. Offers go-karting and quad biking. *Go-karting from Rs440 per person, quad biking from Rs1,380 per person (one hour). Open daily from 09.00.*

Parc Aventure Chamarel; ↘ 234 5385; f 234 5866; e parcaventure@intnet.mu; www.parc-aventure-chamarel.com. An elaborate obstacle course through the forest, with rope bridges, climbing nets etc. The course takes around 2½ hours to complete. Wear long trousers, trainers, gloves and insect repellent. There is a minimum age requirement of 6 years. Also on offer are mountain biking, hiking, kayaking and canyoning. *Open Thu–Tue. Reservation necessary.*

The following private estates offer activities such as hiking, quad biking and 4x4 tours. For more information see the *What to see* section of the relevant chapter.

Eastern Mauritius

Domaine du Chasseur Anse Jonchée; ↘ 634 5097; f 634 5261; e dchasseur@intnet.mu; www.dchasseur.com

Southern Mauritius

Val Riche Nature Reserve Bel Ombre; ↘ 623 5615; f 623 5616

Western Mauritius

Casela Nature and Leisure Park Royal Rd, Cascavelle; ↘/f 452 0693; f 452 0694; e casela@intnet.mu; www.caselayemen.com

Central Mauritius

Domaine les Pailles Les Guibies, Pailles; ↘ 286 4225; f 286 2140; e domaine.sales@intnet.mu; www.domainelespailles.net

Domaine de l'Etoile Royal Rd, Moka; ↘ 433 1010; f 433 1070; e cieletnature@drbc-group.com

MAURITIUS BY BIKE

Hallam Murray

A British newspaper article on Mauritius rounded off with the following sentence: 'If you're not into sun, sea, sand and snorkelling … Terminal Boredom.' What a sad reflection on the author, for few islands of its small size could offer more variety in the way of adventure travel. Mauritius may not have the infrastructure for independent travel outside the well-defined tourist areas along the north and west coasts, but one hardly ever meets another tourist. For most independent travellers this is a positive advantage.

Although there is a local bus service between towns, with a couple of weeks to spare by far the most exciting way to explore the island is by bike. These are available cheaply from a small range of cycle shops in Port Louis. Our reasonable-quality mountain bikes (built in Taiwan) cost us about £100 each (there were no suitable bikes for hire) and we could have sold these back to the shop had we wanted to. We could of course have carried our own bikes out from England.

Gears are essential, for the interior of the island is mountainous, but most of the coastal paths and roads (largely paved) are reasonably flat with just a few hills to help keep one fit. However, it is essential to bring back panniers and a front bag from home, for no cycle shop was able to provide more than a wire or plastic front basket and a back rack with a spring-loaded bar. Talk of 'circumnavigating' the island and exploring inland by bike and you will get raised eyebrows.

We carried a tent but used it rarely (usually on a beach) for we were carrying Quin – our three-year-old son who adored the adventure. Instead we made use of spontaneous hospitality, small and reasonably cheap hostels and, in one case, in Mahébourg, a Reparatice order of nuns. But there are many parts of the island without conventional places to stay, so it is important to be prepared.

December and January, when we travelled, is the hottest part of the year, just at the beginning of the rainy season. This is the time when most exotic flowers are in bloom – crimson bottle brushes, purple lotus, and cacti in multifarious colours. Finest of all are the flaming scarlet flamboyants, also called the 'fleur de l'année' because these trees always flower at the new year. At times we got extremely hot, but we tended to picnic or rest during the hottest hours of the day. Inland it was cooler, especially in the few remaining tracts of indigenous forest around the Black River Gorges.

Each day had its surprises and excitements which would have passed us by had we not been on bikes. On one occasion we found ourselves in a Hindu cremation ground surrounded by sweet-smelling frangipani. Whether you are interested in the fascinating and varied colonial history of Mauritius, or in its flora or fauna, or simply in the wonders of tropical coastlines, coral reefs, cliffs and mighty ocean waves, this has to be the finest way of exploring what Joseph Conrad once called 'the sugary pearl of the Indian Ocean'.

BEACHCOMBER 'SPORT AND NATURE' Beachcomber's Le Shandrani Hotel runs a daily programme of sports and nature activities which cater for all levels of fitness. It's open to non-residents and bookings can be made via Le Shandrani (❧ *603 4343, ext 4540*).

The programmes, which last either a full day or half day, are an ideal way to see beautiful parts of the island, whilst doing some exercise. Some of the programmes are suitable for children. Full-day trips cost around Rs2,000 per person, including lunch and a snack. Half-day trips are around Rs1,200 per person, including a snack. The weekly programme is as follows:

Monday and Thursday: Ile aux Aigrettes/Ylang Ylang (full day)
Canoe from the hotel to Ile aux Aigrettes; visit the nature reserve; canoe from Ile aux Aigrettes to Bois des Amourettes; lunch at Domaine de l'Ylang Ylang; bike and hike around the *domaine*; return by minibus to hotel.

Tuesday: Biking (half day)
Bike from hotel to Le Bouchon.

Wednesday and Saturday: Canyoning at Eau Bleue (full day)
Canyoning at Eau Bleue; picnic lunch; bike from Eau Bleue to Rivière La Chaux; canoe from Rivière La Chaux to Mahébourg; return by minibus to hotel.

Friday: Sport Ylang Ylang (full day)
Canoe from hotel to Treize Cantons; run cross-country to Lion Mountain; lunch at Domaine de l'Ylang Ylang; hike around Bambous Mountains; bike back to hotel.

Sunday: Lion Mountain (half day)
Minibus to Ferney; hike up Lion Mountain; return by minibus to hotel.

Part Two

MAURITIUS AND ITS DEPENDENCIES

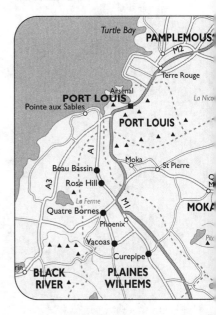

Chasalia boryana

5

Port Louis

Port Louis looks best from the sea. It is a booming city that combines new buildings with old, contrasting with the spires and peaks of the threadbare mountain range behind. In the centre is Pouce, poking 811m into the sky like Jack Horner's thumb. On its left is Pieter Both, a peak named after a Dutch notable who drowned in the bay, distinguished by the boulder balanced precariously on its tip. To the right the city's boundary extends along a switchback of daunting crags: Snail Rock, Goat Rock, Spear Grass Peak and Quoin Bluff. The sheer sides of Signal Mountain (323m) dominate the western flank of the town.

Solid Victorian warehouses and modern concrete towers, like sawn-off skyscrapers, crowd the flat expanse of the city. Houses claim the land right up to the foothills of Pouce Valley, leaving open spaces only on the plain of the Champ de Mars and the isolated 86m-high hill in the middle of the city, on which perches the battered vulture of a fort called the Citadel. Tall royal palms have somehow survived the city's growth to form an avenue of greenery leading from the waterfront up the centre of the Place d'Armes to Government House.

The city was first settled by the Dutch but was named Port Louis in 1722 by French settlers. The name was chosen either to honour the then young King Louis XV (1715–74) or to link the settlement with Port Louis in Brittany from which, at that time, French seamen sailed for India. When Mahé de Labourdonnais arrived here in 1735, however, the harbour was still being called Port Nord-Ouest.

In 1735, dense vegetation covered the area, except for land cleared between where the theatre now stands and the Chien de Plomb at the bayside, which was the ships' watering point.

There were 60 mud huts thatched with palm leaf in this clearing, the homes of the French East India Company staff. Soldiers lived in makeshift shelters of straw. The stream running down from Pouce Mountain formed a swampy gully dividing the plain in two. The right side, as viewed from the sea, became the residential area while the left was given over to commerce.

A statue of Mahé de Labourdonnais stands overlooking the harbour he created. This is a national monument, erected in 1859 at the entrance to the Place d'Armes, where it is isolated on a roundabout in the midst of a daily scrum of traffic. Nearby, a stone set into the patch of lawn at the foot of the palm trees commemorates the 250th anniversary of his founding of Port Louis. City status was conferred on the town by Queen Elizabeth II in 1966.

Port Louis is the seat of government and the most populous town in Mauritius, with some 15% of the island's population. Those with French pretensions call it *Por' Louie*, whilst those with English affectations say *Port Loo-iss*. Others compromise and pronounce it *Port Loo-ee*.

It is a city of boundless charm that has preserved a village soul, perhaps because the crowds of people who descend from the plateau towns during the day to work leave the city alone at night. Its streets are empty then, echoing with the sound of

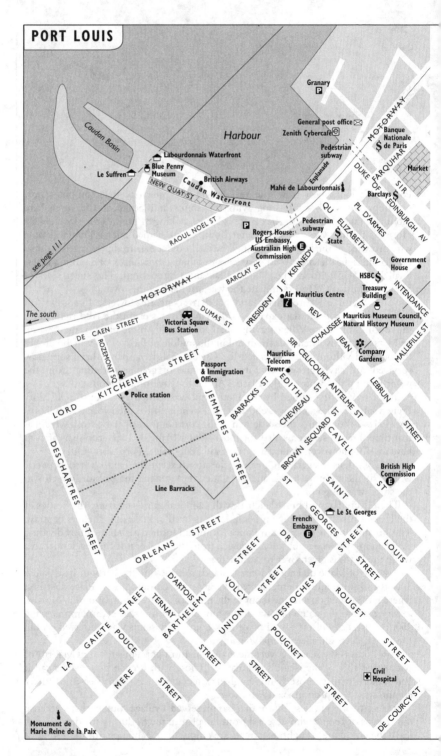

PORT LOUIS

Granary

Caudan Basin

Harbour

General post office
Zenith Cybercafe

MOTORWAY

Banque Nationale de Paris

DUKE OF FARQUHAR

SIR

Market

Pedestrian subway

Esplanade

Labourdonnais Waterfront

Le Suffren
Blue Penny Museum
British Airways

Caudan Waterfront

NEW QUAY ST

Mahé de Labourdonnais

Barclays

QU

PL D'ARMES

DUKE OF EDINBURGH AV

RAOUL NOEL ST

Rogers House:
US Embassy,
Australian High
Commission

Pedestrian subway

ELIZABETH AV

State

Government House

see page 111

MOTORWAY

BARCLAY ST

J F KENNEDY ST

HSBC

INTENDANCE

Treasury Building

PRESIDENT

Air Mauritius Centre

REV

ST

The south

DUMAS ST

Victoria Square
Bus Station

DE CAEN STREET

Mauritius Museum Council,
Natural History Museum

SIR CELICOURT ANTELME ST

CHAUSSEE

JEAN

Company Gardens

MALLEFILLE ST

ROZEMONT SQ

KITCHENER STREET

STREET

Passport
& Immigration
Office

Mauritius
Telecom
Tower

BARRACKS ST

EDITH

CHEVREAU ST

LEBRUN

Police station

JEMMAPES

STREET

BROWN SEQUARD ST

CAVELL

STREET

LORD

DESCHARTRES

Line Barracks

SAINT

British High
Commission

ST

Le St Georges

GEORGES

 STREET

LOUIS

French
Embassy

DR

A

ORLEANS STREET

STREET

D'ARTOIS STREET

VOLCY

STREET

DESROCHES

ROUGET

STREET

GAIETE STREET

TERNAY

BARTHELEMY

UNION

POUGNET

STREET

Civil
Hospital

LA

POUCE

MERE

STREET

STREET

STREET

DE COURCY ST

Monument de
Marie Reine de la Paix

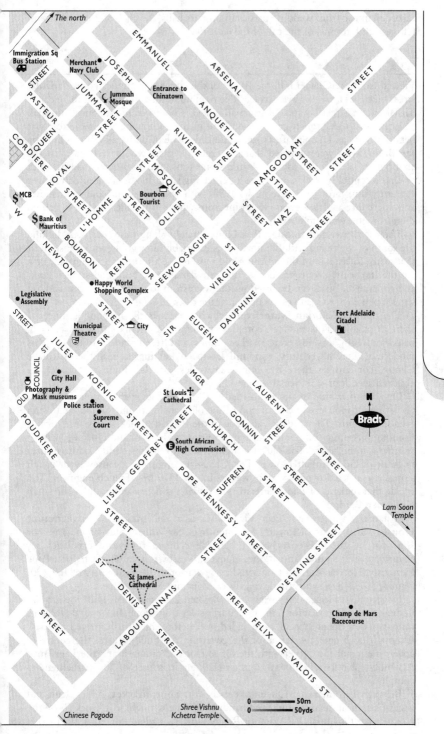

The north

Immigration Sq
Bus Station

Merchant
Navy Club

Jummah
Mosque

Entrance to
Chinatown

EMMANUEL STREET

ARSENAL STREET

STREET

JOSEPH ST

JUMMAH STREET

PASTEUR STREET

CORDIERE

QUEEN STREET

ROYAL STREET

L'HOMME STREET

ANQUETIL STREET

RIVIERE STREET

MOSQUE STREET

OLLIER

RAMGOOLAM STREET

NAZ STREET

STREET

STREET

MCB

Bank of
Mauritius

Bourbon
Tourist

NEWTON

BOURBON

REMY ST

DR SEEWOOSAGUR

VIRGILE ST

DAUPHINE

Happy World
Shopping Complex

Legislative
Assembly

STREET

Municipal
Theatre

City

SIR

SIR EUGENE

Fort Adelaide
Citadel

JULES

OLD COUNCIL ST

City Hall

Photography &
Mask museums

Police station

Supreme
Court

KOENIG STREET

MGR

St Louis
Cathedral

CHURCH STREET

GONNIN

LAURENT STREET

N

Bradt

POUDRIERE

South African
High Commission

LISLET GEOFFREY STREET

POPE HENNESSY STREET

SUFFREN

STREET

STREET

STREET

D'ESTAING STREET

Lam Soon
Temple

STREET

ST DENIS

St James
Cathedral

LABOURDONNAIS STREET

FRERE FELIX DE VALOIS ST

Champ de Mars
Racecourse

0 ___ 50m
0 ___ 50yds

Chinese Pagoda

Shree Vishnu
Kchetra Temple

Port Louis

5

recorded music from wedding parties in upstairs halls, the click of dominoes from Chinese club rooms, or the call of the *muezzin*.

AROUND TOWN

Viewed from the Citadel hill, the layout of the city is uncomplicated: rectangular street blocks as far as the eye can see. The road up to the **Citadel** used to be called Ti-Mountain Street because of its small hill. It is now a continuation of Jummah Mosque Street. A French post existed here in the 18th century but the fort was begun in 1835 and named after Queen Adelaide, wife of William IV. It was built by the British who were worried that the French settlers would revolt against the abolition of slavery. Its solid, volcanic stone walls and two-tiered rooms, built around a central barrack square, are a depressing sight. It was abandoned for over a century until brought to life in the 1980s with open-air sound-and-light shows and pop concerts. It's a great viewpoint from which to see the city but if you go there at night, wrap up warmly.

The motorway cuts through Port Louis, straight along the waterfront, linking the south of the island with the north. It is invariably slow going with a rush hour that seems to last half of the morning and most of the afternoon. On one side of it are the **harbour**, deepwater docks, modern warehouses, bulk fuel-storage tanks and containers. Boats can be hired on the waterfront to tour the harbour and, on ships' open days, to visit vessels tied up at the docks.

The opulent **Caudan Waterfront** which overlooks the harbour is indeed a sight to behold. This modern complex includes apartments, offices, a cinema, bank, museum, casino, craft market, shops and restaurants. Amidst all this modernity, an 18th-century windmill has been left intact, near the Astrolabe Centre. For families there is a mini train (rides cost Rs30) and a play area for children aged four–15. (See also page 114.)

On the other side of the main road is the **city**. Facing the **Place d'Armes**, Government House is at the far end of the old parade ground, announced by an avenue of palms. The roads at each side of the Place d'Armes' lawns are Duke of Edinburgh Avenue (on the left, facing Government House) and Queen Elizabeth Avenue (on the right). The old thoroughfares of Royal Street and Chaussée meet in front of Government House. The Chaussée, originally a causeway of rough stones constructed over a swamp, was rebuilt in 1779 by a French engineer. The trickle that remains of Pouce Stream runs down a concrete gully under the small **Chaussée Bridge**.

A statue of a matronly Queen Victoria stands at the entrance to **Government House**, with a statue of a nearly forgotten man, Sir William Stevenson, governor 1857–63, in the forecourt behind her. He claimed the same privileges for Mauritian officials that British ones enjoyed. Nearby is a statue of Sir John Pope Hennessy. He was the most outstanding governor of the latter part of the 19th century (1883–89), sympathetic to calls of Mauritius for Mauritians.

Government House dates back to 1738 when Labourdonnais built the ground floor and the wings that form the forecourt's sides from stone. In General Decaen's time, wooden upper storeys were added, just before the British arrived in 1810. Although no longer the home of the governor, the building is at the centre of government since, together with the office block adjoining it and the Legislative Assembly Chamber behind it (built in 1965), it is part of the parliamentary complex.

Between Farquhar and Queen streets is Port Louis **market**, selling fruit and vegetables, meat, fish, clothing and handicrafts. The wrought iron work above the entrance has the initials VR (Victoria Regina) intertwined in it. In 2004, the market buildings were completely renovated. As a result, the market lost some of its grubby charm and a greater proportion of it (mostly the first floor) was taken over by souvenir stalls. It may not feel as 'authentic' as it once did but it is still an exciting, bustling place, which offers an insight into the everyday lives of Mauritians. (See also pages 113–14.)

The road beside the government buildings (Intendance Street) leads past the **Treasury** (a national monument) into Gillet Square (Place Foch), with its incongruous Parisian wrought-iron street lamp preserved on a traffic island. Across the road is the **theatre**, restored to look like another Victorian warehouse but with its colonnaded front a sharp contrast to the mediocre buildings around it. It was opened in 1822 with a production by a Creole amateur troupe of *La Partie de Chasse de Henri IV* and is said to be the oldest theatre in the southern hemisphere.

The days of its popularity as an opera house have passed and it is now only by chance that you'll be able to see inside since it is invariably closed and shuttered. The interior has been restored to evoke its days of grandeur with an awning suspended from the ceiling to give a false dome on which have been painted some heavily touched-up, tubby Victorian cherubs around the names of European composers, some familiar, some forgotten. The crest of Mauritius is above the proscenium arch. The occasional productions that the theatre puts on today are mostly amateur Creole musicals, depending on the rhythms of local *séga* music to emphasise stories of liberation – quite a contrast to the European operas of its heyday.

City Hall, built in 1962, is a few yards away up Jules Koenig Street, on the right. Outside is a concrete block tower without walls, with steps spiralling up its interior to the clock at the top. This represents the fire towers formerly used by watchmen to overlook the town's wooden buildings. There is a library in City Hall open to the public.

Beyond City Hall on the right-hand side is a **police station** and the **Supreme Court** (a listed building), with the **Cathedral Square** on the left. Now used as a car park, the square contains the remains of a fountain dating to 1788, an obelisk, and what appears to be a statue of a medieval king, St Louis, erected in 1896.

The Roman Catholic **St Louis Cathedral** is the third church on this site. Built in 1932 in awesome twin-towered imitation Gothic, it replaced the previous one, demolished in 1925. An earlier church dating from 1756 was destroyed by a cyclone. The **Episcopal Palace**, a 19th-century mansion with airy verandas more suited in style to the tropics than the cathedral, stands beside it.

At the end of Pope Hennessy Street is the **Champ de Mars Racecourse**. People still promenade here as they did in the 19th century, although joggers and children have taken the place of crinolined ladies and their beaux. There is a statue of King Edward VII in the centre (with birds nesting in the crook of his arm) and the tomb of Malartic (governor, 1792–1800) at the far end. This is a striking setting for racing with a backdrop of gaunt mountains like a natural amphitheatre for the drama played out on the plain. (See also page 90.)

The Champ de Mars has been a racecourse since the Mauritius Turf Club was founded by an English army officer, Colonel Edward Draper, in 1812. He oversaw the building of the track on what was then the army parade ground. At first, only horses belonging to the English garrison were ridden by young army officers, until the French settlers showed interest and entered their own horses. By 1837, horse racing was firmly established. Today the Mauritians' love of gambling ensures that races are always well attended.

The **Shree Vishnu Kchetra Temple** is in a tranquil location in St Denis Street, which runs parallel to the Champ de Mars, one block from it. It serves

Hindus and Tamils. Shoes have to be removed and left by the bench a few yards inside the gate. The older Hindu temple is simply laid out with bright paintings and statues and places for offerings of coconuts and incense. Worshippers toll the bell to wake the gods.

In the same compound is a new Tamil temple and an ancient, sacred peepul tree (*Ficus religiosa*, known as a bo-tree in Sri Lanka). The temple is closed for five minutes at midnight when it is considered a dangerous time to disturb the gods.

The Anglican **St James Cathedral** has its entrance on Poudrière Street. As a cathedral this is a disappointment, since it looks more like a small New England mission church with its single, cream-plastered spire. It was built in 1828, incorporating the 2m-wide walls of the original building, a French powder magazine. Its stoutness made it a useful cyclone shelter in the last century. Inside it has a wooden ceiling and wood-panelled walls with commemorative tablets set in them. Services in English are held on the second and fourth Sunday every month; except during times of worship, the cathedral is closed.

On the north side of the Champ de Mars, at the corner of Dr Eugene Laurent and Corneille Streets, is the **Lam Soon Temple**, which is actually two temples. The newer one, built in the 19th century, is in the foreground, a curious adaptation of British colonial architecture to Confucian Buddhist needs, the columns of the veranda painted red and gold and the interior devoted to worship. The centre altar is extravagantly carved while the interior walls are simple. Lists in Chinese showing the names of the temple's sponsors are posted on the exterior walls.

The ancient custodian makes a point of telling visitors the temple is independently run and depends on offerings for its upkeep, indicating the offertory box. Once you've put something in, you're invited to walk through to the more dilapidated wooden temple beyond. Its frail female keeper bangs a gong to announce your visit, but the radio keeps playing pop music and the neon light she switches on chases away the atmosphere of the gloomy interior. This temple doubles as a commercial enterprise, selling not only incense sticks and flags but also soft drinks and pickles. Business, according to the old custodian, is brisk on race days. The temple is open from 06.00 to 14.00 daily.

The **Jummah Mosque**, with its 'wedding cake' architecture, is, unsurprisingly, on Jummah Mosque Street. The mosque extends an entire block, its white towers and friezes imposing grace on the clutter of lock-up shops beneath its balconies. Its huge teak doors are priceless, ornately carved and inlaid with ivory. Tourists can only glimpse the marble-cloistered mysteries within. The *muezzin's* call from the minaret before dawn is the signal not only for prayer but for the cacophony of the city to erupt. This mosque, built in the 1850s, is the island's most impressive. It opened when Muslims (inaccurately called Arabs in those days) formed an exclusive merchant group in the neighbourhood.

Just beyond the mosque in Royal Street is **Chinatown**, a clutter of stores, warehouses and restaurants, its shops bright with the plastic and chrome knick-knacks much in demand by modern-day Mauritians. Each door opens off the street into a retail or wholesale business of some kind. There are small, not very pleasant, eating places in side streets and a hint at night of an inscrutable underworld, which, although it won't affect the visitor, lurks behind closed shutters. The location of Chinatown so near to the mosque has caused some tension between the two communities, which at its height resulted in the burning down of the Chinese-run Amicale Casino.

If you're a sailor or can find one to take you in, don't miss the **Merchant Navy Club** at the harbour end of Rivière Street. The lights from the veranda of this colonial mansion shine across its garden, offering a welcome to seafarers of all nationalities and ranks. Although its facilities are for the benefit of seamen, visitors may obtain permission from the Resident Welfare Officer to look around. The club opened originally in 1857 as the Mauritius Sailors' Home, becoming the Merchant Navy Club a century later. It is famed among mariners as one of the best of its kind in the world. The setting is perfect, offering tranquil sanity in the midst of the heat and bustle of the port. The premises spread the width of the entire street block, with a lounge bar and veranda, a restaurant for snacks, rooms for table tennis, billiards and darts, loggias and garden alcoves, badminton, volleyball and outdoor movies. It is open daily from 09.00 to 23.00.

Along Jemmapes Street from the Victoria Square bus station are the **Line Barracks**, whose foundations go back to the early days of the French occupation, when they housed 6,000 men, as well as rebel colonists after the French Revolution. A police station, the police headquarters and the traffic branch are there now.

There are some small wooden mansions from the French period in the block between Poudrière Street and St George Street. There is also a large number of embassies and high commissions in the area. (For details see *Chapter 3, Consular help*, page 86.)

Air Mauritius has its own building, **Air Mauritius Centre**, in President John F Kennedy Street. The smart arcade of shops on the ground floor is known as **Paille en Queue** shopping centre and contains a **tourist information** office (see page 110). Reservations and reconfirmations for Air Mauritius flights can be made in the ground-floor ticket office. (For further details of this and other airline offices, see pages 50–2.)

Chaussée Street has shops and offices on one side, and the **Company Gardens** and the **Mauritius Museum Council** (formerly the Mauritius Institute) on the other. The Company Gardens derives its name from its connection with the French East India Company in the 18th century, when it was created from the marshland around the Pouce Stream. For ten years after the fire of 1816, which destroyed half of Port Louis, it was the site of the town market. Although it is less than a hectare in area, the garden seems larger, with its narrow paths, flowerbeds, shrubs and ponds. There are numerous statues, some of which are national monuments, including one of Adrien d'Epinay, planter, lawyer and campaigner against the abolition of slavery, and Léoville l'Homme, poet. The importance of the garden as the city becomes more built-up is recognised both by the public, who enjoy the benches in the shade of its trees, and by the municipality.

Signal Mountain between Plaine Lauzon and the city marks the western end of the mountain range around Port Louis. A beacon used to be kept alight on its summit at night, and flags hoisted there during the day as a guide for approaching vessels. At the foot of the mountain is the **Marie Reine de la Paix monument** and its pleasant gardens, where the first Mauritian bishop was consecrated in 1989. The Edward VII Boulevard provides a spectacular view of the city and harbour.

Sainte-Croix, a suburb of Port Louis nestling below Long Mountain, is famous for its church, a modern-style replacement of the original, with its shrine containing the body of **Père Laval** (see page 116).

GETTING THERE AND AWAY

The **Immigration Square bus station** is at the end of Pasteur Street, still known by city denizens as Hospital Street, because of the hospital that was in the square. It is difficult to know which bus queue to join since there are limited signs and no enquiry office, but other passengers are helpful. Buses from here serve the north of the island and include an express service to Grand Baie.

The **Victoria Square bus station** is off Dumas Street. Buses leave throughout the day bound for central towns, such as Curepipe, from where you can get buses to the south (including the airport) and west. The long, dilapidated, two-storey building used to be the main railway station and offices.

Apart from the traffic jams, it's easy to get to Port Louis by **car** as the motorway goes right through the city. The most convenient car park for the centre, market and waterfront is **The Granary**, on the harbour side of the highway. From the waterfront there's a pedestrian subway to the city.

Taxis are more expensive in Port Louis than elsewhere and the attitude of the drivers is more predatory. Be sure to negotiate a reasonable fare. There is a taxi stand at Place d'Armes and one at the Victoria Square bus station.

TOURIST INFORMATION

There is a **tourist office** (*208 6379. Open Mon–Fri 09.00–16.00, Sat 09.00–12.00, closed Sun*) in the Paille en Queue Arcade on the ground floor of the Air Mauritius Centre in President John F Kennedy Street. They can't make arrangements for you but they have a healthy supply of leaflets and basic information.

For the location of **embassies** and **high commissions**, see page 86.

WHERE TO STAY

Category B: upmarket

Labourdonnais Waterfront Hotel (109 rooms) Caudan Waterfront; * 202 4000; f 202 4040; e lwh@intnet.mu; www.labourdonnais.com. By far the most elegant accommodation in the city, overlooking the harbour. Caters largely for business guests. Rooms have AC, TV, phone, minibar and safe. Facilities include a pool, casino, health centre, business centre and elaborate conference facilities. *Dbl/sgl from Rs10,400/8,000 BB.*

Category C: mid range

Le Suffren Hotel and Marina (100 rooms) Caudan Waterfront; * 202 4900; f 202 4999; e info@lesuffrenhotel.com; www.lesuffrenhotel.com. This new hotel, which targets business travellers, has a nautical theme and overlooks the harbour. The elegantly decorated rooms have either harbour or mountain views and are equipped with AC, TV, phone, safe, minibar and tea/coffee facilities. There is a manmade beach area, pool, restaurant and bar. *Dbl/sgl from Rs5,800/4,400 BB.*

Le Saint Georges (80 rooms) 19 St Georges St; * 211 2581; f 211 0885; e resa.hsg@intnet.mu; www.blue-season-hotels.com. Centrally located hotel popular with businesspeople. Comfortable en-suite rooms with AC, TV and phone. Only the suites have a safe and minibar. B/fast is served in the restaurant on the first floor and there is a delightful ground-floor bar and café. *Dbl/sgl from € 74/57 BB.*

Category D: budget

Bourbon Tourist Hotel (16 rooms) 36 Jummah Mosque St; * 240 4407; f 242 2087. Probably the best budget option, located above shops opposite Chinese warehouses. Rooms are twin with shower and toilet, some with AC and TV. The rooms are bright and large and the atmosphere is friendly and welcoming. Although it's noisy during the day, at night all is quiet, unless wedding celebrations erupt with firecrackers and dance music from one of the upstairs halls nearby. There is a first-floor restaurant and bar in case of emergency, but since the hotel is on the edge of Chinatown there are plenty of places to eat in the area. *Dbl without AC from Rs700 BB, dbl with AC from Rs800.*

City Hotel (formerly the Ambassador) (20 rooms) 8A Sir S Ramgoolam St; * 212 0466; f 208 5340. A hotel whose lethargic character can be guessed by the sign over its entrance which still announces it as the Ambassador several years after the name changed. The rooms are small and gloomy but air-conditioned. Dbl rooms have baths, singles have showers. Charmless. There is a restaurant. *Dbl/sgl from Rs690/575 BB.*

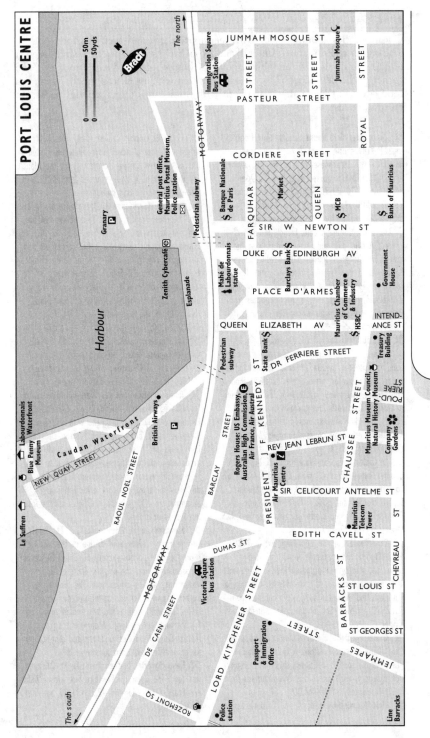

WHERE TO EAT

Cheap eateries abound: snack-bars, *samoussas* sellers, and even fast-food outlets. The corner of Emmanuel Anquetil and Royal Streets is the place for street food at night, with stools to sit on while enjoying Chinese soups and *mine* (noodles). The corner of the next block is for rice and chicken with an African touch. There is a food court in the Caudan Waterfront with numerous outlets serving snacks, ice creams and fast food.

Black Steer Grill House Caudan Waterfront; ☎ 211 9147. Cuisine: grills. A large, modern American-style steakhouse. Popular for its Sunday lunch buffet. *Main courses from Rs175. Open Mon–Sat 12.00–23.30, Sun 12.00–14.30 and 18.00–23.00. Happy hour 17.30–19.00.*

La Bonne Marmite 18 Sir William Newton St; ☎ 212 2403. Cuisine: Creole, French, Indian, Chinese. A café, pub and restaurant in one. The café is on the ground floor behind which is the Rocking Boat Pub (see *Nightlife* opposite). The restaurant is upstairs in a grand room with table d'hôte and à la carte menus. *Main courses from Rs95. Open Mon–Fri for lunch. Reservation recommended.*

Café du Vieux Conseil Old Council St; ☎ 211 0393. Cuisine: French, Creole. In a restored cobbled lane, opposite the theatre. Al fresco dining and an almost Mediterranean atmosphere. Excellent food and service. The menu lists only a few dishes and is changed frequently, but there is sufficient variety, including vegetarian specialities and Australian beef. *Main courses from Rs150. Open daily for lunch.*

Le Capitaine Caudan Waterfront; ☎ 213 0038. Cuisine: seafood, Creole, Indian. A good location by Port Louis's standards, overlooking the harbour. Superb seafood and good service. *Main courses from Rs225, seafood platter for two from Rs1,725. Open daily 11.00–23.00.*

Carri Poulé Duke of Edinburgh Av; ☎ 212 4883. Cuisine: Indian, Creole. A sophisticated restaurant serving well-prepared Indian dishes with a Mauritian touch, not the stereotyped offerings of European 'Indian' restaurants. *Main courses from Rs125. Open Mon–Sat for lunch, Fri–Sat for dinner.*

Chinatown Deli Emmanuel Anquetil St; ☎ 240 0568. Cuisine: Chinese. Although called a 'deli' ('because the food is delicious', says the manager), this is a mid-range restaurant. *Main courses from Rs90. Open daily 11.00–22.00.*

First Restaurant Cnr Royal and Corderie Sts; ☎ 212 0685. Cuisine: Chinese. Tasty, reasonably priced dishes in pleasant surroundings. Regarded as one of the best Chinese restaurants on the island. Try the roast duck. *Main courses from Rs90. Open Tue–Sun for lunch and dinner.*

La Flore Mauricienne 10 Intendance St; ☎ 212 2200. Cuisine: French, Creole. This well-known bar, café and restaurant first opened in 1848. There is a smart open-air terrace, a buffet restaurant and an elegant dining room. The accent is on European cuisine and clientèle. French pastries are a speciality. Patronised by regulars, so some feel it has a cliquish atmosphere. *Main courses from Rs175. Open Mon–Fri 08.30–17.00, Sat 08.30–14.00.*

Lai Min Restaurant Royal St; ☎ 242 0042. Cuisine: Chinese. Smart, air-conditioned restaurant on the edge of Chinatown. *Main courses from Rs100. Open daily for lunch and dinner.*

Tandoori Restaurant and Snack-bar Victoria Sq; ☎ 212 0031. Cuisine: Indian, Creole, Chinese. Features a daily changing menu with a dozen different dishes, often including venison and hare. Ingredients are fresh from the market and prepared in the traditional way. There is a good selection of wines, properly stored. A great discovery for those keen on a local culinary adventure at a bargain price. *Open until the last bus leaves at around 20.00.*

Namasté Caudan Waterfront; ☎/f 211 6710. Cuisine: north Indian. Fine cuisine in the historic setting of the old observatory building. The décor is fascinating, with the original walls of the observatory adding atmosphere. The food is authentic and delicious, carefully prepared with spices imported from India. Live Indian music on Fri, Sat and Sun evenings. *Main courses from Rs320. Open Mon–Sat for lunch and dinner, Sun for dinner. Reservation recommended.*

Kentucky Fried Chicken Chaussée St. Cuisine: fast food. The usual chicken fare but with a halal certificate. *Open Mon–Fri 09.30–21.00, Sat–Sun 10.00–21.00.*

NIGHTLIFE

The shortage of **bars** in Port Louis has a precedence in history. In 1722, there were 125 drinking shops known to the police. The French governor, Ternay, found this excessive and closed all but 30, eventually reducing that number to four.

The **Keg and Marlin** (✆ *211 6821*) at the Caudan Waterfront has a British pub ambience, except you can sit outside on the waterfront and not freeze. Above it is **Secrets Discotheque** (✆ *210 3833*), open at weekends. Also at the Caudan Waterfront is **Port Latino** cocktail bar and nightclub. **Latitude 20 Bar** at the Labourdonnais Waterfront Hotel is another popular watering hole. The **Rocking Boat Pub** at La Bonne Marmite restaurant has been skilfully designed to project the ambience of a European drinking den with low lighting, dark décor and a cocktail bar with stools for the steadier drinkers.

The **Caudan Waterfront Casino** (✆ *210 2191*) is open daily except Monday. The slot machines are open 10.00–02.00 and the tables 20.00–04.00.

OTHER PRACTICALITIES

MONEY AND BANKING Branches of the major **banks**, including HSBC (*Place d' Armes;* ✆ *203 8333*) and Barclays (*Sir William Newton St;* ✆ *207 1800*), can be found near Place d'Armes, a short distance from the harbour.

COMMUNICATIONS The **General Post Office** (✆ *208 2851;* f *212 9640. Open Mon–Fri 08.15–11.15 and 12.00–16.00, Sat 08.00–11.45, closed Sun*) is near the harbour at the end of Sir William Newton Street.

There are plenty of **payphones** in Port Louis, especially around the Caudan Waterfront. **Telephone** calls can also be made and **faxes** sent and received at **Mauritius Telecom** (*Telecom Tower, Edith Cavell Street;* ✆ *203 7000*).

For **internet access**, try **Zenith Cybercafé** (✆ *208 2213*) in the Astrolabe Centre on the waterfront. For details see pages 80–1.

MEDICAL CARE The **Civil Hospital** (✆ *212 3201*) is on Volcy Pougnet Street.

WHAT TO DO

ORGANISED TOURS

Citirama (*Yiptong Hse, Royal Rd, Cassis;* ✆ *212 2484;* f *212 1222;* e *citirama@intnet.mu; adult/child Rs350/200*) Offers a special coach tour of Port Louis daily, except Sundays, from 09.30 and also every weekday afternoon at 13.30. The three-hour tour departs from the town's waterfront, finishing up in the Chaussée area 'where you can spend the rest of the day shopping'. It is an effortless way to see the 24 tourist attractions listed, including City Hall, St Louis Cathedral, Line Barracks, Company Garden and the Citadel.

Harbour cruise (*Bassin des Chaloupes;* ✆ *211 9500; adult/child Rs40/30; operates Tue–Fri 10.00–18.30, Sat–Sun 11.00–18.30, closed Mon*) Leaves from the Bassin des Chaloupes, near the main entrance to the Labourdonnais Waterfront Hotel and the Blue Penny Museum.

SHOPPING Shops in Port Louis are typically open Monday–Friday 09.30–17.00 and Saturday 09.00–12.00. A few open on Sunday morning.

The market between Queen and Farquhar Streets is open Monday–Saturday 06.00–18.00 and Sunday 06.00–12.00. There is a fantastically colourful fruit and vegetable market, which contains two intriguing *tisane* (herbal remedy) stalls. Both have been there for generations and claim to offer a cure for every imaginable ailment, from rheumatism to cellulite, with their unassuming bundles of twigs and leaves. Their cures have become so well known that they now take orders from overseas via email. On the opposite side of Farquhar Street is the meat and fish market.

Above the fruit and vegetable market, on the first floor, is the place for bargain souvenirs, although you may have to look hard to find items made in Mauritius. The colourful bags, wooden objects and spices are largely imported from Madagascar or Africa. Pickpockets are said to operate around the market and, although the atmosphere isn't threatening, the tenacious sales techniques can be rather tiresome. You are expected to barter.

The **Caudan Waterfront** (↘ *211 6560*) contains a vast range of shops: jewellery, fashion, carpets, crafts and souvenirs, some of which are duty free. Opening hours are Monday–Saturday 09.30–12.30, Sunday 09.30–12.30. It's relatively hassle-free shopping with no real hard sell, although prices may be a little elevated. There is a **craft market** within the Caudan Waterfront, not far from the casino, where you can see artisans at work. The **Mauritius Glass Gallery** has an outlet here (↘ *210 1181*). Spices, sugar products, tea, art and locally produced essential oils are also on sale.

The **National Handicraft Promotion Agency** has a shop in the Astrolabe Centre, where you can be sure of buying locally made products (see also *Giving something back*, pages 84–5).

HORSE RACING At the historic Champ de Mars racecourse. The season lasts from May until the end of November/early December, with race days usually every Saturday. (For more information see *Chapter 4, Horse racing*, page 90.)

CINEMA **Star cinema** (↘ *211 5361*) in the Caudan Waterfront complex has three screens showing international films.

THEATRE The tourist office can provide information about productions at the theatre on Sir William Newton Street, or try contacting the theatre direct (↘ *212 1090*).

ART The **Galérie d'Art de Port Louis** in Mallefille Street holds occasional exhibitions of local artists' work. There also are several commercial art galleries in Port Louis: **Galerie Hélène de Senneville** and **Galerie du Chien de Plomb** in Le Caudan Waterfront, and **Galerie Danielle Poisson** at 21 Jemmapes Street.

WHAT TO SEE

MAURITIUS MUSEUM COUNCIL (*Chaussée St;* ↘ *212 0639;* f *212 5717*) A complex containing a number of museums, including a natural history museum, an historical museum, a cultural centre and a public library.

NATURAL HISTORY MUSEUM (*Mauritius Museum Council, Chaussée St;* ↘ *212 0639;* f *212 5717;* e *mimuse@intnet.mu; admission: free; open Mon, Tue, Thu, Fri 09.00–16.00, Sat–Sun 09.00–12.00*) A very popular museum whose most famous display is a goose-down clad dodo replica. Numerous other displays on animals, birds and marine life, extinct or otherwise, are to be seen. A winding staircase at the back of the building leads to a first-floor gallery that opens into the magnificent

Mauritius holds a special place in the affections of stamp collectors since the first stamps issued there are now among the greatest rarities in the philatelic world. In 1993, at an auction in Zurich, a buyer paid the equivalent of US$3.3 million for 'the crown jewel of philately', an envelope – 'the Bordeaux cover' – with two stamps on it, sent from Mauritius to a Bordeaux wine importer in 1847. This is the only cover known with the two values (one penny and twopence) of the Mauritius 'Post Office' series.

Mauritius was the first British colony to use adhesive postage stamps, and was only the fifth country in the world to issue stamps, in 1847. The first 1,000 postage stamps (500 at a penny value and 500 at twopence) were produced by Joseph Barnard, a watchmaker and jeweller of Port Louis, who engraved the dies on a copper plate and laboriously printed the stamps one at a time, direct from the engraving. Despite his skills as a craftsman, the results were very primitive compared with the famous penny blacks of Britain. They also contained an error. Instead of the words POST PAID he engraved POST OFFICE in the left-hand margin.

The stamps were released on 21 September 1847. On the same day, Lady Gomm, the governor's wife, used a considerable number of the orange-red one-penny value on invitations to a ball at Le Réduit. Only 15 one-penny stamps and 12 of the blue twopenny value are believed still to exist.

Barnard was instructed to produce further stamps in 1848. To facilitate printing, he engraved each stamp 12 times on the plate. The result was that no two stamps were identical, although they had the correct words POST PAID on them. These stamps, which were in use until 1859, are also highly prized among collectors.

Another fascinating rarity turned up in a philatelist's collection in 1994. Two twopenny blue stamps postmarked 9 November 1859 revealed spelling errors. One shows 'Maurituis', the other 'Mauritus'. The issue appears to have been withdrawn from circulation the same day. Being unique, the stamps are priceless.

After 1859, mass-produced stamps, printed in Britain, were issued. However, stocks of frequently used stamps were often exhausted before fresh supplies arrived from London. Consequently, the lower-value stamps were surcharged, creating more stamps of interest to collectors.

The first pillar boxes were erected in Port Louis in the early 1860s. Special date stamps for mail collected from them were used from 1885 to 1926 in Port Louis, Beau Bassin, Curepipe, Mahébourg and Rose Hill. Examples of such cancellations are rare.

Other historical events have also given Mauritius stamps special value. Airmail services were launched to Réunion in 1933 and to Rodrigues in 1972. The first use of aerogrammes in Mauritius was on 27 December 1944.

Today, used postage stamps and first-day covers are sold in shops selling tourist souvenirs in Port Louis and Curepipe, and stamps can be bought in the General Post Office and at the Postal Museum in Port Louis.

library. Here magazines and newspapers can be read, books borrowed, and the history of Mauritius studied in its excellent reference section.

PHOTOGRAPHY MUSEUM (*Old Council St;* ✆ *211 1705;* f *212 9640;* e *photomuseemaurice@yahoo.com. Admission: Rs100. Open Mon–Fri 10.00–12.00 and 13.00–15.00*) In a restored street on the opposite side of Jules Koenig Street to the theatre. A private museum containing old cameras and prints of Port Louis in colonial days, many showing horse-drawn taxis. One photograph, dated 1956, shows the last passenger train leaving Curepipe for Port Louis.

BLUE PENNY MUSEUM (*Le Musée, Caudan Waterfront;* ☎ *210 8176;* f *210 9243;* e *bluepennymuseum@intnet.mu; www.bluepennymuseum.com; adult/child Rs150/80; open Mon–Sat 10.00–17.00, last entry is at 16.30*) The stamp collection displayed here includes the famous 'Post Office' stamps issued in 1847 (see box *Philatelist's heaven*, page 115). Paintings, photos, documents and nautical charts from the island's colonial days are also on display.

POSTAL MUSEUM (*Quay St;* ☎ *213 4812;* e *pohqs@intnet.mu; admission: free; open Mon–Fri 09.00–16.00, Sat 09.00–11.30*) At the entrance are two pillar boxes painted a deep salmon pink instead of the usual red. A leaflet about the museum states that letters posted in these boxes are cancelled with a special cachet. Inside, the neatly laid out museum displays cancelling machines, letter boxes and vending machines, as well as stamps. The really famous rare stamps that you see here are reproductions. Souvenir packs of stamps, letter openers, paperweights and other objects with a postal theme are on sale.

PÈRE LAVAL'S SHRINE (*Ste-Croix;* ☎ *242 2129*) Father Jacques Desiré Laval (known locally as Père Laval) was born in France in 1803 and brought up in a strict religious atmosphere, qualifying as a medical doctor before becoming a priest. In 1841, he arrived in Mauritius as a missionary and converted thousands of recently freed slaves to Catholicism, becoming known as the Apostle of the Blacks. He died on 9 September 1864. He was beatified in 1979, following Pope John Paul II's visit to Mauritius, and is regarded as the island's 'national saint'. He is venerated by followers of all faiths who attribute miraculous healing powers to his name. Throughout September, and particularly on the anniversary of his death, people from around the world flock to his tomb in Ste-Croix, many in hope of a miracle healing.

The tomb can be visited at any time of year. A rather gaudily coloured plaster effigy covers it. Ste-Croix is a suburb of Port Louis and is easily reached by bus from the Immigration Square bus station.

6

Northern Mauritius

Northern Mauritius is divided into two districts: Pamplemousses in the west and Rivière du Rempart in the east.

The coast of Pamplemousses is largely given over to tourism and includes the lively resort of Grand Baie. Its boundary is the mountain range encircling Port Louis, with Crève Coeur, behind Pieter Both, as its southernmost village. It cuts through the sugar plantations east of Pamplemousses town and runs northwards to the coast at Pointe aux Canonniers.

Rivière du Rempart is a compact district of contrasts, encompassing the tourist hot spots to the east of Grand Baie, the industrial/agricultural area of Goodlands and the rugged northeast coast around Poudre d'Or. The town of Rivière du Rempart is in the east of the district, originally named Rampart River for its steep banks.

The importance of sugar in the north of Mauritius gave rise to the construction of the island's first railway line in 1864. The Northern Line, which connected Port Louis to Pamplemousses and Flacq, was used to transport sugar to Port Louis. It stopped carrying passengers in 1956 and was closed down completely in 1964.

BAIE DU TOMBEAU TO POINTE AUX PIMENTS

The elbow of land just north of Port Louis is named **Baie du Tombeau** (Tomb Bay), in memory of George Weldon, an English merchant who was drowned there in 1697. He was not alone in his fate and treasure hunters are convinced that treasure lies in this bay, a legacy of the many ships wrecked in its waters. If ferreting for treasure doesn't interest you, then there is little to keep you in Baie du Tombeau. Apart from a rather disappointing beach, there is a flourishing village community, tenement block estate and knitting factory.

Back on the main road from Port Louis to the north, you pass through the village of **Arsenal**. Although locals are quick to point out the link with the English football team of the same name, the name actually comes from the munitions stores which the French had here.

Inland from Arsenal is the small village of **Pamplemousses**, which is home to the Sir Seewoosagur Ramgoolam Botanic Gardens, one of Mauritius's best-known tourist attractions (see *What to see*, pages 133–5). Near the gardens is the **Comptoir des Mascareignes** (see page 133 a new complex of shops aimed at tourists. There is a café here (see page 120 as well as a bureau de change.

The **Church of St François** in the village of Pamplemousses was built in 1743 and is one of the oldest on the island. Its cemetery contains the tomb of Abbé Buonavita (1752–1833), who was Napoleon's almoner (distributor of alms) on St Helena. He settled in Mauritius after Napoleon's death in 1821. Villebague, Governor of Mauritius from 1756 to 1759, is also buried here. In the grounds of the **Town Hall** is the **Bassin des Esclaves**, where it is said slaves were washed before being sold.

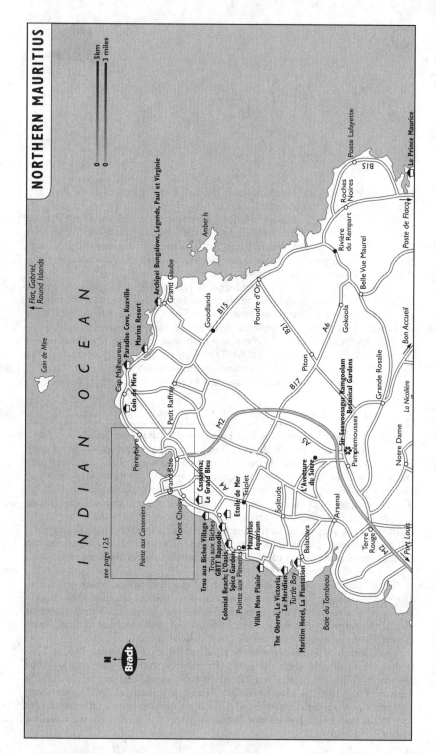

NORTHERN MAURITIUS

INDIAN OCEAN

↑ Flat, Gabriel,
Round Islands

Coin de Mire

0 ——— 5km
0 ——— 3 miles

Pointe aux Canonniers

see page 125

Mont Choisy

Pereybère

Grand-Baie

Casuarina; Le Grand Bleu

Trou aux Biches Village
Trou aux Biches
GBTT Rapsodie;
Colonial Beach; L'Oasis;
Spice Garden
Pointe aux Piments

Villas Mon Plaisir

The Oberoi, Le Victoria;
Le Meridien;
Turtle Bay
Maritim Hotel, La Plantation

Mauritius Aquarium

Etoile de Mer
Fiolet

Solitude

L'Aventure
du Sucre

Arsenal

Balaclava

Terre
Rouge

Port Louis

Baie du Tombeau

Cap Malheureux
Coin de Mire

Paradise Cove, Kuxville
Marina Resort

Archipel Bungalows, Legends, Paul et Virginie

Grand Gaube

Amber Is

Goodlands

B15

Poudre d'Or

Petit Raffray

M2

Pamplemousses

Sir Seewoosagur Ramgoolam
Botanical Gardens

B17

Piton

A5

Notre Dame

Gokoola

Grande Rosalie

La Nicolière

Grand Rosalie

Rivière
du Rempart

Belle Vue Maurel

Roches
Noires

B15

Poste Lafayette

Poste de Flacq

Le Prince Maurice

B21

A6

Bon Accueil

N

Bradt

Not far from Pamplemousses, among the cane fields, with their cairns of stones piled high by slaves, is the village of Calebasses. The Creole saying 'When you are old, we'll send you to Calebasses' came about because of the home for old people there.

Back on the coast near **Balaclava**, **Turtle Bay** is a marine park which offers good snorkelling. The ruins of a **French arsenal** are here and, further north, at **Pointe aux Piments**, lie the remnants of the **Batterie des Grenadiers**. Some of the most impressive ruins are within the grounds of the Maritim Hotel. Non-residents can obtain permission to visit them at the security hut by the entrance.

Inland, on the main road from Port Louis to the north, is **Solitude**, an industrial estate and former sugar plantation where diversification has opened up the area to industry.

WHERE TO STAY Many of the hotels that line this area of coast, particularly the luxury and upmarket ones, are fairly isolated, wedged between cane fields and the sea. Most have excellent facilities and are within walking distance of other hotels but there is no popping out to local shops and bars on foot.

Category A: luxury

The Oberoi (48 rooms, 28 villas) Turtle Bay, Balaclava; ☎ 204 3600; f 204 3625; e reservations@oberoi.intnet.mu; www.oberoihotels.com. Officially opened in April 2001, the Oberoi is a member of 'Leading Small Hotels of the World'. Celebrities were quick to discover the hotel, which prides itself on excellent service and guest privacy. Thoughtful architecture uses natural materials to recreate the charm of a village set in 20 acres of tropical gardens. The luxurious accommodation includes 18 villas with private pool. Interior design is natural elegance with memorable touches like the woven sugarcane headboards, sunken bath and tropical garden in the bathroom. It'll leave you planning to redecorate when you get home! Rooms are equipped with everything you need, including a DVD/CD player (DVDs/CDs are available at the library). There are stunning swimming pools, tennis courts, a watersports centre and a large spa offering all sorts of pampering, including free yoga and tai chi classes. The food is, of course, excellent. It's a romantic, relaxation-focused retreat rather than a family hotel. *Dbl and sgl from € 700 BB, villas with pool (dbl/sgl) from € 1,250 BB.*

Category B: upmarket

Maritim Hotel (221 rooms) Turtle Bay, Balaclava; ☎ 204 1000; f 204 1020; e info.mau@maritim.de; www.maritim.com. Completely refurbished and enlarged in 2000, the hotel stands in 25ha of tropical gardens containing 18th-century ruins. The elegant rooms and suites are equipped with AC, TV, phone, minibar, safe and balcony/terrace. Bathrooms are rather small. There is a choice of restaurants (see page 120) and bars, plus a 9-hole golf course, watersports, dive centre, tennis and horseriding. High standards without too many frills makes this good value for money. Very popular with Germans. *Dbl/sgl from Rs8,820/5,860 BB.*

Le Victoria Hotel (248 rooms) Pointe aux Piments; ☎ 204 2000; f 261 8224; e victoria@bchot.com; www.levictoria-hotel.com. A Beachcomber property whose rooms are some of the most spacious on the island (standard rooms are 60m²). It also has suites and family apts. All are equipped with AC, TV, phone, minibar, safe, tea/coffee facilities and balcony/terrace. Three restaurants, including 1 Italian. There are the usual free watersports, a dive centre, floodlit tennis courts, a large swimming pool and a kids' club. Guests can use the golf course at Trou aux Biches Hotel. Being such a large hotel, it can feel a little impersonal but the beach here is excellent and the facilities and room sizes make it ideal for families. *Dbl/sgl from Rs8,008/5,512 HB, family apt (2 adults, 2 children) from Rs9,400.*

Le Meridien (198 rooms) Village Hall Lane, Pointe aux Piments; ☎ 204 3333; f 204 3344; e resa@lemeridien.mu; www.mauritius.lemeridien.com. The rooms and suites are in 3 blocks of 3 storeys on either side of an impressive lobby area. The buildings aren't particularly pretty but all rooms have a sea view and are spacious, with room for children. Perks which you don't find in all hotels of this kind are tea/coffee facilities and an ironing board. There are 3 restaurants, 4 bars, a pool, tennis courts, a gym and spa, as well as the usual free watersports, including water skiing. Children are well catered for with a kids' club and babysitting service. *Dbl and sgl from € 265 RO.*

🏠 **La Plantation** (270 rooms) Turtle Bay, Balaclava; ✆ 204 3000; f 261 5709; e resa.plantation@apavou-hotels.com; www.apavou-hotels.com. Set in 8 acres at the centre of the bay.

Category C: mid range

🏠 **Spice Garden Hotel** (26 rooms) Pointe aux Piments; ✆ 261 0741; f 261 0740; e spicegarden@intnet.mu; www.hotelspicegarden.com. An attractive hotel with rooms arranged in a 3-storey block overlooking the pool. All rooms are en suite and have AC, TV, phone, safe, minibar and balcony/terrace facing the sea. Facilities include a restaurant, bar, spa and free non-motorised watersports. *Dbl/sgl from € 115/70 HB.*

Category D: budget

🏠 **Villas Mon Plaisir** (43 rooms) Coastal Rd, Pointe aux Piments; ✆ 261 7471; f 261 6600; e villasmp@intnet.mu; www.villasmonplaisir.com. One of those small hotels budget travellers hope to find and seldom do. In a quiet cul-de-sac with access to the beach, the hotel has cosy en-suite rooms with AC, including 3 family rooms. All have phone and balcony/terrace overlooking the pool. There is a small bar and a restaurant with sea view. Some non-motorised watersports are free and

The rooms and suites have AC, TV, phone, safe and balcony/terrace. There are 4 rooms equipped for the disabled. There is a choice of restaurants and bars around a generous pool. Also available are watersports, a dive centre, a spa, tennis courts, a small fitness centre, a kids' club and a nightclub. A lively hotel with plenty going on. *Dbl/sgl from € 238/161 HB.*

🏠 **Colonial Beach Hotel** (43 rooms) Coastal Rd, Pointe aux Piments; ✆ 261 5187; f 261 5427; e cbeach@intnet.mu; www.blue-seasons-hotels.com. Colourful is the first word which springs to mind, thanks to the tropical décor! There are 40 en-suite rooms and 3 family apts, with AC, TV, phone and balcony/terrace. Facilities include a restaurant, bar, pool, TV/games room and a good beach. *Dbl/sgl from € 98/74 HB.*

there is a dive centre next door. Very good value. *Dbl/sgl from € 76/50 HB.*

🏠 **L'Oasis** (22 apts) Pointe aux Piments; ✆ 265 5805; f 265 5207; www.maurinet.com/oasis-gb.html. Self-catering studios and apts equipped with AC and kitchenette (fridge, cooker, etc). The stark white units face the sea and are fronted by a small pool. It also has a restaurant and a decent beach. *Studio from € 38 (2 people), 2-bedroom apt from € 63 (4 people), 3-bedroom apt from € 76 (6 people).*

✖️ **WHERE TO EAT** There is a small supermarket in Pointe aux Piments and numerous snack vendors. Most of the hotels in this area have restaurants which are open to non-residents.

✖️ **Le Fangourin** L'Aventure du Sucre, Beau Plan; ✆ 243 0660. Cuisine: Creole, French. Set in the grounds of the old Beau Plan sugar factory, which now houses a sugar museum. Dining is indoors, on the terrace or in an air-conditioned room, all of which overlook the attractive gardens. Snacks, as well as meals, are on offer. *Main courses from Rs300. Open daily 09.00–17.00.*

✖️ **Café Valse de Vienne** Powder Mill Rd, Pamplemousses; ✆ 243 0560. Cuisine: Austrian, German. Near the main entrance to the gardens, opposite the Church of St François. Has a pleasant atmosphere and serves excellent pastries. *Salads from Rs80. Open daily 09.00–20.00.*

✖️ **Café le Mascarin** Comptoir des Mascareignes, Royal Rd, Pamplemousses; ✆ 787 3136. Cuisine: Creole, snacks. Opposite the car park at the botanical gardens. A range of snacks, salads and crêpes.

Inexpensive. Open Mon–Sat 09.30–18.30, Sun 10.00–14.00.

✖️ **La Marée** Maritim Hotel, Turtle Bay; ✆ 204 1000. Cuisine: Creole, European, seafood. Stunning setting right on the beach where you can watch the chef barbecue your chosen fish or meat. *Main courses from Rs300 to Rs1,900. Open daily for lunch, Tue–Sun for dinner. Reservation recommended.*

✖️ **Le Soleil Couchant** Royal Rd, Pointe aux Piments; ✆ 261 6786. Cuisine: Creole, French, Chinese, seafood. Menu offers a wide range of reasonably priced dishes. *Main courses from Rs90. Open daily for lunch and dinner.*

✖️ **Villas Mon Plaisir** Coastal Rd, Pointe aux Piments; ✆ 261 7471. Cuisine: Creole, Chinese. Unpretentious restaurant with views of the ocean. Good value for money. *Buffet from Rs450, three-course set menus from Rs350. Open daily for lunch and dinner.*

From Pointe aux Piments the coast road runs parallel to the main road, through the extended hamlet of **Trou aux Biches** (Hole of the Does), so named because there is supposed to have been a small watering hole here frequented by female deer. In contrast, Trou aux Cerfs (Hole of the Stags) at Curepipe was said to be used by the males of the species.

Despite falling victim to extensive tourism development, Trou aux Biches retains much of its Mauritian charm. A far quieter alternative to Grand Baie, it features a good beach, excellent snorkelling and a wide range of accommodation and restaurants. The northern end of Trou aux Biches seems to almost blend into **Mont Choisy**, which boasts one of the best beaches in the area. The beach curves around a large bay lined with casuarina trees, stretching to **Pointe aux Canonniers**. This area is extremely popular with locals and the beaches can become busy on weekends.

Inland from Trou aux Biches is **Triolet**, which boasts the largest **Hindu temple** in Mauritius. It is an amalgamation of seven temples added to the original Maheswarnath Temple, built in 1857. As soon as you arrive, an elderly gentleman will probably appear out of nowhere to give you a guided tour. A donation to the temple is usually all that is required in exchange. He may seem eccentric but he appears to know his stuff.

WHERE TO STAY
Category B: upmarket

Trou aux Biches Village Hotel (197 rooms) Trou aux Biches; ☏ 204 6565; f 265 6611; e trouauxbiches@bchot.com; www.trouauxbiches-hotel.com. Guests checking into this Beachcomber hotel are given a map of the property, which consists of thatched cottages scattered in over 40ha of gardens. There is a wonderful feeling of space and the stretch of beach in front of the hotel is enormous. The rooms and family apts have a homely feel and are well equipped, with AC, TV, phone, safe, minibar, tea/coffee facilities and balcony/terrace. There are lots of free watersports and a dive centre. Residents have free use of the 9-hole golf course across the road (green fees for non-residents are Rs550). The hotel has 2 restaurants, a kids' club and a casino, as well as a gym, tennis courts, a hairdresser and beauty centre. Fantastic facilities and

Category C: mid range

Casuarina Hotel (109 rooms) Trou aux Biches; ☏ 204 5000; f 265 6111; e casuarina@intnet.mu. Across the road from the beach, the hotel is a mass of white, fairy-tale thatch cottages, round like toadstools. The rooms are well presented with AC, TV, minibar and balcony/terrace. The 15 apts have 2 bedrooms, a living/dining area, kitchenette and bathroom. They sleep up to 2 adults and 4 children (1 room with 2 sets of bunk beds), although 6 may be a bit of a squeeze. Kitchens are well equipped

one of the best beaches on the island. Dbl/sgl from Rs10,712/7,436 HB.

Hotel Le Canonnier (247 rooms) Pointe aux Canonniers; ☏ 209 7000; f 263 7864; e canonnier@bchot.com; www.beachcomber-hotels.com. Extensively refurbished in 2005, the hotel claims to be the best value 4-star option on the island. It is a large, family-friendly hotel, set on a peninsula surrounded by sea on 3 sides. The rooms have AC, TV, minibar, safe and balcony/terrace. Standard rooms have shower only. There are some interesting ruins in the 7ha of tropical gardens: a lighthouse (now housing the kids' club), cannons and an old fortress. Extensive facilities, always something going on and very child friendly. Dbl/sgl/family apt (2 adults, 3 children) from Rs8,112/5,408/10,712 HB.

and even have a proper cooker complete with oven. There is a restaurant, bar, pool, tennis court, kids' club and many watersports are included. Dbl/sgl from €170/127 HB, apt from €141 RO.

Coralia Mont Choisy (88 rooms) Mont Choisy; ☏ 265 6070; f 265 6749; e montchoisy@intnet.mu; www.accorhotel.com. Formerly the PLM Azur Hotel, the new management haven't got around to removing the old PLM Azur Hotel sign. In fact, there are quite a few alterations that they haven't found time to make. The exterior of the hotel and public areas could do with a makeover. Efforts have been made to spruce up the rooms with new furnishings, although it is not entirely convincing. The rooms are en suite with AC, TV, phone, minibar, safe and tea/coffee facilities. There are 2 restaurants, a bar, pool, tennis courts and a good range of watersports. *Dbl/sgl from € 184/138 BB.*

🏠 **Tarisa Resort** (75 rooms) Coastal Rd, Mont Choisy; ☎ 265 6600; f 265 5193;

Category D: budget

🏠 **Etoile de Mer Hotel** (31 rooms and studios) Coastal Rd, Trou aux Biches; ☎ 265 7856; f 265 6895. No frills accommodation across the road from the beach. The accommodation is clean, although the hotel is looking a little run down. There's an open-air restaurant and pool. *Dbl from Rs1,450 HB.*

🏠 **Le Grand Bleu** (50 rooms and apts) Coastal Rd, Mont Choisy; ☎ 265 5812; f 265 5842; e reservation@legrandbleuhotel.com; www.legrandbleuhotel.com. Basic accommodation across the road from the beach. Small apts with kitchenette (fridge but no cooker) and 26 en-suite rooms. All have AC, TV, phone, minibar and balcony/terrace. The rooms are noticeably newer than the apts. There are 2 small pools, a decent garden and a restaurant. Activities and watersports at additional cost. *Dbl/sgl from € 60/42 HB, suites from € 80 HB.*

🏠 **La Cocoteraie** (19 rooms and apts) Coastal Rd, Mont Choisy; ☎ 265 5694; f 265 6230; e cocoteraie@intnet.mu; http://cocoteraie.amltd.net. Across the road from the Coralia Mont Choisy and 5 mins' walk from the beach. Five dbl rooms and 14 studios and apts, most of which have self-catering facilities. Most have balcony/terrace and some have AC. Rates include a daily maid service and linen. There's a good restaurant (see below) and a small pool. *Dbl from Rs970 RO (Rs1,170 with AC), studio from Rs1,170 (Rs1,440 with AC), 2-bedroom apt from Rs1,700.*

🏠 **Grand Baie Travel & Tours Beach Villas** Coastal Rd, Mont Choisy; ☎ 265 5261/2; f 265 5798; e resagbtt@intnet.mu; www.gbtt.com. Offers self-catering accommodation at 3 establishments around Trou aux Biches and Mont Choisy. They are well maintained and prices include linen and daily maid service but no meals. Bookings for all 3 can be made at the GBTT address above. They also

e tarisa@intent.mu. Opened in 2003, this hotel targets the growing market of tourists from India, a fact which is reflected in the atmosphere and décor. It is across the road from Mont Choisy Beach. The rooms have AC, TV, minibar, safe, tea/coffee facilities and balcony/terrace. Other facilities include a pool, sauna, bar and some free non-motorised watersports. There are 2 restaurants, including the Tandoor (see opposite), which serves fine north Indian cuisine. *Dbl/sgl from Rs4,200/2,850 HB.*

organise excursions.

🏠 **GBTT Villas Mont Choisy** (15 apts) Coastal Rd, Mont Choisy. Across the road from the beach. Five studios and 10 apts all with AC, bathroom (shower only), safe, well-equipped kitchen (hob, microwave etc) and terrace. Apts have 2 dbl rooms of a good size and a living/dining area. Interiors feel a bit old but there is a nice little pool. *Studio/apt from Rs1,140/1,780 RO. Extra bed for adult/child Rs230/105 per night.*

🏠 **GBTT Beach Villas** (14 apts) Coastal Rd, Mont Choisy. On a rocky stretch of beach but good beaches are only a few mins' walk away. Studios and apts with AC, bathroom (shower only), living/dining area, safe, very well-equipped kitchen (kettle, toaster, hob, microwave etc) and balcony/terrace. Arranged in a semi-circle around a pool, facing the sea. Apts have 2 dbl bedrooms and can take an extra bed, studios are very spacious and can easily accommodate a third person (extra bed prices as per Villas Mont Choisy). *Studio/apt from Rs1,575/2,550 RO.*

🏠 **GBTT Rhapsodie** (4 apts) Coastal Rd, Trou aux Biches. The apts are on the seafront, all with 2 dbl bedrooms, AC, bathroom (shower only), living/dining area, safe, TV, well-equipped kitchen and balcony/terrace. An extra bed can be added (for price see Villas Mont Choisy). *Garden-view apt from Rs2,925 RO, sea-view apt from Rs3,250 RO.*

🏠 **Les Filaos Village** (13 studios) X-Club Rd, Pointe aux Canonniers; ☎ 263 7482; f 263 7916; e nathanfilao@intnet.mu; www.filaosvillage.8k.com. Neatly furnished accommodation 2km from Grand Baie. En-suite studios with AC, TV, phone, equipped kitchenette and sea-facing balcony/terrace. Facilities include a restaurant, pool and some free non-motorised watersports. *Dbl/sgl from € 90/70 BB.*

✂ **WHERE TO EAT** For self-caterers there's the **Choisy Royal Supermarket**, in a colourful building at the southern end of the main road through Mont Choisy

(Coastal Road); also **Chez Popo** at the Pointe aux Piments end of Trou aux Biches.

✖ **La Cravache d'Or** Coastal Rd, Trou aux Biches; ☎ 265 7021; f 265 7020. Cuisine: French, Creole, seafood. On the seafront at the southern end of Trou aux Biches. Upmarket with excellent seafood and exceptional views. *Main courses from Rs450. Open daily for lunch and dinner. Reservation recommended.*

✖ **La Coco de Mer** Coastal Rd, Trou aux Biches; ☎ 505 0240. Cuisine: Seychelles Creole. A charming, jolly restaurant serving traditional Seychelles dishes, such as octopus curry with coconut and crab with rum sauce. The Seychelles-style beef is excellent. Guests can even try fruit bat curry, provided it is pre-ordered! The *séga* music, the colourful décor and the authentic cuisine all contribute to the experience. *Mains from Rs300, Saturday evening buffet superb value at Rs300. Open Tue–Sun for lunch and dinner.*

✖ **La Cocoteraie** Mont Choisy; ☎ 265 5694. Cuisine: Creole. Relaxed atmosphere, clean restaurant and good food. *Main courses from Rs250. Open daily for lunch and dinner.*

✖ **L'Espadon** Trou aux Biches; ☎ 204 6565. Cuisine: seafood. On the beach in front of Trou aux Biches hotel, with tables in the sand. Choose your fish and watch it grilled in front of you. A la carte menu daily except Thursday, when a buffet is served. *Main courses from Rs800, mixed seafood grill from Rs950. Open daily for lunch and dinner.*

✖ **Le Pescatore** Coastal Rd, Mont Choisy; ☎ 265 6337. Cuisine: Creole, European, seafood. A good upmarket option right on the seafront with superb seafood. *Main courses from Rs500. Open daily for lunch and dinner.*

✖ **Pizza n' Pasta** Coastal Rd, Mont Choisy; ☎ 265 7000; www.pizzanpasta.biz. Cuisine: Italian. Good-quality food using home-grown herbs and vegetables where possible. The pizzas are cooked in a wood-fired oven and good-quality imported wines and cigars are available. A lot of thought has gone into the Italian décor and the gardens, which contain fish ponds, ducks and chickens. *Pizza from Rs150 and pasta from Rs200. Happy hour (18.00–19.00 daily) is particularly good value with 50% off food and drinks. Open daily for lunch and dinner.*

✖ **Souvenir Snack** Coastal Rd, Mont Choisy; ☎ 265 7047. Cuisine: Creole, Chinese, snacks. Cheap, tasty food and speedy service. *Snacks from Rs40. Open Mon–Sat 07.00–21.00, Sun 07.00–14.00.*

✖ **Tarisa Tandoor** 1st Fl, Tarisa Resort, Coastal Rd, Mont Choisy; ☎ 265 6622. Cuisine: north Indian. Large upmarket Indian restaurant with opulent décor. *Mains from Rs300. Open Wed–Mon for lunch and dinner. Reservation recommended.*

✖ **Hidden Reef** Coastal Rd, Pointe aux Canonniers; ☎ 263 0567. Cuisine: French, Creole. Popular little restaurant and open-air bar on the road to Grand Baie. Clean, trendy and well run, with good value daily specials. *Main courses from Rs250. Open Mon–Sat for lunch and dinner.*

✖ **Wakamé** Coastal Rd, Pointe aux Canonniers; ☎ 263 9888; www.wakamerestaurant.com. Cuisine: Asian. A stylish, modern restaurant serving fine Asian cuisine à la carte, including sushi and a range of vegetarian options. *Main courses from Rs250. Open Wed–Mon for lunch and dinner. Reservation recommended.*

GRAND BAIE

Just within the boundaries of Rivière du Rempart, **Grand Baie** gapes inland beyond **Pointe aux Canonniers**, providing a deep and sheltered bay, often as calm as a lake. It is the place for watersports, self-catering accommodation, and a selection of hotels and restaurants that are among both the worst and best in the island. It is the only area blatantly devoted to mass tourism and consequently has earned the affectionate nickname of 'The Mauritian Côte d'Azur'.

Grand Baie is the safety valve of Mauritius – the place where ordinary tourists, and locals, can go to let off steam without having to pretend to be wealthy jetsetters. Unfortunately, over the years this has resulted in a lowering of the usual excellent standards of the hospitality industry in Mauritius. While Grand Baie has developed, with many bars and restaurants, into a fun place to stay if you like a lively after-beach life, courtesy, warmth and style have been sacrificed. Petty crime is also a by-product of the development, so visitors are advised to be vigilant.

However, there is plenty to do in Grand Baie. All manner of excursions and watersports can be arranged by one of the many activity operators with offices here, and the bars and restaurants which line the bay make it a great place for an evening out.

At the western end of Grand Baie is a very colourful **Tamil temple** covered with statues of gods. If you like temples, it is one of the best Tamil examples on the island.

GETTING THERE AND AWAY The **bus stop** in Grand Baie is on the coastal road, just outside the Highlights Boutique and La Jonque Restaurant. Buses operate regularly between here and the Immigration Square bus station in Port Louis, including an express service which departs every hour. Non-express buses also link Grand Baie to the other coastal villages of the north and east, including Pereybère, Cap Malheureux, Mont Choisy and Trou aux Biches.

TOURIST INFORMATION There is no tourist office as such but there are countless travel agencies who arrange excursions and who can give advice. Everyone in Grand Baie is very keen to share their wisdom on hotels, boat trips and tours but remember that they are wise to tourists and that their cousin almost certainly owns the hotel, boat or tour company which they recommend.

WHERE TO STAY There is certainly no shortage of accommodation in Grand Baie; as well as hotels, there are copious apartments and houses to rent. Much of the accommodation is cheap and cheerful.

David Sullivan reported: 'To stay cheaply in Grand Baie walk around with luggage or backpack. Some sharp-looking young locals will offer to arrange your accommodation. Places in town, one or two blocks away from the waterside, cost half or less than the price of anything on the bay and lots of them are available. Bargain down and prices are well within the *budget* range.'

Category A: luxury

The Royal Palm Hotel (84 suites) Coastal Rd, Grand Baie; ☎ 209 8300; f 263 8455; e royalpalm@bchot.com; www.royalpalm-hotel.com. Located at Grand Sable, adjoining Grand Baie, this is the flagship of the Beachcomber group and a member of 'Leading Hotels of the World'. The luxurious suites are on 3 storeys. They're thoughtfully decorated with colonial-style furnishings and have all the features that you would expect from a world-class hotel, including personal butler service and internet access in the suites. There are excellent sports facilities and most watersports are free. Service is first-class and no wonder — the hotel claims that staff outnumber guests by three to one. The atmosphere is peaceful with an air of self-satisfied superiority — photos of the celebrities who have stayed here adorn one wall, reminding you how lucky you are to be there. *Dbl/sgl from Rs26,104/18,200 HB.*

Category C: mid range

Le Mauricia (197 rooms) Coastal Rd, Grand Baie; ☎ 209 1100; f 263 7888; e mauricia@bchot.com; www.beachcomber-hotels.com. A lively, centrally located hotel. Rooms have AC, TV, phone, safe, minibar and balcony/terrace. The bathroom is partitioned off within the bedroom, which, depending on who you're travelling with, could be a problem. The beach area is rather small but pleasant. Extensive facilities include a shopping centre, 2 pools, a gym, spa, tennis, a kids' club and a nightclub. The usual watersports are on offer and there's a dive centre. The building isn't pretty but this is a popular, mass-market hotel with lots going on. *Dbl/sgl from Rs7,072/4,836 HB.*

Merville Beach Hotel (169 rooms) Coastal Rd, Grand Baie; ☎ 263 8621; f 263 8146; e merville@naiade.com; www.naiade.com. En-suite rooms, either in an unattractive 3-storey block or thatched cottages (superior and family rooms). All have AC, TV, phone, minibar, safe and balcony/terrace. Facilities include a pool, tennis, gym,

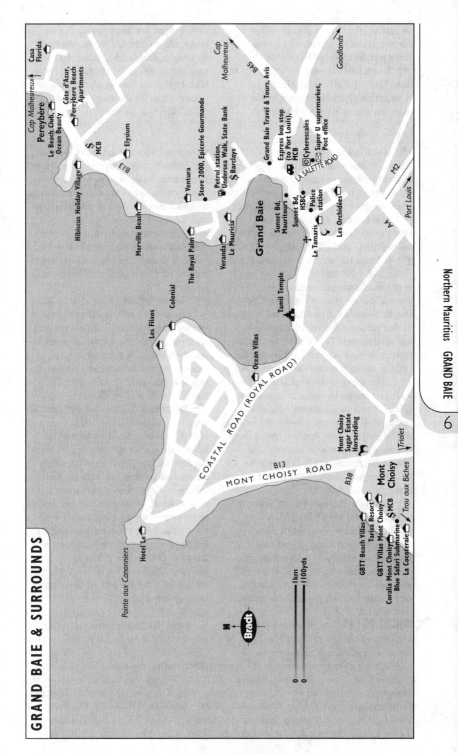

GRAND BAIE & SURROUNDS

Casa Florida

Cap Malheureux Pereybère

Côte d'Azur, Ocean Beauty
Le Beach Club, Ocean Beauty
Pereybère Beach Apartments

Hibiscus Holiday Village

$ MCB

B13

Elysium

B13

Merville Beach

Ventura

Store 2000, Epicerie Gourmande

Petrol station, Undersea Walk, State Bank
$ Barclays

Les Filaos

Colonial

The Royal Palm

Veranda
Le Mauricia

Grand Baie

Sunset Bd, Mauritours
Sunset Bd, HSBC
Police station
Le Tamaris

Grand Baie Travel & Tours, Avis

Express bus stop (to Port Louis), MCB

@ Cyberescales
✉ Super U supermarket, Post office

LA SALETTE ROAD

Les Orchidées

Cap Malheureux

B45

Goodlands

M2

Port Louis

A4

Ocean Villas

Tamil Temple

Pointe aux Canonniers

COASTAL ROAD (ROYAL ROAD)

Hotel Le

Mont Choisy Sugar Estate Horseriding

Triolet

B13

MONT CHOISY ROAD

B38

GBTT Beach Villas
Tarisa Resort
GBTT Villas Mont Choisy
$ MCB
Coralia Mont Choisy
Blue Safari Submarine
La Cocoteraie

Mont Choisy

Trou aux Biches

N

Bradt

0   1km
0   1100yds

the usual watersports and a dive centre. There is a nice wide beach. Entertainment every evening. *Dbl/sgl from Rs7,680/5,160 HB.*

🏠 **Veranda Hotel** (94 rooms and apts) Coastal Rd, Grand Baie; ☎ 263 8015; f 263 7369; e verandahotel@veranda-resorts.com; www.veranda-resorts.com. Recently refurbished hotel near the centre of Grand Baie. Rooms have AC, TV phone, minibar, safe, tea/coffee facilities. Apts also have a kitchenette. Facilities include 2 restaurants, 2 pools, tennis courts, fitness centre, boutiques and a good beach. Prices include some watersports and access to facilities at other Veranda Group hotels. *Dbl/sgl from €200/140 HB.*

Category D: budget

🏠 **Colonial Coconut** (34 rooms) Coastal Rd, Grand Baie; ☎ 263 8720; f 263 7116; e ccoconut@intnet.mu; www.blue-season-hotels.com. Out of town en route to Pointe aux Canonniers. Simply furnished en-suite twin, dbl and triple rooms in thatched bungalows, with ceiling fan and balcony/terrace. Facilities include a restaurant, bar and pool. *Dbl/sgl from €82/63 HB.*

🏠 **Le Tamaris** (15 apts) Coastal Rd, Grand Baie; ☎ 263 5488; f 263 5269; e tamarisgb@mauritours.intnet.mu; www.mauritours.net. Centrally located across the road from the beach. There are 13 studios and 2 apts on the first and second floors of an unremarkable building, above shops. There is no lift and therefore no access for those with limited mobility. Apts are meant to take up to 2 adults and 2 children, with the children sleeping in the lounge area, but this would be a squeeze. The studios and apts are en suite and have a small kitchenette equipped with crockery, TV, AC and balcony. A linen service is provided every other day. There is a common lounge area and a b/fast area, where continental b/fast is provided. The accommodation lacks character but it is clean and good value for central Grand Baie. *Dbl/sgl from Rs1,200/900 BB.*

🏠 **Ocean Villas** (31 rooms and apts) Coastal Rd, Grand Baie; ☎ 263 8567; f 263 3055; e resa@ocean-villas.com; www.ocean-villas.com. A modern complex with a range of good value accommodation, including 3- and 4-bedroom self-catering apts, studios and dbl rooms. All have TV, phone and en-suite facilities. AC is available as an extra in most. Dbl rooms have tea/coffee facilities, studios have a kitchenette and the villas have a good kitchen, complete with proper cooker and oven. Villas accommodate up to 9 people but prices are according to the number of guests, so you don't pay for 6 when there are only 2 of you. There's a pool, snack bar and BBQ facilities. Excursions and watersports can be arranged (payable). The very comprehensive website offers online booking. *Dbl from €40 BB, studio (2 adults, 2 children) from €44 RO, villa (1–9 people) from €38 per person RO.*

🏠 **Hotel Les Orchidées** (29 rooms) Grand Baie; ☎ 263 8780; f 263 8789; e orchidees@intnet.mu; www.hotel-les-orchidees.com. Centrally located hotel, two streets back from the seafront. Comfortable en-suite rooms with AC, TV and phone. It has a restaurant and pool. Guests receive a discount at some local restaurants. Good value option. *Dbl/sgl from €56/45 BB, €82/58 HB.*

🏠 **Ventura Hotel** (32 rooms and apts) Coastal Rd, Grand Baie; ☎ 263 6030; f 263 7479; e info@hotelventura.net; www.hotelventura.net. Behind a row of shops with the main road, private bungalows and large gardens between it and the beach. The rooms, studios and 2-bedroom family units are in 2-storey blocks grouped around a pool. All come with AC, TV and phone, and most have a balcony/terrace. There are 2 restaurants, 1 Creole and 1 Indian. There's a pool and guests receive a discount on watersports at the Centre Nautique de Grand Baie. Excellent facilities for a hotel in this price range. *Dbl/sgl from Rs2,275/1,400 BB , family apt from Rs675 per person BB. HB supplement Rs260 per person per night.*

✖ **WHERE TO EAT** Diners are spoilt for choice in Grand Baie, with restaurants offering a variety of cuisine to suit all budgets. Most are open daily for lunch and dinner but prices and standards vary greatly.

For self-caterers there is a **Store 2000 supermarket** (*open Mon–Sat 07.30–19.30, Sun and public holidays 07.30–12.00*) on the coastal road at the Pereybère end of town. A little further into Grand Baie is the **Epicerie Gourmande** (☎ *269 1123. Open Mon–Thu 09.30–19.00, Fri–Sat 09.30–20.00, Sun 09.00–12.00*), which sells a range of fine food and treats. There is also a large and well-stocked **Super U supermarket** (*open Mon–Thu 09.00–20.30, Fri–Sat*

09.00–21.00, Sun and public holidays 09.00–13.00), which is clearly signposted and just inland from the centre of Grand Baie.

Here is a selection of Grand Baie's restaurants:

✖ **L'Assiette du Pêcheur** (also Phil's Pub) Coastal Rd; ☎ 263 8589. Cuisine: Creole, Chinese, vegetarian, seafood. *Mains from Rs180. Lunch and dinner daily.*

✖ **Café de la Plage** Sunset Bd; ☎ 263 7041. Cuisine: seafood, grills. Doesn't look particularly smart but this cheerful seafront restaurant serves excellent seafood. Tanks of live prawns, crayfish and lobsters are on display to assist diners in choosing their meal (although this may put the squeamish off their food altogether). There is a well-stocked bar and a *séga* show on Sat evenings. *Main courses from Rs150. Open daily 09.45–22.00.*

✖ **Le Capitaine** Coastal Rd; ☎ 263 6867. Cuisine: seafood. Romantic setting overlooking the bay. Superb seafood platter. *Mains from Rs200. Open Mon–Sat for lunch and dinner. Reservation recommended.*

✖ **La Charette** Coastal Rd; ☎ 263 8976. Cuisine: Creole, Indian, Chinese, European. Fairly smart, with a view of the bay. *Set menus from Rs250. Open daily for lunch and dinner.*

✖ **Don Camillo** Coastal Rd; ☎ 263 8540. Cuisine: Italian. Informal and popular. *Pizzas from Rs170.*

✖ **Ebisu** Coastal Rd; ☎ 263 1035; ☏ 263 1034. Cuisine: Japanese. On the same site as La Langouste Grisée and has also won awards. A selection of fine imported wines is available. *Three-course menus from Rs750. Open daily 10.00–22.00.*

✖ **Fusion** Coastal Rd; ☎ 269 1338. Cuisine: French, Japanese, seafood. New restaurant/bar (opened in November 2004) just out of town, above Epicerie Gourmande. Its trendy 'zen' décor wouldn't look out of place in central London, but it seems a little odd in this tropical island setting. Eclectic menu, from sophisticated French dishes to sushi. *Main courses from Rs400. Open Tue–Sat for dinner.*

✖ **Hong Kong Palace** La Salette Rd; ☎ 263 6308/0019. Cuisine: Chinese. A large restaurant on the first floor of the Happy World Complex across the car park from the Super U supermarket. Interesting, elegant décor but the location above the car park isn't exactly atmospheric. *Main courses from Rs200. Open daily for lunch and dinner.*

✖ **La Jonque** Coastal Rd; ☎ 263 8729. Cuisine: Chinese, Creole. Popular, centrally located restaurant

offering a good choice of dishes. *Main courses from Rs120, set menus for two people from Rs300. Open daily for lunch and dinner.*

✖ **Keg and Marlin** La Salette Rd; ☎ 269 1591. Cuisine: European, grills. At the Super U shopping centre near the Hong Kong Palace. In the style of an English pub. Has a big-screen TV, which shows sport. *Mains from Rs200. Open daily 12.00–late.*

✖ **La Langouste Grisée** Coastal Rd; ☎ 263 1035; ☏ 263 1034. Cuisine: seafood, French. Award-winning upmarket seafood restaurant. *Seafood platter for two people from Rs1,850. Open 10.00–22.00 daily.*

✖ **Luigi's** Coastal Rd; ☎ 269 1125. Cuisine: Italian. Just out of town, next to Epicerie Gourmande. Offers plenty of choice, from homemade pizza and pasta to sumptuous seafood dishes with a Mediterranean twist. *Pizza from Rs150, pasta from Rs165, other main courses from Rs300. Open Tue–Sun for lunch and dinner.*

✖ **La Méditerranée** Coastal Rd; ☎ 263 8019. Cuisine: Creole, French, seafood. Popular, unpretentious restaurant. *Main courses from Rs160, set menus from Rs200. Open Mon–Sat for lunch and dinner.*

✖ **Palais de Chine** Coastal Rd; ☎ 263 7120. Cuisine: Chinese. *Mains from Rs120. Open daily for lunch and dinner.*

✖ **Sakura** Coastal Rd; ☎ 263 8092. Cuisine: Japanese. Take-away available. The décor could do with some sprucing up but the food is excellent, particularly the *tepanyaki. Main courses from Rs300. Lunch and dinner, closed Sun lunch. Reservation recommended for weekends.*

✖ **Sunset Café** Sunset Bd; ☎ 263 9602. Cuisine: European snacks and lunches. European atmosphere, right on the seafront. *Salads from Rs150. Open daily 08.30–19.00.*

✖ **Taj Mahal** Coastal Rd; ☎ 263 4984. Cuisine: Indian. *Main courses from Rs150. Open Tue–Sun for lunch and dinner. Reservation required for dinner.*

✖ **Le Tanjore** Ventura Hotel, Coastal Rd; ☎ 263 6030. Cuisine: Indian, Chinese. Not as smart as the Taj Mahal. *Main courses from Rs150. Open daily for lunch and dinner.*

NIGHTLIFE Most hotels in the mid range and upmarket categories organise evening entertainment in the form of live bands, *séga* nights or themed evenings. However, for nightlife outside of the hotels, Grand Baie is really the only place to go. Entry to almost all the nightclubs is around Rs100–150.

Bars, like **Banana Café** (✆ 263 8540), with loud music and sand on the floor, are open all day until late, closing only when they feel like it. Banana Café soon becomes a favourite for most visitors to Grand Baie. Lounging in comfy chairs and twiddling your feet in the sand certainly has its appeal. Next door, behind Don Camillo Restaurant, is **Zanzibar** (✆ 263 3265), a popular nightclub that opens from 22.00 until late Wednesday–Saturday. It has an African theme and plays a variety of music. **Keg and Marlin** (✆ 269 1591) at the Super U supermarket complex is modelled on an English pub. There is big-screen TV showing sport, live music on Friday and Saturday evenings, and ladies' night on Wednesday.

Other lively bars in the centre of town include **Phil's Pub** (✆ 263 8589), **Le Privé** (✆ 263 8766) and **L'Alchémy** (✆ 263 5314). **Stardance** nightclub (✆ 263 9188) opens at 23.00 and is free for women on Wednesdays. **El Diablo** (✆ 263 7664) seems to be Grand Baie's most popular nightclub, with two bars and three dance floors. There's a touristy nightclub with nautical décor at **Le Mauricia Hotel** which is open daily until the early hours, with theme nights on Saturdays. Entry is payable (about Rs400) for non-residents, free for residents.

OTHER PRACTICALITIES

Money and banking Perhaps because there are so many opportunities to spend money in Grand Baie, there are several bank counters that are open outside normal bank hours, enabling visitors to change travellers' cheques or to withdraw cash. Most are open Monday–Saturday 08.00–18.00 and Sunday 09.00–14.00. There are numerous ATMs in Grand Baie, mostly along the coastal road.

Communications The **post office** (*open Mon–Fri 08.15–16.00, Sat 08.15–11.45*) is in the Richmond Hill Complex next to the Super U supermarket on La Salette Road. There are numerous **payphones** in Grand Baie.

For **internet access** try **Cyberescales** on the corner before the Super U supermarket or **Cyber Pirate** (✆ 263 1757) in the Espace Ocean Building on Coastal Road. For details see pages 80–1.

PEREYBERE

The coastal road from Grand Baie to Cap Malheureux passes through **Pereybère**, which offers a pleasant bay and beach, popular with locals at weekends. It is quieter than Grand Baie but is growing rapidly and with just 2km separating the two it probably won't be long before they meet in the middle.

WHERE TO STAY The majority of the accommodation in the area is aimed at budget travellers. There is a particularly healthy population of self-catering apartments.

Category C: mid range

Hibiscus Holiday Village (15 rooms) Coastal Rd, Pereybère; ✆ 263 6891; f 263 8553; e hibisvv@bow.intnet.mu; www.hibiscushotel.com. Accommodation is in bungalows in a pretty garden on the beach side of the road. Small, basic but clean rooms with AC, TV, phone, minibar and terrace. The restaurant is on the water's edge (see opposite) and there is a private manmade beach with sun loungers to make up for the lack of natural beach. Some watersports are included and there's a dive centre. A good location but a little over-priced. Dbl/sgl from

Rs2,580/2,040 BB or Rs3,150/2,400 HB.

Ocean Beauty (10 rooms) Pointe d'Azur La, Pereybère; ✆ 263 6000; f 263 3055; e resa@ocean-villas.com; www.ocean-villas.com. A new boutique hotel on the beach at Pereybère. The en-suite rooms are modern and equipped with AC, TV, safe and balcony/terrace. The suites have a second bedroom. There is a pool and some watersports are free. There is no restaurant although for independent travellers this offers the opportunity to sample local eateries. Dbl/suite from €85/145 BB.

Category D: budget

🏠 **Elysium** (8 rooms) Coastal Rd, Pereybère; \/f 269 1102; e info@hotelelysium.com; www.hotelelysium.com. An intimate little hotel, great for the independent traveller who doesn't feel compelled to stay right on the beach. The hotel is set back down a lane among houses and is signed from the coast road. The beach and shops are within walking distance. The rooms vary from standard to 'junior suite' (the main difference being size) and are priced accordingly. The rooms are clean and fresh, with en-suite shower, AC and minibar. Some have a balcony; only the suites have TV. There is a decent pool and a terrace restaurant serving lunch. Dinner is not available here but it is an easy walk to several restaurants. Good value. *Dbl/sgl from Rs2,490/1,915 BB.*

🏠 **Le Beach Club** (21 apts) Coastal Rd, Pereybère; ☎ 263 5104; f 263 5202; e beachclub@intent.mu; www.le-beachclub.com. Clean, colourful studios and apts on the seafront. Accommodation is equipped with en-suite facilities, AC, TV, kitchenette, phone, safe and balcony/terrace. Rooms are cleaned daily and all linen is provided. There is a bar, pool table and table tennis. B/fast is available. *Studio/2-bedroom apt from Rs1,200/3,100 BB.*

🏠 **Casa Florida** (85 rooms and apts) Mont Oreb Lane, Pereybère; ☎ 263 7371; f 263 6209; e florida@intnet.mu; www.casaflorida.net. Set back down a lane 5 mins' walk from the beach and the centre of Pereybère. The rooms, self-catering studios and apts are set in an attractive garden. Studios have a bedroom and a kitchen, apts have 2 bedrooms and a kitchen. Superior rooms have AC and TV. There is a restaurant, a pool and tennis courts (rackets and balls aren't supplied). A good option for budget travellers who appreciate comfort and quiet. *Dbl/sgl from Rs1,190/995 BB, studio (2 people) from Rs1,190 BB, apt (4 people) from Rs1,840 BB, superior room (2 people) from Rs1,750 BB. HB supplement Rs275 per person.*

🏠 **Côte d'Azur Hotel** (21 rooms and apts) Coastal Rd, Pereybère; ☎ 263 8165; f 263 6353; e cotedazur@intnet.mu; www.hotelcotedazur.com. A range of accommodation across the road from the beach. 14 en-suite rooms with TV, phone, minibar, tea/coffee facilities and balcony. 2 studios with bathroom, phone and kitchenette. Five 2-bedroom apts with kitchenette, living area, TV and balcony. There's also a 2-bedroom suite with dining room, living area, TV, stereo, kitchen, jacuzzi and balcony. The restaurant specialises in seafood. *Dbl from €40 RO, studio (2 people) from €42 RO, apt (4 people) from €48 RO, suite (3 people) from €51 RO.*

🏠 **Pereybère Beach Apartments** (15 apts) Coastal Rd, Pereybère; \/f 263 8679; e beachapt@intnet.mu. Studios and 2-bedroom apts in the centre of Pereybère, across the road from the beach. All have en-suite facilities and equipped kitchenette; most have balcony/terrace. Accommodation is clean and well furnished but the studios appear newer. Daily maid service is included. *Studio (2–3 people) from Rs600 RO, apt (4–5 people) from Rs1,100 RO. AC supplement is Rs100 per day.*

✖ WHERE TO EAT

✖ **Cafeteria Pereybère** Coastal Rd; ☎ 263 8539. Cuisine: Chinese, Creole, European. Eat-in or take-away. Wide choice of snacks and meals, right beside beach. *Set menus from Rs200. Open daily 10.30–22.30.*

✖ **Pereybère Café** Coastal Rd; ☎ 263 8700. Cuisine: Chinese, Creole, European. Also take-away. *Set menus for 2 people from Rs270. Open daily for lunch and dinner.*

✖ **Nirvana** Coastal Rd; ☎ 262 6711. Cuisine: Indian. About 1km north of Pereybère. Excellent food in elegant surroundings. Pricey but worth it. *Main courses from Rs250. Open Mon–Sat for lunch and dinner. Reservation recommended.*

✖ **Les Pieds dans l'Eau** Hibiscus Holiday Village; ☎ 263 8553. Cuisine: Creole, European, seafood. Right on the beach. *Creole BBQ and séga show on Sunday evening costs Rs540. Seafood buffet on Friday is* Rs650. Open daily for lunch and dinner.

✖ **Pizzeria Pereybère** Coastal Rd; ☎ 263 9488. Cuisine: Italian. Centrally located across the road from the beach. *Good pizzas from Rs140.*

✖ **Sea Lovers** Coastal Rd; ☎ 263 6299. Cuisine: French, seafood, Creole. Fantastic new upmarket restaurant in a converted seafront home at the northern end of the public beach. Elegant indoor and outdoor dining – the tables on the huge terrace have great sea views. There is an excellent choice of wines and a relaxing bar. The best place in the area to treat yourself to a memorable meal. *Main courses from Rs250, seafood platter for 2 people from Rs1,900. Open daily for breakfast, lunch and dinner.*

✖ **Wangthai** Beach Hse, Coastal Rd; ☎ 263 4050. Cuisine: Thai. Tasty, authentic Thai cuisine. *Main courses from Rs200. Open Tue–Sat for lunch, daily for dinner.*

NIGHTLIFE Pereybère is far less lively than Grand Baie by night but it does have one claim to fame – a karaoke bar. **Julie Bar** on the coast road (✆ *269 0320*) caters not only for frustrated sopranos but also for sports fans with a large TV screen. On Saturday evenings there's a *séga* show.

CAP MALHEUREUX TO GRAND GAUBE

Cap Malheureux is the most northerly point of Mauritius, 22km from Port Louis. It was there that the British landed in 1810, although no monument marks the site. From Cap Malheureux, the view of **Coin de Mire** (Gunner's Quoin) shows the wedge shape that gave the island its name (the quoin was the wedge used to steady a cannon). There is a picturesque bright-red Roman Catholic chapel close to the beach, Notre Dame Auxiliatrice. Services are held on Saturdays at 18.00 and Sundays at 09.00. During the week from about 13.00, cheerful fishermen gather round a set of scales near the church, weighing, sorting and selling their catch of colourful fish.

Heading east from Cap Malheureux, the coastal road turns inland through stone-encrusted patches of cane, touching the coast again briefly at **St François** before reaching **Grand Gaube**. *Gaube* or *goab* is the local word for an inlet or bay. This small village is still very much a fishing community and groups of fishermen can be seen relaxing in the evenings with a game of *boules* or dominoes by the beach. As yet largely untainted by tourism, there is an exceptionally pleasant atmosphere of the 'real Mauritius'.

Grand Gaube is somewhat isolated, but the industrial town of **Goodlands** is not far inland. **Historic Marine**, makers of wooden ship models, is on the St Antoine Industrial Estate. Visitors can watch the models being made in the workshop and buy the finished products on site (see page 133).

WHERE TO STAY
Category B: upmarket

Paradise Cove Hotel (67 rooms) Anse La Raie, Cap Malheureux; ✆ 204 4000; f 204 4040; e pcove@intnet.mu; www.paradisecovehotel.com. Intimate, romantic hotel providing high standards of accommodation and service. Enjoys an enviable position on a peninsula, which means the beaches are essentially private. Accommodation is in 2- and 3-storey complexes around a small cove with a glittering white beach. Rooms are tastefully decorated and equipped with AC, TV, phone, internet access, safe, minibar and balcony/terrace. As well as the usual free watersports, guests receive 1 free catamaran cruise. There are tennis courts, a pool, a spa, a gym and a dive centre. Lots of luxuries and being small it has a cosy feel, and no ugly scrums for the buffet as in some of the larger resorts. There are 2 restaurants, including the fabulous La

Belle Créole right on the water (see opposite). *Dbl/sgl from Rs13,416/10,036 HB.*

Legends (198 rooms) Grand Gaube; ✆ 698 2222; f 698 4222; e resa@naiade.com; www.naiade.com. Formerly Le Grand Gaube, the hotel was taken over by Naiade and reopened in November 2002 after an extensive refurbishment. The entire hotel is based on the principles of Feng Shui. Rooms are well equipped, with AC, TV, phone, internet access, safe, minibar, tea/coffee facilities and balcony/terrace with sea view. There are 4 restaurants, a spa, a dive centre, tennis courts, a golf driving range, and kids' and teenagers' clubs. Certainly no shortage of entertainment for the family, and there is a good beach. *Dbl/sgl room from Rs12,240/8,280 HB, dbl/sgl suite from Rs19,140/12,930 HB.*

Category C: mid range

Kuxville (25 apts) Coastal Rd, Cap Malheureux; ✆ 262 7913; f 262 7407; e kuxville@intnet.mu; www.kuxville.de. 25 self-catering bungalows, studios and apts with bathroom, kitchen and AC. There is a

daily maid service. There is no restaurant but there is a romantic spot for lounging under thatched parasols on a spit alongside the tiny beach. Some watersports, a dive centre and kitesurfing are available. Run by a German couple with a conspicuously German atmosphere. *Studio from €85 RO, apt (2–4 people) from €90, bungalow (2–4 people) from €100. Prices are based on two people sharing, each extra adult is €20 per day or €10 for children under 12.*

🏠 **Marina Resort** (122 rooms) Coastal Rd, Anse La Raie; ✆ 204 8800; f 262 7650; e marina@veranda-resorts.com; www.veranda-resorts.com. Mid-range all-inclusive hotel. The rooms, bungalows and family units, which include 2 rooms with disabled facilities, have AC, TV, phone, minibar, safe and balcony/terrace. There are 2 restaurants, a big pool, tennis, mini-golf, a gym, kids' club, watersports and a dive centre. There is entertainment every evening. A lively, family-friendly hotel in a quiet spot with good views of Coin de Mire. *Dbl/sgl from €246/172 Al.*

🏠 **Paul et Virginie Hotel** (81 rooms) Coastal Rd, Grand Gaube; ✆ 288 0215; f 288 9233; e pauletvirginie@veranda-resorts.com; www.veranda-resorts.com. This Veranda Group hotel opened in May 2000 on the site of the Island View Club Hotel. It's well laid out, with thatched blocks of 2 and 3 storeys housing the en-suite rooms. All rooms have AC, TV, minibar, safe and sea-facing balcony/terrace. There are 2 restaurants overlooking the sea, 2 pools, a shop and a floodlit tennis court (across the road). A small museum tells the tragic love story of Paul and Virginie. There's a kids' club and the rooms, especially the superior ones, have plenty of space for a child or two. Non-motorised watersports are free and bikes can be hired. Good value for money. *Dbl/sgl from €206/145 HB.*

🏠 **Coin de Mire Hotel** (90 rooms) Coastal Rd, Bain Boeuf, Cap Malheureux; ✆ 262 7302; f 262 7305; e coindemire@veranda-resorts.com; www.veranda-resorts.com. Recently renovated hotel across the road from the beach and a fantastic lagoon. 24 standard and 66 superior rooms, all with phone, safe, ceiling fan, tea/coffee facilities and balcony/terrace. Only superior rooms have AC. There are 2 decent pools, tennis courts, a restaurant and a colourful garden. There are some free watersports. Activities, such as bike hire, can be arranged and guests can use facilities at 4 other Veranda hotels, including Paul et Virginie. Not bad value given the facilities and location. *Dbl/sgl from €116/81 HB.*

✖ **Category D: budget**

🏠 **Archipel Bungalows** (10 rooms and apts) Calodyne, Grande Gaube; ✆ 283 9518; f 283 7910; e info@archipelhotel.com; www.archipelhotel.com. A variety of sea-facing accommodation. For self-caterers there are 3-bedroom bungalows and a 2-bedroom apt, all with fan. There are also a few AC dbl rooms. All have en-suite shower and balcony. Facilities include a restaurant, pool and free kayaks. Excursions can be arranged. *Dbl/sgl from Rs1,280/1,150 BB.*

WHERE TO EAT

✖ **La Belle Créole** Paradise Cove Hotel, Anse La Raie, Cap Malheureux; ✆ 262 7983. Cuisine: Creole, European. In a stunning setting on the beach. Very upmarket with prices to match. *Open daily for lunch and dinner.*

✖ **Restaurant Amigo** Pavillon, Cap Malheureux; ✆ 262 8418. Cuisine: Creole, European, seafood. On the B45 road which heads inland from Cap Malheureux towards Port Louis. Sooner or later the owner is bound to boast to you that Jacques Chirac has been there, so I'll spoil the surprise and tell you now. *Medium price range. Open Mon–Sat for lunch and dinner.*

✖ **Le Coin de Mire** Cap Malheureux; ✆ 262 8070. Cuisine: Creole, seafood. In a lovely position opposite the red church. *Mains from Rs110. Open daily 10.30–22.00.*

NORTHERN OFFSHORE ISLANDS

COIN DE MIRE This distinctively shaped island lies 4km from the north coast and can be visited on excursions arranged by hotels or travel agents, although landing is tricky. There is a cave on the island called **Madam's Hole**, which was used by the British navy in the 19th century for target practice. Graceful white *paille en queues* (tropic birds) can be seen soaring around the black cliffs.

FLAT, GABRIEL, ROUND, SERPENT AND AMBER ISLANDS Off the northern coast beyond Coin de Mire are Flat, Gabriel, Round, Serpent and Amber Islands. **Flat Island** has a lighthouse and good snorkelling and is visited by groups on picnics from hotels. Dr Ayres, writing in a scientific paper published in 1865, said: 'In Flat Island we find the fossilised remains of an extensive forest consisting of stumps of trees closely planted about 2ft high, hollow in the centre to the base, and some of them 2ft in diameter.' **Gabriel Island** is also a popular stop-off point for cruises and excursions.

It is difficult to land on **Round Island** by boat because of strong currents and a permit is required to do so since it is a nature reserve. The island, which is kidney-shaped, not round, and about 1.5km² in area, is some 22km from Mauritius. Its flora and fauna are fascinating as much of it is rare, having evolved in isolation without the attentions of the early colonists. (See also pages 34–5.)

Neighbouring **Serpent Island**, a large barren rock with no serpents or snakes, also known as Parasol Island, is a sanctuary for birds.

Amber Island is so called because of the ambergris which used to be found there. The ill-fated *St Géran* was wrecked on the Amber Island reefs in 1744 with heavy loss of life. The tragedy inspired the Mauritian love story of *Paul et Virginie*, written by Bernadin de St Pierre. A monument commemorating the disaster was erected at Poudre d'Or in 1944 and artefacts recovered from the ship can be seen at the Naval Museum in Mahébourg (see pages 154–5).

POUDRE D'OR TO RIVIÈRE DU REMPART

The name **Poudre d'Or** could have derived from gold found in the region or, more likely, from the golden powder sands found here. Virginie, the fictional heroine of St Pierre's novel, *Paul et Virginie*, is supposed to have been washed ashore on this coast, prompting Mark Twain to observe wryly that it was 'the only one prominent event in the history of the island, and that didn't happen'.

Poudre d'Or is a fishing village with a public picnic area and a sturdy building built in 1864 as a chest hospital. Excursions to Amber Island leave from here.

The road down the east coast passes between cane and tobacco fields to reach **Rivière du Rempart**. This town has many cyclone-proof concrete houses as well as two old wooden mansions, opposite each other, that have managed to survive all of the progress and storms. Inland, the oddly named village of **Gokoola** takes its name from the town of Gokul, between Delhi and Agra in India.

WHAT TO DO

Many hotels offer or can arrange excursions, activities and watersports, as do the numerous travel agents in Grand Baie. Cruises to the nearby islands and deep-sea fishing are particularly popular. Try **Mauritours** in the Sunset Boulevard complex, Grand Baie (✆ *263 6056*) or alternatively, go directly to the offices of the activity operators. For more information on the activities listed below, see *Chapter 4, Activities*.

SPORTS
Scuba diving The reefs off the northern coast and the islands off Cap Malheureux offer some of the best diving in Mauritius. There are many scuba-diving operators in the north of the island catering for all levels and experience.

Snorkelling The best snorkelling in northern Mauritius is in the lagoons at Turtle Bay, Trou aux Biches, Pereybère and Grand Baie.

Other undersea experiences For those who don't want to dive, it is possible to experience underwater life on an undersea walk or in a submersible, such as the Blue Safari Submarine (see page 96). The north is where these activities take place.

Deep-sea fishing Although the west coast is reputed to be the best for deep-sea fishing, several companies offer trips off the northern coast.

Watersports The north of the island, Grand Baie in particular, has the island's greatest range of watersports.

Golf There is a nine-hole course at **Trou aux Biches Village Hotel**.

Horseriding Most hotels and tour operators can arrange horseriding. One of the island's best riding stables is at the **Mont Choisy Sugar Estate** (✆ *265 6159*) near Grand Baie (see page 91).

HIKING AND ADVENTURE SPORTS
Yemaya Adventures (*Grand Gaube;* ✆ *752 0046*) Based in Grand Gaube and offers hiking, mountain biking and sea kayaking (see also page 98).

Le Domaine de Labourdonnais (*Mapou;* ✆ *266 1533;* f *266 6415;* e *ciaglabo@intnet.mu; www.vergersdelabourdonnais.com*) Guided walking and cycling tours of a 40ha orchard a few kilometres inland from the north coast. The tour includes a visit to the anthurium greenhouses, the plant nursery and the craft shop for a tasting of fruit juices and purées.

SPA TREATMENTS
Surya (*Coastal Rd, Pereybère;* ✆/f *263 1637;* e *surya_mauritius@yahoo.co.uk; www.geocities.com/surya_mauritius; Indian head massage from Rs800, body massages from Rs1,400; open daily 09.00–19.30*) This Ayurvedic spa between Grand Baie and Pereybère offers a range of relaxing massages and treatments. As well as one-off treatments, programmes lasting from three days to three weeks are available.

SHOPPING Grand Baie, and Sunset Boulevard in particular, is crammed with boutiques, reminiscent of any touristy beach resort. Some of the jewellery shops here are duty free. There are various souvenir shops at the Super U supermarket in Grand Baie, including a **Mauritius Glass Gallery** outlet (✆ *269 0376*).

There is a **National Handicraft Promotion Agency** (NHPA) shop at the SILWF Compound (✆ *263 5423*). For more information on the NHPA see *Giving something back*, pages 84–5.

At **Historic Marine** in Goodlands (✆ *283 9304;* f *283 9204;* e *hismar@intnet.mu; www.historic-marine.com. Open Mon–Fri 08.30–17.00, Sat–Sun 08.30–12.00*), visitors can tour the model-ship workshop and buy finished models in the shop. Prices range from €50 to €4,200. The **Comptoir des Mascareignes** (✆ *243 9900. Open Mon–Sat 09.30–18.00, Sun 10.00–14.00*) complex opposite the botanical gardens at Pamplemousses has a number of shops selling handicrafts, clothing, jewellery and model ships and planes..

WHAT TO SEE

SIR SEEWOOSAGUR RAMGOOLAM BOTANIC GARDENS (*Pamplemousses;* ✆ *243 3531; admission: free; gardens open daily 08.30–17.30*) Formerly known as the Royal Botanic Garden, this is one of the island's most popular tourist attractions, located 11km northeast of Port Louis. Most hotels and travel agents offer tours to the gardens and they are easily accessible from Port Louis by bus from the Immigration Square bus station. There are also buses from the coastal towns of the north. Buses stop on the main road and the garden is a five-minute walk away. On Sundays it is popular with picnickers.

The garden covers 60 acres so a guide or good map is essential to get the most out of it. Official guides (with a badge) are available by the main gate and the entrance from the car park. Their guided tours cost Rs50 per person for up to four people, Rs40 per person for larger groups. It is by no means obligatory to have a guide and their sales pitch can sometimes be rather pushy. Unofficial guides (no badge) operate within the garden and may approach you. The booths at the main gates, which are only open on weekdays, sell comprehensive guidebooks on the gardens (Rs125).

The fence and gates at the entrance are scrolled in wrought iron and gained a first prize in the International Exhibition at London's Crystal Palace in 1862. The gate was a gift from François Liénard, a Frenchman, born in India in 1783, who lived in Mauritius. There is a memorial obelisk to him in the garden.

The garden's origins go back to 1729 when a French colonist acquired about half the present site, then called Mon Plaisir. Mahé de Labourdonnais bought it in 1735 and created a vegetable garden (to the left of the present main entrance) beside his own residence, Château de Mon Plaisir, to supply vegetables to his household, the town and visiting ships. The garden was also used as a nursery for plants imported from Europe, Asia and South America. Mulberry bushes were planted in the hope of starting a silkworm industry but were replaced by *bois noir* (*Albizia lebbeck*), to be turned into charcoal for use in the manufacture of gunpowder for the island's defence.

When, in 1770, the garden became the private property of Pierre Poivre, administrator of the island, Pamplemousses flourished. He cultivated spices such as nutmeg and cloves, as well as ornamental trees. In 1810, the garden reverted to government ownership and was neglected by the British until James Duncan was appointed director in 1849. He introduced many of the palms including the royal palms (*Roystonea regia* and *Roystonea oleracea*), which add a majestic splendour to the main avenue. Thousands of eucalyptus trees were planted in the garden after the malaria epidemic of 1866, for transplanting in swamps to dry them out and reduce mosquito-breeding grounds. Since 1913 the garden has been under the control of the Ministry of Agriculture.

Today the garden boasts 500 species of plant, of which 80 are palms and 25 are indigenous to the Mascarene Islands. The numerous highlights include the impressive giant water lilies (*Victoria amazonica*), which float like giant baking tins in a rectangular pond. Their flowers open for two days only, from the late afternoon to the following morning. On the first day they are cream-coloured with a heady fragrance, on the second they are pink. Another pond contains the white and yellow flowers of the lotus (*Nelumbo nucifera*), which is held in veneration by Hindus. The betel nut palm (*Areca cathecu*) grows nearby. Its orange fruit contains the betel nut which is sliced, mixed with lime paste, wrapped in the leaf of the vine (*Piper betel*) and chewed. It's a cancer-causing stimulant which depresses the appetite and stains the gums and lips an alarming red. The talipot palms (*Corypha umbraculifera*) are said to flower once every 40 to 60 years with over 50 million tiny blooms, reaching a height of 6m above the tree. After waiting so long to flower just once, the tree dies.

The **Château de Mon Plaisir** looks impressive but lightweight, perhaps because it is not the original home of Labourdonnais but an English-built office mansion, now used for administration. The nearby **sugar mill** is also a reconstruction. Former Prime Minister and Governor General Sir Seewoosagur Ramgoolam was cremated outside the mansion and his ashes scattered on the Ganges, in India. In front of the château are trees planted by visiting royal and political dignitaries, such as Nelson Mandela.

The **tortoise pen** houses Aldabra tortoises, first brought to the gardens in 1875 from Aldabra Island to protect them from being wiped out by seabirds (when young) or being eaten by humans (when older). The **stag park** contains the *Cervus timorensis russa* deer, first introduced in 1639 from Batavia.

Animals to be seen at liberty include the indigenous fruit bat (*Pteropus niger*), two species of rat (the brown Norway rat and the black arboreal Asiatic rat), and the Madagascar tenrec (*Centetes sp*). The large, black butterfly with blue windows on its wings is the *Papilio manlius*.

Indigenous birds include the moorhen (*Gallinula chloropus pyrrhorrhoa*), with its red bill, and the green-backed heron (*Butorides striatus rutenbergi*). The small greyish bird in groups with a 'tip-tip-tip' call is *l'oiseau Manioc* (*Malacirops borbonicus mauritianus*). Species of the *Phelsuma* lizard may be seen on palm trees.

There are several **monuments** in the garden including a stone slab which the sentimental believe marks the grave of the fictitious lovers, Paul and Virginie. Their creator, Bernadin de St Pierre, is remembered with a bust.

L'AVENTURE DU SUCRE (*Beau Plan, Pamplemousses;* ✆ *243 0660;* f *243 9699;* e *aventure.sucre@intnet.mu; www.aventuredusucre.com; admission: adult/child Rs250/125; open daily 09.00–18.00; guided visits are included in the admission price*) In 1999, the Beau Plan sugar factory, which had been operating since 1895, closed down. In October 2002, it was converted into a fascinating high-tech museum covering the history of sugar, the history of Mauritius and the process of sugar production. The exhibits on slavery and the treatment of slaves and runaways are particularly thought provoking. In fact, the museum provides one of the most comprehensive and digestible histories of Mauritius available on the island. The visit culminates in a tasting of export-quality sugar and rum. Sugar products and other souvenirs are on sale at the shop. Guided visits are at 11.00 and 14.30 and last for one hour but the modern, detailed displays are easy to follow without a guide. Allow approximately two hours for self-guided tours, including tasting. There is a restaurant, Le Fangourin, which serves snacks and meals (see page 120).

MAURITIUS AQUARIUM (*Coastal Rd, Pointe aux Piments;* ✆ *261 4561;* f *261 5080; www.mauritiusaquarium.com; admission: adult/child/family (2 adults, 2 children) Rs195/95/525; open Mon–Sat 09.30–17.00, Sun and public holidays 10.00–16.00*) Opened in 2004, the aquarium has filled an important gap in the island's attractions. It has been thoughtfully designed and, unusually, the tanks are undercover outdoors, allowing you to view the fish and corals under natural light. It is a good opportunity to see some of the creatures you'll observe while snorkelling or diving off Mauritius but in the aquarium they have handy labels. Favourites include the Picasso triggerfish (*Rhinecanthus aculeatus*), domino fish (*Dascyllus aranus*) and sea horses (*Hippocampus kuda*). There are freshwater fish too, such as the carp caught locally by the manager. Children will enjoy the touch pool. There is a small souvenir shop and snack-bar. The fish are fed daily at 11.00.

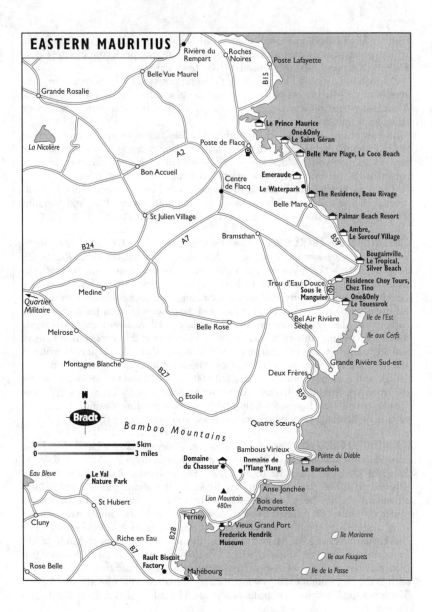

EASTERN MAURITIUS

Rivière du Rempart
Roches Noires
Poste Lafayette
Belle Vue Maurel
Grande Rosalie
B15
La Nicolière
Poste de Flacq
A2
Bon Accueil
Le Prince Maurice
One&Only Le Saint Géran
Belle Mare Plage, Le Coco Beach
Centre de Flacq
Emeraude
Le Waterpark
St Julien Village
Belle Mare
The Residence, Beau Rivage
Bramsthan
Palmar Beach Resort
B24
A7
Ambre, Le Surcouf Village
B59
Bougainville, Le Tropical, Silver Beach
Medine
Trou d'Eau Douce
Résidence Choy Tours, Chez Tino
Sous le Manguier
Quartier Militaire
One&Only Le Touessrok
Belle Rose
Bel Air Rivière Sèche
Ile de l'Est
Melrose
Ile aux Cerfs
Montagne Blanche
B27
Deux Frères
Grande Rivière Sud-est
Etoile
B59
N
Bradt
Quatre Sœurs
Bamboo Mountains
0 ———— 5km
0 ———— 3 miles
Bambous Virieux
Pointe du Diable
Domaine du Chasseur
Domaine de l'Ylang Ylang
Le Barachois
Eau Bleue
Le Val Nature Park
Lion Mountain 480m
Anse Jonchée
St Hubert
Ferney
Bois des Amourettes
Ile Marianne
Cluny
Vieux Grand Port
Frederick Hendrik Museum
Riche en Eau
B28
Ile aux Fouquets
Rose Belle
B7
Rault Biscuit Factory
Mahébourg
Ile de la Passe

7

Eastern Mauritius

The district of Flacq occupies most of the east of the island, which for our purposes extends from Roches Noires in the northeast down to Bois des Amourettes in the southeast.

Much of eastern Mauritius was covered with ebony forest when the Dutch settled here in the 17th century, but it didn't take them long to start felling the trees to make a road northwards from their settlement at Grand Port. The French continued attacking the forests, using the timber to build ships and houses. The land is now primarily devoted to agriculture and the area boasts two of the island's largest sugar estates.

The beaches around Belle Mare are glorious, and have attracted swarms of upmarket hotels. Nevertheless, there is sufficient mid-range and budget accommodation in the area.

The uninhabited Ile aux Cerfs, off Trou d'Eau Douce, is one of the best-known tourist attractions of the east, with its miles of beaches, new championship golf course and copious watersports facilities. The area south of Trou d'Eau Douce is largely undeveloped owing to the lack of beaches. Driving along this coast is a real pleasure, with the road sandwiched between the sea and unspoilt fishing villages.

ROCHES NOIRES TO BELLE MARE

South of Rivière du Rempart is the bulge of **Roches Noires**, with weekend houses – *campements* – facing the turquoise sea. The term *campement*, according to the hefty pictorial souvenir book *Living In Mauritius*, 'originally referred to a weekend house made of *ravenala* and straw. Whole families – and most of their belongings – used to move from the Upper Plateau to 'go camping' in the summer months. Nowadays the word is applied to the ever-multiplying concrete villas that house the tourists.'

In summer, this coast is pleasant, but it suffers from strong southeast winds in winter. Pedlars on motorbikes, loaded with goods of every description, travel the roads selling their wares to women working in the fields who can't go to town to shop.

From Roches Noires the road trickles down the east coast, passing through **Poste Lafayette**. The coast around Lafayette is lined with casuarinas, bent by the winter winds. There are some beaches but the sea is rougher than in other areas and they don't compare to those further south. Lafayette is named after one of the surveyors who helped the Abbé de la Caille draw up the first detailed map of the island. Another surveyor, d'Esny, has several points named after him, including one in the bay of Poste de Flacq. The town of **Poste de Flacq** is little more than a road junction, although there is a petrol station. Don't be surprised to see kiosks selling oysters around here; they are farmed on this coast.

The heart of the Flacq district is **Centre de Flacq**, a town of about 15,000 inhabitants. Its courthouse and post office are housed in a well-maintained, French-style colonial building, listed as a national monument.

Belle Mare and the surrounding area offer some of the island's best beaches. Belle Mare Beach itself is true postcard material, with a long white-sand beach, shallow turquoise waters and a border of casuarina trees. The old **lime kiln** among the trees is one of many along this coast, where coral was burnt over casuarina wood fires to extract the lime. Sadly, the large upmarket hotels which have begun to dominate this area of coast in recent years have brought with them jet skis, banana boats and water-skiing tourists. At times, you strain to hear the gentle lapping of the ocean over the wailing of outboard motors.

The eastern beaches are not easily reached by bus but a taxi is inexpensive from anywhere on the east coast. One of the best things about the area is that whilst there are hotels on the beach side of the road, the opposite side is still the domain of small farmers, who seem to tend their modest crops at all hours of the day. Vegetables such as onions, chillies and aubergines are the main crops, grown for sale at local markets.

WHERE TO STAY

Category A: luxury

Le Prince Maurice (89 suites) Poste de Flacq; 413 9100; f 413 9130; e resa@princemaurice.com; www.princemaurice.com. A luxury hotel in a quiet location. 76 junior suites, 12 senior suites and 1 'princely suite', some of which are on stilts over the water. All are superbly appointed with fabulous facilities including DVD player, private fax and jacuzzi. Most senior suites have a private pool. There are 2 restaurants, one of which is a small floating restaurant. Other amenities include a spa, squash court, fitness centre, watersports, library, kids' club and free access to Belle Mare Plage Golf Club. *Dbl/sgl from Rs19,656/14,768 BB.*

One&Only Le Saint Géran (163 rooms) Poste de Flacq; 401 1688; f 401 1668; e info@oneandonlylesaintgeran.mu; www.oneandonlyresorts.com. This member of 'Leading Hotels of the World' boasts 148 luxurious junior suites, 14 ocean suites and 'the villa', an extravagant 2-bedroomed monument to self-indulgence. The junior suites have a view of either the sea or lagoon and, as well as the usual first-class facilities, feature a DVD/CD player, internet access via the TV and butler service. One junior suite is suitable for disabled guests. There are 3 lavish restaurants, including the Spoon des Iles, which serves innovative international cuisine at heart-stopping prices. Facilities include a casino, a Gary Player-designed 9-hole golf course and a Givenchy Spa, which offers such vital services as 'herbal wraps', 'skin peeling' and 'special lifting objectives'. Free watersports include water skiing and small-game fishing. There are 5 tennis courts, a gym offering personal training and a dive centre. As well as a kids' club, there is one for teenagers. *Dbl/sgl from €800/540 HB, but rising to €1,200/810 in high season.*

Category B: upmarket

Belle Mare Plage Golf Hotel and Casino Resort (256 rooms) Belle Mare; 402 2600; f 402 2616; e resa@bellemareplagehotel.com; www.bellemareplagehotel.com. Extensively refurbished in 2002, this sprawling resort stretches along a pristine beach. As well as 235 rooms and suites, there are 20 luxurious 2- and 3-bedroom villas and a presidential villa. There are 2 rooms with disabled facilities. The accommodation is stylish and comfortable, with the usual upmarket amenities. The villas are particularly impressive, each with private pool and butler service. There are 4 restaurants, including the first-class Blue Penny Café (see opposite). A popular hotel with golfers, who take advantage of the 2 18-hole championship courses (see opposite). Also available are a choice of pools, a fitness centre, spa, tennis, watersports and a kids' club. Good value for money. *Dbl/sgl from Rs11,440/8,008 HB, dbl/sgl junior suite from Rs14,040/9,828 HB.*

Le Coco Beach (333 rooms and villas) Belle Mare; 415 1010; f 415 1888; e info@lecocobeach.mu; www.lecocobeach.com. You'd be forgiven for thinking this was a theme park rather than a hotel, with its unrelenting Calypso-carnival décor and roller-blading staff. From 2006, it will become an all-inclusive resort. The 204 rooms and 129 villas are all en suite with AC, TV, phone, minibar, safe, tea/coffee facilities and balcony/terrace. The emphasis is on constant entertainment, with numerous bars, a disco (open every night), cabarets and fashion shows. A huge range of activities is available, including watersports, 6 tennis courts, a 9-hole pitch-and-putt golf course and horseriding. A family-friendly hotel where children are kept busy by the kids' and teenagers' clubs. *Dbl/sgl from € 240/180 Al.*

🏠 **The Residence** (163 rooms) Belle Mare; ☎ 401 8888; f 415 5888; e hotel@theresidence.com; www.theresidence.com. The entrance is suitably grand for a hotel which is impressive in every way. The style is intended to be that of a colonial palace. The rooms and suites are spacious and beautifully decorated, equipped with everything you need, including butler service. The bathrooms here deserve special mention – they are superb. Surprisingly for a modern luxury hotel, not all the rooms face the sea but those with a view of the garden are cheaper. There are 3 restaurants, including the unforgettable La Plantation (see page 140) right on the beach. Facilities include an excellent kids' club, tennis courts, many free watersports (including water skiing) and a fabulous spa. There's also a helipad. Free fruit and chilled water whilst you're on the beach is a nice touch. The service is incredible, even by Mauritian standards. *Dbl/sgl from € 428/292 HB, dbl/sgl suite from € 584/438 HB.*

Category C: mid range

🏠 **Palmar Beach Resort** (70 rooms) Coastal Rd, Belle Mare; ☎ 415 1041; f 415 1043; e palmar@veranda-resorts.com; www.veranda-resorts.com. An informal Veranda Group hotel on a superb stretch of beach. The well-maintained en-suite rooms are equipped with AC, TV, phone, minibar, safe

Category D: budget

🏠 **Emeraude Hotel** (60 rooms) Coastal Rd, Belle Mare; ☎ 415 1107; f 415 1109; e htl.emeraude@intnet.mu; www.blue-season-hotels.com. Across the road from the northern end of the beach, white cottages with thatched roofs are scattered in a pleasant garden. However, the buildings are a little run down. The en-suite rooms are simply furnished with AC and phone. As well as a restaurant, there's a pizzeria by the pool, a TV room and free non-motorised watersports. Staff are very friendly and it's not bad value. *Dbl/sgl from € 84/68 HB.*

🏠 **Le Surcouf Village** (35 rooms) Coastal Rd, Belle Mare; ☎ 415 1800; f 212 1361;

✕ WHERE TO EAT

✕ **Blue Penny Café** Belle Mare Plage Golf Hotel and Casino Resort; ☎ 402 2600. Cuisine: European. Far from being a café – this is an exclusive restaurant

🏠 **Beau Rivage** (170 rooms) Belle Mare; ☎ 402 2000; f 415 2020; e brivage@intnet.mu; www.naiade.com. A large resort hotel whose rooms and suites are in 3-storey buildings with thatched roofs. Rooms are very spacious, colourful and equipped with the usual facilities of an upmarket hotel: AC, TV, phone, safe, minibar, etc; suites have a jacuzzi. All rooms face the sea and have a balcony/terrace. It has a spa, an impressive pool with palm trees seemingly growing in it, tennis courts and a gym. Free watersports include water skiing. Buffets in the main restaurant can be rather hectic; the alternatives are Mediterranean, Indian/Chinese and seafood restaurants. *Dbl/sgl from Rs16,980/10,710 HB.*

🏠 **Hotel Ambre** (246 rooms) Coastal Rd, Belle Mare; ☎ 401 8000; f 415 1594; e resa.ambre@intnet.mu; www.apavou-hotels.com. A large hotel on a good stretch of beach. The rooms and suites are comfortable with AC, TV, phone, minibar and balcony/terrace. There is a choice of restaurants and bars, as well as a nightclub. Facilities include a large pool, watersports, tennis and a balneotherapy and fitness centre. At the very bottom end of upmarket. *Dbl/sgl from € 234/159 HB.*

and balcony/terrace. There are 2 restaurants, 2 bars, a pool, fitness and beauty centre, kids' club and a good choice of free watersports. Bike hire is available and guests have use of the facilities at other Veranda hotels. *Dbl/sgl from € 198/143 HB.*

e surcouf@intnet.mu; www.lesurcouf.com. Cottage-style complex at the southern end of Belle Mare beach. The en-suite rooms have AC, TV, phone and balcony/terrace. The 6 family rooms have a dbl bedroom and a sitting room with 2 sgl sofa beds. There are also 2 suites for up to 6 people with 3 bedrooms, 2 bathrooms, a kitchen, a living/dining area and 4 balconies; one has a jacuzzi, one has a pool. In all accommodation bedrooms have AC. Facilities include some free non-motorised watersports, a restaurant, pool and evening entertainment. *Dbl/sgl from Rs2,040/1,293 HB.*

which is likely to offer you one of the finest dining experiences of your life. Chef Michael Scioli produces unforgettable dishes, and if you are lucky enough to be served by Oliver Prodigson, you can consider that you have been served by the finest head waiter on the island. It is worth ordering tea at the end of your meal just to see the elaborate preparation, where the leaves are meticulously weighed at your table in hand-held scales. *A dégustation menu will set you back around Rs2,820. A la carte main courses from Rs860. Open Mon–Sat 19.30–22.00.*

✗ **Deer Hunter** The Legend Golf Course, Belle Mare; ☎ 402 2600. Cuisine: Creole, European. If you've seen enough of the beach, this may be the restaurant for you, with its sweeping views of the golf course. You may even spot a deer drinking at one of the lakes. *Main courses from Rs500. Open daily for breakfast, lunch and dinner.*

✗ **La Plantation** The Residence Hotel, Belle Mare; ☎ 401 8888. Cuisine: Creole, seafood. Built in the style of a planter's house, perched on the beach away from the main body of the hotel. A great place to treat yourself. The food is as fantastic as the setting and the service is both friendly and slick. *Set menu from Rs1,400, à la carte main courses from Rs320, rising to Rs1,400 for lobster. Open daily for lunch and dinner.*

✗ **Symon's Tropical Restaurant** Coastal Rd, Belle Mare; ☎ 415 1135. Cuisine: Creole, Chinese, Indian, seafood. Also does take-away and there's a lively bar. *Main courses from Rs220. Open daily 11.00–midnight.*

✗ **Chez Manuel** St Julien Village; ☎ 418 3599. Cuisine: Creole, Chinese. Just off the A7 between Centre de Flacq and Quartier Militaire. A good escape from the coast. Offers plenty of choice. *Main courses from Rs120, set menus from Rs220. Open Mon–Sat for lunch and dinner.*

TROU D'EAU DOUCE

The fishing village of **Trou d'Eau Douce** is an early Dutch settlement. The **Puits des Hollandais**, meaning Well of the Dutch, is an extinct crater well still used for fresh water and Trou d'Eau Douce refers to this freshwater spring although, since it is pronounced *Tro do-doo*, some historians have assumed it is named after the dodo, which lived in this region.

Off Trou d'Eau Douce lies **Ile aux Cerfs**, an uninhabited island which has been transformed into a tourist attraction, with miles of beaches, numerous watersports and a handful of restaurants. It is marketed as a 'paradise island' and is a popular excursion but many travellers find it too touristy and overpriced. The island has a total area of 300ha, much of which has been transformed into the recently built Ile aux Cerfs Golf Course (see *Chapter 4, Golf,* pages 89–90).

If you walk far enough around from the boat landing area, you should be able to find a quiet spot on the beach. Once you've settled down, it probably won't be long before a passing gentleman offers you a pineapple or coconut. It's almost worth the Rs40 just to watch him expertly hack the pineapple into the classic ice cream cone shape (see also *What to do*, page 143).

⌂ WHERE TO STAY
Category A: luxury

⌂ **One&Only Le Touessrok** (200 rooms) Trou d'Eau Douce; ☎ 402 7400; f 402 7500; e info@oneandonlyletouessrok.mu; www.oneandonlyresorts.com. This hotel has long been one of the most upmarket hotels on the island and was extensively refurbished in 2002. There is a range of first-class accommodation, including 98 newly built suites on a private island linked by a bridge to the mainland. The rooms are luxuriously appointed with all mod cons and have superb sea views. There are 3 sumptuous 3-bedroom villas with private pools. It has all the facilities you would expect of a luxury hotel and guests enjoy free use of the Ile aux Cerfs Golf Course (see page 90). *Dbl/sgl from €660/445 HB, dbl/sgl suite from €720/485 HB.*

Category B: upmarket

⌂ **Le Tropical** (60 rooms) La Pelouse, Trou d'Eau Douce; ☎ 480 1300; f 480 2302; e resa@naiade.com; www.naiade.com. A cosy, friendly hotel with 58 sea-view rooms and 2 garden-view family units. All are pleasantly decorated and equipped with AC, TV, phone, minibar, safe and balcony/terrace.

The restaurant has wonderful sea views and there is a pool and a gym. There is a twice-daily free boat shuttle to Ile aux Cerfs, as well as watersports facilities. There is a dive centre nearby. It just creeps into this category on price, but is more of a mid-range property. *Dbl/sgl from Rs8,100/5,430 HB.*

Category C: mid range

🏠 **Hotel Bougainville** (50 rooms) Coastal Rd, Trou d'Eau Douce; ☎ 480 2206; f 480 2432; e resa.bougainville@apavou-hotels.com; www.apavou-hotels.com. A recently refurbished, informal hotel. The en-suite rooms have AC, phone and terrace. 16 of the rooms are designed for families (2 adults and 2 children). There are 2 restaurants and a pool. Pedaloes and kayaks are available but other watersports (payable) take place at Hotel Ambre. *Dbl/sgl from € 148/100 HB.*

🏠 **Silver Beach** (60 rooms) Coastal Rd, Trou d'Eau Douce; ☎ 480 2600; f 480 2604; e silverbeach@intnet.mu; www.silverbeach.mu. A fairly unattractive building on a lovely stretch of beach. Rooms have AC, TV, phone, minibar, safe and balcony/terrace. The bungalows sleep 2 adults and 2 children. Facilities include a restaurant, pool, regular evening entertainment and some free non-motorised watersports. *Dbl from Rs4,472 HB (an extra Rs150 per person for sea view).*

Category D: budget

🏠 **Résidence Choy Tours** (3 rooms) Coastal Rd, Trou d'Eau Douce; ☎/f 480 0144. No-frills accommodation in an apt block over shops. The studios are equipped with bathroom, kitchenette and balcony. Excursions can be organised. *Studio (2 people) from Rs850 RO, Rs1,000 with AC.*

🏠 **Chez Tino** (3 studios) Coastal Rd, Trou d'Eau Douce; ☎ 480 2769. These basic studios come with kitchenette, fan, TV and balcony. *Dbl/sgl from Rs700.*

✖ WHERE TO EAT

✖ **Chez Tino** Coastal Rd, Trou d'Eau Douce; ☎ 480 2769. Cuisine: Creole, Chinese, seafood. Unassuming but popular restaurant on the first floor, with sea views. Offers a wide choice of inexpensive dishes. *Main courses from Rs125. Open Mon–Sat 09.30–14.30 and 19.00–21.30, Sun 09.30–14.30.*

✖ **Le Four à Chaux** Coastal Rd, Trou d'Eau Douce; ☎ 480 1036. Cuisine: Creole, seafood. Upmarket seafood restaurant at the northern end of the village serving imaginative dishes. Have heard excellent reports. *Main courses from Rs275. Open daily for lunch, Fri–Sat for dinner.*

✖ **Resto Sept** Trou d'Eau Douce; ☎ 480 2766. Cuisine: Creole, Indian, Chinese, seafood. On the first floor of a Creole house in the village. The owner, Prem Beerbul, also organises excursions to Ile aux Cerfs. *Main courses from Rs60, set menus from Rs200. Open daily 09.30–15.00 and 18.00–23.00.*

✖ **Sous le Manguier** Coastal Rd, Trou d'Eau Douce; ☎ 480 0192/3855. Cuisine: Creole. Tiny table d'hôte restaurant opposite the church, which also offers internet access and fax facilities. Traditional, home-cooked food highly recommended by locals. *A set menu will cost you Rs350 plus tax (15%) and includes aperitif, starter, main course, dessert, wine and a digestif (after-dinner drink). Open daily for lunch, dinner on reservation.*

OTHER PRACTICALITIES

Communications There is a **post office** in the centre of Trou d'Eau Douce. Sous le Manguier restaurant opposite the church in the village (☎ *480 0192/3855*) has two **internet** terminals and **fax** facilities. For details see pages 80–1.

SOUTH OF TROU D'EAU DOUCE TO BOIS DES AMOURETTES

Travelling south from Trou d'Eau Douce, the road heads inland and passes through the village of **Bel Air Rivière Sèche** before turning back towards the coast and crossing over the **Grande Rivière Sud-est**.

At the mouth of the river is a charming fishing village. There is a small waterfall where the river dives into the sea, which is often visited during tourist boat trips. It can also be reached on foot. Follow the signs marked GRSE to the parking area and it's a 15-minute walk.

Across the river is the village of **Deux Frères** (Two Brothers), with another village, puzzlingly called **Quatre Sœurs** (Four Sisters), a little further on. The scenery along this road is beautiful, with sugarcane clinging to the impossibly steep slopes of the **Bamboo Mountains** on one side and fishing boats huddling together in turquoise water on the other.

The mountain range descends to the sea at the headland of **Pointe du Diable** (Devil's Point), where the ruins of French batteries are listed as a national monument. Cannons here date from 1750–80 and were used to guard two wide gaps (North and Danish Passages) in the reef. The devil of this point was said to be responsible for upsetting the magnetic compasses of ships passing the headland.

The road follows the coast around the edge of the peninsula, from where **Ile aux Fouquets** and **Ile de la Passe** are visible. An unmanned lighthouse on Ile aux Fouquets marks the rocks at the southern entrance through the reef into Grand Port. During the battle for Grand Port, Ile de la Passe was captured by the British, who kept the French flag flying to lure in French vessels. Ruined fortifications remain on the island.

Back on the mainland, at **Bambous Virieux** you can see the results of a project to replant mangroves. The British removed the mangroves, which once lined this area of coast, following the malaria epidemic of 1866. Nature trails through the mangrove forest begin at Le Barachois Restaurant and last about an hour.

Close to **Bois des Amourettes** (Young Lovers' Wood) are bulk fuel storage tanks, their installation financed by the Russians. Legend says that French soldiers used to duel over the girls they met here. Swords have been found in the vicinity of the cave and rock known as **Salle d'Armes** down on the sea's edge.

⌂ WHERE TO STAY
Category C: mid range

⌂ **Domaine du Chasseur** (5 chalets) Anse Jonchée; ☏ 634 5097; f 634 5261; e dchasseur@intnet.mu; www.dchasseur.com. Back-to-nature-style accommodation in this stunning reserve in the mountains above Vieux Grand Port. Simply furnished chalets with 1 bedroom, a bathroom, sitting area and balcony, plus 1 suite with 2 bedrooms. Le Panoramour Restaurant boasts superb views (see below). Celebrities have already discovered this retreat but those of a sensitive disposition should avoid the hunting season. Dbl/sgl from Rs4,000/3,200 BB. (See also *What to see*, opposite.)

Category D: budget

⌂ **Le Barachois** (16 rooms) Anse Bambous; ☏ 634 5643; ☏/f 634 5708; www.lebarachois.com. Rustic accommodation near Pointe du Diable. En-suite rooms in thatched buildings on the water with AC and a small terrace. The coast here is far from the idyllic beaches for which Mauritius is known, instead mangroves grow at the water's edge and there is no lagoon. This in itself has its attractions: tranquillity and natural beauty. Shellfish are farmed here, some of which are served in the restaurant (see below). There is also a small pool. Nature trails through the mangrove forest start here. Dbl from €90 HB.

✖ WHERE TO EAT

✖ **Le Barachois** Anse Bambous; ☏ 634 5643. Cuisine: Creole, seafood. Specialises in crabs, oysters and lobsters, which are farmed on site. You can walk off your lunch on the nature trail. Main courses from Rs220, set menus from Rs1,600. Open daily for lunch.

✖ **Le Panoramour** Domaine du Chasseur; ☏ 634 5097. Cuisine: Creole, European, game, seafood. Set high in the Bamboo Mountains, diners enjoy superb views down to the coast. Specialities include dishes using every imaginable part of the estate's deer and wild boar. Snacks from Rs125, main courses from Rs500; expect to pay around Rs575 for venison steak and Rs500 for roast wild boar. Open daily 08.00–16.30.

✖ **Domaine de l'Ylang Ylang Restaurant** Anse Jonchée; ☏ 634 5668. Cuisine: Creole, European, game. Like the restaurant in neighbouring Domaine du Chasseur, the menu features venison and wild boar dishes. A tranquil, pretty location. Main courses from Rs220. Open daily 09.30–16.30.

MARKETS There is a market in **Centre de Flacq** on Wednesdays and Sundays.

ILE AUX CERFS For those whose hotels don't provide trips to Ile aux Cerfs, there are other ways of getting there. Almost every second person you pass in Trou d'Eau Douce will offer to take you there but be wary, as their service may not be reliable, particularly when it comes to bringing you back again. Operators with good reputations include the Vicky Boat (↘ 419 2902) and Resto Tours (↘ 419 2766).

A number of operators offer full-day group excursions to Ile aux Cerfs, which usually include a barbecue and a visit to the waterfall at Grande Rivière Sud-est. Vicky Boat and Resto Tours both offer trips of this kind.

THEME PARK
Le Waterpark and Leisure Village (*Coastal Rd, Belle Mare;* ↘ *415 2626;* f *415 2929;* e *commercial@lewaterpark.intnet.mu; admission: adult/child Rs350/185; open daily 10.00–17.30*) An amusement park with numerous waterslides and fairground rides, located amidst the agricultural land opposite the public beach. Entrance fees allow access to all waterslides but there are additional fees for each dry ride, for example bumper cars cost from Rs50 per ride.

YACHTING/CATAMARAN CRUISES Catamaran cruises and sailing trips frequently depart from Trou d'Eau Douce, usually stopping off at Ile aux Cerfs. For details see *Chapter 4, Sailing,* pages 96–7.

DEEP-SEA FISHING While the east coast is not as highly regarded for deep-sea fishing as the west coast, fishing trips are available. See *Chapter 4, Deep-sea fishing,* page 92.

DOMAINE DE L'YLANG YLANG (*Anse Jonchée;* ↘ *634 5668; exploring the estate on foot costs Rs75 per person (including map) and Rs300 by jeep; tours of the small perfume distillery cost Rs25 per person; open daily 09.00–17.00*) The estate is just off the road to Domaine du Chasseur and is well signposted. Plants such as lemon grass, pink pepper and eucalyptus are grown and distilled to produce essential oils. However, the estate is best known for its Ylang Ylang essential oils and perfume, made from the flowers of the same name. It takes an incredible 50kg of these flowers to make just one litre of perfume (no wonder it's a little pricey). A range of their products is on sale – Ylang Ylang essential oil costs from Rs230 for 10ml to Rs1,580 for 100ml. There is a restaurant specialising in game (see opposite).

DOMAINE DU CHASSEUR (*Anse Jonchée;* ↘ *634 5097;* f *634 5261;* e *dchasseur@intnet.mu; www.dchasseur.com; admission Rs100, guided hike Rs300, quad biking Rs1,000 for one hour*) About 2,350 acres of the Bamboo Mountains form the privately owned Domaine du Chasseur game park and nature reserve. Nature trails wind through the forest, which is home to Javanese deer, wild boar, monkeys, hare, and the famed Mauritius kestrel. The area can be explored on foot or by jeep (except when hunting is in progress). Hunting is also available, with guns and guides provided (see *Chapter 4, Hunting,* page 91). Wild kestrels are fed by the game warden in the car park at 16.00. There is a good restaurant (see opposite) and rustic accommodation is available (see opposite).

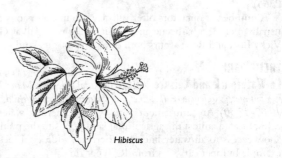
Hibiscus

8

Southern Mauritius

The south extends from historic Vieux Grand Port in the southeast to Baie du Cap River, on the border between the districts of Savanne and Black River, in the southwest.

Saved by a lack of beaches, the south of Mauritius has avoided much of the tourist development that has taken place elsewhere. The southeast is most visitors' first experience of the island, having arrived at the international airport at Plaisance. Many simply pass through the area, returning only to catch another flight, yet there is so much for the visitor to see.

The ruins and monuments around Vieux Grand Port attest to its dramatic past: the first landings of the Dutch in 1598 and the naval battle between the English and French in 1810. Nearby is the south's main town, Mahébourg, a sleepy fishing community crammed with colourful old houses.

There is a small beach resort around Pointe d'Esny and Blue Bay, with a good selection of accommodation. Just off the coast here is Ile aux Aigrettes, a nature reserve run by the Mauritius Wildlife Foundation, which is well worth a visit.

Savanne is the southernmost district of Mauritius, stretching westwards from the sugar-growing village of Savannah along a coast that is the island's most rugged. Cane fields interspersed with fishing villages dominate the coast, while the interior around Grand Bois is tea-growing country. In 2004, this area changed for ever when the Bel Ombre Sugar Estate, prompted by the downturn in the sugar industry, allowed three upmarket hotels to be built on some of its coastal land. Thankfully the hotels were built in such a way as to minimise any negative impact on the local area and the community. For visitors looking for tranquillity, the area now offers a peaceful alternative to the north and east coasts.

VIEUX GRAND PORT AND MAHEBOURG

Vieux Grand Port was named Warwyck Bay in 1598 by the Dutch, who made two attempts to establish a colony here before they left in 1710. The French named the bay Port Bourbon and planned to have the headquarters of the French East India Company there, although after a feasibility study they chose Port Louis instead.

Port Bourbon then became Port Sud-est and slipped into decline. Governor Decaen visited the harbour in 1804 and sensed its vulnerability. He abandoned the manning of the old Dutch posts and built a new town on the opposite side of the bay. Mahébourg, after Mahé de Labourdonnais, was his original name for this new town but he soon changed it for reasons of diplomacy to Port Imperial. He renamed Port Louis at the same time, as Port Napoleon.

When the British tried to take Grand Port in August 1810 they were soundly beaten. Both sides used subterfuge but the French were more successful. They managed to move the buoys marking the passage through the reef, causing British vessels to run aground. The victory of the French is recorded at the Arc de

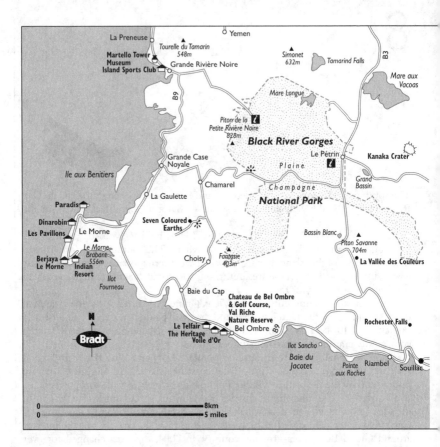

Triomphe in Paris. Four months later, however, the island capitulated and Port Imperial became Mahébourg again.

The barracks master at Mahébourg from before 1837 and until at least 1858 was a Waterloo veteran called J S Sedley (1794–1867). Mr Sedley was said to be a son of the Duke of Kent and thus an elder half-brother of Queen Victoria. Since he lived in Mahébourg for so long, it is possible he left descendants, who could be distant cousins of the British (and many other) royal families.

The crouching lion of **Lion Mountain** (480m) guards the bay around **Vieux Grand Port**, the site of the first Dutch settlement. Some of the oldest buildings in Mauritius, with foundations dating back to the 17th century, are to be found in this town. The ruins of the Dutch **Fort Frederick Hendrik** are located in a park at the northern end of the town. The park also contains the **Frederick Hendrik Museum**, which tells the story of the Dutch on the island (see *What to see*, page 154).

About 3km south of Vieux Grand Port, on the coastal side of the road at **Ferney**, is an obelisk, erected on 20 September 1948, to commemorate the landing of the Dutch 350 years before to the day. Bodies of the Dutch settlers are buried at the foot of Lion Mountain.

Mahébourg (pronounced *Mayberg* by some, *Mah-ay-bour* by others) is the main town in the south of the island, a laid-back fishing community of some 20,000. Its development suffered through the malaria epidemic in 1866 which drove coastal town-dwellers to the hills.

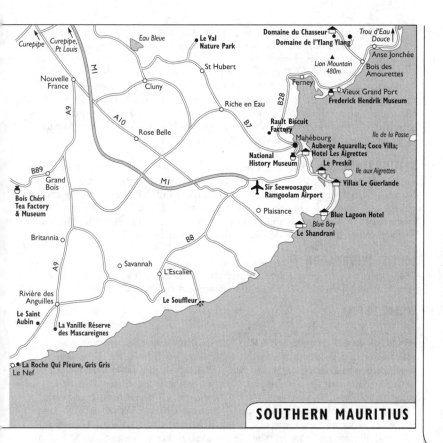

SOUTHERN MAURITIUS

However, Mahébourg has prospered since it was described in a 1973 guide as 'a down-at-heel town lined with small shops where friendliness of service has to substitute for sophistication of goods'. Rue Shivananda has recently acquired a rather smart **promenade** (Esplanade Sir Charles Gaëtan Duval), which, provided it's one of Mahébourg's rare non-windy days, is a good spot from which to watch the fishermen.

The **market** is between Rue de la Colonie and Rue de Labourdonnais, at the northern end of town. The **police station**, **banks** and **petrol station** are on Rue des Créoles, which is a continuation of Royal Road.

One of the town's main attractions is the **National History Museum** (formerly the Mahébourg Naval and Historical Museum), which lies about 1km south of Mahébourg on the main road (see *What to see*, pages 154–5). About 1km north of Mahébourg is the **Rault Biscuit Factory**, which has been producing manioc biscuits since 1870. The short guided tour is fascinating (see *What to see*, page 155).

On a headland at the northern end of Rue Shivananda is **Pointe des Régates**, where there is a memorial to the French and English killed 'during the engagement off Ile de la Passe 20–28 August 1810'. This was erected in 1899 and lists the names of the vessels that took part.

To the south of Mahébourg lies **Ile aux Aigrettes**, an island nature reserve managed by the Mauritius Wildlife Foundation. Many of the plants found there grow nowhere else and there is a good chance of seeing pink pigeons, one of the rarest birds in the world. (See also pages 35–6 and 154.)

Blue Bay, to the south of Mahébourg, offers a good beach, fabulous lagoon and a range of accommodation. The only disadvantage to the hotels here is that they can suffer from aircraft noise.

The **Sir Seewoosagur Ramgoolam International Airport** lies just inland, at **Plaisance**. It's a small but modern airport with good facilities (see page 59). On the airport site in 1875, an English primary-school teacher who worked in Mauritius dug up the bones of a dodo. The teacher, George Clark, had patiently searched for years to find dodo remains and the results of his work are the restored skeletons in museums around the world.

GETTING THERE AND AWAY The **bus station** in Mahébourg is at the northern end of Rue Shivananda and there is a **taxi stand** nearby. Buses operate regularly between Mahébourg and Curepipe, via the airport and Rose Belle. Passengers can change in Curepipe for onward journeys to Port Louis and the north coast. Direct buses between Mahébourg and Port Louis are less frequent. There are also buses from Mahébourg to Centre de Flacq, Blue Bay, Souillac and Le Val.

TOURIST INFORMATION There is no tourist office in either Vieux Grand Port or Mahébourg but the people are very friendly and helpful. If you are staying in the area, your hotel should be able to offer advice and arrange excursions.

WHERE TO STAY

Category B: upmarket

Le Shandrani (327 rooms) Blue Bay; ☎ 603 4343; f 637 4313; e shandrani@bchot.com; www.beachcomber-hotels.com. The road to the hotel follows the airport runway then twists and turns through sugarcane fields. The rooms, which include 36 family apts, are spread through spacious grounds. They all face the sea and are well equipped, including AC, TV, phone, minibar and tea/coffee facilities. Despite the hotel's regular renovations, some rooms feel a little dated. Family apts are thoughtfully designed, with a separate en-suite bedroom with TV for up to 3 children under 12. Those with restricted mobility should note that there are two steps in superior rooms. There are 4 restaurants, a 9-hole golf course, 2 pools, tennis, watersports, bike hire, kids' club and a spa. Recent additions are a sailing school and a kitesurfing school. Interestingly, there are 3 types of beach: bay, lagoon and ocean. Lots of facilities, but you do get some aircraft noise. *Dbl/sgl from Rs8,840/6,084 HB.*

Category C: mid range

Le Preskil Beach Resort (200 rooms) Pointe Jérome, Mahébourg; ☎ 604 1066; f 631 0774; e reservation@lepreskil.mu; www.lepreskil.com. Formerly La Croix du Sud, the hotel was fully renovated in 2003 and now features Creole architecture. The location is stunning and very private – on a peninsula with views to Ile aux Aigrettes across a shallow, protected turquoise lagoon. All rooms are en suite with AC, TV, phone, internet access, minibar, safe and tea/coffee facilities. There is 1 room with disabled facilities. The standard rooms are small but well decorated. The 'duo' rooms are designed for couples and the finish seems somehow more luxurious than in other rooms. The cottages are great but try to get one with direct beach access if you can. Free watersports include water skiing; there are 2 pools, a restaurant, a gym and a spa offering massage. The hotel is popular as a base for windsurfing and kitesurfing, and as a departure point for trips to Ile aux Aigrettes. Aircraft noise does not seem to be an issue here – aircraft can be seen in the skies above the area but are usually too high to be heard at the hotel. Le Preskil can arrange accommodation at one of their rural lodges (Lodges Andrea and Lodges Exil) for those who wish to trade the beach resort for true tranquillity (for further information, see below). *Dbl/sgl from €180/135 HB.*

Lodges Andrea (10 lodges) c/o Le Preskil; ☎ 604 1066; f 631 0774; e reservation@lepreskil.mu; www.lepreskil.com. The lodges are set on a cliff top among the canefields of the Union Sugar Estate east of Souillac. The lodges are modern and have sea view, fan, tea/coffee facilities. At the time of writing, a pool is being built. Children under 12 are not accepted to stay at the lodges.

Lodges Exil (10 lodges) c/o Le Preskil; \ 604 1066; **f** 631 0774; **e** reservation@lepreskil.mu; www.lepreskil.com. Rural lodges set in the forest near Rivière des Anguilles. There is a waterfall nearby, where guests can swim. As getting away from it all is the aim, there is no TV in the rooms but guests can walk, cycle or birdwatch in the forest. Refreshingly, there is no quad biking or off-road driving – the only motorised vehicle is the lodge's transfer vehicle. Children under 12 are not accepted to stay at the lodges.

Category D: budget

Villas le Guerlande (17 rooms and apts) Pointe d'Esny, Blue Bay; \ 631 9882; **f** 631 9225; **e** guerlande@intnet.mu; www.leguerlande.com. Simple accommodation on the beach opposite Ile aux Aigrettes. Nine en-suite rooms, some with kitchenette. Eight bungalows with 2 bedrooms, kitchenette, living area, bathroom, fan and terrace. Airport transfers are included for stays of 3 nights or more. The restaurant specialises in Creole cuisine. *Dbl from Rs2,070 BB, bungalows (4 people) from Rs3,300 BB.*

Auberge Aquarella (10 rooms) 6 Rue Shivananda, Mahébourg; \ 631 2767; **f** 631 2768; **e** aquarellaamu@email.com; www.aquarellamu.com. Simple but spotless accommodation in the gardens of the Borsato family home on the seafront. Eight dbl rooms, 1 family room and 1 'suite' for up to 4 people. The rooms have en-suite shower and balcony but only the 'suite' has a TV. One thatched bungalow is particularly cute – the one that's almost dipping its toes in the water. In 2005, there were plans to

Blue Lagoon Beach Hotel (72 rooms) Pointe d'Esny, Blue Bay; \ 631 9046; **f** 631 9045; **e** blbhotel@intnet.mu; www.bluelagoonbeachhotel.com. In pleasant gardens overlooking the lagoon, just 10km from the airport. Clean, colourfully decorated en-suite rooms with AC, TV, phone, minibar, safe and balcony/terrace. The restaurant offers a range of cuisine and BBQs are held by the pool. There are some free non-motorised watersports, tennis court and regular excursions. Gets some noise from the airport. *Dbl/sgl from Rs3,740/2,470 HB.*

install AC in some rooms. B/fast is served in the dining room overlooking the bay. Traditional Mauritian evening meals can be provided if booked in advance. Airport transfers and excursions can be arranged. Good value for money. *Dbl/sgl from Rs1,200/1,100 BB.*

Coco Villa (19 rooms) Rue Shivananda, Mahébourg; \ 631 2192; **f** 631 2192; **e** cocovilla20@hotmail.com; www.mahecocovillas.net. An unattractive 3-storey block on the seafront with 17 dbl en-suite rooms and 2 2-bedroom self-catering apts. The apts and most rooms have a balcony with sea view. It lacks character, is run down and we have heard mixed reports about the service. *Dbl/sgl from €33/24 BB.*

Hotel les Aigrettes (19 rooms) Rue Chaland, Mahébourg; \/f 631 9094; **e** saidadhoomun@hotmail.com. A hotel in the centre of town. Rooms have AC, TV, phone and balcony. There is a restaurant and excursions can be arranged. *Dbl/sgl from €20/15 BB.*

✕ WHERE TO EAT
There are a dozen or more snack vendors around the bus station in Mahébourg and in front of the nearby vegetable market.

✕ Restaurant Le Phare Rue Shivananda, Mahébourg; \ 631 9728. Cuisine: European, Indian, Creole, seafood. Near the junction with Rue Suffren, opposite the promenade. The most upmarket place to eat in Mahébourg. *Mains from Rs225. Open daily for lunch and dinner daily, closed Sun in June and July.*

✕ Monte Carlo Rue de la Passe, Mahébourg; \ 631 7449. Cuisine: European, Chinese, seafood. Relaxed restaurant near the bus station. *Main courses from Rs150. Open daily for lunch and dinner.*

✕ Le Jardin de Beau Vallon Beau Vallon; \/f 631

2850; **e** beauvallon.fvl@intnet.mu. Cuisine: Creole, European. A table d'hôte restaurant in a refurbished colonial house set in pleasant, peaceful gardens between the SSR International Airport and Mahébourg. *Prices are mid range. Open daily 09.00–22.00. Reservation recommended.*

✕ Chez Patrick Royal Rd; \ 631 9298. Cuisine: Creole, Chinese, Italian. Popular with locals for its traditional Creole dishes. *Snacks from Rs60, salads from Rs70, main courses from Rs100. Open daily for lunch and dinner. Reservation recommended.*

OTHER PRACTICALITIES

Communications The **post office** is on Rue des Créoles. For **internet access** try **Cybersurf Internet Exchange** on Rue Labourdonnais (\ *631 4247*). For details see pages 80–1.

Heading southwest towards Souillac from the busy area around the airport, you step back into a far more traditional, rural Mauritius of cane fields and small village communities.

The village of **L'Escalier** takes its name from Baron Daniel l'Escalier, a French officer. There is a road here, which winds through the Savinia sugar plantation to **Le Souffleur**, a blowhole formed in the rocks of the coast. (See *What to see*, page 155.)

Rivière des Anguilles (Eel River) has the atmosphere of a country village, with plenty of fruit and vegetable stalls and pavement vendors. There is even what could be the smallest discotheque in the world, a room open to the street, only large enough for an old-fashioned jukebox and two youngsters dancing carefully in front of it. Just south of the town is **La Vanille Réserve des Mascareignes**, formerly known as the La Vanille Crocodile and Tortoise Park (see *What to see*, pages 155–6).

North of Rivière des Anguilles is the immaculately maintained **Britannia Sugar Estate** (part of the Lonrho group). In front of the estate factory are neat ornamental gardens and orderly fields of miniature pineapples, part of the estate's diversification programme. The odour of warm sugar pervades the air and workers swathed in protective clothing tend the sugar crop.

Further north on the main road (A9) is the turning to **Grand Bois**, which is surrounded by fields of tea bushes belonging to the **Bois Chéri Tea Estate**. One can only marvel at the women who work in the fields plucking the tea leaves with mechanical precision. Their speed and dexterity is even more amazing when you consider how meagre the rewards are. They work from 04.00 to midday and are paid about Rs3 per kg picked, which on a good day may be 80–100kg. Some of the ladies have become tired of being the subject of countless photographs, so it is advisable to ask permission. The leaves they pick are transported to the nearby Bois Chéri Tea Factory, which has produced tea since 1892. It is worth taking a guided tour of the factory and museum, followed by a tea tasting. (For details see *What to see*, page 157.)

Off the road to Souillac, 2km south of Rivière des Anguilles, is **Le Saint Aubin**, an attractive colonial house built in 1819, which has been transformed into a wonderful restaurant (see opposite). You can also visit the anthurium nursery, learn about vanilla and rum production and enjoy the tropical gardens (see page 157). The anthuriums are of the *andreanium* type and have been grown in the region for nearly 200 years, but it is only during the past 30 years that the growing of anthuriums has become the first horticultural industry in Mauritius. The wax-like leaf (actually the flower spathe) is normally pink although some varieties are blood red and others white. The plants, which bloom all year, are grown in humid, warm conditions under vast awnings of netting. Each year the nursery, one of a dozen on the island, exports 600,000 flowers to Europe, Réunion and South Africa. Flat boxes of anthuriums can be bought at florists and at the airport by departing visitors.

The fishing town of **Souillac** lies midway between the east and west corners of the island. It is named after Vicomte de Souillac, governor of Mauritius from 1779 to 1787, who encouraged settlers to develop the south of the island. There is a ponderous Roman Catholic church here, along with a village market and the **Telfair Gardens**.

Charles Telfair was a British planter who arrived with Governor Farquhar in 1810 and took over the sugar factory at Bel Ombre. He published pamphlets on his enlightened treatment of slaves which only won him censure from abolitionists.

He was a keen amateur botanist. The garden bearing his name is somewhat windswept and bereft of charm, being mostly lawn, badamier (Indian almond) and banyan (*Ficus benghalensis*) trees. There are pavilions for picnics, but bathing in the sea below the garden is dangerous because of currents.

Just east of Souillac, at **Le Nef**, is the site of the house where **Robert Edward Hart**, half-French, half-Irish Mauritian poet and writer, spent his last years. In 1967, the house was turned into an evocative free **museum**. In 2002, the Mauritius Museums Council was forced to rebuild the house because of its poor condition, however it has been kept as close to the original as possible. (See *What to see*, pages 156–7.)

Hart is buried in the cemetery on the point across the bay. He shares it with Baron d'Unienville, a 19th-century historian, and with a number of British and French soldiers and drowned seamen whose tombs have been defaced by the fierceness of the elements. Bones were even scattered around the graveyard by the cyclone of 1962.

Inland from Souillac are **Rochester Falls**. The falls are signed from the main road just west of Souillac and reached on foot by following signposts through cane fields. Fed by water flowing down from the Savanne Mountains, they are not high but reveal vertical columns created in the rocks by the constant pounding of the falling water.

Also inland from Souillac, about 10km north of the town, is **La Vallée des Couleurs**, an exposed area of the stratum under the earth's crust, similar to the Seven Coloured Earths at Chamarel. (See *What to see*, page 157).

On the coast just beyond Le Nef is **Gris Gris**, a viewpoint where black cliffs drop away sharply. There is a beach where swimming is dangerous, despite the apparent shallow lagoon formed by the reef that runs close to the shore. The name *Gris Gris* is associated with local witchcraft. A pavilion (and unsophisticated public toilet) look out to sea. There is also a restaurant, some snack vendors and a small shop selling postcards and ice cream. There are deep chasms in the cliffs surrounding the beach which lead to a distinctive headland known as **La Roche Qui Pleure** (The Crying Rock), so called because one of the rocks here is said to resemble a crying man. You can walk out on the headland to look for the face but take care, as the path is steep and the rocks uneven. The rock that you're looking for is on the furthest point, facing out to sea. When the waves roll in water drenches his face and he is then crying.

8

WHERE TO EAT

Le St Aubin Rivière des Anguilles; ☎ 625 1513. Cuisine: Creole, seafood. The table d'hôte menu uses home-grown ingredients to create delicious local dishes, such as heart of palm salad, freshwater prawns with watercress, Creole chicken with rice and pineapple mousse. A good selection of wines is available too. *Set menus from Rs775. Open daily for lunch.* The *Route du Thé* includes lunch here (see *What to see*, page 157).

Restaurant Le Gris Gris Gris Gris; ☎ 625 4179. Cuisine: Creole, seafood. Small but airy budget restaurant. *Main courses from Rs150. Open daily 12.00–17.00.*

Le Batelage Village des Touristes, Coastal Rd, Souillac; ☎ 625 6083; ☎/f 625 6084; e lebatelage@intent.mu. Cuisine: European, Creole,

seafood. Very good food in an open-air restaurant overlooking the water. It turns into a piano bar on Friday evenings and features a *séga* show on Saturdays. *Main courses from Rs150. Open daily 12.00–17.00 and 18.00–21.30. Dinner on reservation only.*

Rochester Restaurant Coastal Rd, Souillac; ☎ 625 4180; f 625 8429. Cuisine: Creole, Indian, European. The sort of restaurant every traveller hopes to find. In December 2004, Mr and Mrs Appadu converted the front room of their home into this tiny restaurant (6 tables). It is clean, beautifully decorated, has a well-stocked bar and serves a wide range of delicious traditional food. Excellent value. *Main courses from Rs250. Open daily 11.00–15.00 and 18.00–21.30.*

The village of **Riambel** is said to derive its name from the Malagasy word for 'sunny beach'. It marks the beginning of a long rugged beach that stretches up to **Pointe aux Roches**. Swimming here is dangerous because of currents and rocks – the signs on the beach leave you in no doubt, 'if you bathe here, you may be drowned'.

Just off Pointe aux Roches, in **Baie du Jacotet**, is **Ilot Sancho**. During the preliminary forages of the British in 1810, the French battery on this coral islet was captured and a French colonist taken hostage in exchange for supplies. Rumours of treasure buried on the island have never been proved. It is now covered in scrub.

The road continues along the coast, passing through yet more cane fields and fishing villages. Close to the **St Martin Cemetery** is a cairn monument recalling the landing of survivors from the wreck of the steamer *Trevessa*, which foundered in 1923 on its way to Australia. The cigarette-tin lid which was the measure for the daily water ration of the survivors during their ordeal at sea is an exhibit at the National History Museum (see *What to see*, pages 154–5).

As you continue along the coast, you enter the domain of the **Bel Ombre Sugar Estate**. The Bel Ombre factory has now closed, although sugarcane is still grown here and transported to other factories for processing. In 2004, the estate allowed three luxury hotels to be built on some of its coastal land, along with a championship **golf course** (see page 90). The development of this area has included a new road, making this part of the island more accessible. The **Château de Bel Ombre**, a colonial house across the road from the coast, has been converted into a restaurant (see opposite). Although there was some objection from local communities to the tourism development of the area, this appears to have been controlled by a government policy of compensation and a requirement for the hotels to recruit at least 40% of their staff from the area.

Hills roll down to the scruffy beach at **Baie du Cap**. A church on a hillock overlooks the sea here, which is shallow for a long way out. There is also a picnic pavilion and a quiet beachside village, whose inhabitants work in the cane fields or as fishermen. On the road to **Choisy**, a village in the hills behind Baie du Cap, there are good views of the sea; look back before you get to **Chamarel**.

The boundary with the Black River district is the Rivière du Cap, which reaches the sea at the long inlet of Maconde.

WHERE TO STAY
Category B: upmarket

La Voile d'Or Hotel and Spa (181 rooms) Allée des Cocotiers, Bel Ombre; ☎ 623 5000; f 623 5001; e info@voiledor.com; www.voiledor.com. This hotel has an atmosphere of grandeur and is reminiscent of a Moorish palace, thanks to the Arabic and Portuguese theme used in the design. The rooms and suites have an exotic flavour and all the facilities of a top-class hotel. The hotel is family friendly – unlike most upmarket hotels, it offers family rooms and over 50% of rooms are interconnecting. However, couples needn't fear that their holiday will be ruined by other people's children – an effort is made to keep one side of the hotel, including one pool, for couples. The spa is impressive and continues the Arabic/Portuguese theme. There are several pools, including one in the kids' club, tennis courts, the usual free watersports, mini-golf, gym and a beauty salon, where Tina draws exquisite *mehendi* (see page 156). Guests can even produce their own mementos in the pottery workshop or blend their own perfume at the perfumery. Guests in club rooms and suites have access to the executive club facilities, namely a colonial clubhouse with pool and business facilities. There are 3 restaurants, including the sophisticated Le Gavroche des Tropiques (see opposite). The 4 bars include a circular den contained in one of the turrets of the building, which doubles as a nightclub. *Dbl/sgl from Rs12,000/7,800 HB, family rooms from Rs17,400.*

The Heritage Golf & Spa Resort (160 rooms) Coastal Rd, Bel Ombre; ☎ 601 1500; ℹ 601 1515; e heritage@veranda-resorts.com; www.veranda-resorts.com. The Veranda Group's flagship hotel, on the Bel Ombre Sugar Estate. The African-inspired design is used to great effect throughout, from the bedrooms to the spa. There are 154 rooms, 5 suites and 1 villa with private pool. The standard rooms have a suite-like feel, with first-class facilities and a large balcony/terrace. Facilities include 3 bars, 3 restaurants, 2 pools, tennis, gym, watersports, a hairdresser, a kids' club and a nursery. The spa offers all manner of pampering — massage, relaxation areas, pools, steam rooms and a sauna. For golfers, the stunning Château de Bel Ombre golf course opposite the hotel will be hard to resist (see page 90). Excursions to the Val Riche Nature Reserve behind the hotel are also popular with guests (see page 154). Unusually for a hotel of this quality, a premium all-inclusive (AI) package is available, which includes wine and spirits, a daily massage at the spa, golf, scuba diving, dinner once a week at La Compagnie des Comptoir fine-dining restaurant and an excursion to Val Riche. If you plan to indulge yourself while in Mauritius, the AI package could be a very economical way of doing so. *Dbl/sgl from €320/225 HB or from €560/345 AI.*

Le Telfair (158 rooms) Coastal Rd, Bel Ombre; ☎ 601 5500; ℹ 601 5555; e info@letelfair.com; www.letelfair.com. Set on the Bel Ombre Sugar Estate, everything about this hotel evokes colonial times, giving the impression you are a guest at the vast home of a wealthy, 19th-century sugar baron. The hotel is built on either side of the Citronniers River and is spread over 15ha. The rooms are housed in 2-storey villas of 6 or 8 rooms, which means the hotel is unlikely to feel crowded. All of the rooms are enormous and unusually light and airy; they feature AC, TV, DVD, phone, safe, minibar, tea/coffee facilities and balcony/terrace. There are 3 impressive restaurants, where food is prepared in front of the diners. Some will be relieved to find there are no buffets. Don't miss the sophisticated Cavendish Bar, complete with pianist, cigar lounge and reading area. The facilities are first class: a Six Senses spa (one of the best on the island), tennis, gym, watersports and kids' club. Guests can use the Golf du Château championship golf course (see page 90). *Dbl/sgl room from Rs13,832/9,672 HB, dbl/sgl suite from Rs17,472 HB.*

✖ WHERE TO EAT

✖ **Château de Bel Ombre** Bel Ombre; ☎ 623 5620; www.domainedebelombre.mu. Cuisine: European. Creative cuisine in the refined setting of the beautifully restored château, which dates from the early 1800s. *Main courses (lunch) from Rs400, main courses (dinner) from Rs700. Open Mon–Sat for lunch, Fri–Sat for dinner. Reservation recommended.*

✖ **La Compagnie des Comptoirs** Heritage Golf and Spa Resort, Bel Ombre; ☎ 601 1500; ℹ 601 1515. Cuisine: French, Mauritian. A romantic, fine-dining restaurant under the patronage of French chefs, Laurent and Jacques Pourcel. The à la carte menu is creative and the service is excellent. The restaurant is open air, set on a deck over a large pool. *Expect to pay about Rs2,100 for a meal including wine. Open daily for dinner. Reservation required.*

✖ **Le Gavroche des Tropiques** Voile d'Or Hotel and Spa, Bel Ombre; ☎ 623 5000; ℹ 623 5001. Cuisine: French cuisine adapted for the Mauritian climate and produce. This fine-dining restaurant is under the patronage of Michel Roux junior and is based on its namesake in London, where both the head chef and the maître d'hotel have previously worked. *Set menu from Rs1,950, à la carte mains from Rs700. Open for lunch and dinner, closed Sun and Tue. Fri evening – food and wine dégustation. Reservation recommended.*

✖ **Gin'ja** Le Telfair Hotel, Bel Ombre; ☎ 601 5500. Cuisine: Asian, seafood. A stylish, modern restaurant overlooking the ocean, with tables in the sand. Refined, exotic cuisine with an Asian twist. *Reservation recommended.*

✖ **Green Palm** Coastal Rd, Riambel; ☎ 625 7777. Cuisine: Creole, Indian, seafood, take-away. About 2km west of Souillac. There is little choice in the area for those on a limited budget but I have heard very mixed reports about this one. *Prices are mid range. Open daily 10.00–22.00.*

WHAT TO DO

MARKET Mahébourg market is on Mondays. It's near the bus station, between Rue de la Colonie and Rue de Labourdonnais.

SPORTS

Scuba diving Several hotels around Blue Bay offer diving. For more information see *Chapter 4, Activities*.

Sailing/catamaran cruises For details of companies offering cruises and yacht charter in the area see *Chapter 4, Activities*.

Deep-sea fishing The south is less well known for deep-sea fishing than other areas, but it is still available. For more information see *Chapter 4, Activities*.

Kitesurfing Le Shandrani Hotel has a kitesurfing school catering for all levels of experience and ability. For more information see *Chapter 4, Activities*.

NATURE RESERVES

Ile aux Aigrettes (*Excursions arranged via White Sand Tours or your hotel, or* ✎ *631 2396 (reservations); www.ile-aux-aigrettes.com; admission: adult/child Rs600/250*) This coral islet is a nature reserve managed by the Mauritius Wildlife Foundation (MWF). Conservationists are working to restore it to its original state by clearing exotic species of plant and replacing them with native ones. As well as seeing fascinating plants, giant Aldabra tortoises and cannons left by the British during World War II, visitors also have a good chance of spotting rare pink pigeons.

The boat leaves from Pointe Jérome, about 500m south of Le Preskil Hotel at Blue Bay. One of the MWF staff will take you on a guided tour of the island and talk you through the flora, fauna and history. Being a coral island, it is very hot and do remember to take mosquito repellent. There is a small exhibition on the flora and fauna of the Mascarenes, with a disturbingly large section on extinct species. (For more information see pages 35–6.)

Tours start at 09.30, 10.00, 10.30 and 13.30 (mornings only on Sundays and public holidays) and last about one hour. It is money well spent as not only is the tour fascinating, but part of the fee goes towards the continuation of the MWF's work. There is also a small shop on the island, where the money you spend benefits their conservation projects.

Val Riche Nature Reserve (*Bel Ombre;* ✎ *623 5615;* f *623 5616; quad biking and 4x4 tours [3 hours] Mon–Sat 09.30 and 14.30; hiking and mountain biking [2 hours] Mon–Sat 09.00*) A nature reserve of 3,500 acres bordering the Black River Gorges National Park, and which offers fantastic scenery and the opportunity to see wildlife, such as deer and Mauritius kestrels. Activities include hiking, mountain biking, quad biking and 4x4 tours. During the tours, expert commentary on the flora and fauna is provided by a qualified guide. Bookings can be made through most tour operators.

WHAT TO SEE

FREDERICK HENDRIK MUSEUM (*Vieux Grand Port* ✎ *634 4319; admission free; open Mon–Sat 09.00–16.00, Sun 09.00–12.00, closed public holidays*) Charts the history of the Dutch on the island.

THE NATIONAL HISTORY MUSEUM (*Royal Rd, Mahébourg;* ✎ *631 9329; admission free; open Wed–Mon 09.00–16.00*) On the main road just south of Mahébourg is the French colonial mansion built in 1722 which houses the museum formerly known as the Mahébourg Naval and Historical Museum. It is here that, in 1810, wounded British and French naval commanders, Willoughby and Duperré, were brought for medical treatment.

The battle is described in the museum, which contains relics from numerous ships that have been wrecked off Mauritius over the years, including *Le Saint Géran*. The tragedy was the inspiration for the love-story, **Paul et Virginie**, by Bernardin de St Pierre. Paul attempts to save his beloved but, for the sake of modesty, she refuses to remove her heavy clothing and is drowned. Accounts of the shipwreck tell of other women making the same terminal decision.

In the grounds of the museum are the wooden huts of the **Village Artisanal**, which is run by the Ministry of Arts, Culture, Leisure and Reform Institutions. Local artisans can be seen at work and a range of handicrafts is on sale at the National Handicraft Promotion Agency (NHPA) shop (see *Chapter 3, Giving something back*, pages 84–5).

BISCUTERIE H RAULT (BISCUIT FACTORY) (*Mahébourg;* ↘ *631 9559;* f *631 9192; adult/child Rs85/60; open Mon–Fri 09.00–15.00*) Since 1870 this small, family-run business has been producing biscuits made from manioc (a local root vegetable). A guided tour explains the process from raw vegetable to finished biscuit. The staff of six women and two men still do everything by hand. The ingredients are weighed on a set of scales made in Liverpool, UK, in 1869 and the biscuits are cooked over burning sugarcane leaves. The tour culminates in a tasting of the biscuits in various flavours – chocolate, coconut, custard and cinnamon. The factory is about 1km north of Mahébourg follow the signs after Cavendish Bridge (don't be put off by the narrow residential streets lined with corrugated iron).

LE VAL NATURE PARK (*Cluny;* ↘ *633 5051;* f *633 5139; adult/child Rs50/25; open daily 09.00–17.00*) Cluny is on the old Mahébourg–Curepipe road (B7). There are 2ha of palm tree-lined alleys and spring-fed ponds where watercress is cultivated and freshwater prawns are reared. Anthurium flowers are grown for export to Europe and Japan. There is also a deer park, endemic plants and birds and a restaurant.

LE SOUFFLEUR (*Admission: free; open Mon–Fri 07.00–16.00, Sat 07.00–12.00*) The sea used to spout spectacularly from this blowhole at high tide. Erosion has deprived it of the power it had 150 years ago when a writer remarked that 'it roared furiously to a height of fully sixty feet', though it still roars a little when the tide is high.

LA VANILLE RÉSERVE DES MASCAREIGNES (*Senneville, Rivière des Anguilles;* ↘ *626 2503;* f *626 1442;* e *crocpark@intnet.mu; www.lavanille-reserve.com; adult/child Rs180/78 weekdays, Rs135/55 weekends and public holidays; open daily 09.30–17.00*) Located just south of the town of Rivière des Anguilles, the park was created in 1985 by an Australian zoologist as a crocodile farm. Nile crocodiles are still bred here for their skins (there are some 2,000 of them) but the park has grown into a mini-zoo with Japanese macaques, numerous reptiles, deer, koi carp and wild boar. La Vanille also boasts the world's largest captive group of giant Aldabra tortoises (127 adults in 2006). They roam in a large open space where visitors can walk freely amongst them. Watch out for 'Domino', the largest of them, a male aged approximately 92 years and weighing some 273kgs. The park now has an insectarium, where over 23,000 species of butterflies and beetles are displayed. The cool, shady walkways through the lush forest make this an ideal excursion on a hot day. Because spraying would upset the ecology, there are mosquitoes too, but repellent can be bought at the shop, which also sells crocodile-skin goods.

There is a licensed restaurant, the only place in Mauritius where crocodile meat is on the menu. Low in cholesterol, the meat tastes like a combination of chicken

Alexandra Richards

The art of *mehendi*, or henna tattooing, has been practised for thousands of years and is very much a part of Hindu and Muslim tradition, particularly in marriage ceremonies. Immigrants to Mauritius brought their tradition and skills with them, and visitors to the island are likely to see young Mauritian women with their hands and feet beautifully decorated. There is now a growing number of skilled henna artists offering *mehendi* to tourists wanting to follow the trend set by numerous celebrities, such as Madonna and Naomi Campbell.

The origins of *mehendi* are unclear, although it is believed to have originated in Mesopotamia before being introduced to India in the 12th century. The leaves of the henna bush (*Lawsonia inermis*) are harvested, then dried and crushed to make a fine powder. It is then mixed with rosewater or essential oils, cloves and water to make a paste. The henna paste seen in Mauritius uses plants grown on the island. The henna artist applies the paste to the skin in intricate patterns. After a few hours the paste crumbles away, leaving the skin temporarily stained in a shade between orange and brown. The tattoo gradually fades and usually disappears completely between one and three weeks later. The trick to prolonging the life of the tattoo is to ensure the paste remains moist while on the skin. This is done by spraying it with water or a mixture of lemon juice and sugar.

Mehendi is typically applied to the hands and feet and almost any design can be drawn by a skilled henna artist. Indian and Pakistani designs are often very ornate, giving the appearance of a lace glove or stocking. They traditionally reflect nature and include leaves, flowers and birds. Middle Eastern designs are mostly made up of floral patterns, while north African *mehendi* is typified by geometric shapes. Today these styles are often mixed, and some artists now use Chinese and Celtic symbols.

For weddings, it is traditional for the female friends and family of the bride-to-be to spend several hours, or even days, preparing her *mehendi* and discussing the forthcoming marriage. The *mehendi* is intended to charm and seduce the bridegroom, and in Hindu tradition his initials may be hidden among the designs for him to find on the wedding night.

One of the island's best *mehendi* artists is Tina Ramma. Having learnt her skills from her mother, Tina has been practising *mehendi* for 15 years and has a qualification in the field. She works both from home (☏ *725 8269/626 1954;* e *aramma@sil.int.mu*) and from the beauty salon at the Voile d'Or Hotel and Spa (☏ *623 5000*). Prices range from Rs300 to Rs5,000 depending on the size and intricacy of the design.

and fish. Expect to pay around Rs430 for crocodile steak, sweet and sour crocodile or crocodile curry. The meat comes from the tail of three-year-old crocodiles and is part of the commercial side of the park.

Feeding time (see the crocs leap out of the water for chicken carcasses) is on Wednesday at 11.30. Guided tours on the hour, every hour. Some of the park is wheelchair accessible, including the tortoise area.

ROBERT EDWARD HART MEMORIAL MUSEUM (*Le Nef;* ☏ *625 6101; admission free; open Wed–Mon 09.00–16.00*) This museum on the site of Hart's home offers the visitor a very personal insight into the life and work of this well-known Mauritian poet. In 2002, the original house was destroyed for safety reasons and a replica built in its place. The interior has been left, as far as possible, as it was when Hart died. Quotes from Hart's work are displayed, as are personal belongings such as photographs, a pith helmet, his OBE (1949) and his *Légion d'Honneur* (1950). The museum is next to Telfair Gardens; follow the signs and don't be put off by the route through narrow residential streets.

BOIS CHÉRI TEA FACTORY *(Bois Chéri, Grand Bois;* ↘ *617 9109; factory tour plus tea tasting: adult/child Rs200/90; tea tasting only: Rs115; open Mon–Fri 08.30–15.30, Sat 08.30–11.30)* This working tea factory turns 40 tonnes of tea leaves into ten tonnes of tea per day. Guided tours take you through the whole process, from the drying of the leaves when they are first received through to the flavouring of the tea and finally the packaging. There is also a museum which charts the history of tea and exhibits various machines which have become obsolete over the 115 years that the factory has been in production. A short drive brings you to a chalet where you can taste a number of the teas produced in the factory, such as vanilla, coconut and mint flavours, while enjoying magnificent views down to the coast. Packets of tea are on sale in the shop. Tour buses seem to arrive around 11.00 and it can get busy at this time. It may be wise to phone ahead. See also *La Route du Thé* below.

LE SAINT AUBIN *(Rivière des Anguilles;* ↘/f *625 1513;* e *lesaintaubin@intnet.mu; admission: adult/child Rs200/90)* A picturesque colonial house, built in 1819, where visitors can take a tour of the anthurium nursery and rum distillery. Vanilla is grown here and the complicated processes involved in its production are explained. There is a small shop selling souvenirs, including vanilla, sugar, rum and tea.

The restaurant here is excellent (see page 151). See also *La Route du Thé* below.

LA ROUTE DU THÉ (THE TEA ROUTE) *(*↘ *626 1513;* f *626 1535;* e *lesaintaubin@intnet.mu; Rs1,150 per person, including lunch)* A combined tour, allowing you to visit three sites linked to the Bois Chéri Tea Estate. Unless you are on an organised tour, transport is not provided between the three points and you must make your own way. The route begins at Domaine des Aubineaux near Curepipe, a colonial mansion built in 1872 as the home of the estate's owner. The interior contains furniture and photographs from the period (see page 180). The second stop is Bois Chéri Tea Factory for a guided tour and tasting (see above). Finally, lunch is provided at Le Saint Aubin (see page 151). The main advantage of the combined tour is that it works out cheaper than visiting the three separately.

VALLÉE DES COULEURS *(Souillac;* ↘ *622 8686; adult/child Rs150/75; open daily 09.00–16.30)* About 10km north of Souillac lies this multi-coloured exposed area of earth, similar to the Seven Coloured Earths of Chamarel. It is far less visited than Chamarel and claims to have 23 colours of earth as opposed to seven. There is a walking circuit, a picnic area with views to the coast and a café.

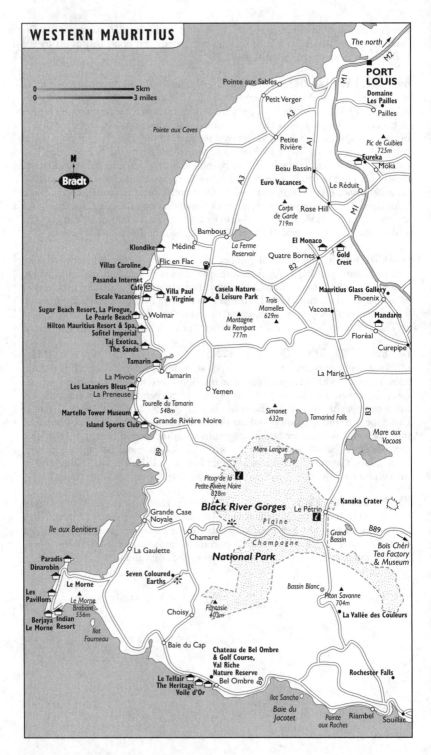

WESTERN MAURITIUS

0 _____ 5km
0 _____ 3 miles

Bradt

N

PORT
LOUIS

Pointe aux Sables

Petit Verger

Domaine
Les Pailles
Pailles

Pointe aux Caves

Petite
Rivière

Pic de Guibies
725m

Eureka
Moka

Beau Bassin

Euro Vacances

Le Réduit

Corps
de Garde
719m

Rose Hill

Bambous

La Ferme
Reservoir

Klondike — Médine

El Monaco

Villas Caroline — Flic en Flac

Quatre Bornes

Gold
Crest

Pasanda Internet
Café

Villa Paul
& Virginie

Casela Nature
& Leisure Park

Mauritius Glass Gallery
Phoenix

Escale Vacances

Trois
Mamelles
629m

Sugar Beach Resort, La Pirogue,
Le Pearle Beach

Wolmar

Vacoas

Mandarin

Hilton Mauritius Resort & Spa,
Sofitel Imperial

Montagne
du Rempart
777m

Floréal

Taj Exotica,
The Sands

Curepipe

Tamarin

La Mivoie

Tamarin

La Marie

Les Lataniers Bleus
La Preneuse

Yemen

Simonet
632m

Tamarind Falls

Tourelle du Tamarin
548m

Martello Tower Museum

Grande Rivière Noire

Mare aux
Vacoas

Island Sports Club

Mare Longue

B9

Piton de la
Petite Rivière Noire
828m

Kanaka Crater

Black River Gorges

Le Pétrin

Grande Case
Noyale

Plaine

B89

Ile aux Benitiers

Chamarel

Champagne

Grand
Bassin

Bois Chéri
Tea Factory
& Museum

La Gaulette

National Park

Paradis
Dinarobin

Seven Coloured
Earths

Bassin Blanc

Piton Savanne
704m

Les
Pavillons

Le Morne

Le Morne
Brabant
556m

La Vallée des Couleurs

Berjaya
Le Morne

Indian
Resort

Choisy

Fantasie
403m

Ilot
Fourneau

Baie du Cap

Chateau de Bel Ombre
& Golf Course,
Val Riche
Nature Reserve
Bel Ombre

Rochester Falls

Le Telfair
The Heritage
Voile d'Or

Ilot Sancho

Baie du
Jacotet

Pointe
aux Roches

Riambel

Souillac

9

Western Mauritius

The district of Black River covers the west coast of Mauritius, extending from the southwest, by Baie du Cap, northwards to the boundary of Port Louis. It was called Zwarte River by the Dutch and Rivière Noire by the French, who created the district in 1768. The river itself is not black, so the name probably refers to the black rocks of its bed and banks.

Black River is mostly mountainous and sparsely populated, its inhabitants employed in fishing, tourism and sugar. It has no towns, only village communities, and is the most 'African' part of the island. Creole lifestyle dominates, with Catholic churches rather than Hindu temples providing the focal point for communities. The region is also famed for its *séga* music and dancing.

The Black River Gorges National Park is by far the island's largest nature reserve. For walkers and nature lovers, the park offers spectacular scenery and wildlife.

The west is the driest and sunniest of the island's coasts and it boasts dramatic sunsets. Its climate, combined with some superb beaches, makes this a popular weekend escape for Mauritians. There is also plenty of accommodation for visitors, particularly around Flic en Flac.

The west is the best coast for deep-sea fishing. This is particularly so around the area of Grande Rivière Noire, where the ocean floor drops away to a great depth, attracting large predators to feed on smaller fish.

MORNE BRABANT TO TAMARIN

The sheer cliff of the square-shaped **Morne Brabant** (556m) rises dramatically out of the southern peninsula, dominating the west coast of the island with its looming presence. The Dutch believed that fish caught from the waters around the Morne were poisonous. Runaway slaves took refuge on it and, in the 19th century, fearing that the police party sent to tell them slavery was abolished had come to capture them, threw themselves off the summit to their deaths below. A sadness haunts the mountain still.

A few luxury hotels now lie at the foot of the Morne; it is a breathtaking setting between the austere cliff and the gentle beaches.

From the village of **La Gaulette** on the coast road, there is a clear view of Le Morne Brabant. The foothills of the island's highest mountain, **Piton de la Petite Rivière Noire** (Little Black River Mountain – 828m), reach down to the road. A French soldier called Noyale retired to the area on the coast now known as **Case Noyale**. He was renowned for his hospitality and built a rest house at **Petite Case Noyale**, but was murdered by runaway slaves.

There is a turning next to the church at **Grande Case Noyale** that leads to **Chamarel** and into the **Black River Gorges National Park**. It is a steep, winding road with spectacular views of the coast, Le Morne Brabant, **Ile aux**

Bénitiers and the countless colours of the lagoon. About 6km from the coast is the village of **Chamarel**. There are two popular restaurants in the vicinity, Le Chamarel just before the village and the Varangue Sur Morne a further 4km towards the national park. Both have splendid views. (See *Where to eat*, page 162.)

Taxi drivers repeat the words '**seven coloured earths of Chamarel**' as a litany that will bring them business. There is, indeed, an exposed heap of colourful clinker on a private estate just south of Chamarel village. The piles are remarkable for being an exposed part of the stratum under the earth's crust. The 'seven colours' are best seen with the sun on them. Some people marvel at them whilst others are disappointed having heard so much hype. Also on the estate is an impressive waterfall, which plunges 100m down a sheer cliff face. (See *What to see*, page 167.)

Chamarel is famous for its **coffee**, although buying a sample is not as easy as you may think as most is sold to hotels or Curepipe supermarkets. There is a shop at Le Chamarel Restaurant which sells it, as does the souvenir shop at the 'seven coloured earths'.

The Chamarel road continues up to the forest plateau of **Plaine Champagne**, at 737m above sea level. A track off the road leads to the **Alexandra Falls** car park, from where it is a 50m walk to the viewpoint. Not only can you see the falls, but also the coast. The area is part of the nature reserve and glimpses of deer, monkeys and mongoose are likely.

Returning to the coast road, mountains are the main feature of the landscape on the drive towards Port Louis. Beyond the Black River mountain range is **Simonet** (632m), in the Vacoas mountain range, overlooking the plain between Montagne du Rempart and Yemen to the sea at Tamarin. By the coast is **Tourelle du Tamarin** (548m), but it is the profiles of the upturned, udder-like **Trois Mamelles** (629m) and the mini-Matterhorn, **Montagne du Rempart** (777m), which are so impressive. They are visible from almost anywhere on the western coast, haunting the visitor with their omnipresence.

In the village of **Grande Rivière Noire**, the Black River Aviary is hidden away near the wooden Creole building which houses the **police station**. Visitors are not allowed, except by arrangement, as this is a sponsored scientific project run by the Mauritius Wildlife Foundation to encourage the breeding of rare species of birds which might otherwise become extinct. However, Mauritius kestrels can often be seen flying around the area having ventured from their nesting boxes.

The road to **Tamarin** runs through salt pans where salt is dried by solar evaporation. The air is despairingly still. The Tamarin peak stands out behind the drying ponds like a giant salt cellar. The beach at Tamarin has waves, unlike many of the northern and eastern beaches, and so is popular with surfers.

WHERE TO STAY
Category A: luxury

Dinarobin Hotel (172 rooms) Le Morne Peninsula; 401 4900; f 401 4901; e dinarobin@bchot.com; www.dinarobin-hotel.com. A brilliantly designed all-suite Beachcomber hotel, opened in 2001. The emphasis is on relaxation and luxury, as is reflected in the sumptuous spa, one of the island's best. The 2-storey thatched villas are arranged in horseshoe shapes facing the beach, each with one suite on the ground floor and one above. The junior suites have a light, airy bedroom and sitting area, plus a huge bathroom. The presidential suites have a separate sitting room with dining area. All suites have a large covered veranda looking out to sea. Rooms have everything you'd expect, including internet access, iron and tea/coffee facilities. There are 3 restaurants, including an excellent Italian, a generous pool and a kids' club. If the calm here becomes too much you can head next door to the livelier Paradis and use the facilities or eat at one of the restaurants; there is a regular shuttle service. Dinarobin is brilliantly managed by the charming Gilbert Staub, former assistant manager at the top-class Royal Palm. *Dbl/sgl from Rs18,408/12,740 HB.*

Category B: upmarket

🏠 **Paradis Hotel** (299 rooms) Le Morne Peninsula; ☎ 401 5050; f 450 5140; e paradis@bchot.com; www.paradis-hotel.com. Renovated in 2001, this huge Beachcomber resort boasts an 18-hole golf course, deep-sea fishing, dive centre and 4 restaurants (see page 162). The hotel is fronted by 5km of beach and uses lots of traditional materials, like wood and thatch. Rooms have the usual upmarket facilities and are particularly spacious; there are also 13 luxury villas. Sports are free, except golf (green fees are around Rs250 for residents), scuba diving, deep-sea fishing and mountain biking. There is a kids' club. Guests can use many of the facilities, including the restaurants, at the Dinarobin Hotel. *Dbl/sgl from Rs14,248/9,932 HB.*

🏠 **Berjaya Le Morne** (200 rooms) Le Morne Peninsula; ☎ 450 5800; f 450 5675; e salesm@berjaya.intnet.mu; www.berjaya-mauritius.com. Malaysian-style 2-storey villas each house 4 rooms. The villas are packed so close together that their dark wood finish and red composition roofs make them seem top heavy in the flat expanse of grass between beach and road. Rooms have the usual upmarket facilities but without the opulence of some. There is plenty of entertainment, including a casino, and a good stretch of beach. *Dbl/sgl from Rs8,760/6,000 HB.*

Category C: mid range

🏠 **Island Sports Club Hotel** (66 rooms) Grande Rivière Noire; ☎ 483 5353; f 483 6547; e islsprt@intnet.mu. Its published aim is 'to offer 5-star personalised service with 4-star comfort at a 3-star price'. This translates into rooms with large bathrooms, AC, TV, phone and safe in villa blocks around a pool. It has a restaurant, tennis courts, a gym and some free watersports, as well as a boat shuttle to Martello Beach. Deep-sea fishing (the hotel's speciality), catamaran cruises and diving are all payable. *Dbl/sgl from Rs4,500/2,925 HB.*

Category D: budget

🏠 **Les Lataniers Bleus** (3 villas) La Mivoie, Rivière Noire; ☎ 483 6541; f 483 6903; e latableu@intnet.mu; www.leslataniersbleus.com. There are 3 clean, simple villas, each with 2 to 5 bedrooms. You can either rent the whole villa or just

🏠 **Indian Resort** (349 rooms) Le Morne Peninsula; ☎ 401 4200; f 450 4011; e resa.indian@apavou-hotels.com; www.apavou-hotels.com. The island's largest hotel carries an Indian theme. This is a mass-market hotel offering innumerable activities. Rooms are equipped with AC, TV, minibar and safe. Four rooms have disabled facilities. Unusually for a hotel in this category, standard rooms do not have bathrobes, beach towels or tea/coffee facilities. It's almost as if standard rooms are designed to be 'no-frills' in terms of service. There are 7 restaurants and unusually guests on half board can eat in any without a supplement. Other facilities include kids' and teenagers' clubs, 5 bars, a fitness centre, a spa and a mass of sporting facilities. The hotel is home to Club Mistral, a kitesurfing school, catering for beginners to professionals. *Dbl/sgl €270/182 HB, family room (2 adults, 2 children) from €338 HB.*

🏠 **Les Pavillons** (149 rooms) Le Morne Peninsula; ☎ 401 4000; f 450 5248; e resa@naiade.com; www.naiade.com. Popular hotel on a good stretch of beach. Rooms and suites are in 2-storey colonial-style villas. They have AC, TV, minibar, safe, tea/coffee facilities and sea-facing balcony/terrace. There are 3 restaurants and a pool overlooking the lagoon. Plenty of free watersports, a dive centre, tennis, a fitness centre and a kids' club. *Dbl/sgl from Rs11,100/7,560 HB.*

🏠 **Tamarin Hotel** (67 rooms) Tamarin; ☎ 483 6927; f 483 6581; e linda@blue-season-hotels.com; www.blue-season-hotels.com. Recently renovated by its new owners, the hotel now has an Art Deco theme. Rooms are spacious, with en-suite facilities, AC, phone and balcony/terrace. The 2-bedroom villas also have TV, minibar and kitchenette, while the suites have a separate living room. There are 2 restaurants, a pool, some watersports and a kids' club. *Dbl/sgl from €154/107 AI.*

1 bedroom. The location is quiet – on the beach at La Preneuse. Each villa has a living room, kitchen, dining area, TV and phone. There is a pool and a good table d'hote restaurant. *Dbl room from Rs2,645 BB, villa from Rs5,750 (4 people) BB.*

✖ WHERE TO EAT

✖ **Epicerie Gourmande** Royal Rd, Tamarin; ☎ 483 8735. Cuisine: European. An upmarket delicatessen selling a good range of tasty treats, most of which originate from France. *Open Mon–Sat 08.30–18.30.*

✖ Blue Marlin Paradis Hotel, Le Morne Peninsula; ↘ 401 5050. Cuisine: European, seafood. Gourmet food overlooking the sea. Upmarket atmosphere, not for the budget conscious. *Main courses from Rs350. Open daily for lunch and dinner. Reservation necessary for dinner.*

✖ La Ravanne Paradis Hotel, Le Morne Peninsula; ↘ 401 5050. Cuisine: Creole. Between Dinarobin and Paradis, overlooking the water. *Main courses from Rs340. Open daily for dinner. Reservation necessary.*

✖ Domino Restaurant Le Morne; ↘ 551 0206. Cuisine: Creole, Chinese, seafood. Popular restaurant on the slopes of Le Morne with superb views. *Medium price range. Open daily for dinner.*

✖ Le Chamarel Chamarel; ↘ 483 6421. Cuisine: Creole, European, game, seafood. You feel perched on the edge of the world as you sit on the veranda overlooking forest, plain and sea. The menu is extensive. It's advisable to book, and tour groups stop here on Wednesday and Saturday from about 13.00. There is a small souvenir shop. *Set menus from Rs665. Open Mon–Sat for lunch.*

✖ La Varange sur Morne Coeur Bois; ↘ 483 5710. Cuisine: Creole, European, game, seafood. If you can get a table on the open side of the restaurant or outside there are wonderful views of the surrounding mountains and down to the coast. You do need to book for lunch. It is a popular stop for organised tours, which tend to arrive at about 13.30. There are usually no tour groups on weekends. *Expect to pay around Rs800 for three excellent courses. Open daily for lunch daily, dinner by arrangement.*

✖ Zucca Ruisseau Creole, Rivière Noire; ↘ 483 7005. Cuisine: Italian, seafood. The Italian chef prepares a good range of dishes, including homemade pasta. *Main courses from Rs200. Open daily for lunch and dinner.*

✖ Niu Ruisseau Creole, Rivière Noire; ↘ 483 7118. Cuisine: Japanese, Asian. Modern, upmarket restaurant offering specialities such as sushi, tempura shrimps and Peking duck. *Main courses from Rs300. Open daily for lunch and dinner.*

✖ Pizzadelic Ruisseau Creole, Rivière Noire; ↘ 483 7003. Cuisine: Italian. Also take-away. Wide range of homemade pizzas. *Pizza from Rs175. Open daily for lunch and dinner.*

✖ La Bonne Chute La Preneuse; ↘ 483 6552. Cuisine: European, Creole, seafood, game. With an unimpressive entrance by the petrol station on the main road, in a shed-like building. Open for at least 10 years, it has a reputation for good food, although some travellers report an air of nonchalance. *Main courses from Rs180. Open Mon–Sat for lunch and dinner.*

WOLMAR AND FLIC EN FLAC TO PORT LOUIS

A few kilometres off the main road to Port Louis (A3), Wolmar and Flic en Flac have seen considerable development over recent years with hotels and holiday houses multiplying at an alarming rate. The village of **Wolmar** has largely disappeared and luxury hotels now dominate this stretch of coast, giving it an air of exclusivity. **Flic en Flac** has a broader range of accommodation and all the trappings of a tourist resort: restaurants, travel agents, souvenir shops and a casino.

Despite the rows of Spanish Costa-style holiday homes opposite, the Flic en Flac public beach remains unspoilt and is a popular place for Mauritians at weekends. There are public toilets and an old lime kiln, and people sometimes camp by the beach among the casuarina trees.

The name Flic en Flac is thought to come from Old Dutch, an onomatopoeic word for the sound of hands slapping goatskin drums. Say it quickly.

The main road to Port Louis cuts from the coast through cane fields, bypassing the smoking chimney of the Médine factory and the village of **Bambous**, named after the bamboos that once grew there. **La Ferme Reservoir** is below **Corps de Garde** Mountain (719m), on the edge of the Black River district. The road continues to Port Louis, joining the motorway just outside the city.

TOURIST INFORMATION There is no tourist information office in Flic en Flac, but the **Flic en Flac Tourist Agency** (↘ 453 9389; f 453 8416; e ffagency@intnet.mu; www.fftourist.com. Open Mon–Fri 08.30–17.00, Sat 08.30–13.00) on the Coastal Road at the northern end of town has leaflets, can answer questions and organise accommodation, car/scooter/bike hire and excursions.

WHERE TO STAY

Category A: luxury

🏠 **Taj Exotica Resort and Spa** (130 rooms); Wolmar; ☎ 403 1500; f 453 5555; e exotica.mauritius@tajhotels.com; www.tajhotels.com. The epitome of luxury. Believe it or not, the most basic accommodation here is a 163m² villa with private pool, outdoor dining area, open-air garden shower, plasma TV, DVD/CD, internet, minibar, safe and 24-hour butler service. The enormous presidential villa is on the beach and has 2 bedrooms, each with plasma TV and DVD/CD surround sound. There are 2 restaurants, including one specialising in Pan-Asian and Indian cuisine. The spa offers a range of treatments, including Ayurvedic therapies. There are the usual watersports, tennis and a kids' club. A hotel designed for relaxation rather than family fun. *Dbl/sgl from € 800/500, presidential villa from Rs4,200 (4 people). Beachfront villa supplement Rs100 per person per night.*

Category B: upmarket

🏠 **Hilton Mauritius Resort and Spa** (193 rooms) Wolmar; ☎ 403 1000; f 403 1111; e info_mauritius@hilton.com; www.hilton.com. Forget all images that you have of Hilton hotels as concrete monstrosities in smoggy city centres. This is a new, architecturally striking hotel with grand gardens and public areas; it is particularly beautiful at night when torches are lit around the grounds. The sea-facing rooms and suites include 2 rooms with disabled facilities. Rooms have all that you'd expect from a first-class hotel and are decorated in neutral colours. There are lots of activities during the day and entertainment every evening. The 4 restaurants include one Thai (see page 164). The spa offers all manner of pampering and there are plenty of land and watersports available. There is a kids' club. A popular hotel for conferences, which are most common between May and September, should you wish to avoid them. *Dbl/sgl from Rs17,120/13,000 HB.*

🏠 **Sofitel Imperial Hotel** (191 rooms) Wolmar; ☎ 453 8700; f 453 8320; e sofitel@intnet.mu; www.sofitel.com. I blinked when I saw the outside of this hotel – it looks like a temple in Thailand. There is a serenity within and, architecturally, it is unlike the usual beach resorts. The rooms and suites have all the facilities of an upmarket hotel, including 24-hour room service. New family rooms have recently been built in a separate area away from the main building. There are 4 restaurants, a pool, gym, tennis, watersports, a dive centre and a new spa. *Dbl/sgl from € 365/260 BB.*

🏠 **Sugar Beach Resort** (238 rooms) Wolmar; ☎ 453 9090; f 453 9100; e info@sugarbeachresort.mu; www.sugarbeachresort.com. Colonial-style architecture and manicured lawns create the desired impression of a sugar estate. The rooms, suites and beach villas are well equipped but with smallish bathrooms in standard rooms. The vast lawns put a fair distance between the rooms and the beach, except for the beach villas. There is a huge restaurant, which makes buffets good exercise, and a smaller Mediterranean one. Facilities include a fitness and beauty centre, watersports, kids' club and teenagers' club. A popular conference venue. *Dbl/sgl from € 290/200 HB.*

🏠 **La Pirogue** (248 rooms) Wolmar; ☎ 453 8441; f 453 8449; e info@lapirogue.mu; www.lapirogue.com. A long-overdue renovation in 2004 has vastly improved this large hotel, which first opened in 1976. The rooms are in cottages spread over a large area. They are meant to resemble traditional fishing boats, although they look more like static turtles. Rooms have AC, TV, minibar, phone, tea/coffee facilities and terrace. There is a choice of restaurants, including the romantic Paul et Virginie seafood restaurant (see page 165). There is entertainment day and night, a popular casino, a new pool and a dive centre. Guests can use some of the facilities at neighbouring Sugar Beach. It remains a mass-market hotel that has hosted such sophisticated events as 'Miss Pirogue', 'ideal couple' and crab-racing contests. *Dbl/sgl from € 270/180 HB.*

Category C: mid range

🏠 **The Sands Resort** (93 rooms) Wolmar; ☎ 403 1200; f 453 5300; e thesands@intnet.mu; www.thesands.info. Less luxurious than many of its exclusive neighbours, but extremely comfortable and welcoming. The rooms are modern and particularly large, with huge en-suite bathrooms (with bath and shower), AC, TV, phone, minibar and safe. All rooms face the sea. There is a spa offering massage and beauty treatments. The pool is fairly small but there is a good stretch of beach. The hotel seems to target couples and there is no kids' club. There are 2 restaurants (see page 165), a bar, a dive

9

centre and some watersports are included. Unusually for a hotel of this type, the Sands welcomes outsiders, including locals, to their entertainment evenings. Friday night dinner, entertainment and dancing are particularly popular with locals, who mingle with the hotel guests. If meeting Mauritians in a social setting appeals to you, then this may be the place to do so. *Dbl/sgl from Rs7,300/4,410 HB.*

🏠 **Le Pearle Beach Hotel** Coastal Rd, Flic en Flac; 📞 453 8428; f 453 8405; e pearle@intnet.mu. This old, tired hotel is due to undergo major renovations in 2006 and reopen as an upmarket hotel, the details of which were unavailable at the time of writing.

Category D: budget

🏠 **Klondike Hotel** (31 rooms) Coastal Rd, Flic en Flac; 📞 453 8333; f 453 8337; e klondike@intnet.mu. At the northern end of Flic en Flac. Cottages house 20 clean rooms with AC, TV, minibar and phone. There are also 11 bungalows with kitchenette (4–8 people). There is a good pool and a newly created beach, as well as a restaurant and bar. Regular live entertainment with a barbecue and séga show on Saturdays. Some free watersports, a dive centre and tennis court. Good value accommodation, popular with German guests. *Dbl/sgl from Rs3,000/2,200 HB, 2-bedroom bungalow (4 people) from Rs2,600 BB.*

🏠 **Escale Vacances** (18 apts) Coastal Rd, Flic en Flac; 📞 453 5002; f 453 5082; e ffagency@intnet.mu, www.fftourist.com. Across the road from the beach. Self-catering duplexes with 1 bedroom, shower, living room with sofa-bed and equipped kitchenette (microwave, fridge etc), AC, TV and balcony/terrace. They sleep up to 2 adults and

🏠 **Villas Caroline** (74 rooms) Coastal Rd, Flic en Flac; 📞 453 8411; f 453 8144; e caroline@intnet.mu. Has expanded over the years to 68 rooms and 6 self-catering bungalows for either 2 or 4 people. Rooms have AC, TV, phone, minibar and balcony/terrace. Bungalows also have a well-equipped kitchen. Public areas are very pleasant, with a pool, open-air international restaurant, speciality Indian restaurant (see opposite), bar and shop. There is a fantastic beach that is separated from the main strip of beach. Live music daily except Sunday and a BBQ and séga show on Saturdays. Limited free watersports but there is a dive centre, where English and German are spoken. Good value accommodation in an excellent location. *Dbl/sgl from Rs4,255/3,450 HB.*

2 children under 12. Six have sea view and are slightly more expensive, but they also get some road noise. Facilities include a good pool, private parking, daily maid service and 24-hour reception. Internet access is available. Clean, modern accommodation, centrally located. Good value, especially for families. *Apt from € 40 RO.*

🏠 **Villa Paul et Virginie** (13 rooms) Sea Breeze Lane, Flic en Flac; 📞 453 8537; f 453 8159; e pauletvirginie@email.com; www.geocities.com/villapauletvirginie. In a quiet spot in the village of Flic en Flac, a 5-min walk from the beach. New owners have completely refurbished the hotel and there are now 12 bright en-suite rooms with AC and phone, each one with a different décor. There is also an en-suite family room with kitchen (up to 6 people). The hotel has a pool, a TV room and a restaurant serving Creole, French and Italian cuisine (see opposite). *Dbl and sgl from € 40 BB, family room from € 80.*

✗ **WHERE TO EAT** For self-caterers there is a **Spa supermarket** in the Pasanda Village complex near the Flic en Flac Beach (*open 08.30–20.00 Mon–Sat, 08.00–13.00 Sun*). There is also a small supermarket next to the Sea Breeze Restaurant on the coast road and another in the group of shops beyond the Flic en Flac Mall, on the way out of town.

✗ **Le Bois Noir** Flic en Flac Mall; 📞 453 8820. Cuisine: Chinese, Creole. Also take-away. For the budget conscious. *Main courses from Rs100. Open Fri–Wed for lunch and dinner.*

✗ **Ginger Thai** Hilton Resort; 📞 403 1000. Cuisine: Thai. The Thai chef here conjures up excellent dishes. Elegant setting with tables indoor and out. *Very plush with prices to match. Open daily for dinner. Reservation necessary.*

✗ **Golden Beach Restaurant** Coastal Rd, Flic en Flac; 📞 453 5620. Cuisine: Chinese, Indian, European. Across the road from the main beach. Smart, airy dining area and friendly staff. *Main courses from Rs150. Open Wed–Mon 11.00–22.00.*

✗ **Mer de Chine** Flic en Flac Beach; 📞 453 8208. Cuisine: Chinese. Small open-air budget restaurant on the beach. It's not particularly clean and is very popular with flies. *Main courses from Rs100. Open Tue–Sun for lunch and dinner.*

✕ **Moti Mahal** Villas Caroline; ➊ 453 8411. Cuisine: Indian. Good food overlooking the pool. *Main courses from Rs150. Lunch and dinner, closed Mon and Thu. Reservation recommended.*

✕ **Le Papayou** Flic en Flac Mall; ➊ 453 9826. Cuisine: Creole, Chinese, pizza, snacks. Also take-away. Simple but modern and spotless with good-value food. *Continental breakfast Rs120, pizza from Rs70, other main courses from Rs140. Open daily 09.00–22.00.*

✕ **Paul et Virginie Restaurant** La Pirogue Hotel; ➊ 453 8441. Cuisine: seafood. Upmarket open-air dining on the beach. *Main courses from Rs400. Lunch and dinner, closed Thu and Sun evening.*

✕ **Sea Breeze** Coastal Rd, Flic en Flac; ➊ 453 9241. Cuisine: Chinese, Creole, European. No view but good food, smart décor and a relaxed atmosphere. *Main courses from Rs100. Open Wed–Mon for lunch and dinner.*

✕ **Spices Restaurant** The Sands Resort, Wolmar; ➊ 403 1200. Cuisine: Creole, French. Upmarket à la carte restaurant. *Main courses from Rs375. Open Sun for lunch, Tue–Sun for dinner.*

✕ **Villa Paul et Virginie Restaurant** Sea Breeze Lane, Flic en Flac; ➊ 453 8537. Cuisine: Italian, Creole, French. Also take-away. A good option with tasty pizzas, grilled fish and paella. Live music Wed and Sat evening. *Main courses from Rs220. Open daily for lunch and dinner. Reservation recommended.*

OTHER PRACTICALITIES

Money and banking The Flic en Flac Mall has a Mauritius Commercial Bank with an ATM. There is also a State Bank ATM at the Pasadena Village.

Communications The **Pasanda Internet Café** at the Spa Supermarket in Flic en Flac (➊ *453 5631*) offers fax, scanning, photocopying, CD burning and international phonecards, as well as internet access. For details, see pages 80–1.

WHAT TO DO

SPORTS

Deep-sea fishing The island's first deep-sea fishing clubs were set up around the area of Grande Rivière Noire as the deep waters here provide ideal conditions. There is now a good choice of operators based in the southwest of the island. For more information see *Chapter 4, Activities*.

Scuba diving The southwest and west coast has excellent diving sites for all levels of experience, including a number of shipwrecks. There is a good choice of diving operators to choose from around Flic en Flac and Le Morne. For more information see *Chapter 4, Activities*.

Kitesurfing Indian Resort at Le Morne Peninsula is home to Club Mistral (➊ *401 4263;* e *mauritius@club-mistral.com; www.club-mistral.com*), a kitesurfing school catering for all levels of experience and ability. For more information see *Chapter 4, Activities*.

Golf The 18-hole course at Paradis Hotel is open to non-residents. A new 18-hole course is due to open in April 2006 as part of the Tamarina Golf Estate and Beach Club on the Médine Sugar Estate. For more information see *Chapter 4, Activities*.

Go-karting/quad biking Available at **Kart Loisir** at Petite Rivière (➊ *233 2223;* f *233 2225;* e *kartloisir@intnet.mu. Open daily from 09.00*). Go-karting costs from Rs440 per person, quad biking costs from Rs1,380 per person for one hour.

Horseriding Available at **Les Ecuries de la Vieille Cheminée** at Chamarel and **Le Ranch** near Rivière Noire. For more information see *Chapter 4, Activities*.

Alexandra Richards

In the early hours of the morning of Sunday 21 February 1999, Joseph Reginald Topize, better known as Kaya, was found dead in a high-security police cell.

His death brought Mauritius to a standstill but, more importantly, it revealed how important it is for the government to address potential racial tension.

Kaya was a popular Rastafarian singer, an important Creole figure known throughout the Indian Ocean islands and beyond. His group, Racinetatane, was responsible for launching *Séggae*, a blend of reggae and *séga*, in the late 1980s.

In early 1999, the Mouvement Républicain (MR) began a campaign for the decriminalisation of cannabis smoking. On 16 February, a concert was held in support of the campaign and Kaya was asked to perform.

The following day, he and eight others were arrested for smoking cannabis in public. All but Kaya denied the charge and were released. Kaya admitted it and was sent to a high-security cell at Line Barracks, known locally as Alcatraz.

He was granted bail of Rs10,000 but his family could not raise the money. Surprisingly, the MR did not attempt to pay the bail, although Kaya had performed for free at their concert.

When his body was found in the cell, it was clear that he had died of head injuries and an autopsy later confirmed this. News of Kaya's death, apparently a result of police brutality, swept through the island. Groups of protesters gathered, and by the afternoon there were widespread riots. Severe rioting continued for three days. Police stations were attacked and buildings set alight all over Mauritius. Hundreds of police officers and rioters were injured during the unrest, many by gunshot wounds. Several people were killed.

News of Kaya's death spread to Réunion too, where I was living at the time, and I vividly remember the anger amongst the Creole population there.

The unrest in Mauritius began to take on a political and racial tone. Creoles vented their frustration at what they considered to be their disadvantaged position in society and rebelled against the Indo-Mauritian-dominated authorities.

Something positive did come out of Kaya's death – it forced politicians to acknowledge the discontent of the Creole community and a government department was set up to address their concerns. The events were a reminder that Mauritius's ethnic cocktail, which is an asset in so many ways, can also be an explosive mixture. It seems that politicians have learnt their lesson and realise that constant efforts must be made to listen to and involve all communities.

Parc Aventure (*Chamarel;* ☎ *234 5385;* f *234 5866;* e *parcaventure@intnet.mu; www.parc-aventure-chamarel.com; open Thu–Tue; reservation necessary*) An elaborate **obstacle course** through the forest, with rope bridges, climbing nets etc. The course takes around 2¹/₂ hours to complete. Wear long trousers, trainers, gloves and insect repellent. There is a minimum age requirement of six years. Also on offer are **mountain biking, hiking, kayaking** and **canyoning**.

SPA TREATMENTS Life Care Spa Club in Flic en Flac (☎ *453 9999;* e *lifecare@intnet.mu*) specialises in Japanese massages and mud baths.

SHOPPING Flic en Flac has lots of touristy shops, selling cheap clothing and souvenirs. There are two shopping malls: the Flic en Flac Mall at the northern end of town and the new Pasadena Village opposite the police station near Flic en Flac Beach. The abundance of tourists in the area means that shopkeepers tend to try it on when it comes to price. A few words of Creole usually do the trick (see *Language*, pages 325–6).

Beyond Flic en Flac Mall, on the way out of town on the right, there are two model ship shops. **Pirate Ship Models** (↘ *453 9028*) has lots of choice and is open Monday–Saturday 09.30–17.30. The smaller **Superbe Ship Shop** is almost next door.

Ruisseau Creole (↘ *483 800; www.ruisseaucreole.com*) is a large new shopping centre at Rivière Noire, which targets the tourist market and well-heeled Mauritians. It opened in June 2005 and has shops selling jewellery, clothing, handicrafts and art, as well as restaurants (see page 162) and bars. The shops are open Monday–Saturday 09.30–18.30.

WHAT TO SEE

MARTELLO TOWER MUSEUM (*La Preneuse Rd, Grande Rivière Noire;* ↘ *583 0178;* e *foemau@intnet.mu; adult/child Rs50/10; open Tue–Sat 09.30–16.30, Sun 09.30–13.30*) In the 1830s the British built five Martello Towers, with sturdy walls and cannons, to protect the island. They were in the process of negotiating the abolition of slavery, a proposition which faced hefty resistance from the French sugarcane planters, who relied on slave labour. The British feared a rebellion by the planters may be followed by a French invasion and so built the towers, which have come to symbolise the abolition of slavery. The tower at Rivière Noire has opened as a museum, where a short video is followed by a guided tour.

CASELA NATURE AND LEISURE PARK (*Royal Rd, Cascavelle;* ↘/f *452 0693;* f *452 0694;* e *casela@intnet.mu; www.caselayemen.com; adult/child Rs150/50; open daily 09.00–17.00 Apr–Sep, 09.00–18.00 Oct–Mar*) Access is off the Black River road between Tamarin and the turning to Flic en Flac. There are 1,500 birds of 150 different species, as well as tigers, monkeys, wallabies and other zoo favourites. Well-known residents include the rare pink pigeon. The layout of the park is spacious, giving shaded walks through the 85 aviaries. Also available are 4x4 tours of the nearby Yemen Reserve, quad biking (Rs1,380 for one hour), Tilapia fishing (Rs35 for ½ hour) and mini-golf (Rs45). The tigers are fed at 11.30.

THE SEVEN COLOURED EARTHS (*Mare Anguilles, Chamarel;* ↘ *622 6177; admission Rs60; open daily 07.00–17.00*) Signed from the village of Chamarel, a track through the private estate leads first to the waterfall then on to the coloured earths. Both attractions involve parking the car for a short walk. The track is lined with the Arabica coffee plants for which the area is known and 'heart of palm salad trees'. The Chamarel Waterfall is the island's highest and tumbles 100m down a sheer cliff face. The track continues to the second car park. A viewing platform allows you to see the denuded earth from on high. Specimens of the coloured earths in glass tubes are on sale in the small shop. There is also a snack-bar, serving simple three-course meals for around Rs250.

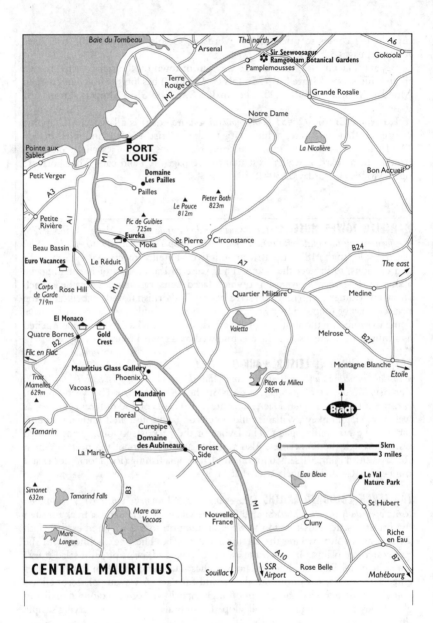

CENTRAL MAURITIUS

Baie du Tombeau

The north

Arsenal

Sir Seewoosagur
Ramgoolam Botanical Gardens

Gokoola

A6

Pamplemousses

Terre
Rouge

Grande Rosalie

M2

Notre Dame

La Nicolière

PORT
LOUIS

Pointe aux
Sables

M1

Petit Verger

Domaine
Les Pailles

Bon Accueil

A3

Pailles

Pieter Both
823m

Petite
Rivière

Le Pouce
812m

A1

Pic de Guibies
725m

Eureka

St Pierre

Circonstance

Moka

B24

Beau Bassin

Le Réduit

Euro Vacances

The east

Corps
de Garde
719m

Rose Hill

A7

Quartier Militaire

Medine

M1

El Monaco

Valetta

Quatre Bornes

Melrose

B27

Gold
Crest

B2

Flic en Flac

Montagne Blanche

Trois
Mamelles
629m

Mauritius Glass Gallery

Etoile

Phoenix

Piton du Milieu
585m

N

Vacoas

Bradt

Mandarin

Floréal

Tamarin

Curepipe

0   5km

Domaine
des Aubineaux

0   3 miles

La Marie

Forest
Side

Eau Bleue

Le Val
Nature Park

Simonet
632m

B3

Tamarind Falls

St Hubert

Mare aux
Vacoas

Nouvelle
France

Mare
Longue

Cluny

Riche
en Eau

A9

A10

B7

Souillac

SSR
Airport

Rose Belle

Mahébourg

10

Central Mauritius

Two districts make up central Mauritius: Plaines Wilhems to the south and west of centre and Moka to the north and east.

At around 600m above sea level, the centre of the island is noticeably cooler and wetter than the coast. Temperatures are generally 3–5°C lower so a visit to the centre can be a welcome break from the heat of the beaches.

The central plateau is characterised by extinct volcanic craters, lakes, rivers and waterfalls. Some of the island's most spectacular scenery lies within the Black River Gorges National Park, which protects Mauritius's remaining forests and offers good opportunities for hiking.

Another attraction which draws tourists to the centre is the abundance of discount clothing and souvenir shops in the plateau towns. These towns are largely residential, linked to each other and to Port Louis by the motorway that cuts through the centre of the island.

PLAINES WILHEMS

Although Plaines Wilhems has had settlers since 1690, officially it only became an inhabited district in 1877. Since then it has burgeoned into the island's most densely populated region, with at least 30% of Mauritius's population living in the plateau towns of Beau Bassin, Rose Hill, Quatre Bornes, Phoenix, Vacoas, Floréal and Curepipe. Historians differ as to how it got its unusual name. Perhaps it came from two Dutchmen, called Wilhelm, who settled there in 1690, or from one Dutchman called William Willemsz, or from a marooned German pirate, Wilhem Leiching, whom the French found there in 1721.

The district begins as a thin wedge between the Port Louis and Black River districts. It follows the motorway southwards, widening gradually around the plateau towns. In the south, beyond Curepipe, it borders the districts of Grand Port and Savanne. The northern part of Plaines Wilhems is largely residential, while the south is characterised by tea plantations, forests and reservoirs.

Plaines Wilhems was sparsely populated until 1861, when a cholera epidemic caused the first exodus from Port Louis of people seeking a healthier climate and swelled the population to 28,020. The malaria epidemic of 1866–68 accelerated the drift.

This migration resulted in ghettos. Whereas Port Louis had been a cosmopolitan mixture, the races here divided to form new towns. Those of French origin settled in Curepipe, whilst the upper class of the Indian and Creole population chose Rose Hill. The division between social/ethnic groups was emphasised by the trains, which had three separate classes, and were used by the plateau town dwellers to commute every day to Port Louis. Now the settlements from Beau Bassin to Curepipe have merged into a single, built-up area, and people travel by car or classless bus. The divisions remain by tradition.

Buses from Port Louis to Curepipe take either the trunk road or the more interesting main road that leads straight up the hill to **Beau Bassin**, revealing Mauritius's own brand of suburbia. The town takes its name from a pool in the area. It has a small municipal park, **Balfour Gardens**, overlooking the **Plaines Wilhems Gorge**, where there is a waterfall. Across this valley is Le Réduit (see *Around Le Réduit*, pages 178–9). **La Tour Blanche**, a white manor house built in 1834, lies to the south of the garden. This is where Charles Darwin stayed during his visit in 1836. At the other side of the town are the island prisons, the police training school and the college of education.

Beau Bassin and **Rose Hill** are intertwined, sister towns separated only by a stroke, since they are run with a joint town hall as Beau Bassin/Rose Hill. They are mainly residential without large-scale industries. Taken as one town, it has a larger population (over 90,000) than Curepipe, and is second only to Port Louis.

Although Beau Bassin/Rose Hill was declared a town in 1896, it was not until 1927 that it was decided to build its **town hall**. This resulted in the series of linked, two-tiered pavilions that lie off the main road just outside the centre of Rose Hill. As well as the town hall, the complex includes the largest **theatre** in the Indian Ocean region, with an extravagant rococo interior of gold leaf and maroon plush. When it opened in 1933, the first performance was a movie and the theatre became known as **The Plaza**, although from 1934 stage shows and cultural events have taken place frequently. There is also an art gallery in the complex.

The **British Council** office and library is on Royal Road in Rose Hill, with a director appointed in 1987 to revive the Council's work after a period of reduced activity. (See page 86 for further details.)

Royal Road is the main street through the town, on which you'll find **banks**, **shopping malls** and **payphones**.

A number of solid Victorian buildings have been preserved amidst the lock-up shops and apartment blocks of this bustling town. Some say its name comes from the rosy glow of sunset on Corps de Garde Mountain behind it, whilst others claim the town, being on a hill, was named after Rose, the mistress of the landowner. **Corps de Garde** Mountain (719m) won its name because a French military post was established on it to control the bands of runaway slaves in the region.

GETTING THERE AND AWAY The **bus station** in Rose Hill is at Place Margéot. There are regular buses from Victoria Square in Port Louis to Rose Hill, and some continue via the other plateau towns to Curepipe. There are also buses linking Rose Hill and Centre de Flacq.

⌂ WHERE TO STAY
Category D: budget

⌂ **Euro Vacances** (12 rooms) 8 Rue Poivre, Beau Bassin; ✆ 466 3524; f 465 1022. Comfortable en-suite rooms with fan, TV, phone and minibar. *Dbl/sgl from Rs750/650 BB.*

✗ WHERE TO EAT

✗ **Le Pékinois** Cnr Royal and Ambrose Sts, Rose Hill; ✆ 454 7229. Cuisine: Chinese, grills. *Main courses from Rs90. Open Tue–Sun for dinner.*

QUATRE BORNES

The main road from Rose Hill (Royal Road) takes you to the St Jean's Church roundabout, where you can either continue to Phoenix and Curepipe or turn right to Quatre Bornes. The town was so named as four former sugar estates (Bassin, La Louise, Palma and Beau Séjour) shared a common four-point boundary.

With a population of over 78,000, Quatre Bornes has developed on either side of the main road as the centre of five residential communities. The emergence of a large middle class in the area is apparent from the presence of modern shops, two bookshops, supermarkets and good-quality restaurants and snack-bars. It aspires to resemble High Street, UK or Main Street, USA.

The **market** is centrally located on St Jean Road, the main road through the town, and is open on Thursday and Sunday. It is reputed to be one of the best markets in Mauritius. There are plenty of discount clothing shops on the same road, especially in the **Orchard Centre**, which is just west of the market. A little further on is the **police station**, near the Total **petrol station**. **Payphones** are to be found near the bus station. The **banks** are mostly on St Jean Road, including a branch of Mauritius Commercial Bank with an **ATM**, opposite the market. There is also a branch of HSBC on the corner of Avenue des Rosiers and Avenue des Palmiers, near the market.

GETTING THERE AND AWAY The **bus station** is roughly in the middle of St Jean Road, near the junction with Victoria Avenue. There are regular buses to and from Port Louis via Rose Hill and Beau Bassin. Buses also depart from Quatre Bornes for Curepipe, Baie du Cap and Wolmar (via Flic en Flac).

TOURIST INFORMATION The independently run website, www.quatre-bornes.com, is a good source of information.

WHERE TO STAY
Category D: budget

Gold Crest Hotel (59 rooms) Georgetown Bldg, St Jean Rd; ✆ 454 5945; f 454 9599; e crestel@intnet.mu. Opened in 1986 as a business hotel, in the centre of town above a shopping complex. There is a lift up to the wood-panelled bar and reception lobby on the third floor. The en-suite rooms have AC, TV and phone, and overlook the central plaza. It has a restaurant (see below) and a conference room. Dbl/sgl from € 48/40 BB.

El Monaco (92 rooms) 17 St Jean Rd; ✆ 425 2608; f 425 1072; e elmo@intnet.mu; www.el-monaco.com. Set back from the main road, the hotel is a warren of en-suite rooms of different vintages (the hotel was begun in 1971), with fan, TV and phone. It has a restaurant, pool and conference room. A basic hotel catering for tour groups from Réunion. Dbl/sgl from Rs1,265/1,035 BB.

WHERE TO EAT

Le Bon Choix St Jean Rd; ✆ 465 3856. Cuisine: Creole. Popular restaurant serving reasonably priced food. Main courses from Rs140. Open daily for lunch and dinner.

Rolly's Steak & Seafood House St Jean Rd; ✆ 464 8264. Cuisine: European, Chinese, grills. On the first floor of the building next to the Gold Crest. Serves good steaks imported from Australia. Mid range in price and quality. Open daily for lunch and dinner.

Happy Valley St Jean Rd; ✆ 454 9208. Cuisine:

Chinese. Eat-in and take-away. Main courses from Rs150. Open Mon–Sat for lunch and dinner.

King Dragon La Louise; ✆ 424 7888. Cuisine: Chinese. At the west end of St Jean Rd. Clean and pleasant. Main courses from Rs150. Open Wed–Mon for lunch and dinner.

Gold Crest Hotel St Jean Rd; ✆ 454 5945. Cuisine: Indian, Chinese, Creole, European. Pleasant AC restaurant serving a wide range of dishes. Main courses from Rs200. Open daily for lunch and dinner.

OTHER PRACTICALITIES

Communications Orchard Cybercafé (✆ 424 0575) is in the Orchard Centre. There is also an internet café in the **town hall** on St Jean Road (✆ 454 8054). For details see pages 80–1.

South of Quatre Bornes lies another residential area, **Vacoas** (pronounced Vak-wa). It was named 'Les Vacoas' in the 18th century after the pandanus trees (known locally as vacoas) that grew in the region.

A sister town of Phoenix, it obtained municipal status in 1968. Residential and agricultural, it produces mainly vegetables and has some light industry. The heart of the town is a crossroads with a **taxi stand**, a **public toilet**, a **petrol station** and the **municipality building**.

The British presence in Mauritius lingered on at Vacoas with a land-based communications station on St Paul Avenue, and with British instructors training the men of the Special Mobile Force, which has its headquarters in Vacoas. The frightfully British **Gymkhana Club** on Suffolk Road originally opened in 1849 as a polo club for officers. It now has an 18-hole golf course (see page 90), tennis courts, swimming pool, squash courts, gym, snooker table and a modern clubhouse with a view of the golf course. It also has a restaurant with a stage, a lounge bar and library. The atmosphere is of a well-run establishment with dedicated, long-serving staff. Temporary membership is available to visitors on a daily or monthly basis.

Phoenix is an industrial area, with Mauritius Breweries producing their Phoenix and Stella beers at **Pont Fer**. Maurifoods is also there, and the colonial house close to its factory complex is the Phoenix Youth Training Centre. Pont Fer also has a **Mauritius Glass Gallery** workshop, where bottles, lamps and ornaments are made from recycled glass (see *What to see*, page 179).

✗ **WHERE TO EAT** On the road to Floréal from Phoenix there is a **Continent supermarket**.

✗ **Mandarin Restaurant** Royal Rd, Vacoas; ✆ 696 4551. Cuisine: Chinese. Popular restaurant with tables around a dance floor. *Medium price range. Open daily for lunch and dinner.*

OTHER PRACTICALITIES

Communications **Cyber Surfer** internet café (✆ *696 4878*) on Avenue St Paul in Vacoas offers internet access at reasonable rates. For details see pages 80–1.

FLORÉAL

Members of the diplomatic corps live in Floréal, in country houses set in large gardens on leafy lanes, which give the English stranger the impression of being in Haslemere. Appropriately, the British High Commissioner resides here but the main consular office is now on the seventh floor of the Cascades Building, Edith Cavell Street, Port Louis. Floréal is a comparatively new community, having been begun by Governor Hesketh Bell during his tenure (1916–24).

Bargain-hunting is probably the visitor's main reason for stopping here. One place that is of particular interest to shoppers is the **Floréal Knitwear Factory**, which has a boutique in Mangalkhan, selling export-quality, locally made knitwear.

Floréal Square on John Kennedy Street houses shops (mostly clothing, but also jewellery, art and carpets), a café (see below) and the fascinating **Floréal Textile Museum** (see *What to see*, page 180).

More expensive, but just as popular, are the duty-free diamond shops, such as Adamas in Mangalkhan. (See also page 73.)

WHERE TO STAY
Category D: budget

Mandarin Hotel (98 rooms) G Guibert St; ↘ 696 5031; f 686 6858. An extraordinary-looking bright-pink hotel, built like a castle. It's Chinese-run with an indifferent attitude and is pretty run down. The en-suite rooms are basic and in need of refurbishment. It has a restaurant. *Dbl/sgl from Rs728/504 BB.*

WHERE TO EAT

Epicerie Gourmande Royal Rd, Floréal; ↘ 697 5429. Cuisine: European. A branch of the upmarket chain of delicatessens, which sells a good range of tasty treats, most of which originate from France. *Open Mon–Sat 08.30–18.30.*

La Clef des Champs Queen Mary Av, Floréal; ↘ 686 3458. Cuisine: French with a Creole accent. An upmarket restaurant in a converted house, which caters for Floréal's diplomatic residents and well-heeled gourmets. *Main courses from Rs400. Open Mon–Sat for lunch and dinner. Reservation recommended.*

Koh-I-Noor Réunion Rd, Floréal; ↘ 689 6093. Cuisine: Indian. *Main courses from Rs200. Open daily for lunch and dinner.*

Floréal Café Floréal Sq, I John Kennedy St, Floréal; ↘ 698 8040. Cuisine: European. Homemade meals, light snacks and pastries. *Open Mon–Fri 09.30–17.30, Sat 09.30–16.00.*

CUREPIPE

Many writers have seen Curepipe as a dismal place. Mark Twain described it as 'the nastiest spot on earth'. Michael Malim, writing in the 1950s book *Island of the Swan*, which caused a stir in Mauritius when it was published, said 'it seems drowned in some immemorial woe … stricken and inconsolable'. Mauritians themselves say there are two seasons in Curepipe: 'the rainy season and the season of rains'. In fact, its annual rainfall matches London's. It can be humid ('God – the dankness of it all,' wrote Malim) and temperatures as low as 7°C have been known there.

Perhaps its off-putting publicity is a campaign by residents to keep visitors away. They like their privacy. The avenues of the residential areas are lined with tall bamboo hedges, hiding the old, French-style, verandaed villas, wooden cottages and concrete, cyclone-proof houses. Streets have no names displayed, nor numbers on the houses, so only those familiar with the town will find their way around. It is not a welcoming place, with its grim market building of upturned culverts. The town seems to have no heart, either geographically or spiritually.

Its origins go back to the 18th century when it was a halt for travellers from one side of the island to the other. The usual story is that travellers stopped to smoke there, after which they would clean (cure) their pipes. However, its name is more likely to have come from a village in France. It was a military post in the 1830s and had a small hotel. In 1858, the population was just 200, but an invasion of new residents was prompted by the cholera and malaria epidemics of the 1860s. The population now stands at around 80,000.

The **town hall** overlooks a large compound of open square and gardens with the **Carnegie Library** and the former railway station, now used by the Central Water Authority, close to it. Close by are the Roman Catholic **Ste Thérèse Church** and the **casino**. The formal **gardens**, with lawns, flowerbeds and pathways, soften the administrative square and provide relief from the chaos of the open-air market nearby. The gardens include a memorial to Abbé de la Caille, the 18th-century surveyor of the island, and a romantic statue of Paul and Virginie, which is a bronze replica of Mauritian sculptor Prosper d'Epinay's original. There are other listed national monuments in Curepipe, notably the grim stone building of **Royal College**, the island's most prestigious school, and the **war memorial** in front of it.

10

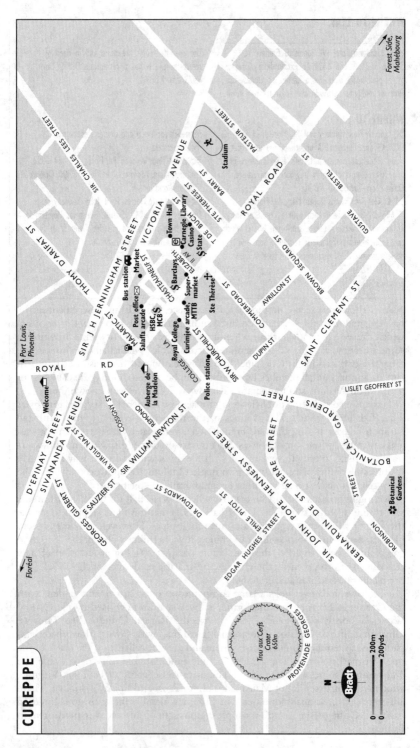

CUREPIPE

Forest Side,
Mahébourg

Stadium

PASTEUR STREET

ROYAL ROAD

BESTEL ST

GUSTAVE

Town Hall
Carnegie Library
Casino
State
Barclays
Market
Bus station
Post office
Super-
market
Ste Thérèse
HSBC
MCB
Curimjee arcade
MTTB
Salaffa arcade
Royal College
Police station

VICTORIA AVENUE

STE THERESE ST
T DE BUCH ST
BARRY ST
ELIZABETH AV
CHASTEAUNEUF ST
J F KENNEDY ST
SIR J H JERNINGHAM STREET
THOMY D'ARIFAT ST
SIR CHARLES LEES STREET
BROWN SEQUARD ST
AVRILLON ST
COMMERFORD ST
DUPIN ST
SAINT CLEMENT ST
SIR W CHURCHILL ST

Port Louis,
Phoenix

ROYAL RD

Welcome

Auberge de
la Madelon

MALARTIC ST

RAMOND ST

COSSIGNY ST

SIR VIRGILE NAZ ST

SIR GILBERT SAUZIER ST

GEORGES GILBERT

SIVANANDA AVENUE

D'EPINAY STREET

Floréal

COLLEGE LA
SIR WILLIAM NEWTON ST
DR EDWARDS ST
EMILE PITOT ST
EDGAR HUGHES STREET
SIR JOHN POPE HENNESSY STREET
BERNARDIN DE ST PIERRE STREET
LISLET GEOFFREY ST
BOTANICAL GARDENS STREET
ROBINSON STREET

Botanical
Gardens

Trou aux Cerfs
Crater
650m

PROMENADE GEORGES V

N

Bradt

0   200m
0   200yds

It is tempting to wonder if the **market** building will ever be declared a national monument; it is certainly a unique feature of Curepipe's skyline, with its concrete pipes pointing upwards. In its foyer are kiosks selling local dishes, with eating booths behind the partitions. The **public toilets** are closed for cleaning every day, 06.00–06.30, 10.30–10.45, 15.00–15.15 and 17.15–17.30. Be warned.

Curepipe is another popular town for shopping. As well as the usual discount clothing and duty-free jewellery shops, there are numerous handicraft outlets, including several model ship shops.

Curepipe has its own small **Botanical Gardens** to the southwest of the centre. The **Forestry Department** (↘ 675 4966) offices next door are where permission can be sought to visit the nature reserves of the interior.

The unsightly spread of Curepipe can be seen from the hills around the extinct volcanic crater of **Trou aux Cerfs**, at 650m above sea level. To get there from the centre of Curepipe, follow Sir John Pope Hennessy Street for about 800m, then turn right into Edgar Hughes Street. It is a short climb to the crater. The inside of the crater is wooded and it is possible to climb the 85m to the bottom. If you've been to Réunion you won't be overly impressed by the crater, but the views are far reaching. The panoramic view takes in the plateau towns and the mountains to the north and northwest, including the three cones of **Trois Mamelles** (629m). There is a meteorological station of futuristic design poised by the crater, as though mooning for its architectural soulmate, the market complex.

On the road from Curepipe to the motorway is the **Millennium Monument**, an 18m-high tower made of no fewer than 3,500 dark blue basalt stones, some six or seven million years old. It was erected by the Ministry of Arts and Culture to 'celebrate the passage of the Republic of Mauritius into the third millennium'.

GETTING THERE AND AWAY The **bus station**, which adjoins the market on Sir J H Jerningham Street, is the island's busiest. Buses from Port Louis to Curepipe leave from the Victoria Square bus station. There are regular buses to Mahébourg, via Rose Belle and the airport. Buses also depart from Curepipe for Centre de Flacq, Souillac, Grand Bassin (via Bois Chéri) and Wolmar (via Flic en Flac). The best place to find a **taxi** is on Chasteauneuf Street.

TOURIST INFORMATION There is no tourist office in Curepipe. There are some travel agents that may be able to help, provided your query is pretty simple. You could also try logging onto www.curepipe.org for information on the town.

🏠 WHERE TO STAY
Category D: budget

🏠 **Auberge de la Madelon** (15 rooms) Sir John Pope Hennessy St; ↘ 676 1520; f 676 2550; e madelon@intnet.mu. Just north of the town centre. Simple but clean en-suite rooms with fan, TV and phone. Good value. *Dbl/sgl from Rs600/550 BB*

or Rs650/600 with AC.

🏠 **Welcome Hotel** (11 rooms) Royal Rd; ↘ 675 3265. North of Curepipe on Royal Rd in the direction of Rose Hill. Basic rooms, some with en suite. *Dbl and sgl from Rs500 BB.*

🍴 WHERE TO EAT
The **Prisunic supermarket** near the town hall stocks all the essentials. For cheap snacks, try the stalls around the market.

🍴 **La Potinière** Hillcrest Bldg, 18 Sir Winston Churchill St, Curepipe; ↘ 676 2648. Cuisine: French, crêpes, Creole, snacks. Claims to be the oldest restaurant in Mauritius. Has a sophisticated summery atmosphere. *Main courses from Rs175. Open*

Mon–Sat for lunch, Thu–Sat for dinner. Reservation recommended.

🍴 **Le Gaulois** Dr Ferrière St, Curepipe; ↘ 675 5674. Cuisine: Creole, French. Great for people-watching because of its corner location on the road leading

175

to the post office and bus station. Table d'hôte and à la carte menus. Plenty of plastic but clean. *Main courses from Rs190. Open Mon–Sat 11.00–17.00.*

✕ **Nobby's** Royal Rd, Curepipe; ✆ 676 1318. Cuisine: European, Creole, grills. *Main courses from Rs220. Open Mon–Sat for lunch and dinner.*

✕ **Chinese Wok** Royal Rd, Curepipe; ✆ 676 1548. Cuisine: Chinese. *Main courses from Rs100. Open Mon–Sat for lunch and dinner.*

✕ **Pizza Hut** Manhattan Mall, Victoria Av, Curepipe; ✆ 670 1010. Cuisine: Italian.

OTHER PRACTICALITIES

Communications The **post office** is near the market and offers poste restante. **Internet access** is available at the **Carnegie Library** (for details see pages 80–1) at a cost of Rs0.50 per minute.

Money and banking Banks, including branches of Barclays, HSBC and Mauritius Commercial Bank, are found on Royal Road, in the centre of town.

BLACK RIVER GORGES NATIONAL PARK AND AROUND

Access to the Black River Gorges National Park from Curepipe and Vacoas is via **La Marie**. There is a memorial here to the hapless English adventurer Matthew Flinders who, having helped explore and map Australia, stopped off in Mauritius in 1803, unaware that the British and French were at war. He was arrested by the French and imprisoned on Mauritius for six years.

Along the road (B3) to the national park are two important bodies of water. The reservoir of **Mare aux Vacoas** is the largest in Mauritius, a mountain lake at 600m above sea level, surrounded by pine forest and traveller's palms. Unlike many of the reservoirs it can be visited by road and is a popular spot for local fishermen. Further on through the forest, where deer abound, there is a motorable track leading to **Mare Longue**, another reservoir. The track passes through the shorn terrain of tea plantations and through woods where monkeys leap excitedly out of the way of the occasional car. It is possible to hike from the main road on forest trails to reach the seven cascades of **Tamarind Falls**. This is a restricted area so permission is required from the Forestry Department in Curepipe.

The main road continues southwards, passing into the Black River Gorges National Park, and reaches a crossroad at **Le Pétrin**. This is on the eastern edge of the park and there is a visitors' information centre here with picnic facilities.

Black River Gorges is the largest national park in Mauritius (6,574ha) and protects the remaining native forests on the island. It is home to many of the rare endemic plants and birdlife, and offers spectacular natural scenery and excellent walks. However, some areas where conservation projects are in progress are off-limits to visitors. These areas are clearly marked. For detailed information, including a map of the national park, see *Chapter 2*, pages 32–4.

At Le Pétrin, the turning to the east leads to **Grand Bassin**, a natural lake in the crater of an extinct volcano at 702m above sea level. It is regarded as sacred by Hindus, who come here regularly to leave offerings of fruit and incense on small pedestals on the lake's edge. Japanese macaque monkeys and birds watch carefully from a distance, before raiding the fruit left for the gods. The lake is also known as **Ganga Talao** (Lake of the Ganges) as the Hindus believe that it is linked to the Ganges by an underground stream. There are temples around the lake, containing ornate statues of gods.

Sadly, Grand Bassin now features on the itineraries of all tour operators and coaches of tourists tend to arrive from late morning and throughout the afternoon. When I last visited in 2005, I was shocked by the changes that had taken place. Scores of tourists were lining up for a Hindu blessing, each returning to the coach proudly sporting a token *tika* (red dot) on their forehead. Early morning and late afternoon are the best times to visit. Shoes should be removed before entering any of the temples.

During the festival of **Maha Shivaratree**, in honour of the god Shiva, is when Grand Bassin really comes into its own. For several days during February/March hundreds of thousands of Hindus make the journey to the lake, where they leave offerings for Shiva and take holy water from the lake to purify their bodies. Traditionalists make the pilgrimage following an all-night vigil, dressed in white and carrying the *Kanwar*, a highly decorated wooden structure which they make themselves. Nowadays it is not unusual to see families making the journey by car but the number of pilgrims on foot lining the roads is still an incredible sight.

The nearby **Kanaka Crater** can only be reached by hiking along a trail off the road that goes beyond Grand Bassin towards **Bois Chéri**. This is the entrance to tea-growing country, with hills up to 500m above sea level covered with the close-cropped bushes. This area is covered in *Chapter 8, Southern Mauritius*.

MOKA

This district is part of a plateau of scrub, sugarcane and, in the midlands area, tea. It caters for the educational overspill of Port Louis, with the University of Mauritius and the Mahatma Gandhi Institute, and also contains the president's official residence at Le Réduit.

Coffee was planted here when it was introduced from Al Makha in Yemen, hence the name Moka. Its boundary runs along the mountains ringing the south of Port Louis to Pieter Both, then skirts below La Nicolière Reservoir, across Nouvelle Découverte Plateau – embracing the agricultural centre of the island – to the outskirts of Curepipe and Rose Hill.

The approach to Moka is by the two-lane motorway that links Port Louis with the residential plateau towns. After crossing the St Louis Stream, the road passes through **Pailles**, a suburban community with a church, temple and mosque overshadowed by **Pailles Hill** (225m) and the peaks of the **Moka mountain range**. The countryside opens up as the road begins to climb, with hills on the left and the flats of **Coromandel** on the right.

Pailles has become widely known since the opening of **Domaine Les Pailles**, an extraordinary creation by a Mauritian who has converted previously unutilised land into a kind of educational theme park. A whole day can be spent there discovering the old ways of living via a series of exhibits that recreate old traditions. There are four upmarket restaurants on the estate, a riding stables and a casino. (For details see pages 178 and 180.)

Further south along the motorway, a road branches off to the left beneath **Junction Peak** to the residential sprawl of **Moka**, **St Pierre** and **Circonstance**. The motorway continues, skirting around the university and leaving the Moka district at the Cascade Bridge. The range of hills between Moka, St Pierre and Port Louis consists of the bush-covered **Guiby**, **Berthelot**, **Junction** and **Mount Ory** peaks, rising to 500m.

Off to the right, just after the road to Moka crosses the rubbish-clogged Moka River, is a lane leading to **Eureka**, a colonial house open to the public and where accommodation is available. Although it has the appearance of a fine French colonial house with its 109 doors and windows and encircling veranda, it was built by an Englishman, with the help of a French carpenter, at the beginning of English colonisation. It gained its name when Eugène Leclézio, a wealthy lawyer and planter, cried 'Eureka' as his bid to buy the house at auction in 1856 was accepted. (See also *What to see, Where to stay* and *Where to eat*, page 178.)

10

WHERE TO STAY
Category C: mid range

Eureka (7 rooms) Moka; 433 8477; f 433 4951; e eurekamr@intnet.mu; www.maisoneureka.com. Accommodation is available in 3 guesthouses and 4 guest rooms in converted historic buildings in the grounds of Eureka, a colonial house built in 1830. The guesthouses are slightly more rustic than the rooms but are equipped with dbl bedroom, bathroom and kitchenette. The en-suite rooms have been refurbished to a high standard and are in a separate building, with a shared lounge and kitchen. Only the rooms, and not the guesthouses, have TV. If you want to escape the heat of the coast for a few days, then this is a good option. On balance, the rooms offer better value for money than the guesthouses, unless privacy is particularly important to you. *Guesthouses and rooms from Rs3,450 BB.*

WHERE TO EAT

Escale Creole Moka; 433 1641. Cuisine: Creole. Delicious traditional table d'hôte menus are prepared using only fresh ingredients. Since it is rare for a visitor without personal contacts to be able to enjoy real Creole food, this is a 'must-try' to complete your Mauritian experience. *The set menu prices are mid range. Meals must be booked a day in advance.*

Le Ravin Eureka, Moka; 433 4501; f 433 4951; e eurekamr@intnet.mu; www.maisoneureka.com. Cuisine: Creole, French. Fine-dining restaurant, which also serves light meals and snacks. Decorated in a colonial style, with some seating by the river. *Three-course meals from Rs690. Open Mon–Fri for lunch, dinner on reservation.*

Domaine les Pailles Les Guibies, Pailles; 286 4225. Has the following upmarket restaurants, each beautifully decorated and serving excellent food. *Three-course set menus from Rs500.*

Indra Cuisine: Indian. *Open Mon–Sat for lunch and dinner.*

Clos St Louis Cuisine: Creole, European. *Open Mon–Sat for lunch, Fri–Sat for dinner.*

Fu Xiao Cuisine: Chinese. *Lunch and dinner, closed Sat lunch.*

La Dolce Vita Cuisine: Italian. *Less formal than the others with a terrace overlooking a swimming pool. Open daily 11.00–17.00 and for dinner on Wed, Fri, Sat and Sun.*

AROUND LE REDUIT

The **University of Mauritius** at Le Réduit was created in 1965 with the help of a £3 million grant from the British government.

Together with a large school of agriculture, the university has a centre for medical studies, a school of administration and a department of law, as well as a school for industrial technology and a computer centre. The student population varies from year to year, according to financing, but is limited to 3,000.

In the same area are the Sugar Research Institute, the Institute of Education, the Examinations Syndicate, the College of the Air and the Ministry of Agriculture. The **Mahatma Gandhi Institute**, for the study of Indian and African cultures, is within walking distance of the Le Réduit campus.

In 1748, the French governor built a small wooden fort, surrounded by a ditch and stone walls, on a 290m-high bluff between two rivers. It was to serve as a redoubt (*réduit*) for women, children and valuables of the French East India Company if ever the island was invaded.

La Brillane, who was governor from 1776 to 1779, added a central block with two wings, and the date of his addition (1778) is carved on a plaque above the front door. **Le Réduit** became the official residence of the governors from then on, with Government House in Port Louis used as a residence only during the winter theatre, racing and social season.

Part of the house was destroyed by a cyclone in 1868 and it was extended considerably during the 19th century, particularly when Napier Broome was governor (1880–83). During his tenure, the first telephone line in Mauritius was installed, to connect Government House with Le Réduit. A special stop was made at Le Réduit by trains bearing officials when the governor was working at home. Governor Bell (1916–24) erected a small, stylised white temple in the grounds, dedicated to the creator of Le Réduit, from 'his grateful successors'.

Camphor and badamier trees line the drive that curves up to the entrance of the two-storied mansion, with its columns, verandas and mix of Victorian and French architecture draped in bougainvillaea. The gardens in the 132ha estate are overlooked by a wide terrace joining the two wings of the house.

The French botanist, Aublet, laid out the original gardens, which were later gradually anglicised by British governors and their wives. One British governor called the house 'our prison between the ravines' and the point between the gorges is called **Le Bout du Monde** (end of the world).

As it is now the residence of the president, the house and grounds of Le Réduit are no longer open to the public. Apparently the president is not keen on tourists strolling around his backyard, scrutinising his flowerbeds. However, there is one day a year when visitors can get past the charming armed gentlemen on the gate – the residence is usually open to the public on the last Sunday in August.

The eastern part of the Moka district is sparsely populated, with **Quartier Militaire** on the main road (A7) the only settlement of any size. It was once a military post offering protection to travellers against attacks by runaway slaves. After passing through Quartier Militaire the road continues to Centre de Flacq and the east coast.

WHAT TO DO

HIKING The Black River Gorges National Park provides the island's best opportunities for hiking and seeing wildlife. For more information see above, *Chapter 2, Black River Gorges National Park,* pages 32–4 and *Chapter 4, Hiking and adventure sports,* pages 97–8.

HORSERIDING One of the island's best equestrian centres is at **Domaine les Pailles**, just off the motorway between Port Louis and Moka. Treks are an ideal way to see the dramatic surrounding countryside. For more information see *Chapter 4, Activities.*

CASINOS The **Casino de Maurice** (✆ *675 5012. Open Mon–Fri 21.00–04.00, Sat–Sun 13.00–04.00*) is near the town hall in Curepipe. **Le Grand Casino** (✆ *211 0452*) at Domaine les Pailles is open every evening.

SPA TREATMENTS Spa Viva at 102 St Jean Rd, Quatre Bornes (✆ *467 8907/8;* e *spaviva@intnet.mu*) offers massages and beauty treatments.

SHOPPING The towns of the centre are now well known to tourists in search of bargain clothing and souvenirs. For more information see *Chapter 3, Shopping,* pages 72–5

WHAT TO SEE

MAURITIUS GLASS GALLERY (*Pont Fer, Phoenix;* ✆ *696 3360;* f *696 8116;* e *mgg@intnet.mu; admission free; open Mon–Sat 08.00–17.00*) The workshop at Pont Fer produces handmade glass ornaments from recycled glass and aims to promote environmental awareness. Glass-blowing demonstrations take place throughout the day except 12.00–13.00 and there is a shop selling the products.

FLORÉAL TEXTILE MUSEUM (*Floréal Sq, 1 John Kennedy St, Floréal;* \f *698 8007;* e *floreal-sq@intnet.mu; adult/child Rs100/50*) The textile industry is a pillar of the Mauritian economy, employing over 250,000 people, and this is where you can see what their work involves. The museum is modern and, in addition to the usual displays, there is a film in English, French, German and Italian. There are guided tours every hour.

BOTANICAL GARDENS (*Curepipe; free; open daily 06.00–18.00*) The Botanical Gardens in Curepipe are a miniature Pamplemousses. There is a small lake in which nandia palms can be seen growing. It is a pleasant place in which to recover from the cacophony of Curepipe.

DOMAINE DES AUBINEAUX (*Curepipe;* \ *626 1513;* f *626 1535;* e *lesaintaubin@ intnet.mu; adult/child Rs200/90*) An attractive colonial house built in 1872 as the home of the owners of the Bois Chéri Tea Estate. Visitors can take a guided tour of the interior, which contains much of the original furniture and family photographs. The guide will explain the history of the family and the estate, as well as significant points in the island's past. There is a small gift shop, selling locally made soap, rum and tea. Domaine des Aubineaux can be visited as part of the *Route du Thé*, which also includes a visit to the Bois Chéri Tea Factory and lunch at Le Saint Aubin (see page 157).

DOMAINE LES PAILLES (*Les Guibies, Pailles;* \ *286 4225;* f *286 2140;* e *domaine.sales@intnet.mu; www.domainelespailles.net; guided tour of the domaine: adult/child Rs95/45, guided tour plus horse-carriage ride and 4x4 tour: adult/child Rs670/335; open daily 09.00–16.30*) Just 3km from Port Louis, this has to be one of the best days out in Mauritius. The *domaine* gives visitors an insight into the island's past, with its recreation of an 18th-century ox-driven sugar mill, a working rum distillery from 1758 and other exhibits, such as aloe weaving and coffee grinding. There is also a spice garden and a tropical forest. It has four fantastic restaurants, as well as a shop, swimming pool and the island's biggest casino. The vast reserve can be explored on horseback or in a 4x4, whilst shorter journeys are made by horse-drawn carriage or the estate's train. Quad biking is also on offer.

DOMAINE DE L'ETOILE (*Royal Rd, Moka;* \ *433 1010;* f *433 1070;* e *cieletnature@drbc-group.com; www.cieletnature.com*) Another estate which has opened to the public in recent years. The forests, which are home to deer and many species of bird, can be explored on foot, and by quad bike or 4x4. Archery is also available, using animal-shaped targets dotted around the forest. There is a table d'hôte menu serving Mauritian cuisine.

EUREKA (*Moka;* \ *433 8477;* f *433 4951;* e *eurekamr@intnet.mu; www.maisoneureka.com; adult/child under 12 Rs175/free; open Mon–Sat 09.00–17.00, Sun 09.00–15.30*) A Creole mansion, built in 1830, which is now open to the public and also offers accommodation in cottages in its grounds (see page 178). It is set in a park overlooked by the Moka Mountain Range and crossed by the Moka River. Visitors are free to explore the grounds and swim in the river, which has several small waterfalls. The house is decorated in colonial style with antique furniture, some of which was produced by the French East India Company. Every detail is designed to take you back to that era. There are guided tours of the house to view the period furniture. A typical Creole lunch can be provided. (See also *Where to stay* and *Where to eat*, page 178.)

Island Dependencies of Mauritius and British Indian Ocean Territory

AGALEGA

Agalega is situated between the Seychelles and Mauritius, west of the Mascarene Ridge, about 1,206km north of Mauritius and 563km south of the Seychelles. There are actually two islands (North and South), separated by a sandbank which can be forded at low tide. Taken as one, the island is 24km long but not more than 3.25km wide.

North Island is elongated and has the main coconut mill on it; pear-shaped South Island is used as the administrative centre. There are nearly 300 people living on Agalega, which is administered by the Outer Islands Development Corporation as an island plantation producing coconut oil. It is almost entirely covered with coconut palms and some casuarinas. The highest points are sand dunes of 15m: **Grand Mountain** on South Island and **Emmerez Mountain** on North Island.

The islands were named by the Portuguese after the nationality of their discoverer, Juan de Nova, who was a Spanish Galician serving the King of Portugal. Galega or A'galega means Galician. At the time of the British takeover they were occupied by the captain of a French privateer, licensed by General Decaen to cultivate and harvest coconuts, using slaves from Madagascar. The importance of coconut oil to Mauritius resulted in the island being left alone to continue production by various French concession holders.

From the 1930s, exploitation of Agalega was by Mauritian/Seychellois companies until the government of Mauritius took over control in 1975, paying Rs13.2 million in compensation. In 1982, the Outer Islands Development Corporation was formed, with responsibility for all the islands of the State of Mauritius, except for Mauritius itself and Rodrigues. A board of government officials and knowledgeable citizens was set up with a general manager to run the corporation.

In Agalega, the resident manager is responsible for a working population of 180 to 200, including administration staff, police, meteorologists, teachers, medical personnel and approximately 150 labourers. These include carpenters, masons, gardeners and the coconut cultivators employed on contract. Wives and children make up the additional population.

The entire population is Roman Catholic and Creole. Culturally they have been much influenced by the Seychelles connection and Radio Seychelles is better received than MBC. Consequently, their language is a mix of Mauritian and Seychelles Creole. *Séga* and sport (there are two football clubs) are their main diversions. The staple diet is rice and fish, with a liberal amount of coconut milk in curries and sweet preparations.

It recently came to light that Agalega could be set to change forever. In 2004, Ireland Blyth Limited (IBL) announced plans to build the island's first hotel

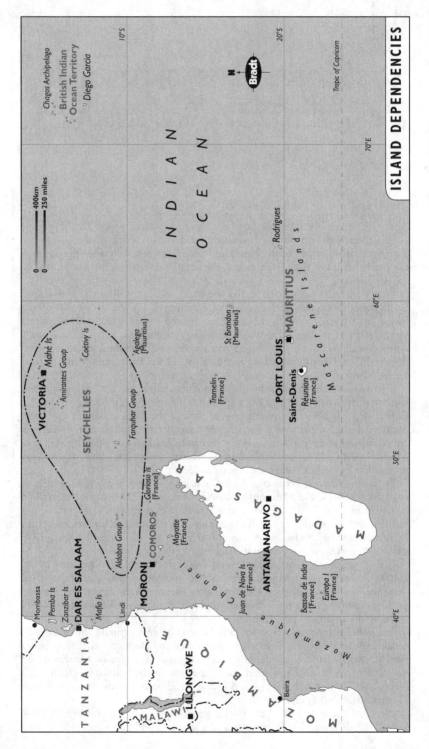

ISLAND DEPENDENCIES

complex, with between 15 and 25 chalets. The company's new airline, Catovair, will commence flights between Mauritius and Agalega once the hotel is open. Few details of the development were available at the time of writing but, if successful, visitors to Mauritius could soon be adding a few days in Agalega to their itineraries.

ST BRANDON

In Mauritius, reference to '**Les Iles**' means the St Brandon archipelago, also known as the Cargados Garayos Islands. These lie 395km northwest of Mauritius, forming an arc from south to north, its convex side facing towards the east. There are 22 low-lying islands, parts of which are sometimes submerged, as well as numerous reefs and sandbanks. Eight of the islands are in the south of the arc, where the biggest (at 12.2ha) is **Cocos Island**. **Albatros** is 48km to its north. Between the two is **Raphael Island** (10.1ha), which is the administrative centre, also sometimes known as Establishment Island.

From 1546, the islands were shown on Portuguese charts as São Brandao, which is puzzling since St Brandon is an Irish saint. The Portuguese also called them Cargados Garayos, deriving the name from Coroa dos Garajãos, meaning reef of seabirds.

The islands abound with birds and in the past guano was the main export. In 1862, cotton was tried, without success. Cyclones, problems with fresh water, and the harsh conditions of life (no women) also affected the islands' development. Since the 1830s, the richness of the fishing grounds has been exploited and in 1910 there were 100 fishermen based in the islands.

Fish is still king, salted and dried for export to Mauritius. Fishermen are engaged by the Outer Islands Development Corporation, which manages St Brandon, on a four to six months' contract. Their working day begins at dawn and by 07.00 they are at sea. After they have returned with their catch, the fish have to be gutted, cleaned and put in the salt beds.

The fishermen, several dozen of them from Mauritius, Rodrigues and the Seychelles, lodge in barracks. Raphael (Establishment) Island has a modest chapel, a house for the administrator and his staff, a hangar for the salt fish, a community hall and a shop.

Beaches of soft, white, powdery sand, waving palm trees and translucent lagoons with thousands of seabirds living undisturbed make St Brandon seem a tropical island paradise. Perhaps it is, but not for the fishermen who have to work there in isolation from family and girlfriends.

There have been surveys and proposals with a view to making the St Brandon Islands a new tourist destination. Perhaps it will happen, but not just yet.

TROMELIN

Mauritius claims sovereignty over Tromelin but France occupies it and Madagascar wants it. It is a flat, sandy, barren place, less than 2km long and about 640m wide. It lies between the St Brandon archipelago and Madagascar, actually closer to Madagascar than Port Louis, which is 482km away.

It was known in the 18th century as Ile aux Sables or Sandy Island. In 1761, a French vessel was shipwrecked on the reef which extends from its southern point. The whites in the crew built a boat and reached Madagascar safely. They left 80 blacks on the island, promising to return. It was 15 years before a French chevalier, M Tromelin, landed and found seven women living there. They were the only survivors, having existed on shellfish, turtle and brackish water. He took them to Mauritius.

11

Mauritius's claim to ownership is based on the capitulation terms of 1810, as Tromelin was regarded then as a dependency of Mauritius. Also, there are guano-gathering permits granted by the British colonial government in 1902. Fishing rights were claimed in 1980 by an act of the Mauritius parliament.

THE CHAGOS ARCHIPELAGO

The Chagos Archipelago, together with Desroches, Farquhar and Aldabra, formerly part of the Seychelles group, now constitute the British Indian Ocean Territory (BIOT). They lie 1,930km northeast of Mauritius, south of Gan in the Maldives. Visits by individuals are difficult to arrange.

SIX ISLANDS This group of six low islands arranged in a horseshoe shape is 109km from Diego Garcia. When they were dependencies of Mauritius, they were harvested for coconuts as well as supplying pigs, poultry and fat-tailed land crabs. They are connected by shoals and access is difficult because of the reefs and breakers.

PEROS BANHOS A cluster of a score of small islands which form the largest group of the Chagos Archipelago, Peros Banhos forms a basin of 29km in length, north to south, and 19km in breadth from east to west. The main one is about 3km long. They were also known as the Iles Bourdés after a M de Bourdé, who is credited with discovering them after the Portuguese had named them.

In the mid 19th century, these islands were a flourishing fishing station and establishment for the manufacture of coconut oil, under Mauritian ownership and employing 125 people.

SALOMON ISLANDS Known as Les Onze Iles, being 11 in number, the Salomons were named after a ship called *Salomon*. They form a basin with a safe anchorage for vessels of small draught. Their soil is rich in coconut trees, which used to be harvested by resident Mauritians.

In the last century, these islands were noted for a rare tree called *faux gaiac*, which grew to a height of 40m, and was a deep chocolate colour, with sound wood when old. Fresh water could be obtained from wells. Turtles used to be found there but not so many fish, due to the presence of seals.

TROIS FRÈRES Actually four small islands, connected by shoals. Coconuts grow on all of them and fish, turtles and fresh water are all to be found. Nearby, between this group and Six Islands, are **Eagle** and **Danger** Islands. All used to provide coconut oil for the Mauritius market.

DIEGO GARCIA The name of the archipelago used to be Bassas de Chagos, after the largest island of the group, which was known as Chagos, or Gratiosa, as well as by the name which has survived today, Diego Garcia.

The island is in the form of a serpent bent double, its interior forming a broad, steep, coral wall standing in the ocean. This encompasses a lagoon which is itself a large natural harbour and safe anchorage. The island is 28.5km² in area with a steep coral reef all around, except at the entrance to the lagoon.

The French exiled leprous slaves to Diego Garcia from Mauritius claiming that the turtle, which would be their sole diet, would restore them to good health. In 1792, an English merchant ship sent two Indian crew members ashore for water and some of the leper residents – women as well as men – met them and showed them to a well. When the master of the ship learned of the encounter, he made the seamen stay on the island and sailed away as fast as he could.

After the British takeover in 1810, the exiling of leprosy sufferers was discontinued and some 300 migrants, including Europeans, went voluntarily from Mauritius to set up a saltfish trading company and to plant and harvest coconuts. The settlement flourished peacefully for 150 years, with produce being ferried to Mauritius, from whence came the imported goods the settlers needed to live.

By 1965, the population of the entire Chagos Archipelago had grown to some 900 families, representing 2,000 inhabitants. The islands were dependencies of Mauritius and the *îlois* – the Creole term for the Chagos islanders – conducted trade with Mauritius through an irregular ferry link. They were content with their simple and presumably happy existence.

In the countdown to independence, Britain decided to detach Diego Garcia and the nearby islands from Mauritius, virtually taking them over a second time. The politicians in Mauritius were obliged to agree because, being a colony, they had little choice and gaining independence was their priority.

Three million pounds in development aid was the reward while Mauritius stipulated two conditions for letting Britain keep Diego Garcia: it would be used for communication purposes only, and the atoll would be returned to Mauritius if Britain no longer needed it.

Having signed the agreement, Britain created a new colony: the British Indian Ocean Island Territory. The Chagos islanders were bemused but they did not have long to wait. The ferry service linking them to Mauritius was stopped, the sole employer of labour was bought out by the British and the copra plantation was closed down. Work ceased, and so did food imports. To survive, the *îlois* had to leave.

Less than a year later, the BIOT was leased to the United States of America for 'defence purposes'. By then it was nominally uninhabited and both the British and North American public were kept in the dark about the real situation. The lease to the US is for 50 years, with an option for a further 20 years.

Now Diego Garcia is the main US military base in the Indian Ocean, with superb port facilities, the latest in communications systems and a 3,600m runway capable of handling, and fuelling, B52 bombers. The coconuts have been replaced with a nuclear arsenal.

When politicians in Mauritius realised what had happened, a cyclone of protest and controversy raged. After years of angry negotiations, Britain acknowledged that the Chagos islanders, who had been forcibly displaced from their homes, were entitled to better treatment than being abandoned in the backstreets of Port Louis. Compensation was paid in 1982, but mainly to the Mauritian government, who had to accommodate the islanders.

In November 2000, the *îlois* won an historic victory in the English High Court, which upheld their right to return to their homeland. However, the British government declared that this ruling had to be balanced with their treaty obligations to the US and affirmed that the right to return excluded Diego Garcia. Furthermore, the UK and US both said it was not their responsibility to arrange for the Chagos islanders to return.

In June 2002, the British Foreign and Commonwealth Office completed a feasibility study into resettlement of the islands and concluded that it would be difficult, precarious and costly. Harvard resettlement expert, Jonathan Jenness, commented that the study's conclusions were 'erroneous in every assertion'.

In October 2003, the Chagos islanders were dealt another blow with the High Court in London denying them compensation for their ordeal on the basis that the claim had come too late.

Finally, on 10 June 2004, the British government passed an order banning anyone from setting foot on the Chagos Islands. This effectively cancelled out the victory that the Chagos islanders had won in the High Court in 2000.

Despite these major setbacks, the Chagos islanders are continuing their fight. They are challenging the order that the British government made in 2004 with a judicial review and have applied for their case to be heard at the European Court of Human Rights in Strasbourg.

Part Three

RODRIGUES

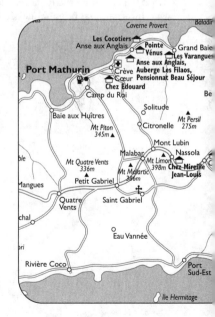

Country An integral part of Mauritius, with its own regional assembly

Location 560km northeast of Mauritius

Size Rodrigues has an area of 108km²; it is 18km long (west–east) and 8km at its widest point (north–south). It is roughly equivalent in size to the British Channel Island of Jersey and is surrounded by 14 satellite islets.

History Discovered by Arabs, then Portuguese explorer Diego Rodrigues, in 1528. Some believe Diego Fernandez de Pereira got there first in 1507. The first settlers were French Huguenots fleeing France, who arrived in 1691. The French colonised the island in 1725; the British took it in 1809. A dependency of Mauritius until 1968, it's now a part of Mauritius.

Nature Valleys and forest with rare wildlife and nothing dangerous; rugged coastline, beaches and coral reefs.

Climate Generally warmer and drier than Mauritius. In summer (November to April), temperatures range from 29°C to 34°C, and in winter (May to October) from 15°C to 29°C. Subject to drought, winds from the southeast and prone to cyclones.

Capital Port Louis

Population Approximately 37,000; 98% of Creole origin

Economy Based on subsistence agriculture and fishing. Tourism and handicraft production are growing.

Language Creole is the everyday language; French is widely spoken and English much less so

Religion 97.5% of the population is Roman Catholic. Anglicans, Adventists, Hindus, Muslims and Rastafarians form a minority.

International telephone code +230

Time GMT+4

Electricity 220 volts

12

Background Information

OVERVIEW

Rodrigues is remote, a part of Mauritius but 560km further east. Its predominantly Roman Catholic Creole population sometimes feels closer to the Seychelles than to the Indo-Mauritian-dominated Mauritius. That's a contention visitors are often made aware of as Rodriguans speak freely about the neglect of their isolated backwater.

There's something stark about the island and things are decidedly low key. It is not a tropical paradise but those in search of something offbeat will find it a fascinating, peaceful place to explore, with a people whose shy friendliness is genuine. Life here is refreshingly slow and uncomplicated. Being such a small community, it has a delightful intimacy and sense of security. After just a few days on the island, I began to bump into people whom I had already met and no-one was ever too busy to stop for a chat.

As they are administratively linked, much of the information about Mauritius in *Chapters 1–3* is relevant to Rodrigues.

GEOGRAPHY

Like the other Mascarenes, Rodrigues is of volcanic origin – albeit more recent than Mauritius and Réunion – having been created some 1½ million years ago. Its landscapes of steep hills, plunging valleys and scattered rocks create the impression that it is much larger than it is. The two highest points are Mont Limon, a mere 398m, and Mont Malarctic at 386m.

There are no impressive mountains and no imposing rock formations. Large rivers and lakes are also absent. Nor are there many impressive beaches. But where Rodrigues wins hands down is in the quality of its marine environment. The island is entirely surrounded by reefs, which offer some of the best underwater experiences available in the Indian Ocean. A vast lagoon (200km²) shelters some of the best beach and reef areas. Among its many coral caves is the often-visited, 795m-long Caverne Patate, near Plaine Corail. The other caves are far less well known.

Much of the island features grass or scrub-covered slopes, some of which are rocky with black cliffs. At Plaine Corail, in the southwest, the landscape is especially harsh and barren. The remaining woodlands are severely degraded and cover only certain hillsides around the Solitude–Citronelle–Cascade Pigeon area. The higher reaches of the hilly interior are often covered by mist, at which time the surrounds take on a dreamy, sultry ambience.

The tumbling Cascade Pigeon River offers some of the island's more attractive scenery. While much of the coast features rocky shores, there are also some pleasant, sandy beaches on the east coast, like St François and Trou d'Argent.

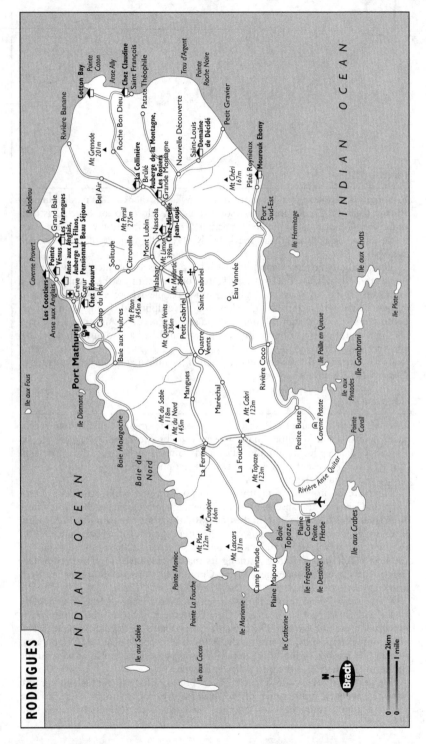

RODRIGUES

INDIAN OCEAN

INDIAN OCEAN

Île aux Fous
Île Diamant
Baie Malagache
Pointe Manioc
Pointe La Fouche
Île aux Sables
Île aux Cocos
Île Marianne
Île Catherine

Caverne Provert
Baladirou
Rivière Banane

Pointe Coton
Anse Ally
Trou d'Argent
Pointe Roche Noire

Cotton Bay
Chez Claudine
Saint François
Patate Théophile
Roche Bon Dieu
Mt Grenade 201m
La Collinière
Brûlé
Auberge de la Montagne,
Les Rosiers
Grande Montagne
Nouvelle Découverte
Saint-Louis
Domaine de Décidé
Pâté Reynieux
Mourouk Ebony
Petit Gravier

Les Cocotiers
Anse aux Anglais
Grand Baie
Pointe Vénus
Les Yarangues
Anse aux Anglais,
Auberge Les Filaos,
Pensionnat Beau Séjour
Crève Cœur
Chez Edouard
Port Mathurin
Bel Air
Solitude
Camp du Roi
Mt Persil 275m
Citronelle
Mont Lubin
Nassola
Malabar
Mt Limon
Mt Malartic 398m
Mt Mandarin 390m
Chez Mireille
Jean-Louis
Mt Chéri 167m
Port Sud-Est
Île Hermitage
Île aux Chats
Île Plate

Baie aux Huîtres
Mt Piton 345m
Mt Quatre Vents 336m
Petit Gabriel
Saint Gabriel
Quatre Vents
Eau Vannée
Rivière Coco
Île Paille en Queue
Île Gombrani
Île aux Pintades

Baie du Nord
Mangues
Maréchal
Mt du Sable 118m
Mt du Nord 145m
Mt Cabri 123m
Petite Butte
Caverne Patate
Pointe Corail

La Ferme
La Fouche
Mt Topaze 123m
Rivière Anse Quitar
Plaine Corail
Pointe l'Herbe
Île aux Crabes

Mt Plat 122m
Mt Coupier 166m
Mt Lascars 131m
Camp Pintade
Plaine Mapou
Baie Topaze
Île Frégate
Île Destinée

N

Bradt

2km
1 mile

0
0

When the first settlers arrived on Rodrigues, they found an island largely swathed in woodland and populated by a bizarre ensemble of animals. These included two species of giant tortoises (similar to those now surviving on Aldabra), herds of dugong in the lagoons and a variety of endemic birds.

Most conspicuous of these were the Rodrigues solitaire (*Pezophaps solitaria*), the island's answer to the Mauritian dodo. These extraordinary creatures shared their Mauritian cousins' fate and were soon exterminated. Trade in the two species of giant tortoise began in 1736. Fifty years later, they too were extinct.

Of 17 endemic species of vertebrate, just three remain: the Rodrigues warbler (*Acrocephalus roderICana*), Rodrigues fody (*Foudia flavicans*) and the Rodrigues fruit bat (*Pteropus rodericensis*).

The two surviving endemic bird species are both threatened. The greyish Rodrigues warbler is classed 'endangered' and the population was estimated in 1999 to be 150. This marks a significant improvement since 1974, when a survey recorded just 32 warblers.

The pretty yellow and orange Rodrigues fody is classed as 'vulnerable' and numbered approximately 911 individuals in 1999. In 1974, the population was down to around 50.

To see the endemic birds, go to the woods around Cascade Pigeon River or Solitude, not too far from Port Mathurin. You should find both within half an hour.

The endemic Rodrigues fruit bat is the last remaining indigenous mammal. It is very rare, numbering around 3,000. Once, these famed 'blonde bats' were on the verge of oblivion. They were down to a population of 120 during the mid 1970s when the late Gerald Durrell and the Jersey Wildlife Preservation Trust (now the Durrell Wildlife Conservation Trust) undertook a collecting expedition to Rodrigues and Mauritius (see box on page 192). Thanks to the intensive captive breeding efforts which followed the JWPT expedition, the bat population has increased substantially. They can usually be seen from about 16.00 in the trees which line the road near Solitude, between Port Mathurin and Mt Lubin.

The outlook for the Rodrigues fody is bright, provided that their forest habitat is safeguarded. The warbler's future is less sure as the population remains at a critically low level. The fruit bat has made significant progress since the 1970s but the risk of a localised catastrophe, such as a cyclone, remains.

ENDANGERED FLORA Of 49 endemic plants, eight are extinct and 38 threatened, seven of which are down to only two or three specimens each. These include the Rodrigues hibiscus, saved from extinction after specimens were located in faraway colonial collections around the globe (especially in Hawaii). This was done after only two were found to remain on Rodrigues itself. One of the world's rarest plants, 'café marron' (*Ramosmania heterophylla*), is Rodriguan. A lone specimen remains in the wild on the island, just off the road near Citronelle, where it is carefully fenced in. In 1986, cuttings were sent to Kew, where one took root.

Many of the island's indigenous plants are shared with the other Mascarenes, where they are usually more numerous. Two such orchids are *Angraecum mauritianum* and the much smaller *A. pectinatum*, which lacks the long spur common to many *Angraecoid* orchids.

A threatened liana distributed throughout the Mascarenes, 'liane savon' (*Gouania mauritania* var. *mauritania*), has tiny star-shaped blooms.

The critically endangered shrub, 'bois d'ortie' (*Obetia ficifolia*), is shared only with Réunion, where it is known to be pollinated by a single, endangered species

Lee Durrell

In a nutshell, saving animals from extinction is our mission. According to the World Conservation Union, some 6,000 animals are currently threatened to varying degrees. When Gerald Durrell founded the Jersey Zoo in 1959, he chose the dodo as the trust's symbol, vowing that its tragic story would never be repeated. Most of the target species we have selected may be viewed as 'flagship' animals, meaning those able to inspire efforts by people to help other species, or those which are likely to canonise environmental ethics among local people. When your target species is used to symbolise a healthy environment, people invariably come up with ideas concerning environmental management. Projects then develop from grassroots level and the DWCT acts in an advisory capacity. We use captive breeding as a safety net, to buy time, while attempting to implement habitat protection within the species' natural range. So we view captivity as a temporary state, not an end in itself.

When we first visited Mauritius and Rodrigues in 1976, indigenous birds had been reduced to 11 species, including the world's rarest pigeon, falcon and parrot all teetering on the brink of extinction. Off the Mauritian coast, Round Island was the bleak, barren home of eight species of reptiles, including the world's two rarest snakes. Nearby Rodrigues had suffered drought and cyclones in addition to manmade indignities. The Rodrigues fruit bat was considered the world's rarest bat, and of the bird species, only two remained. Small conservation efforts were underway but the international zoological community largely regarded the Mascarenes as paradise lost. With the encouragement of the Mauritian government and the support of the International Council for Bird Preservation, the DWCT (then the Jersey Wildlife Preservation Trust) mounted an intense conservation campaign, spearheaded by John Hartley and Trust Conservation Field Officer Carl Jones, in Mauritius.

The most radical step in our programmes is releasing captive-bred animals into their natural range. This is necessary when natural recovery of wild populations is not happening in spite of our efforts to protect and manage them in their natural habitats. We've had tremendous success in Mauritius, where we carried out intensive work on birds like the Mauritius kestrel, once down to only four individuals. Today, more than 600 kestrels live in the wild, and currently they even nest in people's gardens. Another Mauritian bird which we brought back from the brink is the pink pigeon, of which we have bred and released in excess of 250. Subsequent outside interest led the Mauritian government to set up a national park in the last remaining natural forest, Black River Gorges.

Our best example of management of wild animals in their natural habitat is seen on Round Island, off Mauritius. Some time ago sailors had introduced goats and rabbits on to this little island. These animals destroyed most of the unique flora and consequently a fascinating ensemble of endemic reptiles were gravely threatened. These include the large Telfair's skink, one of my favourite animals. After we procured the 'safety net' of reptiles for captive breeding, we had to deal with the 'politics and practicalities' of restoring the island. That took ten years, but we eventually eliminated the goats and rabbits with the help of, among others, the New Zealand Department of Conservation (then the New Zealand Wildlife Service). Almost immediately, Round Island's flora began recovering dramatically. Subsequent studies have revealed that the reptile populations have increased beyond all expectations.

The world-renowned Durrell Wildlife Conservation Trust has enjoyed spectacular success with its Mascarene-related projects. Author Lee Durrell is the trust's Honorary Director. For details of how you can help the DWCT in their work, see Chapter 3, Giving something back, pages 84–5.

of butterfly. Another rare shrub shared with the other Mascarenes is the 'bois de chenille' (*Clerodendron heterophyllum*); growing to 3–4m high, it bears small clusters of white flowers. The hardwood tree 'bois rouge' (*Eleaodendron orientale*), which attains a height of 5–20m, is often used to make furniture.

The 'bois jaune' tree (*Ochrosia borbonica*), more common on the other Mascarenes, bears white flowers reminiscent of – but smaller than – those of the frangipani.

REFORESTATION The Mauritius Wildlife Foundation (MWF) has been doing marvellous work in Rodrigues, with help from the Mauritius government. A nursery has been established at Solitude, where all the native Rodriguan plant species are being propagated.

According to Colin Barbery, a Kew-trained botanist who has worked with MWF, the main cause of the alarming decline of many native plants is introduced rats – not the ubiquitous goats one sees all over the island. Barbery showed me seed samples from several indigenous plant species, to illustrate his point: rats had gnawed these to the extent that none would be able to germinate.

'Even the local pandanus (screwpines), which are endemic and which appear plentiful, are threatened because of the extensive rat damage,' Barbery said. Indeed, one does not see any young pandanus about. Like many of the threatened plant species, it has been used for centuries by Rodriguans in their daily lives. Whilst many of the plants have a medicinal purpose, the leaves of the pandanus are used for weaving. The MWF is currently working on community projects to boost the numbers of such plants, with the help of villagers who take responsibility for the young plants. In the long term, both the plants and the villagers will benefit.

Very noticeable in the remaining Rodriguan woods is the high proportion (97%) of exotic vegetation. In particular, eucalyptus, sisal and lantana have taken over large tracts of land. However, the MWF and Mauritian government are hard at work, weeding out the alien vegetation and replanting saplings of other fast-growing trees, particularly those which are indigenous.

Visiting a nursery like the one at Solitude is certainly encouraging, and well worth the effort if you want to see the endemic and indigenous flora up close. When seeing the extent of the reforestation programmes and the commitment of the MWF staff and volunteers, one can't help but feel positive about the future of Rodriguan flora.

ABUNDANT SEABIRDS ON OFFSHORE ISLANDS The idyllic Ile aux Cocos is an island sanctuary and breeding ground for huge populations of seabirds. Common noddies (*Anous stolidus*) and lesser noddies (*A. tenuirostris*) are present in their thousands, nesting on casuarina ('filao') trees wherever space permits. The bridled tern (*Sterna anaethetus*) and the graceful fairy tern (*Gygis alba*) are also present. Part of Ile aux Cocos is fenced off to protect the ground-nesting sites of bridled terns.

The nearby Ile Aux Sables is a recognised nature reserve islet for a few pairs of fairy terns. Visitors may snorkel nearby after leaving Ile aux Cocos but setting foot on Ile aux Sables is forbidden. According to Ian Sinclair and Olivier Langrand, who co-authored the excellent field guide *Birds of the Indian Ocean Islands*, common tern (*Sterna hirundo*) and wedge-tailed shearwater (*Puffinus pacificus*) are also often seen there.

For information on excursions to Ile aux Cocos, see page 211.

HISTORY AND POLITICS

Rodrigues shares its history with Mauritius although it was discovered later, in 1528, and retained the name of its Portuguese discoverer, Diego Rodriguez,

12

throughout Dutch, French and British colonisation. Some historians maintain that it was actually discovered earlier, in 1507, by another Portuguese seafarer, Diego Fernandes de Pereira.

The Dutch paid little attention to Rodrigues and the first known settlers were French, although they came during the Dutch period. These were nine French Protestants fleeing from France, led by François Leguat. They had actually been trying to reach Ile Bourbon (Réunion) but stumbled upon Rodrigues in 1691 and found the island covered in luxuriant vegetation, with an abundance of birds and tortoises. After two years, the settlement broke up and Leguat was arrested on the orders of the Dutch governor of Mauritius.

In 1725, France decided to colonise Rodrigues in the name of Louis XV and sent eight soldiers, 13 planters and 15 slaves. The colonisation was unsuccessful, although some of the slaves remained when the French left. The French noted that Rodrigues suffered from more cyclones and higher winds than Ile de France, and had a difficult approach through rocks and shoals to the harbour they called Port Mathurin.

The first permanent settler was a master mariner, Germain le Gros, who arrived in September 1792 to engage in fishing and trading. He was followed in 1793 by Michel Gorry and Philibert Marragon, who had visited previously in 1791. Marragon and his wife lived at L'Orangerie until both died on Rodrigues in 1826.

In the time-honoured manner of expatriates living on a small island, the three French settlers distrusted each other and soon fell out. Marragon was civil agent for the French government, a position that did not deter him from entertaining and welcoming the crews of British ships when they put in for water and food, much to Le Gros's annoyance.

The fraternisation of the settlers on Rodrigues with the British made the new governor of Ile de France, General Decaen, keen to replace Marragon and the others with his own island's unwanted lepers. The plan failed. Marragon remained and the lepers went to Diego Garcia.

Marragon conducted a census in 1804 which shows the island's population as 22 whites (about half of them actually of mixed race) and 82 slaves. The majority of the slaves were from Mozambique, yet nearly a third (24) were born in Rodrigues.

In 1794, Britain decided to capture Ile de France, but their attempts were limited to foraging expeditions to Rodrigues. They wanted to take Rodrigues too, and concentrated on building up good relations with the settlers by paying for their supplies instead of looting. By August 1809, they had no qualms about making their intentions known and landed the first of the forces being assembled to capture Ile de France: 200 infantry and 200 sepoys (Indian soldiers trained by the British).

The occupation of Rodrigues began enthusiastically, with Colonel Keating, who was in command, writing home: 'These are some of the most delightful valleys I ever saw and the soil naturally rich in one of the finest climates in the world capable of producing every sort of vegetation and there is a sufficient quantity of land already cleared for cultivation and the feeding of cattle.' Keating imported cattle and slaves from Madagascar as more British troops assembled.

In July 1810, a force of 4,000 left Rodrigues and went on to capture Bourbon (Réunion) from the French. Following their unexpected defeat at Vieux Grand Port in August, the British gathered a large force in Rodrigues for their successful assault on Ile de France in December 1810. After that, the British occupied Rodrigues until April 1812 when they withdrew, leaving behind most of the 300 slaves they had imported. British rule of Rodrigues was confirmed by the Treaty of Paris in May 1814.

The first British settler was a young man called Thomas Robert Pye, a lieutenant of the marines at a loose end, who was sent by Governor Farquhar in 1821. He stayed only two years. When slavery was abolished, those slaves who had not emancipated themselves already promptly left their owners and squatted on crown land. They finally settled in the mountains where their descendants still live today.

In the mid 19th century, several Europeans or near-Europeans settled in Rodrigues, mostly in the lowlands. They included shipwrecked sailors and minor British civil servants who liked the island. Some of the British married Rodriguan women while others had affairs with them and, as the saying goes in Rodrigues, 'left one or two portraits behind'.

The portraits and the mixed-blood population were centred around Port Mathurin, Baie aux Huîtres, Grand Baie and La Ferme. When the first steamer arrived in the 1890s, so did more settlers, including Indian and Chinese traders. By 1970, the Chinese owned 90% of all the shops on the island.

The growth of the population was rapid. As there were more men than women at first, most women had several partners, their children being raised as the children of the man of the moment. At the end of the 19th century, the population was 3,000. Twenty years later this had become 6,573. The population almost doubled in subsequent 20-year periods, becoming 11,385 in 1944, 18,587 in 1963 and 32,000 in 1981.

Rodrigues was administered as a dependency of Mauritius during the 158 years of British rule. Like a poor relation, it was mostly forgotten or neglected, with occasional official reports warning of the consequences of too large a population.

Since 1968, it has been an integral part of Mauritius. For many years Rodrigues sought greater autonomy over its affairs and on 12 October 2002 the newly created Rodrigues Regional Assembly met for the first time. The Assembly is made up of 18 members, plus its chairperson. At present the *Organisation du Peuple Rodriguais* (OPR) has a majority of ten members. While the assembly may initiate legislation, this must pass through the Mauritian National Assembly to become law. For further information, visit the Assembly's website: http://rra.gov.mu.

ECONOMY

Fishing and agriculture provide the livelihood of Rodriguans although the young hanker for employment either with government or in commerce, not as independent entrepreneurs. There is no vibrant private sector as in Mauritius.

Onions and garlic are grown for export to Mauritius and maize (the staple) and chicken are produced for home consumption. Livestock (cattle, pigs, sheep) are also reared for the Mauritian market. Octopus is dried and fish salted for export.

The traditional system of farmers growing maize and beans, helping each other with harvesting and existing on a barter basis has died out. People have become money and subsidy minded. As a district of Mauritius, social benefits filter through to the island from central government and international aid agencies.

A decline in agriculture over the last decade has resulted in a boom in small handicraft units, which is being encouraged by the growth of tourism. Some large Mauritian industries (beer, poultry, wood) have also set up operations on Rodrigues.

The island's fishing industry is organised on a co-operative basis under the auspices of the Rodriguan Fishermen's Cooperative Federation. Fish is delivered to the area co-operative for distribution and sale on the island or for cold storage at the plant in Port Mathurin. Training in fishing methods, assistance with boat and equipment purchase, catch monitoring and marketing, and foreign aid funding are all provided under various schemes to sustain a viable fishing industry.

The tourism industry in Rodrigues is gradually being developed and has the potential to become one of the island's greatest income earners. The airport has been expanded and several mid-range hotels have been built, some of which are managed by groups with several hotels in Mauritius. Rodriguans have, by and large, reacted positively to the establishment of tourism, with many families opening their homes to offer guesthouse-style accommodation. However, according to locals in 2005, tourism in Rodrigues was off to a slow start and the island was not receiving the number of visitors that had been expected.

It is vital that tourism in Rodrigues is developed gradually and thoughtfully. The Rodriguan way of life will be vulnerable to overdevelopment and the island's already stretched resources, water and waste disposal in particular, will be further tested. Rodrigues will never compete with Mauritius's beaches, luxury hotels and first-class service. Nor should it try to. It has a charm of its own, which will attract visitors who will relish the island as it is.

LANGUAGE AND EDUCATION

Creole is the everyday language but educated Rodriguans also speak French. English has been neglected, with the result that young Rodriguans' aspirations to work in government service (for which a credit in English is compulsory) are thwarted. Efforts are being made to improve the standard of English teaching in schools.

The main school in Port Mathurin is a joint venture between the Roman Catholic and the Anglican churches. There is a large state secondary school at Maréchal in the centre of the island, which is attended by pupils from all over Rodrigues.

RELIGION

The Roman Catholic faith is very strong and is the religion of the majority, although perhaps less than 97.5%, which is the figure usually quoted. Other active religions are Anglican, Adventist, Muslim and Hindu.

Creoles and Chinese form the Roman Catholic community, although some Chinese are members of the Anglican Church. There are no Buddhists. The Muslim community is small, mostly traders, but supports a mosque in Port Mathurin. There are a few Rastafarians in the interior village communities.

Witchcraft is also practised in the traditional Afro-Creole manner of believing in the efficacy of certain potions, charms, herbs, fortune telling and the warding off of evil.

EVERYDAY LIFE AND CULTURE

Rodriguans pride themselves on their hospitality and refer to their remote haven as the 'anti-stress' island. It's certainly worth taking time to see some of the towns, villages and scenery and to get a feel for Rodriguan lifestyle.

Most of the people live either off the sea or the land. The crops cultivated – onions, garlic, chillies, potatoes and maize – are not the same as on Mauritius. As a result, the countryside bears no resemblance to that of Mauritius, but reminds many of the Transkei in southern Africa, with deep green valleys, cultivated lands, and herds of livestock (cattle, goats, and pigs).

Maize cobs are left to dry on roofs, which is very reminiscent of Africa and something that is not seen in Mauritius. Sausages, left to cure in the sun, are also often seen on rooftops. The rather uninspiring but neatly built square houses one sees so much of in the countryside are government subsidised, built using coral bricks and designed to be cyclone-proof.

SHOALS RODRIGUES

Tom Hooper

Shoals Rodrigues is a Mauritian non-governmental organisation, which developed from the Shoals of Capricorn Programme, a three-year initiative led by the Royal Geographical Society.

The new organisation was established in March 2001 to continue the marine research, education and training activities on Rodrigues. With the combination of these three disciplines good progress is being made towards discovering more about the seas around Rodrigues and promoting sustainable resource use and marine conservation.

The Shoals Centre is based at Pointe Monier, on the outskirts of Port Mathurin, alongside the government agencies which have responsibility for the sea, such as the Coastguard, the Fisheries Protection Service and the Fisheries Research and Training Unit. Our work focuses on collecting information about the Rodrigues lagoon and seas which can be used to improve the management of the important fishery resources and protect the biodiversity and health of the marine ecosystem.

The Shoals Rodrigues Centre is run by a committed group of young Rodriguans with the help of a British marine biologist, Emily Hardman. Our work on the reef fisheries, zooplankton populations and the effects of land-based sediments have all been developed in collaboration with foreign experts. In addition we are carrying out an extensive programme of coral reef surveys to monitor the health of the reef ecosystem.

With training in the scientific collection and analysis techniques this local team is working towards building up important long-term data sets. Many new skills and techniques have been taught to a wide range of people on the island. These range from first aid, lifesaving and diving qualifications to marine tourist guide training. We also regularly visit fishing villages to give first aid and swimming training to fishermen and to discuss marine ecology and resource use.

Shoals Rodrigues is also a thriving centre for young people who come to learn more about the marine environment through 'Club Mer'.

The work of Shoals Rodrigues is supported by private donations, as well as a variety of organisations in Mauritius and abroad: the United Nations Development Programme GEF-SGP, the British and Australian high commissions, Barclays Bank, the US National Fish and Wildlife Foundation, the Sea Trust and the European Union as well as others.

Visitors are welcome to come and see the work of the organisation at Pointe Monier. Contact Eric Blais (✆ *831 1225*). If you would like to help or find out more please see our website at www.shoals-rodrigues.org.

Tom Hooper is a highly respected British marine biologist, specialising in reef fisheries. For details of how you can help Shoals Rodrigues, see Chapter 3, Giving something back, pages 84–5.

12

Water is very scarce in Rodrigues. Most villages have a communal water tank, which is filled every two weeks. In the early evening families walk to the nearest tank to fill their buckets, which will last them, their animals and their crops until the following evening.

In late afternoon, fishermen can be seen sailing to shore in their pirogues and bringing in their nets, whilst at low tide groups of women wade out to the reefs to fish for octopus. This requires a great deal of skill as the octopus are well camouflaged.

One of the highlights of the week for most people is the market at Port Mathurin on Wednesday and Saturday, where much of the home produce is sold.

On weekend evenings the island vibrates to the sound of traditional music at nightclubs, hotels, community 'balls' and private celebrations. Dancing is a vital part of the Creole culture but the European influence is obvious: the *Scottish*, *polka*, *laval* (the waltz) and *quadrille* are still danced today, mainly by the older generation. The traditional *Séga-tambour* has its roots in Africa and Madagascar. The *séga* of Rodrigues is said to be closer to its original form than that of Mauritius, thanks to its isolation from external influences. It is also known as the *séga coupé* because the only couple on the dance floor is continually separated by other male and female partners cutting in.

The European influence can also be seen in the musical instruments, namely the accordion, which gave rise to the *séga-kordion*. However, there is now concern amongst the older generation that the tradition of accordion playing is at risk, as few young people are learning to play the instrument. With the help of the European Union, a programme to teach the accordion to youngsters has been established. The Franco-Malagasy legacy to the Rodriguan folk group is a series of simple instruments, such as the drum, the *maravanne* (a small box filled with dry seeds), the triangle and the *bobre* (musical bow).

One of the highlights of the Rodriguan calendar is Fish Day on 1 March, when celebrations throughout the island mark the first day of the dragnet fishing season. *Banané*, or New Year (from *Bonne Année*), is also a time for festivities, which typically last for a week. Families eat their fattened pigs and there is a drinking contest known as 'Le Roi boire'.

✚ HEALTH AND SAFETY

There is no malaria on Rodrigues so you need not take prophylaxis. The advice on inoculations for Mauritius (see pages 52–3) applies equally to Rodrigues.

Insect repellent is necessary as mosquitoes are abundant. Strong sunblock is essential. Water is drinkable in hotels but, as in Mauritius, can cause upsets. It is advisable to drink bottled water.

There is one hospital on the island, the Queen Elizabeth Hospital (✆ 831 1521) at Crève Cœur on the outskirts of Port Mathurin. In emergencies they will send an ambulance. Medical care is also available at the Mont Lubin Clinic (✆ 831 4403) and La Ferme Clinic (✆ 831 7202). There is a pharmacy (✆ 831 2279. *Open Mon–Sat 07.30–16.30, Sun 07.30–11.30*) in Rue de la Solidarité, Port Mathurin.

A huge plus factor on Rodrigues is safety: crime, it would appear, is virtually absent. There are three prison cells, which are hardly ever occupied. Nevertheless, caution cannot be a bad thing, especially for women.

An urban legend on Rodrigues is the story of two men who stole a pig in Port Mathurin and dressed the pig up with an old jacket and floppy hat. They then walked alongside the pig, holding its front legs so it could 'walk' with them on its hind legs, down the road. When anyone passed by the bizarre threesome, the thieves loudly asked the pig why 'he was so drunk again'. Apparently, their mission succeeded.

Hitchhiking on Rodrigues is a safe and easy way of getting around as it is the custom to pick anyone up who is thumbing a lift – no questions asked. Of course, you should exercise due caution when accepting a lift from a stranger.

13

Practical Information

i TOURIST INFORMATION

For information before you go, contact the Mauritius Tourism Promotion Authority, either in your home country or in Mauritius (for contact details see pages 42–3). The MTPA produces a small booklet called *Rodrigues: le Guide*, which contains useful addresses. There is plenty of useful information on the MTPA website: www.rodrigues-island.org.

There is no tourist office in Rodrigues. The best source of information is **ARTO** (Association of Rodrigues Tour Operators), Complex la Citronelle, Rue Max Lucchesi, Port Mathurin (↘ *831 2801;* f *831 2800;* e *ecotours@intnet.mu*). They should be able to give you a copy of the MTPA guide to Rodrigues, which you can also obtain directly from the MTPA.

MAPS Maps (also French magazines) are available in the small library, which is near Pension Ciel d'Eté on Rivière Cascade Pigeon just off Rue Johnston in Port Mathurin.

TOUR OPERATORS

The sense of going somewhere 'off the beaten track' begins as soon as you try to get to Rodrigues. As yet, very few tour operators feature the island.

France

Jet Tours 38 Av de l'Opera; 75002 Paris; ↘ 01 47 42 06 92; f 01 47 42 57 02; www.jettours.com

Germany

Trauminsel Reisen Summerstrasse 8, D–82211 Herrsching, Munich; ↘ 08 1529 3190; f 08 1529 31920; e info@trauminselreisen.de; www.trauminselreisen.de

Italy

Kuoni Gastaldi Tours 1 Mura di S Chiara, 16128 Genova; ↘ 010 59991; f 010 594438

South Africa

Unusual Destinations 12 George St, Bryanston, Johannesburg; ↘ 011 706 1991; f 011 463 1469; e info@unusualdestinations.com; www.unusualdestinations.com

Switzerland

Stohler Tours 81 Av Louis-Casai, 1216 Geneva-Cointrin; ↘ 022715 1900; e info@stohler.com; www.stohler.com

UK

Partnership Travel Marlborough House, 298 Regents Park Rd, London N3 2TJ; ↘ 020 8343 3446; f 020 8349 3439; e info@partnershiptravel.co.uk; www.partnershiptravel.co.uk

Rainbow Tours 64 Essex Rd, London N1 8LR; ↘ 020 7226 1604; f 020 7226 2621; e info@rainbowtours.co.uk; www.rainbowtours.co.uk

Sunset Travel 4 Abbeville Mews, 88 Clapham Park Rd, London SW4 7BX; ↘ 020 7498 9922; f 020 7978 1337; e info@sunsettravel.co.uk; www.sunsetfaraway.com

RED TAPE

ENTRY REQUIREMENTS As for Mauritius. See pages 42–3.

HELP

CONSULAR HELP Only Britain and France have honorary consulates in Rodrigues. For other countries, see *Mauritius high commissions, embassies and consulates*, in *Chapter 3, Practical Information*, page 47.

UK (Mrs Suzanne Auguste) CARE-CO Centre, Camp du Roi; ↘ 832 0120; e brhonconrod@intnet.mu

France (Mr Benoit Jolicoeur) Jean-Tac; ↘ 831 1760

EMERGENCY SERVICES
Police emergency	999
Police station	Port Mathurin: 831 1536
Fire station	Port Mathurin: 831 1588

GETTING THERE AND AWAY

BY SEA The *Mauritius Pride* links Mauritius and Rodrigues three times a month. The journey takes about 36 hours to Rodrigues but only 24 hours on the way back. There are two classes, *'loisirs'* (seats) and *'excellence'* (cabins). Expect to pay from around US$110 (Rs3,300) per person return for a seat and US$160 (Rs4,800) per person return for a cabin. Children under 12 receive a 50% discount.

The *Mauritius Trochetia* makes one journey per month between Mauritius and Rodrigues. Prices for second-class cabins start from US$180 (Rs5,400) per person return.

For information on either service, contact the Mauritius Shipping Corporation in Mauritius (↘ *210 5944*) or Island Service in Rodrigues (↘ *831 1555*).

BY AIR Air Mauritius flies regularly between Mauritius and Rodrigues, with at least four flights per day in peak season and two per day in low season. The new airline, Catovair (see page 49) offers six flights per week between Mauritius and Rodrigues.

In 2002, Rodrigues began receiving its first international flights, with Air Mauritius operating twice-weekly flights from Réunion. This is a major development for the island and it is hoped that it will provide a boost to the fledgling tourism industry.

Demand for flights from Mauritius as well as Réunion is high and reservations need to be made well in advance, and reconfirmed. The return airfare from Mauritius is expensive for non-citizens at around Rs5,500 return, and from Réunion around €400 (Rs14,000). However, it is possible to include Rodrigues on an Air Mauritius ticket from Europe to Mauritius at a reduced add-on rate, if it is bought prior to flying to Mauritius. Alternatively, tourists can soften the blow by buying the air ticket from a travel agent in Mauritius (instead of from Air Mauritius or overseas), when it comes lower as part of a package that includes accommodation.

For non-Mauritian passport holders, the check-in procedure at Sir Seewoosagur Ramgoolam Airport for flights to Rodrigues is as for international flights. Passports must be shown even though this is a domestic flight, although there is no departure tax to pay. It is advisable to check in early, otherwise your seat may be given to someone on standby. The luggage allowance is just 15kg.

Flying time between Mauritius and Rodrigues is 1 hour 20 minutes. The ATR42 has 48 seats and not much leg or arm space, so keep your hand baggage small.

Air Mauritius can be contacted at the airport (↘ *832 7700*; f *832 7321*) or at their office in the ADS Building on Rue Max Lucchesi in Port Mathurin (↘ *831 1558*; f *831 1321*; e *jhung@airmauritius.com*).

ON ARRIVAL/DEPARTURE The first sight of Rodrigues, in the dry season, is of parched hillsides with cactus-like vegetation and box-type houses dotted all over an inhospitable landscape. The airport is at the opposite end of the island to the main town.

When I first visited Rodrigues in 2002, the airport terminal was a tiny, one-storey building, with spectators waiting obediently behind the perimeter fence where jeeps and buses are parked. The person at the immigration desk had a hand-written list of the passengers due to arrive on each flight, and he checked the names off one by one. With the introduction of international flights, things have changed. There is now a smart, new terminal building with duty-free shops and immigration and customs procedures have been formalised in line with those in Mauritius (see pages 44–5).

Getting to your hotel Most hotels and guesthouses will provide airport transfers for a fee, usually around Rs500–800. If you haven't pre-arranged transport you can take a bus or one of the jeeps or vans that come to pick up hotel guests. The Supercopter bus that operates between the airport and Port Mathurin for arrivals and departures costs Rs100.

WHAT TO TAKE

Take light, casual cotton clothing. Bathing costumes and T-shirts are acceptable everywhere. Remember beach shoes to protect your feet against sea urchin spines whilst swimming. Pack some long trousers or similar for the more upmarket hotels and restaurants in the evenings. Comfortable trainers with a sturdy grip are sufficient for the hiking trails.

$ MONEY AND BANKING

Hotels and most guesthouses and restaurants accept the major credit cards. Opening hours for banks are typically Monday–Friday 09.15–15.15 and Saturday 09.15–11.15.

Barclays Bank Rue de la Solidarité, Port Mathurin; ↘ 831 1553
State Bank Rue de la Solidarité, Port Mathurin; ↘ 831 2066
State Bank Rue Max Lucchesi, Port Mathurin;

↘ 831 1642
Mauritius Commercial Bank Rue Max Lucchesi, Port Mathurin; ↘ 831 1833
Indian Ocean International Bank Rue François Leguat, Port Mathurin; ↘ 831 1591

GETTING AROUND

INBOUND TOUR OPERATORS The following agencies can provide transfers, excursions and activities, as well as car hire:

RodTours (affiliated to MauriTours of Mauritius) Camp du Roi, Port Mathurin; ↘ 831 2249; f 831 2267; e rodtours@intnet.mu
2000 Tours Rue Morrison, Port Mathurin; ↘/f 831

1894; e 2000trs@intnet.mu
Beracca Tours Baie aux Huîtres; ↘ 831 2198
Ebony Tours Rue de la Solidarité, Port Mathurin; ↘ 832 3351; f 832 3355; e ebony@intnet.mu

Rotourco Pl François Leguat, Port Mathurin; ☎ 831 0747; f 832 0747; e rotourco@intnet.mu; www.rotourco.com

Ecotourisme Rue Max Lucchesi, Port Mathurin; ☎ 831 2801; f 831 2800; e ecotours@intnet.mu

🚗 **DRIVING** During the 1990s, roads were improved and many more vehicles imported. Regulations for drivers are as for Mauritius. Take care as there are many steep, windy, narrow roads which are not lit at night. Four-wheel drive vehicles are common and are best suited to the conditions. There is no coastal road around the island; you have to keep climbing back up to the centre to get almost anywhere. There is only one petrol station on the island, in Port Mathurin, so keep an eye on the fuel gauge.

In addition to the inbound tour operators above, the following offer **car hire**:

Comfort Cars Rue Père Gandy, Port Mathurin; ☎ 831 2092/1603; f 831 1609

Spring Lovers Car Rental Petit Gabriel; ☎/f 831 4431

Scooters, motorbikes and **bicycles** can also be hired. However, be wary – some people hire out these vehicles without having the necessary permits.

TAXIS There is just a handful of taxis on the island and they do not drive around looking for clients. Your best chance of finding one is at the bus station in Port Mathurin.

🚌 **BUS** The **bus station** is on the outskirts of Port Mathurin at the east end of Rue de la Solidarité. It's on the seafront beyond the Winston Churchill Bridge. On one side are buildings housing snack-bars and stalls selling an array of goods. The bus stops are on the other side, with the bus number and destination marked on each. The network is far-reaching as much of the population is without a car, but timetables are pretty 'flexible' and buses stop running at about 17.00. Travelling by bus is inexpensive: the maximum price for a ticket is usually around Rs15. Don't forget to raise your hand or clap in order to stop the bus.

HITCHHIKING Hitchhiking around Rodrigues is an absolute pleasure, because it's the 'done thing' to pick up anyone thumbing for a lift. You should, however, exercise due caution when accepting a lift from a stranger.

🏠 **ACCOMMODATION**

Although there are much-discussed plans to further develop tourism in Rodrigues, the industry is in its infancy. There are just a few small hotels on the island and no tourism training school, so if you are hoping to find accommodation and service of mainland Mauritian standards, you will be disappointed.

However, visitors who are looking to experience a unique island way of life will be delighted. Perhaps the best way to achieve this is to stay with a family or rent a house from a local, or at least eat a home-cooked meal at one of the many table d'hôte restaurants. Plenty of Rodriguans now offer this type of accommodation and dining, and in October 2001 the *Association des Gîtes, Chambres et Table d'Hôtes* came into being. Their leaflet is available from the MTPA in Mauritius and from inbound tour operators in Rodrigues. Details of some of the establishments are given in the following *Where to stay* and *Where to eat* sections.

Lack of crime and limited accommodation mean that opportunities for camping holidays are still many. Some of the best spots are around the beaches of the east coast.

Please note that as water is so scarce in Rodrigues, all of the hotels ask you to limit the amount that you use.

BUS?

Buses are privately owned and wistfully named: *Air Jumbo Jet* was typical. Buses go to the beach only on Sundays.

At Mangue Village, I found the only restaurant in Rodrigues open on Sunday, Chez Jean. Raw, mottled red sausages, traditional to Rodrigues, hung from a wrought-iron fence to cure among the scarlet leaves of poinsettias. There were no prices on the menu as Jean, the proprietor, charges according to his mood. My bill was the equivalent of £3.70 for a spicy sausage starter, fish with ginger, and a beer. As I left, Jean must have felt he had charged too much for I was presented with a bottle of his own bilious green chilli sauce as a souvenir.

At the road junction where the Ho Tu Nam store, Chez Ah Kong, Mrs Wong Tong's grocery and Jameson Begue's bar and bakery constitute the village centre, I waited for a bus back to town. Mr Begue, the baker, sold me a hot sponge cake and advised me to walk.

The breeze tempered the heat of the sun and the climb was gentle to Quatre Vents, a hilltop village with views of both north and south coasts and the constant, reassuring blue where sea and sky merge. I asked a group of farmers sitting on the steps of the grocer's shop when the next bus was due.

'No bus,' one of them said cheerfully. 'You'll have to walk.'

'There's a short cut to Oyster Bay,' said a boy when he saw my look of despair. 'You can get a lift to town from there. I'll show you.'

We set out through an avenue of trees along a grass path that opened up to a hillside of green sloping down to the coast. Oyster Bay seemed a long way off. At an isolated house where tanned, flaxen-haired children played in the garden, the boy invited me to meet his family. I gave them the cake and they presented me with another bottle of chilli sauce, brimful with whole chillies and garlic.

It took us an hour to reach Oyster Bay. A bus pulled up on the main road. It was the one that had taken me to the town from the airport a week before. The driver smilingly refused payment.

The next day, on the plane back to Mauritius, the pilot warned us before take-off: 'It is strictly forbidden to carry fish on flights from Rodrigues.' I looked at my bag. All I had from Rodrigues were two bottles of chilli sauce.

From an article by Royston Ellis for The Sunday Telegraph.

PHOTOGRAPHY

Most visitors prefer to purchase and develop film in their home country. Film and development are expensive in Rodrigues and are available at Citronelle Fotolab in the Rogers Centre on the corner of Rue Max Lucchesi and Rue Mamzelle Julia in Port Mathurin (✆ *831 1555*).

COMMUNICATIONS

POST The main post office is in Rue de la Solidarité, Port Mathurin (✆ *831 2098. Open Mon–Fri 08.15–16.00, Sat 08.00–11.30*). There are small post offices in Grande Montagne, La Ferme, Rivière Coco and Mt Lubin.

TELEPHONE To call Rodrigues from overseas, after dialling the international access code dial 230 followed by the seven-digit number beginning with 831. From Mauritius, dial 095 followed by the seven digits.

There are coin-operated payphones in Rodrigues – at the airport, in Port

Mathurin and also some villages, like La Ferme, Quatre Vents, Mont Lubin and Port Sud Est. Cardphones are now fairly widespread throughout the island.

Phone calls can be made and faxes sent at Mauritius Telecom in Rue Johnston, Port Mathurin (℩ *831 1816. Open Mon–Sat 07.30–15.30, Sun 07.00–12.00*). You can also buy phonecards (*télécartes*) here. Many hotels and guesthouses now have fax machines.

Mobile phone coverage is not good in Rodrigues; even if your mobile works in Mauritius it is unlikely to work here.

Useful telephone numbers
Administration office   Port Mathurin: 831 1515

ⓔ INTERNET ACCESS/EMAIL There is a shortage of internet cafés and many of those that have opened in recent years have had a very short lifespan. The only internet café in Port Mathurin is currently **Rodnet Cybercafé** (*Patricio Bldg, Pl François Leguat;* ℩ *831 0747. Open Mon–Fri 08.30–16.30, Sat 08.30–13.00*). Internet access costs Rs3 per minute or Rs300 for five hours. Scanning, faxing, CD/DVD burning and photocopying are also available.

PORT MATHURIN

This is an attractive, well laid-out town with the access road (Rue de la Solidarité) running its length (1,700m) and emerging to cross over reclaimed land and on to the residential village at **Baie aux Huîtres** (Oyster Bay).

Rodrigues's new regional assembly has replaced the British-influenced street names of Port Mathurin with names with a French flavour. However, many people still use the British street names, so both are included on the map of Port Mathurin opposite.

Parallel to Rue de la Solidarité, on the waterfront, is Rue Wolfert Harmensz. Three other streets also run parallel northeast to southwest: Rue François Leguat, Rue Max Lucchesi and Rue Victoria, giving the town a depth of about 300m. The streets linking them at right angles are leafy lanes lined with neat houses, many of them colonial wooden bungalows behind well-trimmed hedges.

A walk down Rue de la Solidarité leads past the colonial **house of the administrator** (built in 1873), with a cannon outside the gates and the gardener acting as security guard. The new administrative offices are opposite. Facing Barclays Bank and almost hidden by one-storey houses are the six miniature minarets of the **Noor-ud-Deen Mosque**, rebuilt in 1979–81.

On Rue Wolfert Harmensz, behind Rue de la Solidarité, are the **port, customs office** and a **public toilet**. At the port, opposite Rue Morrison, is a **war memorial** with three rifles forming a tripod and two cannon shafts beside them. The inscription reads: '*Aux engagés volontaires Rodriguais 1914–18, 1939–45*' (For the Rodriguans who served 1914–18, 1939–45).

At the western end of Rue Wolfert Harmensz is the slaughterhouse, where the white-painted buildings are marked PORC, CABRIS and BOEUF (pigs, goats and cattle). The **market** takes place in the street outside the slaughterhouse on Wednesday and Saturday mornings. The road is lined with stalls selling all manner of homemade and home-grown goodies: chutneys, drinks, woven baskets and hats, fruit and vegetables. For many locals this is the highlight of their week and a chance to catch up on the island's gossip. It's worth getting up early to see the market at its busiest, around 08.00.

The **St Barnabas Anglican Church** and school complex is at the eastern end

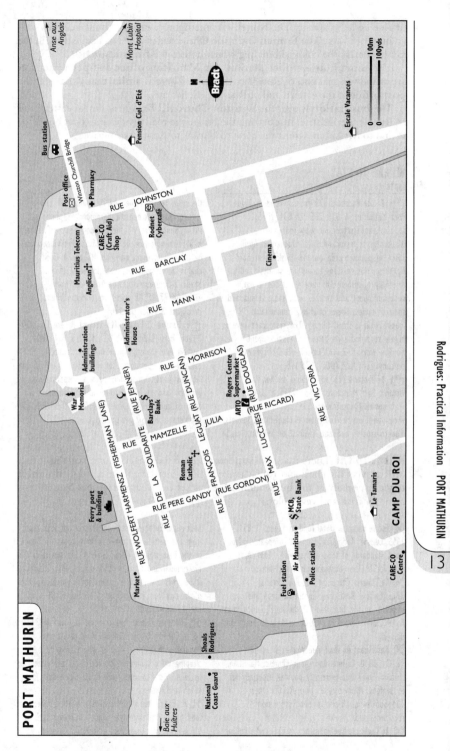

PORT MATHURIN

Anse aux Anglais

Mont Lubin Hospital

Bus station

Winston Churchill Bridge

Post office

Pharmacy

Pension Ciel d'Eté

RUE JOHNSTON

Mauritius Telecom

CARE-CO (Craft Aid) Shop

Anglican

Rodnet Cybercafe

RUE BARCLAY

Cinema

RUE MANN

Administration buildings

Administrator's House

War Memorial

RUE (RUE JENNER)

RUE MORRISON

RUE DE LA SOLIDARITE

Barclays Bank

RUE MAMZELLE

LEGUAT (RUE DUNCAN)

Rogers Centre

ARTO Supermarket

(RUE DOUGLAS)

(RUE RICARD)

RUE WOLFERT HARMENSZ (FISHERMAN LANE)

Roman Catholic

JULIA

FRANÇOIS

RUE MAX LUCCHESI

RUE VICTORIA

Ferry port & building

RUE PERE GANDY (RUE GORDON)

Le Tamaris

Market

CAMP DU ROI

Shoals Rodrigues

Fuel station

Air Mauritius

MCB, State Bank

Police station

CARE-CO Centre

National Coast Guard

Baie aux Huîtres

Escale Vacances

100m
100yds

13

of Rue de la Solidarité. The church is contemporary in style (built in 1977) with an interior tower. The **Roman Catholic Church** is in Rue Mamzelle Julia, in the same block as the colonial building which houses the **fire station**.

The **court house, police station, Air Mauritius office** and **petrol station** are at the western end of Rue Max Lucchesi. There is a **pharmacy** opposite the **post office** at the eastern end of Rue de la Solidarité.

The **bus station** is over the **Winston Churchill Bridge** at the far eastern end of Rue de la Solidarité. Just beyond the bridge the road divides into two; one leads inland to Mt Lubin, whilst the coast road leads to Anse aux Anglais.

WHERE TO STAY
Category D: budget

Escale Vacances (23 rooms) Fond la Digue, Port Mathurin; ☎ 831 2555; f 831 2075; e escal.vac@intnet.mu; www.rodrigues-island.org/escalesvacanes.html. Opened in April 1997, in a quiet area on the outskirts of Port Mathurin. The en-suite rooms are spotless and tastefully furnished; 18 have AC. It has a bar, swimming pool and terrace with table tennis and snooker tables. There is also a comfortable TV lounge with a small library. The restaurant here is highly regarded (see below). *Dbl/sgl without balcony from Rs2,400/1,500 HB. Dbl/sgl with balcony from Rs2,700/1,625 HB.*

Le Tamaris (15 apts) Camp du Roi, Rue Victoria, Port Mathurin; ☎ 831 2715; f 831 2720; e letamaris@intnet.mu; www.mauritours.net/rodrigues/letamaris.html. Spotless, modern studios and apts (with 2 or 3 bedrooms) in the town centre, owned by MauriTours. All have a well-equipped kitchenette, bathroom, TV, phone and sitting/dining area. All the bedrooms have AC. There is a restaurant (see below) and accommodation can be booked on room only, BB, HB or FB. Good-quality accommodation, ideal for self-caterers. *Studio/2-bedroom apt/3-bedroom apt from €51/64/77 RO. All prices are per apartment. Breakfast €4 per person.*

Pension Ciel d'Eté (15 rooms) Rivière Cascade Pigeon, Port Mathurin; ☎ 831 1587; f 831 2004. Just off Rue Johnston, near the bus station. A colonial-style guesthouse set in pleasant gardens with labelled plants. Simple but clean and spacious rooms, with fan and en-suite bathroom. The restaurant is open to guests only. *Dbl/sgl Rs800/500 BB. HB supplement Rs150 per person.*

WHERE TO EAT
There is a small **supermarket** in the Rogers Centre on the corner of Rue Max Lucchesi and Rue Mamzelle Julia. Snack vendors are dotted all over town, especially at the bus station. The market on Wednesdays and Saturdays is great for fruit and vegetables.

Escale Vacances Hotel Fond la Digue; ☎ 831 2555. Cuisine: Rodriguan, Chinese, European, seafood. Good standards of food and service. *Main courses from Rs90. Open daily for lunch and dinner.*

Le Tamaris Camp du Roi, Rue Victoria; ☎ 831 2715. Cuisine: Rodriguan, European. Clean and pleasant, on the first floor of the hotel. *Lunch from Rs140, dinner from Rs190. Open daily for lunch and dinner.*

Restaurant du Quai Rue Wolfert Harmensz; ☎ 831 2840. Cuisine: Rodriguan, Chinese, Mauritian, seafood. Small but extremely popular, especially for its seafood. *Main courses from Rs100. Open Tue–Sun for lunch and dinner. Reservation recommended.*

Le Capitaine Rue Johnston; ☎ 831 1581. Cuisine: Rodriguan, European, seafood. It may not look much from the outside but the chef here cooks up some of the best seafood dishes around. The service is professional and friendly. After dinner on a Saturday it becomes the place to dance the night away. *Dish of the day from Rs60. Open Mon–Sat 10.00–15.00 and 17.00–22.00.*

Paille en Queue Rue Francois Leguat; ☎ 831 1616. Cuisine: Creole, Chinese. Also take-away. Popular with locals, many of whom seem to be sleeping off a hangover. Wouldn't win any prizes for hygiene. *Main courses from Rs80. Open daily for lunch and dinner.*

Le Ranch Rue Victoria; ☎ 831 0440. Cuisine: fast food. Small American-style snack-bar. *Meals such as chicken nuggets and chips from Rs35. Open daily.*

The island's fish shape has its head in the east and its forked tail in the west. The bay at **St François** is its mouth. The road from the airport at the western corner of Rodrigues to Port Mathurin winds over the spine of mountains in the island's centre. These spines run north to south with deep ravines between them and offer breathtaking views down to the coast.

The airport is at **Plaine Corail**, aptly named for the coral plain on which the airstrip is built. The quickest route to Port Mathurin and the east is via **La Fouche**, **Quatre Vents** and **Mont Lubin**. From La Fouche you can also head north or south to the coastal roads. The north coast road takes you through **Port Mathurin** as far as **Grand Baie**, whilst the southern equivalent ends at the Mourouk Ebony Hotel in **Pâté Reynieux**. Both offer picturesque drives through villages and smallholdings, where cattle and pigs can often be seen rummaging on the seashore. Mangroves have been replanted along both coasts and can be seen in various stages of development.

The road to the north coast passes through **La Ferme**, where a school and church serve scattered dwellings. It was at this unassuming church that Pope John Paul II celebrated mass on 15 August 1989. Along the north coast, octopus can often be seen left out to dry and many of the houses sell seafood at the door. Also on this road, at **Pointe la Guele**, is the island's only (usually empty) **prison**, an unassuming blue and white building with fantastic sea views.

Beyond Port Mathurin is **Crève Coeur**, where there is a **Hindu temple** dedicated to Shiva. Further along the coast is the pretty bay of **Anse aux Anglais**, which has a sandy beach and plenty of places to stay. Scores of local ladies can often be seen walking out into the lagoon to catch octopus.

Almost all the island's roads lead to **Mont Lubin** before branching off in different directions. On the road from Port Mathurin to Mont Lubin, the **Queen Elizabeth Hospital** is on the right and the **meteorological station** is on the left. Opposite the meteorological station is a shrine, **La Reine de Rodrigues**, built in 1954, with magnificent views over Port Mathurin and out to sea. On the same road around the area of **Solitude**, you're likely to see rare **Rodrigues fruit bats** in the late afternoon.

In the centre of the island is **Mont Limon**, Rodrigues's highest point at 398m. From the road there is a short path leading to the summit, which offers far-reaching views around the island. Nearby, just south of the main road, is **St Gabriel**, which boasts the island's largest church. It was built from limestone blocks from 1934 onwards by devoted parishioners who carried the coral, sand and cement on foot.

At **Petit Gabriel** is a small bright blue and red corrugated-iron dwelling, which doubles as **Calypso Artisanat** (☎ *831 6171*) and the Boulauck family home. Mme Boulauck, who sits behind an ancient sewing machine, weaves hats and bags from vetyver and aloe leaves, whilst her husband makes an array of powerful chutneys (Rs40 per jar). He has recently created one especially for tourists – without chillies. M Boulauck speaks good English and will happily explain to you how the goods are made.

There is no road along the east coast but this is where the island's best **beaches** are found. They are easily reached on foot and almost always deserted. (See page 215.)

WHERE TO STAY
Category C: mid range

Pointe Vénus (54 rooms) Mont Vénus; ☎ 832 0104; f 832 0101; e infos-resa @ pointevenus.intnet.mu; www.mauritours.net/rodriuges/pointevenus.html. Opened in 2004, this is now the island's most upmarket hotel, offering the equivalent of 4-star accommodation and facilities. The hotel is about 3km from Port Mathurin, set back 100m from the coast road, overlooking the ocean. The rooms are well appointed, with AC, TV, phone, minibar, safe, tea/coffee facilities and balcony/terrace. For families, there are apts designed to take 2 adults and 2 children. There are 2 restaurants, a bar, 2 pools (one for children), gym, dive centre and kids' club. Activities such as deep-sea fishing can be organised. There is no beach to speak of but there is a good beach in front of Les Cocotiers, about 500m away. *Dbl/sgl from € 186/130 HB.*

🏠 **Les Cocotiers Hotel** (42 rooms) Anse aux Anglais; ✆ 831 1058; f 831 1800; e lescocotiers@intnet.mu; www.mauritours.net/rodrigues/lescocotiers.html. Belongs to MauriTours and is managed by Naiade who have numerous hotels in Mauritius. Fully refurbished in January 1999, it now offers some of the best-quality accommodation in Rodrigues. The standard en-suite rooms are comfortable, with AC, TV and phone, however, the hotel prefers to use these for Mauritian guests only. Overseas guests tend to stay in superior rooms, which are larger and have a minibar, safe and balcony/terrace with sea view. The suites are very large with 2 bedrooms, 2 bathrooms, fully equipped kitchen and sitting/dining room — ideal for families. The hotel has an open restaurant, bar, 2 pools, a jacuzzi, small gym,

hairdresser, some free watersports, regular evening entertainment and a good beach. There is a very pretty coral reef just off the coast. *Superior dbl/sgl from € 154/108 HB.*

🏠 **Cotton Bay Hotel** (48 rooms) Pointe Coton; ✆ 831 8001; f 831 8003; e cottonb@intnet.mu; www.cottonbayhotel.com. The en-suite rooms and 2 suites are housed in sea-facing bungalow-style buildings. Rooms have AC, TV, phone, minibar and safe. It has a small swimming pool, restaurant, games room, tennis court, dive centre and some watersports facilities. There are pleasant beaches in the area but it's an unattractive, windswept location. I've heard several reports of indifferent service and poor food. Horseriding is available (see page 212). *Dbl/sgl from Rs5,500/4,125.*

🏠 **Mourouk Ebony Hotel** (30 rooms) Pâté Reynieux, Mourouk; ✆ 832 3351; f 832 3355; e ebony@intnet.mu; www.mouroukebonyhotel.com. Perched on a hillside facing a vast lagoon and Ile aux Chats. A very popular, friendly hotel, so book well in advance. The rooms are housed in neat, red-roofed chalets set in beautiful gardens. Rooms are simply furnished with en-suite facilities, AC and fridge. Three rooms have a phone. There is a good restaurant with a bar, and a small pool. Activities include windsurfing and there are mountain bikes for hire, as well as a dive centre. *Dbl/sgl from Rs3,980/2,620HB.*

Category D: budget

🏠 **Chez Edouard** (3 rooms) Crève Coeur; ✆ 831 1665. Just east of Anse aux Anglais. As yet there is no sign marking the entrance to the house but it is easily recognisable: as you climb out of Anse aux Anglais, it is a large white house on the left with a red garage door and a low wall painted like a Friesian cow. The family let 2 dbl rooms and one family unit with 2 dbl rooms and 1 sgl, which sleeps up to 6 (it feels slightly older than the other rooms). All the accommodation has its own private entrance, en-suite facilities, kitchenette, TV and fan. The rooms are spotless and have been lovingly decorated by the owners right down to the handicrafts and shells. M and Mme Edouard are incredibly enthusiastic and eager to please their guests. Mme Edouard prepares delicious Rodriguan meals. *Dbl from Rs500 RO. Breakfast Rs50 per person, dinner Rs150. Airport transfers are Rs700 both ways.*

🏠 **Auberge Anse aux Anglais** (21 rooms) Anse aux Anglais; ✆ 831 2179, f 831 1973; e aubergehung@yahoo.com. Coming from Port

Mathurin, turn right after Seth mini-market and the hotel is on your left. The rooms have en-suite facilities and phone, most have AC and 3 have a minibar. Rooms are spacious with whitewashed walls and a small balcony/terrace. Facilities include a restaurant, an open-air TV lounge and a pool. *Dbl/sgl with fan from Rs1,725/1,095 HB, dbl/sgl with AC from Rs2,070/1,325.*

🏠 **Auberge Les Filaos** (14 rooms) Anse aux Anglais; ✆ 831 1644; f 831 2026; e filaos@intnet.mu. Opposite Auberge Anse aux Anglais. The location is quiet and the gardens are a good place to relax. There are 10 en-suite rooms, 4 with shared bathroom. Rooms are stark but spacious with ceiling fan and balcony/terrace. There is a simple, clean restaurant and a pool. *Dbl/sgl from Rs900/600 BB.*

🏠 **Pensionnat Beau Séjour** (5 rooms) Anse aux Anglais; ✆ 831 1753; f 831 1754. Enquire in Seth mini-market; rooms are above it. Five simple rooms with fan, 3 of which are en suite. There is a shared terrace with a view of the sea. *En-suite* dbl/sgl from Rs850/400 BB, dbl/sgl with shared bathroom from Rs800/350 BB. HB supplement Rs75 per person.

🏠 **Les Varangues** (1 villa, 3 apts) Grand Baie; ☎ 832 0022; e reser@lesvarangues.com; www.lesvarangues.com. Offers a fully furnished 3-bedroom villa and 3 apts (2 studios and a 2-bedroom flat). Accommodation is simply furnished but comfortable and clean. Table d'hôte meals can be provided. Villa/2-bedroom apt/studio from Rs3,500/2,100/1,400 per night RO. HB supplement Rs350 per person.

🏠 **Chez Claudine** (4 rooms) St-François; ☎/f 831 8242; e cbmoneret@intnet.mu. In a tranquil spot on one of the island's best beaches. Fantastic views of the ocean and there are some great coastal walks in the area. Immaculate rooms with shared bathroom. There is a TV lounge. Dbl/sgl from Rs1,800/900 HB.

🏠 **La Collinière** (5 rooms) Brûlé; ☎/f 831 8241; e lacolliniere@yahoo.co.uk; http://lacolliniere.site.voila.fr. Comfortable guesthouse accommodation in a modern home with tropical gardens and views of the ocean. The rooms are simply furnished and clean. All have en-suite facilities and 3 have a balcony. There are good walks in the area and the table d'hôte serves excellent Creole and seafood dishes. Dbl/sgl from Rs1,400/900 HB.

🏠 **Auberge de la Montagne** (5 rooms) Grande Montagne; ☎ 831 4607; e villa@intnet.mu. A stay with the charming Baptiste family is truly memorable. The accommodation is basic – 3 of the rooms are en suite, 2 have shared bathroom. Françoise Baptiste is a superb chef and prepares excellent table d'hôte meals. The family are very knowledgeable and much can be gained from the conversation at dinner, particularly as they speak good English. Dbl/sgl from Rs1,400/600 HB.

🏠 **Les Rosiers** (5 rooms) Grande Montagne; ☎ 831 4703; f 831 1894; e 2000trs@intnet.mu. Spacious en-suite rooms, most with 1 dbl and 1 sgl bed, fan, TV and terrace. Very comfortable and clean. Owners also do table d'hôte meals. Dbl/sgl from Rs1,400/800 HB.

🏠 **Domaine de Décidé** (2 villas) Batatrana, Nouvelle Découverte; ☎ 262 6708, f 262 8283; e fmloc@intnet.mu. Two comfortable self-catering Creole-style houses, in a quiet park off the road to Gravier, in the southeast. Each cottage has 4 twin rooms, 2 bathrooms, a kitchen and a terrace. Serviced by a maid. Pretty, but may be too isolated for some. Prices vary but are around Rs750 per person RO.

🏠 **Chez Mireille Jean-Louis** (2 rooms) Nassola; ☎ 831 4615. Two en-suite dbl rooms. There is a TV lounge. Meals can be provided in the family home. Dbl/sgl from Rs1,000/520 HB.

Houses for rent Large, clean houses can be rented per night or per week. Prices vary. If there are only two of you, the owners may arrange for you to share a house with other visitors.

🏠 **Jean-Louis Limock** Anse aux Anglais; ☎ 831 1653. If his house is occupied he can arrange other accommodation.

🏠 **Karl Allas** Mont Lubin; ☎ 831 1473. Rents a floor of his house.

✖ **WHERE TO EAT** All villages have a small general store, where you can buy essentials. Larger shops stocking food can be found in Anse aux Anglais, La Ferme and Port Mathurin.

In family homes There is nothing like good old home cooking and, luckily for us, some Rodriguan families have opened up their homes for table d'hôte dinners. The following will serve up a traditional gastronomic delight if you reserve beforehand. Expect to pay around Rs200 per person for lunch or dinner.

✖ **Auberge de la Montagne** Grande Montagne; ☎/f 831 4607
✖ **Gladys Rivière** Camp du Roi; ☎ 831 1934
✖ **Sylviane Limock** Anse aux Anglais; ☎ 831 1653

✖ **Chez Claudine** St-François; ☎/f 831 8242
✖ **La Collinière** Brûlé; ☎/f 831 8241
✖ **Les Rosiers** Grande Montagne; ☎ 831 4703
✖ **Chez Mireille Jean-Louis** Nassola; ☎ 831 4615
✖ **Eliane Prudence** Maréchal; ☎ 831 6560

Restaurants

✕ La Marmite Resto Crève Coeur; ☎ 831 1689. Cuisine: Rodriguan, Mauritian and Indian. The owner of this cheerfully decorated restaurant is a schoolteacher during the day and chef by night, cooking with his wife. Good friendly service and great food – most people come back for more. *Main courses from Rs95. Open daily for lunch and dinner.*

✕ Le Récif Caverne Provert; ☎ 831 1804. Cuisine: Chinese, Rodriguan. Popular, smart place with evening entertainment on the weekends. *Medium price range. Open Thu–Tue for lunch and dinner.*

✕ John's Resto Mangues; ☎ 831 6306. Cuisine: Rodriguan, Chinese, seafood. Small plain restaurant but wonderful seafood dishes (prawns, crab, oysters etc) and a well-stocked bar. Interior and terrace seating. Very good reputation. *Main courses from Rs110. Open daily for lunch, dinner on reservation.*

✕ Le Printemps Quatre Vents; ☎ 831 6585. Cuisine: Rodriguan, Chinese, European, seafood. A small restaurant, lots of plastic but clean. *Main courses from Rs100, crayfish from Rs275 (min 500g). Open daily for lunch and dinner. Reservation recommended.*

NIGHTLIFE On weeknights Port Mathurin is transformed into what resembles a ghost town by about 20.30. There is a **cinema** on Rue Victoria; the films are mostly in French and tickets cost Rs70.

There is regular live entertainment (traditional music and dance) at the **Cotton Bay Hotel** on Friday and Saturday nights, at the **Mourouk Ebony** on Wednesday and Saturday and at **Les Cocotiers Hotel** on Saturday.

Le Récif (☎ *831 1804*) at Caverne Provert, near Anse aux Anglais has *séga* on Friday evenings and a disco on Saturdays. **Hermitage** disco (☎ *831 4641*) in Mont Lubin is open on Saturday nights.

WHAT TO SEE AND DO

As part of its campaign to promote Rodrigues as a destination to appeal to sensitive travellers, the MTPA has produced a glossy leaflet with a section on what to do and see. The list is short but pinpoints some of the charms of the island. The activities can be organised by a tour operator or hotel.

- Hiking/trekking/mountain biking
- Rod and line fishing or accompanying fishermen when they pick up lobsters, crab and octopus from the *casiers* left overnight in the lagoon
- Visit Caverne Patate (the cave) at Plaine Corail; guide essential
- Visit local people in their homes. It is possible to stay with them and sample home cuisine.
- Boat trip to Ile aux Cocos, a haven for seabirds
- Experience the *séga-tambour*, the island's folkloric dance
- Enjoy Rodriguan fish and seafood in local restaurants

CAVERNE PATATE There are many caves in the west of the island but Caverne Patate, near Petite Butte, is the only one open to the public. The cave is 600m long and 18m below sea level. It takes around 30 minutes to walk through the maze of contorted stalactites and stalagmites. When the cave was discovered many bones of the extinct Rodrigues solitaire were found.

A permit to visit the cave, which costs Rs200, has to be obtained from the administration office on Rue Morrison in Port Mathurin (☎ *831 1504*). The permit should be shown to the guide on arrival (a guide is obligatory). If you go on an organised excursion, this should all be handled for you.

The guide will compare the rock formations to various famous people and objects but little insight is gained into the geological origins of the cave. The experience is also diminished by the poor quality of the torches. Warm clothes and sturdy shoes should be worn. Guided tours depart daily at 09.00, 10.30, 13.00 and 14.30.

OFFSHORE AND COASTAL EXCURSIONS The excursion to **Ile aux Cocos** is unquestionably the most popular day trip available and should cost around Rs700. It is a shallow sand bar with coconut palms, casuarina trees and colonies of terns and noddies.

Most hotels and tour operators organise full-day trips, which include a barbecue lunch. Apart from admiring the seabirds you can relax on the unspoilt beach and swim in the shallow lagoon. Although most operators offer snorkelling as part of the trip, the flat, sandy bottom provides little of interest.

Certain areas of the island are bird nesting sites and so are off-limits to visitors. However, some unscrupulous guides lead their groups through the breeding colonies, which disturbs the birds. Some of the adult birds can become agitated and aggressive, so please avoid these areas.

On the return trip the boats head into the wind and the crossing can be long, wet and cold. Some boats now come ashore at Pointe Diable to meet a minibus, which is a more comfortable option.

Ile aux Chats (Cat Island) is an uninhabited islet in the vast lagoon fronting the Mourouk Ebony Hotel. A full-day excursion there organised by the hotel costs Rs800 and includes a beach barbecue. You can stop off for diving/snorkelling at Gouzoupa *en route* (see pages 214–15).

SPORTING ACTIVITIES The following companies can arrange activities such as hiking, fishing and bike rental:

RodTours (affiliated to MauriTours of Mauritius) Camp du Roi, Port Mathurin; ✆ 831 2249; f 831 2267; e rodtours@intnet.mu
2000 Tours Rue Morrison, Port Mathurin; ✆/f 831 1894; e 2000trs@intnet.mu
Beracca Tours Baie aux Huîtres; ✆ 831 2198

Ebony Tours Rue de la Solidarité, Port Mathurin; ✆ 832 3351; f 832 3355; e ebony@intnet.mu
Rotourco Place François Leguat, Port Mathurin; ✆ 831 0747; f 832 0747
Ecotourisme Rue Max Lucchesi, Port Mathurin; ✆ 831 2801; f 831 2800; e ecotours@intnet.mu

Hiking There are several possible trails into the interior, where gorges, hills and deep valleys beckon keen hikers. No special skills are required, as grading is mostly moderate or easy.

Some trails commence near the hotels, such as behind the Mourouk Ebony (Anse Mourouk). The hotels and tour operators will advise keen hikers on routes and can organise local guides.

A 5km trail starts at Anse Mourouk and runs uphill to Grande Montagne. First the trail leads to Montagne Chéri, a viewpoint over the vast lagoon to one side and the Mourouk Gorge on the other. Continue further uphill through a small village, with a few houses, herds of goats and cattle. The last part of the trail covers wooded terrain and ends at the broad, paved road leading to the Grande Montagne police station. The trail can be done in reverse for those who don't want to walk continuously uphill. Public bus services are available at either end of the trail.

Mt Limon and Mt Malartic offer good opportunities for hiking, while the pristine beach of Trou d'Argent is a fairly easy 30-minute walk from the coastal village of St-François. Other good walks include Port Mathurin to Grand Baie and on to Pointe Coton and Port Mathurin to Baie du Nord.

Guided hikes can be organised by the inbound tour operators (see pages 201–2). Eco-évasion (for contact details see page 213) offers guided hikes in the island's nature reserves for Rs250 per person.

Horseriding Cotton Bay Hotel (*Pointe Coton;* ⤷ *831 3000*). There are only three horses, which are kept in unfortunate conditions. Be wary – the equipment is in an extremely poor state; very few hats are available so a good fit is unlikely and the instructor is not qualified, nor does he speak English.

Mountain biking Mt Limon and Mt Malartic offer good mountain biking. For bike hire, contact **Club Osmosis** (*Mourouk Ebony Hotel, Pâté Reynieux;* ⤷ *832 3051;* f *832 3355;* e *osmosis@intnet.mu; www.osmosis-rodrigues.com*).

Windsurfing/kitesurfing Available through **Club Osmosis** (*Mourouk Ebony Hotel, Pâté Reynieux;* ⤷ *832 3051;* f *832 3355;* e *osmosis@intnet.mu; www.osmosis-rodrigues.com*).

Deep-sea fishing

BDPM Mont Fanal; ⤷/f 831 2790; e birgit.dirk@intnet.mu
Blue Dynamite Fishing Mourouk; ⤷ 832 3351; f 625 4300; e contact@bluedynamite.mu. I am told that the deep-sea fishing around the island is relatively poor. Expect to pay around Rs1,250 per person per day.

Scuba diving and snorkelling Having never been affected by industrial pollution, the reefs around Rodrigues offer rewarding scuba diving and snorkelling. Many people believe that the underwater experiences to be had there are superior even to those around the outer Seychelles or Maldives. Furthermore, some insist that divers need not even use scuba gear, because even without it they can see such a stunning array of underwater life.

Snorkelling excursions can be arranged by many of the island's hotels and cost around Rs150 per person. This includes boat trips to and from the reefs.

The island's dive sites and dive centres are best suited to qualified divers with a reasonable amount of experience. Rodrigues lacks the shallow, clear, sandy-bottomed sites which beginners need and the instructors at the dive centres tend to focus on leading rather than teaching. However, both dive centres do offer resort courses for beginners.

Reef Beneath Aquatic specialises in activities associated with marine eco-tourism. They have knowledgeable staff and good equipment. They organise guided coastal walks, picnics around the reef, snorkelling and diving. Contact Eric Blais (⤷ *831 1225*).

Warning to divers Scorpionfish, lionfish (firefish) and stonefish are all common around Rodrigues and are highly venomous. Striped catfish and banded eels are present too. Wear gloves as protection from anemones on wrecks and watch out for black-spined sea urchins.

Dive centres The dive centres below offer a range of diving options and packages. The following is a guide to the prices you can expect to pay:

Single dive: Rs920 (qualified), beginner's resort course (pool lesson and sea dive): Rs1,100, night dives: Rs1,200, five-dive package: Rs4,000. These rates include equipment.

Bouba Diving Centre Mourouk Ebony Hotel, Pâté Reynieux; ⤷ 832 3063; f 832 3355; e ebony@intnet.mu. Run by NAUI instructor Benoit de Baize. Fully equipped to cater for 6 divers at a time.

Cotton Dive Centre Cotton Bay Hotel, Pointe Coton; ⤷ 831 8001; f 831 8003; e diverod@intnet.mu. Run by Jacques and Marie-Jose Degremont (CMAS 2-star instructor and CMAS-3 star diver, respectively); both are PADI dive masters.

Caters for 10 divers at a time. Prices on request from the dive centre. The dive centre closes in July and August.

Eco-évasion Pointe Monier, Port Mathurin; ✆ 831 2368; e contact@rodrigues-eco-evasion.com;

www.rodrigues-eco-evasion.com. Run by Richard, a CMAS 2-star instructor and PADI dive master. Offers diving and snorkelling trips, boat trips to the outlying islands and guided nature walks.

Top dive sites

Grande Paté Near Port Mathurin, this site is outstanding for its coral gardens at depths of 8–28m.

Grand Bassin Beyond the waters of the pass, there are some superb sites at around 20–25m with large table corals. Occasional sightings of white-tipped reef sharks, large groupers and jacks are reported. The two islets of **Ile aux Sables** and **Ile aux**

CORALS OF RODRIGUES

Tom Hooper

The corals on the reef slopes of Rodrigues are in very good condition, with around 140 different species of coral represented. Compared to places such as Indonesia or the Great Barrier Reef, this biodiversity is quite low. A coral reef is made up of countless individual animals called polyps. These invertebrate animals manufacture their skeleton from calcium in the seawater.

The following species are commonly found in Rodrigues:

FAVIA This coral grows in huge mounds known as 'massive' formations. When alive it is a brown or green colour. Its polyps are translucent and come out at night to feed. They are very sensitive and can quickly retract back into the skeleton if they sense movement such as a fish about to take a nip of their tentacles.

PAVONA Has a form which resembles leaves. The corallites are on both sides and have a very clear spider shape. They are brown in colour and are often found in muddy habitats such as around the channel at Port Mathurin, which is quite unusual for corals.

FUNGIA These are called mushroom corals as they resemble field mushrooms with their disc shapes and radiating vanes. This coral has only one polyp with many bright green tentacles. Unlike other corals, this one does not stay cemented to the reef, but is free living and will be moved around by the waves.

POCILLOPORA This is a coral with very fine branches. Sometimes these corals are a beautiful pink colour. Their bumpy corallites can look like popcorn!

STYLOPHORA These corals live all around the tropics. Their larvae can travel for hundreds, if not thousands of miles.

GONIASTREA This is one of the toughest corals and is often found in places where other corals cannot survive. It can tolerate long exposure to the sun and muddy conditions. The skeleton looks a bit like honeycomb.

ACROPORA This is the fastest-growing coral. With a very light and delicate skeleton the fingers of some branching shapes can grow 10cm a year. This group has a wide variety of shapes with forms which are branching, mounds, fingers and flat plates.

PORITES This group are often large, rounded and dense balls. They are very slow growing, with a coral taking up to 50 years to reach the size of a football. Some huge colonies which reach the size of a car are thousands of years old and are sometimes cored to yield climatic information.

CARE-Co, formerly known as Craft-Aid, is a non-profit, non-government organisation with a centre for handicapped people (blind, deaf, and physically handicapped) founded in 1989 by Paul Draper MBE, one of two British expats living on the island.

The project's aim is to provide creative and remunerative employment, as well as education, for people with disabilities. There are no shareholders in the organisation, and profits are shared among the workforce. Surplus is reinvested.

Suzanne Auguste, originally from Scotland, is the second British expat living on the island and runs the educational aspect of the project, the Gozague Pierre-Louis Centre. The school, which opened in 1994, is privately run for hearing and visually impaired children who, because of their handicap, are unable to benefit from the formal education offered by their local primary school. The centre also provides the island's only hearing and sight tests. Suzanne is qualified to carry out hearing tests, but since there is no optician on the island specialists must come over from Mauritius. All the equipment, books and stationery are financed by private donation.

After completing their education, the youngsters are employed in the CARE-Co workshop and receive all the conditions of employment that anyone else would.

The only items made on Rodrigues which are sold further afield than Mauritius are the jewellery made at the CARE-Co Centre. The items are made from coconut and ox bone and include a variety of necklaces, hair slides, bracelets, earrings (for pierced and non-pierced ears), brooches, key rings and pendants. They are all very striking. Fencing, souvenirs, handicrafts and furniture are also made.

Latest on the agenda is a project involving Rodriguan honey. The honey has already had huge success and won second prize at the international London Honey Show in 2000 and third prize in 2001. CARE-Co now supplies Air Mauritius with honey for in-flight meals. Paul hopes to build on this success and begin production of goats' cheese.

With 45 employees, CARE-Co is one of the island's largest private sector employers. Production activities are carefully chosen to fit in with the ability of the handicapped people to manage the work. The human benefits of CARE-Co both to individuals and Rodriguan society are evident but immeasurable.

To arrange to visit the CARE-Co workshop at Camp du Roi in Port Mathurin contact Mary François or Suzanne Auguste (✆ 831 1766; f 831 2276). There are two CARE-Co shops where you can purchase jewellery and souvenirs, one adjoining the workshop and one in Rue de la Solidarité. The shops and the workshop are both open Monday–Friday 08.00–16.00, while the Rue de la Solidarité shop is also open Saturday 08.00–12.00.

For further details of how you can help CARE-Co's vital work, see *Giving something back*, pages 84–5.

Cocos lie within an extensive fringing reef and can be visited at high tide. Both offer good diving and snorkelling, but go with skippers familiar with the area or else the chances of being shipwrecked are alarming here.

Pointe Coton At depths of 4–5m the diving is spectacular.

Off Port Sud-est People dive in the passage near the entrance to the barrier reef. Diving is best along the cliff, at 4–18m.

Gouzoupa Opposite Mourouk Ebony Hotel, this is an excellent site (depth 2–17m). There is a good chance of seeing large shoals of jacks, parrot fish and surgeon fish, and the area is rich in branching and other formations of coral. There are currents, so the site is best visited when there is little tide and conditions are calm.

Grand Baie Has excellent varieties of coral and fish (depth 2–20m).

Shipwrecks There are many wrecks around the reefs which ring Rodrigues. Those around the southern reefs include *Quatre Vingt Brisants*, *Clytemnesra* (1870) and *Nussur Sultan*. Northwest of Port Mathurin are the *White Jacket* (1871) and *Traveller*.

BEACHES Aside from **Ile aux Cocos**, the best beaches on Rodrigues itself are on the east coast at **Pointe Coton**, **Mourouk** and around **St François**.

Owing to the small number of tourists present at any time on Rodrigues, none of the glorious beaches is ever crowded. This makes it ideal for those in search of solitude, privacy and relaxation in a secluded setting.

Trou d'Argent ('Silver hole') must surely be the most beautiful beach on Rodrigues itself and is one of the island's postcard images. You can get to the long, unspoilt beach of St François by bus or car, from where a 30-minute walk will take you to the small cove of Trou d'Argent. Head through the gates to the right of the small hut at the southern end of the Baie de l'Est and you are on the path to Trou d'Argent.

The coastline between **Gravier** and St François is dotted with small beaches. To walk this stretch of coast takes around three hours but involves some clambering over rocks in places.

SHOPPING FOR SOUVENIRS Rodrigues is not a souvenir hunter's paradise. If you want to shop til you drop, stick to Mauritius or Réunion. That said, there has been a recent increase in the number of people involved in the handicraft industry, which today provides employment to some 700 Rodriguans. They're involved in basketry, hat-making, textile-based crafts like embroidery, coconut crafts and jewellery. Food processing, souvenir articles, woodcarvings, straw collages and screenprinting have also developed of late. The Rodrigues branch of the National Handicraft Centre acts as co-ordinator and facilitates the development of the industry by hosting workshops, seminars and training sessions.

The hats you can buy in Rodrigues are made from fibre of vetyver, pandanus, coconut or latanier leaves. Basketry also utilises bamboo or sisal. Other items made from these materials include cradles, baskets, briefcases, tablemats, lampshades, letter holders and so on. In Port Mathurin, as well as the market, there are several roadside kiosks and curio shops which sell local handicrafts and food preserves, including hellishly hot chillies, mango and tamarind.

When doing your souvenir shopping, bear in mind that it is well worth supporting **CARE-Co** (see box *CARE-Co*, opposite).

13

Trochetia blackburniana

Part Four

REUNION

Country An overseas department of France

Location Island in the western Indian Ocean, south of the Equator and north of the Tropic of Capricorn

Size 2,512km²

History Discovered by Arab and Malay sea traders around the 10th century, then by the Portuguese. In 1642, it was annexed for France but remained uninhabited. The first settlers were exiled from Madagascar in 1646. After Napoleon Bonaparte surrendered to Britain in 1810, Britain received Réunion but showed no interest in the island and never assigned a governor to it. The island was handed back to France after the Treaty of Paris in 1814. In 1848, the island's name was changed to Réunion. On 19 March 1946 Réunion was declared a *Département d'Outre-Mer* (overseas department) and it remains one of France's last colonies.

Climate The island features some 200 microclimates. Broadly speaking, the climate around the coast is tropical while in the mountainous uplands it is temperate. The hot and rainy summer lasts from November to April, while the remaining months are cooler and drier. Cyclones may occur from January to March.

Nature Réunion has the highest mountains in the Indian Ocean, one of the world's most active volcanoes, more remaining natural forests than on the other Mascarenes, black volcanic beaches in the south and east, white sandy beaches on the west coast, coral reefs, rare birds and waterfalls in abundance.

Visitors 430,000 tourists in 2004, 80% from France. Visitors come all year round; busiest times coincide with French school holidays.

Capital St-Denis

Government The island is administered by a *préfet* (prefect), who is delegated by the French government

Population 776,948 (July 2005), mostly Creole (blend of Franco-Africans, but also groups with Indian and Chinese origins). Substantial community of metropolitan French.

Economy Since the mid 1990s tourism has taken over from traditional industries as the main currency earner. Most goods are imported from France, while local products are exported to France by agreement. Traditional exports are geranium and vetyver oils, sugar and vanilla. Inflation and unemployment are high, with rates exceeding those of mainland France.

Language French is the official language. Creole spoken in daily life but French used in more formal situations. English barely spoken outside tourist industry.

Religion Christianity, Hinduism, Islam, Buddhism. Some islanders adhere to tribal lore.

Currency The euro (€)

Rate of exchange £1 = €1.46, US$ = €0.84, MRs38 = €1

International telephone code +262

Time GMT +4

Electricity 220 volts

Weights and measures Metric system

14

Background Information

GEOGRAPHY

Réunion is situated in the western Indian Ocean, 700km east of Madagascar. Mauritius, the nearest and oldest of the Mascarenes, lies 200km to its northeast.

Réunion's volcanic birth is estimated to have started some 2½ million years ago. First to rise up from the Indian Ocean floor was its oldest and highest peak, the formidable Piton-des-Neiges (Snow Peak – 3,069m), said to have become extinct about 500,000 years ago. It is the highest mountain in the western Indian Ocean but, despite its name, snow is very rarely seen on its peak.

More recently (about 380,000 years ago), the aptly named Piton-de-la-Fournaise (Furnace Peak) evolved. It stands at 2,631m and is one of the world's most active volcanoes. Since 1998, the volcano has erupted almost every year. The lava tends to flow down the eastern slope of the volcano, spilling into the sea and modifying the coastline with every eruption.

The two mountain ranges and three vast natural amphitheatres known as 'cirques' (Cilaos, Mafate and Salazie) account for much of the island's rugged interior. Converging at the 2,991m summit of Le Gros Morne, the amphitheatres give Réunion its wildly dramatic appearance, as well as breathtaking hiking trails, waterfalls, forests and gorges.

Réunion retains more original forest than do the other Mascarenes. Where there are accessible tracts of arable land, fields of geranium, vetyver and sugarcane are cultivated. Tucked away between the ravines, on small patches of level ground called 'ilets', are vineyards and lentil fields.

The inhospitable interior means that the majority of the population is concentrated in towns along the narrow coastal plains. Réunion does not have the abundance of wide sandy beaches that Mauritius enjoys but there are both black and white sand beaches along the west and south coasts. Coral reefs and lagoons are also dotted along the west and south of the island.

CLIMATE

The island lies in the path of moist tropical weather pattern circulations, rainfall being highest in the eastern region. In fact, a world record for rainfall of over 12m in a year was claimed in the 1980s for Takamaka, a gorge in Réunion's interior uplands.

Waterfalls are numerous and a prominent feature of the scenery, especially in the many steep ravines. In the amphitheatre of Salazie, for example, there are around a hundred waterfalls, plunging like silvery ribbons down sheer, green cliffs.

The weather along the coast is pleasant almost all year round, although in winter the southeasterly trade winds can make the south coast unbearably blustery. Summer, which is hot and humid, is from November to April with rains peaking from January to March. Cyclones may strike between January and March, as they

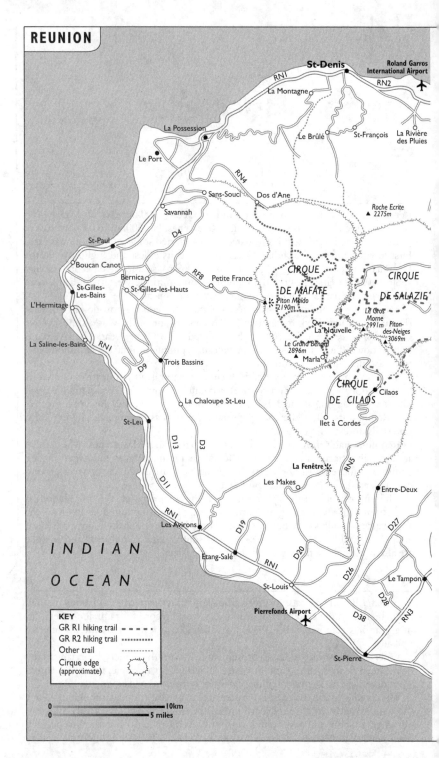

REUNION

St-Denis

Roland Garros
International Airport

La Montagne

RN1

RN2

La Possession

Le Brûlé

St-François

La Rivière
des Pluies

Le Port

RN4

Sans-Souci

Dos d'Ane

Roche Ecrite
▲ 2275m

Savannah

D4

St-Paul

Boucan Canot

RF8

Petite France

CIRQUE
DE MAFATE

CIRQUE
DE SALAZIE

Bernica

St-Gilles-les-Hauts

St-Gilles-
Les-Bains

L'Hermitage

Piton Maïdo
2190m

Le Gros
Morne
2991m

Pitons-
des-Neiges
3069m

La Saline-les-Bains

RN1

La Nouvelle

D9

Trois Bassins

Le Grand Bénard
2896m

Marla

CIRQUE
DE CILAOS

Cilaos

D13

D3

La Chaloupe St-Leu

St-Leu

Ilet à Cordes

La Fenêtre

RN5

D11

Les Makes

Entre-Deux

RN1

Les Avirons

D19

D27

D20

INDIAN

Etang-Salé

RN1

D26

Le Tampon

OCEAN

St-Louis

D28

RN3

Pierrefonds Airport

D38

KEY
GR R1 hiking trail – – – –
GR R2 hiking trail ·········
Other trail
Cirque edge
(approximate)

St-Pierre

0 ——————— 10km
0 ——————— 5 miles

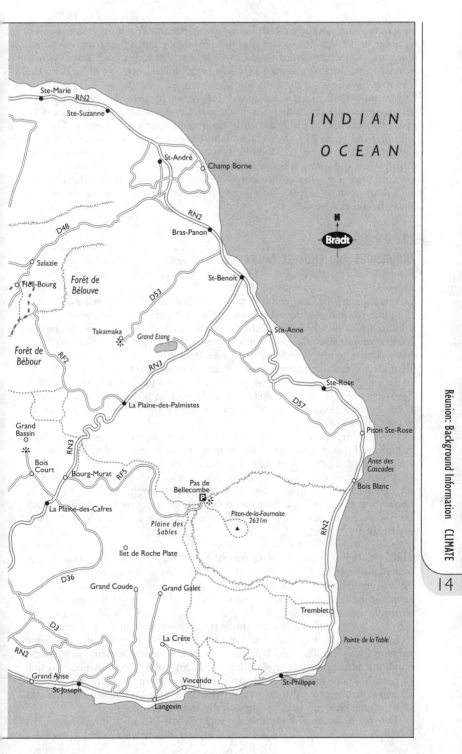

INDIAN

OCEAN

Bradt

Ste-Marie
RN2
Ste-Suzanne
St-André
Champ Borne
RN2
D48
Bras-Panon
Salazie
Forêt de
Bélouve
Hell-Bourg
St-Benoît
D53
Ste-Anne
Takamaka
Grand Etang
Forêt de
Bébour
RF2
RN3
Ste-Rose
D57
La Plaine-des-Palmistes
Piton Ste-Rose
Grand
Bassin
RN3
Anse des
Cascades
Bois
Court
Bourg-Murat
RF5
Bois Blanc
Pas de
Bellecombe
La Plaine-des-Cafres
Piton-de-la-Fournaise
2631m
Plaine des
Sables
RN2
Ilet de Roche Plate
D36
Grand Coude
Grand Galet
Tremblet
D3
La Crête
Pointe de la Table
RN2
Grand Anse
Vincendo
St-Philippe
St-Joseph
Langevin

may in the whole of the western Indian Ocean region. (For more information on cyclones in the Mascarenes, see page 4–5. For the cyclone information telephone line, see page 252.) Winter (May to October) is cooler and drier. Winter temperatures, aside from being very low in the mountains, also drop along the windward east coast.

During winter nights, frost and ice occur in the high mountains as temperatures fall to freezing point. In the interior, winter days start at around 4°C, rising to about 15°C by midday, whilst summer days are fairly warm, 15°C in the morning and up to 25°C by midday. Temperatures along the west coast average around 21°C in winter to 31–35°C in summer. Skies along the west coast are usually clear and sunny, whereas a blanket of mist and clouds invariably descends over the rest of the island in the mid-afternoon. The numerous microclimates mean that when there is rain on the coast it can be completely clear in the interior uplands, and vice versa.

FLORA AND FAUNA

INDIGENOUS AND ENDEMIC FAUNA *Note 'Indigenous' pertains to something found in Réunion and on the other Mascarene Islands, whilst 'endemic' means something found only in Réunion.*

Surprisingly little has been documented of Réunion's natural history. Just like the other Mascarenes, this island was once inhabited by an ensemble of animal oddities, most of which were birds. From detailed accounts left by the earliest settlers, we can glean that Réunion's original inhabitants included large, flightless birds similar to the Mauritian dodo and Rodriguan solitaire. Like them, the Réunion species, also referred to as 'solitaire', was roughly the size of a turkey. To its detriment, it was very trusting, having evolved in a predator-free environment. Some experts are now of the opinion that the solitaire of Réunion was possibly a large, aberrant, terrestrial ibis. In any case, it was swiftly exterminated along with at least a dozen other endemic birds.

It would appear that the extinct species were dependent on the lowland rainforests, because these were felled long ago for agriculture and timber, whereas Réunion's upland rainforests are still in magnificent shape.

Absent (as is the case also on Mauritius and Rodrigues) are indigenous, terrestrial mammals; neither are there any native amphibians. Of Réunion's known endemic reptiles, all but two have been exterminated. The survivors are both colourful species of day gecko: *Phelsuma inexpectata* and *P. bourbonas*. Neither is particularly common.

BIRDS As Réunion retains more natural forest than most other Indian Ocean islands, its endemic birds have fared better than those elsewhere in the region. Today, nine species are still fairly plentiful. A short walk in places such as Roche Ecrite or the fabulous Bébour Forest should reveal the likes of Réunion cuckoo-shrike, Réunion bulbul, Réunion stonechat, Réunion grey white-eye and Réunion olive white-eye. Only the cuckoo-shrike is somewhat uncommon and furtive.

Easier to see in Réunion than on Mauritius is the elegant little Mascarene paradise flycatcher. The land bird best known to locals is the Réunion harrier, a handsome black and white raptor often seen soaring over lush vegetation in search of prey. It is also found on Madagascar but is less common there. Locally, it is known as the *papangue*. Also shared with Mauritius is the Mascarene swiftlet, flocks of which can be seen wheeling energetically around their nesting caves.

Two small, threatened seabirds are high on the lists of visiting birders: the Réunion black petrel (*Pterodroma atterima*) and the Barau's petrel (*Pterodroma*

Considering the large number of invasive exotic plants which have run rampant in Réunion, it is refreshing to note that one of these pests, the Goyavier (*Psidium cattleyanum*), is actually extremely useful.

Introduced from eastern Brazil, the goyavier is a fairly nondescript shrub which grows to a height of 8m. Its deep red fruit somewhat resembles a miniature guava. It is an excellent source of Vitamin C.

After being picked, the fruit tastes quite acidic, but innovative Réunionnais have found many uses for it.

For starters, goyavier cocktails are hallucinatory! Alternatively, try the exceedingly potent rum punch flavoured with it. Goyavier jam, too, is really tasty. So significant has this fruit become in Réunion, that there is even a two-day Goyavier festival, held every June in La Plaine-des-Palmistes.

baraui). Both are virtually confined to Réunion and breed in the inhospitable heights of Piton-des-Neiges, which they leave just before dusk for nocturnal foraging jaunts far out at sea.

Sometimes, however, fledgling petrels which are not familiar with artificial lights in coastal buildings fly into the buildings. Many are killed in this way and a campaign is underway to foster an awareness of the petrels' plight. People are requested, if they find injured petrels, to bring them to local experts who then treat and release the birds back into the wild. Owing to their rarity, the precise nesting locations of these petrels are kept secret, known only to a few dedicated ornithologists.

A third highly localised, small seabird is the Mascarene shearwater (*Puffinus atrodorsalis*), thought to inhabit only the Mascarenes and Comoros.

The national bird is the white-tailed tropic-bird, or *paille en queue*, often seen flying gracefully in the vicinity of its sheer nesting cliffs.

FLORA with Sabine Deglise

Nobody who visits the lush montane forests in places such as Bébour-Bélouve, La Roche Ecrite, Cilaos (Plateau du Matrum), Salazie and Maïdo can fail to leave impressed. The same applies to the heathlands higher up, such as those of Brûlé de St-Paul, Maïdo and Grand Bénard, at about 1,600–2,400m.

Thanks to the inaccessibility of most of the interior uplands, large tracts of Réunion's original forest still remain intact. The habitat types which have suffered most at the hands of man are lowland evergreen rainforests (everywhere, but especially in the eastern half) and the much drier scrub and woodlands of the west. Some 98,972ha of forest are under the care of the Office National des Forêts (ONF), which controls about 39% of Réunion. The French state presides over the coastal environment. The island's only nature reserve is Mare Longue.

Réunion has some 700 indigenous plant species, of which 161 are endemic. (Mauritius has 150 endemics and Rodrigues 42.) There are several impressive botanical gardens around the island, where endemic and indigenous plants can be seen. At the Conservatoire Botanique Nationale de Mascarin, above St-Leu, visitors can enjoy guided walks around the gardens with experienced botanists or ecologists (see page 307).

Commonly seen on the forest floor in humid places is the fern *Marattia fraxinea*. It is shared with Mauritius, Madagascar and the Comoros. Much more impressive is the tree fern *Cyathea borbonica*, which dominates the 5,146ha Bébour-Bélouve forest area. It attains a height of 10m and is also found in Mauritius. One bamboo, *Nastus borbonicas*, is endemic and easily identifiable by its papyrus-like clusters of leaves.

In dry western Réunion are two endemic succulents, although they aren't common. The one you're most likely to see is the aloe, *Lomatophylum locrum*, which bears yellow and dull-orange flowers.

There are many orchids endemic to the western Indian Ocean islands and, of these, some seven species are unique to Réunion. Most are now very rare. Indigenous orchids tend to have white blooms, with many flowering from December to March. *Angraecum mauritanium* is also found in Mauritius and, like other 'comet' orchids, it features a very long spur. Presumably, it is pollinated by hawk moths as other 'comet' (angrecoid) orchids are. *Aeranthes arachnites* is less showy and is shared with the other Mascarenes. The diminutive *Bonniera appendiculata* is extremely rare and endemic, with blooms shaped like a very thin starfish.

Some of the palms local to the Mascarenes are on the verge of extinction. An exception is the attractive *Hyophorbe indica*, endemic to Réunion. Today, it's still quite plentiful. The same applies to the large, endemic 'latanier rouge' (*Latania lontaroides*), which has fan-shaped leaves with a distinct reddish hue. However, the 'white palm' (*Dictosperma album*, also found in Mauritius) is virtually extinct in the wild, because it is often used for heart of palm salad. That said, it has been cultivated very successfully.

Hibiscus are well represented in the Indian Ocean islands. Two rare species are unique to Réunion and Mauritius. Both are now protected. *Hibiscus boryanus* has scarlet or orange-red flowers, while those of *H. columnarus* are a bright yellow.

The shrub *Ruizia cordata* is possibly Réunion's best-known endemic, because it is used as a 'flagship' species, to educate the public about the plight of endangered life forms. It is highly endangered and its silvery leaves are used in certain Tamil rituals. Unfortunately, researchers have not yet determined what the shrub's pollinators are.

Foetidia mauritanium is an endemic hardwood used for construction. Its pungent wood is apparently not attacked by termites, hence its popularity, and as a consequence, its rarity. *Mimusops maxima*, which bears round green fruit and oozes white latex, is another endangered and endemic hardwood.

Two endangered shrubs – *Pouzolia laevigata*, used for treatment of fever, and *Obetia ficifolia*, which is shared with Rodrigues – are known to have their own, specific pollinator butterfly species. The extreme rarity of these shrubs means that their pollinator butterflies are also endangered.

One of the most striking hardwoods is the 'guineafowl tree', *Tarenna borbonica*. Its oval leaves are covered in whitish spots, hence the name. Another distinctive hardwood is the endemic tamarind, *Acacia heterophylla*. In Bélouve especially, this silvery tree is abundant and it is the preferred wood for furniture production.

Sabine Deglise guides visitors around the Conservatoire Botanique Nationale de Mascarin, where she has been working in plant conservation and studies for several years.

HISTORY

From about the 10th century, Arab and Malay traders occasionally stopped by on Réunion. They never settled because the island lacked a large harbour and protected lagoons, which featured so prominently on Mauritius.

The Portuguese were the next to arrive. First was explorer Tristan da Cunha, who accidentally landed in the area in 1507 and named the island Santa Apollonia. In 1512, Pedro de Mascarenhas renamed it Mascareigne, the name still applied to the island group as a whole. The Portuguese did not settle.

The first French arrival was in 1642, when a French East Indiaman landed, planted the French flag and departed. The French, meanwhile, had claimed nearby *with Mario Serviable*

On 20 December 1998, the 150th anniversary of the Abolition of Slavery was celebrated in Réunion.

However, abolition of slavery on this particular French colony proved to be a convoluted process. Initially, slavery had been banned outright in 1794 by the First French Republic. But slave owners balked, maintaining that one stroke of a pen could not simply eliminate all their investments involved in labour purchases (at least not without compensation). Napoleon therefore reinstated slavery.

When the French monarchy was abolished in 1848 and the Second Republic came into being, the question of banning slavery arose once again in the light of the French motto – 'Liberty, Equality and Fraternity'.

So on 27 April 1848, slavery was abolished for a second time, but with the necessary compensation to slave owners. When the French commissioner arrived on 13 October to announce the new law, he was refused permission to set foot on the island. The following day, he declared that although slavery had been abolished according to the law passed in April, slaves would have to return to work and finish harvesting the crops; only after that was their freedom to be discussed.

This situation was strikingly different from those in Martinique and Guadeloupe, where slaves heard about the new law on 22 May and immediately demanded instant freedom, announcing that they would never again work as slaves. To drive the point home, they promptly set about burning down some of their (former) owners' houses and business premises.

Eventually, on 20 December 1848, slavery on Réunion was abolished in practice. Former slaves were not only granted liberty, but France also gave them equality, as citizens with full civil rights.

Madagascar, where they established several ill-fated settlements, notably in the giant island's southeast at Fort Dauphin.

It was from Fort Dauphin that Réunion's first settlers came, in 1646. The then Governor of Madagascar, Sieur Pronis, exiled a dozen-odd troublesome Frenchmen to Réunion. They were left there to fend for themselves and lived in caves around what is now St-Paul.

A fleet of five French ships brought more settlers in December 1649. The island's name was then changed to Ile Bourbon, after Colbert Bourbon, who had founded the French East India Company. Twenty French volunteers and 42 Malagasy slaves, under Etienne de Regnault, established the island's first permanent settlement.

By the late 1600s, Réunion had become a prominent pirate base, as international seafaring riff-raff realised the island was conveniently removed from the French military machine. Well-known pirate captains (including the likes of Captain William Kidd) ruled that no weapons were to be brought ashore and that no treasure was to be buried on the island. In 1713, the French East India Company arrived in full force, sinking many of the pirate vessels. Aiming to make the island profitable, they set up a garrison and brought in hundreds of African and Malagasy slaves from 1715 to 1730, despite contravening their own regulations by doing so. The slaves were put to work on coffee, cotton and spice plantations.

In 1735, Bertrand Mahé de Labourdonnais arrived in the Mascarenes to administer Ile Bourbon and Ile de France (Mauritius) simultaneously, on behalf of the French East India Company. He was responsible for a mini industrial revolution in Réunion, building schools, roads, clinics and a successful export infrastructure. Labourdonnais held his position until 1746, when he left for India. In June 1764, the French East India Company collapsed and the French crown assumed control of its assets. Ile Bourbon was virtually forgotten during the French Revolution. It then fell under the jurisdiction of the Colonial Assembly and, in 1794, was finally renamed Ile de la Réunion. Slavers who had not been ousted from their feudal landlord positions insisted on referring to it as Ile Bonaparte, after Napoleon.

In 1806, Réunion's agriculture was demolished by a cyclone and the island was rendered wholly dependent on France. Four years later, after Napoleon surrendered to British forces, Réunion was ceded to Britain. On 9 July 1810, the British navy arrived and set about establishing a Royal Marine garrison. They did not assign a governor to Réunion, preferring to invest effort and resources in Mauritius and the Seychelles. Following the signing of the Treaty of Paris (1814) by the British and the French, Réunion, then known as Ile Bonaparte once again, was handed back to France.

France invested heavily in the island: towns were established, the sugar industry was developed and immigration was actively encouraged. With the birth of the Second French Republic in 1848, the name 'Réunion' was reinstated. Slavery was abolished in 1848, spelling the liberation of some 63,000 slaves (see box *The Abolition of Slavery: A Unique Case*, page 225). The subsequent lack of labour meant that the Colonial Assembly indentured Indians, Chinese and Arabs between 1848 and 1855.

From 1850 to 1870, the island flourished and the economy boomed, thanks to the sugar industry and the island's location on the trade routes between Europe, India and the Far East. This period of prosperity was followed by a dramatic decline, attributable to two main causes. Firstly, the opening of the Suez Canal in 1869 removed the need for ships to circumnavigate Africa in order to reach the Far East. Secondly, the use of sugarbeet in Europe, in lieu of expensive imported sugar, dealt a severe blow to the sugar industry. An exodus to Europe ensued.

The two World Wars drained Réunion significantly. In World War I, about 15,000 Réunionnais left to fight in Europe. During World War II, Nazi Germany blockaded the French island colonies. Consequently, nothing left or arrived in Réunion for two years and the island declined into a state of famine. By the end of 1942, that abominable blockade was broken. On 9 March 1946, the French government officially declared Réunion a *Département d'Outre-Mer*. Today Réunion remains a department of France and thereby a member of the European Union.

GOVERNMENT AND POLITICS

Réunion, together with Martinique, Guadeloupe and French Guiana, is a French *Département d'Outre-Mer (DOM)*, or overseas department. It is administered by a *préfet* (prefect), who is appointed by the French government The island elects five deputies to the National Assembly and three representatives to the Senate. General and Regional councils for Réunion are elected every six years. The most popular political parties, and thereby the most powerful, are the Partie Communiste de la Réunion (Communist Party of Réunion) and the Partie Socialiste (Socialist Party).

The white and Indian communities are substantially better off than the Creole population, which causes underlying socio-economic tensions. The economic well-being of Réunion and containment of these tensions depends heavily on continued financial assistance from France. Although there are groups who would like to see independence for Réunion, the majority of the population is aware that this would mean forfeiting the financial benefits of their association with France, something which they are not prepared to do.

In many ways Réunion is similar to Hawaii in terms of its economic history, although unlike Réunion, Hawaii had a native population when it was discovered by westerners. Réunion was first settled by a small group of Europeans, who subsequently brought in large numbers of slaves to work plantations of coffee and spices. Attention was then turned to sugar.

Following the abolition of slavery in 1848, Tamil labourers were recruited. In the late 19th century, Chinese and Muslim (Gujarati) immigrants came. Like Hawaii, Réunion began exporting sugar and fruit, particularly pineapples. Floriculture (notably of anthuriums) was developed, as were fisheries and tourism. Today, the fishing and tourism industries are still growing, not yet having been developed to their full potential.

FISHERIES Réunion's fishing industry has benefited greatly from the fact that stocks in the Indian Ocean are in better condition than in other waters. Tuna and swordfish are filleted and exported by airfreight to France, Italy and the UK. Red tuna is exported to Japan, a new market for the island. Réunion also has some barren islets around which Patagonian toothfish and lobsters are caught and frozen for export.

SUGAR The only industry in Réunion which has been developed to its full potential (in terms of land usage and technology) is the now-subsidised sugar industry. Réunion sells its sugar above world market prices, which is possible because the industry is subsidised.

TOURISM The target that Réunion hoped to achieve by the year 2000 was only 500,000 tourists per annum. They fell slightly short with 430,000 arrivals and the number was still at this level in 2004. However, of the total number of visitors, 44% stayed with friends or family. Despite efforts to encourage more English-speaking and German visitors, the vast majority (80%) are from metropolitan France; 8.6% are from neighbouring Mauritius.

At present, tourism is the industry which holds the largest potential for growth. The limited amount of English spoken on the island is a stumbling block, although attempts are being made to increase English teaching in Réunion and to expose Réunionnais students to Anglophone countries by sending them on exchange visits. And I have to say, in the seven years that I have been visiting Réunion the amount of English spoken by those working in tourism has noticeably increased.

Also standing in the way of tourism development is the limited number of airlines flying to Réunion. Almost all long-haul flights are via France or Mauritius. Réunion is very under-marketed in the Anglophone world and in the Far East. Mauritius has become a well-known holiday destination but few people outside of France even know of Réunion's existence.

FOOD Réunion's food industry is flourishing. Foodstuffs exported are largely tropical fruits, spices and rum. Business is booming for the local gift parcel courier service, Colipays, which delivers parcels of fruit, sweets and flowers around the world. Most are sent to France, either by Réunionnais who have relatives there or by expatriate French.

Concerns like Coca-Cola arrived in the 1950s, to be followed later by other soft drinks, alcoholic beverages and a range of dairy products. Many are now manufactured locally under French patents.

UNEMPLOYMENT There is a very high rate of unemployment in Réunion, currently around 33%. According to the French Catholic dictum, the lowest economic strata in society must not be left in the lurch. So even if people don't have jobs, they are still provided with homes and are accorded a set minimum revenue (the *Revenue Minimum d'Insertion*), which enables them to survive. This leads to many people not really needing or wanting to work and increasingly those who do go out and find jobs do so for the sake of dignity, not finances. One sees fewer people out on the streets in Réunion than is the case in Europe, not simply thanks to the RMI but also because there is still a strong sense of family solidarity in Réunion. People will take in the homeless.

The reason why there has not been a large-scale social outburst yet is that at least a third of the declared unemployed earn revenue through moonlighting. So there are actually lots of informal jobs being done by people who then do not declare their income. With the French system being utilised for remuneration, salaries are high. An employer must also pay the employee's pension fund, retirement plan and health insurance, so keeping workers is very costly. For this reason the labour-intensive concerns have started pulling out of Réunion. An example is Levi (jeans), which closed its factory because of the high cost involved in running it. In the UK, for instance, labour is at least 50% lower in terms of cost.

INVESTMENT OPPORTUNITIES All this means that Réunion, while not being a viable alternative for labour-intensive concerns, is actually very suitable for capital-intensive businesses. There are great incentives for such investors, who are assisted by tax elimination schemes and direct subsidies.

An example is a business involved in the manufacture of ophthalmic products. They have a staff of 12, the most junior of whom has a French vocational qualification. The whole concern is computerised, so need for labour is minimal. People who should consider investing in Réunion are those involved with the manufacture and export of high-value products in capital-intensive situations.

Those who wish to learn more about investment opportunities might want to obtain copies of *L'Eco Austral*, a bimonthly economic newspaper, or visit the Industrial Development Board's website: www.cpi.asso.fr.

Finally, anything manufactured in Réunion gets the prestigious 'Made in France' label, which inspires confidence among consumers.

Alain Chung Wee works with International Investments in the Comité de Pilotage de l'Industrie de l'Ile La Réunion.

PEOPLE

The faces of today's Réunionnais attest to the racial diversity of their ancestors. About 40% of the population is Creole (of mixed African/European origin), whilst Europeans make up around 35%, Indians 20% and Chinese 3%.

It is often hard to pinpoint the ethnic origin of Réunionnais, but colloquial terms are freely used by the locals to describe themselves: a *Cafre/Cafrine* is a black man/woman of African origin, a *Malbar/Malbaraise* is an Indian man/woman, a *yab* is a white Creole, usually from the interior, and *Zarab* refers to a Muslim. The locals refer to the white French who live on and visit the island as *Zoreilles*, which literally means 'ears' in Creole. The word is thought to originate from the French slavers straining to understand the Creole spoken by their slaves. Some believe in a less palatable explanation – that the French used to cut off the ears of their slaves, who therefore referred to the whites as *Zoreilles*.

with Mario Serviable and Sophie Annette

Today, Réunion's population is about 775,000, most of whom are Creole. 'We Creoles tend to view ourselves as the light of the world,' says Mario Serviable. 'We're a relatively recently established people, and because various Asian, European and African elements were involved in creating the contemporary Creole people, we believe that all those cultural worlds are ours. In other words, your creed and culture are mine too. We adapt freely from other cultures, assimilating the best aspects of those cultures into our own. And we do not close our doors, hearts or frontiers to anyone.'

Urban Réunionnais tend to be more affluent, educated and Westernised than their rural counterparts, who are noticeably more reserved, poorer and traditional.

'Many Réunionnais feel that our society could serve as an example of how people can live together in tomorrow's world,' suggests Mario. He maintains that Réunionnais Creole society surpasses even the Brazilian model when it comes to an example of how various social groups can live together harmoniously. 'Sure there are visible economic differences, but Réunion is the most affluent society in the western Indian Ocean region,' he explains. 'For that reason, people from the other islands tend to come here, many hoping to stay.'

But things are less rosy than they might seem on the surface.

'The plight of islands is a complex one,' Serviable says. 'Everyone thinks islands are preserved bunkers of happiness in which people don't have to work. But actually, islands are very difficult to live on. Réunion is an agricultural island, and because of finite resources we simply cannot accommodate too many more immigrants. Every year, 11,000 people complete their school education. But there are only jobs for about 2,500 of them,' he explains.

According to economists, some 40% of the working public are unemployed, living on social security similar to the dole.

'But just because they are unemployed, it doesn't mean they don't work,' adds social worker Sophie Annette. The French social security system, operating as it does, has led to many people being demotivated when it comes to seeking employment. Salaries are extremely high so it costs employers dearly to keep staff. Therefore, Réunion is best suited to small business concerns which are not labour-intensive.

Mario Serviable is a Réunionnais academic who was involved in the English translation of But Big is Bountiful, *a book about the history of Réunion. Sophie Annette is a social worker based in St-Gilles-les-Bains.*

LANGUAGE

As in Mauritius, the Creole language is a powerful unifying force amongst Réunionnais of every ethnic origin. French is the island's official language and is spoken by the majority of the population in formal situations, but amongst friends and family the user-friendly Creole is favoured. It is not identical to the Creole of neighbouring Mauritius but there are similarities as both derive largely from French with some African, Malagasy and local terms thrown in. There is no grammar and the language is written phonetically, according to the writer's whims.

Réunionnais have been battling for some time to have Creole recognised as a language and taught in schools. When I taught in Réunion it was very clear that the pupils confused Creole and French without realising it, thereby dragging their marks down when it came to examinations (which are all taken in French). Many people campaigned for Creole to be taught in schools so that children would grow up treating it as a separate language from French. Thankfully, in 2002 the first trainee teacher of Creole qualified at the University of St-Denis and Creole will now be an optional subject on the school curriculum.

Although it is taught in schools, very little English is spoken in Réunion. Anglophone visitors are still a novelty, so locals patiently make every effort to help and to understand those who struggle to communicate in French.

For some handy Creole phrases see *Appendix 1, Language*, pages 325–6.

RELIGION

The majority of the population (about 86%) is Roman Catholic. Many of the island's towns are named after saints, and roadside shrines line every route. However, many Réunionnais follow more than one religion. For this reason, Tamil festivals, such as Cavadee, and Hindu festivals, like Dipavali, are celebrated with great enthusiasm. Chinese New Year is also welcomed with a great deal of noise and festivities.

Some descendants of the Malagasy still practise ancient rites, like summoning the spirits via a living family member, particularly on All Saints' Day, the Christian festival. You may come across people who have been baptised into the Roman Catholic Church and who go to mass, but seek help from a Malagasy spirit or Hindu god in times of trouble. Sorcery (*gris gris*) is also practised on the island. In St-Pierre, the grave of the famous sorcerer and murderer, Sitarane, continues to be visited by those seeking his assistance (see box *Le Sitarane*, page 290).

Roadside shrines where the colour red dominates are a familiar sight in Réunion. They are dedicated to Réunion's national saint, Saint Expédit, who is usually depicted as a Roman legionnaire. The saint is revered by Réunionnais of all faiths, who generally turn to Saint Expédit when they want revenge or to put a curse on someone. It is fascinating how an originally Christian concept has been distorted to incorporate beliefs in sorcery and superstition. (See also box *Saint Expédit*, page 323.)

EDUCATION

The education system is the French model, with primary schools, *collèges* (10–15 years) and *lycées* (15–18 years). State-run schools in Réunion suffer from the same problems as those in mainland France (*la Métropole*), such as overcrowded classes, underfunding and poor morale amongst teachers. Both teachers and pupils follow French counterparts by striking at regular intervals.

The University of St-Denis gained university status in 1982 and offers a good range of courses, including modules in Creole studies, Creole-language classes and tropical environment studies. There are over 11,500 students at the university.

It is possible for foreign students to study at the University of St-Denis on an exchange programme, although competition for places can be fierce. The ERASMUS programme allows students already at university in the European Union to study for a year in another European university, which of course includes St-Denis. Speak to your university or contact the University of St-Denis (✆ 0262 938322; f 0262 938006; e rei@univ-reunion.fr). The International Student Exchange Programme provides similar opportunities for students in the US. For more information visit www.isep.org.

To my people, culture is an important issue. Our island is part of France and, as such, culture is one of the few domains in which we have been able to develop an identity of our own – a vibrant cultural life based on influences adopted from various parts of the world. Culture in Réunion is not a show prepared for tourists. It's our way of life. But visitors are always more than welcome to join in.

Réunion represents a great example of the 'melting pot' phenomenon. Following its discovery, representatives from several nationalities arrived, each bringing with them aspects of their own heritage. Europeans and Malagasy came first. The first child born on the island was half French, half Malagasy. Many of the earlier European settlers were pirates, while Malagasy, and later Africans, were brought in as slaves. Following the abolition of slavery, labourers from south India were brought in to work the fields. Muslims, northern Indians and Chinese came too, in search of economic opportunities. As mixed marriages have always been the norm, no Réunionnais can claim to have 'both feet from the same continent'. That is the crux of the 'melting pot', of how our culture came into being.

MUSIC Currently, the dominant musical trend is to fuse international styles with two traditional styles – *séga* and *maloya*.

Séga is the better known of the two, having been around for many years. It's what folk groups usually play in hotels. *Séga* blends tropical rhythms with European instruments like violin, accordion and the banjo. Such bands also include Mambo, Quadrille and Mazurka in their acts. Today, the big names in *séga* are still Jacqueline Farreyrole and the Troupe Folkloric de la Réunion. A new band, Pat'Jaunes, is in the process of reviving *séga*.

Maloya is the style directly from our African roots. Instruments used are exclusively percussion and drums. Vocals tend to be plaintive and repetitive, with similarities in places to the Blues. Recently *maloya* has enjoyed tremendous international popularity and artists have been accorded much exposure. The most renowned *maloya* artists include Gramoun Lele and Daniel Waro. Also of note are Firmin Viry and Roi Caf'. Leading popular bands who integrate *maloya* with other (Western) styles are Zabouk (jazz *maloya*), Baster and Oussanoussava (electric *maloya*), Natty Dread (local reggae), Joe Sparring and Rapidos (rock *maloya*), Ragga Force Filament (local Ragga) and Flash Gordon (local urban funk).

We also enjoy music from the other islands, for instance *Cassiya* from Mauritius, or *Zouk* from the Caribbean islands.

Big names who have performed here include James Brown, Jimmy Cliff and Lucky Peterson. We host various music festivals combining performances by foreign and local artists. Best known of these is KabaRéunion, held each October over ten days to celebrate the World Music Movement. (See box *KabaRéunion*, page 308.) There's also the Jazz Festival of Château-Morange, held each winter. You may also have the chance to attend one of the numerous concerts simply entitled '*Kabar*', which are organised by associations, clubs, neighbourhoods or private individuals. These are normally free and feature mostly unknown musicians from Réunion. The atmosphere is decidedly 'underground'. *Kabars* are usually advertised only by means of small posters or word of mouth.

Among the live music venues, special mention must be made of St-Gilles's open-air theatre. Built like a Roman amphitheatre, it can accommodate 1,000 people and is a landmark of Réunionnais cultural life. Some venues allow for excellent opportunities to get a feel for our 'underground' music scene: The Palaxa in Jeumon Cultural District of St-Denis; the Bato Fou in Rue de la République, St-Pierre and the Séchoire de Piton St-Leu outside St-Leu host shows on a regular basis.

Obtaining music The best option in Réunion for CDs is Mega Top music shop at 40 Rue Alexis de Villeneuve in St-Denis and 65 Rue des Bons Enfants in St-Pierre. In your home countries, CDs featuring Réunionnais music should be available in the World Music sections of record stores and can be ordered over the internet via websites such as www.amazon.com.

Didier Annette used to run Réunion Promotion International. He is currently based in France.

ARCHITECTURE European settlers brought with them European styles of architecture, which can now be seen side by side with traditional Creole buildings. In some cases, the two styles are blended in the one building. Both Mauritian and Réunionnais Creole architecture utilise the *lambrequin*, a carved wooden or metal fringe adorning the roof.

Thanks to energetic conservation efforts on the part of the French Government, Creole architecture tends to be better preserved in Réunion than it is in Mauritius. Particular efforts have been made to restore and maintain Réunion's many delightful *'ti cases*, the humble dwellings of ordinary Creole families. These are typically small, single-storey, wooden homes painted in bright colours, featuring shuttered windows, a corrugated-iron roof and decorative *lambrequin*. The best examples of these are found in Hell-Bourg, Entre-Deux, Cilaos and Rivière St-Louis.

15

Practical Information

WHEN TO VISIT

Cyclone season, January to March, is best avoided. Even if a cyclone does not strike, rains are plentiful at this time. If hiking is on your itinerary, you may prefer to visit in winter (April to October) as trails can become impassable after the heavy rains of summer. Accommodation for hikers becomes very booked up during the winter, so try to book well in advance.

The other factor to consider is the French school holidays. Flights and hotels tend to be very full at any time which coincides with school holidays in mainland France (*la Métropole*): Christmas, Easter and from July to September.

HIGHLIGHTS

Unlike most island destinations, it is Réunion's interior, not its coastline, that draws visitors back year after year.

For many, **hiking** is *the* reason for visiting Réunion, which boasts over 1,000km of well-maintained trails. The island's three **Cirques**, formed by the collapse of ancient volcanic craters, are a hiker's dream, with spectacular mountainous scenery punctuated by thundering waterfalls. **Mafate** is the most remote of the cirques and only accessible on foot or by helicopter. It can, however, be seen from the spectacular viewpoint at **Piton Maïdo**. For non-hikers the cirques are still a 'must-see', not least for their spectacular scenery and cool, clean mountain air. The Cirques of **Cilaos** and **Salazie** can be reached by road. The pretty town of Cilaos is set in a basin surrounded by mountains and is known for its thermal springs. Salazie is the wettest and greenest of the cirques, with numerous waterfalls and pretty Creole villages, such as **Hell-Bourg**, rated one of the most beautiful in France.

High on your list of things to do in Réunion should be hiking up **Piton-de-la-Fournaise**, one of the world's most active volcanoes – provided it's not erupting at the time, of course. Keen hikers will also enjoy the two-day climb of **Piton-des-Neiges**, which can be timed so you arrive at the summit to watch the sun rise over the Indian Ocean.

If hiking doesn't appeal or you are short of time, you needn't miss out on seeing the interior – **helicopter rides** over the island are becoming increasingly popular.

Réunion offers all manner of **adventure sports** and **activities** – climbing, canyoning, mountain biking, horseriding and paragliding to name but a few. For water-based activities try **scuba diving** at St-Gilles-les-Bains or **surfing** at St-Leu.

Those seeking **culture** will be spoilt for choice. The **Creole people** are incredibly friendly and only too happy to share aspects of their culture with visitors. Head to a nightclub in St-Pierre and locals will be only too pleased to teach you to dance the *séga*, *zouk* or *maloya*. You can't leave Réunion without sampling the delicious **Creole cuisine** – try *cari ti-jacques* or *rougail saucisses*. Follow your meal with a *rhum arrangé* (fruit-infused rum). There are festivals all year round:

highlights include **Tamil fire-walking** ceremonies and the **Abolition of Slavery** celebrations on 20 December.

Thanks to the well-maintained coastal road, you can drive around the island in one day but there is plenty to see along the way so allow more time if you can. **St-Denis** offers a European café culture in a tropical setting and some good examples of colonial and Creole **architecture**. The northeast, around **St-André**, is the place to learn about **vanilla** production, with guided tours offered at the Maison de la Vanille and Cooperative de la Vanille.

Between **St-Philippe** and **Ste-Rose** is where you will see the remnants of past **lava flows** and the path they took down the eastern face of Piton-de-la-Fournaise to the sea. The coast in this area is rugged – lava cliffs constantly pounded by the ocean. **St-Pierre** is the hub of the south coast and certainly worth a visit. It has a lively nightlife, some great **restaurants** and the daily **markets** are one of the best places on the island to pick up souvenirs. If you can time your visit to include the large Saturday morning street market, all the better.

At the end of an active couple of weeks in Réunion, spend a few days relaxing on the **beaches** around St-Gilles-les-Bains or snorkel in the lagoon at L'Hermitage.

ℹ GATHERING INFORMATION

The Comité du Tourisme de la Réunion (CTR) is based in St-Denis at Place du 20 Décembre 1848 (☏ *0262 210041;* f *0262 210021;* e *ctr@la-reunion-tourisme.com*).

They publish numerous useful information booklets on the island, including the invaluable *Run Guide*, which contains contact details of hotels, restaurants, tourist attractions, activity operators, etc.

The CTR's mission is to market the destination abroad so everyday enquiries during your stay on the island should be directed to the regional tourist offices. The CTR works in conjunction with French tourist offices abroad, who should be able to give you information and advice on Réunion.

FRENCH TOURIST OFFICES

Information about any of the following tourist offices can be found on www.franceguide.com.

Australia Maison de la France, Level 20, 25 Bligh St, Sydney NSW 2000; ☏ +61 2 9231 5244; f +61 2 9221 8682; e info.au@franceguide.com

Belgium Maison de la France, 21 Av de la Toison d'Or, 1050 Brussels; ☏ +32 2 505 3828; f +32 2 505 3829; e info.be@franceguide.com

Canada Maison de la France, 1981 Av McGill College, Suite 490, Montreal, Quebec H3A 2W9; ☏ +1 514 288 2026; f +1 514 845 4868; e canada@franceguide.com

Germany Maison de la France, Zeppelinallee 37, D-60325 Frankfurt; ☏ +49 69 9759 0494; f +49 69 9759 0495; e info.de@franceguide.com

Italy Maison de la France, 7 Via Larga, 20122 Milan; ☏ +39 02 584 8656; f +39 02 584 86222; e riccardo.avanzi@franceguide.com

South Africa Maison de la France, Oxford Manor, 196 Oxford Rd, Ilovo 2196, Johannesburg; ☏ +27 11 268 0498; f +27 11 770 1666; e mdfsa@frenchdoor.co.za

Spain Maison de la France, 18 Plaza de España, Torre de Madrid – 8a Plta, 28008 Madrid; ☏ +34 91 548 9738; f +34 91 541 2412; e jesus.bravo@franceguide.com

Switzerland Maison de la France, Rennweg 42, CH–8023, Zurich; ☏ 0900 900 699; f +41 1 217 4617; e info.zrh@franceguide.com

UK 178 Piccadilly, London W1J OAL; ☏ 020 7399 3512; f 020 7493 6594; e info@franceguide.com

USA Maison de la France, 444 Madison Av, 16th Fl, New York, NY 10022; ☏ +1 514 288 1904; f +1 212 838 7855; e info.us@franceguide.com

The CTR's website (*www.la-reunion-tourisme.com*) is also packed with information. For other useful websites see *Appendix 3, Further Information*, pages 332–5.

TOUR OPERATORS

Tour operators specialising in the Indian Ocean islands are able to secure special low-cost airfares to Réunion, as well as competitive rates on accommodation. Many offer a stay in Réunion combined with a visit to Mauritius, the Seychelles or Mayotte. Unfortunately, there are few tour operators outside of France that offer package holidays to Réunion. Some of these are listed below.

UK

Rainbow Tours 64 Essex Rd, London N1 8LR; ℡ 020 7226 1004; f 020 7226 2621; e info@rainbowtours.co.uk; www.rainbowtours.co.uk
Partnership Travel Marlborough Hse, 298 Regents Park Rd, London N3 2TJ; ℡ 020 8343 3446; f 020 8349 3439; e info@partnershiptravel.co.uk; www.partnershiptravel.co.uk
Sunset Travel 4 Abbeville Mews, 88 Clapham Park Rd, London SW4 7BX; ℡ 020 7498 9922; f 020 7978 1337; e info@sunsettravel.co.uk; www.sunsetfaraway.com

Australia

Beachcomber Tours 1344 Gympie Rd, Aspley, Queensland 4034; ℡ +61 07 3862 8588; f +61 07 3862 8599; e reservations@beachcomber.com.au; www.beachcomber.com.au

Germany

Alizee Kirschbaümleboden 30, D-79379 Mühlleim; ℡ +49 07 6311 0982; f +49 07 6311 0721; e Schumacher@inselreunion.de; www.inselreunion.de
Marco Polo Reisen Reisstr 25, 80992 Munich; ℡ +49 08 9150 0190; f +49 08 9150 01918
Trauminsel Reisen Summerstr 8–82211, Herrsching; ℡ +49 08 1529 3190; f +49 08 1529 31920; e info@trauminselreisen.de; www.trauminselreisen.de

Italy

Alke Viaggi 80 Via Marco Polo, 00154 Rome; ℡ +39 06 574 2020; f +39 06 575 8854; e booking@alkeviaggi.com; www.alkeviaggi.com
Cormorano 3 Via A Battisti, 58015 Orbetello; ℡ +39 05 6486 0309; f +39 05 6486 3848; e info@cormorano.it; www.cormorano.it

Seven Days 155/15 Via Filadelfia, 10137 Turin; ℡ +39 011 327 1476; f +39 011 365 203; e sevendays@seven-days.com; www.seven-days.com

South Africa

Passport To Pleasure 195 Oak Avenue, Ferndale, 2194 Randburg; ℡ +27 011 886 0760; f +27 011 886 1490; e brian@passport-to-pleasure.co.za; www.passport-to-pleasure.com
Sun & Sandals PO Box 2513, Edenvale 1610, Johannesburg; ℡ +27 011 616 7705; f +27 011 616 7716; e info@sunandsandals.com; www.sunandsandals.com
Unusual Destinations PO Box 97508, Petervale 2151, 12 George St, Johannesburg; ℡ +27 011 706 1991; f +27 011 463 1469; e info@unusualdestinations.com; www.unusualdestinations.com

Spain

Dimensiones Jacometrezo 4-11, 28013 Madrid; ℡ +34 91 531 6007; f +34 91 521 4254; e gsanchez-matas@viajesdimensiones.com; www.viajesdimensiones.com
Kuoni 17-1 Paseo Infanta Isabel, 28014 Madrid; ℡ +34 91 538 2700; f +34 91 538 2727; e grupos@kuoni.es; www.kuoni.es
Orixa Viatges 228 Arago, 08007 Barcelona; ℡ +34 93 487 0022; f +34 93 487 2459; e orixa@orixa.com; www.orixa.com

Switzerland

Nouvelles Frontières 10 Rue de Chantepoulet, 1201 Geneva; ℡ +41 022 906 8080; f +41 022 906 8090; e geneve@nouvelles-frontieres.ch

RED TAPE

ENTRY REQUIREMENTS The entry requirements for Réunion are the same as those for France. Holders of European Union passports do not need a visa for a stay of up to three months but do need to carry a valid passport or identity card. Some other nationalities, for example South African passport holders, require a visa. The French Embassy or Consulate in your home country will be able to provide up-to-date information and handle visa applications. All visitors must be in possession of a return ticket.

STAYING ON Those who do not need a tourist visa but who wish to stay longer than three months should apply for a *carte de séjour* (residence permit). French bureaucracy makes this far harder than it should be and applications are usually only accepted if you have been offered a job on the island or cannot leave for medical reasons. You will need to go to the *Préfecture* in St-Denis armed with copious documents, including certified translations of your birth certificate, a letter from your potential employer, passport photos, etc. The requirements change regularly so it is best to check with the Service d'Etat Civile et des Etrangers at the *Préfecture* (\ *0262 407580. Open Mon–Fri 08.00–14.00*).

IMMIGRATION There are two channels – one for European Union passport holders and one for all other nationalities. Staff are generally helpful and efficient.

CUSTOMS

Incoming visitors are permitted to import free of duty the following:

Cigarettes	200
Spirits	1 litre
Wine	2 litres of wine, ale or beer
Perfume	50g of perfume and about 25cl of eau de toilette
Coffee	500g
Tea	100g
Medicines	Quantities corresponding to the duration of stay

Plants and animals Restrictions on the importation of plants vary and each case is treated individually. Contact the Direction des Services Vétérinaires (\ *0262 420997;* f *0262 420583*). They also handle requests for the importation of pets. Cats and dogs must be microchipped, have a valid anti-rabies certificate and health certificate. Other requirements vary depending on the country of origin.

GETTING THERE AND AWAY

BY AIR The vast majority of visitors arrive by air, from Africa, Europe or other Indian Ocean islands. The main airport is Roland Garros International Airport, which is 11km east of the main town, St-Denis (see pages 239–40). The airport at Pierrefonds, in the south of the island, only handles flights within the Indian Ocean (for more information see page 240).

From Europe The only direct flights from Europe to Réunion are from France and take 11 hours from Paris. A number of airlines have introduced flights from regional airports in France. These flights are considerably more expensive during high season, ie: French school holidays. If you are travelling from any other part of Europe you will need to fly to France to connect with an onward flight. However, most airlines offer special fares for the flight to Paris if you are carrying on to Réunion. Alternatively, you could fly to Mauritius and on to Réunion from there.

Air France Ten flights per week from Paris to St-Denis.

Air Austral Seven flights per week from Paris, two flights per week from Lyon and one from Marseille.

Corsair Six flights per week from Paris and one flight per week from Lyon and Marseille.

From Africa

Air Austral Two flights weekly from Johannesburg; duration from four hours. Also flights from Nairobi, Harare and Madagascar (Antananarivo and Tamatave).

Air Madagascar Several flights per week from various destinations in Madagascar, including Antananarivo and Tamatave.

From the Indian Ocean islands

Air Austral Several flights daily between Mauritius and St-Denis. At least six flights per week from Mauritius to Pierrefonds. Also several flights per week from the Seychelles, Mayotte and Comoros (Moroni) to St-Denis.

Air Mauritius Several flights daily between Mauritius and St-Denis. Daily flights from Mauritius to Pierrefonds.

Catovair A new airline launched in September 2005 by IBL Aviation, part of the IBL Group. Currently only flies between Mauritius and Rodrigues but intends to expand its network in 2006 to include flights between Rodrigues and Réunion.

From the US To Paris by any airline and then as above. Air Mauritius can arrange visits of two to three days to Réunion as extensions to holidays in Mauritius. For Air Mauritius details see pages 50–1.

Airline offices in Réunion

✈ **Air France** Indian Ocean Office, 7 Av de la Victoire, BP 845, 97477 St-Denis; ☎ 0262 403838; f 0262 403840; www.airfrance.com. Also at 10 Rue François de Mahy, 97410 St-Pierre; ☎ 0262 250606

✈ **Corsair** 37 Rue Juliette Dodu, 97400 St-Denis; ☎ 0262 948282; f 0262 409672

✈ **Air Austral** 4 Rue de Nice, BP 611, 97472 St-Denis; ☎ 0262 909090; f 0262 909091; e reservation@air-austral.com; www.air-austral.com.

Also at 14 Rue Archambaud, 97410 St-Pierre; ☎ 0262 962696; f 0262 354649

✈ **Air Madagascar** 31 Rue Jules Auber, 97461 St-Denis; ☎ 0262 210521; f 0262 211008

✈ **Air Mauritius** 13 Rue Charles Gounod, 97400 St-Denis; ☎ 0262 948383; f 0262 941323; e airmauritius@wanadoo.fr; www.air-mauritius.com. Also at 7 rue François de Mahy, 97410 St-Pierre; ☎ 0262 960600.

BY SEA Few cruise ships stop off at Réunion, although the number is rising. Lots of glamorous French yacht owners keep their vessels in St-Gilles-les-Bains and may be looking for crew if you're lucky. Try asking at the local tourist office or around the port, where everyone seems to know each other.

For details of regular sea links between Mauritius and Réunion see page 52.

+ HEALTH

Although there are mosquitoes on Réunion, they are not malarial so you don't need prophylaxis. However, watch out for malarial symptoms developing if you've just arrived from a malarial area such as Madagascar.

No inoculations are compulsory but medical practitioners recommend the usual: hepatitis A, typhoid, tetanus and polio.

Medical care is excellent, conforming to French standards throughout the island. For hospital treatment you need to be referred by a doctor – ask at your hotel or look in the *Yellow Pages* (*Pages Jaunes*). You can usually turn up at a doctor's surgery and be seen fairly promptly without an appointment. Medical care is expensive and European visitors should carry a completed E111 form in order to take advantage of reciprocal agreements and to claim refunds of fees. The form can be obtained from post offices in your home country.

Water is officially safe to drink throughout the island but can cause minor upsets. It's best to stick to mineral water, which costs around € 1.00 per 2-litre bottle, and avoid ice in drinks. You should be particularly careful to avoid tap water after heavy rains or cyclones, as the supply can be contaminated. As with any tropical country, try to peel or wash fruit before eating it.

As in Mauritius, there is an uncomplicated attitude to sex and AIDS has arrived on the island.

SAFETY

Violent crime is rare. However, there are some nasty tales of hikers disappearing in the cirques, particularly Mafate. If you plan to hike it is best to go in a group and make sure that you tell someone what route you are taking and how long you expect to be away.

Be wary in bars and nightclubs as a large number of both locals and visitors tend to drink excessively, which can lead to tension.

Women attract a lot of unwanted attention in Réunion. A pair of sunglasses can be very helpful as it enables you to avoid eye contact. Women should not walk alone at night. When I lived in Réunion, I was followed several times by both lone men and groups on my way home in the evenings, even whilst driving on one occasion.

Knowledge of French or Creole helps in such situations and a few firm but polite words are usually sufficient. There have been incidences of women being attacked on quiet stretches of beach (even during the day), so try to make sure that you remain within sight of other people.

As in Mauritius, stray dogs can be a problem, particularly as they tend to hang around in packs. As well as being a potential danger to pedestrians, they can cause traffic accidents, so be wary whether on foot or in a vehicle. Should a dog show aggression towards you, I am told that an umbrella opened in its general direction is a good deterrent.

There are usually one or two shark attacks off the coast of Réunion each year, so avoid swimming alone or at the mouths of rivers. Lagoons are the safest places. Sharks are said to be more likely to attack in the early mornings and evenings.

DISABLED TRAVELLERS

Réunion is better equipped than neighbouring Mauritius for disabled travellers. By law, all hotels of a certain size and classified three-star or above must have some rooms equipped for the disabled. However, some hotels with fewer than three stars also have rooms for the disabled.

WHAT TO TAKE

Don't forget that Réunion is part of France so visitors from EU countries should carry a completed E111 form (see *Health*, above).

Credit cards are widely accepted and travellers' cheques easily changed at the many banks. You should be able to buy everything that you need in Réunion, although it is likely to be more expensive than in your home country. Mosquito repellent and suncream are essential. Sockets take two-pin continental plugs, so carry an adaptor if necessary.

Take light, comfortable clothing, with a smart-casual outfit for dinner in hotels. Include beachwear for the coast, not forgetting beach/swimming shoes to protect your feet from sea-urchin spikes and sharp coral. Some warm clothing will come in handy for the evenings, particularly in the interior. For the mountains (which can get very cold) you'll need rain gear and really warm clothing; and also good hiking boots if you plan to explore the trails.

As ever, travel insurance is essential. If you plan to partake in any of Réunion's many activities, such as canyoning or paragliding (see *Chapter 16*, *Activities*), make sure your travel insurance covers this.

MAPS Tourist maps of the island are normally available at all tourist offices, as well as at the Maison de la Montagne (see page 255). Many hotels also have a supply. For hikers, map 4402 RT is widely available in Réunion and should be sufficient for most routes. However, if you want detailed maps for hiking, it's best to get them in advance: contact the Institut Géographique National, 107 Rue de la Boétie, 75008 Paris, France. For more information, see *Hiking*, pages 254–6.

$ MONEY AND BANKING

The transition from the French franc to the euro seems to have gone relatively smoothly in Réunion. The main French banks, such as Crédit Agricole and BNP Paribas, have branches in all the main towns. Banks are generally open Monday–Friday 08.00–16.00. ATMs are widespread on the coast and you can withdraw money using Visa, MasterCard, Cirrus and Eurochèques. Credit cards are widely accepted in shops, restaurants and hotels. If you're travelling to the interior, take sufficient cash with you as here there are very limited banking facilities.

The currency exchange rates in April 2006 were as follows: £1 = €1.44, US$1 = €0.81, MRs38 = €1.

BUDGETING Réunion is an expensive destination because so many goods are imported. However, markets and roadside stalls sell fruit, vegetables and handicrafts at very reasonable prices. Eating out in restaurants is not cheap but *camions bars* (mobile snack bars) are a good option for those on a budget, serving everything from *samoussas* to pizzas.

You can keep accommodation costs low by staying in *meublés de tourisme* (furnished flats), *chambres d'hôtes* and *gîtes* (see *Accommodation*, pages 243–5). There is an excellent, inexpensive bus service. *Taxis collectifs*, which take passengers until the car is full, are far cheaper than ordinary taxis as you pay a proportion of the fare.

If you are staying in one of the island's more upmarket hotels, expect meals and drinks to be pricey. There are no all-inclusive resorts on the island. Bars and nightclubs are also expensive: most clubs charge around €12–15 for entry and drinks are often around €8.

Finally, you are bound to be tempted to try some of the many outdoor activities on offer in Réunion, so allow for some extra expenses.

ON ARRIVAL/DEPARTURE

ROLAND GARROS AIRPORT The airport, which is named after a French aviator born in Réunion (1888–1915), is 11km east of St-Denis (☎ *0262 488068;* e *arrg.dir@reunion.cci.fr; www.reunion.aeroport.fr. For flight information,* ☎ *0262 281616*). Although relatively small, this is a well-organised airport. There are souvenir shops, a post office, a bank and ATMs in the entrance hall of the terminal building.

15

The bank and post office are open on weekdays and Saturday mornings, but close for lunch. There is also a very helpful tourist information desk with lots of leaflets, including the invaluable *Run Guide*. Next to the desk is a touch-screen information point – follow the instructions on the screen and it gives you details of hotels (which you can then telephone free), transport, entertainment, etc. The restaurants and bars are upstairs. The departure lounge has a duty-free shop and snack-bars. The main car-hire companies, including Budget, Avis, Hertz and Europcar are represented at the airport, with offices in a separate building on the right-hand side of the car park as you exit the terminal building. See *Getting around* below for further details.

Luggage Baggage reclaim is located just beyond immigration. For a trolley you will need a €1 coin, which you will get back when you return it.

Getting to your hotel There is a shuttle bus service (*navette*) between Roland Garros Airport and St-Denis city centre (Line M), which makes 12 return trips daily between 07.00 and 20.30. The journey takes around 15 minutes and costs €4.

A taxi to the centre of St-Denis costs between €18 and €24. Fares are higher after 20.00. If you can't find a taxi, which may be the case on a public holiday or at night, ⟍ 0262 488383.

PIERREFONDS AIRPORT The south of the island is now conveniently linked to neighbouring Indian Ocean islands by flights to and from Pierrefonds Airport, 7km west of St-Pierre (⟍ *0262 968000;* e *aerorport.pierrefonds@wanadoo.fr; www.grandsubreunion.org. For flight information,* ⟍ *0262 967766*).

A regular bus service connects the airport to the main bus station in St-Pierre. Buses leave St-Pierre 1½ hours before each flight departs and leave the airport one hour after each flight arrives. Taxis between the airport and St-Pierre cost around €15.50. Car rental can also be arranged in the terminal building.

GETTING AROUND

INBOUND TOUR OPERATORS Inbound tour operators meet visitors on behalf of hotels and overseas tour operators. They can arrange transport, accommodation, excursions and activities with multilingual guides.

Bourbon Tourisme 90 Av de Bourbon, 97434 St-Gilles-les-Bains; ⟍ 0262 330870; f 0262 330879; e bourbon.tourisme@travel-run.com
Connections Réunion 53 Route de Domenjod, 97490 Ste-Clotilde; ⟍ 0262 931398; f 0262 931399
Mille Tours 9 bis Rue Sarda Garriga, 97460 St-Paul; ⟍ 0262 225500; f 0262 226469; e milletours.individuel@wanadoo.fr;

http://milletours.com
Nouvelles Frontières Résidence Claire I, 31 Pl Paul Julius Bénard, 97434 St-Gilles-les-Bains; ⟍ 0262 331199; f 0262 331198; e receptif.run@nouvelles-frontieres.fr; www.nf-reunion.com
Objectif 28 Rue Summer, 97434 St-Gilles-les-Bains; ⟍ 0262 330833; f 0262 242680; e Objectif.Reunion@wanadoo.fr

COACH TOURS

Souprayenmestry 2 Rue André Letoulec, Ste-Thérèse, 97419 La Possession; ⟍ 0262 448169; f 0262 449162; e transports-souprayenmestry@wanadoo.fr. Offers guided tours in comfortable, AC coaches. They leave early in the morning, picking up passengers from all the main towns along the west coast, from

St-Pierre to St-Denis. The programme is the same each week: Tue – Salazie, Thu – island tour, Fri – Piton-de-la-Fournaise, Sat – Cilaos. Each tour costs €15 per adult, €8 per child. Ask at the nearest tourist office or contact them directly.

Hilary Bradt

If you rent a car you feel you should use it each day – such a pity in a lovely island like Réunion, where the hiking is superb and the bus service excellent. In the two weeks that we were there we travelled by bus, hitchhiking and on foot, and saw everything we wanted to see.

The yellow buses, or *cars jaunes*, are great. Each bus stop displays the timetable (so it is easy to plan your day), buses arrive on time, their destination is clearly displayed on the front, and the driver will make an unauthorised stop if you are caught out between official bus stops.

The only problem with buses is that they are infrequent on some routes (about every two hours around St-Philippe, for instance) so hitchhiking is a useful alternative. We (two women) found it easy and fun – and very good for our French, even if the Creole accent put a strain on our understanding.

DRIVING Réunion's roads are overcrowded. Driving through towns such as St-Denis and St-Pierre during peak hours can be exasperating. The coastal road between St-Leu and St-Gilles-les-Bains is prone to very heavy traffic and there are invariably long queues around l'Hermitage.

Driving is on the right and road markings are as in France. The roads are well maintained but the standard of driving is frighteningly bad at times. Every year over 100 people are killed on the island's roads and the situation is not improving. For many young Réunionnais a car is a status symbol and they seem to believe that the faster they drive, the more their image benefits. The speed limit on the dual carriageway that runs along much of the west coast is 110km/h, although you wouldn't know it. Drink-driving is a real problem and some people even smoke *zamal* (locally grown marijuana) whilst at the wheel. Stray dogs also cause their fair share of accidents, so keep your eyes peeled. Don't be put off hiring a car! It is one of the best ways to see the island and gives you valuable independence. Just be vigilant.

Car hire Most visitors will hire cars for at least one day whilst on the island. Car hire can be arranged either through your hotel, tour operator or directly. The main car-hire companies have desks at Roland Garros Airport. Cars can be hired on a daily basis plus mileage or for longer periods with unlimited mileage. Air conditioning costs extra (and uses more petrol) but is a real blessing in the summer. Petrol prices are uniform throughout the island (€1.25 per litre in July 2005).

The requirements vary but the minimum age for car hire is usually 21 years and you must have held a driving licence for two years. You will be asked to pay in advance and provide a deposit. Do check that the insurance cover that comes with the car is fully comprehensive (*tous risques*). Some car-hire companies may try to tell you that no firm offers fully comprehensive insurance – not true. Make sure you know what 'excess' you will have to pay if you cause an accident; some companies keep costs down by scrimping on insurance.

Expect to pay around €50–55 per day (one–three days) for a Peugeot 206 or about €100–110 per day for a 4x4. As noted above, air conditioning is extra.

Car-hire companies

ADA Location 39 Rue Ruisseau des Noirs, 97400 St-Denis; ☎ 0262 215901; f 0262 418940; airport, ☎ 0262 488183; e info@ada-reunion.com; www.ada-reunion.com

Avis-SGM 83 Rue Jules Verne, BP 8, 98721 Le Port; ☎ 0262 421599; f 0262 439513; airport, ☎ 0262 488182; e resa@avis-reunion.com; www.avisreunion.com

15

Budget 2 Rue Pierre Aubert, ZI du Chaudron, 97490 Ste-Clotilde; ⊃ 0262 289200; f 0262 289300; airport, ⊃ 0262 280195; e budget.resa@caille.com; www.budgetreunion.com

Europcar Gillot la Ferme, 97438 Ste-Marie; ⊃ 0262 931415; f 0262 931414; airport, ⊃ 0262 282758; e europcar@runnet.com; www.europcar-reunion.com

Hertz Locamac 7 bis Rue de la Pépinière, ZAE la Mare, 97438 Ste-Marie; ⊃ 0262 532255; f 0262 532634; airport, ⊃ 0262 280593; e reservations@hertzreunion.com; www.hertzreunion.com

ITC Tropicar 207 Av Général de Gaulle, 97434 St-Gilles-les-Bains; ⊃ 0262 240101; f 0262 240555; www.itctropicar.com

National Citer 65 Bd du Chaudron, 97490 Ste-Clotilde; ⊃ 0262 974974; f 0262 488799; airport, ⊃ 0262 488377; e citer.sd@foucque.fr; www.citer.re

Campervan-hire companies

Réunion Dodo Campers 7 Rue des Palmiers, Le Tampon; ⊃/f 0262 596698; e dodocampers@wanadoo.fr; www.dodocampers.com

Réunion Evasion 55 Rue Jules Reydellet, La Bretagne; ⊃ 0262 523108; f 0262 525641; e info@reunion-evasion.com; www.reunion-evasion.com

Motorbike/moped hire Take extra care on the roads on a motorbike or moped, as drivers are not courteous. Hire is by the day and usually includes unlimited mileage, with reduced rates for seven days or more. You will need to leave a deposit and, as with cars, check that you are happy with the insurance cover provided.

Expect to pay around €35 per day for a 125cc moped (one–seven days) and €65–70 per day for a 600cc motorbike (one–seven days).

Locascoot 203 Rue du Général de Gaulle, 97434 St-Gilles-les-Bains; ⊃ 0692 858830; e gonzo@wanadoo.fr; www.runweb.com/locascoot

Max Moto 10 Av Gaston Monerville, 97400 St-Denis; ⊃ 0262 211525; f 0262 214566

Moto Rencontre 84 Rue Archambaud, 97410 St-Pierre; ⊃ 0262 250935; e moto.rencontre@wanadoo.fr; www.moto-rencontre.com

TAXIS Taxi stands are usually situated in town centres, often near the bus station. Taxis are numerous but quite expensive. They don't tend to hang around looking for passengers in the evening, so you'll probably need to order one and there is a surcharge after 20.00. Most taxis have meters but it's not a bad idea to negotiate a fare beforehand, otherwise you may be charged 'tourist rates'. A cheaper option is a *taxi collectif* (shared taxi). The driver waits until the car is full before leaving, then each passenger pays a proportion of the fare. The only disadvantage is that you could be waiting a while in quieter areas for the taxi to fill up, and they only run during the day.

Taxi firms

In and around St-Denis

Roland Garros Airport Taxis ⊃ 0262 488383
Allo Taxi ⊃ 0262 854134
Taxis Express ⊃ 0262 417890
Taxis GTD ⊃ 0262 213110
Taxis Paille-en-Queue ⊃ 0262 292029
Taxis Plus ⊃ 0262 283774

St-André

Taxis Léopard ⊃ 0262 460028

St-Benoît

Taxis les Marsouins ⊃ 0262 505558

St-Pierre

Taxis Saint-Pierrois ⊃ 0262 385484

Le Tampon

Taxi rank ⊃ 0262 271169

St-Louis

RUN Taxis m 0692 663061

St-Leu

Taxi rank ⊃ 0262 348385

St-Paul	Cilaos
Taxis de la Buse ✆ 0262 456434	**Taxi Figuin** ✆ 0262 391945
Taxis de St-Paul ⌯ 0692 863996	

BUS Travel between towns is provided by the excellent bus service (*cars jaunes*). Buses are a reliable, easy and cost-effective way to get around the island. *Cars jaunes* are easily distinguished from the buses which operate within towns because, as the name indicates, they are bright yellow.

To give you an idea of prices, a ticket from St-Denis to St-Pierre costs €4.20, and from St-Denis to St-Benoît €2.80. Local bus etiquette dictates that you should get on at the front and off at the back. Don't forget to validate your ticket by putting it in the machine as you get on, and keep hold of it as on-the-spot checks are frequent. Stops are mostly on request, so you will need to clap your hands to signal that you want to get off.

Listed below are bus routes with the duration of each journey. On the main routes buses are regular (every one to two hours) and service is from around 05.00 to 19.00. On quieter routes (like the east coast) buses are less frequent and operate from around 07.00 to 17.30. Fewer buses run on Sundays and public holidays. Each bus stop displays a timetable so planning is easy. The French for bus station is *gare routière*.

Line A	St-Denis to/from St-Pierre (express): 1hr 35min	**Line F**	St-Denis to/from St-Benoît (express): 50min
Line B	St-Denis to/from St-Pierre (coastal road): 1hr 40min	**Line G**	St-Denis to/from St- Benoît: 1hr 30min
		Line H	St-Benoît to/from St-Pierre via les Plaines: 2hr 30min
Line C	St-Denis to/from St-Pierre (inland): 2hr 20min	**Line I**	St-Benoît to/from St-Pierre via St-Philippe: 2hr 30min
Line D	St-Denis to/from St-Paul: 1hr 50min	**Line L**	St-Pierre to/from Entre-Deux: 30min
Line E	Chaloupe St-Leu to/from St-Pierre: 1hr 40min		

Please note, Lines J (St-André to/from Salazie) and K (Cilaos to/from St-Pierre) no longer operate.

If you need more information, current fares, schedule updates or timetables, contact the following coach/bus stations:

St-Denis ✆ 0262 415110	**St-Paul** ✆ 0262 225438
St-André ✆ 0262 468000	**Le Port** ✆ 0262 550311
St-Benoît ✆ 0262 501069	**St-Pierre** ✆ 0262 356728
St-Leu ✆ 0262 349532	**St-Joseph** ✆ 0262 560390
St-Louis ✆ 0262 268205	

HITCHHIKING Hitchhiking in Réunion is relatively easy but women should not attempt it alone. It's an excellent way of meeting the locals, practising your French and learning more about the island. You may end up doing a fair amount of walking but on such a beautiful island this is no hardship.

ACCOMMODATION

As there is only a limited number of hotels on Réunion, accommodation should preferably be booked well in advance, particularly if you are travelling during peak season (November–January, March–April, July–October). Try to book at least six weeks prior to departure.

Accommodation in Réunion is divided into 'classified' and 'unclassified', with a star rating system applied to the classified hotels. It is this star system, devised by the French government, which is used in this guide. Star ratings are allocated by the *préfet*.

The prices indicated in this guide are per night, based on two people sharing, unless otherwise indicated. A tax (*taxe de séjour*), calculated on the room rate and the duration of your stay, is payable when you settle your account. It is usually around €1 per room per night. Please use them as a guideline only as prices change regularly and the ones shown here are the lowest public rates offered by a hotel. Prices may rise considerably during the high season. As in Mauritius, the board basis is indicated, either all-inclusive (AI), full board (FB), half board (HB), bed and breakfast (BB) or room only (RO). (For definitions of these terms see page 66.)

There are no five-star hotels on Réunion and the service does not compare to that in Mauritius, but accommodation with plenty of character is easy to find. As well as hotels there are guesthouses (*gîtes de France*), furnished flats (*meublés de tourisme*), rural farm inns (*fermes auberges*), mountain huts/lodges (*gîtes de montagne*), guesthouses/huts on hiking trails (*gîtes d'étape*), 'VVF' holiday villages and youth hostels (*auberges de jeunesse*).

GÎTES DE FRANCE Classified guesthouses of reasonable standard, found throughout Réunion. Can be booked as per *gîtes ruraux* (see below).

GÎTES RURAUX (*For bookings, contact Relais Départemental des Gîtes de France, 5 Rue Rontaunay, 97400 St-Denis;* ↘ *0262 907890;* f *0262 418429;* e *resa@reunion-nature.com; www.iledelareunion-nature.com; Open Mon–Thu 09.00–17.00, Fri 09.00–16.30, Sat 09.00–12.00*) Self-catering accommodation, with owners living on the property but not in the house itself. They carry the 'Gîtes de France' label and there are 123 on the island. Prices are between €180 and €575 per *gîte* per week for between two and 14 people.

CHAMBRES D'HÔTE These are not self-catering and the owner lives in the house; some also offer table d'hôte meals. Staying in such accommodation is a marvellous experience as the owner and guests all dine together. Double rooms cost from €23 per night on BB. Table d'hôte meals start at around €14 (very worthwhile). Can be booked as per *gîtes ruraux* (see above).

MEUBLÉS DE TOURISME (*Fédération Réunionnaise des Offices de Tourisme et Syndicats d'Initiative [FROTSI], 18 Rue Ste-Anne, 97400 St-Denis;* ↘ *0262 217376;* f *0262 218447;* e *frotsi@wanadoo.fr; www.officesdetourisme-reunion.com*) There are 93 furnished flats and villas, classified from one to four stars. Guides to furnished accommodation, published annually, are available at tourist offices. Most insist on a minimum stay of at least two nights. Rates often depend on length of stay. No meals are provided.

FERMES AUBERGES (*Relais Agriculture et Tourisme, 24 Rue de la Source, BP 134, 97464 St-Denis;* ↘ *0262 942594;* f *0262 213156;* e *chambreagi-cda-97@wanadoo.fr; www.agro-tourisme-reunion.com*) There are 15 farms offering accommodation. The *Chambre d'Agriculture* publishes a brochure called *Bienvenue à la Ferme*. Double rooms cost from around €40 on BB, meals from around €14.

GÎTES DE MONTAGNE (*For bookings, contact Maison de la Montagne, 5 Rue Rontaunay, 97400 St-Denis;* ↘ *0262 907878;* f *0262 418429;* e *resa@reunion-nature.com; www.iledelareunion-nature.com; Open Mon–Thu 09.00–17.00, Fri 09.00–16.00, Sat 09.00–12.00*) There are 30 of these, mostly on hiking trails. Expect to pay from €13 per person per night.

GÎTES D'ETAPE Often in small villages; those with the Gîtes de France label are usually better in quality. Dinners and breakfasts prepared by hosts. No self-catering. Can be booked as per *gîtes de montagne*, see above.

REFUGES (rest huts) Basic. No self-catering, as meals (dinners, breakfasts) are prepared by host.

CAMPSITES There are very few campsites in Réunion and camping in state forests (just about all forests) is prohibited.

VVF Villages Vacances Familles (family holiday villages) (*Village de Corail, 80 Av de Bourbon, 97434 St-Gilles-les-Bains;* ✆ *0262 242939;* f *0262 244102;* e *contact@villages-des-australes.com; www.villages-des-australes.com*) There is one in St-Gilles-les-Bains offering 129 fairly basic self-catering flats. You need to become a member of the VVF organisation to stay here but you can arrange this at the time of booking. Reservations are made direct with the VVF. Self-catering studio flats cost from €46.

AUBERGES DE JEUNESSE There are three hostels on the island, in Hell-Bourg (✆ *0262 474131*), Entre-Deux (✆ *0262 395920*) and Bernica, above St-Gilles-les-Bains (✆ *0262 228975*). To use these you need to buy a membership card, which can be done at the hostel or by contacting Auberges de Jeunesse Ocean Indien, 5 Rue Rontaunay, 97400 St-Denis (✆ *0262 411534;* f *0262 417217;* e *ajoi@wanadoo.fr; www.ajoi-reunion.com*). Expect to pay around €12–15 for a dormitory bed.

See also *Chapter 16, Hiking*, pages 254–6

� EATING AND DRINKING

Eating in Réunion is a pleasure. There is such variety, with Creole, Chinese and French restaurants in almost every town. Surprisingly, Indian cuisine is far harder to find.

Traditional Creole food is slightly spicy and includes elements from French and Indian culinary styles. The mainstay of Creole cuisine is the *cari* – fish, meat or poultry in a tasty sauce packed with spices. It is eaten with rice and *grains* (beans or lentils) and accompanied by *rougail*, a kind of spicy chutney often made with tomatoes, onions and chillies. Tuna, shark and swordfish make delicious *cari*, as do *camarons* (large freshwater prawns). *Cari poulet* (chicken *cari*) and *rougail saucisses* (a spicy pork sausage in a tomato-based stew) are a good inexpensive option. *Cari ti-jacques* (curried young jackfruits) is very traditional, as are duck with vanilla and *cabri massalé* (masala spiced goat stew). If you're feeling adventurous, look out for *cari tang* (curried tenrec – similar to a hedgehog), although this is rarely seen on menus nowadays.

For traditional food in a family atmosphere, try a table d'hôte. If you're on a tight budget, there is a very healthy population of *camion bars* (mobile snack bars) on the island, serving inexpensive filled baguettes, *samoussas* and other light meals.

Most towns have fish sellers on the seafront. If you have access to a kitchen, there is nothing better than cooking freshly caught tuna or shark. Try to buy it in the morning though, because the stalls are not refrigerated and fish that has sunbathed for eight hours is more than a little risky.

Whilst there are plenty of tasty options for seafood lovers, vegetarians are not well catered for on the island. Restaurants with a French flavour usually serve a variety of salads, whilst vegetarian Creole fare includes *achards* (spicy, pickled vegetables) and *brèdes* (a mixture of greens).

15

translated by Alexandra Richards

Here are two of the most popular examples of Creole cuisine, as prepared by culinary wizard Mamie Javel, who has written a Creole cookbook and runs one of the island's top restaurants, Relais des Cîmes in Hell-Bourg (see page 322).

COCONUT CHICKEN

Cooking time = 30 minutes
Ingredients (serves 4):

1 chicken (1.5 kg)	100g grated coconut
6 ripe tomatoes	½ teaspoon turmeric
3 large onions	20 peppercorns
5 cloves of garlic	3 cloves
1 sprig of thyme	4 tablespoons of oil
25cl fresh or tinned coconut milk	salt to taste

Method: Cut chicken into pieces. Finely chop the onions and tomatoes. Crush the garlic, peppercorns and cloves. Heat the oil in a large pan and lightly brown the chicken pieces. Add the onions, garlic, peppercorns and cloves. When the onions have softened, add the tomatoes. Cook until the mixture has reduced, then add the turmeric. Stir continuously and add a glass of water. Cover and allow to simmer for 20 minutes. Finally, add the coconut milk. Serve sprinkled with grated coconut.

VANILLA TROUT

A speciality in Hell-Bourg, Cirque de Salazie, where you can also catch your own trout which will then be prepared for you.

Cooking time = 20 minutes
Ingredients (serves 4):

4 trout, each weighing 200g	butter to taste
50cl crème fraîche	soya sauce
½ vanilla pod	salt and pepper to taste
2 cloves of garlic	

Method: Clean trout, salting the insides. Grill fish for five minutes on each side. Just before they are cooked, sprinkle a few drops of soya sauce over each fish, turn and heat again for two minutes. Meanwhile, prepare the vanilla cream.

Crush the garlic cloves. Cook in butter on low heat. Add cream, making sure that it doesn't stick to the pan. Slice the vanilla pod lengthways, using the knife to scrape the vanilla seeds from the pod into the sauce. Then add the rest of the pod to the mixture. Stir continuously. Season with salt and pepper.

Presentation: Pour the vanilla cream on to the plates and place the trout on top. Pour a tablespoon of heated rum over each trout and light. Serve with mixed vegetables.

On Sundays Réunion goes for a picnic. We're not talking a wicker hamper filled with a few scotch eggs and some cheese sandwiches. This is picnicking on the grandest scale, a real family affair. Réunion is equipped with excellent picnic facilities, not merely tables but also barbecue areas. From the beaches to the forests, people can be seen picnicking, some arriving as early as 10.00 to claim their favourite spot and prepare their *cari*. If you are ever invited to join in, don't miss the opportunity.

As in Mauritius, rum – as a by-product of the sugar industry – is big business.

Rhum arrangé is made by adding fruit and spices to white rum and allowing it to ferment for several months. You are likely to be offered a *rhum arrangé* at the end of your meal in most restaurants or alternatively a *Punch* (pronounced 'ponsh'), which also has rum as the main ingredient but is more fruity and less powerful.

When in a bar you may hear people ordering '*une Dodo*'. This is not as ridiculous as it sounds – the local brand of beer is called '*Dodo*'. It is usually the cheapest beer on offer and is very popular. Just take care not to order '*un dodo*'; not even the most skilled of barmen can produce one of those.

WORKING HOURS, PUBLIC HOLIDAYS AND FESTIVALS

Offices are typically open Monday–Friday 08.00–12.00 and 14.00–18.00. Shops open Monday–Saturday 08.30–12.00 and 14.30–18.00. Some food shops are open on Sunday mornings. State administrative offices are a law unto themselves, many opening for very limited hours. For example, the *Préfecture* in St-Denis opens Monday–Friday 08.00–14.00.

PUBLIC HOLIDAYS Public holidays in Réunion are as follows:

New Year's Day	1 January
Easter Monday	variable (March/April)
Labour Day	1 May
1945 Victory	8 May
Ascension Day	variable (May)
Whit Sunday	variable (May)
Bastille Day	14 July
Assumption	15 August
All Saints' Day	1 November
1918 Armistice	11 November
Abolition of Slavery	20 December
Christmas Day	25 December

FESTIVALS AND FAIRS
January/February/March
Fête du Miel (honey), La Plaine-des-Cafres, January (duration: seven days)
Thaipoosam Cavadee (Tamil festival), January/February (variable)
Chinese New Year, January/February (variable)
Tamil fire-walking ceremonies, throughout the island, January/February

April/May/June
Varusha Pirappu (Tamil New Year), April
Fête du Vacoas, St-Benoît, April (duration: seven days)
Fête de la Vanille, Bras-Panon, May (duration: ten days)
Sacred Heart (Roman Catholic pilgrimage), St-Leu, June
Fête des Goyaviers, Plaine-des-Palmistes, June (duration: two days)
Festival of Music, main towns, 21 June
Comedy festival, main towns, June
Fête de la Randonnée (hiking), throughout the island, June

July/August/September
Bastille Day, throughout the island, 14 July
Tamil fire-walking ceremonies, August
La Salette (Roman Catholic pilgrimage), St-Leu, August

October/November/December

Flower show, Le Tampon, October (duration: two weeks)
Dipavali (Hindu Festival of Light), November
Fête du Curcuma (turmeric), St-Joseph, November
Fête des Lentilles (lentils), Cilaos, November
Foire de St-Pierre, St-Pierre, December (duration: ten days)
Fête des Letchis (lychees), St-Denis, December (duration: seven days)

SHOPPING

Réunion is not a bargain-hunter's paradise. Clothing here tends to be imported from France and is therefore expensive. Parts of St-Denis and St-Gilles and, to a lesser extent, St-Pierre are reminiscent of fashionable Parisian streets with their chic boutiques and effervescent French sales assistants.

The only bargains to be had are in the wonderful local markets. St-Paul claims to have the biggest and best weekly market, which takes place on Fridays. The markets in St-Pierre are also worth a visit. Sadly, few of the handicrafts on sale are made in Réunion. The majority come from Madagascar and even Indonesia. A lot of work has recently been put into promoting Réunionnais handicrafts and they are gradually becoming more readily available, both in small souvenir shops and the markets. The French for handicrafts is '*artisanat*'.

Worthwhile souvenirs include geranium oil, rum, vanilla and products made from woven pandanus (*vacoas*) leaves. Vanilla is best bought direct from producers or tourist offices. The vanilla sold in the markets is often from Madagascar; it is cheaper but is said to be of inferior quality.

MARKETS

St-Denis	Grand Marché daily, Petit Marché daily except Sunday
St-Benoît	Saturday 05.00–12.00
St-Pierre	covered market daily, street market Saturday 05.00–12.00
St-Louis	daily
St-Leu	Saturday 07.00–12.00
St-Gilles-les-Bains	Wednesday 07.30–12.00
St-Paul	Friday 06.00–18.00, Saturday 05.00–12.00

ARTS AND ENTERTAINMENT

Local tourist offices should be able to tell you what's going on while you're in Réunion. I also recommend obtaining a copy of *L'Attitude*, a glossy lifestyle magazine published bimonthly and sold in newsagents. It has sections on music, theatre, restaurants, exhibitions and sport, as well as a regular slot on tourism, reviewing worthwhile excursions and activities. Also useful is the free monthly publication, *Pages Noires*, which is widely available in bars. It is devoted to nightlife and has details of the coming month's concerts, as well as what the bars and nightclubs will be offering. *Kwélafé* is a similar publication, which covers live music, shows, cinema, exhibitions, etc.

THEATRE AND DANCE The arts in Réunion have benefited greatly from financial grants from France. Cultural events happen throughout the year – plays, music, dance, and even stand-up comedy. Several theatre troupes are well established on the island: Théâtre Vollard, Théâtre Talipot and Compagnie Act 3 are the best known. Théâtre Talipot has participated in the Edinburgh Festival and in South Africa's Grahamstown Arts Festival.

To find out who is performing when you're in Réunion, contact the ODC (local cultural office) (✆ *0262 419300; www.odcreunion.com*). There are numerous theatres, including the open-air theatre in St-Gilles-les-Bains, a wonderful setting. Most publish a programme for the coming season, which you can get hold of at the tourist offices.

ART GALLERIES The best of Réunion's many galleries is the Museum Léon Dierx, at 28 Rue de Paris in St-Denis (✆ *0262 202482*) (see page 271). The focus of the permanent exhibition is modern and contemporary art, including works by the likes of Gauguin, Picasso, Bernard, Maufra, Erro and Chen Zen. At 26 Rue de Paris is Artothèque du Département, which is also worth a visit.

If you want to buy art try the following: Galerie Cadre Noir at 11 Rue de Paris in St-Denis (✆ *0262 214488*), Le Grenier des Artistes at the Forum in St-Gilles, and Galerie Vincent at 32 Chemin Archambaud, St-Pierre.

LITERATURE Despite the work of organisations such as ADER (Association for the Promotion of Réunionnais Authors) and MCR (Cultural Movement of Réunion), Réunion's literature is little known beyond the Mascarene Islands.

The first novel written by a Réunion-born author and set on the island was *Les Marrons* by Louis-Timagène Houat, published in Paris in 1844. Houat was an abolitionist and *Les Marrons* provides a detailed portrait of Réunion society in 1833, condemning slavery and racism. As do many later Réunionnais novels, *Les Marrons* explores the themes of runaway slaves and romance between a black slave and a white woman.

'Colonial novels' thrived at the height of colonial expansion (1920–30), when authors such as Marius-Ary Leblond attempted to exalt the virtues of the colony. Marius-Ary Leblond was the pseudonym used by two cousins, George Athenas and Aimé Merlo, who published 20 novels and over 250 articles under that name. *Ulysse Cafre* (1924) tells the story of a slave who goes in search of his son, revealing the clash between black magic and Christianity.

The 1970s saw the birth of what is known as the 'Réunionnais novel', dealing with Creole issues throughout the island's history. Well-known authors publishing from the 1970s to the present include Anne Cheynet, Axel Gauvin, Agnès Gueneau and Jean-François Sam-Long. Sam-Long's novel, *Madame Desbassyns*, draws on the life story of the plantation owner of the same name, who is said to have been a particularly cruel woman. The true story of Madame Desbassyns is told at the Museum de Villèle at her former estate near St-Gilles-les-Hauts (see page 308).

The poet, Leconte de Lisle, is undoubtedly the best known of Réunion's literary figures. He was born in St-Paul in 1818 and went on to be admitted to the prestigious *Académie Française*. He is buried in the seafront cemetery in St-Paul. If you are able to read French, you can find his works, and many more, in any of the island's bookshops.

NIGHTLIFE St-Denis, St-Gilles-les-Bains and St-Pierre are the three towns where people head for a night out. St-Pierre wins hands down as far as I'm concerned – it is the only town with lots of bars and clubs that still offer a genuine local, tropical flavour. If French Riviera is more your style, then St-Gilles-les-Bains has exactly what you want. The numerous nightclubs there cater almost exclusively for French holidaymakers. St-Denis has a real mixture and you're likely to bump into English-speaking students from the university. Wherever you go out, prepare to dance to an eclectic mixture of musical styles, likely to include *séga*, *zouk*, reggae and *maloya*, as well as French, British and American chart music. (For more information on local music see *Chapter 14, Culture*, pages 231–2.)

Throughout the island there are bars offering regular live music. To find out what's going on when, pick up a copy of *Pages Noires* from a bar (see page 248).

Casinos are popular with locals and are found in St-Denis, St-Gilles-les-Bains and St-Pierre. Going out in Réunion is not cheap. Entry to nightclubs is expensive, typically around € 12, and drinks too are costly.

PHOTOGRAPHY

Réunion offers superb opportunities for the amateur photographer, in particular its stunning landscapes. It is courteous to ask people before taking their photo and it is particularly important to do so when you visit the island's interior, where people are less accustomed to the eccentricities of tourists. Film and developing are readily available but both tend to cost more than in Europe. (See also box, *Photographic tips*, pages 78–9.)

MEDIA AND COMMUNICATIONS

MEDIA Local newspapers and magazines are in French. You may be able to find international newspapers on sale in St-Denis's larger bookshops. The island's main newspapers are *Le Quotidien* and *Le Journal de l'Ile de la Réunion*. Both offer free classified advertising on certain days of the week.

Télé 7, *Télé Mag* and *Visu* all have weekly television and radio guides. There are two state television channels run by Réseau France Outre-Mer, RFO1 and RFO2, which include programmes from France. Independent channels are Antenne Réunion, Canal Réunion, TV4 Réunion and TV Sud. Almost all programmes are in French but RFO1 broadcasts the news in Creole on Saturdays at 12.30.

There are two RFO state radio stations, plus numerous others, such as Kreol FM and Radio Arc-en-Ciel.

MAIL All towns of any size have a post office which is open Monday to Friday and until midday on Saturday. Some close for lunch. Poste restante is handled at the main post office in St-Denis, on the corner of Rues Juliette Dodu and Maréchal Leclerc.

The postal codes for the main towns are as follows:

St-Denis	97400	St-Gilles-les-Bains	97434
St-Benoît	97470	St-Paul	97460
St-Philippe	97442	La-Plaine-des-Cafres	97418
St-Joseph	97480	La-Plaine-des-Palmistes	97431
St-Pierre	97410	Cilaos	97413
Le Tampon	97430	Salazie	97433
St-Leu	97436		

TELEPHONE Telecommunications are straightforward. To call Réunion from abroad, use the IDD code 262 followed by the nine-digit number. All land line numbers begin with 0262 and mobile numbers begin 0692. There are plenty of public payphones and most take phonecards (*télécartes*), which are sold in post offices, newsagents and shops displaying the sign.

By far the cheapest way to make international calls is to buy an *outre-mer* phonecard. You can make calls from any touchtone phone by first dialling a free-phone number, then the code on the back of the card. France Telecom offers a similar service.

If you own a mobile phone you should be able to use it in Réunion, via the local networks, SFR and Itinéris. You should confirm with your service provider before travelling that your phone will work. Parts of the interior have very patchy reception.

FAX There are plenty of offices offering fax services and hotels will usually send/receive them on your behalf for a fee.

e INTERNET ACCESS/EMAIL Although increasingly used in homes, schools and businesses, public email facilities are surprisingly rare. If you are resident on the island, your local *médiathèque* should provide free internet access but you'll need to prove that you live in the surrounding area. Prices at internet cafés vary but you can expect to pay €4–12 per hour. Internet access is available at the following:

St Denis

B@Bookafé 82 Rue Juliette Dodu; ☏ 0262 209480. *Open Mon–Fri 09.00–08.30, Sat 09.00–19.00.*
La C@se à Hello 68 Rue Juliette Dodu; ☏ 0262 941955. *Open Mon–Sat 10.00–20.00.*

St Benoît

Le Web Kafé Place Antoine Roussin; ☏ 0262 929672; f 0262 929673. *Open Mon–Fri.*

St-Pierre

Espace Multimédia 81 Rue Archambaud; ☏ 0692 776873. *Open Mon–Sat 09.00–19.00.*
Jet Set Bar 32 Bd Hubert Delisle; ☏ 0262 328366; www.jetset-bar.com. *Open Mon–Thu 11.00–midnight, Fri–Sat 11.00–02.00 and Sun 14.00–midnight.*

St-Leu

Point Run Rue du Commandant Legros, St-Leu; ☏ 0262 348772; f 0262 348794. *Open Mon–Fri 08.30–12.00 and 13.30–18.00, Sat 08.30–12.00.*

St-Gilles-les-Bains

Hotwave Cybercafé 37 Rue de Général de Gaulle; ☏ 0262 240424. *Open Mon–Sat 10.00–19.00.*
Chez Loulou 84 Rue Général de Gaulle, St-Gilles-les-Bains; ☏ 0262 244636. This bakery/snack bar has 1 internet terminal. *Open daily except Sun evening.*

Cilaos

Video Club 3 Salazes 40 Rue St Louis; ☏ 0262 318395. Also has photocopying facilities, videos, DVDs and a games room. *Open Tue–Sun 10.00–12.00 and 14.00–21.00.*

Salazie

Cyber C@se Creole L'Orchidée Rose, 26 Rue Olivier Manes, Hell-Bourg; ☏ 0262 478722. Can also burn digital photos onto CD and DVD. *Open daily 09.00–22.00.*
Cyber Salazie Rue Georges Pompidou, Salazie; ☏ 0262 477524. Also has photocopying and faxing facilities and sells phonecards. *Open Tue–Sun 10.00–22.00.*

CULTURAL SENSITIVITIES

Although beachwear is fine for a coastal resort, it may be frowned upon away from the beach. For women, it will also attract unwanted attention. If visiting temples or mosques, dress conservatively and remove your shoes before entering. For women, it is a good idea to carry a long-sleeved top and sarong, just in case. You may be asked to remove leather items when visiting Hindu temples and you may be requested to cover your head at certain mosques.

The large number of young, single mothers in Réunion is likely to shock most visitors. Sadly, the pregnancies are all too often the result of incest and sexual abuse. Domestic violence is also a problem and frequently goes undetected.

If you see strange objects on the side of the road, such as red pieces of material, coconut, or parts of chickens, resist the temptation to interfere with them. They are often left by people practising black magic and are part of a spell. Keep your eyes on the road as many local drivers will swerve to avoid such objects, for fear of being cursed.

It is perhaps also useful to know that, for some superstitious Réunionnais, various actions must be avoided in order to prevent attracting bad spirits. These include burning hair, burning a shoe or putting wood in a cross shape on the fire.

HELP

CONSULAR HELP As Réunion is not an independent country, few countries have diplomatic representation on the island. The following are honorary consulates:

Belgium 72 Av Eudoxie Nonge, BP32, 97491 Ste-Clotilde; ☎ 0262 979910; f 0262 291664; e chantel@runnet.com

Germany 9c Rue de Lorraine, 97400 St-Denis; ☎ 0262 216206; f 0262 217455; e h.mellano@wanadoo.fr

India 266 Rue Maréchal Leclerc, 97400 St-Denis; ☎ 0262 417547; f 0262 210170; e congendia@guetali.fr

Italy Apt 111, Résidence les Lataniers, 12 Rue Rouget Delisle, 97419 La Possession; ☎/f 0262 222889

Norway 44 Rue Paul Verlaine, Zic 2, BP111, 97823 Le Port; ☎ 0262 433048; f 0262 432248

Spain 64 Rue du Lagon, 97436 St-Leu; ☎ 0262 348351; f 0262 348304

Switzerland 107 Chemin Crève-Cœur, 97460 St-Paul; ☎/f 0262 455574

In the event of a serious problem, British and American visitors should contact their respective embassies in Paris.

UK 35 Rue du Faubourg, St-Honoré, 75383 Paris; ☎ 01 44 51 31 00; f 01 44 51 31 27

US 2 Av Gabriel, 75008 Paris; ☎ 01 43 12 22 22; f 01 42 66 97 83

EMERGENCY SERVICES
☎ **Police** 17
☎ **Ambulance** 15
☎ **Fire service** 18

☎ **Coastguard** 0262 434343
☎ **Mountain rescue** 0262 930930

OTHER USEFUL TELEPHONE NUMBERS
☎ **Directory enquiries** 12
☎ **Weather forecast** 30 50 (from a land line); 0892 680808 (from a mobile phone)
☎ **Cyclone information** 0897 650101

☎ **Volcano information** 0262 275292; 0262 275461 (recorded message)
☎ **Hiking trail information** 0262 373839
☎ **Traffic information** 0262 972727

16

Activities

Réunion's beaches may not be world class but its list of sporting activities certainly is. Activities have become big business in Réunion, so there are usually several operators to choose from, and it is good to know that reputable operators must adhere to French safety standards.

MULTI-ACTIVITY COMPANIES

Below are the contact details of a few multi-activity operators and an indication of the kinds of activities that they can arrange.

Centrale de Reservation Loisirs Accueil Nature et Campagne 5 Rue Rontaunay, 97400 St-Denis; ☎ 0262 907878; f 0262 418429; e resa@reunion-nature.com; www.iledelareunion-nature.com. This snappily named organisation is the central reservations office used by many activities companies and should be able to help with most queries. Can arrange hiking, canyoning, climbing, horseriding, mountain biking, rafting, hang gliding, 4x4 excursions and helicopter trips. *Open Mon–Thu 09.00–17.00, Fri 09.00–16.00, Sat 09.00–12.00.*

Austral Aventure 16 Av Amiral Lacaze, Hell-Bourg, 97433 Salazie; ☎ 0262 324029; f 0262 472430; e austral-aventure@wanadoo.fr; www:creole.org/australaventure/index.html. Hiking, canyoning, climbing, paragliding and mountain biking.

Ducrot Daniel 30 Chemin des Trois Mares, 97413 Cilaos; m 0692 659067; e ducrotd@wanadoo.fr; www.canyoning-cilaos.com. Hiking, canyoning and mountain biking.

Jean-Yves Hervet 26 Av des Moutardiers, Plateau Caillou, 97460, St-Paul; ☎/f 0262 324568; e jyhervet@wanadoo.fr. Hiking, white-water rafting and mountain biking.

Maham Nature Treks Pl Artisanale, 97433 Hell-Bourg, Salazie; ☎/f 0262 478282; m 0692 865067; e maham@chez.com; www.chez.com/maham. Hiking, climbing, canyoning,

mountain biking, microlighting and paragliding.

Parc du Maïdo Route du Maïdo, 97423 Petite France; ☎ 0262 325252; f 0262 325200. Hiking, mountain biking, mini-bobsleigh and archery.

Réunion Sensations Apt 3, 1 Rue de la Plage, 97434 St-Gilles-les-Bains; ☎ 0262 331758; f 0262 243402; e reunion.sensations@wanadoo.fr; www.reunionsensations.com. Large professional company (est 1989) offering a wide range of products and qualified staff. Offices and shops in St-Gilles and Cilaos. Hiking, canyoning, abseiling, mountain biking, climbing and bungee jumping.

Ric à Ric 13 Rue du Général de Gaulle, 97434 St-Gilles-les-Bains; ☎ 0262 332538; f 0262 331999; e ricaric@canyonreunion.com; www.canyonreunion.com. Canyoning, white-water rafting and climbing.

Run Evasion 23 Rue du Père Boiteau, 97413 Cilaos; ☎ 0262 318357; f 0262 318072; www.run.evasion.voici.org. Hiking, canyoning, climbing and mountain biking.

Tropic Rando 58 Chemin Eucalyptus, Bois Rouge, 97460 St-Paul; ☎ 0262 719242; e manu.baglin@ilereunion.com. Hiking, canyoning, white-water rafting and mountain biking.

Vincent Terrrisse 131 Rue du Four à Chaux, 97410 St-Pierre; m 0692 245658; e iles.d.aventures@wanadoo.fr; www.ilesdaventures.org. Hiking, climbing and canyoning.

16

Réunion's rugged interior makes it the best hiking destination in the western Indian Ocean. More than 1,000km of trails criss-cross the island's mountains.

Opened in 1997, the **Maison de la Montagne** (Mountain House) in St-Denis is the central reservations office for accommodation in rural areas. Here visitors can obtain all the necessary information about hiking trails, accommodation along the routes, grading of routes and other activities on offer in rural areas. As yet, their literature is available only in French; however, the maps are useful and the staff speak English. They also provide itineraries, which can be booked as packages. (For contact details see *Accommodation for hikers*, opposite.)

The trails are well managed and marked according to the official French system. The two **Grande Randonnées hiking trails** (GR R1 and GR R2) are marked with red and white paint. Other footpaths are indicated in red and yellow. The **GR R1** trail, known as *Le Tour du Piton-des-Neiges*, is a complete circle, which covers the north of Cirque de Cilaos, passes through Hell-Bourg and around Cirque de Salazie, then into Mafate and back to Cilaos via the Col du Taïbit. **GR R2**, or *La Grande Traversée de l'Ile*, cuts across the island from St-Denis to the coast near St-Philippe, via the Cirques, Entre-Deux, the Plaines and Piton-de-la-Fournaise. The trails classified as Sentiers Marmailles are easy walks of less than three hours, designed to be suitable for children. There are 42 listed in a book, *Sentiers Marmailles*, published by the Office Nationale des Forêts. For details of other publications on hiking, see *Appendix 3, Further Information*, pages 332–5.

Even for organised hikes, you must bring along your own backpack, sleeping bag, torch, Swiss army knife, crockery, cutlery, toiletries (including loo paper), warm clothing, appropriate footwear (sturdy hiking boots), rain gear, sun protection and any personal medication.

If you are hiking independently, it is advisable to ring the Maison de la Montagne beforehand to check that your proposed route is open. A good **map** is essential: 4402 RT is ideal for most hikes as it covers Cirque de Mafate, Cirque de Salazie and the northern part of Cirque de Cilaos, including the whole of the GR R1 trail. It is widely available from the Maison de la Montagne and tourist offices. To obtain maps prior to travel, contact: Institut Géographique National, 107 Rue de la Boétie, 75008 Paris, France. (See also the map of the cirques on page 314.)

Always let someone know where you are going and how long you plan to be away. Avoid hiking alone. Do check the weather forecasts and make sure that you are well prepared and equipped. If the worst does happen, the following are the official **distress signals** (helicopters do fly across the island regularly):

- Arms raised above your head in a 'V' shape
- Red flare
- Red square and a white circle

The gendarmerie nationale has a 24-hour emergency line, ☏ 0262 930930.

See also box *Day hikes around Hell-Bourg*, page 320. For literature on hiking see *Appendix 3, Further Information*, pages 332–5.

GUIDED HIKES There is a number of state-certified guides and organisations operating in the mountains, the best of which is **Maham Nature Treks** (see page 253 for contact details). Maham is staffed by Tim Techer and Alice Deligey, who are the best-known mountain guides in Réunion and who both speak good English.

Expect to pay around €40–60 per person per day for a guided hike with the following companies or the multi-activity companies listed on page 253.

Anne Le Garrec 44 lot des Pêcheurs, 97434 St-Leu; m 0692 058262. Mountain guide who speaks English, French and German.
Luc Grondin 5 Rue Evariste de Parny, 97480 St-Joseph; \/f 0262 561548
Olivier Thevenot 5 Rue Philibert, 97400 St-Denis; \/f

0262 943524; e olivier.thevenot@wanadoo.fr; http://monsite.wanadoo.fr/OTS. Mountain guide who speaks English, French and Spanish.
Rando Run 2 Impasse des Acacias, 97427 Etang-Salé-les-Bains; \/f 0262 263131;
e gilbert.aureche@wanadoo.fr; www.randorun.com

🏠 **ACCOMMODATION FOR HIKERS** There are numerous options open to hikers but remember to book well in advance. Most can be booked through the **Maison de la Montagne** in St-Denis (*5 Rue Rontaunay, 97400 St-Denis;* ✆ *0262 907878;* f *0262 418429;* e *resa@reunion-nature.com; www.reunion-nature.com. Open Mon–Thu 09.00–17.00, Fri 09.00–16.00, Sat 09.00–12.00*).

The following types of accommodation are available in rural areas: *gîtes de montagne, gîtes d'étape, gîtes ruraux, chambres d'hôte, fermes auberges* and *refuges* (rest huts). For details see *Chapter 15, Accommodation*, pages 243–5.

Gîtes de montagne/gîtes d'étape
These mountain houses/huts are the most plentiful type of accommodation on hiking routes and are often the only option in remote outposts. Thanks to the central reservations system you can book them in advance, at the following offices:

- **Maison de la Montagne** in St-Denis (see contact details above)
- **All tourist offices**

Reservations must be made well in advance to avoid disappointment (they prefer it if people book six months before travelling, particularly for high-season months), with payment preferably two weeks before arrival. Late reservations may be accepted, as there are often last-minute cancellations. Meals can be arranged through the caretakers, at least a day in advance, by phone. Pay for your meals directly, in cash.

Note that *gîtes de montagne* and *gîtes d'étape* are basic, dormitory-type accommodation. Some visitors have arrived to find that other guests have hogged all the blankets and pillows for themselves, but this is rare. Most do not have hot water and a few don't have showers, so they really are only suitable as overnight stops.

All gîtes provide two blankets, a pillow and two sheets per person. Some kitchen utensils and a gas cooker are provided as well (speak to caretakers). Lighting in gîtes is usually by means of solar power.

Below is a list of mountain gîtes, with the approximate price per person per night. Please note that child prices usually apply to children under 12 years of age.

Piton-de-la-Fournaise
🏠 **Volcan** Mr Picard; ✆ 0262 511742. 57 beds. *Adult/child* € 14/9.50. *Breakfast* € 5, *dinner* € 15.

Roche Ecrite
🏠 **Plaine des Chicots** Mr Bonald; ✆ 0262 439984. 36 beds. *Adult/child* € 14/9.50. *Breakfast* € 5, *dinner* € 15.

Basse Vallée
🏠 **Basse Vallée** Mr Bénard; ✆ 0262 373625. 16 beds. *Adult/child* € 14/9.50. *Breakfast* € 4.50, *dinner* € 14.50.

Piton-des-Neiges
🏠 **Caverne Dufour** Mr Dijoux/Mr Morel; ✆ 0262 511526. 67 beds. *Adult/child* € 14/9.50. *Breakfast* € 4.50, *dinner* € 13.50.
🏠 **Bélouve** Mr Rosset; ✆ 0262 412123; e gite.belouve@wanadoo.fr. 33 beds, 2 dbl rooms. *Adult/child* € 14/9.50, *dbl room* € 32. *Breakfast* € 5, *dinner* € 14.

Rivière des Remparts
🏠 **Roche Plate** Mrs Morel; ✆ 0262 591394. 31 beds. *Adult/child* € 14/9.50. *Breakfast* € 5, *dinner* € 16.

Mafate

🏠 **Aurère** Mr Boyer; ☎ 0262 550233. 14 beds, 3 dbl rooms. *Adult/child* € 14/9.50, *dbl room* € 32. *Breakfast* € 4, *dinner* € 13.50.

🏠 **Marla** Mrs Hoareau; ☎ 0262 437831. 16 beds, 4 dbl rooms. *Adult/child* € 14/9.50, *dbl room* € 32. *Breakfast* € 5, *dinner* € 14.

🏠 **Roche Plate** Mrs Robert; ☎ 0262 436001. 24 beds. *Adult/child* € 14/9.50. *Breakfast* € 4.50, *dinner* € 14.

🏠 **Grand Place Cayenne** Mr C Thomas; ☎ 0262 438542. 16 beds, 2 dbl rooms. *Adult/child* € 14/9.50, *dbl room* € 32. *Breakfast* € 4.50, *dinner* € 14.

🏠 **Ilet à Bourse** Mrs M Thomas; ☎ 0262 434393. 16 beds, 2 dbl rooms. *Adult/child* € 14/9.50, *dbl room* € 32. *Breakfast* € 5, *dinner* € 14.

🏠 **La Nouvelle 1** Mr A Begue; ☎ 0262 436177. 12 beds, 5 dbl rooms, 10 4-person bungalows. *Adult/child* € 13.50/10.50, *dbl room* € 31, *4-person bungalow* € 60. *Breakfast* € 6, *dinner* € 20.

🏠 **La Nouvelle 2** Mr Oréo; ☎ 0262 435857. 12 beds, 1 dbl room. *Adult/child* € 13.50/9.50, *dbl room* € 31. *Breakfast* € 4, *dinner* € 14.

🏠 **La Nouvelle 3** Mr S Bègue; ☎ 0262 434310. 22 beds. *Adult/child* € 13/9. *Breakfast* € 4, *dinner* € 13.

Salazie

🏠 **Salaozy** Maham; ☎ 0262 478282. 16 beds, 1 dbl room. *Adult/child* € 14/9.50, *dbl room* € 32. *Breakfast* € 4.50, *dinner* € 14.50.

CANYONING

Canyoning, or abseiling down waterfalls, is becoming increasingly popular amongst thrill-seekers in Réunion. The island, with its innumerable waterfalls and spectacular gorges, boasts the ideal landscape. Canyoning starts at around € 45 per half day, € 55 per full day. For details of multi-activity operators that organise canyoning, see page 253.

🚴 MOUNTAIN BIKING

Mountain bikes are all the rage in Réunion and are available for hire in most activity centres. The island has over 1,400km of marked trails, which meet French

---

CANYONING IN REUNION

Duncan Guy

Like it or not, in Réunion they – and you – speak French. If you go canyoning, it's unlikely that needing the vocabulary to understand the answer to a question such as 'which road to Le Tampon?' is as crucial as understanding things like *Pied droit là* – 'right foot here'.

The reason is simple – you're harnessed to abseiling gear, dangling from a rock. The sound of the waterfall next to which you're lowering yourself is deafening, so the quicker you can click that *pied* means 'foot' and *droit* means 'right' and *là* means where the operator is pointing, the better.

Canyoning down the tumbling mountain streams, high in the Cirques, is thrilling. You look at each piece of crashing river and wonder – do I go through this? Next minute you're through it. When you're padded with wetsuits, the rocks are nothing to bump past. But you sometimes feel a bit heavy in the water, especially while swimming across the deep, dark pools after diving in through the shower of a waterfall.

All the way down the shady river, the steep, high walls of the canyon enable only a peep of sky view. The smoothness of the rock gives the idea that powerful river erosion has taken place here. You're minute, a midget, so it's important to take the right steps – and understand the instructions.

Duncan Guy is a South African journalist and author, based in Johannesburg. He went canyoning in Cilaos in 1998.

Cycling Federation standards. Popular trails are around Maïdo, Entre-Deux, Cilaos, Salazie, Piton-de-la-Fournaise and the coast around Ste-Rose.

The French for mountain bike is *VTT* (*vélo tous terrains*) (pronounced *vay-tay-tay*). The Centrale de Reservation Loisirs Accueil Nature et Campagne in St-Denis can supply information on the many routes throughout the island and arrange bike hire (for contact details see page 266). You will also see suggested routes marked on large boards in many tourist areas.

Once a year, usually in November, Réunion plays host to one round of the Mega Avalanche international series of downhill mountain-bike races. The races in this series are unusual for the downhill discipline as they are mass-start races of up to 25km. Packages which include flights, accommodation and bike transport are available from mainland France. For more information visit www.avalanchetrophy.com.

The going rate for hire is around €5 per hour, €11 per half day, €20 per day. Helmets and gloves are extra. Some companies organise group rides, which cost around €40 per half day and include instructor, gear and insurance.

Descente VTT Telenavette BP 54, 97862 St-Paul; m 0692 211111; e info@descente-vtt.com; www.descente-vtt.com
Rando Bike 100 Route du Volcan, 28ème km, 97418 La Plaine-des-Cafres; ✆ 0262 591588; f 0262 353478; e bertil@favron.org; www.favron.org
Rando Réunion Passion 13 Rue du Général de Gaulle, 97434 St-Gilles-les-Bains; ✆ 0262 242619; f 0262 245026; e randoreunion@outremeronline.com; www.vttreunion.com

VTT du Lagon 8 Av des Mascareignes, St-Gilles-les-Bains; m 0692 239982; e vttdulagon@wanadoo.fr
VTT Réunion 35 Rue Maximin Lucas, 97425 Les Avirons; ✆ 0262 380197
3 Athlon 1/3 Pl Julius Bénard, 97434 St-Gilles-les-Bains; ✆ 0262 245556; f 0262 331603; e 3a.st-gilles@wanadoo.fr; www.3athlonscycles.com

🐎 HORSERIDING

On horseback is the ideal way to explore Réunion's rugged interior. Rides can be arranged for just an hour, a half day, a full day or several days. Some of the establishments around La Plaine-des-Cafres offer rides to the volcano, Piton-de-la-Fournaise.

Riding schools vary considerably in standard, although instructors are usually qualified. Although most establishments are affiliated to the French Equestrian Federation, many are reluctant to loan hats, even if they have them. If you insist, you will usually get one, which is important as the terrain in the interior is invariably rocky and uneven. An hour's ride will usually cost around €14–16, a half day €45–50, a full day €90–100.

Alti Merens 120 Rue Maurice Kraaft, 97418 La Plaine-des-Cafres; ✆ 0262 591884; m 0692 041238. A very picturesque place to ride and the 8 Merens horses from the Pyrenees are ideally suited to the rough ground. Can offer a 2-day ride to the volcano, with accommodation and meals, if booked in advance.
Centre Equestre de la Fenêtre 31 Route de Mont Plaisir, 97421 Les Makes; ✆ 0262 378874
Centre Equestre du Maïdo 350 Route du Maïdo, 97423 Le Guillaume; ✆/f 0262 324915. Plenty of well-cared-for horses and equipment.
Centre Equestre de la Montagne Chemin Couilloux, St-

Bernard, 97417 La Montagne; ✆/f 0262 236251; e cem@runedit.com; www.equimontagne.com
Club Hippique de l'Hermitage Zac Hermitage, Chemin Ceinture, 97434 St-Gilles-les-Bains; ✆ 0262 244773; f 0262 330048. Lots of very chic French regulars, so it feels a bit cliquey. Closed on Mon. Rides along the beach are available and cost around €25 (1½ hours).
Ecuries de Notre Dame de la Paix 41 Chemin de la Chapelle, Notre Dame de la Paix, 97418 La Plaine-des-Cafres; ✆ 0262 593449; m 0692 614679; e antoine-patrick.lauret@wanadoo.fr

Ecurie du Relais 75 Manapany-les-Hauts, 97480 St-Joseph; ✆ 0262 567867; f 0262 566270

Ecuries du Volcan Bourg-Murat, 97418 La Plaine-des-Cafres; m 0692 066290; f 0262 355445

Ferme Equestre Auberge des Avirons 59 ter, CD 11 Pont Neuf, 97425 Les Avirons; ✆/f 0262 380940; www.fermedupontneuf.fr.st

Ferme Equestre du Grand Etang RN3, Pont Payet, 97470 St-Benoît; ✆ 0262 509003; f 0262 509835; m 0692 868825; e riconourry@wanadoo.fr. A

huge range of rides offered, including treks of up to 7 days. Mountain biking is also available.

Haras du Cap 124 Route Hubert Delisle, 97416 Chaloupe St-Leu; ✆ 0262 547617; m 0692 823576; www.harasducap.com

Pony Club Equirun 37 Allée Montignac, 97427 Etang-Salé; ✆ 0262 265252; f 0262 355645. More of a riding school than a trekking centre, but it does offer rides through Etang-Salé forest.

✓ GOLF

Although not a popular sport amongst locals, Réunion boasts a few beautiful courses. All the clubs offer trolley and club hire, as well as lessons. In all cases, the green fees shown for weekends also apply on public holidays. Lessons cost in the region of €20 for 30 minutes.

Golf du Bassin Bleu 75 Rue Mahatma Gandhi, Villèle, 97435 St-Gilles-les-Hauts; ✆ 0262 555358; f 0262 554801; e club@golfbassinbleu.com; www.golfbassinbleu.com. 18-hole par-72 course. Has a restaurant serving lunch. *Green fees €34 weekdays, €40 weekends. Open daily.*

Golf Club du Bourbon 140 Les Sables, 97427 Etang-Salé; ✆ 0262 263339; f 0262 263840; e golfclubbourbon@wanadoo.fr. Beautiful 18-hole

par-72 course with hordes of tropical plants. Attractive clubhouse with a restaurant (closed Mon) and swimming pool. *Green fees €42 for 18 holes, €28 for 9 holes. Open daily except Mon morning.*

Golf du Colorado 52 Zone de Loisirs du Colorado, 97417 La Montagne; ✆ 0262 237950; f 0262 239946; e GCC4@wanadoo.fr. 9-hole par-68 course. Snack-bar. *Green fees for 18 holes €20 weekdays, €28 weekends. Open daily except Mon morning.*

4X4 EXCURSIONS

The going rate for excursions in 4x4 vehicles is around €90–95 per person per day (usually including lunch).

Kréolie 4x4 4 Impasse des Avocats, 97414 Entre-Deux; ✆/f 0262 395087; e kreolia@wanadoo.fr

MICROLIGHTING

Microlighting offers a bird's-eye view of some of the island's greatest assets. The French for microlight is *ULM* (*Ultra Léger Motorisé*) (pronounced *oo-el-em*).

Felix ULM RUN Base ULM Cambaie, 97460 St-Paul; ✆ 0262 430259; m 0692 873232; f 0262 4556308; e felixulm@wanadoo.fr; www.felixulm.com. *Lagoon €60, Cirque de Mafate €60, Mafate/Salazie/Cilaos €140, Mafate/Salazie/Cilaos/volcano €160.*

Les Passagers du Vent Base ULM, ZI de Cambaie, 97460 St-Paul; ✆ 0262 429595; m 0692 687055; f 0262 422234; e contact@ulm-reunion.com; www.ulm-reunion.com. *Introductory flight €30, Cirque de Mafate €55, Mafate/lagoon €100.*

PARAGLIDING

Paragliding is very popular, particularly in the hills above St-Leu. Beginners glide in tandem with an instructor. The French for paragliding is *parapente*. Expect to pay around €60–65 for an introductory flight over the lagoon (a descent of about 800m).

Air Lagon Parapente 10 Rue de l'Océan Indien, 97436 St-Leu; ☎ 0262 349114; m 0692 875287; e jcbetemps@wanadoo.fr; www.airlagon-parapente.com

Azurtech 3 Impasse des Plongeurs, La Pointe des Châteaux, 97436 St-Leu; ☎ 0262 349189; m 0692 850400; f 0262 380186; e contact@azurtech.com; www.azurtech.com

Bourbon Parapente I Rue Terre Tabaillet, 97424 Piton St-Leu; ☎/f 0262 341834; m 0692 875874; e master@bourbonparapente.com; www.bourbonparapente.com

Lit d'Air 36 Allée de l'Avé Maria, 97400 St-Denis; ☎ 0262 247817; m 0692 600123; f 0262 409819; e john.jourdain@wanadoo.fr

Modul'Air Aventure 26 Ruelle des Bougainvilliers, 97434 St-Gilles-les-Bains; m 0692 040404; f 0262 338449; e nicodid@wanadoo.fr; www.modulair-parapente.com

Parapente Réunion 103 Rue Georges Pompidou, 97436 St-Leu; ☎ 0262 248784; m 0692 606760; f 0262 248715; e info@parapente-reunion.fr; www.parapente-reunion.fr

SKY DIVING

Paraventure Reunion Route de l'aéroport de Pierrefonds, 97410 St-Pierre; m 0692 023239; f 0262 398640; e paraventure@wanadoo.fr; www.paraventure-reunion.com. Offers tandem jumps with an instructor from €200 and training courses, including 3 jumps with an instructor, from €560.

BUNGEE JUMPING

Bungee jumpers leap from the Pont d'Anglais Suspension Bridge between Ste-Anne and Ste-Rose. The organisers need to have a group of people jumping on each occasion, so you may not be able to jump until several days, or even weeks, after your initial enquiry. Réunion Sensations can arrange bungee jumping (for contact details see page 253).

HELICOPTER RIDES

If your time on Réunion is limited, a helicopter ride is a great way to see the island. The most popular flights cover the island's main attractions: the volcano, the cirques, the coast, Trou de Fer, etc. Prices are in the range €150–260 per person, depending on the itinerary.

Corail Hélicoptères Aéroport de Pierrefonds, 97410 St-Pierre; ☎ 0262 222266; m 0692 006666; f 0262 267670; e info@corail-helicopteres.com

Helilagon Altiport de l'Eperon, 97467 St-Paul; ☎ 0262 555555; f 0262 228678; e heliglagon@helilagon.com; www.helilagon.com

SURFING

Surfing is very popular in Réunion and an international championship competition is held annually at St-Leu. Surfers should seek the advice of locals before leaping into the water as the majority of shark attacks are on surfers. For more information contact the Surf League (☎ 0262 243310). (See box *Surfing in Réunion*, page 297.)

Expect to pay around €25 for a one-hour individual lesson or €15 for a group lesson. The following surf schools cater for all levels, from children to competition training.

Billabong Surf School 9 Rue de Lys, 97434 St-Gilles-les-Bains; ☎ 0692 315316; f 0262 330353; e billabong.surfschool@wanadoo.fr

Ecole de Body Board et Surf des Roches-Noires 4 bis Lot des Charmilles, 97434 St-Gilles-les-Bains; ☎/f 0262 246328; m 0692 860059

Ecole de Surf Extreme Sud and Surf Shop 7 Pl de la Principauté d'Andorre, 97427 Etang-Salé-les-Bains; ☎/f 0262 266702; e extremesud1@hotmail.com

Glissy Ecole de Surf 15 Rue de la Plage, 97434 St-Gilles-les-Bains; ☎ 0262 331313; e b.glissy@wanadoo.fr

⤴ WATER SKIING

Ski Club de St-Paul 1 Rue de la Croix, 97460 St-Paul; ☎ 0262 454287; f 0262 212288. Caters for all levels of ability. *Open daily 09.30–18.30.*

OTHER WATERSPORTS

Planch'Alizé Plage de la Saline, 97422 La Saline-les-Bains; ☎ 0262 246261; f 0262 339284. Hire of windsurfers, kayaks, pedaloes and snorkelling equipment.
Blue Sail Local 6a, Port de Plaisance, 97434 St-Gilles-les-Bains; ☎/f 0262 331739;

e bluesail_reunion@yahoo.fr; www.bluesail-reunion.com. Hire of jet skis, catamaran cruises.
THIM Nautique 165 bis Rue du Général de Gaulle, 97434 St-Gilles-les-Bains; ☎ 0262 242324; e thim.loc@wanadoo.fr; www.thimloc.com. Boat and jet ski hire.

⚠ SAILING

The majority of private yachts are kept in the marinas at St-Gilles-les-Bains and St-Pierre, where you may be able to organise sailing trips on an ad hoc basis. Alternatively, contact one of the following companies:

Batoloc Port de Plaisance, 97434 St-Gilles-les-Bains; ☎/f 0262 334867; www.rj73.com/batoloc. Boat hire, plus fishing trips.
Bleu Indien 7 Rue Andromède, Le Mont Roquefeuille, 97434 St-Gilles-les-Bains; m 0692 853753; f 0262 443776; e bleu_indien@hotmail.com;

www.bleuindien.com. Boat hire, plus fishing and scuba-diving gear.
Blue Sail Local 6a, Port de Plaisance, 97434 St-Gilles-les-Bains; ☎/f 0262 331739; e bluesail_reunion@yahoo.fr; www.bluesail-reunion.com. Hire of jet skis, catamaran cruises.

⤲ SCUBA DIVING

The best diving is on the west coast, around St-Leu and St-Gilles-les-Bains. It is not as good as the diving in the other Mascarenes but is worth trying nonetheless.

All dive centres cater for all levels. Expect to pay around €40–50 for an introductory dive of about 20–30 minutes. Dives for those with experience cost around €40 or €250 for six dives. Snorkelling trips, with equipment supplied, can usually be arranged by dive centres for around €20.

If you don't speak French, check before you book that the dive centre can provide an English-speaking instructor as it's essential that you understand the safety instructions.

⤲ **Abyss Plongée** 7 Bd Bonnier, 97436 St-Leu; ☎/f 0262 347979; e plongeur@abyss-plongee.com; www.abyss-plongee.com
⤲ **Aress** 4 Rue de Villèle, St-Gilles-les-Bains; ☎ 0262 242330; f 0262 242333; e aress@wanadoo.fr; www.aress.free.fr
⤲ **Atlantis** 3 Impasse des Plongeurs, 97436 St-Leu; ☎ 0262 347747; f 0262 349692; e altantisplongee@wanadoo.fr; www.atlantisplongee.com
⤲ **Bleu Marine Réunion** Port de Plaisance, 97434 St-Gilles-les-Bains; ☎ 0262 242200; f 0262 243004; e bleu-marine-run@wanadoo.fr; www.bleu-marine-reunion.com

⤲ **Bleu Océan** 25 RN1, 97436 St-Leu; ☎/f 0262 349749; e bleuocean@bleuocean.fr; www.bleuocean.fr
⤲ **Corail Plongée** Port de Plaisance, 97434 St-Gilles-les-Bains; ☎ 0262 243725; f 0262 244638; e info@corail-plongee.com; www.corail-plongee.com
⤲ **O Sea Bleu** Enceinte Portuaire, 97434 St-Gilles-les-Bains; ☎ 0262 331615; f 0262 243168; e osea.bleu@wanadoo.fr; www.reunion-plongee.com
⤲ **Réunion Plongée** 13 Av des Artisans, 97436 St-Leu; ☎/f 0262 347777; e clubhouse@reunionplongee.com; www.reunion-plongee.com
⤲ **Sub Excelsus** 1 ZA Pointe des Châteaux, 97436 St-Leu; ☎/f 0262 347365; e excelsus@wanadoo.fr; www.chez.com/excelsus

A SEVEN-DAY HIKE COVERING THE VERY BEST OF REUNION

Alice Deligey

To get a feel for what Réunion has to offer hikers, one needs at least two days, because spending a night in the Cirque of Mafate, which you can only reach on foot, is a must.

Mafate is a mysterious place, which I would advise people to explore for two, or even three days. So when we start our week-long treks on Wednesday, from Hell-Bourg (Cirque de Salazie), the first place we hike to is Mafate. That takes roughly 4¹/₂ hours, along which a highlight is the tamarind forest. Accommodation is in the gîte at Plaine aux Sables.

On Thursday, we then do a six-hour hike to Cilaos via the Col du Taibit, taking in magnificent places like the 2,991m Le Gros Morne (Great Mountain). We overnight in Cilaos. Many people just do these first two days, as it's the best way to experience Mafate.

On Friday morning, we have time for discovering Cilaos village. Then, we hike for 3¹/₂ hours to Piton-des-Neiges (3,069m), Réunion's highest mountain. Of course, this is the one mountain most hikers want to scale. We overnight in the basic gîte on Piton-des-Neiges.

On Saturday we get up early to climb to the peak of Piton-des-Neiges to see a spectacular sight: the sunrise over the Indian Ocean. From this peak, you can see everywhere on Réunion. And you should have seen the red of the lava flows from Piton-des-Neiges during the recent eruptions! After taking in the sunrise, we go back down to the gîte, have breakfast and hike to Cirque de Salazie along the trail called Cap Anglais. Through the mineral world to the tropical forest, we reach Hell-Bourg, a typical Creole village (seven hours, it's the longest day). We overnight in Hell-Bourg.

On Sunday, we take our visitors on a three-hour hike around interesting places in Cirque de Salazie, where we place emphasis on local culture. We visit a rural home, where you can see how people live in the mountains and learn all about the history and plants of the area. Again, we overnight in Hell-Bourg.

Monday involves a five-hour hike over the Cirque de Salazie, to the Bélouve Plateau, where we visit the beautiful Bélouve tropical forest. We'll also enjoy a brilliant view of the spectacular Trou de Fer waterfall.

Finally, we complete the wonderful hike, from where we take road transport to the gîte of the volcano, Piton-de-la-Fournaise, our accommodation for the night.

On the last day, we take visitors on the volcano crater hike (six hours). Afterwards, we get them to St-Leu, St-Gilles or St-Denis, where they can recover at the beach!

Prices are seven days/six nights €659; two days/one night €138 (including certified mountain guide, all meals and Creole dinner, accommodation and transport). Contact Maham (see page 253) by fax, phone or email for more information.

Alice Deligey is a leading mountain guide. She lives in Hell-Bourg and is one of the founder members of Maham Nature Treks.

DEEP-SEA FISHING

In 2003, a female fishing world record was achieved in the waters off Réunion, when Catherine Lavit caught a blue marlin weighing 551kg. Other fish caught off Réunion include bonito, tuna, wahoo, dorado, shark and swordfish.

The French for deep-sea fishing is *la pêche au gros*. Expect to pay around €80–90 per person per half day and €50 for those who don't want to fish but just go along for the ride. Drinks and light refreshments are often included.

Réunion Fishing Club 10 Enceinte Portuaire, 97434 St-Gilles-les-Bains; ☏ 0262 243610; f 0262 243946; e reunion.fishing.club@wanadoo.fr; www.reunionfishingclub.com

Réunion Pêche au Gros 5 Chemin Souris Blanche, 97426 Trois-Bassins; ☏ 0262 333399; f 0262 338221; e info@reunion-pecheaugros.com; www.reunion-pecheaugros.com

The following are private boats which operate deep-sea fishing trips from the Port de Plaisance, St-Gilles-les-Bains:

Alpha ☏ 0262 240202
Blue Marlin m 0692 652235
Maevasion m 0692 852346

Oceana II ☏ 0262 343917
Pêche Passion Sud m 0692 253377

GLASS-BOTTOM BOATS

These are a good way for non-divers to see the marine environment and are suitable for children of any age.

Le Grand Bleu Port de Plaisance, 97434 St-Gilles-les-Bains; ☏/f 0262 332832; e info@reunioncroisieres.com; www.reunioncroisieres.com. Two large boats and a bubble boat, all with underwater viewing. Trips last 1¹/₂ hours and depart at least 5 times daily. Dolphins are often seen in the early morning. The large boats can feel a bit crowded. *Adult/child* € 16/9.50.
Visiobul Réunion Port de Plaisance, 97434 St-Gilles-les-Bains; ☏ 0262 243704; f 0262 333062; e visiobulreunion@wanadoo.fr; www.visiobul-reunion.com. Three smaller boats with trips lasting 30 mins. *Adult/student/child* € 12/10/7. *Open daily from 08.00.*

17

Northern Réunion

As the Roland Garros International Airport and the department's main city, St-Denis, are located on the north coast, it is the starting (and end) point of most Réunion holidays. The far north of Réunion is generally defined as the area around St-Denis, extending inland to St-François, Plaine d'Affouches and the wonderful hiking area of Roche Ecrite, on the northern edge of the Cirque de Salazie.

ST-DENIS

Founded in 1668, this attractive coastal city in northern Réunion is home to around 140,000 inhabitants. St-Denis took over as capital from St-Paul in 1738, after being declared as such by the then governor Mahé de Labourdonnais. Understandably, people continue to refer to St-Denis (pronounced *san de-nee*) as the capital, although it has long been a county town.

St-Denis is bordered by the sea to the north and backed by high, green mountains to the south, so its setting is very appealing. The simple grid system makes it an easy place to explore.

It is possible to see the town's main attractions in a day's walkabout. **Le Barachois**, once a port, is a good place to start, with its cannons left over from the days of war with the British. The upmarket bars and restaurants in the area really come to life in the evenings. At **Place Sarda Garriga** (named after the governor who published the decree abolishing slavery) you'll see the statue of Roland Garros, a famed St-Denis-born aviator after whom the international airport is named.

St-Denis is perfect for lovers of history and architecture, with a wealth of old buildings. The **Préfecture**, the island's administrative offices near Le Barachois, is in an attractive former French East India Company building, constructed in 1735. On Avenue de la Victoire is the Tuscan-style **Cathédrale de St-Denis**, which was begun in 1829. Further along is the impressive **old town hall**, lighting up the street with its sunflower-yellow exterior. In front of it is the **Monument aux Morts**, erected in 1923 in honour of the Réunionnais casualties of World War I. **Rue de Paris** is lined with wonderful **colonial buildings**; on the corner of Rue Félix Guyon stands the opulent, much-photographed Creole mansion of the Secretary General.

The main **market** (*Grand Marché*) and its smaller counterpart (*Petit Marché*) are both on Rue Maréchal Leclerc, which also boasts a fine Creole building, the home of former French Prime Minister, Raymond Barre. In the same street is the city's mosque, **La Grande Mosquée**, which was the first Islamic religious building to be constructed in France (1905).

At the far southern end of Rue de Paris is the **Jardin de l'Etat**, established by French botanists after the property was bought in 1767 by an Officer Cremont. This is also where you will find the **Musée d'Histoire Naturelle** (Natural History Museum).

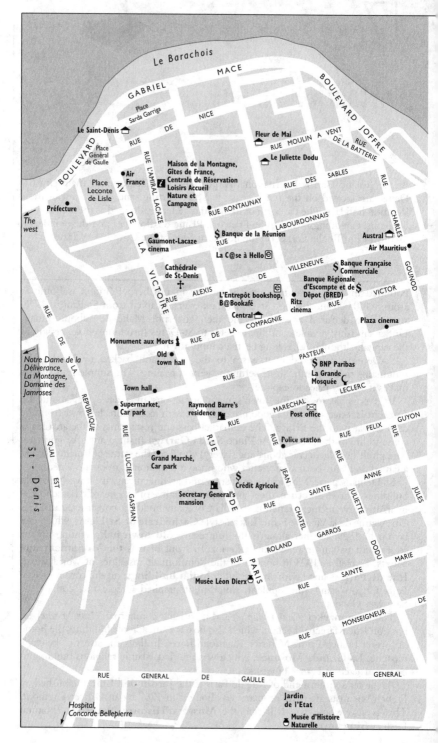

Le Barachois

MACE

GABRIEL

BOULEVARD JOFFRE

NICE

DE

Place
Sarda Garriga

RUE

Le Saint-Denis

Fleur de Mai

RUE MOULIN A VENT

RUE
DE LA BATTERIE

BOULEVARD

Place
Général
de Gaulle

Le Juliette Dodu

Air
France

Maison de la Montagne,
Gîtes de France,
Centrale de Réservation
Loisirs Accueil
Nature et
Campagne

RUE DES SABLES

RUE

Place
Leconte
de Lisle

DE

AV

Préfecture

RUE L'AMIRAL LACAZE

The
west

CHARLES

RUE RONTAUNAY

LABOURDONNAIS

LA

Banque de la Réunion

Austral

Gaumont-Lacaze
cinema

RUE

Air Mauritius

VICTOIRE

La C@se à Hello

VILLENEUVE

Banque Française
Commerciale

GOUNOD

DE

Cathédrale
de St-Denis

Banque Régionale
d'Escompte et de
Dêpot (BRED)

VICTOR

RUE

ALEXIS

L'Entrepôt bookshop,
B@Bookafé

Ritz
cinema

RUE

RUE

DE

Central

Plaza cinema

Monument aux Morts

RUE DE LA COMPAGNIE

LA

Old
town hall

PASTEUR

RUE

DE

BNP Paribas

RUE

RUE

RUE

La Grande
Mosquée

Town hall

LECLERC

REPUBLIQUE

Supermarket,
Car park

Raymond Barre's
residence

MARECHAL

Notre Dame de la
Déliverance,
La Montagne,
Domaine des
Jamroses

QUAI

EST

RUE

Post office

RUE FELIX

GUYON

RUE

St - Denis

LUCIEN

RUE

Police station

RUE

Grand Marché,
Car park

JEAN

ANNE

GASPIAN

DE

Crédit Agricole

SAINTE

JULIETTE

JULES

Secretary General's
mansion

RUE

CHATEL

GARROS

DODU

ROLAND

MARIE

RUE

PARIS

SAINTE

DE

Musée Léon Dierx

RUE

MONSEIGNEUR

RUE

RUE

GENERAL

DE

GAULLE

RUE

GENERAL

Hospital,
Concorde Bellepierre

Jardin
de l'Etat

Musée d'Histoire
Naturelle

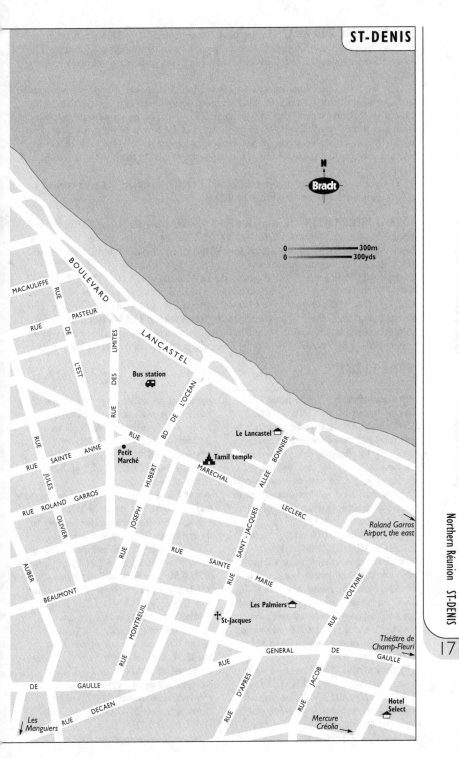

ST-DENIS

GETTING THERE AND AWAY During peak hours traffic in St-Denis can be pretty intimidating for the uninitiated, especially with its intricate one-way system. The town is small enough to explore on foot and Le Barachois is a good place to leave your car.

The *cars jaunes* **bus station** is just off Rue Maréchal Leclerc, between Boulevard de l'Océan and Rue des Limites. This is where you will arrive if you get the shuttle bus from Roland Garros Airport (see pages 239–40). The bus routes are displayed here and there are regular buses to St-Pierre, via the towns of the west coast, and to St-Benoît on the east coast. St-Denis city buses are a good way of getting around, except during rush hour. Timetables are available from the bus station or the tourist office.

Taxis are easy to find at the bus station but are expensive. Shared taxis (*taxis collectifs*) also depart from the bus station.

TOURIST INFORMATION The **tourist office** (*syndicat d'initiative*) is at 27 Rue Amiral Lacaze, 97400 St-Denis (0262 418300; f 0262 213776; e otinord@wanadoo.fr. *Open Mon–Sat 08.30–18.00*). It has lots of useful information and literature, and the staff are helpful and speak English.

At 5 Rue Rontaunay is the **Maison de la Montagne** (0262 907878; f 0262 418429; e resa@reunion-nature.com; www.reunion-nature.com. *Open Mon–Thu 09.00–17.00, Fri 09.00–16.00, Sat 09.00–12.00*), which can organise accommodation in rural areas and hiking. The **Centrale de Réservation Loisirs Accueil Nature et Campagne** is also here and offers information on activities, as well as a reservation service. **Gîtes de France** is represented too, also with a central reservations service.

WHERE TO STAY
Classified hotels

Concorde Bellepierre **** (55 rooms) 91 bis Allée des Topazes, Bellepierre, St-Denis; 0262 515151; f 0262 512602; e commercial@concorde-bellepierre.com; www.concorde-bellepierre.com. St-Denis's only 4-star option is slightly removed from the hustle and bustle, being in a residential area overlooking the city. The rooms are modern, with AC, TV, phone, minibar and safe. Rooms equipped for the disabled are available. There is a restaurant and a pool. *Dbl/sgl from € 160/140 BB.*

Le Saint-Denis *** (118 rooms) 2 Rue Doret, St-Denis; 0262 218020; f 0262 219741; e resa.stdenis@apavou-hotels.com; www.apavou-hotels.com. Smart hotel centrally located, near Le Barachois. Comfortable, spacious rooms with AC, TV, phone and minibar. Rooms equipped for the disabled are available. Facilities include conference rooms, snack-bar, restaurant (see page 268) and swimming pool. Caters for business travellers. *Dbl/sgl from € 165/116 BB.*

Mercure Créolia *** (107 rooms) 14 Rue du Stade, Montgaillard, St-Denis; 0262 942626; f 0262 942727; e H1674-GM@accor-hotels.com; www.runisland.com/mercure. Large, modern hotel 3km from the centre with impressive views of the city. Rooms have AC, TV, phone, minibar and safe. Rooms

equipped for the disabled are available. Facilities include a large pool, jacuzzi, sauna, conference room and car park. The restaurant specialises in Creole and French food. *Dbl from € 135 RO.*

Austral Hotel *** (53 rooms) 20 Rue Charles Gounod, St Denis; 0262 944567; f 0262 211314; e hotel-austral@wanadoo.fr; www.multimania.com/hotelaustral. In the centre of town. Unremarkable but comfortable en-suite rooms with AC, TV, phone and minibar. Rooms equipped for the disabled are available. Facilities include underground parking, a small pool and a restaurant serving b/fast only. B/fasts are good. *Dbl/sgl from € 78/68 RO. Buffet breakfast € 10 per person.*

Le Juliette Dodu *** (43 rooms) 31 Rue Juliette Dodu, St-Denis; 0262 209120; f 0262 209121; e jdodu@runnet.com; www.hotel-jdodu.com. Charming hotel in a beautiful, historic Creole building. The location is central yet quiet. Rooms have AC, TV, phone and minibar. Rooms equipped for the disabled are available. It has a pool, jacuzzi, library and parking. *Dbl/sgl from € 91/75 RO.*

Domaine des Jamroses *** (12 rooms) 6 Chemin du Colorado, 97417 La Montagne; 0262 235900; f 0262 239337; e jamroses@domainedesjamroses.com;

www.ilereunion.com/domainejamroses. 8km from St-Denis centre, in a 2ha park overlooking the sea. Tastefully furnished en-suite rooms with TV, phone, minibar and safe. Rooms equipped for the disabled are available. Facilities include a stylish restaurant (see page 268), pool, jacuzzi, and sauna. *Dbl/sgl from € 130/93 RO.*

🏠 **Central Hotel** ** (57 rooms) 37 Rue de la Compagnie, St-Denis; ✆ 0262 941808; f 0262 216433; e central.hotel@wanadoo.fr; www.ilereunion.com/centralhotel. Comfortable rooms, convenient location. Mainly patronised by Mauritian and Comoran businesspeople. Rooms have en suite, AC, TV, phone and minibar; some have a safe. There is a car park. *Dbl/sgl from € 62/54 BB.*

🏠 **Le Lancastel** ** (136 rooms) 6 Rue Henri Vavasseur, St-Denis; ✆ 0262 947070; f 0262 201205; e resalancastel@apavou-hotels.com; www.apavou-hotels.com. Located across the road from

the sea. Rooms, including some with disabled facilities, have en suite, AC, TV and phone. There is a restaurant, bar and parking. *Dbl/sgl from € 44/41 RO. Breakfast € 5.50 per person.*

🏠 **Marianne** ** (24 rooms) 5 Ruelle Boulot, St-Denis; ✆ 0262 218080; f 0262 218500; e hotel-la-marianne@wanadoo.fr. Rooms are comfortable, with en suite, AC, TV, phone and minibar. Three of the rooms are equipped with kitchenette. There is an underground car park. *Dbl/sgl from € 46/39 BB. Rooms with kitchenette are an extra € 12.*

🏠 **Hotel Select** * (55 rooms) 1 bis Rue des Lataniers, St-Denis; ✆ 0262 411350; f 0262 416707; e hotelselect@wanadoo.fr; www.runweb.com/hotelselect. Comfortable, clean en-suite rooms with AC, TV and phone. It has a small pool and parking. There are rooms suitable for the disabled. *Dbl/sgl from € 45/35 BB.*

Unclassified accommodation

🏠 **Les Manguiers** (20 s/c apts) 9 Rue des Manguiers, St-Denis; ✆ 0262 212595; f 0262 202223; e manguiers@ilereunion.com. Self-catering apts, including 2 equipped for the disabled. All have 1 dbl room, bathroom, sitting area, kitchenette, AC, TV, phone and balcony. Good option for businesspeople staying for lengthy periods. *Apts from € 48 RO.*

🏠 **Fleur de Mai** (10 rooms) 1A Rue du Moulin à

Vent, St-Denis; ✆ 0262 415181; f 0262 941160; e hotelfleurdemai@wanadoo.fr. A charming, flower-bedecked small hotel in a quiet but central location. Spotless en-suite rooms with AC, TV and phone. *Dbl/sgl from € 40/36 BB.*

🏠 **Les Palmiers** (12 rooms) 34 Rue Voltaire; ✆ 0262 203646. Fairly quiet location. *Dbl from € 30 RO. Breakfast € 3.50.*

Classified furnished flats (meublés de tourisme)

🏠 **Bungalows de la Caroline** *** (2 bungalows) 14 bis Chemin de la Caroline, Ste-Clotilde; ✆/f 0262 527298; m 0692 828356; e jean-gonthier@wanadoo.fr; www.meublesdetourisme-reunion.com/caroline. Two self-catering bungalows with 1 dbl room, TV and phone. Garden and pool.

Bungalow from € 53 (2 people).

🏠 **Meublé Bialade** ** (1 apt) 6 Rue Magallon, St-Denis; ✆ 0262 202891; e bialade.gerard@wanadoo.fr. Close to the town centre. Apt for up to 4 people with AC. *Apt from € 260 per week (2 people).*

✗ **WHERE TO EAT** For self-caterers, there is a **Continent hypermarket** between St-Denis and Roland Garros Airport, as well as several smaller supermarkets in town. For eating out, there are numerous restaurants, street vendors, snack-bars, bistros, brasseries and cafés, which are part and parcel of St-Denis's café society. However, finding a restaurant that's open Sunday lunchtime can be a challenge. Below is a cross-section of St-Denis's eateries:

✗ **Bordeaux** 1 bis Av de la Victoire; ✆ 0262 901727. Cuisine: French. *Medium price range. Open daily for lunch and dinner.*

✗ **Chez Piat** 60 Rue Pasteur; ✆ 0262 214576. Cuisine: French. Stylish restaurant, romantic atmosphere. *Main courses from € 15. Lunch and dinner, closed Sat lunch, Mon evening and Sun.*

✗ **La Coquille** 52 Rue Victor MacAuliffe; ✆ 0262

204847. Cuisine: French, seafood. Good range of tasty seafood dishes; mussels are the speciality. *Main courses from € 11. Open 10.00–23.00, closed all day Mon and Tue lunch.*

✗ **Le Corossol** 32 Bd Lancastel; ✆ 0262 214941. Cuisine: Creole, Malagasy. *Medium price range. Open Mon–Sat for lunch and dinner. Reservation recommended.*

✘ **Les Délices de l'Orient** 59 Rue Juliette Dodu; ☎ 0262 414420. Cuisine: Chinese. Large, popular restaurant with a relaxed atmosphere. *Main courses from € 10. Open Tue–Sat for lunch and dinner.*

✘ **L'Igloo Glacerie** Cnr Rues Jean Chatel and Compagnie; ☎ 0262 213469. Cuisine: snacks, ice cream. Huge range of ice creams and sorbets. *Open daily, all day.*

✘ **Les Jamroses** Domaine des Jamroses, 6 Chemin du Colorado, La Montagne; ☎ 0262 235900. Cuisine: French, seafood. Very elegant restaurant, gourmet food and prices to match. *Open daily for lunch and dinner.*

✘ **Les Jardins du Maroc** 90 Rue Pasteur; ☎ 0262 410659. Cuisine: Moroccan. Good reputation. *Main courses from € 13. Open for lunch at weekends, dinner Wed–Sun.*

✘ **Kim Son** 13 Rue Maréchal Leclerc; ☎ 0262 217500. Cuisine: Vietnamese. Small, cosy restaurant and tasty food. *Prices are mid range. Open Mon–Sat for lunch and dinner.*

✘ **Le Labourdonnais** 14 Rue Amiral Lacaze; ☎ 0262 214426 Cuisine: French. Upmarket French favourites, such as foie gras and steak tartare, in a sophisticated atmosphere. *Main courses from € 15. Open Mon–Fri for lunch and dinner, Sat for dinner.*

✘ **Massalé** 30 Rue Alexis de Villeneuve; ☎ 0262 217506. Cuisine: Indian snacks. Eat-in or take-away. Tiny establishment selling delicious *samoussas,* bonbons piments and other tasty bites. *Inexpensive. Open Mon–Sat 10.00–20.30, Sun 11.00–20.30.*

✘ **Mumbai** 79 Rue Pasteur; ☎ 0262 943157. Cuisine: Indian. Good-quality Indian food. *Main courses from € 12. Open Mon–Sat for lunch and dinner.*

✘ **Oasis** Hotel le St-Denis, le Barachois; ☎ 0262 218020. Cuisine: French, Creole. *Main courses from € 9. Open daily 07.00–midnight.*

✘ **Le Pavillon d'Or** 224 Rue Maréchal Leclerc; ☎ 0262 214986. Cuisine: Chinese. Relaxed atmosphere. *Main courses from € 9.50. Open Mon–Sat for lunch and dinner.*

✘ **Le Pekinois** 78 Rue Alexis de Villeneuve; ☎ 0262 200950. Cuisine: Chinese. Popular. *Main courses from € 9.50. Open daily for lunch and dinner.*

✘ **Le Roland Garros** Place du Barachois; ☎ 0262 414437. Cuisine: French, Creole. Handy location, European feel. *Main courses from € 12. Open daily 07.00–midnight.*

✘ **La Saladière** 32 Bd Lancastel; ☎ 0262 214941. Cuisine: French. Stylish and highly regarded. *Main courses for around € 12. Open Mon–Fri for lunch and dinner, Sat for dinner.*

✘ **Via Veneto** Cnr Rues Jules Auber and Ste-Marie; ☎ 0262 219271. Cuisine: Italian, French. *Main courses for around € 12. Open Mon for lunch, Tue–Sat for lunch and dinner.*

NIGHTLIFE The European theme continues into the night in St-Denis, with lots of bars and ice cream parlours open until late. The **bar** of the moment appears to be **Moda Bar** (*75 Rue Pasteur;* ☎ *0262 216829*), with its trendy, modern atmosphere. Other popular drinking holes include **Sí Señor** (*24 Rue de Nice;* ☎ *0262 218006*). Nightclubs include **Le First** (*8 Av de la Victoire;* ☎ *0262 416825*), **Le Hibou** (*Rue Labourdonnais;* ☎ *0262 200066*), **La Loco** (*7 Rue Amiral Lacaze;* ☎ *0262 210745*), which is popular with the university students, and **Palace Salle Candrin** (*Moufia;* ☎ *0262 297555*). Clubs really only get going after 23.00. As in most towns, entry is around € 12.

The **Casino de Saint-Denis** is in Le Barachois (☎ *0262 413333. The slot machines are open daily from 10.00 and the tables Mon–Fri 21.00–02.00, Fri–Sat 21.00–03.00, Sun 21.00–01.00*).

OTHER PRACTICALITIES

Money and banking Many French banking institutions are represented in St-Denis. Currency and travellers' cheques can be changed at all the banks. Most banks have ATMs.

$ **Banque de la Réunion** 27 Rue Jean Chatel; ☎ 0262 400123

$ **Banque Française Commerciale** 60 Rue Alexis de Villeneuve; ☎ 0262 405555

$ **Banque Nationale de Paris Paribas (BNPP)** 67 Rue Juliette Dodu; ☎ 0820 840830

$ **Banque Régionale d'Escompte et de Dêpot (BRED)** 33 Rue Victor MacAuliffe; ☎ 0262 901560

$ **Caisse d'Epargne de la Réunion** 55 Rue de Paris; ☎ 0262 948000

$ **Crédit Agricole** 18 Rue Félix Guyon; ☎ 0262 909100

Communications There is a number of **post offices** in the capital. The main post office (✆ *0262 211212. Open Mon–Fri 07.30–18.00, Sat 08.00–12.00*) is on the corner of Rue Maréchal Leclerc and Rue Juliette Dodu. It also handles Poste Restante.

Public **telephones** are widespread and, as throughout the island, the majority take phonecards (*télécartes*). These can be bought at post offices, newsagents and shops displaying the sign.

For **internet access** try **B@Bookafé** (*82 Rue Juliette Dodu;* ✆ *0262 209480*) or **La C@se à Hello** (*68 Rue Juliette Dodu;* ✆ *0262 941955*). For details see page 251.

Medical care The main **hospital** is on Allée des Topazes, Bellepierre (✆ *0262 905050*) and there are numerous medical practitioners. There are plenty of **pharmacies** – a good starting point is Rue Maréchal Leclerc.

AROUND ST-DENIS

East of St-Denis is the booming district of **Ste-Clotilde**, where the university campus is found. **St-François** is a residential area in the mountains overlooking St-Denis, with a mild climate and lush vegetation. Higher up, at 800m, is **Le Brûlé**, a starting point for hikes on the **Plaine-des-Chicots**, which rises to the **Roche Ecrite** (2,275m). This overlooks the Cirque de Salazie. **La Montagne** is another residential area west of St-Denis, praised for its pleasant climate. The winding road lined with flamboyant trees features some excellent viewpoints.

About 12km east of St-Denis city centre is the village of **Ste-Marie**. There is little to see in the village itself but nearby **Rivière des Pluies** is known for its statue of the **Black Virgin** (*La Vierge Noire*). The statue stands in a tall white shrine to the left of the village church, surrounded by an explosion of flower arrangements and row upon row of candles. People arrive in droves to pray to her for good health, prosperity and protection. The story goes that a runaway slave fled to the place where the shrine now stands. There, the Black Virgin appeared to him, instructing him to hide under a flimsy bush. The slave complied, although the bush was much too small to conceal him properly. Just before the slave hunters reached the spot, the Black Virgin instantly increased the size of the bush, thereby completely covering the runaway. To honour her, the slave then carved the statue and, subsequently, the shrine was erected.

WHAT TO DO

ORGANISED TOURS The **tourist office** (*Office du Tourisme, 27 Rue Amiral Lacaze, St-Denis;* ✆ *0262 418300*) offers organised tours of St-Denis, Ste-Marie and Ste-Suzanne. They operate Monday–Saturday at 09.00 and 15.00, last 1½ hours and cost around €3.

CINEMA There are three cinemas in St-Denis, usually showing international films dubbed into French: **Ritz** (*53 Rue Juliette Dodu;* ✆ *0262 200952*), **Plaza** (*79 Rue Pasteur;* ✆ *0262 210436*) and **Gaumont Lacaze** (*Cnr Rues Amiral Lacaze and Rontaunay;* ✆ *0262 412000*). Tickets cost around €7.

THEATRE The tourist office can provide information on forthcoming productions.

🎭 **Théâtre de Champ-Fleuri** Av André Malraux, St-Denis; ✆ 0262 411141; f 0262 415571; e tcf.administratif@odcreunion.com; www.odcreunion.com

🎭 **Centre dramatique de l'Océan Indien** 2 Rue Maréchal Leclerc; ✆ 0262 203399; f 0262 210160; e centre-dramatique.reunion@wanadoo.fr

SHOPPING In St-Denis, both **Le Grand Marché** (main market) and **Le Petit Marché** (small market) are on Rue Maréchal Leclerc. The main market is open daily and sells mostly handicrafts. The small market has mostly fruit, vegetable, flower and spice stalls (*open Mon–Sat 06.00–18.00, Sun 06.00–12.00*). There are markets in **Le Chaudron** on Wednesday and Sunday mornings, **Le Moufia** on Saturday morning, **La Source** on Thursday morning and **Les Camélias** on Friday morning. You'll find a range of handicrafts at the markets, as well as in the **Galerie Artisanale** at 75 Rue du Karting in the suburb of Ste-Clotilde (✆ *0262 295666*), but prices around St-Denis may be higher than in smaller towns.

HIKING On the outskirts of St-Denis and beyond you'll find picturesque hamlets in breathtaking surroundings. There are plenty of options in terms of hiking trails.

Inland from Roland Garros Airport, southeast of St-Denis, is the waterfall of **Le Chaudron**. Its name comes from the cauldron-like formation into which it plunges. Getting there entails an 8km hike, which takes around two to three hours (grading: moderate).

Hiking trails around **Roche Ecrite** ('written rock') are some of the island's best. The Roche Ecrite forest road is also where you can see most of the island's endemic birds. A 10km, four-hour hike (grading: difficult) takes you to the remote **Bassin du Diable** (Devil's Pond). Alternatively, you could try the 9km, four-hour walk (grading: easy) to **Piton Laverdure**, an extinct volcanic peak, which features a mass of flowers in October and November. A popular and easily reached picnic spot is **Cascade Maniquet** (30 minutes' walk).

The Roche Ecrite walk itself is wonderful, though quite challenging, and can be done in a day. It is, however, recommended that you stay overnight at the Plaine-des-Chicots gîte, which you can book at Maison de la Montagne. If you have a car, you can leave it at the Mamode Camp forest road car park but there have been reports of cars being stolen or damaged here. The first leg, which is the part covered by birding tour groups, involves the three-hour walk to the gîte on the **Plaine-des-Chicots** path (5km), through tamarind and bamboo forest. The second leg is the 4km (1½ hour) one on the Roche Ecrite path. Do this early in the morning for the best weather. From a rocky spur covered with inscriptions (the 'written rock'), you can see the magnificent amphitheatres of Salazie and Mafate. On the way back, stop off at the **Soldiers' Cave (Caverne des Soldats)**, overlooking Rivière des Pluies. Another path leads to **Mare aux Cerfs** (stags' pond).

The energetic (and fairly fit) can continue from Roche Ecrite, west to **Plaine d'Affouches**, which means a three-hour hike past a disused prison, Ilet à Guillaume. You can continue even further, to **Dos d'Ane** village, by taking the path branching off after Ilet à Guillaume. Ardent hikers can confront the steep trail into the Cirque de Salazie. Bring warm clothing since night temperatures are often around freezing point.

GOLF There is a nine-hole course at **La Montagne**. For details see *Chapter 16, Activities*.

WHAT TO SEE

JARDIN DE L'ETAT (*Rue de la Source; admission free*; open *07.00–18.00*) At the southern end of Rue de Paris is this botanical garden, which features 2,000 species from around the world. It is a beautiful, tranquil place in which to spend a few hours.

MUSÉE D'HISTOIRE NATURELLE (*1 Rue Poivre, 97400 St-Denis;* ✆ *0262 200219;* **f** *0262 213393;* **e** *museum@cg974.fr; adult/child €2/1; open Mon–Sat 09.30–17.00*) Natural history museum housed in a colonial building in the Jardin de l'Etat. Exhibits extinct and rare species of the western Indian Ocean, including the solitaire, Réunion's dodo-like bird.

MUSÉE LÉON DIERX (*28 Rue de Paris, 97400 St-Denis;* ✆ *0262 202482;* **f** *0262 218287;* **e** *musee.dierx@cg974.fr; www.cg974.fr; admission: €2; open Tue–Sun 09.00–12.00 and 13.00–17.00*) The museum opened in 1911 in the former bishop's residence. Well worth a visit, it houses original works by the likes of Gauguin, Maufra, Erro, Chen Zen and even Picasso. There is wheelchair access in Rue Ste-Marie.

MUSÉE DE LA VRAIE FRATERNITÉ (*Bd de la Providence, 97400 St-Denis;* ✆ *0262 210671;* **f** *0262 415480; adult/child €2/1; open Wed and Sat 09.00–17.00*) Exhibits are designed to represent the island's different communities.

JARDIN DE CENDRILLON (*48 Route des Palmiers, 97417 La Montagne;* **m** *0692 863288; tours last 1¹/₂ hours and cost €6 per person*) Pleasant private garden. Guided tours are available but must be booked in advance.

Dombeya acutangula

18

Eastern Réunion

The sparsely inhabited eastern region stretches from Ste-Suzanne in the north through St-André and Bras-Panon to St-Benoît, continuing southwards to La Pointe de la Table. It is a lush area of sugarcane, lychee fields and vanilla. In fact, a visit to one of the vanilla estates is one of the highlights of the east. The region includes the awesome active volcano, Piton-de-la-Fournaise.

Although it is the south which has earned the adjective *sauvage* (wild), it could equally be applied to the unspoilt east coast. This is the region which receives the most rain and it is the one into which violent cyclones tear when they rage in the western Indian Ocean between January and March. Most of the east coast consists of black volcanic rock or cliffs, against which rough seas lash continuously. The regular activity of Piton-de-la-Fournaise constantly adds to Réunion's surface area, as lava flows out of the crater towards the eastern coast, solidifying as it hits the ocean.

STE-SUZANNE TO BRAS-PANON

The colonial houses and flowery gardens of **Ste-Suzanne** render the atmosphere somewhat more pleasant than is the case in bustling St-André. It is one of the island's oldest settlements, dating from 1667, and is best known for its **lighthouse**, at the western end of town.

Nearby **Cascade Niagara** is signposted from the southern end of town. The short drive takes you through cane fields and you can park right at the foot of the falls. Although far less impressive than its Canadian namesake, it is a pretty waterfall, 30m high.

St-André is a large industrial town with factories galore. It is the centre of Réunion's Tamil community and therefore the best place to see awe-inspiring **Tamil ceremonies and festivals** such as fire-walking and Cavadee (see pages 70–2).

The main attraction for visitors is the **Maison de la Vanille** on Rue de la Gare, which offers fascinating guided tours explaining the process behind vanilla production (see *What to see*, page 279).

On the coast, a few kilometres from the centre of St-André, is the newly constructed **Parc Nautique du Colosse**. The park is set among the sugarcane fields and features boutiques, eateries, picnic areas and a children's playground. This is also the new home of the local **tourist office**.

About 2km south of St-André is the turning to **Salazie** and **Hell-Bourg** (see *Chapter 21, The Interior*, pages 319–23).

Continuing south along Route Nationale 2 (RN2), you come to **Bras-Panon**, the centre of the vanilla industry (see *What to see*, pages 279–80). The nearby village of **Rivière des Roches** is where much of the island's *bichiques* are fished, a small sprat-like fish usually served in *cari*. In the village is a turning to two beautiful natural pools beneath wooded waterfalls: **Bassin La Paix** and **Bassin La Mer**. About 3km from the RN2, you come to a track that leads to Bassin La Paix, where you can leave your car. It is a short walk through lush woods to the *bassin*. A sizeable waterfall plunges into the deep pool, where a quick dip offers welcome respite from the tropical sun. If you continue uphill for another 30 minutes, you'll arrive at the second pool, Bassin La Mer, arguably even more attractive than the lower one. It's in this area (the tumbling river between the two pools) that people come to do 'water hiking', in other words hiking upstream in the river itself.

Beyond Bras-Panon, on the RN2 to St-Benoît, is a turning to the viewpoint at **Takamaka**. The road winds gradually upwards for about 15km before reaching Takamaka. From the car park, there is a wonderful view of a semicircle of mountains painted with the thin strips of waterfalls. It is the starting point for a walk of 6.5km to the *Electricité de France* platform at Bébour.

TOURIST INFORMATION The **tourist office** in Ste-Suzanne is at 65 Avenue Pierre Mendès-France (⟍ *0262 521354;* f *0262 521363. Open Mon–Fri 08.00–12.00 and 13.00–17.00, Sat 08.00–12.00*). There is also a tourist office in **St-André**, at 25 Parc Nautique du Colosse (⟍ *0262 469163;* f *0262 465216. Open Mon–Fri 09.00–17.00, Sat 09.00–16.00*).

WHERE TO STAY There are no classified hotels in the area but there are *gîtes ruraux* and *chambres d'hôtes*, which can be booked through the Relais Départemental des Gîtes de France (see *Chapter 15, Accommodation*, pages 243–5).

Unclassified accommodation

Ile de France (30 rooms) 50 Rue du Stade, St-André; ⟍ 0262 209411. Basic accommodation.

Dbl from € *36 RO.*

WHERE TO EAT

✕ Le Bocage Chemin Bocage, Ste-Suzanne; ⟍ 0262 522154. Cuisine: French, Chinese, Creole. Peaceful setting by the river. *Main courses from* € *9. Open Tue–Sun for lunch and Tue–Sat for dinner.*

✕ Le Beau Rivage Vielle-Eglise, Champ-Borne; ⟍ 0262 460866. Cuisine: Creole, French. Fairly smart and very popular. *Main courses from* € *12. Open Tue–Sat 10.00–23.00, and Sun for lunch.*

✕ Restaurant Law-Shun 866 Av de Bourbon, St-André; ⟍ 0262 460408. Cuisine: Chinese. Informal. *Main courses from* € *10. Open Mon–Sat for lunch and dinner.*

✕ Le Beauvallon Route du Stade, Rivière des Roches; ⟍ 0262 504292. Cuisine: Creole, Indian. A great place to try local specialities such as *cari bichiques. Main courses from* € *12. Open daily 09.00–15.00, Fri–Sat for dinner. Reservation recommended.*

✕ Le Bec Fin 66 Route National, Bras-Panon; ⟍ 0262 515224. Cuisine: Creole, Chinese. Has earned an excellent reputation thanks to its good food and friendly service. *Main courses from* € *7. Open daily for lunch, Thu–Sat for dinner.*

✕ Vani-La Coopérative de La Vanille, Bras-Panon; ⟍ 0262 517012. Cuisine: Creole, European. A fascinating menu with most of the dishes incorporating vanilla. *Main courses from* € *10. Open Mon–Fri 11.30–15.00.*

ST-BENOIT

Originally built almost entirely of wood, St-Benoît was flattened by a fire in the 1950s and then rebuilt in brick and cement. The town itself is not particularly inspiring; most tourists simply pass through *en route* to the attractions inland.

Rivière des Marsouins runs through the town and *bichiques* are caught at the mouth of the river. The **tourist office** and **banks** (**Crédit Agricole** and **Banque de la Réunion**) are found on Rue Georges Pompidou.

About 10km southwest of the town on the RN3 (towards La Plaine-des-Palmistes) is the turning to **Grand Etang**, a lake once considered sacred by slaves, who would conduct rituals on its shores. There are some pleasant walks here and it is a very popular picnic spot, particularly on weekends. On the same road is the pretty village of **La Confiance**, about 6km from St-Benoît.

GETTING THERE AND AWAY Getting to St-Benoît is not difficult: *cars jaunes* (buses) run regularly to and from St-Denis (Line G) and there are buses to and from St-Pierre, either along the coast road (Line I) or inland via La Plaine-des-Palmistes (Line H).

TOURIST INFORMATION The **tourist office** (*0262 470509. Open Mon–Sat 08.30–17.00*) is at Place de l'Eglise on Rue Georges Pompidou, the main road running through the centre of St-Benoît. The staff are very helpful and speak some English.

WHERE TO STAY
Classified hotels

L'Hostellerie de la Confiance (8 rooms) 60 Chemin de la Confiance, St-Benoît; 0262 509050; f 0262 509727; e hostelleriedelaconfiance.reunion@wanadoo.fr. A few mins inland from St-Benoît, in a former sugar estate. Turn right just after the sign that tells you you're in Confiance. Accommodation with plenty of charm. The rooms, which were once stables, have en-suite bathroom, AC, TV, phone and fridge. It has a pool, garden and an outstanding restaurant (see below). Ideal base from which to explore the east coast and interior. *Dbl/sgl from € 65.50/53.60 RO*.

Unclassified accommodation

Hotel Le Bouvet (7 rooms) 75 Rue Amiral Bouvet, St-Benoît; 0262 501496. Clean, simple en-suite rooms with fan. Has a very good restaurant (see below), a pool and a garden with a view of the sea. *Dbl from € 35 RO*.

WHERE TO EAT
There are large **Cora** and **Champion supermarkets**, both signed from the RN2.

Le Bouvet 75 Rue Amiral Bouvet, St-Benoît; 0262 501496. Cuisine: Creole, French. Attractively decorated with a French ambience. *Main courses from € 12. Open Tue–Sun for lunch, Wed–Sat for dinner*.

Chez Georget 47 Rue Amiral Bouvet, St-Benoît; 0262 502274. Cuisine: Creole, Chinese. Also take-away. Superb *cabri massalé*. *Take-aways from € 5. Open Tue–Sun for lunch, Tue–Sat for dinner*.

Dauphin Gourmand 2 bis Rue Amiral Bouvet, St-Benoît; 0262 504282. Cuisine: Italian, French, Creole. Small, clean and pleasant. *Main courses from € 9. Open Sun–Fri for lunch, Tue–Sun for dinner*.

L'Hostellerie de la Confiance 60 Chemin de la Confiance, St-Benoît; 0262 509050. Cuisine: Creole, European. Excellent food in a peaceful setting. *Main courses from € 11. Open Sun–Fri for lunch, Tue–Sun for dinner*.

OTHER PRACTICALITIES
Communications The **post office** is on Rue Georges Pompidou. **Le Web Kafé** (*Pl Antoine Roussin;* 0262 929672) is a well-equipped internet café with a non-alcoholic bar. It's in the centre of town, behind the church and next to the mediathèque. For details see page 251.

STE-ANNE

About 5km south of St-Benoît on RN2 lies Ste-Anne, a pretty village that has proudly preserved many of its Creole houses.

Just off the main road is the village's highly unusual **church**. The original building, dating from 1857, was rebuilt by Father Daubenberger and his parishioners from 1892. The result is an extravagant pastel pink building embellished with rather odd stone carvings. Next to the church is a small shop called Ilôt Savons, which sells locally made soap.

Just north of Ste-Anne on the RN2 is **La Grotte de Lourdes**, a shrine to the Virgin Mary. It is said that in 1862 a tidal wave hit the area, but the locals hid in a cave and were saved. They built the shrine, which still attracts many pilgrims, as a symbol of their gratitude to the Virgin.

STE-ROSE AND SURROUNDS

On the way from Ste-Anne to Ste-Rose, you pass a large suspension bridge, **Le Pont d'Anglais**, which was built in 1894. Adrenaline junkies now practise bungee jumping from the bridge over the **Rivière de l'Est**. This is also one of many favoured spots for the customary Sunday family picnic.

Surrounded by endless sugarcane fields, **Ste-Rose** is on the shoulder of the Piton-de-la-Fournaise volcano. There's something savage about the coastline here, with its black, rocky cliffs and wild, wild seas. Swimming is not on, but I am told by those in the know that the scuba diving offshore is excellent. (If you do this, make sure you go with very experienced people as the sea is potentially murderous.) In terms of sporting activities, the area is possibly best known for its **mountain-biking** trails (see page 279).

Ste-Rose is essentially a fishing village which has grown up around the harbour. At the harbour is a monument in honour of the defeated British naval commander, Corbett, who died in a battle with the French in 1809. The **post office** is at 184 Route Nationale 2. **Pharmacie Boyer** is at 447 RN2 in Piton-Ste-Rose.

Ste-Rose's big claim to fame is the church of **Notre Dame des Laves**, which is actually at **Piton-Ste-Rose**. On 12 April 1977, Piton-de-la-Fournaise blew its top once again, spewing out a wall of molten lava that rushed directly towards Piton-Ste-Rose. Everything in its path was destroyed: houses, trees and crops. The lava began crossing the road in front of the church. And then the unbelievable happened. The lava separated exactly at the church's front door and forked around it, flowing on either side until the two halves met on the other side of the church and continued towards the sea. Locals thought it was a miracle. Going inside the church and examining the framed photographs and newspaper clippings depicting that incredible event, you can see why. You'll also see a painting of Christ halting the lava. Some strange things have happened on this island.

Next to the church is **La Vierge au Parasol** (the Virgin with the Umbrella). She is easily recognisable, dressed in blue and carrying a blue umbrella, designed to help her in her struggle to protect the local families and crops from the fury of the volcano. The Virgin used to stand just south of **Bois Blanc** but the mayor had her removed just prior to the January 2002 eruption, for fear that she would be destroyed. Local residents were furious and still claim that had she been left there, she would have diverted the lava and they would have had a miracle to rival that of Piton-Ste-Rose.

There's also a waterfall in the area (near Narayanin shop), which according to Creole lore turns a blood red just before the volcano is going to erupt.

Heading south of Ste-Rose, you'll arrive at **Pointe des Cascades**, Réunion's easternmost point. Just below it is **Anse des Cascades**, a beautiful quiet bay, backed on three sides by very high, very steep cliffs. The 'cascades' referred to plummet down the green cliffs into a pool. This is a popular area for local fishermen and colourful fishing boats lie in neat rows along the shore. There's a dense palm grove with several picnic spots and a small restaurant. The bay has a surreal feel and people come here from all over the island to enjoy the natural beauty and remote surrounds. Needless to say, it becomes packed on weekends. Once again, swimming is not safe.

GETTING THERE AND AWAY Ste-Rose lies on the St-Pierre/St-Benoît coastal bus route (Line I) and there is a stop almost directly outside Notre Dame des Laves.

⌂ WHERE TO STAY
Unclassified accommodation

⌂ **Le Joyau des Laves** (4 rooms) Piton Cascades, RN2, Piton-Ste-Rose; ☎ 0262 473400; f 0262 472535; e spielmann@joyaudeslaves.com; www.joyaudeslaves.com. This chambre d'hôte is in a wonderful setting on a hillside overlooking the sea, south of Ste-Rose. The comfortable rooms have en-suite facilities and one is designed to be accessible to the disabled. *Dbl from € 35 BB.*

⌂ **Auberge du Poisson Rouge** (7 rooms) 503 RN2, Piton-Ste-Rose; ☎ 0262 473251. Simply furnished, clean rooms. *Dbl from € 25 RO.*

✗ WHERE TO EAT

✗ **Anse des Cascades Restaurant** Anse des Cascades, Piton-Ste-Rose; ☎ 0262 472042. Cuisine: French, Creole, seafood. Popular restaurant in an idyllic setting. *Dish of the day from € 10. Open Sat–Thu for lunch, dinner on reservation.*

✗ **Auberge du Poisson Rouge** 503 RN2, Piton-Ste-Rose; ☎ 0262 473251. Cuisine: Creole, French, Chinese, seafood. Casual atmosphere. Good reputation for fish dishes. *Main courses from € 10. Open Tue–Sun for lunch, Tue–Sat for dinner.*

✗ **Bel Air** 480 RN2, Piton-Ste-Rose; ☎ 0262 472250. Cuisine: Creole. Informal restaurant, popular with locals. *Set menus from € 12. Open daily 08.00–14.00, dinner on reservation.*

✗ **Deux Pitons** RN2, Piton-Ste-Rose; ☎ 0262 472316. Cuisine: Creole, French. Heart of palm salad and fish *cari* are specialities. *Medium price range. Open Thu–Tue for lunch and dinner.*

✗ **Joyau des Laves** Piton Cascade, RN2, Piton-Ste-Rose; ☎ 0262 473400. Cuisine: Creole. *Table d'hôte from € 16. Open daily for dinner. Reservation only.*

✗ **Restaurant 168** RN2 Ste-Rose; ☎ 0262 472041. Cuisine: Creole, Indian. *Budget prices. Open Tue–Sun for lunch, dinner on reservation.*

NIGHTLIFE On Saturday nights, the energetic might want to try the disco **Roz d'Zil** (*317 RN2, Ravine Glissante;* ☎ *0262 473606*).

SOUTH TO LA POINTE DE LA TABLE

From the road between Ste-Rose and St-Philippe (RN2) you can see the **lava flows** which attest to the fact that Piton-de-la-Fournaise is one of the world's most active volcanoes. Each flow is marked with the date of the eruption from which it originated.

Those from the 1970s and 1980s have been colonised by pioneer plants such as sword ferns, lichens, mosses and a few small herbaceous plants. It is fascinating to walk on the lava and see how these tenacious plants take root in the crevices between slabs of lava.

The flows from 2002 and 2004 are very impressive, still pure black and unchallenged by plants. Amazingly, when I visited in February 2002, a month after the most recent eruption, the lava was still very warm and threw off thick steam when it rained, like a giant sauna. Walking on the solidified lava gives you a chance to admire the coiled patterns of rope lava and appreciate the beauty and drama of this extraordinary place. Do take care, though, as lava is very uneven, sometimes fragile and can be very sharp.

The lava cliffs around **Pointe de la Table** are a perfect example of how the volcano has added tens of hectares to the island's surface area. The views are breathtaking and the furious sea seems locked in a constant battle against the intruding lava.

PITON-DE-LA-FOURNAISE

Most people consider this to be Réunion's single most striking attraction. **Piton-de-la-Fournaise** (Furnace Peak) is one of the world's largest and most impressive shield volcanoes, reaching 2,631m. It is also one of the world's most active, having erupted a number of times in recent years. As activity can last for two weeks or more, the eruptions draw crowds of spectators (at least 20,000 came to see the eruption that began on 8 March 1998). In-depth information on the volcano can be found at the **Maison du Volcan** in La Plaine-des-Cafres (see *What to see*, page 313).

When Piton-des-Neiges was still active, some 300,000 years ago, Piton-de-la-Fournaise rose up to its southeast and the successive layers of lava from both the volcanoes created the eerily lunar Plaine des Sables.

There are several ways of getting to see the volcano, the most popular of which is to drive to Pas de Bellecombe, on the northwestern rim of the caldera, and then to walk to the crater by following a steep path. The fit and energetic can try one of the many hiking trails that lead up to the volcano from various parts of the island. Grading on all of them is difficult. Alternatively, you could see it from the air, as part of an unforgettable helicopter ride over the island. Whichever you choose, don't miss out on seeing the volcano: it is a mind-boggling, primal experience. There is a gîte at Pas de Bellecombe (one of the island's better mountain houses), where visitors can stay overnight.

The drive to the volcano is an adventure its own right. From La Plaine-des-Cafres you climb through an Alpine landscape dotted with cows sporting cowbells, which look as if they should be advertising Swiss chocolate. There are several spectacular viewpoints, including the panorama of Piton-des-Neiges looming over La Plaine-des-Cafres, and perhaps most striking of all, the view of La Vallée de la Rivière des Remparts at **Nez de Boeuf**. This valley, which stretches for 23km, is lined by cliffs rising up to 1,000m and looks almost tunnel-like as you peer down into it. And then you catch sight of a lone village on the valley floor, **Roche Plate**, and are left wondering how people manage to live in such isolation. Certainly, according to the information board at the viewpoint, life is not easy for those villagers, who battle cyclones and landslides on a regular basis.

The landscape becomes gradually stranger until you begin your descent to the barren moonscape that is **La Plaine des Sables**, preceding the volcano crater. Then it's an uphill stretch to **Pas de Bellecombe** (2,311m), which offers a fantastic view of the volcano and outer crater. There is a kiosk displaying information on the volcano and the walks, which is worth reading before you set off as it indicates the routes and their level of difficulty. The building also contains toilets and sells drinks. You can leave your car in the car park whilst you walk to the summit. It is best to set off as early as possible in the morning when the skies are clear because in the afternoon the clouds roll in like a thick fog. You will walk across solidified lava, so take care and make sure you have suitable footwear. Water, some food, suncream and a sunhat are essential, as is some warm clothing.

There is a well-marked path which descends from the car park to the outer crater, with several others branching to the summit and around the rim. From Pas de Bellecombe to the summit, around the crater rim and back to the car park is about 13km, so set aside at least half a day.

In the outer crater, you'll pass the distinctive **Fournica Leo**, which looks like a mini-volcano. As you climb the slopes towards the rim of the volcano, look out for the **Chapelle de Rosemont**, a strange cavern formed from lava.

WHAT TO DO

MOUNTAIN BIKING There are eight mountain-bike trails around Ste-Rose, which vary from 5–44km and are graded according to difficulty. The trails are marked on a large signboard at the Marina Snack-Bar, which you'll find at a conspicuous viewpoint near groves of pandanus trees. Most of the trails start at the four grey reservoirs you'll see up on the slopes above Ste-Rose.

HORSERIDING

Ferme Equestre du Grand Etang RN3, Pont Payet, St-Benoît; ☎ 0262 509003. Offers some very picturesque rides, including treks to the volcano. See Chapter 16, Activities for details.

THEATRE

Compagnie Acte 3 4 Chemin Jean Robert, Boubier-les-Bas, St-Benoît; ☎ 0262 505333

CINEMA

Salle Multimédia Guy Alphonsine 270 Rue de la Gare, St-André; ☎ 0262 466315. A small cinema.

Cristal 15 Rue Montfleury, St-Benoît; ☎ 0262 501098

SHOPPING There are **markets** in **St-André** on Friday morning, **Bras-Panon** on Thursday afternoon and **St-Benoît** on Saturday morning. Roadside stalls selling delicious, locally made honey and jam are a common sight in the east.

WHAT TO SEE

LE DOMAINE DU GRAND HAZIER (*5 le Grand Hazier, Ste-Suzanne;* ☎ *0262 523281;* f *0262 522312; adult/child under 12* €*5/free; on reservation only*) Offers a guided tour of the 18th-century planter's house, surrounded by a large garden containing fruit trees and endemic species.

BOIS ROUGE SUGAR FACTORY/SAVANNA DISTILLERY (*2 Chemin Bois-Rouge, St-André;* ☎ *0262 585974;* f *0262 580651;* e *info@bois-rouge.fr; www.boisrouge.com; combined tour: adult/child* €*8/5.50, distillery only: adult/child* €*3.50/2; all tours are on reservation only; children under 7 are not allowed at the sugar factory*) Just north of St-André, the Bois Rouge sugar factory offers guided tours from July to mid December. Tours of the Savanna Distillery, exploring rum production and ending with a tasting, are available all year except mid December to mid January. Both tours can be provided in English. Combined tours of the sugar factory and the distillery are possible from July to December.

MUSÉE DAN TAN LONTAN (*2208 Chemin du Centre, St-André;* ☎ *0262 584789; admission* €*4; open Tue–Sun 09.00–17.00*) Guided tour of a collection of local antique objects.

LA MAISON DE LA VANILLE (*466 Rue de la Gare, St-André;* ☎ *0262 460014;* f *0262 587016;* e *vanille-adf@wanadoo.fr; www:guetali.fr/maison-vanille; adult/child* €*5/free; open Tue–Sat 09.15–11.15 and 14.15–17.15; closed in Aug*) Offers fascinating guided tours explaining vanilla production past and present. The guide will assume everyone speaks French unless you specify that you'd like the tour in English – they'll be happy to oblige. There is a shop selling vanilla products and other local goods (the vanilla liqueur is delicious). Tours last about 45 minutes.

COOPÉRATIVE DE LA VANILLE DE BRAS-PANON (*21 RN2 Bras-Panon;* `\` *0262 517012;* f *0262 516174; admission* €*4; open Mon–Sat 08.30–12.00 and 14.00–17.00*) Tells the story of vanilla via a guided tour of the factory and a film on the history of vanilla production. Tours last about 45 minutes and are available in English if arranged in advance. There is a shop and a restaurant open for lunch (see page 274).

RIVIÈRE DU MÂT DISTILLERY (*Chemin Manioc, ZI Beaufonds, St-Benoît;* m *0692 674641;* e *visitedistillerie@gqf.com; www.gqf.com; adult/child* €*5/3; open Tue–Sat morning in rum-making season: Mar–Dec; on reservation only*) Historic rum distillery on the Beaufonds sugar estate. One-hour tours of the distillery include a film on rum production and rum tasting.

BANANALAND (*RN2 Bellevue, Piton-Ste-Rose;* m *0692 231127; adult/child* €*3/1.50; open Sun–Fri 09.00–17.00*) Guided tours, lasting about one hour, of a banana plantation. Creole lunch also available. Can also be booked through the central reservation service (`\` *0262 907878*).

19

Southern Réunion

The southern part of the island stretches from the town of St-Philippe in the southeast up to Le Tampon and from there down to Etang-Salé-les-Bains in the southwest.

The bustling coastal town of St-Pierre has deservedly earned the unofficial title of 'capital of the south' and is the gateway to the *'sud sauvage'* (the wild south), the name given to the rugged southeast coast. This is an area which lies in the shadow of Piton-de-la-Fournaise, with a coastline of black volcanic cliffs, the remains of lava flows stopped in their tracks by the sea. By contrast, there are some good white-sand beaches further west around St-Pierre and a large, black-sand beach at Etang-Salé-les-Bains.

The southern towns have plenty of charm and character, generally featuring small, neat Creole-style homes surrounded by colourful gardens. Creole gardens characteristically serve more than just a decorative purpose, containing flowers, medicinal plants, tropical fruit and vegetables intentionally bunched together in each flowerbed. There is a flourishing cottage industry in this region, including Creole furniture, lacework, honey, pâté and cheeses.

ST-PHILIPPE AND SURROUNDS

If you are searching for a remote coastal retreat, then look no further than **St-Philippe**. It is small, peaceful and few tourists spend any time here. This makes it worth staying for a night or two. The town, which is a vanilla and fishing centre, has a backdrop of sugarcane and forested mountains.

St-Philippe has the basic necessities: a few restaurants, a **pharmacy**, a **post office** and a **petrol station**, although no banks. There is a small **supermarket** but the prices tend to be exaggerated, so locals recommend shopping in St-Joseph.

A few kilometres west of St-Philippe is **Le Baril**, where you will find a pandanus-lined coast and two adjacent swimming pools, one fresh water and one which is a corralled area of sea. The best rock-pooling area is to the east of the swimming pool, where colourful fish are often trapped in pools in the volcanic rocks. This is the place to watch rock-skippers (or mud-skippers), an amphibious species of goby. This fish has evolved large, powerful pectoral fins to enable it to escape potential predators by leaping from the sea to the safety of rocks.

The charm of St-Philippe and Le Baril is not the designated sights, of which there are few, but the lava flows and coastal and forest walks. Between St-Philippe and Le Baril is the **Réserve Naturelle de Mare Longue**. Incorporated into this forest area is the *sentier botanique*, a path through a beautiful section of primary forest where the indigenous trees are labelled. A clearly marked Grande Randonnée hiking trail runs straight up the mountainside but you can also take the longer forest road which is easier on the legs and excellent for birdwatching. Bring a picnic and enjoy the flora, fauna and views of this lush region.

For the best views of pounding waves, craggy headlands and graceful tropical birds visit **Cap Méchant**, about 2km west of Le Baril. From here you can walk along the headland, through casuarina trees and vanilla plantations. This is also where you will find **Les Puits des Français** (the wells of the French), the southernmost of a series of mysterious holes in the lava coastline. The origin and purpose of these apparently manmade holes is unknown. Similar holes are at Le Baril (**Puits des Anglais**), La Pointe de la Table (**Puits des Arabes**) and Le Tremblet (**Puits du Tremblet**).

GETTING THERE AND AWAY St-Philippe is easily reached by bus as it lies on the St-Pierre–St-Benoît coastal route (Line I).

TOURIST INFORMATION The **tourist office** (⟍ *0262 371043;* f *0262 371097. Open Tue–Fri 10.00–12.00 and 13.00–17.00, Sat 10.00–16.00, Sun and public holidays 09.00–13.00*) in St-Philippe is next to the town hall at 62 Rue Leconte Delisle, the main coastal road.

WHERE TO STAY
Classified hotels

Hotel Le Baril ** (14 rooms) RN2, Le Baril; ⟍ 0262 370104; f 0262 370762. A cosy, family-run hotel, perched on a typically wild stretch of coast. With very limited accommodation in the area, this hotel gets busy so try to book well in advance. The en-suite rooms (one with disabled facilities) are fairly simple and a little dark, but some have spectacular views of the pounding sea. TVs are available in some rooms on request and there is a TV lounge. There is also a small pool and a good restaurant overlooking the sea (see below). *Dbl/sgl from € 57/51 BB. Sea-view supplement € 5.*

WHERE TO EAT

Hotel Le Baril RN2, Le Baril; ⟍ 0262 370104. Cuisine: Creole, Chinese. A large menu with lots of local specialities. Informal with friendly service and a sea view. *Main courses from € 9. Open daily for lunch and dinner.*

Marmite du Pêcheur RN2, Ravine Ango, St-Philippe; ⟍ 0262 370101. Cuisine: Creole, French, seafood. Tucked away among houses, signed from the main road through St-Philippe. It may not look very special from the outside but this restaurant has a reputation for superb seafood dishes. *Main courses*

from € 10, set menus from € 17 (3 courses). Open Thu–Tue for lunch.

Etoile de Mer Cap Méchant, Basse Vallée; ⟍ 0262 370460. Cuisine: seafood, Creole, Chinese. Large restaurant known for its excellent seafood. *Main courses from € 10. Open daily 11.30–22.00.*

Le Cap Méchant Basse-Vallée; ⟍ 0262 370061. Cuisine: Creole, Chinese. Very popular seafront restaurant. *Main courses from € 10. Open Tue–Sun for lunch. Reservation recommended.*

ST-JOSEPH AND SURROUNDS

The area around St-Joseph is known for its production of turmeric, an important ingredient in *cari*, and for the weaving of pandanus fronds to produce baskets, hats and bags.

Between St-Philippe and St-Joseph is the village of **Vincendo**. There is usually a black-sand beach at La Marine de Vincendo, although its presence depends on the tide.

Further west on the RN2, before you reach St-Joseph, is the turning to **Rivière Langevin**. This is a magical spot. The drive takes you through the village of Langevin, with its colourful Creole houses facing the river. Female residents can often be seen doing their washing on the rocks, whilst the men play dominoes in little huts on the riverbank. The road is lined with picnic tables and there are several restaurants serving Creole food.

You pass a hydro-electric station, then small banana and pineapple plantations. On the left is an adorable little chapel built around a cave, with a shrine to Saint Expédit, typically painted red.

It is a picture-perfect river shrouded by trees, with water bubbling around boulders, pausing in pools and then setting off again towards the sea. You can park and walk a short distance to **Le Trou Noir**, a pool beneath a waterfall, ideal for a refreshing dip. Further along the road, after a steep and winding climb, you can get a close-up view of some more beautiful falls, **La Cascade de Grand-Galet**. The road ends in the pretty village of **Grand-Galet**, above the falls.

St-Joseph is an attractive little town astride the **Rivière des Remparts**. However, it doesn't hold much interest for tourists, other than being an occasional stopover point for people heading eastwards. The **banks**, a **post office**, numerous restaurants and a **medical centre** are on Rue Raphael Babet.

To the east of St-Joseph is **Manapany-les-Bains**, a seaside village with a protected natural swimming pool and a beach.

WHERE TO STAY There are no classified hotels in St-Joseph but there are plenty of furnished flats and houses in the area, some of which are listed below.

Classified furnished flats

La Villa du Barrage, Chez Franco ** 21 Route de Grand-Galet, Langevin, St-Joseph; \/f 0262 372245; e Maillot.Franck@wanadoo.fr. The owner rents out the ground floor of his home overlooking Rivière Langevin. It's a steep climb to the village and you'll need a car to get there. From € 275 per week (4 people).

L'Eau Forte ** 137 bis, Bd de l'Océan, Manapany-les-Bains; \ 0262 563284; e eau-forte@wanadoo.fr; www.eau-forte.fr.st. An apt for 2 people overlooking the bay. From € 40 per night (2 people).

La Case ** 2 Rue Jean Bart, St-Joseph; \ 0262 560750; f 0262 562320; e contact@case.fr; www.case.fr. Modern studio with AC, TV and shared pool. From € 45 per night (2 people).

WHERE TO EAT St-Joseph has the usual well-stocked supermarkets (in this case, Score and Champion), which are just west of the town on either side of the RN2.

Restaurant Le Tagine 23 Chemin de la Marine, Vincendo, St-Joseph; \ 0262 373251. Cuisine: Morrocan. Unremarkable décor but good food. Main courses from € 11. Open Mon–Sat for lunch and dinner, closed Wed evening.

La Bonne Idée 172 Route de la Passerelle, Langevin; \ 0262 562076. Cuisine: Creole, Chinese. Laid-back atmosphere and a varied menu. Main courses from € 10. Open Wed–Mon 10.00–18.00.

Chez Jim 194 Route de la Passerelle, Langevin; \ 0262 565601. Cuisine: Creole, snacks. Also take-away. Informal and friendly, across the road from the river. Set menus from € 7. Open daily for lunch.

La Case 31 Rue Leconte Delisle, St-Joseph; \ 0262 564166. Cuisine: Creole, French, seafood. By far the most upmarket restaurant in the area, in a beautifully renovated Creole house. Serves sophisticated haute cuisine, as well as good-quality Creole dishes. Main courses from € 14. Open daily for lunch, Tue–Sun for dinner.

L'Orient Express 132 Rue Raphael Babet, St-Joseph; \ 0262 562838. Cuisine: Chinese, Creole. Plenty of choice. Main courses from € 10. Open daily for lunch and dinner.

Pizzeria la Gondole Rue Raphael Babet, St-Joseph; \ 0262 561612. Cuisine: Italian. On the main road, just to the west of town. Cosy restaurant serving excellent pizzas and other Italian fare. Good value for money. Open Wed–Sun for lunch and dinner.

Chez Jo 143 Bd de l'Océan, Manapany-les-Bains; \ 0262 314883. Cuisine: Creole, French, Chinese, snacks. Fairly informal with a sea view. Main courses € 10. Open Fri–Wed 09.00–18.00 in winter, 09.00–20.00 in summer.

L'Hirondelle 83 Bd de l'Océan, Manapany-les-Bains; \ 0262 315711. Cuisine: Creole, Chinese, seafood. The décor may not be particularly fancy but the owner prides himself on the quality of his homemade cuisine and only fresh ingredients are used. Main courses from € 9. Open Mon–Sat for lunch, Tue–Sat for dinner.

On the RN2 between St-Joseph and St-Pierre is the turning to **Grande Anse**. This is a stunning bay surrounded by densely wooded slopes, with a wonderful white-sand beach. Swimming, however, is only safe in the purpose-built pool. It's a perfect place for a picnic, with barbecue areas scattered amongst the palm trees. Unfortunately, this means it can be unpleasantly crowded on weekends. There is a cave in the cliffs around which clouds of Mascarene swiftlets wheel and scream excitedly. From the hillside you can see Réunion's only outlying island, **Petit Ile**, a nesting site for birds.

St-Pierre is the largest town in the south, home to some 70,000 people. To call this town bustling is putting it mildly. St-Pierre is especially popular with Réunionnais holidaymakers, who prefer to come here while the French head for glitzy St-Gilles.

The focal point of the town is **Boulevard Hubert Delisle**, the road along the seafront. It is strewn with restaurants, ice cream parlours and bars, as well as a casino. Across the road from the casino is a stretch of white, sandy **beach** – nothing to write home about, but adequate nevertheless. The park in front of the beach has recently undergone a makeover and it is now a very pleasant place to sit, although it still attracts the odd drunk in the evenings. During winter the strong winds around St-Pierre can make the beach a no-go zone. Snorkelling in the lagoon just off the beach is very rewarding and you'll invariably see many people doing just that.

The **harbour**, which is to the east of the beach, has also been expanded and smartened up, with a little help from the European Union. It now boasts a wide promenade and brand new shops. Nearby, opposite the old Café de la Gare, is the **Bassin de Radout**, a dry dock preserved since the 19th century.

The area around the seafront is gradually acquiring a mildly European feel, with designer clothing shops creeping in, but as you climb the hill into the main part of the town that European ambience fades. The town centre, with its numerous (particularly Chinese and Indian) clothing stores, boutiques, bars and restaurants, brings to mind images of urban southeast Asia or Mauritius, rather than Europe. Despite all the recent 'smartening up', St-Pierre remains a Réunionnais town and the people are genuinely welcoming and helpful.

There are plenty of **banks** and pharmacies in town, including a well-stocked and helpful **pharmacy** at the far western end of Boulevard Hubert Delisle. Cazal, on Rue Barquisseau, is a very good **bookshop**. At the seafront end of Rue François de Mahy are the **Air France** and **Air Mauritius** offices (for contact details see page 237).

Further up Rue François de Mahy is an ornate **mosque**. Provided you dress respectfully, you are welcome to visit between 09.00 and midday and from 14.00 to 16.00. The **town hall** at the southern end of Rue Archambaud is worth a look for its colonial architecture. It was formerly a coffee warehouse owned by the French East India Company, built between 1751 and 1773.

There is a **covered market** (*marché couvert*) on Rue Victor le Vigoureux, selling a good range of handicrafts (mostly from Madagascar), as well as fruit, vegetables and spices. On Saturdays, a **street market** operates at the far western end of Boulevard Hubert Delisle (which is blocked off to cars), selling more of the same. Although the market now sells many touristy souvenirs, it is a great place to see locals doing their weekly shop, stocking up on fruit and vegetables, buying live chickens, and – equally important – catching up on the week's gossip. Watch out for the stall that sells delicious, freshly squeezed sugarcane juice. Try to get to the market early – it's all finished by noon.

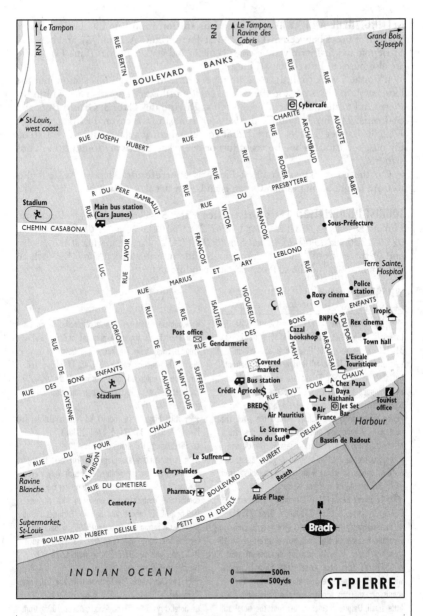

ST-PIERRE

Map labels:

Le Tampon
RN1
RN3
Le Tampon, Ravine des Cabris
Grand Bois, St-Joseph
RUE BERTIN
BOULEVARD   BANKS
St-Louis, west coast
Cybercafé
CHARITE
RUE JOSEPH HUBERT
RUE DE LA
RUE ARCHAMBAUD
AUGUSTE
RUE RODIER
RUE
PRESBYTERE
BABET
R DU PERE RAMBAULT
RUE DU
Stadium
Main bus station (Cars Jaunes)
CHEMIN CASABONA
RUE VICTOR
RUE FRANCOIS
Sous-Préfecture
RUE LAVOIR
RUE FRANCOIS
LE ARY
LEBLOND
Terre Sainte, Hospital
LUC
RUE MARIUS
ET
RUE DE
Police station
Roxy cinema
ENFANTS
Tropic
RUE LORION
RUE DE
RUE ISAUTIER
VIGOUREUX
BONS
BNPI
Rex cinema
R DU PORT
Post office
DES
Cazal bookshop
BARQUISSAU
Town hall
RUE Gendarmerie
MAHY
RUE DES BONS ENFANTS
R SAINT LOUIS
SUFFREN
CAUMONT
Covered market
L'Escale Touristique
RUE DE CAYENNE
Stadium
Bus station
FOUR A CHAUX
Chez Papa Daya
Crédit Agricole
RUE DU
Le Nathania
RUE DU FOUR A CHAUX
BREDS
Air Mauritius
Air France
Jet Set Bar
Tourist office
Le Sterne
DELISLE
Harbour
Ravine Blanche
RUE DU FOUR A
Casino du Sud
Bassin de Radout
R DE LA PRISON
Le Suffren
HUBERT
Les Chrysalides
Beach
RUE DU CIMETIERE
Pharmacy
BOULEVARD
Supermarket, St-Louis
Cemetery
PETIT BD H DELISLE
Alizé Plage
BOULEVARD HUBERT DELISLE
N
INDIAN OCEAN
0   500m
0   500yds
Bradt

Also at the western end of Boulevard Hubert Delisle is the **cemetery**, where Hindu, Chinese and Christian graves lie side by side. The most visited grave of all is that of the African sorcerer and murderer, Simicoundza Simicourba, better known as **Le Sitarane**. (See box *Le Sitarane*, page 290.)

About 10km north of St-Pierre on the RN3 is **Le Tampon**. Many of those who work on the south coast choose to live in or around Le Tampon, which enjoys a cooler climate. The town itself is of little interest, except that it is en route to La Plaine-des-Cafres, and therefore the volcano.

GETTING THERE AND AWAY The main **bus station** is on Rue Luc Lorion. There are regular buses between St-Denis and St-Pierre (Lines A, B and C), and between St-Benoît and St-Pierre via the coast (Line I) and via Les Plaines (Line H). There are also buses to Entre-Deux (Line L).

It's quite a walk (uphill) from the town centre to the main bus station, but the local *bus fleuri* buses do stop there. The *bus fleuri* (flowery bus) operates within St-Pierre and to the outlying villages, such as **Ravine des Cabris**, **Grand Bois** and **St-Louis**. The bus station for the *bus fleuri* is next to the covered market, on Rue François Isautier. Tickets cost € 1.20 if you buy them at a ticket office or € 1.40 on the bus. You can also buy books of five or ten tickets. **Taxis** are found at both bus stations.

On the coast 7km west of St-Pierre is **Pierrefonds Airport**, with flights to/from neighbouring Indian Ocean islands. For details see page 240.

TOURIST INFORMATION The **tourist office** is at 4–5 Galerie Marchande, Boulevard Hubert Delisle (✆ *0262 250236;* f *0262 258276. Open Mon–Fri 08.30–17.15, Sat 09.00–12.30 and 13.00–15.45 and Sun 09.00–11.45*), near the marina at the eastern end of the seafront. There is surprisingly little information on show for such an important town and the staff can be rather indifferent.

☖ WHERE TO STAY
Classified hotels

☖ **Loge Grand Bois** *** (29 rooms) 8–10 Allée des Lataniers, Grand Bois; ✆ 0262 311160; f 0262 311751. In the village of Grand Bois about 8km east of St-Pierre. The hotel is right on the seafront but there is no beach. Rooms are en suite with a well-equipped kitchenette, AC, TV, phone and balcony/terrace. Older rooms are in a 2-storey block, newer rooms are in bungalows around the pool. The pool is of a good size and makes up for the lack of beach. There is a restaurant serving French and Creole cuisine, as well as seafood. A good, quiet, out-of-town option for those with transport. *Dbl/sgl from € 75 RO. Breakfast € 9 per person.*

☖ **Le Sterne Beach** *** (50 rooms) Bd Hubert Delisle, St-Pierre; ✆ 0262 257000; f 0262 257066; e resa-sterne @ ilereunion.com; www.lesterne.com. Centrally located on the main street, across the road from the beach. Is within walking distance of most of St-Pierre's attractions. Comfortable en-suite rooms with AC, TV, phone, safe and balcony/terrace. The rooms are spacious enough but the bathrooms are a little small. Despite regular renovations the hotel still feels a little tired. There's a good restaurant by the pool (see page 288). There is a secure car park and the casino and L'Endroit bar are right next door. One green fee at the Bourbon Golf Club in Etang-Salé is included. *Dbl/sgl € 99/76. Breakfast € 10 per person.*

☖ **Domaine des Pierres** *** (41 rooms) 60, CD26, Route de l'Entre-Deux, St-Pierre; ✆ 0262 554385; f 0262 554390; e domainedespierres@wanadoo.fr;

www.domainedespierres. New accommodation option near Pierrefonds Airport. A pleasant building and grounds, away from the hustle and bustle of St-Pierre. The en-suite rooms have AC, TV, phone and safe. Rooms equipped for the disabled are available. Facilities include a restaurant, bar and pool. *Dbl/sgl from € 98/82 RO.*

☖ **Alizé Plage** ** (6 rooms) Bd Hubert Delisle, St-Pierre; ✆ 0262 352221; f 0262 258063; e alizeplage @ ilereunion.com; www.ilereunion.com/alizeplage.htm. The best location in town, right on the white-sand beach. Very clever use has been made of little space to create comfortable rooms. Each is equipped with en-suite facilities, AC, TV, phone and balcony. Facilities include a fantastic restaurant (see page 288), a bar with regular live music and some free watersports, such as kayaks and pedaloes. *Dbl/sgl from € 76 RO. Breakfast € 8 per person.*

☖ **Les Chrysalides** ** (16 rooms) 6 Rue Caumont, St-Pierre; ✆ 0262 257564; f 0262 252219; e hotel.chrysalides @ wanadoo.fr. About 300m from the beach and town centre in a plain 3-storey building. En-suite rooms with AC, TV and phone. They're spartan but clean. It lacks character but the price isn't bad if there are 2 of you. *Dbl/sgl from € 45 RO. Breakfast € 6 per person.*

☖ **Hotel les Orchidées** * (10 rooms) 3 Rue Jules Ferry, Le Tampon; ✆ 0262 271115; f 0262 277703; e manoir.orchidees @ wanadoo.fr; www.hotel-orchidees.com. Situated away from the heat of the coast, at 600m above sea level. Adequate accommodation but rather dated décor. Simple rooms with TV and minibar. There is a restaurant. *Dbl/sgl from € 35/30.*

🏠 **Hotel Outre-Mer** * (35 rooms) 8 Rue Bourbon, Le Tampon; 📞 0262 573030; **f** 0262 572929; **e** bourbon.henri@wanadoo.fr. Unremarkable, basic but clean rooms with en suite, AC, TV and phone. Rooms equipped for the disabled are available and there is a restaurant. *Dbl/sgl from € 40 RO.*

Unclassified accommodation

🏠 **Chez Papa Daya** (17 rooms) 27 Rue du Four à Chaux; 📞/**f** 0262 256487; **e** chez.papa.daya@wanadoo.fr; www.chezpapadaya.com. Excellent central location, not far from the beach. Cheerful, spotless rooms, some with en-suite facilities and some with AC. There's a well-equipped shared kitchen, as well as a TV lounge and a small garden. Security is good and there is parking for residents. Excellent choice for those on a budget. *En-suite dbl/sgl from € 35/25, dbl/sgl with shared bathroom from € 25/16.*

🏠 **Le Nathania** (14 rooms) 12 Rue François de Mahy, St-Pierre; 📞 0262 250457; **f** 0262 352705; **e** hotel.le.nathania@wanadoo.fr; www.hotel-nathania-reunion.com. Centrally located about 150m from the seafront. All rooms have a TV and fan, some have en-suite facilities and some have AC. Facilities include parking and use of a shared kitchen and laundry. *En-suite dbl from € 25, dbl/sgl*

Classified furnished flats

🏠 **Au Lalou** *** 5 Allée St-Exupéry, Trois Mares, Le Tampon; 📞/**f** 0262 576843; **e** ezan2@wanadoo.fr. Apt for up to 3 people. *From € 39 per night (2 people).*

🏠 **L'Hibiscus** ** 43 Chemin Clain, La Ravine des Cabris; **m** 0692 616385; **f** 0262 497289; **e** hibiscus.reunion@caramail.com. In a village north

🏠 **Le Suffren** (18 rooms) 14 Rue Suffren, St-Pierre; 📞 0262 351910; **f** 0262 259943; **e** hotelsuffren@wanadoo.fr; www.ilereunion.com/suffren.htm. A few mins' walk from the beach and main attractions. Very large but rather soulless en-suite rooms equipped with AC, TV and phone; most have a minibar and all but one have a balcony. It has a restaurant (closed Sundays) and car park. *Dbl/sgl from € 69/55 RO.*

with shared bathroom from € 23/16.

🏠 **L'Escale Touristique** (14 rooms) 14 Rue Désiré Barquisseau, St-Pierre; 📞 0262 352095; **f** 0262 351532; **e** escaletouristique@hotmail.com. All rooms have TV, some have en-suite facilities and some have AC and minibar. A well-equipped kitchen and a laundry are available for use by guests. There is also secure parking. *En-suite dbl from € 23 (€ 33 with AC and minibar), dbl/sgl with shared bathroom from € 23/15.*

🏠 **Tropic Hotel** (16 rooms) 2 Rue Auguste Babet, St-Pierre; 📞 0262 259070. Backpacker-style accommodation. Basic rooms with AC. Can be quite noisy. *Dbl from € 27.*

🏠 **Sud Hotel** (44 rooms) 106 Rue Marius et Ary Leblond, Le Tampon; 📞 0262 270790; **f** 0262 270239. Centrally located with comfortable en-suite rooms with TV and phone. It has a restaurant, bar, pool and pleasant public areas. *Dbl from € 32.*

of St-Pierre. Spacious, newly built house for up to 4 people. *From € 46 per night (2 people).*

🏠 **Les Meublés Saint-Pierrois** * 4 bis Rue Ste-Rose, St-Pierre; 📞 0262 250827; **f** 0262 960243. Self-catering studios in town. Private car park. *From € 39 per night (2 people).*

✗ **WHERE TO EAT** There is a well-stocked **Score Jumbo hypermarket** on the way out of town, at the Centre Commercial du Grand Large, at the far western end of Boulevard Hubert Delisle. There are smaller supermarkets in the town centre. St-Pierre is packed with restaurants to suit all budgets. Just opposite the main beach, on the corner of Boulevard Hubert Delisle and Rue Victor le Vigoureux is a collection of *camions bars* (snack-bars). They serve a great range of inexpensive, tasty food, such as *samoussas*, filled baguettes and *bombons piments*.

I suppose I should also add that just at the entrance to St-Pierre from St-Louis is a branch of McDonald's (they really are everywhere, aren't they?).

Here are some recommended restaurants including a cross-section of culinary styles:

✖ **Alizé Plage** Bd Hubert-Delisle; ☎ 0262 352221. Cuisine: French, Creole, seafood. Has always been my favourite. Superb food overlooking the beach. Tables on the terrace are very romantic, provided it's not one of St-Pierre's windy days. *Set menus from € 20, main courses from € 12. Open daily 10.00–22.00 for lunch and dinner.*

✖ **Bambou** 15 bis Rue Archambaud; ☎ 0262 255866. Cuisine: European, Creole, Italian. There's nothing special about the location but the menu offers plenty of choice. *Main courses from € 10. Open Tue–Sat for lunch, Mon–Sat for dinner.*

✖ **Le Bistroquet** 8 Petit Bd Hubert Delisle; ☎ 0262 250467. Cuisine: French, Creole. Pretty Creole house in a quiet location. Gourmet dishes such as ostrich with *foie gras*. One of St-Pierre's more expensive restaurants. *Main courses from € 14. Open Mon–Fri for lunch, daily for dinner.*

✖ **Le Bora Bora** 89 Bd Hubert Delisle; ☎ 0262 255122. Cuisine: French, Creole. Great location on the seafront at the far western end of Bd Hubert Delisle, opposite the cemetery. A broad selection of dishes, friendly service and a well-stocked bar. Very popular so can get busy. *Main courses from € 10. Open Mon–Sat for lunch and dinner.*

✖ **Le Bubbles** 38 bis Bd Hubert Delisle; ☎ 0262 252190. Cuisine: French, seafood, tapas. Small, cosy bar/restaurant with funky décor using the 'bubble' theme. Excellent cocktail menu. The service is professional and friendly. *Main courses from € 11. Open daily for lunch and dinner.*

✖ **Le Cabanon** 28 Bd Hubert Delisle; ☎ 0262 257146. Cuisine: Italian, French, grills. Fairly large with pleasant décor. *Main courses from € 13. Open Tue–Sun for lunch and dinner.*

✖ **Carpe Diem** 47 Bd Hubert Delisle; ☎ 0262 254512. Cuisine: French. At the western end of the boulevard. Spacious restaurant with additional tables in the courtyard garden area. Creative menu using local ingredients. Specialities include dorado with grapefruit and prawns with chilli and pineapple. *Main courses from € 12. Open Mon–Sat for lunch and dinner.*

✖ **L'Eté Indien** 46 Bd Hubert Delisle; ☎ 0262 255752. Cuisine: European, ice cream, snacks. An excellent buffet lunch daily. *Pizza from € 7.50. Open daily 11.00–22.00.*

✖ **Le Flamboyant** Cnr Rues du Four à Chaux and Désiré Barquisseau; ☎ 0262 350215. Cuisine: Creole, French. Cosy and very popular for its excellent *caris*. *Main courses from € 11. Open Mon–Sat for lunch and dinner, closed Wed evening.*

✖ **Le Fruit à Pain** 14 Rue Victor le Vigoureux; ☎ 0262 356350. Cuisine: French, Creole. Centrally located near the covered market. Cheap and cheerful décor, indoor and outdoor seating. Regular live music and theme nights. Specialities include swordfish *cari*, couscous and chicken with vanilla. Paella is served on Fridays. *Main courses from € 9. Open Mon and Wed–Sat for lunch and dinner.*

✖ **Indyana Steak House** 109 Bd Hubert Delisle; ☎ 0262 252673. Cuisine: grills, seafood, pizza. *Main courses from € 9. Open daily for lunch and dinner.*

✖ **La Jonque** 2 Rue François de Mahy; ☎ 0262 255778. Cuisine: Chinese. Remains popular, although the apparent lack of cleanliness is off-putting. *Main courses from € 7. Open daily for lunch, Wed–Mon for dinner.*

✖ **Malone's** Cnr Bd Hubert Delisle and Rue François de Mahy; ☎ 0262 250222. Cuisine: European, Creole. On a busy (noisy) corner. Regular live music and a rather cliquey atmosphere. *Main courses from € 8. Open daily for lunch and dinner.*

✖ **Le Marin Bleu** 45 Rue Amirale Lacaze, Terre Sainte; ☎ 0262 356165. Cuisine: Creole, French, seafood. Quiet location opposite the seafront in Terre Sainte. Well known for its seafood. *Main courses from € 11. Open Mon–Sat for lunch and dinner.*

✖ **Le Moana** 25 Bd Hubert Delisle; ☎ 0262 327338. Cuisine: French, Creole, Italian. Pleasant restaurant with an airy, tropical feel. Menu offers plenty of choice. *Pizza from € 8, pasta from € 9.50. Open daily for lunch and dinner.*

✖ **La Piscine** Sterne Beach Hotel, Bd Hubert Delisle, St-Pierre; ☎ 0262 257000. Cuisine: Creole, European. Informal dining by the hotel pool. A pleasant setting but not the place to be on one of St-Pierre's windy days. The buffet is good value and the menu offers plenty of choice. *Main courses from € 6, hot buffet from € 10. Open daily for lunch and dinner. Reservation recommended for dinner on weekends.*

✖ **Restaurant Thai** 54 Rue Caumont; ☎ 0262 353095. Cuisine: Thai. Offers good, traditional Thai food and a change from Creole and French cuisine. *Main courses from € 7. Open Tue–Sun for lunch, Tue–Sat for dinner.*

✖ **Utopia** 8 Rue M et A Leblond; ☎ 0262 351583. Cuisine: European. In an old, atmospheric Creole house, with tables inside and in the garden. Upmarket food, a creative menu and vast portions. *Main courses from € 11. Open Mon–Sat for lunch and dinner.*

with *Dominique Vendôme and Richard Thesée*
From my point of view, St-Pierre's nightlife is by far the best on the island. It has an abundance of bars and nightclubs open until the early hours of morning, but perhaps the best thing about going out in St-Pierre is that it retains its Réunionnais feel and has not been transformed into a mini St-Tropez or Ibiza, as is the case in St-Gilles-les-Bains and parts of St-Denis.

There is a string of bars along Bd Hubert Delisle, most of which have live music several times a week. *Les Pages Noires*, stocked by most bars, will tell you which and when.

L'Endroit (0262 252696), next to the casino, has a very clean, European feel. There is a big TV screen where they show sports matches and there is live music on Tuesday, Friday and Saturday. It is closed on Sunday. The dress code here is stricter than in most bars around town and you won't be allowed in wearing flip-flops, shorts or sleeveless tops. **Alizé Plage** (0262 352221), on the main beach, has a relaxed open-air bar with regular live bands; it's open every evening 18.00–02.00. **L'Aquarhum** (0262 391799), on the Petit Boulevard Hubert Delisle, is another trendy, popular watering hole. **Le Malone's** (0262 250222) on the corner of Boulevard Hubert Delisle and Rue François de Mahy claims to be a 'South African pub'. There is indoor and outing seating and it remains very popular, particularly with French military personnel. It is open Monday to Saturday, with regular live music and theme evenings. For **karaoke** divas, there's **Cherwaine's** at 6 Rue Auguste Babet (0262 356949), which also advertises itself as being 'gay friendly'.

Nightclubs don't really get going until after about 23.30 and are open until the early hours, usually Friday and Saturday and on the eve of public holidays. Some open from Wednesday to Saturday. Expect to pay in the region of €12 for entry, which usually includes one drink. The favourite club of the moment is **Africa Queen** (m *0692 703807*) in the old Café de la Gare on Boulevard Hubert Delisle, opposite Rue François de Mahy. It plays a good mix of European chart music and local *séga*, *maloya* and *zouk*. At the other end of Boulevard Hubert Delisle is **Galaxy** (m *0692 901629*), formerly **VIP Club**. **Le Zaza Club** at 16 Rue Méziaire Guignare (0262 964061), also plays a good mixture of European and local music but it can get pretty packed.

Le Pacha (m *0692 719964*) in nearby Terre Rouge is another popular new club, which attracts a lot of teenagers. There are two dance floors, a swimming pool and a terrace. Also out of the town centre are **Le Chapiteau** (0262 310081) at Montvert-les-Bas and **Apollo Night** (0262 495891) in Ravine des Cabris, which is open Saturday night and Sunday afternoon.

The very popular **Casino du Sud** is at 47 Boulevard Hubert Delisle (0262 252696), next to the Sterne Beach Hotel. It's open until 02.00 Sunday–Thursday, 03.00 Friday and Saturday. Slot machines are open daily from 10.00; the tables are open from 21.15 Monday–Saturday and 16.00 on Sunday.

There are two **cinemas** in St-Pierre. For details see *What to do*, page 292.

OTHER PRACTICALITIES

Money and banking Banque Nationale de Paris is on Rue des Bons Enfants. **Crédit Agricole** and **BRED** are both on the corner of Rues du Four à Chaux and Victor le Vigoureux. They all have ATMs. There is also an ATM conveniently located outside the casino.

Communications The main **post office** is on Rue des Bons Enfants. There are several payphones on Boulevard Hubert Delisle, including two near the beach, outside the Alizé Plage.

Alexandra Richards

The place of Le Sitarane in Réunion's history and folklore has been assured by people's unshakable fascination with his story. It is said that he was actually quite a pleasant man, if a little simple, until he was led into crime and black magic by one St-Ange Calendrin.

They formed a gang, which began in 1907 to commit the horrific acts for which they are known. The gang forced their way into their victims' homes, murdered them and used their bodies in black magic rituals. They also took the opportunity to burgle them.

Fear seized the population around St-Pierre and Le Tampon for two years, as the gang repeatedly evaded capture until 1909. Eventually, ten arrests were made. The three ringleaders, St-Ange Calendrin, Sitarane and Fontaine, were condemned to death. However, shortly before the execution, Calendrin's punishment was mysteriously toned down and he was deported to French Guiana. Sitarane and Fontaine were publicly guillotined in St-Pierre in 1909.

Sitarane's tomb still holds both fear and fascination for the local population. Those who dabble in *gris gris* (black magic) visit his grave to ask for assistance in their practices, whilst those who fear black magic ask for his protection. His grave, which is red and black, is almost always strewn with offerings: glasses of rum, cigarettes, pieces of red material and candles.

As you stand at the main entrance to the cemetery, the grave is on the far left near the wall, under a tree. Locals would advise you not to take photos of it, for fear of upsetting the occupant. It is also worth knowing that most locals consider it bad luck to mention Sitarane by name.

Espace Multimédia de St-Pierre (*81 Rue Archambaud;* m *0692 776873*) is a well-equipped computer centre where internet access is available. Nearer the seafront, **Jet Set Bar** (*32 Bd Hubert Delisle;* ✆ *0262 328366*) is a bar with a few internet terminals. For details see page 251.

ST-LOUIS TO L'ETANG-SALE

St-Louis is essentially a residential and industrial town. Despite all the new buildings there, it has retained much of its Creole character and it is one of the few places where you may see bullock carts used, particularly during the sugarcane harvest.

The **Chapelle du Rosaire** here was built in 1732 by Barbe Payet and is the oldest religious building on the island. The chapel is signed from the south of the town and reached via Rue de la Chapelle. St-Louis is the gateway to the **Cirque de Cilaos**, with buses leaving from the station at the southern end of town. Inland from St-Louis, **Entre-Deux** ('between two') is so named because it lies between two rivers, which join and become Rivière Ste-Etienne. It is a pretty village and is one of the best places to see colourful Creole houses and gardens.

About an hour's drive inland from St-Louis is the village of **Les Makes**, which is home to the Indian Ocean's only **Observatory** (see page 293). Beyond Les Makes is **La Fenêtre** (The Window), a viewpoint over the Cirque de Cilaos.

St-Louis is surrounded by fields of sugarcane. The **Gol Sugar Refinery (Sucrerie du Gol)**, which can be seen from the main road to Etang-Salé, was one of the island's first, built in 1816. It is still operational and guided tours are available during harvest season (see page 293).

Opposite the sugar refinery is one of the island's few identified slave cemeteries, **Le Cimtière du Père Lafosse**. Père Lafosse was a priest, an abolitionist and mayor of St-Louis. He is buried in the cemetery, along with some of the island's earliest slaves. His tomb has become a place of pilgrimage, particularly on 20 December, the anniversary of the abolition of slavery.

L'Etang-Salé is the name given to the area encompassing the coastal village of **l'Etang-Salé-les-Bains** and, slightly inland, **l'Etang-Salé-les-Hauts**. The two are separated by the large Etang-Salé Forest.

Etang-Salé-les-Bains is largely a residential area, branching outwards from the main street. It has all the essentials: restaurants, shops, a **post office** and **ATM** facilities (opposite the Floralys Caro Beach). The vast 5km, black-sand beach is popular with locals and tourists alike, although it is noticeably quieter than the beaches around St-Gilles-les-Bains. There are designated swimming areas but the waves can be pretty powerful. Surfers, body-boarders and windsurfers flock here.

TOURIST INFORMATION The **tourist office** (↘ *0262 266732;* f *0262 266792;* e *otsi.run@wanadoo.fr. Open Mon–Fri 09.00–17.00, Sat 09.00–12.00*) is in a former railway station at 75 Rue Octave Bénard, the main road through l'Etang-Salé-les-Bains. They have plenty of literature, including lists of guesthouses and houses to let. Handicrafts are on sale and the staff are helpful.

WHERE TO STAY
Classified hotels

Floralys Caro Beach *** (52 rooms) 2 Av de l'Océan, l'Etang-Salé-les-Bains; ↘ 0262 917979; f 0262 917980; e resa@carobeach.com; www.carobeach.com. In the centre of the village, across the road from the beach. The rooms are in bungalows dotted around a pleasant garden. Some are suitable for families and a few have a

kitchenette. Rooms are equipped with AC, TV, phone, minibar and terrace; deluxe rooms have a safe. It has a large pool, 2 tennis courts, a restaurant and mini-golf. Rooms are on the small side but it's not bad value for money, especially for families. *Dbl/sgl/family apt from € 110/80/120.*

Classified furnished flats

Le Fangourin ** 7 Chemin Petit Bon Dieu, La Rivière St-Louis; ↘/f 0262 391572; e elise.baret@wanadoo.fr; www.lefangourin.com. Two self-catering apts in a house. *From € 244 per week (2 people).*

Les Grains d'Sable ** 5 Rue du Roussillon, l'Etang-Salé-les-Bains; ↘ 0262 271146; f 0262 271805; e grainsdsable@wanadoo.fr. Three self-catering apts in a quiet residential area. *From € 185 per week.*

Camping

Camping Municipal 58 Av Octave Bénard, l'Etang-Salé-les-Bains; ↘ 0262 917586. Facilities are basic

but it's only a short walk to the beach. *Tent sites from € 12.50 per night.*

WHERE TO EAT

Le Bambou 56 Rue Octave Bénard, l'Etang-Salé-les-Bains; ↘ 0262 917028. Cuisine: Italian, seafood. *Main courses from € 11. Open Wed–Mon for lunch and dinner.*

La Carangue 1 Rue Roger Payet, l'Etang-Salé-les-Bains; ↘ 0262 917087. Cuisine: Italian, Chinese. *Informal, with pizzas from € 6. Open Fri–Wed for lunch, Fri–Tue for dinner.*

L'Eté Indien 1 Rue des Salines, l'Etang-Salé-les-Bains; ↘ 0262 266733. Cuisine: Creole, Italian,

Chinese, ice cream. *Pizzas from € 6, other main courses from € 9. Open Tue–Sun 11.00–23.00.*

Luna Rossa Av de l'Océan, l'Etang-Salé-les-Bains; ↘ 0262 265554. Cuisine: Italian. Mostly outdoor plastic seating, with an informal, 'snack-bar' atmosphere. *Main courses from € 9. Open daily for lunch and dinner.*

Le Play Off Golf Club de Bourbon, 140 Les Sables, l'Etang-Salé; ↘ 0262 264349. Cuisine: Creole, European. Beautiful setting in stunning gardens. *Main courses from € 11. Open Tue–Sun for lunch.*

HIKING Experienced, fit hikers may want to tackle the route from St-Joseph to Piton-de-la-Fournaise. It'll take two days, camping overnight or staying at the gîte in Roche Plate. From there, another day's hiking (grading: difficult) eastwards will have you at the Plaine des Sables, then the volcano. Along the Rivière des Remparts route you can still see some of the original wilderness (lowland forests, secluded natural pools, heathland) which once dominated southeast Réunion.

GOLF Golf Club de Bourbon (*140 Les Sables, L'Etang-Salé;* \ *0262 263339;* f *0262 263840;* e *golfclubbourbon@wanadoo.fr; www.golf-bourbon.com*) is situated between St-Louis and l'Etang-Salé-les-Bains, easily reached from the RN1 using the Les Sables exit. Arguably the island's best golf course. A well-maintained 18-hole course with fantastic tropical vegetation. The club covers 75ha and there is an attractive clubhouse, swimming pool and restaurant. For details see *Chapter 16, Activities*.

HORSERIDING There are equestrian centres in St-Joseph, Les Makes, and Etang-Salé. For details see *Chapter 16, Activities*.

CINEMA There are two cinemas in St-Pierre, both showing international films dubbed into French. **Rex**, which is the larger and smarter of the two, occasionally shows foreign-language films (Spanish, Italian etc). Rex is near the town hall, on Rue Auguste Babet (\ *0262 250101*). **Roxy** is at 53 Rue Désiré Barquisseau (\ *0262 353490*). **Eden** is in Le Tampon, at 72 Rue Hubert Delisle (\ *0262 571489*).

THEATRE The **Theatre Luc Donat** (*20 Rue Victor Le Vigoureux, Le Tampon;* \ *0262 272436;* f *0262 571757*) puts on regular plays, dance shows, jazz concerts and classical music recitals. Every year for the first two weeks of June it hosts a comedy festival.

SHOPPING The covered market on Rue Victor le Vigoureux in St-Pierre is open daily and is ideal for souvenir shopping, as is St-Pierre's Saturday-morning street market (see page 284). The markets in St-Louis are open daily.

CAHEB (*83 Rue Kervéguen, Le Tampon;* \ *0262 270227;* f *0262 273554;* e *caheb@geranium-bourbon.com; www.geranium-bourbon.com*) sells essential oils and custom-made perfumes created from local geranium and vetyver.

The village of La Rivière St-Louis is known for its **wood-working** artisans. Their creations can be viewed and purchased at St-Louis Artisanat Bois (*1 RN5 Bois de Nèfles Coco, La Rivière St-Louis;* \ *0262 261375*).

WHAT TO SEE

ECO-MUSÉE AU BON ROI LOUIS (*1 Rue de la Marine, St-Philippe;* \ *0262 371643;* f *0262 371298; adult/child* €*5/2; open Mon–Sat 09.00–12.00 and 14.00–16.30*) Guided visits to a Creole house built around 1850, containing an assortment of antique tools, weapons, furniture, coins, documents and agricultural equipment. Visits last 1½ hours.

LE JARDIN DES PARFUMS ET DES EPICES (*7 Chemin Forestier, Mare Longue, St-Philippe;* \ *0262 370636;* f *0262 371508;* e *fontaine.patrick.e@jardin-parfums-epices.fr; www.jardins-parfums-epices.fr; adult/child* €*6.10/3.10; tours daily at 10.30 and 14.30, on reservation only*) A private garden between Le Baril and St-Philippe, which is more like a chunk of forest, where 1,500 endemic and exotic species grow side by side.

Guided tours (about two hours) explain the origin and use of the plants, be it medicinal, culinary or furniture making. At present tours are offered in French and Danish but they hope to branch out into English soon.

LA MAISON DU CURCUMA (Turmeric House) (*14 Chemin du Rond, Plaine-des-Grègues, St-Joseph;* ☎ *0262 375466;* f *0262 376116; admission €4; open daily 09.00–12.00 and 13.30–17.00; reservation recommended*) In a village above St-Joseph. Guided tours (one hour) explaining the production of turmeric, an important ingredient in Creole cuisine. Also tasting of local products and a shop.

LE JARDIN D'ORCHIDÉE (*12 Rue Léon de Heaulme, St-Joseph;* m *0692 077495; admission free; open Mon–Fri afternoon, 10.00–17.00 on weekends*) An orchid garden open to the public, off the RN2 to the west of St-Joseph. Orchids are on sale.

LE VIEUX DOMAINE (*76 Rue Recherchant, Ravine-des-Cabris, St-Pierre;* m *0692 239530; adult/child €5/2; open Tue–Fri 10.00–17.00; on reservation only*) Those seeking some insight into Creole culture may enjoy a visit to this estate. It features an extensive orchard and a splendid old Creole home.

PARC EXOTICA (*60 CD 26, Pierrefonds, St-Pierre;* ☎ *0262 356545;* f *0262 356544; adult/child €6/3; open Tue–Sun 09.00–12.00 and 13.30–17.00*) A botanical garden packed with fruit trees, orchids, anthuriums and much more. There is also a rock museum.

SUCRERIE DU GOL (*Le Camp du Gol, St-Louis;* ☎f *0262 910547;* e *visitesucrerie@gqf.com; www.gqf.com; adult/child €5/3; on reservation only; children aged under 7 are not allowed*) Claims to be the largest sugar refinery in the European Union. Guided tours of 1½ hours can be organised (in French or English) during harvest season (July–December). Tours take place Tuesday–Saturday at 08.30, 10.30, 13.00 and 15.00. Sugar products are on sale in the shop.

OBSERVATOIRE ASTRONOMIQUE LES MAKES (*18 Rue Georges Bizet, Plaine des Makes;* ☎ *0262 378683;* f *0262 378724;* e *obs.astronomique@wanadoo.fr; www.ilereunion.com/ observatoire-makes; guided tours: adult/child €4/2.50; night observation: adult/child €7.50/4.50; on reservation only*) Observatory about one hour's drive inland from St-Louis, at an altitude of 1,000m. Guided tours take place at 09.30, 10.30, 14.30 and 15.30.

CROC PARC (*1 Route Forestière, l'Etang-Salé-les-Hauts;* ☎ *0262 914041;* f *0262 914100;* e *orizon.reunion@wanadoo.fr; www.crocparc.re; adult/child €7/5; open daily 10.00–17.30*) About 2km from the RN1, between l'Etang-Salé-les-Bains and l'Etang-Salé-les-Hauts. The park is home to over 165 Nile crocodiles (*Crocodylus niloticus*), which are not bred for their skin or meat, but are simply there for the benefit of the public. The gardens are pleasant (many of the plants are labelled), there are copious birds (wild and caged), as well as a small collection of farm animals, a snack-bar and a souvenir shop. Crocodiles don't tend to do very much so a good time to visit is Wednesday or Sunday at 16.00 when they are fed.

294

20

Western Réunion

The western region stretches from Les Avirons in the southwest, all the way up to La Possession. Inland, the scenic Route Hubert Delisle links several small settlements along the western 'heights' from Les Avirons to Bois de Nèfles in the north.

The west coast is Réunion's sea, sun and sand holiday mecca, featuring 27km of beaches. It is the driest part of the island, so more often than not the weather is hot and sunny. Water temperatures generally average 20–26°C.

The coast around the historic town of St-Leu is known for its excellent surfing and black-sand beaches. There are also black-sand beaches at St-Paul but it is the clean, white-sand beaches at Boucan Canot, Roches Noires and l'Hermitage that draw the crowds.

Offshore, particularly around St-Gilles-les-Bains and St-Leu, there are colourful coral reefs, perfect for diving and snorkelling. St-Gilles-les-Bains is Réunion's main tourist resort; it has been developed with tourists in mind and while visitors may enjoy the idea of a French seaside resort in a tropical setting, those seeking an authentic Réunionnais experience will not find it here. As you head north, the coast becomes more rugged and the area around Le Port is primarily industrial. While the west of the island is best known for its coastal resorts, those who head inland will be rewarded with attractive villages, incredible viewpoints and excellent hiking country. In particular, Piton Maïdo provides unforgettable views of the Cirque de Mafate.

ST-LEU

The settlement of St-Leu was created in 1776 and soon became an important beef-rearing and coffee-growing region. By 1806, the population of this prosperous town consisted of 463 free people and 5,352 slaves. A few buildings remain from this era: the **town hall**, formerly a coffee warehouse, and the church, which was begun in 1788. The **Chapelle de Notre Dame de la Salette**, behind the church, was begun during the cholera epidemic of 1859 as a plea for St-Leu to be spared. It was, although thousands died in neighbouring towns.

Today St-Leu is surf city. You're bound to see local and visiting surfers hanging out in the street cafés and at the beach. (See box *Surfing in Réunion*, page 297.) It is also a great spot for diving and a popular area for paragliding.

St-Leu has a noticeably more relaxed air about it than St-Gilles and, although it has some good hotels, it has not been colonised by tourists.

Medical care can be obtained at the **Pharmacie de la Salette**, near which there are doctors' surgeries. **Banque de la Réunion** is at 52 Rue Général Lambert.

Visible from the coast road south of St-Leu, is **Le Souffleur**. When the sea is rough, this blowhole is spectacular.

On the RN1, just north of St-Leu is **La Ferme Corail**, a former turtle farm, where sea turtles are now bred in captivity and studied. It is well worth a visit. See *What to see*, page 307.

TOURIST INFORMATION The **tourist office** (☏ *0262 346330;* f *0262 349645. Open Mon 13.30–17.30, Tue–Fri 09.00–12.00 and 13.30–17.30, Sat 09.00–12.00 and 14.00–17.00*) is on the main street through town, Rue Général Lambert, on the corner of Rue Barrelier. It has an excellent stock of leaflets and offers guided tours of the area.

WHERE TO STAY
Classified hotels

Le Bleu Margouillat *** (14 rooms) Impasse Jean Albany, Zac du Four à Chaux, Saint-Leu; ☏ 0262 346400; f 0262 346415; e info@bleu-margouillat.com; www.bleu-margouillat.com. A real find! A spacious Creole-style mansion on the hillside above St-Leu with wonderful sea views. Entering the hotel is like straying into a celebrity's sumptuous beach villa. Classic mahogany furniture and modern art adorn a huge terrace overlooking a splendid pool. The 12 rooms and 2 suites are beautifully decorated, all with AC, TV, phone and balcony/terrace with sea view. The suites are very private and spacious, ideal for a romantic retreat or for families. There is one room equipped for the disabled. Meals are served around the pool or on the veranda (see page 298). Yves and Wilfred take great pride in their hotel, so first-class standards are assured. They both speak excellent English and so do their staff. *Dbl/suite from € 129/186 RO.*

Hotel Iloha *** (64 rooms) Pointe des Châteaux, St-Leu; ☏ 0262 348989; f 0262 348990; e hotel@iloha.fr; www.iloha.fr. Set on a hill overlooking St-Leu. There are 14 dbl rooms in the main building, 2 with disabled facilities. Bungalows in the garden house 40 superior rooms (20 with kitchenette) and 10 suites for up to 6 guests (with kitchenette). All accommodation has AC, TV and phone. There is a pleasant restaurant around the swimming pool. There are 2 tennis courts and a small shop. Not by the beach, but St-Leu is nearby

and the grounds are a pleasant place to relax. A car is essential. *Dbl/sgl from € 80/69, bungalows from € 148 (3–6 people) RO.*

Hotel Paladien Apolonia *** (129 rooms) Bd Bonnier, St-Leu; ☏ 0262 346262; f 0262 346161; e paladien.apolonia@wanadoo.fr; www.hotel-apolonia.com. In the centre of St-Leu, across the road from the beach. Rooms overlook either the pool or the mountains and are equipped with AC, TV, phone and safe; some have balcony. The sitting area is cleverly separated from the room by sliding doors and so is ideal as a child's bedroom. The restaurant is set around an attractive free-form pool and serves a different themed buffet each evening, including an excellent Creole buffet on Wednesdays. There is entertainment every evening. Facilities include a gym and a kids' club. A range of activities is included, such as guided walks, surfing lessons and mountain bikes. The staff are helpful and make a real effort to speak English. *Dbl/sgl from € 114/71 BB.*

Les Fougères ** (15 rooms) 53 Route des Merles, Le Tévelave, Les Avirons; ☏ 0262 383296; f 0262 383026; e lesfougeres@wanadoo.fr. Cosy accommodation in a quiet, pretty setting on the hills above the coast. Some rooms have TV and minibar, all have a phone. A room equipped for the disabled is available. The restaurant serves French and Creole cuisine and a buffet lunch on Sundays. *Dbl/sgl € 40/35 RO.*

Classified furnished flats

Les Azalées **** 5 Chemin des Azalées, La Chaloupe St-Leu; ☏ 0262 548714. Modern 3-bedroom apt with living area, kitchen, TV and veranda. *From € 385 per week.*

Aux Battants des Lames ** 20 Rue Général Lambert, St-Leu; ☏/f 0262 348018; e battantsdeslames@ifrance.com. Four very comfortable, well-equipped bungalows around a pool. *From € 364 per week (2 people).*

A l'Abri des Flots ** 48 Chemin Quatre Robinets, St-Leu; ☏ 0262 342623; f 0262 341269; e vallee.yannick@wanadoo.fr; http://perso.wanadoo.fr/alabridesflots. Two well-equipped bungalows above St-Leu. *From € 290 per week (2 people).*

Bungalows Murat ** 89 Chemin Dubuisson, St-Leu; ☏/f 0262 348504; e bungalows.murat@wanadoo.fr. Seven bungalows on the hillside above

Jeremy Saville

Réunion, as the Réunionnais will tell you, is the Hawaii of the Indian Ocean. It doesn't offer the diversity of waves that other Indian Ocean destinations do, but there's plenty in the way of impressive, quality surf. There are about 3,000 surfers and 12 surf clubs, and you'll always find many travelling surfers, who come from all corners of the globe, especially Europe, Australia and South Africa.

SEASON The best wave season is during the austral winter (May to October) on the west (leeward) coast. The main surf spots like St-Leu and Etang-Salé are in top gear from March to September. Outside of these times, the offshore trade winds are not as prominent and there is less swell in the Indian Ocean. June and July are usually the most crowded, as the contest circus moves through the island. If you're planning a surfing trip to Réunion, bear that in mind. Summer has reasonable waves on the east coast if you're prepared to take your chances. There are several point/reef and beachbreaks on the east coast, but it's also the favoured haunt of Zambezi and Tiger sharks. The further away from the 'safety belt' of the southwest coast you travel, the greater your chances of coming home without your legs. Most Réunionnais surfers have at least one good shark story to tell.

SURFING SPOTS
- La Gare in St-Benoît is a fickle right that breaks in front of the mouth of the Marsouins River. It's the best wave on the east coast, but sharks are abundant here.
- La Jetée in St-Pierre throws up a powerful right-hander that breaks in front of the harbour wall. Surf here only if you know what you're doing: it's a quality wave but gets blown out easily.
- Etang-Salé has a racetrack of a left (off its black beach) that picks up any hint of a swell. The wave wraps an incredible 90 degrees. Get there in the early morning because it is easily ruined by the wind. If you're into something different, there is a heavy shorebreak further along the beach by the bridge.
- Trois Bassins is a fun utility wave when everything else is flat. Look out for signboards on the road.
- St-Leu has Réunion's best wave – a world-class break in every respect. It's easy to find, being in front of the town of St-Leu. You'll see the reef from the road. Paddle out next to the hut on the beach. Watch out for urchins in the shorebreak and be very, very wary of getting caught inside. A wave for advanced surfers only.
- Roche Noire in the tourist town of St-Gilles is the most popular break on the island. Without a doubt, it's also the worst.
- Les Aigrettes is a shallow left and right that works in a big swell. It's a high-quality wave when at its best. Urchins litter the shorebreak. It is a few kilometres north of Roche Noire, on the same stretch of reef.

It's a sensible idea to take a springsuit for windy days. This will also help prevent coral cuts at shallower spots like l'Hermitage, Les Aigrettes and St-Leu. Localism and intense crowding are occasionally a problem, especially at St-Leu. If you wait your turn and remember your manners, the locals are generally cool. Try *'tu surf comme un singe'* (you surf like a monkey) as a way of breaking the ice!

Jeremy Saville is editor of Zigzag, southern Africa's leading surfing magazine.

Western Réunion ST-LEU

20

St-Leu. From €34 per week (2 people).

🏠 **Le Paille en Queue** ** 153 bis Chemin Dubuisson, St-Leu; ✆ 0262 344645; e schulzy@wanadoo.fr. An apt adjoining the owner's house, 4.5km from the centre of St-Leu. From €280 per week (2 people).

🏠 **Residence des Alizés** ** 48 bis Av des Alizés, St-Leu; ✆ 0262 348912; f 0262 348399; e marie-josee.cornette@wanadoo.fr; www.residencealizes.com. Three apts near the centre of town. From €40 per night (2 people).

✖ **WHERE TO EAT** There is a **Super U supermarket** in the centre of town.

✖ **Aux Bonnes Choses** 73 Rue du Lagon, St-Leu; ✆ 0262 347626. Cuisine: Creole. On the seafront. *Mid-range prices. Open Fri–Sat for lunch and dinner, closed Sunday evening.*

✖ **Le Bleu Margouillat** Impasse Jean Albany, Zac du Four à Chaux, St-Leu; ✆ 0262 346400. Cuisine: French, Creole. Fine food in an elegant setting. *Main courses from €12. Open daily for lunch and dinner. Reservation essential.*

✖ **Casa San Firmin** 3 Rue de la Salette, St-Leu; ✆ 0262 349058. Cuisine: French, Basque. Quaint restaurant serving good food. Excellent paella. *Main courses from €12. Open Tue–Sun for lunch and dinner.*

✖ **Le Lagon** 2 bis Rue du Lagon, St-Leu; ✆ 0262 347913. Cuisine: French, Creole, seafood, snacks. On

the seafront, across the road from the Apolonia Hotel. *Main courses from €9. Open Thu–Mon for lunch and dinner.*

✖ **O-Jacare** 55 Av du Général Lambert, St-Leu; ✆ 0262 348888. Cuisine: European. On a busy stretch of road. *Main courses from €11. Open Mon–Sat for lunch and dinner.*

✖ **Le Stella** Stella Matutina Museum, 6 Allée des Flamboyants, Piton St-Leu; ✆ 0262 340715. Cuisine: French, Creole. Regarded as one of Réunion's best restaurants. *Upmarket food and prices. Open Tue–Sun for lunch.*

✖ **La Varangue** 36 Rue du Lagon, St-Leu; ✆ 0262 347926. Cuisine: Creole, grills. Upmarket restaurant on the seafront. *Main courses from €10. Open Tue–Sun for lunch, Tue–Sat for dinner.*

OTHER PRACTICALITIES
Money and banking/communications The **post office** is near the harbour on Rue de la Compagnie des Indes and has **ATM** facilities. For **faxing**, **secretarial services** and **internet access** try **Point Run** at 14 Rue du Commandant Legros, St-Leu (✆ *0262 348772*). For details see page 251.

ST-GILLES-LES-BAINS AND SURROUNDS

The area around St-Gilles-les-Bains is Réunion's premier beach holiday hangout. The island's best beaches and seaside hotels are here. However, it must be said that even these beaches do not compare with those of Mauritius.

As you head north from St-Leu along the coast, you come to the largely residential area of **La-Saline-les-Bains**. There are decent beaches here, popular for snorkelling, surfing and windsurfing, and they tend to be less crowded than those in St-Gilles-les-Bains.

Continuing north, before you hit St-Gilles itself, you pass the turning to l'Hermitage – arguably the island's prettiest beach. The beach is protected by a long lagoon; the water is clear, shallow and good for swimming.

The bustling town of St-Gilles is packed with restaurants, bars, pubs and trendy nightclubs. It is a playground for hip, young, French holidaymakers, who come to enjoy the sunshine, the sea and the busy nightlife. Many travellers find it too 'commercialised' and crowded; for others it is the ideal way to unwind after hiking in the mountains. You will not get an authentic taste of Réunion in St-Gilles. It is a town built by Europeans for Europeans, a fact captured by one of my Réunionnais friends in his description of it as a *'ghetto zoreilles'* (white people's ghetto). Certainly, it does feel like a mini St-Tropez and traffic congestion is a real problem along this section of coast.

The **harbour** (Port de Plaisance) is also a lively place, where all manner of watersports can be arranged. This is where you'll find the excellent **Aquarium de la Réunion** (see *What to see*, pages 307–8).

About 3km inland from St-Gilles-les-Bains, on the road to St-Gilles-les-Hauts, is the car park that is the starting point for the walk to three waterfalls plunging into pools (*bassins*): **Bassin du Cormoran**, **Bassin des Aigrettes** and **Bassin Bleu**. It's a very pretty walk of about two hours and Bassins des Aigrettes and Bleu are ideal for a quick dip. You will have to take your shoes off and get your feet wet on parts of the walk.

Also on the road to St-Gilles-les-Hauts is the **Village Artisanal de l'Eperon**, where handicrafts and art produced by local artisans are on sale.

GETTING THERE AND AWAY All the towns along the west coast, including St-Gilles-les-Bains, are easily reached on the non-express St-Denis/St-Pierre buses (Lines B and C).

TOURIST INFORMATION There is a well-stocked **tourist office** (\ *0262 440707;* f *0262 550102;* e *odt-saintpaul@wanadoo.fr. Open daily 10.00–18.00, including public holidays*) at 1 Place Paul Julius Bénard, Galerie Amandine, St-Gilles-les-Bains.

WHERE TO STAY
Classified hotels

Le Boucan Canot **** (50 rooms) 32 Rue Boucan Canot, Boucan Canot; \ 0262 334444; f 0262 334445; e hotel@boucancanot.com; www.boucancanot.com. An attractive blue and white Creole-style building in a good location with direct access to Boucan Canot Beach. The rooms and suites are modern and equipped with AC, TV, minibar, safe and balcony. Facilities include a restaurant overlooking the sea (see page 303), pool and regular evening entertainment. *Dbl/sgl from* € *160/130 BB.*

Le Saint Alexis **** (63 rooms) 44 Route de Boucan Canot, St-Gilles-les-Bains; \ 0262 244204; f 0262 240013; e hotel.saintalexis@wanadoo.fr; www.hotelsaintalexis.com. This hotel on the beach at Boucan Canot was extensively refurbished in 2002. All rooms and suites have AC, TV, phone, safe, spa bath, minibar and balcony/terrace. There are 2 pools, a sauna, a gym and a restaurant. *Dbl/suite from* € *140/380 BB.*

Les Villas du Lagon **** (174 rooms) 28 Rue du Lagon, l'Hermitage, St-Gilles-les-Bains; \ 0262 700000; f 0262 700007; e reservation.vdl@villas-du-lagon.com; www.villas-du-lagon.com. Popular resort-style hotel on l'Hermitage Beach. 23 bungalows house the well-maintained rooms, including 4 with disabled facilities and 8 suites. As you'd expect, all have AC, TV, phone, minibar and safe. Plenty of activities: tennis, badminton, gym and some watersports. There are 3 restaurants, a pool and a kids' club. Good feeling of space, with large gardens. *Dbl/sgl from* € *193/154 BB.*

L'Archipel *** (66 rooms) 9 Rue de la Cheminée, Grand Fond, St-Gilles-les-Bains; \ 0262

240534; f 0262 244724; e reservation@archipel-hotel.com; www.archipel-hotel.com. On the road to St-Gilles-les-Hauts, but there is a free shuttle service to the beaches and St-Gilles-les-Bains town centre. The rooms, including 2 with disabled facilities, have AC, TV, phone, minibar and balcony/terrace. There is a pleasant pool, restaurant and tennis. *Dbl/sgl from* € *107/92 RO.*

Mercure Blue Beach *** (56 rooms) Av de la Mer, Les Filaos, l'Hermitage; \ 0262 245025; f 0262 243622; e H1126@accor-hotels.com; www.accorhotels.com. Family-friendly hotel 150m from the beach. Rooms overlook either the pool, garden or car park and are equipped with AC, TV, phone, minibar and balcony/terrace. Standard rooms are on the small side but junior suites are ideal for families as they have a living area with sofa bed, a kitchenette and 2 bathrooms. The hotel has a restaurant, bar, gym, car park and pool, which feels rather overlooked by the rooms bunched around it. *Dbl/junior suite from* € *113/148 RO.*

Les Créoles *** (42 rooms) 43 Av de Bourbon, l'Hermitage; \ 0262 330909; f 0262 330919; e hotel@les-creoles.com. Five mins' walk from l'Hermitage Beach. Rooms with AC, TV, phone, minibar, safe and balcony/terrace lie around a pleasant pool. Rooms for the disabled are available. Very clean and tastefully decorated. It has a good restaurant and regular entertainment. *Dbl/sgl from* € *110/90 BB.*

Grand Hôtel des Mascareignes *** (153 rooms) Les Coquillages, Boucan Canot; \ 0262 243624; f 0262 243724; e resa.ghm@apavou-hotels.com;

20

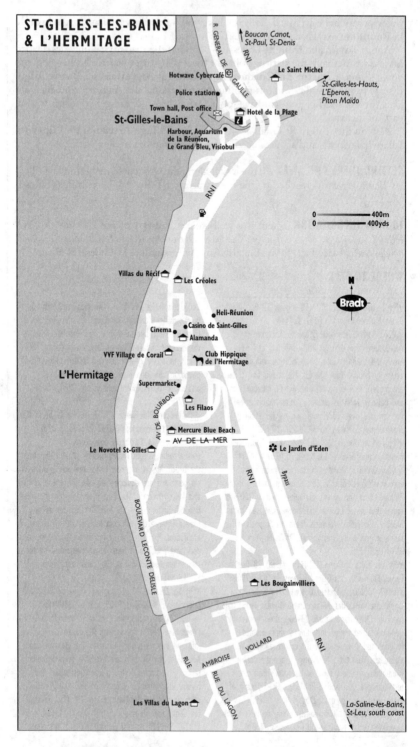

ST-GILLES-LES-BAINS & L'HERMITAGE

Boucan Canot,
St-Paul, St-Denis

Le Saint Michel

Hotwave Cybercafé

St-Gilles-les-Hauts,
L'Eperon,
Piton Maïdo

Police station

Town hall, Post office

St-Gilles-le-Bains

Hotel de la Plage

Harbour, Aquarium
de la Réunion,
Le Grand Bleu, Visiobul

0 ———— 400m
0 ———— 400yds

Villas du Récif

Les Créoles

Heli-Réunion

Cinema

Casino de Saint-Gilles

Alamanda

VVF Village de Corail

Club Hippique
de l'Hermitage

L'Hermitage

Supermarket

Les Filaos

Mercure Blue Beach

— AV DE LA MER —

Le Novotel St-Gilles

Le Jardin d'Eden

RNI

Bypass

AV DE BOURBON

BOULEVARD LECONTE DELISLE

Les Bougainvilliers

VOLLARD

RUE AMBROISE

RUE DU LAGON

Les Villas du Lagon

La-Saline-les-Bains,
St-Leu, south coast

www.apavou-hotels.com. Across the main road from Boucan Canot Beach. Rather dull, stale rooms with AC, TV, phone, minibar and safe (the safe key costs €8 from reception). Despite a recent renovation the hotel still feels in need of updating and the service can be rather indifferent. It has a decent pool, 2 tennis courts, an adequate restaurant and a nightclub. B/fast is rather disappointing. *Dbl/sgl from €124/81 BB*.

⌂ **Le Maharani** *** (55 rooms) 28 Route du Boucan, St-Gilles-les-Bains; ☎ 0262 330606; f 0262 243297; e resa.maharani@apavou-hotels.com; www.apavou-hotels.com. On the seafront with direct access to the beach. Rooms are in a 3-storey building facing the sea and are equipped with AC, TV and phone; most have a safe. It has a generous pool, jacuzzi and regular evening entertainment. *Dbl/family apt from €115/145 RO*.

⌂ **Le Nautile** *** (43 rooms) 60 Rue Lacaussade, La-Saline-les-Bains; ☎ 0262 338888; f 0262 338889; e nautile@runnet.com; www.hotel-nautile.com. Pretty hotel on the beach. Rooms have AC, TV, phone, minibar, safe and balcony/terrace. Facilities include a restaurant, bar, pool, fitness room and car park. Regular evening entertainment. *Dbl from €122/101 BB*.

⌂ **Le Novotel St-Gilles** *** (173 rooms) 123 Av Leconte de Lisle, l'Hermitage; ☎ 0262 244444; f 0262 240167; e H0462-GM@accor-hotels.com; www.accorhotels.com. Sprawling hotel spread through a 3ha garden with direct access to the beach. Rooms have views of either the mountains (and car park!) or the pool. All have AC, TV, phone, safe and minibar, and most have balcony/terrace. Five rooms have disabled facilities. It's a busy hotel, where everyone seems to take advantage of the activities – pool, tennis courts, mini-golf, kayaks, pedaloes and snorkelling equipment. There's a family atmosphere, but the kids' club operates only during French school holidays. *Dbl from €124 RO*.

⌂ **Le Swalibo** *** (30 rooms) 9 Rue des Salines, La-Saline-les-Bains; ☎ 0262 241097; f 0262 246429; e info@swalibo.com; www.swalibo.com. A small, charming hotel, 5 mins' walk from the beach. Rooms are bright and spacious with AC, TV, phone, minibar, safe and balcony. Not much privacy – the balconies and small garden are overlooked by other rooms. Facilities include a restaurant, pool and jacuzzi. Beach umbrellas, kayaks and snorkelling gear are available. *Dbl/sgl from €110/86 BB*.

⌂ **Les Villas du Récif** *** (146 rooms) 50 Av de Bourbon, l'Hermitage; ☎ 0262 700100; f 0262 700107; e hotel@villas-du-recif.fr. Formerly Le Récif, this hotel underwent a transformation in 2004 and is now a very attractive option. The rooms and suites, including 4 rooms for the disabled, are housed in 17 2-storey buildings scattered in a large garden. Rooms have AC, TV, phone, minibar and balcony/terrace. Use of a safe is payable. Facilities include a restaurant, snack-bar, bar, 2 pools, tennis and kids' club. A family-friendly hotel with an emphasis on activities. In a great location, opposite l'Hermitage Beach. *Dbl/sgl from €130 BB*.

⌂ **Les Aigrettes** ** (95 rooms) Chemin Bottard, St-Gilles-les-Bains; ☎ 0262 330505; f 0262 243050; e resa.aigrettes@apavou-hotels.com; www.apavou-hotels.com. On the hillside overlooking St-Gilles. Clean and comfortable sea-facing rooms with en suite AC, TV and phone. Family units (2 standard rooms with shared bathroom) are available. There is a restaurant and a pool. *Dbl/sgl from €92/58 RO*.

⌂ **Alamanda Hotel** ** (58 rooms) 81 Av de Bourbon, l'Hermitage; ☎ 0262 331010; f 0262 240242; e alamanda.hotel@alamanda.fr; www.alamanda.fr. After a much-needed refurbishment in 2002, this 2-star option is now good value. The hotel is close to the casino and nightlife, and 5 mins' walk from the beach. En-suite rooms with AC, TV, phone and balcony/terrace overlook either the pool or small garden. It has a good restaurant, bar and pool. The rooms are small but clean and it is well located. *Dbl/sgl from €86/62 BB, €130/84 HB*.

⌂ **Marina** ** (10 apts) 6 Allée des Pailles en Queues, Lot Champagne, St-Gilles-les-Bains; ☎ 0262 330707; f 0262 330700; e hotelmarina@wanadoo.fr; www.hotelmarinachampagne.com. Modern self-catering studios in pretty gardens 200m from Boucan Canot Beach. Close to shops and public transport. Studios are equipped with TV, AC and phone. *Studio from €52 (2 people) RO*.

⌂ **Le Saint Michel** ** (15 rooms) 196 Chemin Summer, St-Gilles-les-Bains; ☎ 0262 331333; f 0262 331338; e st-michel.hotel@wanadoo.fr; www.blue-season-hotels.com. A small, well-run hotel with neat en-suite rooms with AC, TV, phone and balcony/terrace. There is a restaurant and a pool. *Dbl/sgl from €82/73 BB*.

⌂ **Villa des Songes** ** (12 rooms) 28 Rue Joseph Hubert, St-Gilles-les-Hauts; ☎ 0262 220336; f 0262 550637; e villa.songes@wanadoo.fr; www.villadessonges.fr. A rare find! Elegant yet quaint accommodation in a renovated Creole home on the hillside above St-Gilles. The rooms are beautifully decorated and equipped with all mod cons: en suite, AC, TV, phone and internet access. There is a delightful restaurant serving Creole and French food (see page 303). *Dbl/sgl from €72/60 RO*.

Unclassified accommodation

Les Filaos (44 rooms) 101 Av de Bourbon, St-Gilles-les-Bains; ☎ 0262 245009; f 0262 242809; e les-filaos@wanadoo.fr; www.blue-season-hotels.com. Unfortunately next to a busy road with a nightclub and supermarket in front of it but only a short walk from the beach. Small en-suite rooms with AC, TV, phone, safe and balcony/terrace; studios have a kitchenette. Rooms with disabled facilities are available. It has a pool and bar but no restaurant. *Dbl/sgl from € 84/70 BB, studio from € 95 (2 people) RO.*

Les Bougainvilliers (9 rooms) 27 Ruelle des Bougainvilliers, l'Hermitage; ☎/f 0262 338248; www.bougainvillier.com. Comfortable guesthouse in a quiet spot. Rooms have shower (some have a toilet), fan and fridge, while a few have AC and a terrace. There is a small pool and a communal kitchen. *Dbl from € 37 RO.*

Hotel de la Plage (7 rooms) 20 Rue de la Poste, St-Gilles-les-Bains; ☎ 0262 240637; f 0262 332005. Budget accommodation 100m from Roches Noires Beach. Small, basic rooms, some with AC. En-suite dbl with TV from € 45, dbl with shared bathroom from € 29, sgl with fan from € 26. All rates on BB.

Classified furnished flats

This area has plenty of apartments and villas to let to holidaymakers, many of which represent excellent value for money. Here is a selection:

Résidences St-Gilloises **** 32 Rue St-Alexis, St-Gilles-les-Bains; ☎ 0262 448228; f 0262 449630; e residence-saintgilloise@wanadoo.fr. Very well-equipped ground-floor apt 150m from Roches Noires Beach. Has AC, TV and phone. *Apt from € 363 per week (2 people).*

L'Ilot Vert *** 1 Rue des Salines, La-Saline-les-Bains; ☎ 0262 339211; f 0262 339212; e jean-pierre.fouque@wanadoo.fr; www.a-l-ilot-vert.com. A few mins' walk from the beach. Well-maintained apts around a small pool, all equipped with AC, TV and phone. There is a car park. *Apt from € 65 per night (2 people).*

Senteur Vanille ** & *** Route du Théatre, St-Gilles-les-Bains; ☎/f 0262 240488; e senteurvanille@wanadoo.fr; www.senteurvanille.com. Slightly inland amidst pretty gardens. Accommodation is in elegantly decorated 2-star Creole-style bungalows or in 3-star wooden chalets, all with AC and TV. The chalets are elevated and have a view of the ocean. Fantastic value for money. *Bungalow from € 65 per night for 2 people rising to € 130 per night for 6 people. Chalet from € 75 per night for 2 people, € 130 per night for 6 people. All prices are RO.*

Résidence les Boucaniers ** 29 Rue du Boucan Canot, Boucan Canot; ☎ 0262 242389; f 0262 244695; e les-boucaniers@wanadoo.fr; www.les-boucaniers.com. Nine studios and 6 apts across the road from Boucan Canot Beach, with AC, TV (on request) and balcony/terrace. The accommodation is sea facing and rooms on the first floor have a good view of the coast. One room with disabled facilities is available. Clean and well situated but the kitchenettes are basic. *Studio/4-person apt from € 72/96.*

At Paul & Virginie's ** Apt 8, Résidence Diane, Rue St-Alexis, St-Gilles-les-Bains; ☎/f 0262 294856; e alonabox@wanadoo.fr. Thoughtfully furnished one-bedroom apt in the town centre. *Apt from € 280 per week (2 people).*

Villages Vacances Famille (VVF): family holiday villages

You must be a member of VVF to stay here. For details see *Chapter 15, Accommodation*.

Village de Corail (129 s/c studios) 80 Av de Bourbon, 97434 St-Gilles-les-Bains; ☎ 0262 242939; f 0262 244102; e contact@villages-des-australes.com; www.villages-des-australes.com. Each studio has twin beds, kitchenette, dining area and terrace. Up to 2 extra beds can be added per studio. *Studio from € 46 RO (2 people).*

Youth hostel

One of the island's 3 hostels is in the hills above St-Gilles, at Bernica near St-Gilles-les-Hauts (☎ 0262 228975). To stay there you must have a membership card. For details see *Chapter 15, Accommodation.*

✗ WHERE TO EAT Scores of restaurants are crammed into St-Gilles-les-Bains and the surrounding area. In addition, you'll see numerous snack-bars and, for those who are self-catering, well-stocked supermarkets in the centre of town (**Score, Champion**). There is also a **Score supermarket** in l'Hermitage and a large **Champion supermarket** in La-Saline-les-Bains.

Here is a cross-section of restaurants:

✗ Bois de Couleur Hotel Alamanda, 81 Av de Bourbon, l'Hermitage; ☎ 0262 331010. Cuisine: French, Creole. Creative, sophisticated menu with specialities such as swordfish with lemon and curcuma, and sweet potato cake with coconut and papaya. *Main courses from € 11. Open daily for lunch and dinner.*

✗ Boucan Canot Hotel 32 Rue Boucan Canot, Boucan Canot; ☎ 0262 334444. Cuisine: French, Creole, seafood, grills. Upmarket restaurant, overlooking the water. Specialities include heart of palm salad and grilled lobster. *Main courses from € 12. Open daily for lunch and dinner.*

✗ Chez Go 7 Bd Leconte Delisle, l'Hermitage; ☎ 0262 338261. Cuisine: Creole, Chinese. Eat-in and take-away. *Main courses from € 10. Open Wed–Sun for lunch and dinner.*

✗ Chez Loulou 84 Rue Général de Gaulle, St-Gilles-les-Bains; ☎ 0262 244636. Cuisine: snacks, Creole, French. In a colourful Creole building in the centre of town, opposite Le Forum shopping centre. Excellent bakery which also serves a small range of meals (these vary – just look at the blackboard outside). Good value for money. Also has 1 internet terminal. *Inexpensive. Open daily 07.00–13.00 and 15.00–19.00, closed Sunday evening.*

✗ La Frigousse Villa des Songes, 28 Rue Joseph Hubert, St-Gilles-les-Hauts; ☎ 0262 220336. Cuisine: French, Creole. Tasty food in an elegant but relaxed atmosphere. *Lunch menus from € 15. Open Tue–Fri and Sun for lunch, Tue–Sat for dinner.*

✗ Le Guetali Ilot du Port, St-Gilles-les-Bains; ☎ 0262 242044. Cuisine: seafood, European. Rather smart indoor and outdoor tables with a sea view, plus a trendy bar area. *Main courses from € 11. Open Tue–Sun for lunch and dinner.*

✗ Hacienda Cocobeach Plage de l'Hermitage; ☎ 0262 338143. Cuisine: Creole, European. Trendy restaurant/bar on the beach. *Main courses from € 12. Open Thu–Tue for lunch and dinner.*

✗ Le Laetizia Pl Julius Bénard, St-Gilles-les-Bains; ☎ 0262 244964. Cuisine: Italian, crêpes, snacks. Mid-range restaurant serving good food in a relaxed atmosphere. *Pizza from € 6, pasta from € 7.50. Open daily for lunch and dinner.*

✗ Mayflowers 71 Av de Bourbon, l'Hermitage; ☎ 0262 240997. Three restaurants in one: **La Marmite**

Créole, **Auberge du Bonheur** (Chinese) and **Fuji Ya** (Japanese). Buffet lunch on Sunday. *Main courses from € 8. Open Tue–Sun for lunch and dinner.*

✗ Le Paille en Queue Le Casino, 7 Av des Mascareignes, l'Hermitage; ☎ 0262 244700. Cuisine: French. Elegant décor and gourmet food. *Main courses from € 12. Open Tue–Sun for lunch and dinner.*

✗ Paul et Virginie 15 Route de la Plage, St-Gilles-les-Bains; ☎ 0262 330453. Cuisine: Creole, seafood. Opposite the beach. Known for its seafood platters. *Main courses from € 11. Open Wed–Sun for lunch, Tue–Sun for dinner.*

✗ Le Robinson Le Forum, Rue du Général de Gaulle, St-Gilles-les-Bains; ☎ 0262 242179. Cuisine: Creole, European, ice cream. Inside there is a pub-style atmosphere, plus a courtyard eating area in the centre of the shopping centre. *Main courses from € 9, 3-course menus from € 18. Open daily 07.00–00.30.*

✗ Le St-Gilles Port de Plaisance, St-Gilles-les-Bains; ☎ 0262 245127; www.lesaintgilles.net. Cuisine: European, seafood. Elegant restaurant in an enviable location with a terrace overlooking the marina. Excellent lobster dishes. *Main courses from € 14. Open Tue–Sun for lunch and dinner.*

✗ Les Tipaniers (Chez Dante) 58 bis Rue du Général de Gaulle, St-Gilles-les-Bains; ☎ 0262 242884. Cuisine: Creole, French. Charming atmosphere and excellent food. The menu gives traditional dishes a modern twist. The prawns with vanilla are worth trying. *Main courses from € 12. Open Mon and Wed–Fri for lunch, Wed–Mon for dinner. Reservation recommended for dinner.*

✗ Le Toboggan Plage de l'Hermitage; ☎ 0262 338494. Cuisine: European, Creole, snacks, ice cream. Décor isn't particularly smart but it's right on the edge of the water and the food is very good. Holds jazz evenings fortnightly on a Saturday. *Main courses from € 12.50. Open daily for lunch, Fri–Sun for dinner.*

✗ Le Comptoir Créole Les Coquillages, Boucan Canot; ☎ 0262 255283. Cuisine: Creole, European. Not in the best location (on the edge of a small shopping centre) but it is clean and colourful with good traditional food. *Main courses from € 13. Open Mon–Sat for dinner.*

NIGHTLIFE The harbour in St-Gilles and the town itself are full of bars, whilst most of the nightclubs and the casino are in l'Hermitage. The downside of nightclubbing in Réunion is that it will dent your wallet severely. In the St-Gilles-les-Bains area you can expect to pay in the region of €12–14 for entry and, on top of that, drinks are expensive. Most clubs are open only on weekends, some only on a Saturday night. They tend to get going at around midnight and are open until about 05.00. Most play a mixture of music, but being St-Gilles there is less local music (*séga, zouk* etc) than in St-Pierre, for example.

There are various free publications, available in tourist offices, which will tell you what is going on, where and when in terms of nightlife (see page 248).

Bars are easily found on the main streets of St-Gilles and around the marina. **Cubana Café** (*122 Rue du Général de Gaulle;* ꕯ *0262 332490*) is usually packed. There is a well-stocked bar, a brasserie, a cigar lounge and regular events. Wednesday night is jazz night, while Thursday is salsa night. Other popular spots on Rue du Général de Gaulle include: **Jungle Village** (ꕯ *0262 332193*), **La Rhumerie** (ꕯ *0262 245599*), **Chez Nous** (ꕯ *0262 240808*) and **Pub à Bières** (ꕯ *0262 331665*).

As for nightclubs, **Le Privé** (*1 Av du Général de Gaulle;* ꕯ *0262 240417*) has become *the* place to be seen in St-Gilles. It attracts a lively crowd of young, French partygoers. It is open on weekends and has theme nights during the week. The ever-popular **Moulin du Tango** (*9 Av des Mascareignes;* ꕯ *0262 245390*) is open on Wednesdays as well as Friday and Saturday nights. It is large club, with open-air dance floors and several bars. Other popular nightspots are **Planet Soleil** (*2 Mail de Rodrigues;* ꕯ *0262 331500*), **Caesar's Palace** (*71 Av de Bourbon;* ꕯ *0262 330011*) and **Swing** (*Grand Fond;* ꕯ *0262 244598*).

The **Casino de Saint-Gilles** at l'Hermitage (ꕯ *0262 244700*) is open Monday–Thursday 10.00–02.00, Friday–Saturday 10.00–04.00. The slot machines are open from 10.00 and the tables from 21.00.

OTHER PRACTICALITIES
Money and banking The main banks have branches, with ATMs, on Rue du Général de Gaulle. There are also ATMs outside the post office, at the Score supermarket and at the casino in l'Hermitage.

Communications The **post office** is on Rue de la Poste, near Roches Noires beach. For internet access, try **Hotwave Cybercafé** (*37 Rue du Général de Gaulle;* ꕯ *0262 240424*), which is set back from the main road in St-Gilles-les-Bains. **Chez Loulou** (*84 Rue Général de Gaulle, St-Gilles;* ꕯ *0262 244636*) has one internet terminal in the corner of the bakery. For details see page 251.

ST-PAUL TO LA POSSESSION

St-Paul, the original Réunionnais capital and the site where the first settlers were abandoned, is a favoured weekend escape for residents of St-Denis, as it has the nearest beach to the capital. It's also the centre of Réunion's yachting fraternity, and international yachting events are regularly hosted here.

Of note is the seaside **cemetery**, or **Cimetière Marin**, which has become an unlikely tourist attraction. Signposts guide visitors around the tombs of the famous and infamous occupants. One of these is the notorious pirate, Olivier Levasseur, or **La Buse**, who was hanged in 1730. His tomb features a skull and crossbones. People delving into witchcraft still leave bottles of rum and cigarettes on his grave at night. Some apparently do this in order to communicate with his spirit and find out where he hid his treasure. The late and legendary treasure-hunter Bibique, who was an expert on pirate history, was positive that le Vasseur's treasure is buried in Réunion somewhere. St-Paul-born poet **Leconte de Lisle** (1818–94) is also buried here. Across the road from the cemetery and to the south of town is the **Grotte des Premiers Français**, the cave in which the island's first settlers lived. They were 12 French rebels exiled from Madagascar in 1646.

There are some lovely old **colonial mansions** (now government offices) along the coastal road, Quai Gilbert. Look out for the small **park** with its old French cannons, set up to protect St-Paul but never utilised. There's also a **war memorial** for the Réunionnais soldiers who were killed in both World Wars.

The most important attraction St-Paul holds for visitors is the vibrant street **market**, which residents proudly claim is the island's best. It operates on Friday and Saturday mornings. As well as souvenirs, there is plenty in the way of exotic food and the market is surrounded on three sides by snack-bars.

St-Paul is also the gateway to the picturesque **Maïdo** area in the so-called 'Western Heights', overlooking the west coast. Piton Maïdo (2,190m) affords breathtaking views of the **Cirque de Mafate**. From the coast, you take winding rural roads through cane fields and vegetable plots, after which you pass by the famed **geranium fields** and finally, much higher up, forests. Those forests signal a change in climate, as you enter the cool, green, high-lying area on the lip of the Cirque de Mafate. On the winding RF8 road, halfway between **Le Guillaume** and Piton Maïdo, is **Petite-France**, an area where fields of geraniums (actually a pelargonium plant native to South Africa) are cultivated for their essential oil. Réunion's geranium oil is of the highest quality and so is much sought after in the pharamaceutical/essential oils industry.

It's a slow drive of 30km, but worth it. It's best to reach the viewpoint in the early morning before the clouds roll in. The peaks that you see are **Le Gros Morne** (2,991m) and **Piton-des-Nieges** (3,069m). The villages below are **Roche Plate**, **La Nouvelle** and **Ilet des Orangers**, whose combined inhabitants number some six hundred. It is a mind-boggling sight – a miniature world of isolated communities cupped in a deep crater, untainted by electricity pylons, roads and large buildings. The development of Réunion has passed them by, except for an unreliable water supply that was laid on in 1982. Many of the residents have never seen a car – incredible when you think that just 12km away as the crow flies, people are sitting in a traffic jam on their way to the office.

Further north on the west coast is **Le Port**, Réunion's main harbour, an uninspiring industrial town outside of which is the Nelson Mandela Stadium, where international sporting events are held. Tourists tend to pass through Le Port and **La Possession** on the way to St-Paul or St-Gilles. However, the coast road is impressive, wedged between sheer cliffs and the sea.

WHERE TO STAY
Classified hotels

Lodge Roche Tamarin *** (16 rooms) 142 Chemin Bœuf Mort, La Possession; ↘ 0262 446688; f 0262 446680; e villagenature@wanadoo.fr; www.villagenature.com. Superb new wooden chalets on stilts on the forested hillside above La Possession. Chalets sleep up to 3 people and are rustic yet elegant, with bathroom, TV, phone, kitchenette and veranda. Facilities include a pool, barbecue area, restaurant, shop and conference room. A relaxing hideaway. *Dbl from* € 105 RO.

Unclassified accommodation

La Clé des Champs (5 rooms) 154 Chemin des Barrières, St-Paul; ↘ 0262 323760; f 0262 324573; e lacledeschamps@ilereunion.com; www.ilereunion.com/lacledeschamps. Elegant accommodation in an impressive country house on the hillside above St-Paul, with panoramic views of the coast. En-suite rooms with a classic, country feel. Facilities include a lounge area, table d'hôte restaurant and jacuzzi. *Dbl from* € 95 BB.

🏠 **36 La Baie** ** 36 Rue de la Baie, St-Paul; ✆ 0262 225702; f 0262 455916; e volk-hug@wanadoo.fr. Elegant bungalow on the seafront, sleeps up to 4 people. *Apt from € 420 per week (2 people).*

🏠 **Marie Cascade** ** 46 Rue Frédéric Chopin, La Palmeraie 2, La Possession; ✆/f 0262 322041; e m.cascade@soleil974.com; www.creole.org/cascade. Well-equipped apt in owner's house with 1 bedroom and sofa-bed. Washing machine, TV, phone and small private garden. *Apt from € 268 (2 people).*

✖ **WHERE TO EAT** There are plenty of snack-bars along the seafront in St-Paul, particularly around Quai Gilbert.

✖ **Auberge Gourmande** 120 Chemin Crescence, Tan Rouge, St-Paul; ✆ 0262 327820. Cuisine: Creole, French. The most upmarket option in the area, with views over the coast. Theme evenings are often arranged for Friday and Saturday. Lunches are buffet-style. *Main courses from € 14. Open Wed–Sat for lunch and dinner, Sun for lunch. Reservation recommended.*

✖ **Axel Nativel** Rue G Elizabeth, Dos d'Ane; ✆ 0262 320147. Cuisine: Creole. *Table d'hôte meals from € 18. On reservation only.*

✖ **Chez Doudou** 394 Route du Maïdo, Petite-France; ✆ 0262 325587. Cuisine: Creole. Traditional Creole dishes cooked over a wood fire. *Main courses from € 10. Set menus from € 16. Open Thu–Tue for lunch. Reservation recommended.*

✖ **Restaurant Relais du Maïdo** Route du Maïdo; ✆ 0262 324032. Cuisine: Creole, snacks. *Main courses from € 7, set menus from € 10. Open Tue–Sun for lunch and dinner.*

✖ **Rose Magdeleine** Chemin de l'Ecole, Petite-France; ✆ 0262 325350. Cuisine: Creole. Traditional home-cooked food. *Table d'hôte menus € 15. On reservation only.*

WHAT TO DO

WATERSPORTS All manner of watersports can be organised along the west coast. St-Leu and St-Gilles-les-Bains are the two main areas for scuba diving; St-Leu is where surfers head and St-Paul has a water skiing centre. For details see *Chapter 16, Activities.*

GLASS-BOTTOM BOATS Glass-bottom boat trips depart from St-Gilles-les-Bains. For details see page 262.

HORSERIDING Centre Equestre du Maïdo, on the way to Piton Maïdo, is a good-quality equestrian centre in a very picturesque area. There are also riding centres in St-Leu, Les Avirons and St-Gilles-les-Bains. For details see *Chapter 16, Activities.*

GOLF

✓ **Golf du Bassin Bleu** 75 Rue Mahatma Gandhi, Villèle, 97435 St-Gilles-les-Hauts; ✆ 0262 555358; f 0262 554801; e club@golfbassinbleu.com; www.golfbassinbleu.com. An 18-hole par-72 course, which is open daily with a restaurant serving lunch. For details see *Chapter 16, Activities.*

PARAGLIDING The hills above St-Leu are the most popular area on the island for paragliding. For details see *Chapter 16, Activities.*

ACTIVITY CENTRE

Forêt de l'Aventure Route Forestière des Cryptomérias, Petite France, Maïdo; ✆ 0692 300154; e foretaventuremaido@yahoo.fr; www.foret-aventure.com. An activity centre in the forest with flying-fox slides and rope bridges. Minimum height of 140cm is required. *Admission: € 20 per adult, € 15 per child (under 16 years). Open daily 09.00–17.30, except Tue and Thu, last entry is at 15.30. Reservation recommended.*

THEATRE

Le Théâtre de Plein Air Route du Théâtre, St-Gilles-les-Bains; ☎ 0262 211694; f 0262 243822. The open-air theatre takes 1,000 spectators and has regular performances, particularly of local music. (See box *KabaRéunion*, page 308.)

CINEMA Grand Ecran (☎ *0262 244666*) in l'Hermitage is rather smart. **Ciné Splendid** is a small cinema at 146 Rue Marius et Ary Leblond, St-Paul (☎ *0262 454529*). Tickets cost around €6.

MARKETS There are markets in **St-Leu** on Saturday morning, **St-Gilles-les-Bains** on Wednesday morning and the island's largest market takes place in **St-Paul** all day Friday and Saturday morning.

WHAT TO SEE

FERME CORAIL – CENTRE D'ETUDE ET DE DÉCOUVERTE DES TORTUES MARINE DE LA RÉUNION (*Pointe des Châteaux, St-Leu;* ☎ *0262 348110;* f *0262 347687;* e *info@ tortuemarine-reunion.org; www.tortuemarine-reunion.org; open daily 09.00–18.00*) Just a few years ago this conservation project was a farm, breeding turtles for their meat and shells, which were used to make jewellery and ornaments. Thankfully, since the international ban on this activity, the farm has become a centre for captive breeding and release programmes and the study of the sea turtles of the Indian Ocean. There are seven species of sea turtle in the world and five are found around Réunion.

Most of the turtles here are green sea turtles (*Chelonia mydas*). Once abundant on the island, they are rare now, having been eaten almost to extinction by the early colonisers. The displays are interesting and informative, in French and English. You may be shocked to see trinkets made from turtle shells on sale in the shop, but the shells apparently came from the remaining stock, obtained before the ban. When visited in 2005, the centre was undergoing extensive renovations, aimed to improve turtles' living conditions. Certainly a project worth supporting. Prior to the renovations, admission fees were adult/child €5.50/3.05. These may rise following the renovations.

CONSERVATOIRE BOTANIQUE NATIONALE DE MASCARIN (*2 Rue du Père Georges, Domaine des Colimaçons, St-Leu;* ☎ *0262 249227;* f *0262 248563;* e *cbnm@cbnm.org; adult/child €5/2; open Tue–Sun 09.00–17.00*) Signed from the main road just north of St-Leu. A guided walk around the grounds allows you to see and learn about the island's native flora, as well as spices and plants used for their fruit, seeds or essential oils. Well worth visiting as a 1–2-hour excursion. There is a souvenir shop and a snack-bar. (See also *Flora*, pages 223–4.)

STELLA MATUTINA AGRICULTURAL AND INDUSTRIAL MUSEUM (*6 Allée des Flamboyants, PitonSt-Leu;* ☎ *0262 341624;* f *0262 342041;* e *com.seml@wanadoo.fr; adult/child €6.50/3; combined ticket – Stella Matutina and Maison du Volcan: €10; open Tue–Sun 09.30–17.30, last entry is at 16.45*) Housed in a former sugar factory, this museum tells the story of Réunion's agricultural and industrial development, covering the production of coffee, sugar, rum, spices and perfume. The turning to the museum is on the coast road south of St-Leu. There is an excellent restaurant. Audioguides, available in English, French or German, cost €1.

AQUARIUM DE LA RÉUNION (*Port de Plaisance, St-Gilles-les-Bains;* ☎ *0262 334400;* f *0262 334401;* e *aquarium.reunion@wanadoo.fr; adult/child €7/5; open Tue–Sun 10.00–18.30; last entry 17.30*) Fantastic interactive displays and carefully planned

Western Réunion WHAT TO SEE

20

tanks make this a fascinating aquarium, particularly good for children. Coral, sea horses, barracudas and all the snorkeller's favourites are to be seen in an environment that is intended to be as close as possible to their natural one. It takes at least an hour to have a good look around.

MUSÉE DE VILLÈLE (*Domaine Panon-Desbassyns, St-Gilles-les-Hauts;* ℄ *0262 556410;* f *0262 555191;* e *musee.villele@cg974.fr; open Tue–Sun 09.30–17.30*) A colonial estate, formerly owned by Madame Desbassyns, who is said to have been a particularly cruel plantation owner who mistreated her 300 slaves. Her story inspired Jean-François Sam-Long's novel, *Madame Desbassyns* (see page 249). The Chapelle Pointue (Pointy Chapel), where she is buried, the former slaves' hospital and the garden can be visited free of charge. Guided tours of the Chapelle Pointue and the ground floor of the house (built 1787) can be arranged and cost €2.

LE JARDIN D'EDEN (*155 RN1, l'Hermitage;* ℄/f *0262 338316;* e *jardin.eden@ runnet.com; adult/child €6/3; open Tue–Sun 10.00–18.00*) Exploring this 2ha garden, which focuses on ethnobotany, takes around 1½ hours. There are over 700 species of plant and visitors are likely to see plenty of birds and possibly a chameleon or two. Information booklets are available in English, French and German.

CHOCOLATERIE MASCARIN (*ZI Les Tamarins, 12 Rue Simone Morin, Le Port;* m *0692 687573;* e *visitchoco@gqf.com; www.gqf.com; admission: adult/child €3/1.50; open Tue and Thu, tours on reservation only*) The island's only chocolate factory, where specialities include chocolate combined with locally grown fruit, such as lychees, mango and pineapple. Visits include chocolate tasting and produce can be bought here.

21

The Interior

No visit to Réunion is complete without at least a few days spent exploring the magnificent, mountainous interior.

Visitors cannot fail to be impressed by the island's three natural amphitheatres (the Cirques of Salazie, Cilaos and Mafate), with their imposing green mountains, punctuated by waterfalls plunging down steep gorges. The island's interior also boasts the highest mountain in the Indian Ocean (Piton-des-Neiges, 3,069m) and one of our planet's most active volcanoes, the monstrous 2,631m Piton-de-la-Fournaise (see *Chapter 18, Eastern Réunion*).

There are also the two upland plains: Plaine-des-Palmistes is adjacent to spectacular and vast primary forests, while the much higher Plaine-des-Cafres is surrounded by dairy farms, evoking images of the Swiss Alps in summer. This noticeable resemblance to the Alps is enhanced by quaint mountain villages with charming architecture, a backdrop of imposing slopes and a reputation for producing excellent cheeses.

The best way to explore the interior, particularly the cirques, is on foot. Over 1,000km of hiking trails criss-cross the island, attracting enthusiasts from around the globe. (See *Hiking* in *Chapter 16, Activities*.)

LA PLAINE-DES-PALMISTES

The floriferous village of Plaine-des-Palmistes, in the permanently humid uplands high above St-Benoît, is divided into Premier Village, Deuxième Village and Petite-Plaine.

The magnificent waterfall of **Cascade Biberon**, which tumbles 240m down a sheer mountainside, is easily reached from Premier Village on the RN3. Getting there involves an uncomplicated walk of 3km from the parking area. Most of the goyavier which grows wild in Réunion now comes from this area and, in season, you're bound to see groups of people clambering about in the forests, harvesting the small, red fruit.

The **town hall** and **post office** are on Rue de la République. There's also a **war memorial**, in honour of the soldiers who died in World War I.

South of Plaine-des-Palmistes, just beyond **Col de Bellevue** on the RN3, is a large shrine to **Saint Expédit**, with a statue of the man himself in a Roman legionnaire's outfit. A plaque tells how he was whipped and beheaded on 19 April AD303 for not renouncing Christ. (See box *Saint Expédit*, page 323.)

BEBOUR-BELOUVE FORESTS Plaine-des-Palmistes is the gateway to the fabulous primeval rainforests of **Bébour-Bélouve**. These luxuriant forests constitute the single most important stop in Réunion for naturalists.

Leaving the town for the Bébour-Bélouve forest area, you drive out along Route de la Petite Plaine, towards steep, misty slopes and ridges. *En route*, you pass dairy and vegetable farms, again very reminiscent of Switzerland, Italy or France. The road winds its way steadily uphill; turn right following the arrow pointing to Bébour-Bélouve and you'll see the first slopes swathed in evergreen montane forest.

Dominating these forests are hundreds of thousands of tree ferns, from which the name 'Plaine-des-Palmistes' was (erroneously) derived. For a short distance you then drive along a dirt road, to the sign 'Forêt de la Petite Plaine', where there is a comprehensive information board about the forests of Bébour (5,800ha of primary forest) and Bélouve (889ha of primary forest).

While no wood may be removed from Bébour, tamarind wood can be taken from Bélouve, within reason and under strict supervision. There is also a zone called Canton de Duvernay, where Cryptomeria wood may be extracted. Signs advise the following rules for all the forests: *No litter, no fires, no radios and no removing of indigenous flora.*

Continue past **Canton de Duvernay**, after which you pass the **Col de Bébour** and **Rivière des Marsouins** area to your right, and you'll arrive at another large roadside information board, where a wonderful trail commences into Bébour.

This trail, which can be walked in an hour, involves a level stretch along the mountainside (roughly 1,030m above sea level), so can be managed by almost anyone. I was there in late September, when the ground was carpeted in flowering arum lilies. Now you'll just have to let me gush a bit: this forest is quite unlike any other I have been into, with mosses, lichens and other epiphytes not just festooning the trees, but often clotting on the branches, like enormous, outrageous wigs. Often, these epiphytes have a yellowish or sometimes reddish hue, so the forest is really unusual in that everything appears almost golden, not green. If you search carefully among the epiphytes, you might find some of the indigenous orchids, but they're uncommon.

Also present are most of the birds unique to Réunion. I saw a confiding pair of Mascarene paradise flycatchers, equally inquisitive Réunion bulbuls, Réunion stonechats, Réunion olive white-eye and nesting Réunion grey white-eyes. In the sky above us were Mascarene cave swiftlets, Mascarene martins and a Réunion harrier.

Leaving this magical place, I drove on to Bélouve Forest – quite a distance away. All along the road, you still see miles and miles of primary forest swathing steep, mist-enshrouded slopes and valleys.

When you see increasing numbers of the silvery tamarind trees, you'll know you're approaching Bélouve Forest. There is a point signposted and cordoned off, beyond which vehicles are not allowed. I'm told it's safe to leave your car there. It's a short walk along a road flanked by impressive tamarind forest, to the Gîte de Bélouve. There's a breathtaking viewpoint at the back of the gîte over a wide, deep valley and a disused cable-car station.

GETTING THERE AND AWAY Plaine-des-Palmistes lies on the RN3, which links St-Pierre and St-Benoît. Buses travel the whole route about three times a day (Line H), whilst others just run between Plaine-des-Palmistes and St-Benoît.

TOURIST INFORMATION The **tourist office** (✆ *0262 513992*; f *0262 514533*; e *pat.hautesplaines@wanadoo.fr. Open Mon–Fri 09.00–17.30, Sat, Sun and public holidays 10.00–17.00*) is in the Domaine des Tourelles at 260 Rue de la République, Plaine-des-Palmistes. They can provide a variety of information and organise excursions and activities, such as mountain biking and guided botanical tours.

WHERE TO STAY There are several gîtes in the area and a *ferme auberge* (farm inn). For details see *Chapter 15, Accommodation.*

Classified hotels

🏠 **Ferme du Pommeau**** (15 rooms) 10 Allée des Pois de Senteur, Plaine-des-Palmistes; ✆ 0262 514070; f 0262 513263; e la-ferme-du-pommeau@wanadoo.fr; www.pommeau.com. Comfortable Creole-style en-suite rooms with AC, TV and phone. Rooms equipped for the disabled are available. There is a restaurant and bar, and tours of the farm can be arranged. *Dbl/sgl from € 58/44 RO.*

🏠 **Hotel des Plaines** ** (14 rooms) 280 Rue de la République, 2ème Village, Plaine-des-Palmistes; ✆ 0262 513567; f 0262 5144424. Cosy hotel in the centre of Plaine-des-Palmistes. En-suite rooms with TV, phone, and heater. It has a bar, homely restaurant and TV/video lounge. Rooms can be damp as the area is extremely humid. *Dbl/sgl € 64/52 BB.*

🏠 **Les Azalées** * (36 rooms) 80 Rue de la République, 1er Village, Plaine-des-Palmistes; ✆ 0262 513424; f 0262 281797. Bungalows house clean rooms, with phone and heater. Rooms suitable for the disabled are advertised. There is a bar, games room and TV lounge, but no restaurant. *Dbl from € 45 RO.*

Classified furnished flats

🏠 **Poiny-Toplan** ** (1 villa) 4 Rue Delmas Hoareau, Plaine-des-Palmistes; ✆ 0262 460799; e marlene.poiny-toplan@wanadoo.fr. Pretty Creole-style villa with 6 bedrooms, 2 bathrooms, living room, kitchen and large veranda. Garden and parking. *Villa from € 46 per night (2 people).*

✖ **WHERE TO EAT** Supplies can be bought at the **Chez Alexis supermarket**, near the Shell petrol station in Plaine-des-Palmistes. Most of Plaine-des-Palmistes's restaurants are on Rue de la République, so finding a meal isn't difficult. Here is a selection:

✖ **Café Grègue** 303 Rue de la République, Plaine-des-Palmistes; ✆ 0262 513036. Cuisine: Creole. Good range of traditional fare. *Main courses from € 11. Lunch and dinner, closed Wednesday evening.*

✖ **Ferme du Pommeau** 10 Allée des Pois de Senteur, Plaine-des-Palmistes; ✆ 0262 514070. Cuisine: Creole, French. Excellent home-cooked food at the farm inn. *Set menus from € 14. Open daily for lunch and dinner, closed Sunday evening. Reservation recommended.*

✖ **Mme Grondin** 17 Rue Durau, Plaine-des-Palmistes; ✆ 0262 513379. Cuisine: Creole. *Set menus from € 16. On reservation only.*

✖ **Hotel des Plaines** 280 Rue de la République, Plaine-des-Palmistes; ✆ 0262 513567. Cuisine: Creole, French. A cosy restaurant with a large fireplace. *Main courses from € 11.50. Open daily for lunch and dinner.*

✖ **Les Plantanes** 167 Rue de la République, Plaine-des-Palmistes; ✆ 0262 513169. Cuisine: Creole, Chinese. *Main courses from € 10. Open Tue–Sun for lunch, dinner on reservation.*

LA PLAINE-DES-CAFRES

As you drive away from Plaine-des-Palmistes in a southwesterly direction, the road takes you higher and higher, away from the forests and into a rather desolate-looking expanse featuring harsh, scrubby vegetation and grassland. You'll also see fields of dairy cattle. This is Plaine-des-Cafres, much of which is around 2,000m above sea level.

In the village of **Bourg-Murat**, just north of Plaine-des-Cafres town, is the turning which takes you onto the road to the volcano (RF5, La Route du Volcan), Piton-de-la-Fournaise. This is also where you'll find the **Maison du Volcan** (see *What to see*, page 313).

Many of the towns that line the RN3 between here and **Le Tampon** are named according to their distance from the sea, hence Le Dixneuvième and Le Quatorzième etc. As well as producing cheese, the area is known for its geranium oil and honey.

The town of Plaine-des-Cafres is the starting point for some arduous trekking routes to places like Piton-des-Neiges, of which there are excellent views from here on clear mornings. On the main road you'll find a **post office** and **banks**. The area has a very laid-back atmosphere and, despite nearby attractions like the volcano, does not swarm with tourists. The climate can be pretty chilly, especially when the afternoon clouds smother the area in a cool fog.

If you take the turning towards **Bois Court** at the crossroads in Vingt-troisième, the road will take you to the viewpoint over the gorges of **Rivière des Citrons**. You'll see majestic waterfalls and, way down below, the isolated hamlet of **Grand Bassin**. The energetic can hike the 2km down to Grand Bassin, where there are several gîtes.

TOURIST INFORMATION The **tourist office** (☏ *0262 590982;* f *0262 592218. Open Mon 13.30–17.30, Tue–Sat 08.00–12.30 and 13.30–17.30, Sun 08.30–12.30*) is on the corner of Rues du Volcan and de Genêts in Bourg-Murat.

WHERE TO STAY
Classified hotels

🏠 **Les Géraniums** ** (25 rooms) RN3, 24ème km, La Plaine-des-Cafres; ☏ 0262 591106; f 0262 592183; e hotelgeranium@wanadoo.fr; www.hotel-geranium-runnet.com. Commands panoramic views of Piton-des-Neiges, Bois Court and Dimitile Mountain. Comfortable, spacious en-suite rooms with TV, phone and heater. The atmosphere is peaceful and the staff are friendly. Try to get a room with a mountain view. There is good restaurant (see page 312). *Dbl/sgl 84/68 BB.*

🏠 **L'Ecrin** ** (13 rooms) PK27-RN3, Bourg-Murat, La Plaine-des-Cafres; ☏ 0262 590202; f 0262 593610; e hotel.ecrin@wanadoo.fr; www.hotel-ecrin.fr.st. Conveniently located about 150m from Maison du Volcan and the road to the volcano. Rooms have TV, phone and heater. Rooms equipped

for the disabled are available. It has a restaurant. Sauna and activities can be organised. *Dbl/sgl from € 78/58 BB.*

🏠 **Hotel le Volcan** ** (10 rooms) PK27-RN3, Bourg-Murat, La Plaine-des-Cafres; ☏ 0262 275091; f 0262 591721; e aubvolcan@wanadoo.fr; www.ilereunion.com/hotelvolcan. Simple, cosy accommodation 200m from Maison du Volcan. Rooms with TV, phone, heater and terrace. *Dbl/sgl € 37/28 RO.*

🏠 **Auberge du Volcan** ** (8 rooms) PK27-RN3 Bourg-Murat, La Plaine-des-Cafres; ☏ 0262 275091; f 0262 591721. About 200m from Maison du Volcan. Eight basic en-suite rooms with TV and heater. There is a very pretty restaurant (see below). *Dbl from € 28 RO, dbl/sgl from € 67/47.50 HB.*

Classified furnished flats

🏠 **La Bertha** ** (1 villa) 128 Rue Raphael Douyère, La Plaine-des-Cafres; ☏ 0262 316284. Attractive villa with 3 bedrooms, living room, kitchen

(including dishwasher and washing machine) and garden. *Villa from € 385 per week.*

✖ WHERE TO EAT

✖ **Auberge du Volcan** Bourg-Murat, La Plaine-des-Cafres; ☏ 0262 275091. Cuisine: Creole, French. Quaint, French provincial décor and tasty food. *Main courses from € 11.50. Open 06.30–22.00, closed Sun evening.*

✖ **La Ferme du Pêcheur Gourmand** RN3, 25ème km, La Plaine-des-Cafres; ☏ 0262 592979. Cuisine: French, Creole. Charming table d'hôte restaurant. *Set menus from € 17. Lunch and dinner on reservation only.*

✖ **Les Géraniums** 24ème km, La Plaine-des-Cafres; ☏ 0262 591106. Cuisine: Creole, French. Excellent food and wonderful views. Speciality is a sauce made from geranium mushrooms. *Main courses from € 12. Open daily for lunch and dinner.*

Reservation recommended.

✖ **Relais du Commerson** 2 Route du Volcan; ☏ 0262 275287. Cuisine: Creole, Chinese, grills, snacks. Cheap and cheerful. *Open Thu–Tue 09.00–19.00.*

✖ **Le Panoramic** PK27-RN3, Bourg-Murat; La Plaine-des-Cafres; ☏/f 0262 593612. Cuisine: Creole, French. Next to the Hotel L'Ecrin. *Main courses from € 11. Open Fri–Wed for lunch, daily for dinner.*

✖ **Le Vieux Bardeau** 24ème km, La Plaine-des-Cafres; ☏ 0262 590944. Cuisine: Creole. Elegant restaurant in a charming Creole house, set back from the main road. Superb Creole dishes with a creative twist. *Main courses from € 13. Open Fri–Wed for lunch and dinner.*

NIGHTLIFE Twist Pavillon (✆ *0262 592180*) at 6 Chemin Dorey in La-Plaine-des-Cafres is open on Saturday nights and is a good place to meet the locals.

WHAT TO DO

CHEESE TASTING/BUYING There are several places where you can sample and buy cheeses in the Plaines. One of the best is **Palais du Fromage** (✆ *0262 592715. Open Tue–Sun 10.00–18.00*) on the Route du Volcan in Bourg-Murat.

HORSERIDING There is some fantastic riding country around the Plaines. The equestrian centres around La Plaine-des-Cafres offer treks to the volcano (usually two days). For details see *Chapter 16, Activities.*

WHAT TO SEE

DOMAINE DES TOURELLES (*Rue de la République, Plaine-des-Palmistes;* ✆ *0262 514759;* f *0262 514764;* e *tourelle@guetali.fr; admission free; open Mon–Tue, Thu–Fri 08.30–17.00, Sat–Sun 10.00–17.00*) A wonderful Creole house, built in the 1920s, where all manner of Réunion-made handicrafts and ornaments are on sale.

MAISON DU VOLCAN (*RN3 Bourg-Murat, La Plaine-des-Cafres;* ✆ *0262 590026;* f *0262 591671;* e *maisonduvolcan@wanadoo.fr; adult/child* €*6.50/3; combined ticket – Stella Matutina [see page 307] and Maison du Volcan:* €*10; open Tue–Sun 09.30–17.30, last entry 16.45*) Excellent exhibitions on Piton-de-la-Fournaise and volcanoes in general, including interactive displays, models and videos. Well worth a visit before seeing the real thing, not least because there is a webcam showing what is happening around Piton-de-la-Fournaise.

THE CIRQUES

A substantial portion of Réunion's interior is taken up by three 'cirques' or gigantic natural amphitheatres, which were formed when ancient volcanic craters collapsed. Subsequent erosion by the elements completed the job. The cirques, which differ considerably from each other in scenery and climate, converge at Piton-des-Neiges.

The first inhabitants of the cirques were runaway slaves or *marrons* of Malagasy origin, who fled to the mountains to escape slave hunters. Hence many villages in the cirques have Malagasy names.

CIRQUE DE CILAOS The name 'Cilaos' is derived from a Malagasy word meaning 'the place you never leave'. This is the southernmost and driest of Réunion's cirques, covering roughly 100km². It lies between the island's two highest peaks: **Piton-des-Neiges** (3,069m) and **Grand Bénard** (2,896m). Where remote mountain hamlets now nestle on small, flat plots called *ilets*, runaway slaves once sought shelter.

About 10,000 people live in this cirque, where the climate is conducive to cultivation of lentils (for the nationally popular *cari* dishes), vineyards (for local wine production) and tobacco. The climate is widely renowned as the healthiest of all Réunion's microclimates and the thermal springs there are said to have healing properties (see page 318). Note that evenings, even in summer, can be very cold, whilst the days are normally pleasant, with sunny mornings. Ordinarily, a cloak of mist descends on the town by about 15.00, adding to the dreamy ambience.

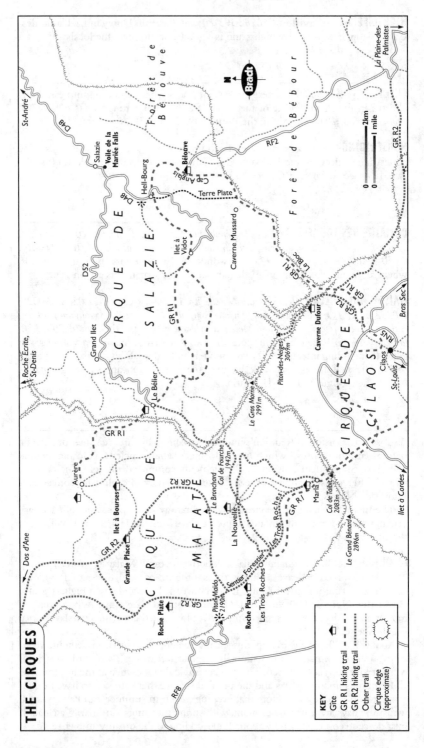

THE CIRQUES

KEY
Gite
GR R1 hiking trail
GR R2 hiking trail
Other trail
Cirque edge (approximate)

St-André
Salazie
Voile de la Mariée Falls
D48
Hell-Bourg
D52
Grand Ilet
Roche Écrite, St-Denis
Le Bélier
GR R1
Aurère
Ilet à Bourses
GR R2
Grande Place
Dos d'Âne
Roche Plate
CIRQUE DE MAFATE
GR R2
Piton Maïdo 2190m
Roche Plate
Les Trois Roches
Sentier Forestier
La Nouvelle
Le Bronchard
Col de Fourche 1942m
GR R2
Les Trois Roches
Maïdo
Col de Taïbit 2083m
GR R1
Le Grand Bénard 2896m
Ilet à Cordes
St-Louis
Cilaos
RN5
CIRQUE DE CILAOS
Bras Sec
Caverne Dufour
Piton-des-Neiges 3069m
Le Gros Morne 2991m
GR R2
GR R1
Le Bloc
GR R1
CIRQUE DE SALAZIE
Ilet à Vidot
Caverne Mussard
Terre Plate
Cap Anglais
Bélouve
Forêt de Bélouve
Forêt de Bébour
RF2
GR R2
La Plaine-des-Palmistes
RF8

N
Bradt

0   2km
0   1 mile

Getting to the town of Cilaos, the largest settlement in the cirques and an absolutely charming place, entails the infamous uphill drive from St-Louis on the coast. I say 'infamous' because this 34km road features 200 sharp hairpin bends and you won't forget negotiating it in a hurry. The trip will take you at least two hours, with stops at awesome viewpoints. Sadly, the road has seen many fatalities, as is evident from the presence of numerous roadside shrines.

Many visitors remark on the similarity of Cilaos's scenery to that of the western European Alps in summertime. This is mostly true of the region around the town of Cilaos itself, which is at 1,200m, but there are also some lush tropical forests.

Cilaos is known for the **embroidery** which is produced there and numerous shops sell locally made examples. The **hospital** (↘ *0262 317050*) is at Les Mares and **Pharmacie des Thermes** is on Rue du Père Boiteau. The **thermal springs** are outside the town, in a steep, densely wooded ravine with lots of grand old oak trees, as well as silky oaks and Norfolk Island pines. The springs were discovered in 1819. The waters, which emerge from the ground at 'bath temperature', are said to cure rheumatism and various other ailments.

Getting there and away If you drive, take your time and take care. Don't be distracted by the view – you'll need all the concentration you can get! Alternatively, you can take the bus, although this may involve at least as many, if not more, heart-in-mouth moments as driving. Buses (Line K) run between St-Pierre and Cilaos, via St-Louis, about six times a day (three times on Sunday).

Tourist information The **tourist office** (↘ *0262 317171;* f *0262 317818;* e *mmocilaos@wanadoo.fr. Open Mon–Sat 08.30–12.30 and 13.30–17.30, Sun and public holidays 09.00–12.00)* is at 2 Rue MacAuliffe. Staff can provide information on trails and local guides, and can book accommodation for any hikes you are planning.

Where to stay
Classified hotels

🏠 **Hotel les Chenêts** *** (47 rooms) 40E Chemin des Trois Mares, Cilaos; ↘ 0262 318585; f 0262 318717; e hotel.les.chenets@wanadoo.fr; www.leschenets.fr. 47 rooms and suites with TV, phone, minibar and safe. Facilities include a restaurant (see page 317), library, internet access, a pool, 2 saunas, a *hammam* (Turkish bath), helicopter pad and baby-sitting service. *Dbl/sgl from* € *110/87 BB.*

🏠 **Tsilaosa** *** (15 rooms) 21 Rue du Père Boiteau, Cilaos; ↘ 0262 373939; f 0262 373938; e su.dijoux@ool.fr; www.tsilaosa.com. A swish new option right in the centre of Cilaos. Romantic en-suite rooms with spa bath, TV, phone and minibar. There is a cosy tearoom open from 14.00. *Dbl/sgl from* € *95/79 BB.*

🏠 **Les Aloès** ** (7 rooms) 14 Rue St-Louis, Cilaos; ↘ 0262 162090; f 0262 318796; e hotel.aloes@wanadoo.fr; www.hotel.aloes.free.fr. Charming Creole building in the centre of Cilaos. Rooms have TV, phone and heater. Rooms for the disabled are available. *Dbl/sgl from* € *64/51 BB.*

🏠 **Bois Rouge** ** (5 rooms) 2 Route des Sources, Cilaos; ↘ 0262 475757; f 0262 317536; e leboisrouge@ilereunion.com; www.ilereunion.com/leboisrouge. Charming Creole house owned by artist and sculptor, Philippe Turpin, with 5 en-suite rooms decorated by the artist. Rooms have en-suite facilities, TV, heating and terrace. There is a cosy lounge with fireplace, a great place to relax after a hard day's hiking. *Dbl/sgl from* € *85/76 BB.*

🏠 **Hotel des Neiges** ** (18 rooms) 1 Rue de la Mare à Joncs, Cilaos; ↘ 0262 317233; f 0262 317398; e reservation@hotel-des-neiges.com; www.hotel-des-neiges.com. About 15 mins' walk from the town centre. Simple rooms of varying sizes, standards and prices all with en-suite facilities and phone. Some also have TV, heating and a balcony. There are 2 restaurants: Le Marla at the hotel and La Grange on the edge of the lake (see page 317). Additional facilities include internet access, a jacuzzi, sauna, snooker and table tennis. Parts of the hotel are a little dark. *Dbl/sgl from* € *60/51 RO.*

21

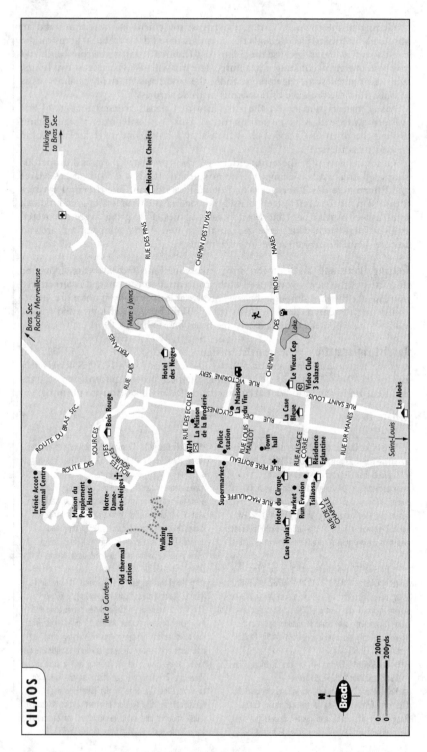

CILAOS

Hiking trail to Bras Sec

Hotel les Chenêts

RUE DES PINS

CHEMIN DES TUYAS

TROIS MARES

Mare à Joncs

Bras Sec Roche Merveilleuse

RUE DES PERTANES

Hotel des Neiges

CHEMIN DES

Le Vieux Cep

Video Club 3 Salazes

RUE SAINT LOUIS

Les Aloès

Saint-Louis

RUE VICTORINE SERY

RUE DES ECOLES

La Maison de la Broderie

La Maison du Vin

RUE DES GLYCINES

La Case Bleue

RUE DR MANES

ATM

Police station

RUE LOUIS MAILLOT

Town hall

RUE ALSACE CORRE

Résidence Eglantine

Tsilaosa

Bois Rouge

RUE DES SOURCES

ROUTE DU BRAS SEC

Irénée Accot Thermal Centre

ROUTE DES SOURCES

Maison du Peuplement des Hauts

Notre-Dame-des-Neiges

ROUTES DES SOURCES

Walking trail

Supermarket

RUE PERE BOITEAU

RUE MACAULIFFE

Hotel du Cirque

Market Run Evasion

Case Nyala

RUE DE LA CHAPELLE

Old thermal station

Ilet à Cordes

N

Bradt

0   200m
0   200yds

316

Le Vieux Cep ** (44 rooms) 2 Rue des Trois Mares, Cilaos; ✆ 0262 317189; f 0262 317768; e le.vieux.cep@wanadoo.fr; www.levieuxcep-reunion.com. Centrally located hotel, recently renovated. The attractive, Creole-style building houses comfortable en-suite rooms with TV, phone, heater and balcony. Rooms for the disabled available. Facilities include an excellent restaurant (see page 318), TV/video lounge, pool, sauna, jacuzzi and table tennis. *Dbl/sgl from* € 79/73 BB.

Hotel Du Cirque * (35 rooms) 27 Rue du Père Boiteau, Cilaos; ✆ 0262 317068; f 0262 318046. An unremarkable hotel, centrally located. Basic rooms, some of which have TV and phone. There is a restaurant serving Creole and Chinese food and a car park. *Dbl/sgl from* € 45.

Unclassified accommodation

La Case Bleue (dormitory – 20 beds) 15 Rue Alcase Corré, Cilaos; ✆ 0262 657496. Backpacker-style accommodation in a gîte run by Run Evasion. Sleeps up to 20 people. *Dormitory bed from* € 13.50. *Breakfast* € 4.50.

Case Nyala (5 rooms) 8 Ruelle des Lianes, Cilaos; ✆/f 0262 318957; e case-nyala@wanadoo.fr; www.case-nyala.com. Charming, Creole house on a quiet street. The rooms are immaculate and beautifully decorated. The public areas are warm and inviting, in particular the dining room. Rooms have en-suite facilities, TV and heating. Guests have use of a communal kitchen. *Dbl/sgl from* € 65/50 BB.

Résidence Eglantine (7 studios) 2–4 Rue Alsace Corre, Cilaos; ✆/f 0262 315772; e residence.eglantine@wanadoo.fr. Well-maintained self-catering accommodation close to the main street. Simple but pleasant studios with kitchenette, TV and heating. There is a communal barbecue. *Studio from* € 50.

Barbin Marie (3 rooms) Chemin du Matarum, Cilaos; ✆ 0262 317689. Guesthouse on a hillside slightly out of town, overlooking the cirque. Run by a charming, elderly couple who always have time for a chat (in French!). En-suite rooms with views of either Piton-des-Neiges or the town of Cilaos. Secure parking. *Dbl/sgl from* € 38/30 BB.

Classified furnished flats

Chez Noé ** 40 Rue du Père Boiteau, Cilaos; ✆/f 0262 317993. Two adjoining flats, centrally located. *Apt from* € 54 per night (2 people).

La Fleur des Sources 3 Rue des Sources, Cilaos; ✆ 0262 317059. Two immaculate adjoining flats in a brightly coloured Creole house with views over Cilaos. *Apt from* € 300 per week (2 people).

✗ **Where to eat** There is a **supermarket** on Rue du Père Boiteau, as well as bakeries, greengroceries and butcher's shops. The covered market (*marché couvert*) on the main street (Rue du Père Boiteau) sells fruit and vegetables, meat, a variety of local jams (goyavier, papaya etc) and sweet Cilaos wine.

✗ **Chez Noé** 40 Rue du Père Boiteau, Cilaos; ✆/f 0262 317993. Cuisine: Creole. Popular restaurant in the centre of Cilaos. Traditional homemade food in an atmospheric setting. The vanilla chicken is delicious. *Main courses from* € 11, 3-course menus from € 20. Open Tue–Sun 10.00–15.00 and 18.00–21.00.

✗ **La Grange** 2 Chemin Saül, Cilaos; ✆ 0262 317038. Cuisine: Creole, French. Owned by the Hotel des Neiges. Fine views from the edge of Mare à Joncs Lake. *Set menus from* € 14. Open Thu–Tue for lunch.

✗ **Le Marla** Hotel des Neiges, 1 Rue de la Mare à Joncs; ✆ 0262 317233. Cuisine: Creole, French. Very tasty *cari ti-jaques* (jack-fruit curry). *Main courses from* € 11. Open daily for lunch and dinner.

✗ **Le Moulin à Café** 68 Rue de la Mare à Joncs, Cilaos; ✆ 0262 318080. Cuisine: Creole, French, grills. Serves afternoon tea, crêpes and ice cream, as well as main meals. *Main courses from* € 10. Open 09.00–22.00, closed Fri evening and Sun.

✗ **Les Physalis** Les Chenêts Hotel, 40E Chemin des Trois Mares, Cilaos; ✆ 0262 318585. Cuisine: French, Creole. Smart yet cosy. *Main courses from* € 14. Open daily for lunch and dinner.

✗ **Petit Randonneur** 60 Rue du Père Boiteau; ✆ 0262 317955. Cuisine: Creole. *Main courses from* € 8. Open 09.00–18.00, closed Tue afternoon and Wed.

✗ **Le Platane** 46 Rue du Père Boiteau; ✆ 0262 317723. Cuisine: Creole, Italian. Neat little restaurant in the centre of town. *Pizzas from* € 6, main courses from € 10. Open Wed–Mon for lunch and dinner.

21

✘ Le Vieux Cep 2 Rue des Trois Mares, Cilaos; ✆ 0262 317189. Cuisine: Creole, French. Wide range of dishes with specialities including duck *cari* with corn and the delicious home-smoked pork with Cilaos lentils. The restaurant's excellent reputation is well deserved. *Main courses from* € 14. *Open daily for lunch and dinner. Reservation recommended, particularly for dinner.*

Other practicalities

Money and banking There is no bank but there is an **ATM** outside the **post office**. To be on the safe side, it is best to bring sufficient cash with you as this is the only ATM in Cilaos and it cannot always be relied upon.

Communications The **post office** is in the main street through the village (Rue du Père Boiteau), not far from the church. **Internet access** is available at **Video Club 3 Salazes** (*40 Rue St Louis;* ✆ *0262 318395*). For details see page 251.

What to do

Spa treatments

Irénée Accot Thermal Centre (*Route de Bras-Sec, Cilaos;* ✆ *0262 317227;* f *0262 317657;* e *thermes-cilaos@cg974.fr; open Mon–Sat 08.00–12.00 and 14.00–18.00, Sun and public holidays 09.00–17.00*) Just above the town of Cilaos, the Irenée Accot Thermal Centre was opened in July 1988, its proprietors having capitalised on the combination of thermal springs and beautiful, tranquil surrounds.

Certain elements in the water, like sodium, magnesium and calcium, are apparently effective in the treatment of complications varying from rheumatism to digestive ailments.

A range of treatments is offered from spa baths (€ 17) to health packages lasting several days. The combination options are good value and typically include two or more of the following: sauna, mineral spa bath, shiatsu, algae or Dead Sea salt treatment and electro-belt massage.

The rates are reasonable, from roughly € 10 per treatment or from € 32 for combined treatments.

Hiking Needless to say, Cilaos has numerous possibilities for those into walking, hiking or lengthy treks. Even if you do only one of the short walks to nearby villages, you can still enjoy some breathtaking views. Two simple options which come to mind here are the roads to **Bras Sec** village and to the **Roche Merveilleuse**, a superb mountain viewpoint overlooking the whole cirque. You can also drive to the base of Roche Merveilleuse and a short climb up some steps takes you to the viewpoint.

For the adventurous, Cilaos is the starting point for the arduous two-day trek to Piton-des-Neiges (see pages 254–6 for more details).

Mountain biking Cilaos is an excellent area for mountain biking. There are two particularly popular routes: the first starts in town, then crosses **Plateau des Chênes** and ends at **Roche Merveilleuse** (grading: moderate). The other starts in **Bras Sec** village, then takes you to **Bras de Benjoin** village and on to Cilaos. **Run Evasion** and **Réunion Sensations** both have mountain bikes and helmets for hire (for contact details see *Chapter 16, Activities*, pages 253–4).

Other outdoor activities Cilaos is a popular area for numerous other activities, especially **canyoning** and **river hiking**. Run Evasion has an outlet in Cilaos, which sells outdoor equipment and can arrange activities. For details of activities and operators, see *Chapter 16, Activities*.

What to see

La Maison de la Broderie (*4 Rue des Ecoles, Cilaos;* \ *0262 317748;* f *0262 318038; admission* €*1; open Mon–Sat 09.30–12.00 and 14.00–17.00*) An insight into the traditional **embroidery** for which the area is known. There is a demonstration workshop and exhibition. Items are on sale.

La Maison du Vin (*34 des Glycines, Cilaos;* \ *0262 317658;* f *0262 317970;* e *lechaidecilaos@wanadoo.fr; wine tasting:* €*2.29; open Mon–Sat 09.00–12.00 and 13.30–16.00*) Guided tours and a short film (in French) exploring the production of wine in the Cilaos area, followed by an opportunity to taste and buy some of the wine.

Maison du Peuplement des Hauts (*5 bis Chemin de Séminaire, Cilaos;* \ *0262 318801;* f *0262 318156; adult/child* €*5/2.90; open Mon–Sat 10.00–12.00 and 14.30–18.00, Sun and public holidays 09.30–11.30 and 13.30–16.30*) Exhibition which tells the story of how the island's interior became inhabited, first by *marrons* (runaway slaves) and later by outcast Réunionnais. It is well worth a visit and the guided tours are highly recommended. There is a small gift shop.

CIRQUE DE SALAZIE The largest of the cirques, Salazie measures about 12km by 9km and has a population of about 8,000. Its name comes from a Malagasy word meaning 'good place to stay'.

The cirque was only settled by European farmers during the mid 19th century, after a hot spring was found at **Hell-Bourg**. A military hospital was established in 1860 to treat soldiers wounded during unrest in Madagascar. Thanks to its pleasant climate, Hell-Bourg became a popular place for coastal inhabitants to visit during the hot months. In 1948, a severe cyclone somehow destroyed the hot spring and Hell-Bourg was all but deserted until 1980, when the government realised its potential value for culture and nature-oriented tourism.

Cirque de Salazie is the greenest of the cirques and is characterised by no fewer than a hundred waterfalls, which drop down incredibly high, steep gorges. Réunion's best-known waterfall, the exquisite **Voile de la Mariée**, or 'Bridal Veil', is in this cirque. Salazie is the most accessible of the cirques, a picturesque 20-minute drive from St-André.

Salazie and Hell-Bourg The drive inland from St-André takes you into increasingly lush and verdant surrounds, along the Rivière du Mât (you also pass through a village of the same name). Then, looming up ahead, are the high gorges, usually shrouded in a mist mantle. You'll know you're approaching the mouth of the cirque when you see several narrow waterfalls, one of which continually showers on to the tarred road, giving you a free carwash. A signpost announces it as *Pisse en l'air* (I don't think that one needs translating!).

Salazie is the area where Réunion's most famed vegetable, the *chouchou* (*Sechium edule*), is cultivated. You will see many small homes surrounded by frames engulfed by this fast-growing climbing plant. The uses for it are many and menus in the area's eateries typically feature everything from *chouchou* stuffed with prawns and melted cheese to *chouchou* cake as a dessert.

The first town you'll come to in the cirque is Salazie itself, but most visitors continue to the smaller town of Hell-Bourg, quite a distance higher up. Few tourists spend any time in Salazie but it does have a small **supermarket** and a **post office** complete with **ATM** and **payphone**. Both Salazie and Hell-Bourg have **pharmacies**.

Hilary Bradt

Hell-Bourg is the centre for hiking in Réunion. Apart from its superb mountain scenery and numerous trails, it's such a pretty village that it invites a stay of a few days even for casual walkers. Be warned, however: it rains a lot in Hell-Bourg and the most popular trails are consequently very muddy. Good rain gear and waterproof hiking boots are a prerequisite.

An information sheet on the walks (*Liste des Balades dans le Cirque de Salazie*) is available from the tourist office in Hell-Bourg (for contact details see opposite). They are also marked on map 4402 RT (St-Denis) in the IGN 1:25,000 series of six maps covering Réunion. It is useful to know that the official French trail system, the Grandes Randonnées, are marked by red and white paint. Other footpaths are indicated in red and yellow.

As a warm-up try **Les Trois Cascades** (one hour there and back) where you'll find a series of waterfalls in a lovely mountain setting, or the four-hour walk (there and back) to **Source Manouilh**. More challenging is the climb up to the top of the escarpment and Bélouve Forest. Beginning at the town hall, this is a two-hour slog up a well-constructed path to the **Gîte de Bélouve** where, disconcertingly, you'll find some parked cars (it is connected by forest road to Plaine des Palmistes). The altitude gain from Hell-Bourg to the gîte is about 500m, so it's hard work but the views and vegetation on the way up are magnificent. The return takes only about an hour.

Once here, you can walk to the famous **Trou de Fer**, a deep pool fed by waterfalls hurtling down the sheer mountainsides that surround it. However, you should allow at least four hours for this walk (there and back). The latter part of the trail can be very muddy and difficult, and although it looks level on the map it is steeply up and down the whole way. So if you are an average hiker you need to leave Hell-Bourg early in the morning to be sure to be back before dark, and be fit enough for a seven-hour walk. It's much better, therefore, to stay in the comfortable dormitories in the gîte. Book as far in advance as possible (`\f` *0262 412123;* e *gite.belouve@wanadoo.fr*).

As you continue on the winding road from Salazie to Hell-Bourg, it is worth stopping at the **Point du Jour** viewpoint for fantastic views of the cirque. There is a map indicating which peak is which.

Nearby is the sign to the lake of **Mare à Poule d'Eau**, which can be reached on foot or mountain bike. This is where the local inhabitants used to come to collect their water. The village of the same name is just a little further on, shortly beyond which are the famous **Voile de la Mariée Falls** (Bridal Veil Falls). The falls are signed and there is space to pull in and admire them from the road as they tumble into the gorge below.

As you travel between Salazie and Hell-Bourg it is worth making the short detour to **Grand Ilet**. It is a pretty, unspoilt village cupped by the cirque's commanding mountains. The village's **Church of St Martin** is a beautiful example of Creole architecture, with its *lambrequin* (filigree-style decoration), its light blue shutters and its tamarind shingle walls. A sign next to the bell tower, which is now in the grounds of the church, tells the building's tortured history – detailing the numerous times it has been destroyed, moved and rebuilt. In the centre of Grand Ilet is a mountain-biking station with a signboard detailing the local trails. **Grand Ilet** is the starting point for hikes to St-Denis via **La Roche Ecrite**, while nearby **Le Bélier** allows access to the hiking trails which connect

Cirque de Salazie and Cirque de Mafate. The viewpoint at **Mare à Martin** provides good views of the cirque and its villages.

In contrast to Salazie, which has little charm, **Hell-Bourg** is picture-postcard-perfect. Residents will proudly tell you that Hell-Bourg was awarded the prestigious title of 'Most Beautiful Village in France' in 2000 (I know, 'in France' still seems odd, doesn't it?). It features small Creole houses with tiled roofs, intricate railings and explosions of colourful flowers in the small gardens and ubiquitous flower boxes. EU money has been made available to restore many of the **Creole houses** to their former glory. The wrought-iron *lambrequins* on the front of the eaves are typical, as are the bright colours.

Hell-Bourg is popular with tourists – there are many **souvenir shops** and numerous good Creole restaurants.

Getting there and away Salazie is easily reached by car or local bus service from St-André along a twisty but well-maintained road. Buses travel regularly between Salazie and Hell-Bourg, except on Sunday.

Tourist information Information about the area, hiking and bookings at *gîtes de montagne* are available from the **tourist office** in Hell-Bourg (*47 Rue Général de Gaulle, Hell-Bourg;* \ *0262 478989;* f *0262 478970;* e *pat.salazie@wanadoo.fr. Open Mon–Thu 09.00–17.00, Fri 09.00–12.00*).

Where to stay

Classified hotels

Relais des Cimes ** (30 rooms) 67 Rue Général de Gaulle, Hell-Bourg, Salazie; \ 0262 478158; f 0262 478211; e relais.des.cimes@wanadoo.fr; www.relaisdescimes.com. Owned by Mamie Javel, the renowned author of a Creole recipe book, the restaurant here is exceptional (see page 322). Now in her eighties, Mamie Javel is still often seen taking charge in the restaurant and bar, although her son has taken over much of the running of the hotel. The rooms are comfortable with en suite, TV, phone and heater; many have superb views. The new rooms are particularly appealing. *Dbl/sgl from* € 65/52 BB.

Unclassified hotels

Le Bananier (12 rooms) 134 Rue Georges Pompidou, Salazie; \ 0262 475705; f 0262 475165. A good basic option in the village of Salazie. Spotless, cosy en-suite rooms. There is a TV lounge, a car park and a good restaurant (see page 322). *Dbl/sgl* € 50/35 RO. Breakfast € 5.50.

L'Orchidée Rose (5 rooms) 26 Rue Olivier Manès, Hell-Bourg; \ 0262 478722; f 0262 478685; e colette@orchideerose.net; www.orchideerose.net. On a quiet back street. Three dbl rooms, 1 triple and 1 family room. All have en-suite facilities and are clean and well furnished. There is a cyber café here. *Dbl from* € 45.50 BB.

Classified furnished flats

Chez Festin ** Impasse Sisayhes 03, Rond-Point, Hell-Bourg; \ 0262 465461. Three-bedroom house with terrace and parking. *From* € 275 *per week (6 people).*

Youth hostel

One of the island's 3 hostels is in Hell-Bourg at 2 Rue de la Cayenne (\ 0262 474131). It has recently been renovated and is a good option for the budget conscious. To stay there you must have a membership card. For details see *Chapter 15, Accommodation.*

✗ Where to eat There are small **general shops** in both Salazie and Hell-Bourg, where you can stock up on food for hiking. The **supermarket** in Hell-Bourg on the corner of Rues Général de Gaulle and Cayenne is probably your best bet.

Le Bananier 134 Rue Georges Pompidou, Salazie; ☏ 0262 475705. Cuisine: Creole, French. No great views but a very pleasant place to eat. Specialities include banana-smoked chicken and fish with banana. *Main courses from €9. Set menus from €16. Open Wed–Mon for lunch, daily for dinner.*

Chez Alice 1 Rue des Sangliers, Hell-Bourg; ☏ 0262 478624. Cuisine: Creole, French, Chinese. Unpretentious restaurant set back on a side street. *Main courses from €9.50, set menus from €13. Open Tue–Sun for lunch and dinner.*

Le P'tit Bambou 166 Rue Georges Pompidou, Salazie; ☏ 0262 475151. Cuisine: Creole, European. Has a terrace overlooking the town hall and church. Specialities include beef with watercress and smoked duck *cari*. *Main courses from €9. Open Thu–Tue for lunch, dinner on reservation.*

Relais des Cîmes 67 Rue Général de Gaulle, Hell-Bourg; ☏ 0262 478158. Cuisine: Creole, French. Arguably the island's best Creole cuisine. Meals are prepared using local products and according to Mamie Javel's famous recipes. Copies of her Creole cookbook are on sale in the restaurant. The décor is unmistakeably French, with red and white checked tablecloths and curtains. The *cari ti jaques boucané* and the *poulet coco* are superb. *Main courses from €11. Dégustation menus (2 starters, 2 main courses and one dessert) from €16. Open daily for lunch and dinner.*

Salaozy 24 Rue Amiral Lacaze, Hell-Bourg; ☏ 0262 478282. Cuisine: Creole. In a charming Creole *case* (house). Traditional cooking on a wood stove. *Set menus from €15. Open daily for lunch and dinner.*

Ti-Chouchou 42 Rue Général de Gaulle, Hell-Bourg; ☏ 0262 478093. Cuisine: Creole, French. Eat-in or take-away. As the name suggests, specialises in chouchou. Popular, so try to book in advance. *Main courses from €9, set menus from €13. Open Sat–Thu for lunch and dinner.*

Other practicalities

Money and banking Neither Salazie nor Hell-Bourg has a bank but there is an **ATM** outside the post office in Salazie.

Communications There are **post offices** in Salazie, Hell-Bourg and Grand Ilet. **Internet access** is available at **Cyber C@se Creole** (*L'Orchidée Rose, 26 Rue Olivier Manès, Hell-Bourg;* ☏ *0262 478722*) and at **Cyber Salazie** (*Rue Georges Pompidou, Salazie;* ☏ *0262 477524*), opposite the post office. For details see page 251.

What to do

Hiking Most of Salazie's visitors come here, at least in part, for the hiking. The offices of the adventure information centre, **Maham**, are in Hell-Bourg. This is the place to arrange long hikes of two to seven days and find information on adventure sports such as canyoning. For details see *Chapter 16, Activities.*

Mountain biking Numerous trails snake around Salazie, Hell-Bourg and Grand Ilet. For more information on mountain biking see *Chapter 16, Activities.*

What to see

Maison Folio (*20 Rue Amiral Lacaze, Hell-Bourg;* ☏f *0262 478098;* e *m.folio@wanadoo.fr; adult/child under 10 €4/free; open daily 09.00–11.30 and 14.00–17.00*) A much-photographed Creole home which has preserved the elegant style of the 19th century. Built in 1870 and renovated in the late 1970s, the house, garden and furniture all accurately reproduce the era. Note that the kitchen and dining room are in a separate building at the back, which was the norm in Creole homes. In the garden, ornamental, medicinal and edible plants are typically bunched together in each flowerbed. The stories told by the present owners provide an interesting insight.

Ecomusée Salazie (*60 Rue du Général de Gaulle, Hell-Bourg;* ☏ *0262 478686;* f *0262 478617;* e *ecomusee-salazie@wanadoo.fr; guided tour [1 hour] €4; admission €2; open daily 09.00–16.00*) Just outside Hell-Bourg on the road to Salazie. A fascinating exhibition of photos, press cuttings and videos on the history of the

Alexandra Richards

As well as the roadside shrines to Christ and the Virgin Mary, there are many dedicated to Saint Expédit, which are typically red. Regarded as the national saint of Réunion, he is revered by Réunionnais of all religions.

Saint Expédit has taken on something of a sinister nature in the island's folklore. He is considered particularly effective and prompt (expeditious) at carrying out requests for revenge by placing curses on people. However, in return he demands payment, otherwise he will punish the person who requested his assistance. For this reason the red shrines are typically smothered by offerings, such as candles, flowers and red material, as well as messages of thanks.

Don't be surprised if you see decapitated statues of Saint Expédit in roadside shrines. The damage is either punishment for an unfulfilled request or has been done in order to break a curse that someone feels has been put on them by the saint.

The story of Saint Expédit is very confused. He is believed by many to have been a Roman legionnaire, named Expeditus, who was beheaded on 9 April AD303 in Malatya (Turkey) for not renouncing Christ.

However, some maintain that this story is a fabrication and that the saint's popularity in Réunion is the result of a misunderstanding. The story goes that at the time of the early colonists, the religious community was having difficulty impressing the importance of its values on the population, so wrote to the Vatican to request some religious relics to help them drive their message home.

Finally, at the end of the 19th century a small wooden box arrived bearing the word *expédit* (despatched). Inside were a few scattered bones. The religious community rejoiced – the relics that they had requested had at last arrived. After some discussion, they concluded that the remains must belong to Saint Expédit, as that was the inscription on the box.

Whichever version you believe, the Church's position is clear. In 1905, Pope Pius X demanded that Saint Expédit's name be struck off the list of martyrs and all images of him removed from churches. By this stage Saint Expédit was already adored throughout Réunion and his popularity has never wavered.

area. The photos and press cuttings provide a particularly good insight into the lives of the early inhabitants. One newspaper article reveals that it snowed in Hell-Bourg on 13 June 1911. In French only.

Creole houses (Cases Créoles) (*Guided tours are arranged via the tourist office;* ☎ *0262 478989 and operate Tue–Fri; tour: €4*) A leaflet on Hell-Bourg's Creole houses and the route you can follow to see them is available at the tourist office and costs €5. Alternatively, you can join a guided walking tour of Hell-Bourg, with a local guide providing information on the architecture, history and residents of the village's Creole homes. At this stage, the leaflet and the guided tour are available only in French.

CIRQUE DE MAFATE Spanning 72km², Mafate is the smallest and most tropical of the cirques. On its northern rim is the **Plaine d'Affouches**, which overlooks St-Denis and the north coast. On its western rim is **Piton Maïdo** (2,190m), which overlooks the dry west coast. To its south lies the Cirque de Cilaos.

Mafate is a wild, sparsely inhabited, mystifying place. Its name has suitably intriguing origins: it is said that a Malagasy sorcerer and runaway slave, named

Mafaty (meaning 'dangerous one'), lived at the foot of **Le Bronchard** (1,261m). He was eventually caught in 1751 by François Mussard, a bounty hunter.

The cirque's first inhabitants were indeed runaway slaves after the agricultural colonisation of the island in the 1730s, then the *Créoles Blancs* (White Creoles) arrived following the abolition of slavery in 1848. Today, approximately 650 people reside in remote mountain hamlets, such as **Marla**, **La Nouvelle** and **Aurère**. They live off the land, in virtual isolation from the outside world. There are no roads, just 100km of walking trails. Supplies such as medication are brought in by helicopter, yet many of the Mafatais have never seen a car.

Visitors need to spend at least two days in Mafate to get a feel for the cirque. Access is on foot from Cilaos, via the **Col du Taïbit**, from Hell-Bourg via the **Col des Bœufs**, and from **Maïdo**, **Sans-Souci**, or **Dos d'Ane**. The easiest option is from Hell-Bourg; even easier is flying in by helicopter. If your time is limited, **Piton Maïdo**, which is accessible by car from St-Paul, provides superb views of the cirque.

There have been some terrible stories of hikers disappearing and even being found murdered in Mafate. Don't panic; this hasn't happened for a while! However, it is always safer to hike with other people, preferably a qualified guide, and a wise precaution is to tell someone where you're going and for how long.

Where to stay Many independent hikers choose to camp in this remote area. It can be a wonderful experience with fabulous starry skies. However, it does get very cold so bring along suitable clothing. If you do camp, be sure to clear up completely when you leave.

The alternatives to camping are *gîtes de montagne* and *gîtes d'étapes*. For details of these, see *Chapter 16, Activities,* pages 255–6.

Where to eat If you're staying in a gîte, you can order breakfast and dinner in advance. You'll need to bring any other food with you, to fuel all that walking. If you run out of snacks, don't despair – there are small food shops in most of Mafate's villages, including La Nouvelle, Marla, Roche Plate, Grande Place les Hauts, Ilet à Malheur, Aurère and Ilet aux Orangers. They are usually closed on Sunday afternoon and Monday morning.

Appendix I

LANGUAGE

USEFUL PHRASES – HOW TO SAY THEM IN CREOLE

To speak Creole, the slightest knowledge of French will be useful for the formalities: for instance, 'Good Morning' is '*Bonzoor*'. Here are some useful phrases that differ from the French. They have been written phonetically (as they should be pronounced).

	Mauritian Creole	Réunionnais Creole
How are you?	*Ki man yeah?*	*Komon ee lay?*
Very well, and you?	*Mwa bee-an, eh oo?*	*Lay la eh oo?*
I'm not well	*Mwa pa bee-an*	*Mi lay pa bee-an*
What is your name?	*Ki oo non?*	*Komon oo apel?*
How old are you?	*Ki arj too on?*	*Kay laz oo nayna?*
What are you doing?	*Ki toe pay fare?*	*Ko sa oo fay?*
I don't understand	*Mwa pa kompran*	*Mi kompran pa*
Speak slowly	*Pa koz tro veet*	*Koz doosmon*
I don't speak Creole	*Mwa pa koz Kreol*	*Mi koz pa Kreol*
I don't know	*Mwa pa konnay*	*Mi konnay pa*
How much is it?	*Koomian sa?*	*Koomian i koot?*
It's too expensive	*Li tro ser*	*Lay tro ser*
Good/That's fine	*Li bon*	*Lay bon*
Where are you going?	*Kot oo pay allay?*	*Oo sa oo sa va?*
I want to go to…	*Mwa oo-lay al…*	*Mi vay allay a…*
Take me to the hotel	*Amen mwa lotel*	*Amen a mwa a lotel*
I want to stay	*Mwa pay restay*	*Mi vay restay*
Would you like a drink?	*Oo poo bwah keek soz?*	*Oo vay bwah keek soz?*
I'd like wine	*Mwa oo-lay do van*	*Mi voodray do van*
What's this?	*Ki etay sa?*	*Ko sa ee lay?*
I love you	*Mwa kontan twa*	*Mi em a-oo*
Goodbye	*Sallaam*	*Na wa/nooa troov*

HOW TO SAY PLACE NAMES IN MAURITIUS AND RODRIGUES

Stressed syllables are shown in bold.

Baie du Tombeau	Beige-tom-**bo**
Beau Bassin	Bo Bas**sa**
Belle Mare	Bel-mar
Case Noyale	Kaz noy-**al**
Curepipe	Kewr-**peep**
Grand Bassin	Gron Bas**sa**
Gris Gris	Gree-gree
Ile aux Aigrettes	Eel-oh-say**gret**

Ile aux Cerfs	Eel-oh-**sair**
Mahébourg	Mayberg *or* Mah-ay-bour
Morne Brabant	Morn Bra**bon**
Port Louis	Por(t) Loo-**ee**
Port Mathurin	Por(t) Ma-to-**ra**
Quatre Bornes	Katr born
Réduit	**Ray**dwee
Rodrigues	Rod**reegs**
Rose Hill	Roh**zill**
Souillac	**Soo**-ee-yak
Triolet	**Tree**-oh-lay
Trou aux Biches	Troo-oh-**beesh**
Trou d'Eau Douce	Troodoh-**doo**
Vacoas	**Va**-kwa

In Réunion (Ray-oo-nee-on), standard French pronunciation applies.

Appendix 2

ACCOMMODATION

IN MAURITIUS AND RODRIGUES The following list summarises the accommodation in Mauritius and Rodrigues that is included in the book. It also indicates the hotel's category, number of rooms and the page number of the relevant description. 'SC' in the number of rooms column indicates that the hotel also offers self-catering accommodation. The categories are as follows:

Category A: luxury Doubles from Rs17,000 (€485) on BB, or Rs18,000 (€515) on HB, per night based on two people sharing.

Category B: upmarket Doubles from Rs7,000 (€200) to Rs17,000 (€485) on BB, or Rs8,000 (€230) to Rs18,000 (€515) on HB, per night based on two people sharing.

Category C: mid range Doubles from Rs2,500 (€70) to Rs7,000 (€200) on BB, or Rs3,200 (€90) to Rs8,000 (€230) on HB, per night based on two people sharing.

Category D: budget Doubles less than Rs2,500 (€70) on BB, or Rs3,200 (€90) on HB, per night based on two people sharing.

For a full explanation of the categories, including the kinds of facilities you can expect, see *Chapter 3, Accommodation*. For exchange rates see *Money and banking* in the same chapter.

Mauritius

Name and location	Category	No of rooms	Page no
Hotel Les Aigrettes, Mahébourg	D	19	149
Hotel Ambre, Belle Mare	B	246	139
Archipel Bungalows, Grand Gaube	D	10/SC	131
Auberge Aquarella, Mahébourg	D	10	149
Auberge de la Madelon, Curepipe	D	15	175
Le Barachois, Anse Bambous	D	16	142
Le Beach Club, Pereybère	D	21/SC	129
Beau Rivage, Belle Mare	B	170	139
Belle Mare Plage Hotel, Poste de Flacq	B	256	138
Berjaya Le Morne, Le Morne	B	200	161
Blue Lagoon Beach Hotel, Blue Bay	C	72	149
Hotel Bougainville, Trou d'Eau Douce	C	50	141
Bourbon Tourist Hotel, Port Louis	D	16	110
Hotel Le Canonnier, Pointe aux Canonniers	B	247	121
Casa Florida, Pereybère	D	85/SC	129
Casuarina Hotel, Trou aux Biches	C	109/SC	121
Chez Tino, Trou d'Eau Douce	D	3/SC	141
City Hotel, Port Louis	D	20	110
Le Coco Beach, Belle Mare	B	333	138–9

Name and location	Category	No of rooms	Page no
La Cocoteraie, Mont Choisy	D	19/SC	122
Coco Villa, Mahébourg	D	19/SC	149
Coin de Mire Hotel, Cap Malheureux	C	90	131
Colonial Beach Hotel, Pointe aux Piments	C	43	120
Colonial Coconut, Grand Baie	D	34	126
Coralia Mont Choisy, Mont Choisy	C	88	121–2
Côte d'Azur Hotel, Pereybère	D	21/SC	129
Dinarobin Hotel, Le Morne	A	172	160
Domaine du Chasseur, Vieux Grand Port	C	5	142
El Monaco, Quatre Bornes	D	92	171
Elysium, Pereybère	D	8	129
Emeraude Hotel, Belle Mare	D	60	139
Escale Vacances, Flic en Flac	D	18/SC	164
Etoile de Mer Hotel, Trou aux Biches	D	31	122
Eureka, Moka	C	7	178
Euro Vacances, Beau Bassin	D	12	170
Les Filaos Village, Pointe aux Canonniers	D	13/SC	122
GBTT Beach Villas, Mont Choisy	D	14/SC	122
GBTT Rapsodie, Trou aux Biches	D	4/SC	122
GBTT Villas Mont Choisy, Mont Choisy	D	15/SC	122
Gold Crest Hotel, Quatre Bornes	D	59	171
Le Grand Bleu, Trou aux Biches	D	50/SC	122
The Heritage Golf & Spa Resort, Bel Ombre	B	160	153
Hibiscus Holiday Village, Pereybère	C	15	128
Hilton Mauritius Resort, Wolmar	B	193	163
Indian Resort, Le Morne	B	349	161
Island Sports Club Hotel, Grande Rivière Noire	C	66	161
Klondike Hotel, Flic en Flac	D	31/SC	164
Kuxville, Cap Malheureux	C	25/SC	130
Labourdonnais Waterfront Hotel, Port Louis	B	109	110
Les Lataniers Bleus, Rivière Noire	D	3/SC	161
Legends, Grand Gaube	B	198	130
Mandarin Hotel, Floréal	D	98	173
Marina Resort, Anse La Raie	C	122	130–1
Maritim Hotel, Balaclava	B	221	119
Le Mauricia, Grand Baie	C	197	124
Le Meridien, Pointe aux Piments	B	198	119–20
Merville Beach Hotel, Grand Baie	C	169	124–6
L'Oasis, Pointe aux Piments	D	22/SC	120
The Oberoi, Balaclava	A	76	119
Ocean Beauty, Pereybère	C	10	128
Ocean Villas, Grand Baie	D	31/SC	126
One&Only Le Saint Géran Hotel, Poste de Flacq	A	163	138
One&Only Le Touessrok, Trou d'Eau Douce	A	200	140
Hotel Les Orchidées, Grand Baie	D	29	126
Palmar Beach Resort, Belle Mare	C	70	139
Paradis Hotel, Le Morne	B	299	161
Paradise Cove Hotel, Anse La Raie	B	67	130
Paul et Virginie Hotel, Grand Gaube	C	81	131
Les Pavillons, Le Morne	B	149	161
Le Pearle Beach, Flic en Flac	-	-	164
Pereybère Beach Apartments, Pereybère	D	15/SC	129

Name and location	Category	No of rooms	Page no
La Pirogue, Wolmar	B	248	163
La Plantation, Balaclava	B	270	120
Le Preskil Beach Resort, Blue Bay	C	200	148
Le Prince Maurice, Poste de Flacq	A	89	138
The Residence, Belle Mare	B	163	139
Résidence Choy Tours, Trou d'Eau Douce	D	3/SC	141
The Royal Palm Hotel, Grand Baie	A	84	124
Le Saint Georges, Port Louis	C	80	110
Le Sands Resort, Wolmar	C	93	163–4
Le Shandrani, Blue Bay	B	327	148
Silver Beach, Trou d'Eau Douce	C	60	141
Sofitel Imperial Hotel, Wolmar	B	191	163
Spice Garden Hotel, Pointe aux Piments	C	26	120
Le Suffren Hotel & Marina, Port Louis	C	100	110
Sugar Beach Resort, Wolmar	B	238	163
Le Surcouf Village, Belle Mare	D	35/SC	139
Taj Exotica Resort & Spa, Wolmar	A	130	163
Tamarin Hotel, Tamarin	C	67	161
Le Tamaris, Grand Baie	D	15/SC	126
Tarisa Resort, Trou aux Biches	C	75	122
Le Telfair, Bel Ombre	B	158	153
Le Tropical, Trou d'Eau Douce	B	60	141
Trou aux Biches Village Hotel, Trou aux Biches	B	197	121
Ventura Hotel, Grand Baie	D	32	126
Veranda Hotel, Grand Baie	C	94/SC	126
Le Victoria Hotel, Pointe aux Piments	B	248	119
Villa Paul and Virgine, Flic en Flac	D	13	164
Villas Caroline, Flic en Flac	C	74/SC	164
Villas Le Guerlande, Blue Bay	D	17/SC	149
Villas Mon Plaisir, Pointe aux Piments	D	43	120
La Voile d'Or Hotel & Spa, Bel Ombre	B	181	152
Welcome Hotel, Curepipe	D	11	175

Rodrigues

Auberge Anse aux Anglais, Anse aux Anglais	D	21	208
Auberge de la Montagne, Grande Montagne	D	5	209
Auberge Les Filaos, Anse aux Anglais	D	14	208
Chez Claudine, St-François	D	4	209
Chez Edouard, Anse aux Anglais	D	3/SC	208
Chez Mireille Jean-Louis, Nassola	D	2	209
Les Cocotiers Hotel, Anse aux Anglais	C	42/SC	208
La Collinière, Brûlé	D	5	209
Cotton Bay Hotel, Pointe Coton	C	48	208
Domaine de Décidé, Nouvelle Découverte	D	2/SC	209
Escale Vacances, Port Mathurin	D	23	206
Mourouk Ebony Hotel, Pâté Reynieux	C	30	208
Pension Ciel d'Eté, Port Mathurin	D	15	206
Pensionnat Beau Sejour, Anse aux Anglais	D	5	208–9
Pointe Vénus, Mont Vénus	C	54	207–8
Les Rosiers, Grande Montagne	D	5	209
Le Tamaris, Port Mathurin	D	15/SC	206
Les Varangues, Grand Baie	D	4/SC	209

IN RÉUNION The following list summarises the accommodation in Réunion that is mentioned in the book. It also includes the number of stars awarded according to the official French system (where applicable), the number of rooms and the page number of the hotel description. 'SC' in the number of rooms column indicates that the hotel also offers self-catering accommodation. For full descriptions of the types of accommodation available in Réunion, see *Chapter 15*, *Accommodation*. For exchange rates see *Money and banking* in the same chapter.

Hotels As a guide, the number of stars equates approximately to the following price ranges:

★★★★	Doubles from € 160 to € 220 on RO, per night based on two people sharing
★★★	Doubles from € 80 to € 160 on RO, per night based on two people sharing
★★	Doubles from € 40 to € 80 on RO, per night based on two people sharing
★	Doubles from € 30 to € 40 on RO, per night based on two people sharing
(no stars)	Doubles from € 20 to € 30 on RO, per night based on two people sharing
u/c (unclassified)	Wide range of prices, but usually doubles less than € 45 on RO, per night based on two people sharing

Name and location	Category	No of rooms	Page no
Les Aigrettes, St-Gilles-les-Bains	★★	95	301
Alamanda Hotel, L'Hermitage	★★	58	301
Alizé Plage, St-Pierre	★★	6	286
Les Aloès, Cilaos	★★	7	315
L'Archipel, St-Gilles-les-Bains	★★★	66	299
Auberge de Poisson Rouge, Piton-Ste-Rose	u/c	7	277
Auberge du Volcan, La Plaine-des-Cafres	-	8	312
Austral Hotel, St-Denis	★★★	53	266
Les Azalées, La Plaine-des-Palmistes	★	36	311
Le Bananier, Salazie	u/c	12	321
Barbin Marie, Cilaos	u/c	3	317
Hotel Le Baril, Le Baril	★★	14	282
Le Bleu Margouillat, St-Leu	★★★	14	296
Bois Rouge, Cilaos	★★	5	315
Le Boucan Canot, Boucan Canot	★★★★	50	299
Les Bougainvilliers, L'Hermitage	u/c	9	302
Hotel le Bouvet, St-Benoît	u/c	7	275
La Case Bleue, Cilaos	u/c	1	317
Case Nyala, Cilaos	u/c	5	317
Central Hotel, St-Denis	★★	57	267
Hotel les Chenêts, Cilaos	★★★	47	315
Chez Papa Daya, St-Pierre	u/c	17	287
Les Chrysalides, St-Pierre	★★	16	286
Hotel du Cirque, Cilaos	★	35	317
La Clé des Champs, St-Paul	u/c	5	305
Concorde Bellepierre, St-Denis	★★★★	55	266
Les Créoles, St-Gilles-les-Bains	★★★	42	299
Domaine des Jamroses, La Montagne	★★★	12	266–7
Domaine des Pierres, St-Pierre	★★★	41	286
L'Ecrin, La Plaine-des-Cafres	★★	13	312
L'Escale Touristique, St-Pierre	u/c	14	287
Ferme du Pommeau, Plaine-des-Palmistes	★★	15	311
Les Filaos, St-Gilles-les-Bains	u/c	44/SC	302

Name and location	Category	No of rooms	Page no
Fleur de Mai, St-Denis	u/c	10	267
Les Floralys Caro Beach, L'Etang-Salé-les-Bains	★★★	52/SC	291
Les Fougères, Les Avirons	★★	15	296
Les Géraniums, La Plaine-des-Cafres	★★	25	312
Grand Hôtel des Mascareignes, Boucan Canot	★★★	153	299–301
L'Hostellerie de la Confiance, St-Benoît	-	8	275
Ile de France, St-André	u/c	30	274
Hotel Iloha, St-Leu	★★★	64/SC	296
Le Joyau des Laves, Piton-Ste-Rose	u/c	4	277
Le Juliette Dodu, St-Denis	★★★	43	266
Le Lancastel, St-Denis	★★	136	267
Lodge Roche Tamarin, La Possession	★★★	16/SC	305
Loge Grand Bois, Grand Bois	★★★	29/SC	286
Le Maharani, St-Gilles-les-Bains	★★★	55	301
Les Manguiers, St-Denis	u/c	20/SC	267
Marianne, St-Denis	★★	24	267
Marina, St-Gilles-les-Bains	★★	10/SC	301
Mercure Blue Beach, L'Hermitage	★★★	56	299
Mercure Créolia, St-Denis	★★★	107	266
Le Nathania, St-Pierre	u/c	14	287
Le Nautile, La-Saline-les-Bains	★★★	43	301
Hotel des Neiges, Cilaos	★★	18	315
Le Novotel St-Gilles, L'Hermitage	★★★	173	301
Orchidées Rose, Hell-Bourg	u/c	5	321
Hotel les Orchidées, Le Tampon	★	10	286–7
Hotel Outre-Mer, Le Tampon	★	35	287
Hotel Paladien Apolonia, St-Leu	★★★	129	296
Les Palmiers, St-Denis	u/c	12	267
Hotel de la Plage, St-Gilles-les-Bains	u/c	7	302
Hotel des Plaines, Plaine-des-Palmistes	★★	14	311
Relais des Cîmes, Hell-Bourg	★★	30	321
Résidence Eglantine, Cilaos	u/c	7/SC	317
Le Saint-Denis, St-Denis	★★★	118	266
Le Saint Alexis, St-Gilles-les-Bains	★★★★	63	299
Le Saint Michel, St-Gilles-les-Bains	★★	15	301
Hotel Select, St-Denis	★	55	267
Le Sterne Beach, St-Pierre	★★★	50	286
Sud Hotel, Le Tampon	u/c	44	287
Le Suffren, St-Pierre	-	18	287
Le Swalibo, La-Saline-les-Bains	★★★	30	301
Tsilaosa, Cilaos	★★★	15	315
Tropic Hotel, St-Pierre	u/c	16	287
Le Vieux Cep, Cilaos	★★	44	317
Villa des Songes, St-Gilles-les-Hauts	★★	12	301
Les Villas du Lagon, L'Hermitage	★★★★	174	299
Les Villas du Recif, St-Gilles-les-Bains	★★★	146	301
Hotel le Volcan, La Plaine-des-Cafres	★★	10	312

Villages Vacances Familles Réunion (VVF)

VVF 'Village de Corail', St-Gilles-les-Bains		129	302

Appendix 3

FURTHER INFORMATION
GENERAL
Books

Adams, Douglas and Carwardine, Mark *Last Chance to See* William Heinemann, London, 1990. Beautifully written and illustrated, including a section on the endangered Mascarene wildlife (especially Mauritian birds).

Ellis, Dr Matthew and Wilson-Howarth, Dr Jane *Your Child Abroad: A Travel Health Guide* Bradt, 2005 (2nd edition). An invaluable guide for those travelling or resident overseas with babies and children of all ages.

Georges, Eliane and Vaisse, Christian *The Indian Ocean* Evergreen, 1998. Many beautiful photos but the information is inaccurate in parts.

Ventor, A J *Where to Dive in Southern Africa and off the Islands* Ashanti Publishing, 1991. Excellent for divers and non-divers alike. Well-written general reviews of all the Mascarenes, plus all the necessary information for divers and snorkelling enthusiasts.

Websites

www.fco.gov.uk/travel Foreign and Commonwealth Office website with up-to-date country-specific advice. Should be consulted prior to travel.

www.dh.gov.uk/travellers Department of Health website giving general travel health advice and country-specific inoculation recommendations. Also, everything you need to know about obtaining, completing and using an E111 form.

www.weddings.co.uk Website providing information on getting married abroad, including lists of necessary documentation and other administrative procedures.

www.africaonline.com News and general information on the region.

MAURITIUS AND RODRIGUES
Books
History

Editions Pacifique *Historical Postcards of Mauritius*.

Riviere, Lindsay *Historical Dictionary of Mauritius* Scarecrow Press, London, 1982.

Vaughn, Megan *Creating the Creole Island, Slavery in 18th-century Mauritius* Duke University Press, 2005. Excellent insight into Mauritius as a land of slaves and their masters.

Natural history

Atachia, Michael *Sea Fishes of Mauritius* Mauritius, 1984.

Durrell, Gerald *Golden Bats and Pink Pigeons* Fountain, 1979.

Michel, Claude *Birds of Mauritius* Mauritius, 1986.

Michel, Claude *Marine Molluscs of Mauritius* Mauritius, 1985.

Michel, Claude and Owadally, A W *Our Environment, Mauritius* Mauritius, 1975.

Owadally, A W *A Guide to the Royal Botanical Gardens, Pamplemousses* Mauritius, 1978.

Sinclair, Ian, and Langrand, Olivier *Birds of the Indian Ocean Islands* Struik/New Holland, 1998. The definitive field guide for birdwatchers visiting the western Indian Ocean. Includes many interesting discoveries made during the 1990s.

Ventor, A J *Underwater Mauritius* Media House Publications, South Africa, 1988.

Language
Goswami-Sewtohul K *A Mauritian Phrase Book* Mauritius, 1981.

Activities
Mountain, A and Halbwachs, Y *The dive sites of Mauritius* Struik, 1996.

Travel guides/tourist booklets
Hildebrand, *Travel Guide to Mauritius* Frankfurt/London, 1985.

MTPA *Mauritius Info Guide* Mauritius Tourism Promotion Authority. General information plus lists of restaurants, hotels and activity operators. Maps of Mauritius and Port Louis. Brief section on Rodrigues. Free.

MTPA *What's on in Mauritius* B&T directories, annually. General information, including activities, shopping and places of interest. Maps of the island, Port Louis, Curepipe and Grand Baie. Free.

MTPA *Rodrigues: your guide* Mauritius Tourism Promotion Authority. Background and practical information, including hotels and restaurants. Map of the island. Free.

General
Andrews, Barry et al *Best of Mauritian Cooking* Times Editions, 1994.

Macmillan, Allister *Mauritius Illustrated (1914)* Editions du Pacifique, 1991.

Mauritius from the Air Nouvelles Editions du Pacifique, 1994.

Ramdoyal, Ramesh *Festivals of Mauritius* Edition Indian Ocean.

Sookhee, Lalita *Mauritian Delights* Mauritius, 1985.

Vaisse, Christian *Living in Mauritius* Editions du Pacifique, 1989.

Newspapers
Mauritius News, 'The first Mauritian Newspaper Overseas' published monthly; 583 Wandsworth Rd, London SW8 3JD; ☎ 020 7498 3066; e editor@mauritiusnews.co.uk; www.mauritius-news.co.uk

Websites
www.gov.mu Mauritian government website with extensive information, including the latest economic news and links to all departments and government bodies.

http://statsmauritius.gov.mu Up-to-date statistics on Mauritius.

www.mauritius.net Mauritius Tourist Promotion Authority website. Contains background and practical information, including visa requirements. Provides details of hotels, restaurants and things to see in Mauritius. Useful information, although the other sites listed tend to be more comprehensive and up to date.

www.servihoo.com General website with news, sport, chat rooms and search engine.

www.mauritius-info.com Designed for tourists and business visitors. Hotel and restaurant contact details can be easily found, as well as the usual background information. The business guide contains listings of company contact details for a multitude of sectors.

www.rodrigues-island.org MTPA website on Rodrigues. General tourist information. Very comprehensive.

www.themauritiusyellowpage.com Directory of businesses. Good in theory but searches do not work as well as they might.

http://metservice.intnet.mu Weather and cyclone information.

www.airmauritius.com Website of the airline. Includes schedule and route details, as well as online booking.

RÉUNION
Books
Natural history
Moyne-Picard, Marylène and Dutrieux Eric *Fonds sous-marins de L'Ile de la Réunion* Ouest France, 1997. Guide to the marine environment around Réunion, plus information on the best dive sites. In French only.

Activities
Colas, Pascal *Le Paradis du Canyoning* Edition Maison de la Montagne. Information on canyoning in Réunion. In French only.

Fédération Française de la Randonnée Pédestre *Topoguide: L'Ile de la Réunion*. Comprehensive guide to the GR R1 and GR R2 trails, including maps. In French only.

Office Nationale des Forêts *Itinéraires Réunionnais* Bat' Karé. Information on hiking and suggested trails. In French only.

Office Nationale des Forêts *Sentiers Marmailles* Bat' Karé. 42 easy walks of less than three hours, designed with children in mind. In French only.

Reynaud, Luc *52 Balades et Randonnées Facile à La Réunion* Orphie. 52 easy and moderate hikes. In French only.

Travel guides/tourist booklets
Comité du Tourisme de la Réunion *Guide des 24 Communes*. Focuses on the places of interest in each of the island's 24 communes. In French only.

Comité du Tourisme de la Réunion *Le Guide Run*. Published annually. Invaluable information on what to see in each region, plus hotel and restaurant contact details. In French and English.

Heissat, Robert and Puget, Anny *Bonjour La Réunion* Les Créations du Pelican, 1993. Colourful photos and text with good sections on culture, natural history and each region. In French only.

General
Gélabert, Serge *La Réunion Fruit d'une Passion* Serge Gélabert, 1998. Largely photos with some text on the island. In French only.

Gélabert, Serge and Javel, Mamy *La Réunion des Mille et Une Saveurs* Serge Gélabert, 1998. Excellent Creole recipe book. In French only.

Grenson, Jan. *La Cuisine de la Réunion* Editions Orphie, 2004. Réunionnais recipes, from *punch* to *cari*. In French only.

Websites
www.la-reunion-tourisme.com Website of the Comité du Tourisme de la Réunion. A must for anyone planning a trip. Packed with information available in English and French about every aspect of the country. Includes calendar of events, tourism statistics and photographs.

www.ilereunion.com General website in French only, with hotel, restaurant and activities information. Useful descriptions of each region and major towns with things to see. Also, weather and traffic information and useful phone numbers.

www.creole.org Aims to give a feel of what Réunion is actually like, with an emphasis on culture. Contains photographs, Creole recipes, accommodation and restaurant information. Mostly in French, although parts are in English.

www.reunion-nature.com Excellent website with information on hiking accommodation and all outdoor activities. Online booking service.

www.reunion-directory.com General tourist information plus a directory of companies in tourism, industry, agriculture and service sectors. Good descriptions and links for hotels. Mostly in French, although some parts are in English.

www.runweb.com Plenty of practical tourist information. Largely in French with parts in English.
www.meteo-reunion.com Weather information for the island, including satellite pictures and cyclone news.

Bradt Travel Guides

www.bradtguides.com

Index

Page numbers in bold refer to major entries; those in italics indicate maps.
*Pages 1–186 refer to **Mauritius**, pages 187–215 to **Rodrigues**,*
*pages 217–324 to **Réunion***